Hebrew between Jews and Christians

Studia Judaica

Forschungen zur Wissenschaft des Judentums

Begründet von
Ernst Ludwig Ehrlich

Herausgegeben von
Günter Stemberger, Charlotte Fonrobert,
Elisabeth Hollender, Alexander Samely
und Irene Zwiep

Volume 77

Hebrew between Jews and Christians

Edited by
Daniel Stein Kokin

DE GRUYTER

ISBN 978-3-11-161995-8
e-ISBN (PDF) 978-3-11-033982-6
e-ISBN (EPUB) 978-3-11-038951-7
ISSN 0585-5306

Library of Congress Control Number: 2022933193

Bibliographic information published by the Deutsche Nationalbibliothek
The Deutsche Nationalbibliothek lists this publication in the Deutsche Nationalbibliografie; detailed bibliographic data are available on the internet at http://dnb.dnb.de.

© 2024 Walter de Gruyter GmbH, Berlin/Boston
This volume is text- and page-identical with the hardback published in 2023.
Typesetting: Integra Software Services Pvt. Ltd.

www.degruyter.com

Contents

Daniel Stein Kokin
Introduction —— 1

Steven D. Fraade
The Torah Inscribed/Transcribed in Seventy Languages —— 21

Alison G. Salvesen
"Hebrew, Beloved of God": The Adamic Language in the Thought of Jacob, Bishop of Edessa (c. 633–708 CE) —— 49

Irven M. Resnick
"Lingua sacra et diabolica": A Survey of Medieval Christian Views of the Hebrew Language —— 67

Gabriel Wasserman
Aramaic – Between Heaven and Earth: On the Use of Aramaic in the Liturgical Life of Medieval European Jewry —— 95

Irene Zwiep
Choice and Determinism at the Crossroads of Early Modern Hebraism —— 125

Saverio Campanini
Learning Hebrew in the Renaissance: Towards a Typology —— 137

Ilona Steimann
Hebraism without Hebrew: Hartmann Schedel and the Conversion of his "Jewish" Books —— 159

Melanie Lange
Hebrew Caught Between? —— 187

Stephen G. Burnett
Luther and Hebrew —— 203

Guido Bartolucci
Hebrew in the Counter-Reformation: The Cases of Caesar Baronius and Gilbert Génébrard —— 219

Stefan Schorch
The Peculiarities of Hungarian Christian Hebraism (16th and 17th Centuries) —— 243

Yael Almog
Reasoning and Exegesis: Hamann and Herder's Notions of Biblical Hebrew —— 275

Thomas Willi
Dalman als Aramaist: Auf der Suche nach der Sprache der neutestamentlichen Welt —— 297

Shalom Goldman
Apostasy, Identity, and Erudition: Paul Levertoff (1878–1954) —— 319

Liora R. Halperin
Metaphors of the Sacred and Profane in Pre-State Zionist Hebrew Discourse —— 337

List of Contributors —— 357

Daniel Stein Kokin
Introduction

At the heart of this volume is the recognition not only that both Judaism and Christianity have deep interest and a long history of engagement with the Hebrew language, but that Hebrew itself has played a significant role in the relations between them. While this may come as no news to those reading these lines, it is nonetheless rare to encounter an academic treatment of this role committed to examining the two religious traditions as equal partners in this story across the *longue durée*. Of course, one volume cannot cover every aspect of this story, and there are inevitably major holes, some that I unsuccessfully tried to fill, others that I may not even have thought of, but in assembling it I have tried to adopt as broad as possible a perspective, and to consider topics that have perhaps not achieved sufficient attention, as well as to place antiquity, the Middle Ages, and modernity, and scholars of Judaism and Christianity, theologians, historians, and others in dialogue with one another. The reader will decide if it has succeeded. The risk, of course, is that each contribution will largely stand or fall on its own, in isolation from the others. But I hope that the articles comprising this volume serve to create and convey something of a common language that will prove stimulating. For it is clear to me that a number of major themes cut across the chronological and disciplinary lines that so frequently divide the objects of our research from one another. After first offering a brief summary of each contribution, I would like then to devote some pages to an exploration thereof, accompanied by some of the various sources, questions, and images that have interested me over the course of the many years during which this volume took shape. I confess at the outset that this will be an impressionistic presentation, but hopefully one that will entice its readers to examine *Hebrew between Jews and Christians* in greater detail.

At the root of any consideration of the place of the Hebrew language among Jews and Christians must be an examination of Hebrew's status as *the*, or possibly merely *a*, language of revelation. Is divine revelation to be understood as inherently Hebraic in character, only incidentally so, or perhaps even at some root level polyglossic? In the first contribution, "The Torah Inscribed/Transcribed in Seventy Languages," Steven Fraade explores the rich early rabbinic meditations on these questions by examining interpretations of the biblical injunction (Deut 27:8) to inscribe

---

Note: My thanks to Benjamin Ratskoff and Clara Vogt for assistance with formatting; to Gabriel Wasserman for numerous astute observations and corrections; and to all the contributors, the publisher, and especially content editor Alice Meroz, for their patience despite unfortunate delays in the preparation of this volume.

the words of the Torah "most distinctly" (*"ba'er heitev"*) as referring to their translation into the seventy languages of mankind, i.e. all human tongues. As Fraade shows, this rabbinic understanding reflects two contrasting approaches to thinking about the revelation-Hebrew-translation nexus. According to one, this translation process is actually essential for drawing out the full meanings and significance of Scripture. For the other, such translation is primarily a concession to the reality of a multilingual world into which some degree of dissemination of Israel's Torah is required. Thus, if one understanding questions, at least to some degree, Hebrew's status or sufficiency as the sole language of revelation, its counterpart clings to and reinforces it. We can summarize the point (and simultaneously "translate" it for translation studies writ large) as follows: can a translation potentially improve upon its original or is it inherently a pale reflection thereof? Fraade concludes that there is no single rabbinic viewpoint with regard to Hebrew's status as prior to, or preferred over, other languages, at least with regard to divine revelation.

In either case, the sources explored by Fraade give witness to a striking rabbinic openness to the revelation and interpretation of Scripture as a potentially polylingual phenomenon. In the second chapter, we examine a related foundational issue, the question of Hebrew's potential status as the original or Adamic language, albeit from the perspective of a rival religious and linguistic community, that of Syriac Christianity.

In her contribution "'Hebrew, beloved of God': The Adamic Language in the Thought of Jacob, Bishop of Edessa (c. 633–708 CE)," Alison Salvesen notes and sets out to explain why, in contrast to nearly all other Syriac writers, Jacob believed that Hebrew was the original and universal human language. Most prominently, she links this rare position to the general theological animosity that abided at the time beween Jacob's Syrian Orthodox Church and that of the "Church of the East" concerning the critical question as to the separate or united character of Christ's human and divine natures. Because the eastern Syrian Church had been strongly influenced by the Greek theologian Theodore of Mopsuestia (350–428 CE), who had derogatively described Hebrew as the language composed of mixed Aramaic and Canaanite elements that emerged when Abraham settled in Canaan, Salvesen posits that Jacob felt compelled to adopt the opposing view.

Alongside this "horizontal" explanation, Salvesen introduces a "vertical" one, namely the special significance of biblical geography and of the patriarch Abraham's Aramean lineage for the Syrian Christians of Jacob's Edessa and environs, which likely rendered the Syriac language less important as an identity marker for them as compared with the Syriac East. When considered from these dual perspective, Jacob's seemingly strange position becomes eminently reasonable.

Salvesen also proceeds to explore some of the signature cases in which Jacob references both "Hebrew etymologies and Jewish exegetical traditions within his vast literary output," further discounting that they reflect potential encounters or relations with contemporary Jews, with whom Jacob would likely have had only limited contact and who would, in any case, have prompted little concern in contrast to both heterodox Christianity and Islam. Finally, Jacob's high regard for the Hebrew language, as reflected in the above-mentioned etymological and exegetical references, ironically induced many modern scholars to mistake him for an actual Hebraist, at a time when this assessment had potential value for raising the perceived status and value of Syriac Studies. In point of fact, Jacob knew very little, if any, Hebrew.

Turning to the medieval period, in his "'Lingua sacra et diabolica': A Survey of Medieval Christian Views of the Hebrew Language," Irven Resnick shows that despite – or precisely because of – its status as a holy tongue for Latin Christians, Hebrew provoked fear, owing both to its perceived magical power and potential for misuse. Evidence suggests that Hebrew was understood to be capable of exorcising demons, curing illness, and providing bodily protection, but at times also took on Satanic associations. Furthermore, Christians were well aware of their Hebrew "language deficit" in comparison with Jews, provoking yet further anxiety. In response, Christians often alleged that Jews had corrupted Hebrew, in some cases adding that its restoration will occur with the return of Jesus.

Resnick is particularly interested in visual evocations of the language through pseudo-Hebrew, speculating that such representations at times linked Christians to Hebrew's primordial sacrality, while on other occasions highlighting the language's corruption and, by extension, that of the Jews. Finally, while the majority of his analysis is concerned with the views of scholarly and religious elites, he closes with an analysis of the appearance of Hebrew in the ritual murder tale *The Passion of Adam of Bristol*, presented here as reflective of popular attitudes. Interestingly, this tale replicates the dual diabolical/sacral theme concerning Hebrew, for while the Jews in the text converse in this language amongst themselves, they fail to acknowledge God when he does as well. For this reason, the tale can also be regarded as an implicit response to, or neutralization of, the Christian "language deficit."

This notion of Hebrew potentially representing for Christians two diametrically opposed valences is nicely matched on the Jewish side by competing conceptions of Aramaic, a theme considered in detail in Gabriel Wasserman's "Aramaic: Between Heaven and Earth." Highlighting the uses medieval European Jews made of this closely-related Semitic tongue, this piece argues that sources from the period discuss Aramaic in two contrasting ways: as either an archaic vernacular, formerly understood by common people; or as a mystical, arcane language of even greater sanctity than Hebrew, owing to the fact that it is understood only by God himself, and not by his angels. Wasserman traces how the notion of the angelic ignorance of Aramaic, which in Talmudic times deterred prayer in the language, came in the Middle Ages to justify it in special circumstances, further observing that it was precisely Aramaic's perceived lowly character early on that paradoxically enabled its later "hyper-sacralizaton."

If the first portion of his study explores the status of Aramaic vis-à-vis Hebrew in general, its second part turns specifically to the two occasions in medieval Ashkenaz on which Aramaic was most prominently deployed in liturgy, the seventh day of Passover, known as Yom Vayyosha', and Shavu'oth. Wasserman explores the continued presence of Aramaic in worship on these dates in light of his earlier suggestions, concluding that it was intended both to create a mystical experience for the worshipper by "[transcending] the limits [of] ordinary language" and symbolically, albeit not directly understandably, to disseminate the respective stories of Yom Vayyosha' and Shavu'oth to the Jewish masses. Through a close of reading of Aramaic piyyutim composed for these occasions, including the famous *Aqdamuth* poem, Wasserman is able to deduce further support for his reconstruction of the likely motivations for this medieval liturgical use of Aramaic. In a final section, this article points to the potential relevance of its discussion for the decision to employ Aramaic as the language of the Zohar and also encourages further study of piyyut as ritual, in addition to merely as literature.

Entitled "Choice and Determinism at the Crossroads of Early Modern Hebraism," Irene Zwiep's contribution positions itself at three points of intersection, at the nexus of the medieval and early modern, the Ashkenazi and Sephardic, and the Jewish and Christian. It begins by emphasizing the often-overlooked tradition of distinctive "Ashkenazi appropriations of Sephardi linguistic lore," for which the correct reading of Scripture (especially pronunciation) served as the key "starting point for grammatical description." Thereafter, it shows how influential this approach was for both the content and structure of the scholarship of two pivotal figures in early modern Hebraism, one Jewish, one Christian: Elijah "Baḥur" Levita (1469–1549) and Johannes Reuchlin (1455–1522). Finally, her article also notes that while the legacy of this Ashkenazi approach to grammar was largely superseded among Christian scholars within a century of Reuchlin, it endured in Jewish contexts down to the Haskalah. In short, Zwiep demonstrates the relevance for Christian engagement with the holy tongue of what we might style "Hebrew between Ashkenazim and Sephardim." Alternatively, it can be suggested, when examining "Hebrew between Jews and Christians," one needs to inquire *which* or *whose* Hebrew.

Drawing upon the extensive autobiographical accounts furnished by early modern scholars – Christian and Jewish alike – concerning their study or teaching of Hebrew, Saverio Campanini sets out in "Learning Hebrew in the Renaissance: Towards a Typology" to explore both the practical models of Hebrew learning present among the first generation of Renaissance Christian Hebraists as well as the intellectual and theological motivations for this study. With regard to the former, he proposes four basic situations: 1) a Christian teacher, 2) a Jewish-convert teacher, 3) a Jewish teacher, or 4) learning directly from books, and inquires at length as to how these categories are reflected and/or intersect in the scholarly biographies of several well-known and lesser-known Hebraists. Concerning the latter, Campanini stresses Kabbalah as the primary factor responsible for the wave of Christian interest in Hebrew at the height of the Renaissance, and explores how Jews responded to this interest, in particular how they attempted to steer Christians towards the much less sensitive study of grammar, which of course only prepared their students to access the Kabbalah on their own. Campanini also offers a number of interesting correctives, rejecting the common assumption of a special climate in Italy in this period particularly conducive to the Jewish teaching of Hebrew to non-Jews and also suggesting that Christians never fully accepted the notion of the holiness of Hebrew.

While we typically associate interest in the collection of Hebrew books with at least some degree of desire to read and directly engage with their contents, Ilona Steimann's study "Hebraism without Hebrew: Hartmann Schedel and the Conversion of his 'Jewish' Books," demonstrates that this need not be the case. A physician and humanist best known for his role in compiling the noted Nuremberg *Weltchronik*, Hartmann Schedel (1440–1514) knew no Hebrew, yet amassed nonetheless a sizeable library of Hebrew texts. Even more striking, he was hardly content merely to own these materials, but invested great effort in their "reshaping," through the addition of both prophetic biblical verses and Christian visual imagery at their respective beginnings and ends. Steimann points out that precisely because Schedel was unable to read the contexts of these works, he couldn't help but conceive of them as in essence "Jewish" objects in need of transformation. Particularly illuminating in this regard is Steimann's contextualization of Schedel's collection practices against the backdrop of the recent expulsion of the Jews from Nuremberg, where he lived. Because no Jews were present by the time of acquisition (which indeed was facilitated precisely by their absence), Schedel's additions can be said to have been "directed inwards, towards the books themselves" and at "Schedel himself." One can thus discern the application of the longstanding rhetoric of conversion present in Nuremberg and elsewhere to these Hebrew books, and perhaps surmise a degree of satisfaction in the ease with which this could be accomplished, especially in light of the pre-expulsion failure of such rhetoric to win more than but a handful of converts. Steimann's study thus reveals the relevance of prevailing patterns in Jewish-Christian relations for the fate of Jewish objects in Christian hands, even objects that could not in any way be read or understood.

As suggested by its title, "Hebrew Caught Between? Sebastian Münster's Edition of Elia Levita's *Sefer ha-Baḥur* as Evidence of Intercultural and Interreligious Dialogue," Melanie Lange's contribution is primarily concerned with the renowned Christian Hebraist and general polymath's 1525 translation of the equally noted Jewish grammarian's 1517/18 *Sefer ha-Baḥur*, assessing the work in the context of the surviving correspondence between Münster and Levita as well as contemporary traditions of Christian Hebrew study. After first stressing Münster's avid pursuit of Jewish-Christian encounter — including his principle of "oculariter videre" ("seeing with one's own eyes"), and his respect for Hebrew and Jewish sources – nicely reflected in his practice of dating his publications according to both the Christian and Jewish calendars, she helpfully notes the mutual dependence between the two figures: Levita benefitted from Münster's dissemination of his scholarship in the non-Jewish world, whereby Münster also served his own career.

Thereafter, she turns directly to the *Baḥur*, or – as Münster entitled it in his translation – *Grammatica Hebraica Absolutissima* itself, before concluding with an analysis of the prominent christological elements in the introductory grammar Münster prefaced to his publication of Levita's treatise. Lange shows how the reception of the Jewish treatise was likely profoundly shaped by its inclusion alongside an explicitly Christianizing text. Thus, Levita's treatise was rendered accessible to the non-Jewish world, but at a very high cost. Hebrew was truly "caught between" and amidst Jewish-Christian controversy.

The significance and reception of Münster's Hebrew scholarship also looms large in the subsequent chapter, "Luther and Hebrew." Here Stephen Burnett takes the great reformer off his pedestal (literally: he opens by noting the numerous statues of Luther one encounters across Germany), to examine afresh the scholarly contexts and community in and among which Luther learned Hebrew, and conducted (and revised) his famous German translation of the Hebrew Bible. What emerges unmistakably here is Luther's "own decades-long disciplined reading of the Hebrew Bible," at least three-times through from start to finish; his general openness to the use of Christian Hebrew scholarship, even in cases of theological disagreement with the authors; and the highly collaborative nature of the translation endeavor, which often featured long discussions involving Luther and his colleagues.

Burnett also treats Luther's deeply ambiguous stance vis-à-vis the Hebrew language as such, as perhaps best reflected in his assertion as to the importance of the noted Jewish Kimhi grammarians, immediately followed by his avowed refusal to be bound by the rules of grammar. Along the same lines, Luther emphasized the incomplete knowledge of Hebrew common to both Jews and Christians and – anticipating many of his Protestant followers – insisted that the "above and below of the rabbis," i.e. the Hebrew vowel points, were but an untrustworthy Jewish invention, preferring to focus instead on Scripture's "inside."

Perhaps most significantly, Burnett shows how during the 1530s Luther became increasingly concerned about the degree to which Jewish biblical interpretation had insinuated itself into Christian biblical scholarship, especially translation. Though Münster was a key target of his wrath, in particular for his willingness to entertain multiple interpretations of Scripture – a rabbinic defect, according to Luther – rather than zeroing in on its single, i.e. Christian, meaning, Luther openly admitted that he himself was not exempt from this tendency. Burnett thus leaves us with a strikingly contradictory Luther. Few, if any, Christians spent as much time reading and translating the Hebrew Bible as did he; few, if any, were as outspoken concerning the theological dangers of this activity.

While the previous two chapters remind us of the tendency to regard Christian Hebraism as primarily a Protestant phenomenon, Guido Bartolucci's consideration of the cases of Caesar Baronius and Gilbert Génébrard offers an important corrective to the common notion of a decline of interest in, and engagement with, Hebrew and the Jewish tradition in the context of post-Tridentine Catholicism. Bartolucci points, for example, to the cardinal Baronius' eclectic, even eccentric, use of Jewish sources, which included references to works that the Catholic Church had recently burnt! He further accounts for Baronius' practice by drawing a distinction between biblical exegesis and consideration of the early history of Christianity. In the former, the drawing upon Hebrew and Jewish sources was problematic for Catholicism; for the latter, their use "was not only permitted, but essential."

With regard to Génébrard, Bartolucci exemplifies the high academic level of the Collège de France in Paris, the only such college that maintained its independence in the Counter-Reformation and remained an important center for the study and teaching of Hebrew. Génébrard used his mastery of Hebrew to challenge his myriad opponents across the theological and geographical spectra as well as in pursuit of his own scholarly interests. He composed the first-ever grammar of rabbinic Hebrew (designed to assist those desirous of reading rabbinic biblical commentaries), translated Jewish historiographical works into Latin, and also explored Hebrew prosody. In addition, he demonstrated particular interest as to the history of the Hebrew vowel markings, in which he struck a rather unique middle position, agreeing as to the lateness of these points, but at the same time showing how Hebrew could legitimately be read without them. Furthermore, in engaging directly with the biblical text, Génébrard aroused great controversy, but managed nonetheless to produce scholarly works so respected that Protestant scholars made use thereof. Hebrew scholarship may have suffered during the Counter-Reformation, but was at times cultivated at a level that matched, and perhaps exceeded, that undertaken by Protestants.

In his contribution, Stefan Schorch takes us to the much less traveled territory of Christian Hebraism in Central and Eastern Europe, focusing in particular on Hungary and Transylvania from the sixteenth to eighteenth centuries. He emphasizes features unique to Hebrew study in these regions during this period, including among members of the Sabbatarian Movement (a Judaizing offshoot of Unitarianism that emerged in late sixteenth-century Hungary) and in the context of scholarship that emphasized links between the Hungarian and Hebrew languages.

For example, as Schorch shows, it was an early Sabbatarian, Miklós Bogáti Fazekas, who produced the first full Hungarian translation of the Psalter, drawing extensively upon Midrash and the Jewish biblical commentary tradition in the process. Subsequently, Simon Péchi translated a wide range of Jewish texts into Hungarian, including the entire Tanakh, Pirkei Avot, and liturgy in the late sixteenth and early seventeenth centuries, and has been described by some modern scholars as one of the leading Hebraists of all time. Schorch links the attainments of Hebrew scholarship in Transylvania at this time to the greater liberty and intellectual freedom that abided there in comparison with other regions of Europe, and to the extensive access enjoyed to Sephardic Jewish culture, thanks to Transylvania's status at the time as an Ottoman vassal state.

With regard to Hungarian itself, Schorch observes that the earliest surviving grammar or grammatical schoolbook for the language, the 1539 *Grammatica Hungarolatina*, draws extensive parallels with Hebrew – thanks to which it arrives at what appears to be the first account of the features that distinguish Hungarian from other European languages. Indeed, on the basis of similarities such as the use of possessive markers and the incorporation of the object into the verbal form, this text concludes that the Hebrew and Hungarian languages are closely related. Such claims appeared also in subsequent Hungarian grammars published in the seventeenth century, and were accompanied by assertions as to Hungarian's status as an oriental and cardinal language that originated at the time of the post-Babelian confusion of the tongues. In certain cases, it seems that some of Hebrew's holiness is even applied to Hungarian. In demonstrating the manner in which early scholars of Hungarian drew upon Hebrew in order to buttress the status of a vernacular language, Schorch's contribution greatly enhances our knowledge of a phenomenon encountered with regard to other emergent languages in the early modern period, e.g. Castilian and Tuscan,[1] while at the same time showcasing the vibrancy of Hebrew study at this time in Hungary and Transylvania.

---

[1] See, for example, Antonio de Nebrija, *Gramatica dela Lengua Castellana*, ed. Ig. González-Llubera (London: Oxford University Press, 1926), 3-4; Claudio Tolomei, *Il Cesano de la lingua toscana*, ed. Maria Rosa Franco Subri (Rome: Bulzoni, 1975), 51.

Turning to late eighteenth-century Germany, Yael Almog's paper ("Hamann and Herder on Hebrew") inquires as to the role played by the Hebrew language in the *Sturm und Drang* literary movement, especially in the context of Georg Hamann (1730–1788) and Johann Gottfried Herder's (1744–1803) respective theories of aesthetics. Almog positions Hamann's inspirational, revelatory approach to reading Hebrew Scripture – what she styles his "theory of imaginative reading" – as a polemic directed against the then-regnant scholarly approach to biblical Hebrew, and further observes how Herder's secularized or naturalized stance (his "hermeneutics of contextualization") differs from that of his friend, in emphasizing the significance of the cultural norms of the society that produced the Bible for comprehension of the Hebrew text.

Hamann, in particular, highlights Hebrew's esoteric and fragmented character as an "invitation" to readers the world over, whom he calls upon to become "Kabbalists," i.e. to fill in the text's gaps through inspiration and faith. As such, Scripture is transformed in essence into a universally subjective text, in which individual perspectives inevitably reflect individual circumstances. While sharing Hamann's assessment as to the obscurity of the Hebrew Bible, for Herder this constitutes an invitation to each individual, not to plumb the depths of their own imagination, but rather to investigate the culture that produced it, concerning which it is possible to arrive at objective truth. Hebrew thus emerges a model for deciphering the foreign. Herder views empathetic identification with the ancient Hebrews as essential for this process and also sings the praises of the unique aesthetic qualities of the Hebrew language in its prime, especially of its poetry, which for him constitutes the key access point to the Hebraic "Denkart," or way of thinking.

For all their differences, both Hamann and Herder's approaches to Hebrew and Scripture also intend to refute any notion of privileged or special "Jewish knowledge," and as such participate in a longstanding tradition of Christian appropriation. Herder, in particular, emphasizes that it is post-exilic Jews who have hybridized and thus corrupted Hebrew, implying that Christians are better positioned properly to appreciate it.

In his highly nuanced contribution, "Gustaf Dalman as Aramaicist: In Search of the Language of the New Testament World," Thomas Willi examines the tension between Hebrew and Aramaic study in the noted late nineteenth- and early twentieth-century theologian, philologist, and orientalist's writings, and explores how it both casts light on his development as a scholar and reflects the scholarly context in which this development took place. In particular, Willi shows that it was Dalman's extensive knowledge of the different strata of Hebrew that rendered participation in Franz Delitzsch's Hebrew New Testament translation project distasteful to him. For while Dalman appreciated philologically that this translation should be in rabbinic

Hebrew, this conflicted with his theological understanding of the New Testament as belonging to the world of biblical literature. Willi further demonstrates that it was Dalman's involvement in the revision of the Delitzsch translation that paradoxically led him to become a pioneer in the study of Aramaic, especially rabbinic Aramaic. On Willi's account, it appears that Hebrew functioned for Dalman at one and the same time as both a bridge and an obstacle to engagement with Judaism.

If Willi's contribution touches tangentially upon the potential missionary value of Christian recourse to Hebrew – the Delitzsch Hebrew New Testament had of course precisely this intention – such concerns are front and center in "Apostasy, Identity, and Erudition," Shalom Goldman's chapter devoted to the fascinating spiritual and scholarly life of Paul Phillip Levertoff (1875–1954). Scion of a Hasidic family, convert to Christianity, and proponent of what he styled "Hebrew-Christianity," Levertoff's productive and eclectic career spanned Poland, Palestine, Turkey, Germany (including a few years teaching at the institute in Leipzig founded by Delitzsch), and England. While offering a valuable summary of Levertoff's life as a whole, this study devotes particular attention to his efforts to create a Hebrew-Christian liturgy and congregation, his role as an educator about Judaism to Christians and about Christianity to Jews, and – most especially – his vast scholarship. For example, Goldman discusses his Modern Hebrew biographies of Jesus and Paul, Hebrew translation of Augustine's *Confessions*, and participation in the Soncino translation of the *Zohar* into English. As demonstrated by Goldman, especially prominent throughout Levertoff's works are his simultaneous efforts to enrich Hebrew literature and scholarship, and to position the Hebrew language (and to some degree Aramaic as well) as a bridge between Judaism and Christianity.

The volume concludes with "Sacredness and Profanity in Modern Zionist Discourses about Hebrew and other Tongues," Liora Halperin's exploration of the paradoxes inherent in Zionism's attempt to re-fashion Hebrew as a national language. Halperin shows that the very attempt to flatten Hebrew's traditional sacrality for both Jews and Christians in order to render it suitable as the Yishuv's vernacular opened it to potential competition from other tongues that could claim various advantages over it. This situation, she further argues, led to Hebrew's re-sacralization, now as a prized and imperiled national possession. Following Giorgio Agamben, she thus suggests that, under Zionism, Hebrew merely came to occupy "a new 'closed-off area' within a broader system that included both sacred and profane elements." In engaging with Zionist efforts to negotiate the national role of Hebrew in a multilingual (Jewish) world, Halperin's piece at this volume's close nicely echoes Fraade's consideration of the rabbinic exploration of the potentially polyglossic character of divine revelation at its outset.

One key issue underlying Fraade's opening contribution – and relevant to this volume as a whole – concerns the character and capacity of Hebrew in comparison with prominent imperial and literary languages. For this reason, I would like here briefly to introduce two later Jewish sources that can profitably be placed in dialogue with it. Midrash Tehillim compares four languages, noting that whereas Roman (i.e. Latin) is best for battle, Greek best for song, and Persian best for lamentation, the Hebrew language is best for prayer.[2] Unlike the sources discussed by Fraade, this passage is concerned not with the role of Hebrew and other languages in the consummation and dissemination of divine revelation (though prayer can perhaps be described as its human counterpart), but rather focuses on their respective strengths in different domains of human activity, which there is no reason not to acknowledge. Nonetheless, the reference to prayer points us toward the human-God relationship and suggests that these four tongues are presented in order of ascending status. As such, it is tempting to see in this list a social justification of Hebrew's importance despite its political irrelevance, and thus a linguistic "response" to Jewish exile and worldly weakness.

If Midrash Tehillim implies that each (or at least many a) language has a particular domain in which it excels, a 1435 letter of R. Elijah of Ferrara instead explores the relationship between Jewish mono- or multilingualism and the successful pursuit of religious text study. This document forms part of the vast literature concerned with the fate of the Ten Lost Tribes and/or Sons of Moses,[3]

---

2 Midrash Tehillim (Buber), Psalm 31 ("R. Yonatan said there are four languages: Latin for battle, Greek for song, Persian for lamentation, Hebrew for prayer"). Translation mine. See Salomon Buber, ed., *Midrash Tehilim: ha-mekhuneh Shoḥer ṭov* (Jerusalem: H. Vagshal, 1976/7). While the dating of this work is uncertain, its existence is attested, at the latest, in the eleventh century. What is translated here as "Hebrew" is actually, in the original Hebrew text, denoted as "leshon Ashurit." That Hebrew is nonetheless intended can be deduced from the earlier, albeit somewhat different version of this passage found in Tractate Megillah of the Jerusalem or Palestinian Talmud 1,10,71b. There the passage closes with the statement: "Assyrian (lit. Ashuri) has a script but no language. Hebrew has a language but no script. They chose for themselves the Assyrian script and the Hebrew language." The identification of the language according to its written character perhaps intends a positive contrast with the ephemeral elements (battle, song, lamentation) for which the rival languages are renowned. I am grateful to Gunter Stemberger for making me aware of this earlier source and providing the translation thereof.
3 Like the Northern Israelite tribes, the Sons of Moses are a legendary lost Jewish population, exegetically inspired by God's suggestion (Exod 32:10; Deut 9:14) during the Golden Calf episode that He destroy the Israelites and instead make Moses directly into a great nation. In the Bible this never takes place, but Jewish folklore gladly took God up on his offer. For a general treatment of the Ten Lost Tribes and for additional bibliography, see Zvi Ben-Dor Benite, *Ten Lost Tribes: A World History* (Oxford: Oxford University Press, 2009). Specifically on the Sambatyon legend, see

in which this folkloristic motif provides an opportunity to reflect upon different forms (attested or fantasized) of Jewish existence.

> The Sons of Moses reside on an island located near the Sambatyon River and across from them is the tribe of Menasseh. Across the Sambatyon River are the tribes of Dan, Naftali, Gad, and Asher. The Sons of Issachar inhabit their own land and have no contact with other men. They excel in the Torah and speak Hebrew, Arabic, and Persian, and are surrounded by fire-worshippers. The tribe of Simeon is at the edge of the south; they too rule over themselves. The tribes of Zebulon and Reuben are on the Euphrates River, some on one side, some on the other side, and they have the Mishnah and Talmud, and speak Hebrew and Arabic. The tribe of Ephraim is to the south of Babylonia and they are heroic fighters, living off of booty. Hebrew is their language.[4]

While this is not the place for a comprehensive analysis of this passage, I wish here to highlight its implicit link between multilingualism and fruitful Torah study. The heroic fighters of Ephraim, living off of booty, appear to know Hebrew alone and are not credited with any scholarly accomplishments. By contrast, the bilingual tribes of Zebulon and Reuben "have the Mishnah and Talmud," and alone of the trilingual "Sons of Issachar" is it stated that they "excel in the Torah." While Hebrew is clearly a prerequisite for Jewish study, it alone – this source seems to argue – does not suffice and requires nourishment from other tongues. For all its linguistic openness, however, the passage does at the same time appear keen to guard against the social pressures that typically accompany multilingualism: the tribe of Issachar is described as being "surrounded by fire-worshippers" and said to "have no contact with other men."

In addition, while not addressed in either of these sources, the specific question as to the relationship between Hebrew and Aramaic (including Syriac, a version of Aramaic) as attested in the contributions of Fraade, Salvesen, Wasserman, and Willi is particularly rich and merits further discussion given the latter's overlapping and historically evolving status as a biblical, vernacular, and liturgical language. From the perspective of Judaism, we might in general describe the challenge posed by Aramaic as follows: how does a particularistic faith community understand the presence in its textual and liturgical midst of a language that constitutes a bridge – sometimes useful, sometimes unwelcome – to the larger non-Jewish world?

Wasserman's indication of the contrasting, and at times coinciding, medieval strategies of the hyper-vernacularization and hyper-sacralization of Aramaic

---

my "Toward the Source of the Sambatyon: Shabbat Discourse and the Emergence of the Sabbatical River Legend," *Association for Jewish Studies Review* 37, no. 1 (April 2013): 1–28.

4 Judah David Eisenstein, ed., *Otsar Masa'ot* (New York: Eisenstein, 1926), 122. Translation mine.

raises the question of its status via-à-vis Hebrew in other historical contexts. For example, a former Israeli colleague once described Aramaic to me as "our Latin," suggesting its role in contemporary Hebrew as akin to that played in English and other European tongues by the West's traditional learned language. Indeed, there are good grounds for the analogy, as both Latin and Aramaic primarily serve today as sources of sophisticated, scholarly vocabulary for related languages in more active use. And yet the Hebrew-Aramaic relationship is far more interesting, since the present situation represents to a large degree a reversal of that which abided in antiquity, when Aramaic served for Jews primarily as the vernacular, with Hebrew the holy language of religious life and study.

Indeed, in light of Aramaic's status as the ancient vernacular, it is interesting to compare my colleague's above comment with the anecdote reported by the Israeli archaeologist Yigael Yadin in his account of the Nahal Hever excavations conducted in 1960 and 1961. Upon viewing letters from the Bar Kokhba revolt discovered there that had been written in Aramaic, David Ben-Gurion is said angrily to have responded: "Why did they write in Aramaic and not Hebrew?"[5] For Ben-Gurion, the value for the Zionist present of an ancient national Jewish uprising was, one could say, squandered by the choice for these missives of the non-uniquely Jewish Aramaic. Ironically, of course, "Bar Kokhba" is itself Aramaic; one can almost imagine Ben-Gurion conditioning (after the fact) support of the rebellion that bore his name on its Hebraization!

The notion of Hebrew as the pure "Jewish" tongue and of Aramaic as spanning the Jewish and non-Jewish remains relevant today for language discourse in the context of contemporary Middle Eastern politics. This was on full display at a public meeting held by then Israeli premier Benjamin Netanyahu and Pope Francis in Jerusalem on the occasion of the latter's May 2014 visit to the Holy Land. When the Israeli premier referred to Jesus as a Hebrew speaker, the pontiff quietly interjected, "Aramaic," to which Netanyahu in turn responded, "He spoke Aramaic, but he knew Hebrew."[6]

In brief, against the backdrop of the contemporary Palestinian nationalist tendency to embrace Jesus as one of their own, Netanyahu's articulation of the *dover 'ivrit* Christian Messiah sought to reaffirm his Jewishness and to enlist him as evidence as to the eternal connection of the Jewish people with the Land of

---

5 Cited in Yael Zerubavel, *Recovered Roots: Collective Memory and the Making of Israeli National Tradition* (Chicago: The University of Chicago Press, 1995), 30.
6 "Pope, Netanyahu Spar over Jesus' Native Language," Reuters (May 26, 2014), accessed June 29, 2021, https://www.reuters.com/article/uk-pope-holyland-jesus-idUKKBN0E618X20140526.

Israel. Thus, whereas Ben-Gurion famously intoned, "The Bible is our mandate,"[7] referring specifically to the Tanakh or Hebrew Bible, here Netanyahu appeared eager to supplement the world of the New Testament. (If Bibi's Zionist backdating was clear but merely implied, it was explicitly stated by one well-known right-wing commentator, who in covering the pope's alleged "outrage," referred to Jesus as an "Israeli Jew."[8]). Undoubtedly aware of the politicization to which Jesus was being subjected, the pope attempted to neutralize the situation. As a language common to both Jews and various Christian communities, and closely linked to both Hebrew and Arabic, Aramaic – *pace* the above-mentioned Bar Kokhba letters – lacks Hebrew's easy association with Jewish nationalism and sovereignty. It also happens to have been Jesus' actual spoken language, according to the current scholarly consensus. Not wishing to contradict the pontiff outright, and probably also well aware of the fundamental accuracy of his statement – the Israeli prime minister had to content himself with the undoubtedly correct, if far-less satisfying, assertion of Jesus' mere Hebrew *knowledge*.[9]

If this episode testifies to Zionism's interest in backdating Hebrew's status as an explicitly national Jewish language, there is at least some indication of a similar, albeit contrasting, tendency among the movement's ultra-Orthodox opponents. The founding Rebbe of Satmar Hasidism, Joel Teitelbaum (1887–1979), asserted in his *Vayoel Moshe* (dating to 1959 or 1960) that even in biblical times, Hebrew had never been a spoken language and that, back then, Aramaic had served as the vernacular.[10] This position matches the contemporary practice of

---

[7] Ben-Gurion made this statement in testimony to the British Peel Commission (Palestine Royal Commission) on Jan. 7, 1937. See Palestine Royal Commission, *Minutes of Evidence Heard at Public Sessions* (London: H.M. Stationery Office, 1937), p. 288. See also his Dec. 6, 1967 letter to Charles de Gaulle, viewable at: https://www.jewishvirtuallibrary.org/ben-gurion-letter-to-french-general-charles-de-gaulle-december-1967 (Accessed June 29, 2021).

[8] Caroline Glick, "Our World: Pope Francis's Unfriendly Visit," *The Jerusalem Post* (May 27, 2014), accessed June 29, 2021, https://www.jpost.com/Opinion/Columnists/Pope-Franciss-unfriendly-visit-354557.

[9] If Netanyahu's concession reflected acknowledgement of the fact that at the time Aramaic was the general vernacular and Hebrew primarily, or at least increasingly, a learned language, it is striking how Glick insisted on precisely the reverse in her gloss on the prime minister's statement: "True, at the time, educated Jews spoke and wrote in Aramaic. And Jesus was educated. But the language of the people was Hebrew. And Jesus preached to the people, in Hebrew" (ibid.).

[10] *Vayoel Moshe*, "Ma'amar leshon ha-kodesh," par. 16, cited in Ari Shvat, "The Commandment to Speak Hebrew and the Use of the Holy Tongue for Secular Matters," *Shema'tin* 177 (Nov.-Dec. 2010), p. 28 (Hebrew), also available at http://www.daat.ac.il/daat/v-articles/shvat-lashon.pdf (Accessed June 29, 2021). I am grateful to Gabriel Wasserman for drawing my attention to this source.

this community, which maintains Yiddish as its vernacular tongue, restricting the use of Hebrew to prayer and the study of holy texts. We might say that in advancing this argument, the late Satmar Rebbe was likewise deploying the Bible as the "mandate" for his rejection of Zionism, including the revival of spoken Hebrew it spearheaded.

Ultimately, at its core, this volume is most concerned to inquire to what degree Hebrew can in fact be positioned "between" Jews and Christians as a language of Scripture and sacrality, as a language of revelation upon which both religious traditions are ultimately dependent. It is of course common to conceive of Hebrew as a perennially Jewish language, for which lesser or greater numbers of Christians periodically cultivate a passion, learn, and attempt to appropriate as their own. There is of course a large degree of truth in this picture. But as there have also been Jewish cultures in which Hebrew has played or plays a very minor or even no role, and moments in the history of Christianity in which Hebrew assumed a rather significant importance, at least on a symbolic and scholarly level, we should be careful not to over-emphasize or essentialize this difference. Indeed, can we not conceptualize the history of Hebrew across the *longue durée* in both religious cultures as a similar one of recurrent revivals and periods of neglect? To be clear, my aim in this proposal is not to minimize the great quantitative difference between the two religious contexts (Jews have obviously used Hebrew more), but to ask if we might frame their overall engagement in somewhat similar terms. Paradoxically, celebration of the modern revival of Hebrew in the context of Zionism and the State of Israel has in many quarters served to cast an unnecessarily dark shadow over Hebrew's past, obscuring the fact that there have been other Hebrew revivals, albeit primarily of Hebrew as a literary, as opposed to vernacular, language. I have in mind here the Hebrew literary revival of medieval Spanish culture or, say, the situation that abided in Southern Italian Judaism. By the early Middle Ages, this culture had well-nigh lost its Hebraic character (epitaphs were only inscribed, and the liturgy recited, in Greek), but towards the close of the first millennium Hebrew literacy made a dramatic comeback as attested in the flowering there of Hebraic literary production. (One might also mention in this regard the modest revival of Hebrew letters that transpired among Jews in late 19th and early 20th century America, which has been overshadowed by that of the Yishuv and subsequent State of Israel.[11])

---

[11] See, for example, Michael Weingrad, *American Hebrew Literature: Writing Jewish National Identity in the United States* (Syracuse, NY: Syracuse University Press, 2011).

Mutatis mutandis, the flowering of Christian Hebraica in early modern Europe has led many non-specialists to discount the significance of medieval Christian engagement with Hebrew, especially as the phenomenon of Christian Hebraica is frequently understood against the backdrop of, and as closely aligned with, Renaissance Humanism. But, again, discounting the issue of the quantity of study or scholarly production, which in any case the further back in time we proceed is to at least a certain extent a question of what has survived in writing, this volume wishes to ask how fundamental a difference divides late antiquity, the Middle Ages, the Renaissance, and beyond in terms of Christian thinking about Hebrew. What, for example, do we do with the albeit little-known, but clearly important, figure of the canon and Cistercian monk Nicolaus Maniacutius or Maniacoria (fl. ca. 1130s–1160s), who in mid twelfth-century Rome achieved a solid command of Hebrew, conducted scholarly exchanges with Jewish scholars (including, it seems, Abraham ibn Ezra), and examined and corrected Latin biblical manuscripts according to the Hebrew text?[12] Even if he was an isolated figure, how fundamentally different is his activity from that of his Renaissance-era counterparts? To ask this question is in essence to inquire concerning Campanini's article in this collection and his claim there as to the significance of the Kabbalah as a motivating factor for Christian Hebrew study. In other words, was the Christian discovery of the Jewish mystical tradition a game-changer, opening up a fundamentally new raison d'être for Christian engagement with both Hebrew and Jewish sources? Or is it best understood as but a new variation on a long-standing theme?

Maniacutius is, however, but one of many possible examples that can be broached here. Campanini's own transcription and analysis together with Giulio Busi of a remarkable set of Hebrew letters exchanged between Marco Lippomano and Meir Crescas around 1420 raises the possibility of far more chronological continuity between Hebraism medieval and early modern,[13] as does my own research

---

12 On Maniacutius, see Cornelia Linde, "Basic Instruction and Hebrew Learning: Nicolaus Maniacoria's *Suffraganeus bibliothece*," *Recherches de Théologie et Philosophie Médiévales* 80 (2013): 1–16; and Marie-Thérèse Champagne, "Christian Hebraism in Twelfth-Century Rome: A Philologist's Correction of the Latin Bible through Dialogue with Jewish Scholars and their Hebrew Texts," *Studies in Church History* 53 (2017): 71–87.
13 Giulio Busi and Saverio Campanini, "Marco Lippomano and Crescas Meir: A Humanistic Dispute in Hebrew," in *Una manna buona per Mantova: Studi in onore di Vittore Colorni per il suo 92 compleanno*, ed. Mauro Perani (Florence: Leo S. Olschki Editore, 2004), 169–202; and Giulio Busi, "Marco Lippomano e Crescas Me'ir: Una disputa umanistica in ebraico," in *L'enigma dell'ebraico nel Rinascimento* (Turin: N. Aragno, 2007), 13–23. The Italian is a slight revision of the original English article.

into the scholarly relationship between Lippomano and Isaac Cohen of Syracuse.[14] And what do we do with a figure like Simone Atumano, the fourteenth-century Greek scholar who produced a new translation of the Hebrew Bible in Greek, as well as a rendering of the New Testament into Hebrew?[15] Once again, at issue here is not whether Atumano represents an isolated case of a Greek Christian Hebraist (though the nature of his activity does indeed raise the question as to whether more Hebraism was present among Greek Christianity than has hitherto been appreciated and/or than our surviving documentation attests), but to what degree a case like his points to the need to conceive of Hebrew as a perennial factor in Jewish-Christian relations.

In any case, it seems clear that both Jews and Christians have used engagement with Hebrew as a means of thinking about, reaching, and also critiquing one another. St. Jerome, in particular, famously bewailed the difficulty of reproducing Hebrew's "hissing, breath-demanding words,"[16] helping spawn a Renaissance-era legend according to which the Church father filed down his teeth in order to do so.[17] Such critique was echoed or reciprocated in reported Jewish ridicule of non-Jewish Hebrew pronunciation.

Resnick's contribution here specifically reminds us that the holiness of Hebrew created the conditions for its subversion as satanic. And the related notion of Hebrew as a negative marker for Jews and Judaism extends down to modern times, in which it has been secularized as suggestive of Jews' alleged foreignness to, and malicious influence upon, their host societies. Witness, for example, this Nazi campaign poster from the 1932 German presidential election (see Figure 1) in which Hindenburg voters are derided as Jews through the use of German font designed to approximate the Hebrew letters, in stark contrast to the Hitler voters, for whom emboldened Gothic script is selected.

As noted, in ending with an examination of internal Jewish discussions concerning Hebrew's relationship with other languages, *Hebrew Between Jews and Christians*' close evokes its opening. However, whereas Fraade's "The Torah Inscribed/Transcribed" was concerned with the translation of revelation – potentially to all mankind – and thus with passage (potential or actual) from Hebrew

---

14 Daniel Stein Kokin, "Isaac ha-Kohen's Letter to Marco Lippomano: Jewish-Christian Exchange and Arabic Learning in Renaissance Italy," *Jewish Quarterly Review* 104.2 (2014): 192–233.
15 On Atumano, see Giorgio Fedalto, *Simone Atumano* (Brescia, 2007).
16 J.N.D. Kelly, *Jerome: His Life, Writings, and Controversies* (New York: Harper & Row Publishers, 1975), 50.
17 Matteo Bossi, *De instituendo sapientia animo* (Bologna, Plato de Benedictis, 1495), sig. P. I, cited in Eugene F. Rice, Jr., *St. Jerome in the Renaissance* (Baltimore: Johns Hopkins University Press, 1985), 205 n. 26.

Figure 1: "Wir wählen Hindenburg! Wir wählen Hitler!" Wahlplakat der NSDAP zur Reichspräsidentenwahl 1932. ("We're voting for Hindenburg! We're voting for Hitler!" Nazi Party election poster for the 1932 German presidential election.) © Deutsches Historisches Museum/S. Ahlers.

to other tongues, Halperin's "Sacredness and Profanity" engages instead with Zionism's attempt to move from traditional Jewish linguistic diversity to Hebraic uniformity. While Zionism has of course achieved great success in re-establishing Hebrew as a mother tongue for millions of people, it has at the same time expanded and thus complicated the language's valences: still alive and well as a holy tongue of Scripture and liturgy, Hebrew now functions in addition as both a sacred national language and a fully secularized vernacular. Paradoxically, in seeking to assert national Jewish control over Hebrew, Zionism has to some degree actually undermined Jewish exclusivity vis-à-vis the language. I came face-to-face with these ironic consequences of the Zionist Hebrew revival in an unforgettable manner some years ago at the Shabbat dinner table of friends in, of all places, Rome. My hosts, observant Jews, speak little to no Hebrew, but are familiar with it as a language of prayer and are fluent in Italian, the de facto official language of the contemporary Catholic Church. Their other guest, an Israeli-Arab Roman Catholic from Haifa, is fluent in Hebrew, but knows no Italian. A Catholic Hebrew-speaker having Shabbat dinner with Italian-speaking Jews in the Eternal City – what an incredible inversion, I thought to myself, and a fascinating moment in the ever-evolving story of "Hebrew between Christians and Jews."

This volume has its ultimate origins in a conference of the same name held all the way back on July 2–3, 2012 in Greifswald, Germany. I am grateful to all those who made their way on that occasion to the university and Hanseatic city on the Ryck and participated in what was, at least for me, a most memorable two days of intellectual exchange. This conference was financed by the Alfried Krupp Wissenschaftskolleg Greifswald and it is my great duty and pleasure to thank the "Krupp Kolleg," and especially its Academic Manager, Dr. Christian Suhm, for their support and encouragement, both with regard to this specific academic meeting and beyond. The University of Greifswald would not be nearly the intellectually stimulating place that it is, were it not for the activities of the Krupp Kolleg. In addition, I would like to express my gratitude to my former Greifswald colleagues, particularly those in the Theology Faculty, for their support, hospitality, and friendship. It is, after all, not every day that an American Jew shows up at a German Protestant Theology Faculty to work. Despite the inevitable difficulties and awkwardness, they succeeded in making my years in Greifswald both enjoyable and productive, and facilitated Jewish-Christian and Jewish-German exchange and collaboration of the highest caliber. Though I no longer serve on the Greifswald faculty, I look back fondly upon the time I spent there and am proud still to consider myself, in some sense, a Greifswalder.

Bibliography

Buber, Salomon. ed. *Midrash Tehilim: ha-mekhuneh Shoḥer ṭov*. Jerusalem: Ḥ. Vagshal, 1976/7.

Busi, Giulio. "Marco Lippomano e Crescas Me'ir: Una disputa umanistica in ebraico." In *L'enigma dell'ebraico nel Rinascimento*, edited by Giulio Busi, 13–23. Turin: N. Aragno, 2007.

Busi, Giulio and Saverio Campanini. "Marco Lippomano and Crescas Meir: A Humanistic Dispute in Hebrew." In *Una manna buona per Mantova: Studi in onore di Vittore Colorni per il suo 92 compleanno*, edited by Mauro Perani, 169–202. Florence: Leo S. Olschki Editore, 2004.

Eisenstein, Judah David, ed. *Otsar Masa'ot*. New York: Eisenstein, 1926.

Glick, Caroline. "Our World: Pope Francis's Unfriendly Visit." *The Jerusalem Post*, May 27, 2014, https://www.jpost.com/Opinion/Columnists/Pope-Franciss-unfriendly-visit-354557.

Kelly, J.N.D. *Jerome: His Life, Writings, and Controversies*. New York: Harper & Row Publishers, 1975.

Palestine Royal Commission. *Minutes of Evidence Heard at Public Sessions*. London: H.M. Stationery Office, 1937.

"Pope, Netanyahu spar over Jesus' native language." *Reuters*, May 26, 2014, https://www.reuters.com/article/uk-pope-holyland-jesus- idUKKBN0E618X20140526.

Rice, Eugene F., Jr. *St. Jerome in the Renaissance*. Baltimore: Johns Hopkins University Press, 1985.

Shvat, Ari. "The Commandment to Speak Hebrew and the Use of the Holy Tongue for Secular Matters." *Shemaʿtin* 177 (Nov.-Dec. 2010): 27-50 (Hebrew).

Stein Kokin, Daniel. "Isaac ha-Kohen's Letter to Marco Lippomano: Jewish-Christian Exchange and Arabic Learning in Renaissance Italy." *Jewish Quarterly Review* 104, no. 2 (2014): 192–233.

"Wir wählen Hindenburg! Wir wählen Hitler!" Deutsches Historisches Museum. Inv.-Nr.: P 62/1072.1.

Zerubavel, Yael. *Recovered Roots: Collective Memory and the Making of Israeli National Tradition*. Chicago: The University of Chicago Press, 1995.

Steven D. Fraade
The Torah Inscribed/Transcribed in Seventy Languages

1 Introduction: The Biblical Base(s)

The following study[1] will look at early rabbinic passages that interpret a set of biblical instructions and narratives regarding the ritual inscription of the Torah (variously understood) on stones soon after the Israelites entered the Land of Israel under Joshua's leadership and following Moses's death. I will do so against the backdrop of the recent plethora of scholarship on multilingualism and translation in ancient Judaism and its broader Greco-Roman cultural context.[2]

---

[1] I had the privilege to present earlier versions of this article to academic audiences at Alfried Krupp Wissenschaftskolleg, Greifswald, Germany, Tel Aviv University (in two formats), Yale University, the Hebrew University of Jerusalem, and the University of Haifa. My thanks to the organizers of those fora and to the faculty and students who provided valuable feedback therein, some of whose specific suggestions are noted below. Special thanks to Daniel Stein Kokin for his perceptive comments and suggestions over multiple readings. After completion of this article, Katell Berthelot kindly shared with me a draft of what was then her forthcoming article, "Rabbinic Universalism Reconsidered: The Roman Context of Some Rabbinic Traditions Pertaining to the Revelation of the Torah in Different Languages," *Jewish Quarterly Review* 108 (2018): 393–421, which deals with many of the same texts, but from a somewhat different contextual perspective. After this article was finally out of my hands, Yair Furstenberg provided some insightful comments that I was only minimally able to incorporate into the printed version.
[2] I will focus on rabbinic texts of Palestinian provenance, making reference to the Babylonian Talmud where relevant. For my own previous publications on these intersecting subjects see as follows: Steven D. Fraade, "Rabbinic Views on the Practice of Targum, and Multilingualism in the Jewish Galilee of the Third–Sixth Centuries," in *The Galilee in Late Antiquity*, ed. Lee I. Levine (New York and Jerusalem: The Jewish Theological Seminary of America, 1992); "Scripture, Targum, and Talmud as Instruction: A Complex Textual Story from the Sifra," in *Hesed Ve-Emet: Studies in Honor of Ernest S. Frerichs*, ed. Jodi Magness and Seymour Gitin, Brown Judaic Studies (Atlanta: Scholars Press, 1998); "Locating Targum in the Textual Polysystem of Rabbinic Pedagogy," *Bulletin of the International Organization for Septuagint and Cognate Studies* 39 (2006); "Before and after Babel: Linguistic Exceptionalism and Pluralism in Early Rabbinic Literature," *Diné Israel* 28 (2011); "עירוב לשונות ורב־לשוניות בארץ ישראל בעת העתיקה: ממצאים ספרותיים ואפיתרפיים," *Leshonenu* 73 (2011); "Language Mix and Multilingualism in Ancient Palestine: Literary and Inscriptional Evidence," *Jewish Studies* 48 (2012); "Moses and Adam as Polyglots," in *Envisioning Judaism: Studies in Honor of Peter Schäfer on the Occasion of His Seventieth Birthday*, ed. Klaus Hermann, Ra'anan S. Boustan, Reimund Leicht, Annette Yoshiko Reed, and Giuseppe Veltri (Tübingen: Mohr Siebeck, 2013); and "The Rehov Inscriptions and Rabbinic Literature: Matters of Language," in *Talmuda De-Eretz Israel: Archaeology and the Rabbis in Late Antique Pales-*

The main biblical base text, for our present purposes, is Deut 27:1–8, part of Moses's final instructions to the Israelites, in the Land of Moab, in preparation for their entry into the Promised Land. As in much of the book of Deuteronomy, Moses's concern is for the continuity of their memory of and adherence to the narratives and laws that constitute the preceding content of that book, especially in preparation for the absence of his charismatic, prophetic leadership and of God's visible presence in their midst:

[1] וַיְצַו מֹשֶׁה וְזִקְנֵי יִשְׂרָאֵל אֶת־הָעָם לֵאמֹר שָׁמֹר אֶת־כָּל־הַמִּצְוָה אֲשֶׁר אָנֹכִי מְצַוֶּה אֶתְכֶם הַיּוֹם:

[2] וְהָיָה בַּיּוֹם אֲשֶׁר תַּעַבְרוּ אֶת־הַיַּרְדֵּן אֶל־הָאָרֶץ אֲשֶׁר־יְהוָה אֱלֹהֶיךָ נֹתֵן לָךְ וַהֲקֵמֹתָ לְךָ אֲבָנִים גְּדֹלוֹת וְשַׂדְתָּ אֹתָם בַּשִּׂיד:

[3] וְכָתַבְתָּ עֲלֵיהֶן אֶת־כָּל־דִּבְרֵי הַתּוֹרָה הַזֹּאת בְּעָבְרֶךָ לְמַעַן אֲשֶׁר תָּבֹא אֶל־הָאָרֶץ אֲשֶׁר־יְהוָה אֱלֹהֶיךָ נֹתֵן לְךָ אֶרֶץ זָבַת חָלָב וּדְבַשׁ כַּאֲשֶׁר דִּבֶּר יְהוָה אֱלֹהֵי־אֲבֹתֶיךָ לָךְ:

[4] וְהָיָה בְּעָבְרְכֶם אֶת־הַיַּרְדֵּן תָּקִימוּ אֶת־הָאֲבָנִים הָאֵלֶּה אֲשֶׁר אָנֹכִי מְצַוֶּה אֶתְכֶם הַיּוֹם בְּהַר עֵיבָל וְשַׂדְתָּ אוֹתָם בַּשִּׂיד:

[5] וּבָנִיתָ שָּׁם מִזְבֵּחַ לַיהוָה אֱלֹהֶיךָ מִזְבַּח אֲבָנִים לֹא־תָנִיף עֲלֵיהֶם בַּרְזֶל:

[6] אֲבָנִים שְׁלֵמוֹת תִּבְנֶה אֶת־מִזְבַּח יְהוָה אֱלֹהֶיךָ וְהַעֲלִיתָ עָלָיו עוֹלֹת לַיהוָה אֱלֹהֶיךָ:

[7] וְזָבַחְתָּ שְׁלָמִים וְאָכַלְתָּ שָּׁם וְשָׂמַחְתָּ לִפְנֵי יְהוָה אֱלֹהֶיךָ:

[8] וְכָתַבְתָּ עַל־הָאֲבָנִים אֶת־כָּל־דִּבְרֵי הַתּוֹרָה הַזֹּאת בַּאֵר הֵיטֵב:

[1] Moses and the elders of Israel charged the people, saying: Observe all the Instruction that I enjoin upon you this day.

[2] As soon as you have crossed the Jordan into the land that the Lord your God is giving you, you shall set up large stones. Coat them with plaster

---

tine, ed. Steven Fine and Aaron Koller, Studia Judaica (Berlin: De Gruyter, 2014). More recently and extensively, see Willem F. Smelik, *Rabbis, Language and Translation in Late Antiquity* (Cambridge: Cambridge University Press, 2013). For the broader recent study of multilingualism in Greco-Roman antiquity, see James N. Adams, Mark Janse, and Simon Swain, eds., *Bilingualism in Ancient Society: Language Contact and the Written Word* (Oxford: Oxford University Press, 2002); James N. Adams, *Bilingualism and the Latin Language* (New York: Cambridge University Press, 2003); Hannah M. Cotton et al., eds., *From Hellenism to Islam: Cultural and Linguistic Change in the Roman near East* (Cambridge: Cambridge University Press, 2009); Arietta Papaconstantinou, ed., *The Multilingual Experience in Egypt, from the Ptolemies to the Abbasids* (Farnham: Ashgate, 2010); Alex Mullen and Patrick James, eds., *Multilingualism in the Graeco-Roman Worlds* (Cambridge: Cambridge University Press, 2012); and Randall Buth and R. Steven Notley, eds., *The Language Environment of First Century Judaea: Jerusalem Studies in the Synoptic Gospels*, vol. 2, *Jewish and Christian Perspectives* 26 (Leiden: Brill, 2014).

[3] and inscribe upon them all the words of this Teaching. When you cross over to enter the land that the Lord your God is giving you, a land flowing with milk and honey, as the Lord, the God of your fathers, promised you –

[4] upon crossing the Jordan, you shall set up these stones, about which I charge you this day, on Mount Ebal, and coat them with plaster.

[5] There, too, you shall build an altar to the Lord your God, an altar of stones. Do not wield an iron tool over them;

[6] you must build the altar of the Lord your God of unhewn stones. You shall offer on it burnt offerings to the Lord your God,

[7] and you shall sacrifice there offerings of well-being and eat them, rejoicing before the Lord your God.

[8] And on those stones you shall inscribe every word of this Teaching most distinctly.[3]

Interpreters have long recognized that two sets of stones appear to be mentioned here.[4] Verses 1–4 would seem to refer to the erection of stelai, large stones with flat surfaces, which are coated with plaster, onto which are to be inscribed the words of "this Teaching," presumably the book of Deuteronomy or some antecedent form thereof. This is to take place soon, if not immediately, after crossing the Jordan River, although the specification, in v. 4, of this occurring at Mt. Ebal (more than a day's travel from the river crossing) would seem to suggest general but not immediate chronological (and geographic) proximity between crossing the Jordan and erecting, plastering, and inscribing the stones.[5] Mt. Ebal is also the site, along with Mt. Gerizim, of the immediately following ritual of blessings and curses as prescribed in Deut 27:11–28:68.

Verses 5–7 of chapter 27 would appear to refer to a different set of stones, altar stones that are unhewn (cf. Exodus 20:21–22), that is, without flat surfaces that can easily be plastered and inscribed. Therefore, to which stones (altar or stelai) does "those stones" of v. 8 refer, the altar stones as the immediate antecedents to that verse or the stelai stones of vv. 2–4 as being more appropriate for inscribing? While we might presume that v. 8 resumes the instructions for writing of vv.

---

[3] Translation from NJPS. "Teaching" here renders *torah*. Except for such citations from NJPS, I will use "Torah," without necessarily implying (pre-mishnaically) that the Pentateuch as a whole is intended. Unless otherwise noted, biblical citations are from NJPS, whereas translations of rabbinic texts are my own.
[4] The Palestinian Talmud (*Soṭah* 7:5, 21d) and the Babylonian Talmud (*Soṭah* 35b) both count three or more (but different) sets of stones.
[5] The Babylonian Talmud (*Soṭah* 36a) considers it a miracle that Israel would have covered so much ground in one day.

2–4, with the building of the altar of unhewn stones in vv. 5–7 being a narrative digression or insertion, it cannot be denied that the immediate antecedent of the stones of v. 8 are those of the altar in v. 6.[6] However we understand the editorial process (and purpose) behind the seemingly composite text as it is canonically composed,[7] later interpreters, already inner-biblically, had to determine how to understand what exactly was prescribed, that is, what was to be inscribed and where. Of course, the passage as we have it does not indicate the purpose of the inscribed stones (whichever they were), except to stress at the end of v. 8 that they were to be inscribed "most distinctly" (בַּאֵר הֵיטֵב), a phrase whose interpretation will preoccupy us shortly. At the very least, we can presume that the publicly inscribed words were intended to be read (and understood), but by whom and for how long?

These seeming textual irregularities and ambiguities in our unhewn scriptural text are smoothed out, as it were, in the account of the fulfillment of these instructions in Josh 8:30–32, but not without leaving other questions unanswered:

[30] אָז יִבְנֶה יְהוֹשֻׁעַ מִזְבֵּחַ לַיהוָה אֱלֹהֵי יִשְׂרָאֵל בְּהַר עֵיבָל:

[31] כַּאֲשֶׁר צִוָּה מֹשֶׁה עֶבֶד־יְהוָה אֶת־בְּנֵי יִשְׂרָאֵל כַּכָּתוּב בְּסֵפֶר תּוֹרַת מֹשֶׁה מִזְבַּח אֲבָנִים שְׁלֵמוֹת אֲשֶׁר לֹא־הֵנִיף עֲלֵיהֶן בַּרְזֶל וַיַּעֲלוּ עָלָיו עֹלוֹת לַיהוָה וַיִּזְבְּחוּ שְׁלָמִים:

[32] וַיִּכְתָּב־שָׁם עַל־הָאֲבָנִים אֵת מִשְׁנֵה תּוֹרַת מֹשֶׁה אֲשֶׁר כָּתַב לִפְנֵי בְּנֵי יִשְׂרָאֵל:

[30] At that time Joshua built an altar to the Lord, the God of Israel, on Mount Ebal,

[31] as Moses, the servant of the Lord, had commanded the Israelites – as is written in the Book of the Teaching of Moses – an altar of unhewn stone upon which no iron had been wielded. They offered on it burnt offerings to the Lord, and brought sacrifices of well-being.

[32] And there, on the stones, he inscribed a copy of the Teaching that Moses had written for the Israelites.

---

6 Compare the covenantal ritual of Exod 24:4–8, which similarly combines the erecting of twelve (cf. Josh 4, below) stelai (but without any mention of writing upon them) and the construction of an altar (presumably of unhewn stones) for sacrifice.

7 Michael Fishbane suggests that vv. 5–7 were inserted here so as to divert attention from the possible idolatrous nature of such erected stones (as *matsevot*; see Deut 16:22) to the more proper form of worship though sacrifice on an altar; see Michael A. Fishbane, *Biblical Interpretation in Ancient Israel* (Oxford: Oxford University Press, 1988), 161–162. Conversely, Jeffrey H. Tigay suggests that vv. 2–4 and 8, stipulating inscribed stelai, serve as brackets to vv. 5–7, stipulating sacrifices, to the effect that "the text makes clear that the terms of the Teaching, and not the sacrifice, constitute the heart of the ceremony"; see Jeffrey H. Tigay, *The JPS Torah Commentary: Deuteronomy* (Philadelphia: Jewish Publication Society, 1996), 250 and 488.

In this passage, with clear reference to the earlier passage in Deuteronomy ("as is written"), the inscribed stelai (or plaster) are not mentioned at all, leaving the only antecedent to "on the stones" to be the unhewn altar stones. It is upon those stones, at Mt. Ebal, that a "copy of the Teaching of Moses" (perhaps referring to the book of Deuteronomy) was inscribed in fulfillment of Moses's prior instructions. Should we presume from the textual sequence that the inscription on the altar stones followed sacrifice thereupon?

Prior to this passage, we find another ritual involving stones, this one without direct reference to Moses's prior instructions (Josh 4:1–8, 19–24). Here, immediately after crossing the Jordan River, God instructs Joshua to have twelve men, representing the twelve tribes, each take a stone from the river, from the places where the priests placed their feet in crossing the parted waters, and to bring them to their night encampment (מָלוֹן) at nearby Gilgal. These stones are to serve as a memorial to the miracle of the parting of the waters of the Jordan as the priests, carrying the Ark of the Covenant, crossed it. In addition, according to 4:9, another set of twelve stones were erected by Joshua in the middle of the river. However, the twelve stones set up at Gilgal are to be a reminder of God's miracle not only to the Israelites, and especially to their children who ask about their meaning,[8] but to "all the peoples of the earth" (כָּל־עַמֵּי הָאָרֶץ) (4:24). These stones, both at Gilgal and in the Jordan, unlike those of Deut 27:1–8, are entirely separate from those with which an altar is built and upon which the words of God's/Moses's Torah are inscribed (according to Josh 8:30–32), but are similarly associated with the crossing of the Jordan and the entering into the Promised Land, with the difference that those that are erected at Gilgal are to be a *permanent* reminder of God's miraculous deeds on behalf of Israel, for the future benefit of both Israel and the other peoples. What is less clear, in the book of Joshua's narration of the fulfillment of Moses's instructions, is what happened to the large plastered stelai upon which, according to the book of Deuteronomy, were to be written, very clearly, the words of the Torah.

2 Sparse Second Temple Retellings

Before turning to our earliest rabbinic sources, it should be noted that the inscribing of the Torah, or a part thereof, whether as Moses's command or Joshua's deed, leaves very few interpretive traces in the Jewish writings of the late Second Temple period that have survived, and none that focus on the manner (or purpose) of the

---

[8] As in Exod 12:26; 13:14; and Deut 6:20.

writing per se. For example, Pseudo-Philo's *Liber Antiquitatum Biblicarum* 21:7–8 harmonistically paraphrases Josh 8:30–35 in conjunction with Deut 27:1–8:

> [7] Et descendit Ihesus in Galgala, et edificavit sacrarium lapidibus fortissimis, et non intulit in eos ferrum sicuti preceperat Moyses. Et statuit lapides magnos in monte Gebal et dealbavit eos et scripsit super eos verba legis manifesta valde. Et congregavit omnem populum in unum, et legit in aures eorum omnia verba legis. [8] Et descendens cum eis levavit supra sacrarium sacrificia pacifica, et hymnizaverunt omnes valde.
>
> [7] And Joshua went down to Gilgal and built an altar with very large stones and did not lift an iron tool to them as Moses had commanded. And he set up large stones on Mt. Ebal and whitened them and wrote on them very plainly the words of the Law. And he gathered all the people together and read out loud before them all the words of the Law. [8] And he came down with them and offered peace offerings on the altar; and all sang many praises.⁹

This retelling resolves several interpretive cruxes in the scriptural sources by carefully differentiating between the plastered and clearly inscribed stone stelai erected on Mt. Ebal, and the sacrificial altar of unhewn stones at Gilgal. By contrast, our only other significant interpretation of our passages from Second Temple times, by Josephus, conflates the two, curiously combining Moses's instructions for reciting the blessings and curses of the covenant at Mts. Ebal and Gerizim with their being written, *by Moses* (perhaps conflating Deut 27:1–8 with vv. 9–10), on a sacrificial altar:

> ἀνέγραψε δὲ τὰς εὐλογίας καὶ τὰς κατάρας αὐτός, ὡς μηδέποτε ἐκλιπεῖν τὴν μάθησιν αὐτῶν ὑπὸ τοῦ χρόνου, ἃς δὴ καὶ τῷ βωμῷ τελευτῶν ἐνέγραψε κατὰ πλευρὰν ἑκατέραν, ᾗ καὶ στάντα φησὶ τὸν λαὸν θῦσαί τε καὶ ὁλοκαυτῶσαι καὶ μετ' ἐκείνην τὴν ἡμέραν οὐκ ἐπενεγκεῖν ἱερεῖον ἕτερον, οὐ γὰρ εἶναι νόμιμον.
>
> These blessings and curses he [=Moses] put on record himself, to the end that their lesson might never be abolished by time, and indeed at the last he inscribed them upon the altar, on either side even where he said that the people were to stand and offer sacrifices and whole burnt-offerings, but after that day they should offer no further victim thereupon, that being unlawful.¹⁰

---

9 For the Latin text, see Daniel J. Harrington, ed., *Pseudo-Philon, Les Antiquités bibliques, tome 1: Introduction et texte critiques*, vol. 229, Sources Chrétiennes (Paris: Éditions du Cerf, 1976), 174. English translation by Daniel J. Harrington in James H. Charlesworth, ed. *The Old Testament Pseudepigrapha*, vol. 2 (New York: Doubleday, 1985), 330.
10 Josephus, *Ant.* 4.307–308 (LCL 4:625). Josephus has one other interesting conflational paraphrase relevant to our subject. In *Ant.* 5.20 (LCL 5:11), in the context of narrating the crossing of the Jordan River under Joshua's leadership (Josh 4), Josephus states: Ἰησοῦς τε τόν τε βωμὸν ἐκ τῶν λίθων ὧν ἕκαστος ἀνείλετο τῶν φυλάρχων ἐκ τοῦ βυθοῦ τοῦ προφήτου κελεύσαντος ἱδρυσάμενος τεκμήριον γενησόμενον τῆς ἀνακοπῆς τοῦ ῥεύματος ἔθυεν ἐπ' αὐτοῦ τῷ θεῷ ("And Joshua, with the stones which each of the tribal leaders had, by the prophet's orders, taken up

Here, clearly, the inscribed words of the Torah, now limited to the blessings and curses, are inscribed on the stones of the sacrificial altar, as might be inferred from the sequence of Deut 27:1–8, and as is understood by Josh 8:30–32. Josephus stresses that the sacrifices at this altar are a *one-time* occurrence, presumably because they are not performed in a central temple, as required by the book of Deuteronomy (e.g., 12:8–12). Once the sacrifices were offered on this single occasion, the altar's only function was to continue to bear the inscription. In contrast to these sparse exegetical "rewritings" of Scripture, the early rabbinic sources to which we now turn are more explicit and direct in engaging the actual words of Scripture in its several locations, producing thereby multiple mishnaic, midrashic, and talmudic understandings of what transpired and why.

3 Mishnah Soṭah 7:5 (MS Kaufmann)

In the context of determining which ritual recitations must be said in Hebrew ("the Holy Language") and which are permitted to be recited in "any language," the Mishnah describes the procedure for the ritual recitation of blessings and curses of Deut 27:15–28:68 (which it deems can be recited only in Hebrew). As a continuation of this narrative, the Mishnah describes the inscribing of stones with the words of Torah as follows:[11]

ואחר כך הביאו את האבנים ובנו את המזבח וסדום בסיד וכתבו עליהן את כל דברי התורה הזאת [ב]שבעים
לשון שנאמר "באר היטב". ונטלו את האבנים ובאו ולנו במקומן.

---

from the river-bed, erected that altar that was to serve as a token of the stoppage of the stream, and sacrificed thereon to God"). There is nothing in Scripture, except perhaps geographic proximity, to suggest that the commemorative stones taken from the Jordan River in Josh 4:1–8 were the ones used to construct the altar in Josh 8:30–32.

11 There are no textual variants of significance between MSS Kaufmann and Parma, or the printed versions. I have treated this and the following rabbinic texts more briefly in Fraade, "Before and after Babel"; "עירוב לשונות"; "Language Mix," 9*–10*. See also Saul Lieberman, *Tosefta Ki-Fshuṭah: A Comprehensive Commentary on the Tosefta, Part 8, Order Nashim* (New York: Jewish Theological Seminary of America, 1973), 699–702; Marc Hirshman, *Torah for the Entire World* (Tel Aviv: Hakibbutz Hameuchad, 1999); Azzan Yadin, "The Hammer on the Rock: Polysemy and the School of Rabbi Ishmael," *Jewish Studies Quarterly* 10 (2003); *Scripture as Logos: Rabbi Ishmael and the Origins of Midrash*, in *Divinations: Rereading Late Ancient Religion* (Philadelphia: University of Pennsylvania Press, 2004); Smelik, *Rabbis, Language*, 29–32; Berthelot, "Rabbinic Universalism," 396–97 with notes.

> And afterward they brought the stones and built the altar and plastered it with plaster. And they wrote on them all the words of this Torah in seventy languages, as it is written, "very clearly" (Deut 27:8). And they took the stones and came and spent the night in their own place.

This mishnaic "rewritten" scriptural narrative is perplexing in several regards, in large part due to its brevity. 1. Contrary to Deut 27 and Josh 8, it suggests that the stones were inscribed *after* the ritual recitation of the blessings and curses. 2. It makes no mention of the stelai of Deut 27, but assumes that the words of Torah were inscribed on the plastered altar stones (in accord with Josh 8 and with Josephus's understanding of where Moses inscribed the blessings and curses, neither of which mentions plaster). 3. After the stones were inscribed, they were removed and brought to the place of the night encampment, presumably at Gilgal, following Josh 4:3,8, with respect to the twelve stones taken from the Jordan River. Were they there reassembled or abandoned? Perhaps the Mishnah reflects an understanding similar to that expressed by Josephus, that the altar stones inscribed with words of Torah could only serve as a sacrificial altar on one occasion. In accordance with the book of Deuteronomy's insistence on a single, centralized place for sacrificial worship, altars prior to the establishment of a centralized place of worship would be deemed temporary and in need of disassembly following their one-time use.[12] Here, as previously, the impracticality of plastering and inscribing unhewn altar stones is not considered.

4. Most striking and significant for our purposes, however, is the Mishnah's concise claim, not only that all of the words of the Torah (presumably the complete Pentateuch) were inscribed on the unhewn plastered altar stones, but that they were so inscribed in "seventy languages," that is, the full roster of human languages (of the seventy nations of Genesis 10, as rabbinically understood), with each nation identified by its language. This is explicitly said to derive from the scriptural words "most distinctly," or "very clearly" (בַּאֵר הֵיטֵב), which phrase had not attracted attention previous to the Mishnah in any of our extant sources. While the verb באר is biblically understood to refer to the physical clarity with which the words of the Torah were to be inscribed,[13] post-biblically the same verb increasingly acquires meanings relating to interpretation, as in to clarify the meaning of a text. Thus, the Mishnah seems to be saying that obtaining the clearest and fullest under-

---

12 See below, n. 42; and Lieberman, *Tosefta Ki-Fshutah*, 701.
13 See Hab 2:2; Ze'ev Ben-Hayyim, "The Contribution of the Samaritan Inheritance," in *Proceedings of the Israeli Academy of Sciences and Humanities* (1969): 166–68.

standing of the meaning of the words of the Torah requires their being inscribed (and read) in all (seventy) human "tongues."[14] Compare in this regard the use of

---

[14] Compare the use of the verb בֵּאֵר in Deut 1:5, understood by medieval exegetes (e.g., Rashi on this verse as on Deut 27:8) to mean that Moses explicated the words of Torah that he taught (to Israel) in seventy languages. See my article, "Moses and Adam as Polyglots," esp. 192–93, for the tradition that the number seventy derives by *gematria* from the word הֵיטֵב. For the typological significance of the number seventy, see Fraade, "Before and after Babel," 39*, n. 18, 48*, n. 41. For the typological significance of the "seventy nations" of Gen 10, see Nahum M. Sarna, *The JPS Torah Commentary: Genesis* (Philadelphia: Jewish Publication Society, 1989), 69, 317. For the association of nationhood with language, each nation having its own language, see Esther 1:22; 3:12; 8:9; Neh 13:23–24; Adele Berlin, *JPS Bible Commentary: Esther* (Philadelphia: Jewish Publication Society, 2001), 76. For the same association, see 4Q266 (4QDᵃ) 11 10. For the maintenance of Israelite identity through the maintenance of Hebrew while slaves in Egypt, see Mek. of R. Ishmael Pisḥa 5: Saul Horovitz and Israel Abraham Rabin, eds., *Mechilta d'Rabbi Ismael* (Frankfurt: J. Kauffmann, 1931), 14–15; but cf. Jacob Z. Lauterbach, ed., *Mekilta de-Rabbi Ishmael*. (Philadelphia: Jewish Publication Society of America, 1934–1935), 1:34–36, following MS Oxford). For its typological significance in later Jewish mysticism, see Moshe Idel, *Old Worlds, New Mirrors: On Jewish Mysticism and Twentieth-Century Thought* (Philadelphia: University of Pennsylvania Press, 2010), 172. On the later expression "seventy faces of (to) the Torah," see Hananel Mack, "The Torah Has Seventy Aspects: The Development of a Saying," in *Rabbi Mordechai Breuer Festschrift: Collected Papers in Jewish Studies*, ed. Moshe Bar-Asher (Jerusalem: Akademon, 1992): 449–62; and Shmuel Askhenazy, "Shivim Panim Le-Torah," in *Alfa Beta Kadimta De-Shmuel Zera* (Jerusalem: 2011): 844–45. For the rabbinic idea that revelation at Sinai was in simultaneously multiple (either four or seventy) languages, see Fraade, "Before and after Babel," 45*–49*. I have not been able to find any reference to "seventy languages" prior to rabbinic literature. I consider *Hebrew Testament of Naphtali* (8:3–6; 9:1) to be a medieval work in its extant form. For the Hebrew text, see Salomon A. Wertheimer, *Batei Midrashot*, 2 vols., vol. 1 (Jerusalem: Rav Kook Institute, 1950–1953), 196. For an English translation, see Harm W. Hollander and Marinus de Jonge, "Appendix I," in *The Testaments of the Twelve Patriarchs: A Commentary* (Leiden: Brill, 1985), 449. Compare *Targum Pseudo-Jonathan* (Tg. Ps.-J.) Gen 11:8; *Pirqe R. El.* 24 (Warsaw ed., 57b; trans. Friedlander, 176–77). Interestingly, the phrase is inscribed in an Aramaic magical bowl (possibly Manichaean): Charles D. Isbell, *Corpus of the Aramaic Incantation Bowls* (Missoula, MT: Scholars Press, 1975); Jason D. BeDuhn, "Magical Bowls and Manichaeans," in *Ancient Magic and Ritual Power*, ed. Marvin Meyer and Paul Mirecki (Leiden: Brill, 1995): 419. My thanks to Sara Ronis for bringing this to my attention. For an early Christian, but possibly Jewishly dependent, reference, see *Pseudp-Clementine, Homilies* 18.4 (brought to my attention by Yakir Paz), where the seventy languages of the seventy nations are linked to the seventy descendants of Jacob who went to Egypt (as per Gen 46:27; Exod 1:5; Deut 10:22). The same association is made in *Tg. Ps.-J.* Deut 32:8, as in Sarna, *Genesis*, 69. For further on seventy languages, see Louis Ginzberg, *Legends of the Jews*, vol. 5 (Philadelphia: Jewish Publication Society, 1953), 194–95, n. 72. For there being 140 nations/languages (brought to my attention by Gideon Bohak), see *Sifre Deut.* 311 (ed. Finkelstein, 352); *Song. Rab.* 6.19 (to 6:8); *Num. Rab.* 9.14; Saul Lieberman, *Greek in Jewish Palestine* (New York: Philipp Feldheim, 1965); Daniel Sperber, *Magic and Folkore in Rabbinic Literature* (Ramat-Gan, Israel: Bar-Ilan University Press, 1994); Ginzberg, 5, 195. For an association between nation and language, already before Babel, see Gen 10:31. Gen 11:7 could be read similarly. For the rabbinic view

מְפֹרָשׁ in Neh 8:8 for Ezra's clear reading of the Torah, rendered as "made distinct" by BDB, as "with interpretation" by NRSV, and as "translating it" by NJPS.[15]

Leaving aside, again, the seeming impracticality of such a vastly multilingual inscription, we might want to speculate on what philosophy of language in general, or of revelatory language in particular, is being suggested or presumed here. The mishnaic text in its extreme but characteristic brevity provides little direct assistance to us in this task.[16] There is, as already noted by Willem Smelik,[17] an irony here, that in the mishnaic context of emphasizing that the ritual recitation of the scriptural blessings and curses was to be in Hebrew alone, the proximate (and in some sources, interlaced) ritual of writing the words of Torah as a whole was to be performed in all seventy languages, an irony with which other rabbinic versions of this tradition, as we shall soon see, appear to wrestle. Which is to say that in all of these regards, the Mishnah is as much interpreting (and interweaving elements of) its three biblical antecedents (Deut 27:1–8; Josh 4:1–8; Josh 8:30–32) as offering up, as it were, its own text for subsequent interpretation.

4 Mishnah Sheqalim 5:1 (MS Kaufmann, with later gloss)

The expression "seventy languages" appears only once elsewhere in the Mishnah, unrelated to the inscribed stones of Deuteronomy and Joshua, but very telling for our purposes nevertheless:[18]

---

that humans spoke seventy languages even before Babel, based on Gen 11:1, see y. (= Jerusalem or Palestinian Talmud) Meg. 1:11 (71b) (ed. Academy of the Hebrew Language, 748), discussed by Fraade, "Before and After Babel, 42*–43*.

15 For the last, see y. Meg. 4.1, 74d and parallels: מפורש זה תרגום ("'clearly,' that is the translation [*Targum*]"), as rendered by Smelik, *Rabbis, Language*, 195. See below, n. 44.

16 The idea seems remarkably similar (*mutatis mutandis*) to Walter Benjamin's conceptions of language and translation, as expressed in his essays, "The Task of the Translator," in *Selected Writings, Vol. 1: 1913–1926*, ed. Marcus Block and Michael Jennings (Cambridge, MA: Harvard University Press, 1997), 253–262; and "On Language as Such and on the Language of Man," in *Selected Writings, Vol. 1*, 62–74. For explication, see Carol Jacobs, *In the Language of Walter Benjamin* (Baltimore: Johns Hopkins University Press, 1999), esp. 75–90.

17 Smelik, *Rabbis, Language*, 32.

18 There are no textual variants of significance between MSS Kaufmann and Parma. The words in parentheses, presumably an explanatory gloss, appear in the printed versions.

אלו הן הממונין שהיו במקדש . . . פתחיה על הקינין (פתחיה זה מרדכי) למה נקרא שמו פתחיה שהיה פותח
בדברים ודורשן ויודע שבעים לשון . . .

> These are the officers who served in the Temple: . . . Petaḥiah was over the bird-offerings. (This same Petaḥiah was Mordechai.)[19] Why was his name Petaḥiah? Because he would "open" (*poteaḥ*) matters, and interpret (*doresh*) them, and/for he knew seventy languages.

As in the previously considered mishnah, seventy languages are again associated, although less directly, with the activity of interpretation, previously expressed by *be'er*, now by *darash* (and *pataḥ*). Although not linked explicitly, Petaḥiah's interpretive renown is associatively connected to his knowledge of seventy (that is, all human) languages.[20] Mordechai, which, according to a second-hand explanatory gloss, is Petaḥiah's cognomen, refers to the person by this name who is mentioned in Ezra 2:2 and Neh 7:7 as being among those who returned with Zerubbabel from the Babylonian Exile. His name is immediately followed by that of Bilshan. However, if the two are taken as one name, then, by a word play it could mean that said Morechai was a master of languages (*ba'al lashon*), or even a mixer of languages (*balal lashon*). Thus, in both mishnaic passages, the knowledge of seventy languages is of assistance (or even necessity) in being able to fully clarify/interpret the meaning of texts or matters in general (*m. Sheqalim*), and of Scripture in particular (*m. Soṭah*).

5 Tosefta Soṭah 8:6–7 (MS Vienna, ed. Lieberman, 205)

We turn next to the Tosefta that is closely connected to Mishnah Soṭah 7:5. As is often the case with Mishnah-Tosefta "parallels," the precise nature of their relationship (and chronological priority) is difficult to determine. To indicate two commonly proposed possibilities, does the Tosefta presume the Mishnah (or

---

19 This gloss is not in MS Kaufmann or the other early manuscripts.
20 For other individuals who are said, in rabbinic literature, to have known all seventy languages, see Fraade, "Before and after Babel," 55*–58*; and Fraade, "Moses and Adam as Polyglots." On this expression, see above, n. 14. For the knowledge of multiple languages as an aid to interpreting Scripture through multilingual word plays, see Fraade, "Before and after Babel," 47*, n. 38; Fraade, "Moses and Adam as Polyglots," 188. For the verb *pataḥ* denoting exegetical activity, see Paul Mandel, "על 'פתח' ועל הפתיחה: עיון חדש", in *Higayon L'Yonah: New Aspects in the Study of Midrash, Aggadah and Piyut in Honor of Professor Yona Fraenkel*, ed. Joshua Levinson, Jacob Elbaum, and Galit Hasan-Rokem (Jerusalem: Magnes, 2006), 49–82, esp. 56.

an antecedent), which it seeks to expand and/or interpret, or does the Tosefta represent the sort of "raw materials" from which the more concise and tightly-structured Mishnah was editorially fashioned?[21] In the present case, either is possible but neither is certain.[22] Therefore, I will treat them as autonomous texts in their own rights. Unlike the anonymous Mishnah, the Tosefta takes the form of *two* accounts of the inscribing of the stones, each attributed to a different (but contemporaneous) tannaitic sage:[23]

[6] ר' יהודה אומ' על אבני מזבח כתבוה. אמרו לו היאך למדו אותן אומות העולם את התורה. אמ' להן מלמד שנתן המקום בלב כל אומה ומלכות ושלחו נוטורים[24] שלהם והשיאו את הכתב מגבי אבנים בשבעים לשון. באותה שעה נתחתם גזר דינם של אומות העולם לבאר שחת.

[7] ר' שמעון או' על הסיד כתבו. כיצד, כירוהו וסדוהו בסיד, וכתבו עליו את כל דברי התורה בשבעים לשון, וכתבו מלמטה "למען אשר לא ילמדו אתכם" וגו', אם אתם חוזרין בכם, אנו מקבלין אתכם.

[6] R. Judah says: They inscribed it [=the Torah] on the stones of the altar. They said to him: How did the nations of the world learn the Torah? He said to them: This teaches that the Omnipresent inspired every nation and kingdom to send their notaries (scribes) and they transcribed the writing from the stones in seventy languages. At that moment the verdict was sealed for the destruction of the nations of the world.

[7] R. Simeon says: They wrote it on plaster. How so? They laid it out and plastered it with plaster, and they wrote on it all the words of the Torah in seventy languages,[25] and they wrote below, "That they teach you not [to do after all their abominations]" (Deut 20:18): "If you [non-Jews] repent, we shall receive you."

Unlike *m. Soṭah* 7:5, which, I have argued (especially in light of *M. Sheqalim* 5:1) understands the recording of the Torah in seventy languages to have an interpretive function (within Israel), both views in the Tosefta understand the purpose of the inscription (or transcription) of the Torah in seventy languages to have been to make it accessible to the (seventy) "nations of the world." Note that *unlike in the Mishnah*, neither R. Judah nor R. Simeon makes reference to "seventy languages" as deriving from the scriptural words בַּאֵר הֵיטֵב ("very distinctly") of Deut

---

21 For discussion of this question, with extensive bibliography of recent scholarship thereto, see Fraade "Before and after Babel," 54*–55*.
22 Cf. Judith Hauptman, *Rereading the Mishnah: A New Approach to Ancient Jewish Texts*, Texts and Studies in Ancient Judaism (Tübingen: Mohr Siebeck 2005), 109–24. She sees our Mishnah as a condensing of our Tosefta; Smelik rejects this view in *Rabbis, Language*, 32, n. 69.
23 Smelik strangely treats what is attributed to R. Judah, but not what is attributed to R. Simeon, in Smelik, *Rabbis, Language*, 31.
24 I read as נוטרים = *notarii*. MS Erfurt has נטירין. See Lieberman's note ad loc.
25 "In seventy languages" does not appear in MS Erfurt.

27:8.²⁶ It may be that in an earlier version of the disagreement between R. Judah and R. Simeon, their dispute was limited to the question of where the words of the Torah were inscribed (stones or plaster), without reference to the nations as readers or copyists of the inscription. Whereas R. Judah is explicit in saying that the words of the Torah were written upon the altar stones, R. Simeon says that they were written upon the plaster, which in light of Deut 27:2,4 would seem to mean on the stelai, but in light of *m. Soṭah* 7:5 could mean on the altar.

In its present redacted setting, R. Judah seems to be saying (the syntax is somewhat ambiguous) that what was written on the stones was the Torah in Hebrew alone, and that God inspired the (seventy) nations to send their (seventy) scribes (*notarim*, notaries) to transcribe (literally, "lift"²⁷) through spontaneous translation the Hebrew writing, each one into the language of his particular nation.²⁸ However, the purpose of making the Torah available to the nations in their own languages was hardly altruistic, but to guarantee their divine punishment for transgressing its laws by denying them the claim that they were innocent by virtue of not having had access to (that is, comprehension of) the Torah in their native tongues. Without such an excuse (that is, with a Torah in their own languages), their doom is *immediately* sealed for their lawlessness, as it were.²⁹

---

26 However, it is likely that the phrase בְּאֵר שַׁחַת ("nethermost pit"; e.g., Ps 55:24) is an ironic word play on בַּאֵר הֵיטֵב ("very distinctly") of Deut 27:8, based on their sharing the consonantal homograph באר.

27 For this understanding of the *hiph'il* of the verb נשא, see Marcus Jastrow, *A Dictionary of the Targum, the Talmud Babli and Jerushalmi, and the Midrashic Literature* (New York: Choreb, 1926), 938, citing our passage. See also Saul Lieberman, *Studies in Palestinian Literature* (Jerusalem: Magnes, 1991), 57–58; Shlomo Naeh, "טובים דודיך מיין׳: מבט חדש על משנת עבודה זרה ב, ה׳," in *Studies in Talmudic and Midrashic Literature in Memory of Tirzah Lifshitz*, ed. M. Bar-Asher, J. Levinson, and B. Lifshitz (Jerusalem: Bialik Institute, 2005): 418, n. 24. Similarly, see Smelik, *Rabbis, Language*, 31 and 168–69. He ignores the view of R. Simeon (the whole Torah written in seventy languages) in t. (= Tosefta) *Soṭah* 8:7. According to the Babylonian Talmud (*Soṭah* 35b), and attributed to R. Judah, the inscription was made directly to the stones, after which it was plastered over. The notaries of the nations came and peeled off the plaster layer, onto which a (reverse) copy of the inscription was impressed, and carried this back (השיאוה) with them to their respective peoples.

28 Alternatively, the Torah is already written in seventy languages on the stones, and notaries simply transcribe the translation that suits their nation. It is a question of whether "in seventy languages" modifies adjectivally "the writing," or whether it modifies adverbially "lifted." I favor the latter as better fitting the word order, but cannot deny the possibility of the former. We will see the same ambiguity in the Palestinian Talmud, but there the wording seems to me to favor the former understanding. For the Babylonian Talmud's understanding of this "lifting," see above, n. 27.

29 Cf. Saul Lieberman, *Hellenism in Jewish Palestine: Studies in the Literary Transmission, Beliefs and Manners of Palestine in the I Century B.C.E. – IV Century C.E.*, 2nd ed. (New York: Jewish Theological Seminary of America, 1962), 201.

By contrast, R. Simeon's understanding is that the Torah in all seventy languages was inscribed on plastered stones (whichever), but that the purpose of so doing was more irenic: the nations whose doom has not yet been sealed now have an opportunity to learn from Israel's Torah, translated into their languages, so that they may have the opportunity to repent (remove their abominations) and be received, rather than be destroyed (as per Deut 20:15–18).

In light of a recent (2012) study of notaries in the Greco-Roman world, particularly in Egypt,[30] more can be said of R. Judah's version of the story. Each such notary, sent by his respective nation (אומה וממלכות), need not have known all seventy languages, but only two: the Hebrew of the Torah and the language of the nation that sent him. That is, at the very least they can be presumed to have been bilingual. It is only collectively that they represented the linguistic totality of seventy languages (necessary, according to the Mishnah, for the full comprehension of the Torah). In real life, of course, such notaries would have had facility in the language of the ruling empire (e.g., Greek, or, in an earlier period, Imperial Aramaic) and their local language (e.g., Egyptian) and the ability to translate between the two in both directions. Thus, the story as attributed to R. Judah places Hebrew (Israel) in the position of the imperial language (and rulers), rather than that of one subject language/people among many, a fantasy of great significance for the privileged place of Hebrew (and the identity of Hebrew speakers, readers, or auditors) among the languages (and peoples) of the world.

I wish to emphasize that this version of the story might be thought of as a clever inversion of the famous story of the translation of the Torah into Greek (the "Septuagint") in Ptolemaic times (mid-third century BCE), as it was surely known to the early rabbinic sages.[31] Rather than the Jerusalemite priesthood sending seventy-two

---

30 Marja Vierros, *Bilingual Notaries in Hellenistic Egypt: A Study of Greek as a Second Language*, Collectanea Hellenistica (Brussels: Koninklijke Vlaamse Academie van België voor Wetenschappen en Kunsten, 2012).

31 See *Mekilta of R. Ishmael Pisḥa* 14 (ed. Lauterbach, 1:111–12); *y. Meg.* 1.9, 71d; *b.* (= Babylonian Talmud) *Meg.* 9a–b; *Mas. Sop.* 1.7 (6–8); *Mas. Sep. Torah* 1:6 (8–9); for the last two sources, see Michael Higger, ed., *Seven Minor Treatises; Sefer Torah, Mazuzah, Tefillin, Zizit, 'Abadim, Kutim, Gerim, and Treatise Soferim II* (New York, 1930), 100-05 and 22–24, respectively. There is extensive scholarly literature on the rabbinic use of this story, which originates with the *Letter of Aristeas* in the mid-second century BCE (but narrating events of a century earlier). Most recently, see Abraham Wasserstein and David J. Wasserstein, *The Legend of the Septuagint: From Classical Antiquity to Today* (New York: Cambridge University Press, 2006); Giuseppe Veltri, "Deconstructing History and Traditions: The Written Torah for Ptolemy," in *Libraries, Translations and "Canonic" Texts: The Septuagint, Aquila and Ben Sira in the Jewish and Christian Traditions*, ed. Giuseppe Veltri, JSJSup (Leiden: Brill, 2006); Moshe Simon-Shoshan, "The Task of the Translators: The Rabbi, the Septuagint, and the Cultural Politics of Translation," *Prooftexts* 27 (2007); and Richard Kalmin, "The Miracle of the Sep-

(but often referred to as seventy) elders from the Land of Israel to Alexandria at the bidding of the Ptolemaic king to produce there a single, authoritative (and possibly inspired) translation into Greek, for the benefit of Jews and non-Jews alike, here the seventy nations, at the bidding (and possible inspiration) of the sovereign of all nations, send each one a notary/translator to the Land of Israel so as to produce seventy[32] different translations of the Hebrew original with, according to R. Judah's telling, disastrous consequences for all but Israel.[33] Compare the expression used here for God's inspiring of the nations, שנתן המקום בלב כל אומה ומלכות (and in the version in the Palestinian Talmud, to be treated shortly: נתן הקב״ה בינה בלב כל אומה ואומה), with that used in *Mas. Sop.* 1:8 for the inspiration of the seventy-two elders gathered by King Ptolemy: נתן המקום עצה בלב כל אחד ואחד ("God placed guidance in the heart of each and every one"). Needless to say, this narrative places the origins of scriptural translation much earlier than Ptolemaic times, in the time of Joshua but in fulfillment of the command of Moses, as if to say that the totality of scriptural translation is a homegrown Israelite innovation, rather than a foreign import. Also, no single translation (e.g., into Greek) is privileged over any other, with the benefit of all such seventy translations to their intended foreign audiences being dubious at best.

6 Mekilta Deuteronomy (Geniza Fragment, ed. Kahana, 345)

We turn next to the last of our tannaitic sources, a Cairo Geniza fragment of a lost commentary to the book of Deuteronomy from the midrashic "school" of R. Ishmael. Discovered by Solomon Schechter and published by him in 1911, it was since lost, no small irony for our purposes, as we shall see. Saul Lieberman improved on Schechter's reconstruction, and it was most recently published by Menahem Kahana.[34] Any interpretations of the fragment must be qualified by recognition of its highly fragmentary and restored nature:

---

tuagint in Ancient Rabbinic and Christian Literatures," in *Follow the Wise: Studies in Jewish History and Culture in Honor of Lee Levine*, ed. Zeev Weiss, et al. (Winona Lake, IN: Eisenbrauns, 2010).
32 There is some ambiguity whether the seventy nations/languages include Israel/Hebrew or not. Needless to say (see above, n. 14), "seventy" is a typological number, regardless of whether it is "actually" sixty-nine, seventy-one, or seventy-two.
33 For the notion that the translation of the Torah into Greek had disastrous consequences for Israel, see *Mas. Sop.* 1:7; *Mas. Sep. Torah* 1:6; *Pesiq. Rab.* 5 (ed. Meir Friedmann, 14b; trans. William Braude, 93; ed. Rivka Ulmer, 51–52).
34 Solomon Schechter, "The Mekhilta Deuteronomy, Pericope Re'eh," in *Tif'eret Ysra'el: Festschrift Zu Israel Lewy's Siebzigsten Geburtstag*, ed. M. Brann and J. Elbogen (Breslau: M. & H.

בו ביום עברו ישראל את הירדן ונטלו את האבנים והעבירום והעמידום וכתבו על [האבנים] אֵת כל דברי התורה [בלשון הקדש]. ר׳ ישמעאל אומ׳ בשבעים לשון כתבו [שנ׳ "באר היטב"]. רבי שמעון בן יוחאי א׳ לא כתבו עליה[ן] א[ל]א את משנה[] תורת משה שנ׳ "ויכתב שם על האבנים את משנה תורת משה" וג׳. ר׳ יוסה בן יוסי אומ׳ משום ר׳ אלעזר בן שמעון לא כתבו עליהן אלא מה שאומות העולם רוצין כגון "כי תקרב אל עיר להלחם עליה וקראת עליה לשלום אם שלום תענך" וג׳. "כי תצור אל עיר ימים רבים" וג׳. על [אבני] [המזב]ח כתבום דברי ר׳ יודה. ר׳ שמעון א׳ על האבנים כתבום. [אמ׳] [ר׳ נרא]ין דברי ר׳ שמעון שאמר על האבנים [כתבום] [שנ׳ "על] האבנים" מדברי ר׳ יודה שאמר על המזבח כתבום. שאלו [על] המזבח כתבום האיך היו אומות העולם רוצין לקרות דין. [ולמטה כת׳] עליהם כת׳ "כל הרוצה לקבל ימין יבוא ויקבל" וגנזום בו ביום.

On the same day that Israel crossed the Jordan, they took the stones, brought them across, and erected them and wrote on [the stones] all the words of the Torah [in the Holy Language]. R. Ishmael says, They wrote in seventy languages, [as it is said, "most distinctly" (Deut 27:8)]. R. Simeon b. Yoḥai says, They did not write on the[m bu]t [a copy] of the Torah of Moses (or: the book of Deuteronomy), as it is said, "And there, on the stones, he inscribed a copy of the Torah of Moses" (Josh 8:32). R. Yose b. Yosi[35] says in the name of R. Eleazar b. Simeon, They did not write on them but that which the nations of the world desired, such as, "When you approach a town to attack it, you shall offer it terms of peace. If it responds peaceably," etc. (Deut 20:10–11); "When you besiege a city for a long time," etc. (Deut 20:19). They wrote them on [the stones] [of the alta]r. These are the words of R. Judah. R. Simeon says, They wrote them on the stones (cf. Deut 27:2–4). [Said] [Rabbi (Judah the Patriarch?) I prefer] the words of R. Simeon, who said, They wrote them on the stones, to the words of R. Judah, who said, They wrote them on the altar. For if they had written them [on] the altar, how could the nations of the world who desired to read the law (been able to do so)? [At the bottom was written] on them: "Whoever wishes to receive right (forgiveness) shall come and receive!"[36] But the very same day they hid them (the stones of the altar) away.

To begin with, unlike the Mishnah and the view of R. Judah according to the Tosefta, the anonymous opening voice of the *Mekilta Deuteronomy* fragment endorses the view that the Torah was inscribed (presumably in Hebrew) on the stelai (or possibly the stones removed from the Jordan River according to Josh 4). By contrast, R. Ishmael, citing Deut 27:8 (and the Mishnah's interpretation thereof), affirms that the Torah was inscribed on the stones (without specifying which) *in seventy languages*. I assume that the only difference between the anonymous opening and R. Ishmael is whether what was actually written on the stones (presumably the stelai) was the Torah (in its entirety) just in Hebrew (anonymous) or in

---

Marcus, 1911); Lieberman, *Tosefta Ki-Fshuṭah*, 700–01; Menahem I. Kahana, *The Geniza Fragments of the Halakhic Midrashim. Part I: Mekhilta d'Rabbi Ishmaʿel, Mekhilta d'Rabbi Shimʿon Ben Yohay, Sifre Numbers, Sifre Zuta Numbers, Sifre Deuteronomy, Mekhilta Deuteronomy* (Jerusalem: Magnes, 2005), 345.

35 As Lieberman notes (*Tosefta Ki-Fshuṭah*, 700, n. 17.), no tannaitic sage by this name is otherwise known to us, whether as Yose or Yosi, the two being variants of the same name.

36 On the difficulties of the text here, see Lieberman, *Tosefta Ki-Fshuṭah*, 701, n. 19.

all seventy languages (R. Ishmael, echoing R. Simeon of the Tosefta). By contrast, I understand R. Simeon of *Mekilta Deuteronomy* to say (following the wording of Josh 8:32) that it was only the book of Deuteronomy (מִשְׁנֵה תּוֹרַת מֹשֶׁה), and not the whole Pentateuch, that was inscribed (presumably on the stelai), leaving unclear whether it was just in Hebrew or in seventy languages.

Strikingly different from any of the views thus far expressed as to how much was inscribed, and without parallel elsewhere, is the view of R. Eleazar b. Simeon, as transmitted by R. Yose b. Yosi, that all that was written (presumably both in Hebrew and the other languages) were several scriptural verses that relate somewhat sympathetically to non-Israelites in time of war.[37] Alternatively, it is only such "universal" laws of warfare that would interest the bellicose nations, with anything else being wasted on them.[38] Since these verses, or at least their being recorded here, are intended for the "ears" of the nations, they are presumably recorded in seventy languages, although this is not stated explicitly. This is reminiscent of Josh 4:24, in which the erecting of commemorative stones is intended for the benefit of "all the peoples of the earth" (כָּל־עַמֵּי הָאָרֶץ). Thus far we have seen three different attitudes toward the non-Jews for whom the translated words of Torah are intended: cynical (only to condemn them), irenic (so they might repent and be "received" by Israel), and apologetic (only to convey to them what they want to hear), the last being possibly insulting or mocking as well.[39]

Again we encounter the persistent question of which stones were written upon, with R. Judah favoring the stones of the altar (as in the Mishnah), R. Simeon favoring the stelai, and Rabbi (Judah the Patriarch?) preferring the words of R. Simeon (the stelai). Rabbi (Judah the Patriarch?) explains his preference for the view of R. Simeon (stelai; contra the Mishnah) as follows: had the words of Torah been written on the stones of the altar, they would not have remained there for long, since the inscribed altar stones would have been removed immediately

---

37 Lieberman (Lieberman, *Hellenism in Jewish Palestine*, 201–02) refers to these as "international law." While we do not know, how many such verses R. Yose had in mind, what is cited being examples of a larger class, we can presume that the challenge of insufficient space for the inscription(s) was significantly mitigated by such a narrow selection of verses. Note that Deut 20:15–18, calling for the genocide of the native nations, is elided in this selection of verses. Compare *Gen. Rab.* 74.15 (ed. Theodor-Albeck, 872–73), where it is said that in David's time, the Edomites and Moabites produced stelai (אסטליות) inscribed with Torah verses (Deut 2:3 and 2:9) that are favorable to these nations in avoiding combat with them.
38 I thank Daniel Stein Kokin for this suggestion.
39 Respectively: R. Judah in the Tosefta, R. Simeon in the Tosefta, and R. Yose b. Yosi in the name of R. Eleazar b. Simeon in *Mekilta Deuteronomy*.

after the one-time sacrifices were completed, as stated in the Mishnah (reflecting Josh 4:3,8). On this reading of Rabbi (Judah the Patriarch?)'s reading of R. Judah, even the irenic view of the public writing of the Torah in seventy languages (on the altar stones), so as to provide an opportunity for the nations to follow the Torah and be received by Israel (as per the added subscript of the inscription), was in reality a cynical, if not duplicitous, ploy, since the altar stones (with the Torah inscribed in seventy languages) did not remain in place for long enough to accomplish that purpose, as the midrash's conclusion confirms in its statement that the altar stones were "hidden away" (*ganzum*, from the same root as *geniza*) on the very same day that they were inscribed. But what of R. Simeon's implied view that the Torah (or at least the book of Deuteronomy), inscribed on stelai, remained accessible to the nations for some time? Did its inscription similarly have a subscript (as per the Tosefta) holding out the hope of the nations' repentance and acceptance? Or was it too simply a cynical ploy? Our fragmentary text eludes us on these questions.

As for the other (non-irenic) views represented here, the inscribing of the Torah in seventy languages was either to condemn the nations for their transgression or to gain their appreciation (however briefly?), or, alternatively, to mock them for their war-making, but not to join with them in the practice of Torah since that opportunity, according to this midrash in its final lines, was not truly provided to them. Perhaps it is an irony of history that Rabbi (Judah the Patriarch?)'s frank uncovering of the duplicitous nature of the seemingly irenic public disclosure of the Torah in seventy languages is found only in this largely unknown ancient midrash, which was itself "hidden away" in the Cairo Geniza in medieval times, only to be discovered (and lost again) much more recently.[40]

---

[40] I have incorporated here some suggestions of Daniel Stein Kokin. Menahem Kahana has argued that at least for some non-legal sections (*Hăazinu* and *Ve-Zo't Ha-berakha*) Mekhilta Deuteronomy is more "universalistic" in its attitude toward non-Jews than is *Sifre Deuteronomy* to the same verses. See "דפים מן המכילתא לדברים פרשיות האזינו וזאת הברכה," *Tarbiz* 57 (1988). See also Menahem Kahana, "The Halakhic Midrashim," in *The Literature of the Sages: Second Part: Midrash and Targum, Liturgy, Poetry, Mysticism, Contracts, Inscriptions, Ancient Science and the Languages of Rabbinic Literature*, ed. S. Safrai, et al. (Assen: Royal Van Gorcum, 2006): 51–52. A similar argument, it seems to me, cannot be made here, in part because the *Sifre*'s commentary to Deut 27:1–8 is not extant.

7 Palestinian Talmud Soṭah 7:5, 21d (ed. Academy of the Hebrew Language, 935–36)

Several familiar traditions, but with some new twists, are found in the Palestinian Talmud, presented as a barayta, as follows:

> תני. על אבני המלון נכתבו. דברי רבי יודה. רבי יוסי אומר. על אבני המזבח נכתבו. מאן דמר על אבני המלון נכתבו בכל יום ויום אומ׳ העולם משלחין נוטריהן ומשיאין את התורה שהיתה כתובה בשבעים לשון. מאן דמר על אבני המזבח נכתבו. לא לשעה היו וגנגזו. עוד הוא מעשה ניסים. נתן הקב״ה בינה בלב כל אומה ואומה והשיאו את התורה שהיתה כתובה בשבעים לשון.

It was taught: [The words of the Torah] were written on the stones of the lodging place (Josh 4:3,8). These are the words of R. Judah. R. Yosi says: They were written on the stones of the altar. [With respect to] the one who says that they were [permanently] written on the stones of the lodging: Every day the nations of the world would send their notaries, who would transcribe the Torah which was written in seventy languages . [With respect to] the one who says that they were written on the altar, [how can this be?] Were they not (there) for only a short time before they were hidden away? [Rather,] this was another miracle. The Holy One, blessed be He, gave insight into the heart of each and every nation so that they transcribed the Torah that was written in seventy languages.

The disagreement over which stones were inscribed with the words of the Torah continues, although here R. Judah is associated with the view that the inscribed stones were those of the night encampment (Josh 4:3,8), presumably the stelai at Gilgal, whereas in the Tosefta he was credited with the view that they were the altar stones at Mt. Ebal. Here that position is attributed instead to R. Yose. In the first case it is assumed that the inscription was on *permanent display*, and that every day (and without rush) the seventy notaries of the seventy nations could transcribe the Torah, each in his own native language.[41] However, this would not seem to be possible according to the view that the Torah was inscribed on the altar stones, since they would have been disassembled and hidden away once the sacrifices had been performed.[42] It is in this event that God needed to inspire the notaries (presumably) so that they could miraculously complete their task of transcription and translation in the shortest possible time. Thus, in either case, whether of inscribing on the altar stones (and being divinely inspired) or on the stelai (and having plenty of time), the notaries would have succeeded at their task of either transcribing or translating the Torah in seventy languages.

---

41 On my understanding of this verb as to transcribe and translate, and of the ambiguous syntax, see above, at and in nn. 27, 28.
42 See above, at and in n. 12.

However, the Palestinian Talmud does not indicate whether the intent of the translations (that is, of God's inspiring the nations or their notaries to transcribe the Torah) was to condemn the nations for their knowing transgressions (as attributed to R. Judah in the Tosefta), or to allow for their repentance and acceptance by Israel (as attributed to R. Simeon in the Tosefta and in *Mekilta Deuteronomy*). My sense is that the tone of the Palestinian Talmud is more irenic than that of either the Tosefta or *Mekilta Deuteronomy*, since it removes the obstacle of insufficient time to complete the task of transcription/translation, whether on altar stones or stelai, without indicating any others.

8 Palestinian Targumim to Deuteronomy 27:8 (Fragmentary Targum MS Paris, ed. Klein, 111)

Finally, let us hear from those who translated the Torah into Aramaic, choosing one example that is representative of the Palestinian tradition.

ותכתבון על אבניא ית כל מילי שבח אוריתא הדא כתב חקק ומפרש טבא מתקרי בחד לישן ומתורגם בשבעין לישן.

> And you shall inscribe upon the stones all of the words of praise of this Torah, in engraved writing and very distinct; to be read in one language and translated into seventy languages.[43]

In rendering the key phrase בַּאֵר הֵיטֵב ("most distinctly"), the Targum employs a double translation, first fairly (but slightly expansively) literal as "in engraved writing and very distinct," before moving on to a more expansive gloss, "to be read in one language and translated into seventy languages."[44] This confirms my earlier understanding of the use of the verb נשא in the *hiphʿil* (by R. Judah in the Tosefta and, less certainly, in the Palestinian Talmud), as denoting that the words of Torah that were written on (and directly read from) the stones were in Hebrew alone, whereas what was "lifted" from the stones by the notaries were spontane-

---

43 Much the same translation is found in other manuscripts of *Fragmentary Targum* (*Frg. Tg.*) and from the Cairo Geniza, as well as in *Tg. Ps-Jon*. However, *Targum Neofiti* (*Tg. Neof.*) and *Frg. Tg.* MS Vatican are slightly different, as I will note below. *Tg. Onqelos*, the *Peshiṭta*, and the Samaritan *Tg.* are all fairly literal, lacking the targumic glosses that I will highlight.

44 For מפרש here as denoting the clarity of writing (and not interpretive exposition), see Michael Sokoloff, *A Dictionary of Jewish Palestinian Aramaic of the Byzantine Period*, 2nd ed. (Ramat-Gan: Bar-Ilan University Press, 2002), 451 ("explicitly written"); Sokoloff, *A Dictionary*, 213 ("engraved writing"). See also above, n. 15.

ous translations into seventy (or sixty-nine) languages.[45] Only the Hebrew was privileged to be inscribed and read aloud (in public?) to all, whereas each of the individual translations was intended for the use of its particular linguistic society alone. Of course, given the relatively compact nature of the targumic translation, most of the questions that are addressed in other rabbinic sources (on which stones was the Torah inscribed?; how much of the Torah was inscribed?; for how long was it on public display?; for what purpose was the Torah made available in translation to the nations?) are not addressed here. That makes all the more remarkable what it *does* address: the difference between what was written on and read directly from the stones (whichever) – the Torah in Hebrew – and what was subsequently translated spontaneously – the seventy translations.[46] Significantly, this is very similar to the rabbinically prescribed practice of *reading* Scripture from a written scroll and orally *reciting* Targum, without such a written aid, as part of the synagogue service.[47] It is as if the written text of the Targum here authorizes its own oral liturgical practice.

9 Conclusions

We have seen two fundamentally different attitudes toward multilingual scriptural translation in the rabbinic texts herein surveyed. The first is typified by the Mishnah (and other early rabbinic texts on the multilingual nature of revelation, as I have discussed elsewhere[48]). According to it, it is in the very nature of the language of revelation (if not of language more broadly[49]) that inter-lingual translation (and maximally/ideally translation into every language) is necessary in order to fully uncover the deep plenitude of scriptural meaning. The second is typified (but with significant variations) by the other rabbinic texts that we have examined as interpre-

---

45 See above, nn. 27, 28, 32.
46 *Tg. Neof.* departs slightly from this translation, being less explicit in this regard: ומתקרא ומתרגם בשבעים לשן ("to be read and translated into seventy languages"). However, this most likely has the same meaning: "to be read [in Hebrew] and [thereafter] translated into seventy languages." The same is true for *Frg. Tg.* MS Vatican.
47 A similar point is made by Smelik, *Rabbis, Language,* 30. For the practice of Targum in ancient synagogues according to rabbinic literature, see Philip S. Alexander, "The Targumim and Rabbinic Rules for the Delivery of Targum," in *Congress Volume Salamanca 1983,* ed. John A. Emerton, VTsup 36 (Leiden: Brill, 1986); and Fraade, "Rabbinic Views on the Practice of Targum".
48 See above, n. 14. For the knowledge of other languages as helpful for the midrashic interpretation of Hebrew Scripture, see above, n. 20.
49 See above, n. 16.

tations of the covenantal-renewal ritual prescribed in Deut 27:1–8 and described in Josh 8:30–32, with assistance from Josh 4:1–8, 19–24. According to it, scriptural revelation, via translation into the languages of the "seventy" nations, defines Israel's often ambivalent relationship to those nations, and thereby its social and cultural identity and status with respect to them. Posed as a question, these two attitudes can be conveyed as follows: does the translation of the Torah into all seventy languages enable its fullest possible meaning(s) to be apprehended, that is, for it to achieve its maximal polyglossic resonance, even if only *within* Israel, or is it simply a utilitarian concession to the nations so as to assure their punishment, enable their repentance (but not really), or, by sharing with them only so much Scripture as they desire/need to know, to gain their favor (however briefly) or, alternatively, to mock them?[50]

Does the recording of the Torah in all seventy languages suggest that Hebrew is just one language among seventy, each one conveying the Torah's meaning in the respective tongue of each people, as the Babylonian Talmud (*Meg.* 18a) in a different context states, "Egyptian for the Egyptians, Hebrew[51] for the Hebrews, Elamite for the Elamites, and Greek for the Greeks"? Alternatively, does the view that only the Torah was inscribed on the stones (whichever), and that the nations had to send their notaries to transcribe and/or translate the text in their own tongues (in some views by divine inspiration), affirm the superior, exceptional status of the Hebrew *original* and the inferior, *derivative* status of all other translations (as well as languages and national identities)? The fact that most of our rabbinic texts do not answer these questions in a monological voice (even the Aramaic Targum provides a "double translation"), suggests that the *polyglossic* nature of revelation might be more closely connected than otherwise thought to its *polysemic* divine origins, human reception, and transmission, which were there, as it were, all along.[52]

---

[50] The question of the extent to which the Torah was intended for all of humankind, or only a select part thereof, is a very old one. See, for example, Ben Sira (ca. 180 B.C.E.), as demonstrated by Seth Schwartz, *Were the Jews a Mediterranean Society? Reciprocity and Solidarity in Ancient Judaism* (Princeton: Princeton University Press, 2009), 45–79; and Hirshman, *Torah*. See also my treatment of the story in *Sifre Deut* 344 (ed. Finkelstein, 400–01), and parallels, in Steven D. Fraade, *From Tradition to Commentary: Torah and Its Interpretation in the Midrash Sifre to Deuteronomy* (Albany: State University of New York Press, 1991), 51–54; and "Navigating the Anomalous: Non-Jews at the Intersection of Early Rabbinic Law and Narrative," in *The Other in Jewish Thought and History: Constructions of Jewish Culture and Identity*, ed. Laurence J. Silberstein and and Robert L. Cohn (New York: New York University Press, 1994): 153–56 (= Steven D. Fraade, *Legal Fictions: Studies of Law and Narrative in the Discursive Worlds of Ancient Jewish Sectarians and Sages* (Leiden: Brill, 2011), 153–56.)
[51] "Hebrew" here may mean something other than the Hebrew of the Hebrew Bible or of the Rabbis, but for present purposes this question need not detain us.
[52] See, in this regard, the following exchange: Steven D. Fraade, "Rabbinic Polysemy and Pluralism Revisited: Between Praxis and Thematization," *AJSR* 31 (2007): 1–40; Azzan Yadin-Israel,

Although this study has focused intensely on the exegetical aspects of the texts considered, as interpretations of both Scripture (already inner-biblically) and (inner-rabbinically) of received rabbinic traditions, they are very much part of a larger multilingual cultural world, as revealed not just by literature, but by the archeological uncovering of ancient inscriptions, coins, and documents.[53] The constant negotiation of "code-switching" and "bilingual interference," and their necessary assumptions about the role and status of each language in relation to and in contact with the others, suggests that what is at stake in the texts we have examined is as much perennial *intellectual* questions of the contested role of language(s) in revelation and its decipherment, as perennial *practical* questions of the contested role of language in the arena of competing social interrelations and identities.

Bibliography

Adams, James N. *Bilingualism and the Latin Language*. New York: Cambridge University Press, 2003.

Adams, James N., Mark Janse, and Simon Swain, eds. *Bilingualism in Ancient Society: Language Contact and the Written Word*. Oxford: Oxford University Press, 2002.

Albeck, Chanoch, and Yehudah Theodor, eds. *Midrash Bereshit Rabbah: Critical Edition with Notes and Commentary*. Berlin and Jerusalem, 1893–1936.

Alexander, Philip S. "The Targumim and Rabbinic Rules for the Delivery of Targum." In *Congress Volume Salamanca 1983*, edited by John A. Emerton. Supplements to Vetus Testamentum 36, 14–28. Leiden: Brill, 1986.

Askhenazy, Shmuel. "Shivim Panim Le-Torah." In *Alfa Beta Kadimta De-Shmuel Zera*, edited by S. A. Tefilinski. Jerusalem: S. A. Tefilinski, 2001.

BeDuhn, Jason D. "Magical Bowls and Manichaeans." In *Ancient Magic and Ritual Power*, edited by Marvin W. Meyer, and Paul Mirecki, 419–34. Leiden: Brill, 1995.

Ben-Hayyim, Ze'ev. "The Contribution of the Samaritan Inheritance." *Proceedings of the Israel Academy of Sciences and Humanities* 3 (1969): 162–72.

Benjamin, Walter. "On Language as Such and on the Language of Man." In *Walter Benjamin, Selected Writings, Vol. 1: 1913–1926*, edited by Marcus Block and Michael Jennings, 62–74. Cambridge, MA: Harvard University Press, 1997.

Benjamin, Walter. "The Task of the Translator." In *Selected Writings, Vol. 1: 1913–1926*, edited by Marcus Block and Michael Jennings, 253–62. Cambridge, MA: Harvard University Press, 1997.

"Rabbinic Polysemy: A Response to Steven Fraade," *AJSR* 38 (2014): 129–41; Steven D. Fraade, "A Response to Azzan Yadin-Israel on Rabbinic Polysemy: Do They 'Preach' What They Practice?," *AJSR* 38 (2014): 339–61.

53 See Fraade, "עירוב לשונות"; "Language Mix." (translations of one another)

Berlin, Adele. *JPS Bible Commentary: Esther*. Philadelphia: Jewish Publication Society, 2001.
Berthelot, Katell. "Rabbinic Universalism Reconsidered: The Roman Context of Some Rabbinic Traditions Pertaining to the Revelation of the Torah in Different Languages." *Jewish Quarterly Review* 108 (2018): 393–421.
Braude, William G., trans. *Pesikta Rabbati*. Yale Judaica Series. New Haven: Yale University Press, 1968
Buth, Randall, and R. Steven Notley, eds. *The Language Environment of First Century Judaea: Jerusalem Studies in the Synoptic Gospels*. Vol. 2. Jewish and Christian Perspectives 26. Leiden: Brill, 2014.
Charlesworth, James H., ed. *The Old Testament Pseudepigrapha*. Vol. 2. New York: Doubleday, 1985.
Cotton, Hannah M., Robert G. Hoyland, Jonathan J. Price, and David J. Wasserstein, eds. *From Hellenism to Islam: Cultural and Linguistic Change in the Roman Near East*. Cambridge: Cambridge University Press, 2009.
Finkelstein, Louis, ed. *Sifre on Deuteronomy*. New York: Jewish Theological Seminary of America, 1969.
Fishbane, Michael A. *Biblical Interpretation in Ancient Israel*. Oxford: Oxford University Press, 1988.
Fraade, Steven D. "A Response to Azzan Yadin-Israel on Rabbinic Polysemy: Do They 'Preach' What They Practice?" *Association for Jewish Studies Review* 38 (2014): 339–61.
Fraade, Steven D. "Before and after Babel: Linguistic Exceptionalism and Pluralism in Early Rabbinic Literature." *Diné Israel* 28 (2011): 31–68.
Fraade, Steven D. *From Tradition to Commentary: Torah and its Interpretation in the Midrash Sifre to Deuteronomy*. Albany: State University of New York Press, 1991.
Fraade, Steven D. "Language Mix and Multilingualism in Ancient Palestine: Literary and Inscriptional Evidence." *Jewish Studies* 48 (2012): 1–40.
Fraade, Steven D. *Legal Fictions: Studies of Law and Narrative in the Discursive Worlds of Ancient Jewish Sectarians and Sages*. Leiden: Brill, 2011.
Fraade, Steven D. "Locating Targum in the Textual Polysystem of Rabbinic Pedagogy." *Bulletin of the International Organization for Septuagint and Cognate Studies* 39 (2006): 69–91.
Fraade, Steven D. "Moses and Adam as Polyglots." In *Envisioning Judaism: Studies in Honor of Peter Schäfer on the Occasion of His Seventieth Birthday*, edited by Klaus Hermann, Ra'anan S. Boustan, Reimund Leicht, Annette Yoshiko Reed, and Giuseppe Veltri, 185–94. Tübingen: Mohr Siebeck, 2013.
Fraade, Steven D. "Navigating the Anomalous: Non-Jews at the Intersection of Early Rabbinic Law and Narrative." In *The Other in Jewish Thought and History: Constructions of Jewish Culture and Identity*, edited by Laurence J. Silberstein and Robert L. Cohn, 145–65. New York: New York University Press, 1994.
Fraade, Steven D. "Rabbinic Polysemy and Pluralism Revisited: Between Praxis and Thematization." *Association for Jewish Studies Review* 31 (2007): 1–40.
Fraade, Steven D. "Rabbinic Views on the Practice of Targum, and Multilingualism in the Jewish Galilee of the Third–Sixth Centuries." In *The Galilee in Late Antiquity*, edited by Lee I. Levine, 253–86. New York and Jerusalem: The Jewish Theological Seminary of America, 1992.
Fraade, Steven D. "Scripture, Targum, and Talmud as Instruction: A Complex Textual Story from the Sifra." In *Hesed Ve-Emet: Studies in Honor of Ernest S. Frerichs*, edited by Jodi Magness and Seymour Gitin. Brown Judaic Studies, 109–22. Atlanta: Scholars Press, 1998.

Fraade, Steven D. "The Rehov Inscriptions and Rabbinic Literature: Matters of Language." In *Talmuda De-Eretz Israel: Archaeology and the Rabbis in Late Antique Palestine*, edited by Steven Fine and Aaron Koller. Studia Judaica, 225–38. Berlin: De Gruyter, 2014.

Fraade, Steven D. "עירוב לשונות ורב־לשוניות בארץ ישראל בעת העתיקה: ממצאים ספרותיים ואפיגרפיים." *Leshonenu* 73 (2011): 273–307.

Friedlander, Gerald, ed. and trans. *Pirke of Rabbi Eliezer (The Chapters of Rabbi Eliezer, the Great)*. London: K. Paul, Trench, Trubner; New York: Bloch, 1916.

Friedmann, Meir, ed. *Midrash Pesikta Rabati*. Vienna, 1880.

Ginzberg, Louis. *Legends of the Jews*. Vol. 5. Philadelphia: Jewish Publication Society, 1953.

Harrington, Daniel J., ed. *Pseudo-Philon, Les antiquités bibliques, Tome 1: Introduction et texte critiques*. Vol. 229, Sources Chrétiennes. Paris: Éditions du Cerf, 1976.

Hauptman, Judith. *Rereading the Mishnah: A New Approach to Ancient Jewish Texts*. Texts and Studies in Ancient Judaism. Tübingen: Mohr Siebeck, 2005.

Higger, Michael, ed. *Seven Minor Treatises; Sefer Torah, Mazuzah, Tefillin, Zizit, 'Abadim, Kutim, Gerim, and Treatise Soferim II*. New York, 1930.

Hirshman, Marc. *Torah for the Entire World* [in Hebrew]. Tel Aviv: Hakibbutz Hameuchad, 1999.

Hollander, Harm W., and Marinus de Jonge. "Appendix I." In *The Testaments of the Twelve Patriarchs: A Commentary*. Leiden: Brill, 1985.

Horovitz, Saul, and Israel Abraham Rabin, eds. *Mechilta d'Rabbi Ismael*. Frankfurt: J. Kauffmann, 1931.

Idel, Moshe. *Old Worlds, New Mirrors: On Jewish Mysticism and Twentieth-Century Thought*. Philadelphia: University of Pennsylvania Press, 2010.

Isbell, Charles D. *Corpus of the Aramaic Incantation Bowls*. Missoula, MT: Scholars Press, 1975.

Jacobs, Carol. *In the Language of Walter Benjamin*. Baltimore: Johns Hopkins University Press, 1999.

Jastrow, Marcus. *A Dictionary of the Targum, the Talmud Babli and Jerushalmi, and the Midrashic Literature*. New York: Choreb, 1926.

Josephus, Flavius. *The Jewish Antiquities, Books 1–19*, translated by Henry St. J. Thackeray et al. Loeb Classical Library. Cambridge, MA: Harvard University Press, 1930–1965.

Kahana, Menahem. *The Geniza Fragments of the Halakhic Midrashim, Volume I: Mekhilta de-Rabbi Ishma'el, Mekhilta de-Rabbi Shim'on Ben Yohay, Sifre Bamidbar, Sifre Zuta Bamidbar, Sifre Deuteronomy, Mekhilta Deuteronomy* [in Hebrew]. Jerusalem: Magnes Press, 2005.

Kahana, Menahem. "The Halakhic Midrashim." In *The Literature of the Sages, Second Part: Midrash and Targum, Liturgy, Poetry, Mysticism, Contracts, Inscriptions, Ancient Science and the Languages of Rabbinic Literature*, edited by Shmuel Safrai, Zeev Safrai, Joshua Schwartz, and Peter J. Tomson, 3–105. Assen: Royal Van Gorcum, 2006.

Kahana, Menahem. "דפים מן המכילתא לדברים פרשות האזינו וזאת הברכה." *Tarbiz* 57 (1988): 180–85 and 200–01.

Kalmin, Richard. "The Miracle of the Septuagint in Ancient Rabbinic and Christian Literatures." In *"Follow the Wise": Studies in Jewish History and Culture in Honor of Lee Levine*, edited by Zeev Weiss, Oded Irshai, Jodi Magness, and Seth Schwartz, 241–53. Winona Lake, IN: Eisenbrauns, 2010.

Lauterbach, Jacob Z., ed. *Mekilta de-Rabbi Ishmael*. Philadelphia: Jewish Publication Society of America, 1934–1935.

Lieberman, Saul. *Greek in Jewish Palestine*. New York: Philipp Feldheim, 1965.

Lieberman, Saul. *Hellenism in Jewish Palestine: Studies in the Literary Transmission, Beliefs and Manners of Palestine in the I Century B.C.E.–IV Century C.E.* 2nd ed. New York: Jewish Theological Seminary of America, 1962.
Lieberman, Saul. *Studies in Palestinian Literature* [in Hebrew]. Jerusalem: Magnes, 1991.
Lieberman, Saul. *Tosefta Ki-Fshuṭah: A Comprehensive Commentary on the Tosefta, Part 8, Order Nashim* [in Hebrew]. New York: Jewish Theological Seminary of America, 1973.
Mack, Hananel. "The Torah Has Seventy Aspects: The Development of a Saying." In *Rabbi Mordechai Breuer Festschrift: Collected Papers in Jewish Studies*, edited by Moshe Bar-Asher. Jerusalem: Akademon, 1992.
Mandel, Paul. "עיון חדש: על 'פתח' ועל הפתיחה", in *Higayon L'Yonah: New Aspects in the Study of Midrash, Aggadah and Piyut in Honor of Professor Yona Fraenkel*, ed. Joshua Levinson, Jacob Elbaum, and Galit Hasan-Rokem (Jerusalem: Magnes, 2006), 49–82, esp. 56.
Mullen, Alex, and Patrick James, eds. *Multilingualism in the Graeco-Roman Worlds*. Cambridge: Cambridge University Press, 2012.
Naeh, Shlomo. "'טובים דודיך מיין': מבט חדש על משנת עבודה זרה ב, ה." In *Studies in Talmudic and Midrashic Literature in Memory of Tirzah Lifshitz*, edited by M. Bar-Asher, J. Levinson, and B. Lifshitz. Jerusalem: Bialik Institute, 2005.
Papaconstantinou, Arietta, ed. *The Multilingual Experience in Egypt, from the Ptolemies to the Abbasids*. Farnham: Ashgate, 2010.
Pirke Rabi Eli'ezer ha-gadol. Warsaw: T.Y. Bamberg, 1852.
Sarna, Nahum M. *The JPS Torah Commentary: Genesis*. Philadelphia: Jewish Publication Society, 1989.
Schechter, Solomon. "The Mekhilta Deuteronomy, Pericope Re'eh." In *Festschrift zu Israel Lewy's siebzigsten Geburtstag*, edited by Marcus Brann and Ismar Elbogen, 187–92. Breslau: M. & H. Marcus, 1911.
Schwartz, Seth. *Were the Jews a Mediterranean Society? Reciprocity and Solidarity in Ancient Judaism*. Princeton: Princeton University Press, 2009.
Simon-Shoshan, Moshe. "The Task of the Translators: The Rabbi, the Septuagint, and the Cultural Politics of Translation." *Prooftexts* 27 (2007): 1–39.
Smelik, Willem F. *Rabbis, Language and Translation in Late Antiquity*. Cambridge: Cambridge University Press, 2013.
Sokoloff, Michael. *A Dictionary of Jewish Palestinian Aramaic of the Byzantine Period*. 2nd ed. Ramat-Gan: Bar-Ilan University Press, 2002.
Sperber, Daniel. *Magic and Folkore in Rabbinic Literature*. Ramat-Gan, Israel: Bar-Ilan University Press, 1994.
Tanakh: The Holy Scriptures: The New JPS Translation According to the Traditional Hebrew Text. Philadelphia: Jewish Publication Society, 2010.
Tigay, Jeffrey H. *The JPS Torah Commentary: Deuteronomy*. Philadelphia: Jewish Publication Society, 1996.
Ulmer, Rivka, ed. *Pesiqta Rabbati: A Synoptic Edition of Pesiqta Rabbati Based Upon All Extant Manuscripts and the Editio Princeps*. Lanham, MD: University Press of America, 2009.
Veltri, Giuseppe. "Deconstructing History and Traditions: The Written Torah for Ptolemy." In *Libraries, Translations and "Canonic" Texts: The Septuagint, Aquila and Ben Sira in the Jewish and Christian Traditions*, edited by Giuseppe Veltri. JSJSup, 147–89. Leiden: Brill, 2006.

Vierros, Marja. *Bilingual Notaries in Hellenistic Egypt: A Study of Greek as a Second Language*. Collectanea Hellenistica. Brussels: Koninklijke Vlaamse Academie van België voor Wetenschappen en Kunsten, 2012.

Wasserstein, Abraham, and David J. Wasserstein. *The Legend of the Septuagint: From Classical Antiquity to Today*. New York: Cambridge University Press, 2006.

Wertheimer, Solomon Aaron. *Batei Midrashot*. Vol. 1. Jerusalem: Rav Kook Institute, 1950–1953.

Yadin, Azzan. "The Hammer on the Rock: Polysemy and the School of Rabbi Ishmael." *Jewish Studies Quarterly* 10 (2003): 1–17.

Yadin, Azzan. *Scripture as Logos: Rabbi Ishmael and the Origins of Midrash*. Divinations: Rereading Late Ancient Religion. Philadelphia: University of Pennsylvania Press, 2004.

Yadin-Israel, Azzan. "Rabbinic Polysemy: A Response to Steven Fraade." *Association for Jewish Studies Review* 38 (2014): 129–41.

Alison G. Salvesen
"Hebrew, Beloved of God": The Adamic Language in the Thought of Jacob, Bishop of Edessa (c. 633–708 CE)

1 Jacob's Biography

The Syrian Orthodox polymath Jacob of Edessa was born in a village near Antioch in Syria, probably sometime in the early 630s CE. From childhood onwards he would only have known a world in which Arab and Islamic rule prevailed. Certainly his own works and the account of his life that appears in medieval authors do not indicate that he was personally affected by any momentous historical events. However, there are hints in his works of the social effects of regime change on the Christians of Syria and Mesopotamia.[1]

No doubt an Aramaic speaker by birth, Jacob learned Greek and Syriac in an ecclesiastical context. Once he had taken monastic vows and had received academic training in the famously learned convent of Qenneshre, his biographers say that he went to Alexandria in Egypt for further study. Having returned to the city of Edessa in northern Mesopotamia, he was made bishop in 684.[2] However, he resigned his see after only four years in office, in reaction to what he perceived as the intolerable laxity of the local clergy and church hierarchy. He retreated to the monastery of Eusebona in Syria where he taught Greek for nine years, but he was then driven out by monks who were hostile to his promotion of Greek. He moved on to Tell 'Adda, a monastery near Aleppo, where he continued to write and teach. He died shortly after being reinstated as bishop of Edessa in 708 CE.[3]

---

1 Robert G. Hoyland, "Jacob and Early Islamic Edessa," in *Jacob of Edessa and the Syriac Culture of His Day*, ed. R.B. ter Haar Romeny (Leiden: Brill, 2008), 16–18.
2 Omert J. Schrier, "Chronological Problems Concerning the Lives of Severus Bar Mašqā, Athanasius of Balad, Julianus Romāyā, Yohannān Sābā, George of the Arabs and Jacob of Edessa," *Oriens Christianus* 75 (1991).
3 A biography of Jacob is preserved in the much later works of Michael the Syrian and Barhebraeus. For Michael, see Jean-Baptiste Chabot, ed., *Chronique de Michel le Syrien, patriarche jacobite d'Antioche (1166–1199)*, 4 vols. (Brussels: Culture et Civilisation, 1963), 4:445–46 (Syriac text);

Note: The present study is dedicated to Mor Gregorios Yohanna Ibrahim, Archbishop of the Syriac Orthodox Church in Aleppo, who hosted a symposium in the city in June 2008 to commemorate the 1300th anniversary of Jacob of Edessa's death in 708 CE. Mor Gregorios was kidnapped in April 2013 by unknown assailants. His fate remains unknown at the time of writing.

2 Jacob and the "Adamic" Language

The question of which language was the one spoken by Adam arises in several Jewish, Christian and Muslim sources in Late Antiquity, including Jacob of Edessa. These sources have been surveyed and discussed by Milka Rubin,[4] Yonatan Moss,[5] and most recently by Sergey Minov in his book on the *Cave of Treasures*.[6] The present study is narrower, focusing specifically on Jacob's interest in Hebrew language and Jewish tradition in his particular historical context.

In contrast to several other Syriac writers,[7] Jacob espoused the theory that Hebrew was the first and universal language before the Tower of Babel. His correspondent John the Stylite of Litarba had asked him two questions: first, whether the Jews/Hebrews (*yūdāyē ʿebrāyē*) were really named after ʿEber (Gen. 10:21,25), and second, whether Hebrew was the original language (*qadmāyā d-lešānē*). Jacob's reponse is that the Hebrews were indeed named after ʿEber, an ancestor of Abraham. ʿEber's descendants had preserved the first, Adamic language when they dwelt in Ur.[8] The term "Hebrews" was *not* derived from the fact that Abraham crossed (*ʿĕbar*) the river Euphrates, a tradition created by an "absurd" (*ṣabārā*) person. Jacob ascribes this error to a misinterpretation of the word περάτης, which can mean either "emigrant," or "one who crosses over," used as an epithet

---

2:71–72 (French translation). The shorter version of Barhebraeus can be found in Joannes B. Abbeloos and Thomas J. Lamy, *Gregorii Barhebraei Chronicon Ecclesiasticum*, vol. 1 (Louvain: C. Peeters, 1872), 289–94. Schrier considers it unlikely that this Vita came from one of Jacob's students, arguing instead that it was written some generations later (Schrier, "Chronological problems," 72).
4 Milka Rubin, "The Language of Creation or the Primordial Language: A Case of Cultural Polemics in Antiquity," *JJS* 49 (1998): 306–33.
5 Yonatan Moss, "The Language of Paradise: Hebrew or Syriac? Linguistic Speculations and Linguistic Realities in Late Antiquity," in *Paradise in Antiquity: Jewish and Christian Views*, eds. Markus Bockmuehl and Guy Stroumsa, 120–37 (Cambridge: Cambridge University Press, 2010).
6 Sergey Minov, *Memory and Identity in the Syriac Cave of Treasures: Rewriting the Bible in Sasanian Iran*. Jerusalem Studies in Religion and Culture 26. Leiden/Boston: Brill, 2020, 272–83. Minov situates *Cave of Treasures* in Miaphysite (= Syrian Orthodox) circles in Northern Mesopotamia under Sasanian control, in the second half of the sixth century or early seventh century.
7 See references in Minov, *Memory and Identity*, 272–83.
8 See William Wright, "Two Epistles of Mar Jacob, Bishop of Edessa," *Journal of Sacred Literature and Biblical Record* NS 10 (1867): 430–60 [pp. *k-k'*]. French translation by Francois Nau, "Traduction des lettres XII et XIII de Jacques d'Édesse," *Revue de l'orient chrétien* 10 (1905): esp. 273–74. Earlier in the same letter (XIII), Jacob had explained to John that the descendants of ʿEber remained in Chaldea after the dispersion from the Tower of Babel, and that these people alone continued to speak the original Adamic language of Hebrew (Wright, "Two Epistles of Mar Jacob, Bishop of Edessa," p. *d*; Nau, "Traduction des lettres XII et XIII de Jacques d'Édesse," 200–202.).

of Abraham in the Septuagint text (Gen. 14:13).[9] Given the "absurd" person's reliance on the LXX text, we can assume that he was a Greek writer:[10] we will return to the matter of his identity later.

John the Stylite's second question to Jacob concerns the status of Hebrew. Jacob replies that Hebrew is indeed the original language of all, and not Syriac/Aramaic "as many people erroneously suppose, even some great and illustrious ones." He says he has much evidence for the antiquity of Hebrew, but there is sufficient proof in the testimony of "Clement the disciple of the apostle Peter"[11] that the single language before the division of tongues was Hebrew, "beloved of God" (*raḥīm l-'alāhā*).[12] Jacob also cites a treatise of Eusebius of Emesa that relies on the names of men before the Flood, and especially the wordplay in Gen 2:23, to demonstrate that Adam's exclamation at the Creation must have been uttered in Hebrew.[13] For the pun *'îš/'iššâ* only works in Hebrew, and not in Syriac (contrast *gabrā/'attā*).[14] Bas Romeny suggests that this "proof" originates from a now lost comment by the fourth-century Syrian Greek bishop Eusebius of Emesa, itself derived from the work of Eusebius' teacher

---

9 The Hebrew and Syriac Bibles have the gentilics *hā'ivrî/ 'ebrāyā* respectively at that point.
10 Many exegetes who used LXX understood the text in a similar way, that Abram was so called because he crossed either the Euphrates or Mesopotamia to enter Canaan: Philo, *Migr. Abr.* §20; Origen, *Selecta in Genesim fragmenta*, PG 12: 113; John Chrysostom, Homilies 35 and 40 (Greek text in *Homilies 1–67 on Genesis*, PG 53: 326, 364, and English translation by Robert C. Hill, *Homilies on Genesis 18–45*. Fathers of the Church 82. Washington, D.C.: Catholic University of America, 2001, 312, 380). In both these sermons, Chrysostom is under the misapprehension that "Abram" means "crossing" in Hebrew and Syriac: no doubt he confused the name with 'Eber. There is similar confusion over the meaning of the names 'Eber and Abram in another homily attributed to John Chrysostom, where it is stated that "Abram" means "crossing" in Hebrew and Syriac, on the basis of the use of the epithet Περάτης (Καὶ γὰρ τὸ Ἀβραμ τῇ Σύρων φωνῇ τὸ πέραν λέγεται: *Sermons 1–9 on Gen*esis, PG 54: 624).
11 In fact a pseudonymous work, the *Recognitions* of Pseudo-Clement. See Bernhard Rehm, ed., *Die Pseudoklementinen. II, Rekognitionen: in Rufins Übersetzung* (Berlin: Akademie-Verlag, 1965), I.30.
12 See Minov, *Memory and Identity*, 274, and n. 93 for the Syriac form of the citation from the Pseudo-Clementine *Recognitions*.
13 Though this work is no longer extant, a similar argument involving the Hebrew words for man and woman appears in an anonymous catena fragment (attested by frag. §314 in Françoise Petit, *La chaîne sur la Genèse. Édition intégrale 1*. Traditio Exegetica Graeca 1 [Leuven: Peeters, 1992]), and §100 in Françoise Petit, *Catenae Graecae in Genesim et in Exodum. 2, Collectio Coisliniana in Genesim*. CCSG 15 [Turnhout-Leuven: Peeters, 1986]). Both are given in R.B. ter Haar Romeny, *A Syrian in Greek Dress. The Use of Greek, Hebrew, and Syriac Biblical Texts in Eusebius of Emesa's Commentary on Genesis*. Traditio Exegetica Graeca 6 (Leuven: Peeters, 1997), 203–206.
14 Wright, "Two Epistles of Mar Jacob, Bishop of Edessa," p. *k'*.; Nau, "Traduction des lettres XII et XIII de Jacques d'Édesse," 274.

and namesake Eusebius of Caesarea.[15] (The rabbinic work Bereshit Rabba (18:4) similarly uses Gen 2:23 as evidence for the originality of Hebrew.[16])

Milka Rubin states that apart from Jacob, almost all Syriac writers support the view that Syriac or Aramaic is the original language of Creation.[17] She argues that this could be due to the desire to promote a separate Syriac cultural identity from the Byzantine Greek church after the Council of Chalcedon in 451.[18] However, all the post-Chalcedonian, pre-medieval Syriac sources she cites come from the Church of the East, which was theologically opposed to Jacob of Edessa's Syrian Orthodox Church over the highly contested matter of whether Christ's human and divine natures were separate or united.[19] These Church of the East sources are the Anonymous Commentary in the Diyarbakir manuscript (early eighth century),[20] Theodore bar Koni (late eighth century), Isho'dad of Merv (ninth century), and the Anonymous Commentary in the Mingana collection (ninth to tenth century).[21]

---

[15] Eusebius of Caesarea, *Praeparatio Evangelica* 11.6.18 (PG 21: 857): ἡ δὲ γυνή, ἐπείπερ εἴρηται ἐκ τοῦ ἀνδρὸς εἰλῆφθαι, καὶ τὴν προσηγορίαν ἐπικοινωνεῖ τῷ ἀνδρί. ΕΣΣΑ γὰρ ἡ γυνὴ λέγεται παρ' αὐτοῖς, ὥσπερ ΕΙΣ ὁ ἀνήρ. ("As for the woman, since it was said that she was taken from the man, she also shares a name with man. For woman is called *essa* among them [i.e. the Jews], as man is called *heis*.") Ter Haar Romeny suggests that Eusebius of Emesa found the transliteration of the Hebrew in this passage from the bishop of Caesarea, or was given it by a (Jewish?) informant: actual knowledge of Hebrew on Eusebius' part is unlikely (*Syrian in Greek Dress*, 59). Eusebius of Caesarea also mentions in the same passage the name Heber (= 'Eber) "who passes over" in connection with the gentilic "Hebrew," "since both a passage and the one who passes over are called in the Hebrew language 'Heber.'" Eusebius presents the "Greek" opinion on the variety of language and its random development in *Praep.Evang* 1.7: Rubin understood the latter to be Eusebius' own view, but in fact it derives from Diodorus Siculus (1.8), as is suggested by the preceding paragraph in *Praep.Evang.* 1.6 ("Language of Creation," 320).
[16] Rubin, "Language of Creation," 311.
[17] See now the critique of the positions of Rubin and Moss by Minov (*Memory and Identity*, 275–77). Minov also expresses some doubt on the authenticity of the views ascribed to Theodore of Mopsuestia by later writers of the Church of the East (277).
[18] Rubin, "The Language of Creation," 327, 33.
[19] The label "Nestorian" was often used in the past. However, the doctrines of the Church of the East had nothing to do with Nestorius. The Church of the East distinguishes between the human and divine natures of Christ, and rejects the title "God-bearer" (Theotokos) used of Mary. The Syrian Orthodox Church, by contrast, stressed one incarnate nature in Christ (hence the modern use of the terms "monophysite" or "miaphysite"). Both the Church of the East and the Syrian Orthodox Church were regarded as heterodox by the (mainly western) churches that had embraced the Confession of the Council of Chalcedon in 451 CE, that Christ was incarnate in two natures, but without mingling, confusion or division.
[20] Lucas van Rompay, ed. *Le commentaire sur Genèse-Exode 9, 32 du manuscrit (Olim) Diyarbakir 22*, CSCO 483–84, SS 205–06 (Leuven: Peeters, 1986).
[21] Abraham Levene, ed. *The Early Syrian Fathers on Genesis. From a Syriac Ms. On the Pentateuch in the Mingana Collection* (London: Taylor's Foreign Press, 1951).

Furthermore, as Rubin notes, all but Theodore bar Koni explicitly attribute to the Greek theologian Theodore of Mopsuestia (350–428 CE) the tradition that Syriac was the original language. Theodore's exegesis was revered above all others in the Church of the East, while his theology was rejected by both Chalcedonians and the Syrian Orthodox Church.

Isho'dad states that according to Theodore, Syriac, not Hebrew, was the first language, and that Hebrew was "a mixed language introduced by Abraham," who had spoken Aramaic in Babylon and in Harran. When Abraham crossed the Euphrates and settled in Canaan, his native Aramaic was mixed up with Canaanite. The blended language formed Hebrew, *'ĕbrāyā*: the implication being that it was named after Abraham's crossing of the Euphrates.[22] Although the original Greek form of Theodore's comment is lost, his fellow Syrian Theodoret of Cyrrhus expresses himself in Greek in almost identical terms to those of Isho'dad's report. Since Theodoret was Theodore's pupil, it is very likely that Theodoret inherited his argument about the derivation of the term "Hebrew" directly from Theodore.[23]

What Jacob says in his reply to John the Stylite about the origin of the name "Hebrew" and the Hebrew language implicitly refutes the negative assessment of Hebrew by Theodore of Mopsuestia and his followers, both Greek and Syriac. So it is likely that Theodore is the "absurd" person that Jacob refers to in his letter to John, and that theological animosity forms an element in Jacob's assessment of the linguistic situation. Thus, although Jacob's view of Hebrew was inherited from earlier tradition (Eusebius of Caesarea, via Eusebius of Emesa), it was very far from being a default position, as Rubin rightly observes: it was deliberately chosen. Neither can its function be detached from Jacob's own religious and political situation. Though Rubin tackles questions of Syrian identity in relation to Byzantium and the Chalcedonian church, arguing that a pro-Syriac stance with

---

22 Jacques M. Vosté and Ceslas van den Eynde, eds., *Commentaire d'Išo'dad de Merv sur l'Ancien Testament. I. Genèse*, CSCO 126, SS 67 (Louvain: Imprimerie Orientaliste L. Durbecq, 1950), 134, line 26–36, line 11.

23 Cf. Rubin, "Language of Creation," 321–22: she notes the pro-Syriac, anti-Hebrew views of Theodoret in *Quaest.Oct.* §§60–62, but not the likelihood that these were derived from Theodore. In *Quaest.Oct.* §62, Theodoret says that περάτης in Gen. 14:13 refers to Abraham's crossing of the Euphrates and corresponds to the "Syriac" word *hebra* and the Hebrew *hebrei* (Theodoret of Cyrus, *The Questions on the Octateuch*, Library of Early Christianity 1, trans. John F. Petruccione and Robert C. Hill [Washington: Catholic University of America Press, 2007]). Moss, "Language of Paradise," 135–36, observes that Theodoret adds a sociolinguistic dimension to his teacher's view.

Theodoret is apparently more positive than Theodore on the subject of Hebrew. He deems it a sacred language (§61), even if not the most ancient, and he does not repeat the disparaging remarks ascribed to Theodore by Isho'dad about the Jewish people being too stubborn and lazy to receive the Scriptures in anything but their own tongue.

regard to the original language of mankind helped create a separate cultural identity for Syriac Christians to mark them out against the Byzantines,[24] she does not take into account the intercommunal aspect of relations between the Syrian Orthodox Church and the Church of the East, nor Jacob's situation in the early Islamic world. Even if the arguments and proofs that Jacob cites were not new, their use in his present context subtly altered their function and purpose. In short, it is likely that Jacob's pro-Hebrew stance was at least in part adopted not only in deference to his authorities "Clement," Eusebius of Emesa, and his favourite pseudepigraphical book, Jubilees, but also in order to oppose the Church of the East's promotion of Syriac/Aramaic as the primeval language under the influence of the "heretic" Theodore of Mopsuestia.[25]

Jacob's position on this question is an isolated one, however much it may have been shaped by the religious controversies of his day. Thus Rubin notes that the later Syrian Orthodox scholars Michael the Syrian and Barhebraeus favoured Syriac as the original language. Similarly, Moss cites the Syrian Orthodox writer Moses bar Kepha as reproducing the argument for Hebrew priority based on Gen. 2:33 in his work *On Paradise*, yet preferring the priority of Syriac (and so approximating the position of the Church of the East writers of his time).[26] However, Moses bar Kepha post-dates Jacob by nearly two centuries, and Michael the Syrian and Barhebraeus were active in the twelfth and thirteenth centuries respectively. Michael's discussion and rejection of Jacob's championing of Hebrew as the primordial language needs to be viewed in the context of the very different historical context of his own time. The lifetimes of all three figures, Moses, Michael and Barhebraeus, fell during the period when the status of Syriac among eastern Christians was threatened by the widespread use of Arabic, the language of heavenly revelation to the Prophet Muhammed. In contrast, the promotion of Arabic as the administrative language of the Caliphate began only a few years before Jacob's death.[27]

---

24 Rubin, "Language of Creation," 327–28.
25 According to Minov's analysis, the Syriac *Cave of Treasures* dates to the period prior to Jacob's career and connects to the Syrian Orthodox Church rather than the Church of the East. It strongly promotes the notion that Syriac/Aramaic was the primordial language and attacks the opposing position as "an ignorant error" (*Memory and Identity*, 272–83, and *Cave*, 24:9–11).
26 Moss, "Language of Paradise," 128–29.
27 Under 'Abd al-Malik (685–705 CE), in c. 700 CE, according to the ninth century Persian writer al-Balādhuri, in his *Futūh al-Buldān* (Michael J. de Goeje, ed. *Liber expugnatio regionum* [Leiden: Brill, 1866], 193). See Arietta Papaconstantinou, "Administering the Early Islamic Empire: Insights from the Papyri," in *Money, Power and Politics in Early Islamic Syria: A Review of Current Debates*, ed. John F. Haldon, 57–74 (Farnham: Ashgate, 2010). She comments that documents in Arabic only became common in the eighth century (69).

Jacob's apparently anomalous position among late antique and medieval Syriac writers on the primordial language is therefore not so strange when seen within his historical and theological context. He draws on the authority of past figures and sources – the ancient Jewish tradition of Jubilees, apostolic Christianity in "Clement," and the "Syrian in Greek dress," Eusebius of Emesa – to find further ground for opposition to the views of scholars in the Church of the East.

3 Jacob the Hebraist?

Did Jacob's evident respect for Hebrew as the Adamic language have any practical implications for him? The statement that Jacob was a triglot, "equally conversant with Syriac, Greek and Hebrew," was made by the Victorian scholar William Wright,[28] and a century later it was repeated by François Graffin.[29] However, Theodor Nöldeke was much more disparaging, noting that Jacob's Hebrew was "sehr, sehr fadenscheinig."[30] Notably, the biography of Jacob preserved in Michael the Syrian and Barhebraeus speaks only of his mastery and promotion of Greek language and learning.[31]

So why did modern scholars believe that Jacob actually knew Hebrew? It must be partially due to the many references to Hebrew etymologies and Jewish exegetical traditions within his vast literary output. Another reason would be Jacob's "high" view of the Hebrew language, as for instance expressed in his Letter XIII to John the Stylite mentioned above. In the late eighteenth and nineteenth century, Syriac was a relatively new and fashionable subject in Europe, thanks to important manuscript discoveries in Egypt, including some early manuscripts of Jacob's own work. Scholars such as Wright were no doubt keen to raise the profile of Syriac studies in the face of the dominance of Greek and Latin authors. Thus Jacob could be portrayed as the Syriac equivalent of St Jerome. But even without an investigation of the sources of Jacob's erudite comments on Scripture, it was clear at an early stage of the enquiry that Jacob's own revisions of several Old Testament books, produced between c. 695–705, involved no consultation of

---

[28] Wright, "Two Epistles of Mar Jacob, Bishop of Edessa," 430.
[29] François Graffin, "Jacques d'Édesse réviseur des Homélies de Sévère d'Antioche d'après le ms. syriaque B.M. Add 12.159," in *Symposium Syriacum 1976, Chantilly, France*, ed. François Graffin and Antoine Guillaumont, 243–55 (Rome: Istituto Pontificio Biblico, 1978): 250.
[30] In Eberhard Nestle, "Jakob von Edessa über den Schem Hammephorasch und andere Gottesnamen. Ein Beitrag zur Geschichte der Tetragrammaton," *ZDMG* 32 (1878): 465–508, esp. 473–74, n. 3.
[31] Nestle, "Jakob von Edessa über den Schem Hammephorasch," esp. 473–74, n. 4.

the Hebrew biblical text.³² If he had been as gifted a Hebraist as Jerome, or even Origen, it would have been an obvious step to use his Hebrew knowledge as a tool in the process of revision. But this is not the case. In fact, in one of his letters he doubts his ability to explain Hebrew expressions to his correspondent.³³

Examples of Jacob's use of Jewish and Hebrew traditions occur in several of his discussions of problems in the biblical text. He wrote letters to learned friends on theological matters; there are later collections of his scholia on the Old Testament; there are marginal notes and scholia that he added to his revision of the Syriac translation of the *Cathedral Homilies* of Severus of Antioch; a Commentary on the Octateuch;³⁴ there are also comments on Hebrew etymologies in his work on the six days of Creation, the *Hexaemeron*, which was written during the last few years of his life.

Jacob often cites "Jewish stories/histories" (*tašʿyātā yūdāyātā*) to explain difficulties in the text of Genesis: it is clear that Jacob used a work closely related to what we know as the book of Jubilees. This latter work is attested in many Hebrew fragments at Qumran and Masada, cited in Greek by Christian writers and translated into Latin, but only preserved in full form in Ethiopic translation.³⁵ Jacob probably had access to a Greek version.³⁶ But of course, despite Jacob's enthusiasm for this work, this does not indicate that he knew Hebrew.

---

32 Although Nau says that Jacob's citation of Job in Letter XIII seems to be a combination of Hebrew and Greek, this is highly unlikely (Nau, "Traduction des lettres XII et XIII de Jacques d'Édesse," 263, n. 1).
33 Nau, "Traduction des lettres XII et XIII de Jacques d'Édesse," 270; Wright, "Two Epistles of Mar Jacob, Bishop of Edessa," p. ḥ.
34 Not yet fully edited and published: see R.B. ter Haar Romeny, "Ephrem and Jacob of Edessa in the Commentary of the Monk Severus," in *Malphono w-Rabo d-Malphone. Studies in Honor of Sebastian P. Brock*, ed. George A. Kiraz, 535–57 (Piscataway, NJ: Gorgias, 2008).
35 See Sebastian P. Brock, "Abraham and the Ravens: A Syriac Counterpart to Jubilees 11–12 and Its Implications," *Journal for the Study of Judaism* 9 (1978): 135–52; William Adler, "Abraham and the Burning of the Temple of Idols: Jubilees' Traditions in Christian Chronography," *Jewish Quarterly Review* 77, no. 2/3 (Oct. 1986–Jan. 1987): 95–117; William Adler, "Jewish Pseudepigrapha in Jacob of Edessa's Letters and Historical Writings," in *Jacob of Edessa and the Syriac Culture of His Day*, ed. R.B. ter Haar Romeny, 49–65 (Leiden: Brill, 2008). Adler argues that Jewish pseudepigrapha became more popular after their exclusion from the canon by Athanasius in the late fourth century: in his Letter XIII, Jacob explains that Athanasius needed to exclude them in order to discourage the heresies of that period, but that in the present day it was possible to use the genuine apocryphal books such as Enoch, which was known and used by the apostles such as Jude (Nau, "Traduction des lettres XII et XIII de Jacques d'Édesse," 206–208; Wright, "Two Epistles of Mar Jacob, Bishop of Edessa," pp. z-ṭ.). See also Jacob's remarks about "the written stories transmitted by the Jews" that are "not false," apparently referring to Jubilees (Nau, "Traduction des lettres XII et XIII de Jacques d'Édesse," 207; Wright, "Two Epistles of Mar Jacob, Bishop of Edessa," p. ṭ.).
36 See Adler, "Jewish Pseudepigrapha in Jacob of Edessa's Letters and Historical Writings," 64, and n. 51.

The following are a few examples typical of his use of Hebrew and Jewish traditions:

a) *Hexaemeron*, ed. Chabot,[37] p. 19: Maḥnim

> [The patriarch Jacob] saw the armies of holy angels there who surrounded him, and even up to the present the Hebrews call the place "Maḥnim." The Israelites built a fortified city in it, where David took refuge when he was fleeing from his son Absalom.

No doubt owing to the use of the term "encampment" earlier in Gen 32:3 in both LXX and Peshitta, Jacob realizes that the toponym Maḥnim in the Peshitta has a similar meaning and is a transliteration of the Hebrew name. There is no indication that he was employing direct knowledge of Hebrew.

b) *Hexaemeron*, ed. Chabot, p. 76: "heavens"

> This word *šēmāyā* (heavens) we use was not part of our Mesopotamian, Aramaic speech. Rather, it is a loanword from the language of the Hebrews that we use regularly as if it were our own expression. Many people who employ it, whether in speech, reading or writing, do not realize this. Since it is a loanword, we do not differentiate it as singular or plural. As for its meaning, we use it in both senses, since we employ exactly the same word and expression as singular and plural. For we say *šēmāyā* for singular and plural alike. We are unable to change the expression because it is as I have said, a loanword, not native to our language. Now, among the Hebrews, who possess the first, Adamic tongue, this expression is used in the singular sense, while also being understood and written in the plural. For they say *šōmā* in the singular, and *šōmāīm* in the plural.[38] And as far as it is possible to compare, this particular expression is a composite form from the term for water. For *mā* is how they say "water" in the singular, and *māīm* in the plural. So as I said, *šōmā* is one heaven, and *šōmāīm* is the plural form . . . This is how this word seems to be formed and pronounced among the Hebrews.

Jacob's discussion of singular versus plural forms of the word "heaven" in Hebrew has some similarities to John Chrysostom's *Homily* 4.10 on Genesis, where the Greek writer remarks on the use of the "plural" for heavens in Hebrew.[39] However,

---

[37] Jean-Baptiste Chabot, ed., *Iacobi Edesseni Hexaemeron, seu in opus creationis libri septem*, CSCO 92, SS 44 (Paris: E Typographeo Reipublicae, 1928–32); Latin translation in and by Arthur Vaschalde, *Iacobi Edesseni Hexaemeron, seu in opus creationis libri septem*, CSCO 97, SS 48 (Paris: E Typographeo Reipublicae, 1932).

[38] In the early manuscript of the *Hexaemeron* presented in Chabot's facsimile edition, given as ܫܡܐ and ܫܡܝܐ. The "Hebrew" for water is transcribed as ܡܐ and ܡܝܡ, with a Greek note ΜΑ in the margin.

[39] PG 53: 43: Λέγουσι τοίνυν οἱ τὴν γλῶτταν ἐκείνην ἀκριβῶς ἠσκημένοι, τὸ τοῦ οὐρανοῦ ὄνομα πληθυντικῶς καλεῖσθαι παρὰ τοῖς Ἑβραίοις, καὶ τοῦτο καὶ οἱ τὴν Σύρων γλῶτταν ἐπιστάμενοι συνομολογοῦσι. (English translation in Robert C. Hill, *Homilies on Genesis 18–45*. Fathers of the Church 82. Washington, D.C.: Catholic University of America, 2001, 57: "Those with a precise

the source of Jacob's unusual transliterations *šōmā* and *šōmayim* is obscure. The Greek transliteration of שמים in the second column of Origen's Hexapla gives the Hebrew as σαμμαϊμ.⁴⁰ Therefore Jacob's use of a *waw* in his Syriac transliteration, indicating the pronunciation *šōmayim*, suggests that this was not the ultimate origin of his comment. Procopius of Gaza's *Commentary on Genesis* does preserve an alternative transliteration, σουμην, in a philological explanation of the word "heaven" in Gen 1.8, but this is not particularly close to Jacob's version either.⁴¹

It is possible Jacob may have been aware of the Hebrew pronunciation of his day, where *qameṣ* was pronounced in the (emerging) Palestinian system as a sound between *a* and *o*, or open *o* (a similar change would take place in Western Syriac as well).⁴² If this is the case, unusually, he may be relying on a first-hand oral source, even a Jewish one, for the pronunciation. He does mention in one letter on the subject of the direction of prayer (the *qibla*) that he himself has witnessed both Jews and Muslims praying in Egypt,⁴³ but there is no indication of direct conversational contact with Jews in his works.

c) Jacob's *Scholion on the Divine Name*, ed. Brière, p. 196/[700]⁴⁴

> They say that the name that the Hebrews use and that is pronounced *'Elōhīm*, is translated as "Maker." In that they know that he is the Maker of all, the Hebrews regard this as the true name. Similarly we Arameans or Syrians, because of our relationship⁴⁵ to them and of

---

knowledge of that language tell us that among the Hebrews the word is used in the plural and those who know the language of the Syrians confirm this.")

40 On Ps 89:30. See Benjamin P. Kantor, "The Second Column of Origen's Hexapla in Light of Greek Pronunciation" (PhD diss, University of Texas, Austin, 2017), 32.

41 Karin Metzler, *Prokop Von Gaza: Der Genesiskommentar. Aus den "Eclogarum in Libros Historicos Veteris Testamenti Epitome" übersetzt und mit Anmerkungen versehen*. GCS 23 Berlin/Boston: De Gruyter, 2016, p. 32: "daher heiße es in hebräischer Sprache auch 'Sumen,' was gefrorenes Wasser anzeigen." Metzler notes that the source of this observation is unidentified. Also Kantor, "Second Column," 217 and n. 257.

42 See Angel Sáenz-Badillos, *A History of the Hebrew Language* (Cambridge: Cambridge University Press, 1996), 111; Edward Y. Kutscher, *The Language and Linguistic Background of the Isaiah Scroll (I Q Isaᵃ)* (Leiden: Brill, 1974), 495 on Jerome's transcriptions *rob* and *gob* for Hebrew *rab* and *gab*.

43 Jacob's Letter XIV to John the Stylite in BL Add. MS 12,272, fol. 124a.

44 Found between Severus of Antioch's *Homiliae Cathedrales* 123 and 124: Maurice Brière, "Scolie (au sujet du nom honorable et secret)," in *Les Homiliae Cathedrales de Sévère d'Antioche. Traduction syriaque de Jacques d'Édesse*, ed. Maurice Brière, PO 29 (Paris: Firmin-Didot, 1960). On 206 [710], Brière reproduces the diagram at the end of the scholion, which contrasts the false and true names of God and Psalm 109 (110): 1 in Syriac, Greek and "Hebrew," i.e. a Greek transliteration of Hebrew.

45 The notion that Syriac is close (a "neighbour") to Hebrew is found in the Syrian Greek writer Eusebius of Emesa (c. 300–360) whose *Commentary on Genesis* is preserved in Armenian: Françoise

our language to theirs, imitated this name that comes from them. We called the Maker of all ʾAlāhā, and likewise also the Ṭayāyē, or Arabs, their neighbours ... Neither the sages of the Hebrews nor the ancient Syrians transmitted [the false form PIPI as the Divine Name], neither did the orators and writers of the Greeks ...

This excerpt is from a very lengthy scholion in which Jacob attacks the use of the nonsense word "*Pīpī*" (ܦܝܦܝ) in manuscripts of the Syrohexapla as an alternative for the normal Syriac title for God, *māryā*, "Lord." He explains that the name *Pīpī* arose out of ignorance, and is connected to the different direction of writing: it arose because Greek scribes misunderstood the Hebrew Tetragrammaton written in square script, and treated it as if it were Greek, hence ΠΙΠΙ. This was then transliterated into Syriac. (It indeed is frequently found in extant manuscripts of the Syrohexapla as a marginal note where *māryā* occurs in the main text.) Jacob regards the "name" *Pīpī* as the invention of Satan, since it misrepresents the Name of God.

His information on the Tetragrammaton may derive ultimately from Origen of Alexandria's comments on the names of God, and there are also some brief comments by Evagrius on ΠΙΠΙ, but Jacob's treatment is far fuller.[46]

Jacob transcribes Hebrew *ʾĕlōhîm* correctly, though he did not need to know any Hebrew to do so, since the transliterations Ἐλωείμ and *ʾElōhīm* can be found in the Greek and Syriac Bibles (e.g. Peshitta Gen. 6:4). As with the "Hebrew" forms that Jacob cites for "heaven" and "soul," he assumes that the similarity between Hebrew and Syriac forms means that Syriac borrowed the word from Hebrew, since in his view Hebrew existed first.

Petit, Lucas van Rompay, and Jos J.S. Weitenberg, eds., *Eusèbe d'Émèse, Commentaire de la Génèse. Texte arménien de l'édition de Venise (1980). Fragments grecs et syriaques*, Traditio Exegetica Graeca 15 (Leuven: Peeters, 2011), 22–23. This may be the source for the remark found in John Chrysostom, following the discussion of the meaning of the name Abram cited above: Πολλὴ δὲ τῇ Σύρων φωνῇ πρὸς τὴν τῶν Ἑβραίων γλῶτταν ἡ συγγένεια (*Sermons 1–9 on Genesis*, PG 54: 624).

46 E.g. Origen, *Selecta in Psalmos* PG 12: 1101–04; and 1269 line 19; *Contra Celsum* VI.32.18, Origen gives Ἰαώ/Ἰά, Σαβαώθ ... Ἀδωναῖον ... Ἐλωαῖον/Ἐλωαΐ; and Paul de Lagarde, ed., *Onomastica sacra*, 2nd ed. (Göttingen: Horstmann, 1887): 229–30, Ἤλ, Ἐλωείμ, Ἀδών, Σαβαώθ, Σαδδαΐ, Αϊὲ ἐσεριέ.

There are several other similar examples of Jacob's reference to "Hebrew" words,⁴⁷ and his high regard for Hebrew can be seen in the *Hexaemeron* when he refers to it as "the ancient and revered language of the Hebrews."⁴⁸

4 Jacob on Hebrew and Jewish Traditions

As for what Jacob's pro-Hebrew stance might have to do with his attitude towards contemporary Jews and Judaism, the answer is: very little. His views on Hebrew and on "Jewish stories" are part romantic, part theological. Any direct personal contact with Jews would have been limited to the four years he was bishop of Edessa, since he spent most of his life in monasteries. The church canons he edited and the canonical issues he rules on in correspondence mention issues of Christian dealings with Jews, but there is nothing new in them compared to the new guidelines for dealing with Muslims (referred to as *Ṭayāyē*, "Arabs" and *Mahgrāyē*, "Hagarenes").⁴⁹ In the late seventh century, Judaism and Judaizing were much less of a threat to Syriac Christians than heterodox Chalcedonian and Nestorian forms of Christianity or, most recently, Islam. So it is likely that Jacob could afford to be relaxed about emphasising the links between his "orthodox" Christianity and the Hebraic past. (This would be comparable to his use of apocryphal books of Jewish origin, now that the "age of heresy" had passed.⁵⁰)

Jacob took Hebrew seriously, but this does not mean he did not have a strong sense of Syriac identity. He spoke with pride about the links between the Hebrew and Syriac languages. Members of the Syriac church in Northern Mesopotamia identified with biblical geography and often self-identified with the family of Abraham via Laban, who lived in Aram-Nahrain, near Harran. Harran was still in existence in Jacob's day, and was close to the heartland of Syriac Christianity and his bishopric of Edessa. (This is perhaps why the name Jacob was so popular

---

47 See Alison Salvesen, "Did Jacob of Edessa Know Hebrew?," in *Biblical Hebrew, Biblical Texts. Essays in Memory of Michael Weitzman*, ed. Ada Rapoport-Albert and Gillian Greenberg, 457–67 (Sheffield: Sheffield University Press, 2001); Alison Salvesen, "Was Jacob Trilingual? Jacob of Edessa's Knowledge of Hebrew Revisited," in *Studies on Jacob of Edessa*, ed. Gregorios Y. Ibrahim and George A. Kiraz, 93–105 (Piscataway, NJ: Gorgias, 2010).
48 Chabot, *Hexaemeron*, 324b.
49 Hoyland, "Jacob and Early Islamic Edessa," 16–18. In contrast, Herman Teule notes that dealings with Jews are not an important theme in Jacob's canons: Herman G.B. Teule, "Jacob of Edessa and Canon Law" in *Jacob of Edessa and the Syriac Culture of his Day*, ed. R.B. ter Haar Romeny, MPIL 18 (Leiden/Boston: Brill, 2008): 96–97.
50 See Adler, "Jewish Pseudepigrapha in Jacob of Edessa's Letters and Historical Writings," 49.

among Syrian Orthodox clergy and monks: it was a name conveniently shared with the Hebrew patriarch in Genesis and with the brother of Jesus, as well as the revered Syriac ecclesiastics Jacob of Nisibis and Jacob Baradaeus.[51]) Jacob's emphasis on this geographical coincidence perhaps meant that the Syriac *language* did not need to be the sole cornerstone of Syrian Orthodox identity.[52]

Rubin may be correct in seeing a direct connection between Jacob and the majority view of the Greek church, that Hebrew was the primordial language. In support of her suggestion, we may note that Jacob's promotion of Greek in Syrian Orthodox monasteries was a contentious issue. As mentioned earlier, he had to leave one institution where he had taught for a decade because of the "hatred" that the monks there had for the "Greeks," meaning presumably the Byzantine Chalcedonians. But Jacob himself had a lively awareness of different languages and their scripts,[53] he had some basic knowledge about Arabic, and could identify differences between Syriac and what we now call Christian Palestinian Aramaic.[54] However, Jacob's choice of supporting evidence for the priority of Hebrew is drawn not from Byzantine Greek writers but from the sub-apostolic writer "Clement," the pre-Chalcedonian Greek Syrian Eusebius of Emesa, and less explicitly from the "Jewish stories" of Jubilees that he favoured.

---

51 Cf. also Jean M. Fiey, *Saints syriaques*, Studies in Late Antiquity and Early Islam 6 (Princeton, NJ: Darwin Press, 2004), 105–11. In the mid-fourth century, Ephrem's older contemporary, Aphrahat, who may have lived in the region of Mosul, describes Jacob three times as 'abūn, "our father" (twice in *Dem.* IV.5 on Prayer, describing Jacob's prayer at Bethel, once in *Dem.* XVI.1). However, in all three places the context may indicate that Jacob is seen as the father of the "People from the Peoples," rather than the ancestor specifically of Syriac Christians. Isaac is also referred to once as 'our father' (*Dem.* XIV.27), in a more indefinite context. Though Aphrahat often describes Abraham as father of many nations (cf. Gen. 17:5), especially of those from all nations who act righteously (cf. *Dem.* XI, on Circumcision), he never refers to Abraham as "*our* father."
52 See Alison Salvesen, "The Genesis of Ethnicity? The Role of the Bible in the Self-Definition of Syriac Writers," *The Harp* 23 (2008): 369–82
53 On the direction of writing, see *Scholion on the Divine Name,* PO 29, ed. Brière, 196 [700], lines 28–30: "Those who write from left to right: the Greeks, Romans, Egyptians and Armenians. Those who write from right to left: the Hebrews, Syrians, Tayāyē and Persians." Compare the very different and theological point made on the basis of the different directions of scripts in *The Cave of Treasures* (Minov, *Memory and Identity*, 272, 281–83).
54 See William Wright, *A Catalogue of Syriac Manuscripts in the British Museum*, vol. 2 (London: Trustees of the British Museum, 1871), 984b. giving a note in Jacob's *Encheiridion* where he distinguishes the use of the particle *yath* in "Mesopotamian Syriac" and "Palestinian Syriac."

5 Conclusion

Jacob's attitude to Hebrew has both vertical and horizontal functions. Vertically, or historically, it reaches back into antiquity and grafts Syrian Orthodox Christians onto a privileged lineage via the Arameans, relatives of the Hebrew patriarchs. Horizontally, or contemporaneously, it marks itself off from other Syriac Christian communities whom Jacob considered heterodox and who took a different view of what the primordial language had been.

Jacob's admiration for Hebrew was unique among the Syriac writers who discuss the language. Not only does he state that Hebrew is the Adamic language, but he often refers to Hebrew words in his works. His stance is likely to represent a reaction against the predominant view of the Church of the East.

As for scholarly contact between Jews and Christians in the period, it is not supported by Jacob's appreciation of Jewish traditions and reference to "Hebrew" etymologies, since both of these are almost entirely received at second- or third-hand. It may only imply that that in the new world order of the late seventh century, it was safe to promote them: Judaism was now seen as much less of a threat to Syriac Christians than Islam was becoming.

Bibliography

Abbeloos, Joannes B., and Thomas J. Lamy. *Gregorii Barhebraei Chronicon Ecclesiasticum*. Vol. 1. Louvain: C. Peeters, 1872.

Adler, William. "Abraham and the Burning of the Temple of Idols: Jubilees' Traditions in Christian Chronography." *Jewish Quarterly Review* 77, no. 2/3 (Oct. 1986–Jan. 1987): 95–117.

Adler, William. "Jewish Pseudepigrapha in Jacob of Edessa's Letters and Historical Writings." In *Jacob of Edessa and the Syriac Culture of His Day*, edited by R.B. ter Haar Romeny, 49–65. Monographs of the Peshitta Institute, Leiden 18. Leiden: Brill, 2008.

Brière, Maurice. "Scolie (au sujet du Nom honorable et secret)." In *Les Homiliae Cathedrales de Sévère d'Antioche. Traduction syriaque de Jacques d'Édesse*, ed. Maurice Brière. Patrologia Orientalis 29. Paris: Firmin-Didot, 1960.

Brock, Sebastian P. "Abraham and the Ravens: A Syriac Counterpart to Jubilees 11–12 and Its Implications." *Journal for the Study of Judaism* 9 (1978): 135–52.

Chabot, Jean-Baptiste, ed. *Chronique de Michel le Syrien, patriarche jacobite d'Antioche (1166–1199)*. 4 vols. Brussels: Culture et Civilisation, 1963.

Chabot, Jean-Baptiste. *Iacobi Edesseni Hexaemeron, seu in opus creationis libri septem*. Corpus scriptorum Christianorum Orientalium 92/Scriptores Syri 44. Paris: E Typographeo Reipublicae, 1928–1932.

Chrysostom, John. *Homilies 1–67 on Genesis*. In *Patrologia Graeca*, vol. 53, edited by J.-P. Migne. Paris, 1862.

Chrysostom, John. *Sermons 1–9 on Genesis*. In *Patrologia Graeca*, vol. 54, edited by J.-P. Migne, cols. 581–630. Paris, 1862.
de Goeje, Michael J., ed. *Liber expugnatio regionum*. Leiden: Brill, 1866.
Eusebius of Caesarea. *Praeparatio Evangelica*. In *Patrologia Graeca*, vol. 21, edited by J.-P. Migne. Paris, 1857.
Fiey, Jean M. *Saints syriaques*. Studies in Late Antiquity and Early Islam 6. Princeton, NJ: Darwin Press, 2004.
Graffin, François. "Jacques d'Édesse réviseur des Homélies de Sévère d'Antioche d'après le ms. syriaque B.M. Add 12.159." In *Symposium Syriacum 1976, Chantilly, France*, edited by François Graffin and Antoine Guillaumont, 243–255. Rome: Istituto Pontificio Biblico, 1978.
Hill, Robert C. *Homilies on Genesis 1–17*. Fathers of the Church 74. Washington, D.C.: Catholic University of America, 1999.
Hill, Robert C. *Homilies on Genesis 18–45*. Fathers of the Church 82. Washington, D.C.: Catholic University of America, 2001.
Hoyland, Robert G. "Jacob and Early Islamic Edessa." In *Jacob of Edessa and the Syriac Culture of His Day*, edited by R.B. ter Haar Romeny, 11–24. Monographs of the Peshitta Institute, Leiden 18. Leiden: Brill, 2008.
Kantor, Benjamin P. "The Second Column of Origen's Hexapla in Light of Greek Pronunciation." PhD diss., University of Texas, Austin, 2017.
Kutscher, Edward Y. *The Language and Linguistic Background of the Isaiah Scroll (1Q Isaᵃ)*. Leiden: Brill, 1974.
Lagarde, Paul de, ed. *Onomastica sacra*, 2nd ed. Göttingen: Horstmann, 1887.
Levene, Abraham, ed. *The Early Syrian Fathers on Genesis. From a Syriac Ms. On the Pentateuch in the Mingana Collection*. London: Taylor's Foreign Press, 1951.
Metzler, Karin. *Prokop von Gaza: Der Genesiskommentar. Aus den "Eclogarum in Libros Historicos Veteris Testamenti Epitome" übersetzt und mit Anmerkungen versehen*. Die griechischen christlichen Schriftsteller der ersten drei Jahrhunderte 23. Berlin/Boston: De Gruyter, 2016.
Minov, Sergey. *Memory and Identity in the Syriac Cave of Treasures: Rewriting the Bible in Sasanian Iran*. Jerusalem Studies in Religion and Culture 26. Leiden/Boston: Brill, 2020.
Moss, Yonatan. "The Language of Paradise: Hebrew or Syriac? Linguistic Speculations and Linguistic Realities in Late Antiquity." In *Paradise in Antiquity: Jewish and Christian Views*, edited by Markus Bockmuehl and Guy Stroumsa, 120–37. Cambridge: Cambridge University Press, 2010.
Nau, François. "Traduction des lettres XII et XIII de Jacques d'Édesse." *Revue de l'orient chrétien* 10 (1905): 197–208, 258–282.
Nestle, Eberhard. "Jakob von Edessa über den Schem Hammephorasch und andere Gottesnamen. Ein Beitrag zur Geschichte der Tetragrammaton." *Zeitschrift der Deutschen Morgenländischen Gesellschaft* 32 (1878): 465–508.
Origen. *Contra Celsum*. In *Patrologia Graeca*, vol. 11, edited by J.-P. Migne, cols. 641–1650. Paris, 1857.
Origen. *Selecta in Genesim*. In *Patrologia Graeca*, vol. 12, edited by J.-P. Migne, cols. 145–280. Paris, 1862.
Origen. *Selecta in Psalmos*. In *Patrologia Graeca*, vol. 12, edited by J.-P. Migne, cols. 1053–1684. Paris, 1862.
Papaconstantinou, Arietta. "Administering the Early Islamic Empire: Insights from the Papyri." In *Money, Power and Politics in Early Islamic Syria: A Review of Current Debates*, edited by John F. Haldon, 57–74. Farnham: Ashgate, 2010.

Petit, Françoise. *Catenae Graecae in Genesim et in Exodum. 2, Collectio Coisliniana in Genesim.* Corpus Christianorum. Series Graeca, 15. Turnhout-Leuven: Peeters, 1986.

Petit, Françoise. *La chaîne sur la Genèse. Édition intégrale 1.* Traditio Exegetica Graeca 1. Leuven: Peeters, 1992.

Petit, Françoise. Lucas van Rompay, and Jos J.S. Weitenberg, eds. *Eusèbe d'Émèse, Commentaire de la Génèse. Texte arménien de l'édition de Venise (1980). Fragments grecs et syriaques.* Traditio Exegetica Graeca 15. Leuven: Peeters, 2011.

Rehm, Bernhard, ed. *Die Pseudoklementinen. II, Rekognitionen: in Rufins Übersetzung.* Berlin: Akademie-Verlag, 1965.

Rubin, Milka. "The Language of Creation or the Primordial Language: A Case of Cultural Polemics in Antiquity." *Journal of Jewish Studies* 49 (1998): 306–33.

Sáenz-Badillos, Angel. *A History of the Hebrew Language.* Cambridge: Cambridge University Press, 1996.

Salvesen, Alison. "Did Jacob of Edessa Know Hebrew?" In *Biblical Hebrew, Biblical Texts. Essays in Memory of Michael Weitzman*, edited by Ada Rapoport-Albert and Gillian Greenberg, 457–467. Sheffield: Sheffield University Press, 2001.

Salvesen, Alison. "The Genesis of Ethnicity? The Role of the Bible in the Self-Definition of Syriac Writers." *The Harp* 23 (2008): 369–82.

Salvesen, Alison. "Was Jacob Trilingual? Jacob of Edessa's Knowledge of Hebrew Revisited." In *Studies on Jacob of Edessa*, edited by Gregorios Y. Ibrahim and George A. Kiraz, 93–105. Piscataway, NJ: Gorgias, 2010.

Schrier, Omert J. "Chronological Problems Concerning the Lives of Severus Bar Mašqā, Athanasius of Balad, Julianus Romāyā, Yoḥannān Sābā, George of the Arabs and Jacob of Edessa." *Oriens Christianus* 75 (1991): 62–90.

ter Haar Romeny, Robert B. *A Syrian in Greek Dress. The Use of Greek, Hebrew, and Syriac Biblical Texts in Eusebius of Emesa's Commentary on Genesis.* Traditio Exegetica Graeca 6. Leuven: Peeters, 1997.

ter Haar Romeny, Robert B. "Ephrem and Jacob of Edessa in the Commentary of the Monk Severus." In *Malphono w-Rabo d-Malphone. Studies in Honor of Sebastian P. Brock*, edited by George A. Kiraz, 535–557. Piscataway, NJ: Gorgias, 2008.

Teule, Herman G.B., "Jacob of Edessa and Canon Law," in *Jacob of Edessa and the Syriac Culture of his Day,* edited by R.B. ter Haar Romeny, 83–100. Monographs of the Peshitta Institute, Leiden 18. Leiden/Boston: Brill, 2008.

Theodoret of Cyrus, *The Questions on the Octateuch.* Trans. John F. Petruccione and Robert C. Hill. Library of Early Christianity 1. Washington: Catholic University of America Press, 2007.

van Rompay, Lucas, ed. *Le Commentaire sur Genèse-Exode 9,32 du Manuscrit (olim) Diyarbakir 22.* Corpus scriptorum Christianorum Orientalium 483–84/Scriptores Syri 205–06. Leuven: Peeters, 1986.

Vaschalde, Arthur, trans. *Iacobi Edesseni Hexaemeron, seu in opus creationis libri septem.* Corpus scriptorum Christianorum Orientalium 97/Scriptores Syri 48. Paris: E Typographeo Reipublicae, 1932.

Vosté, Jacques M., and Ceslas van den Eynde, eds. *Commentaire d'Išoʻdad de Merv sur l'Ancien Testament. I. Genèse.* Corpus scriptorum Christianorum Orientalium 126/Scriptores Syri 67. Louvain: Imprimerie Orientaliste L. Durbecq, 1950.

Wright, William. *A Catalogue of Syriac Manuscripts in the British Museum*. Vol. 2. London: Trustees of the British Museum, 1871.

Wright, William. "Two Epistles of Mar Jacob, Bishop of Edessa." *Journal of Sacred Literature and Biblical Record* NS 10 (1867): 430–60.

Irven M. Resnick
"Lingua sacra et diabolica": A Survey of Medieval Christian Views of the Hebrew Language

A little more than three decades ago, my study 'Lingua dei, lingua hominis: Sacred Language and Medieval Texts,'[1] investigated the development of the Western Christian tradition of three sacred languages. That study determined that it was especially the *titulus* above the Cross identifying Jesus as King of the Jews in Hebrew, Greek, and Latin that supported their shared status as sacred tongues.[2] Furthermore, the Fathers of the Church and their medieval heirs typically identified Hebrew as the primordial language,[3] the *Ursprache* (and sometimes also the *Endsprache*)[4] – the language of God, the angels,[5] and Adam (*lingua Adamica*);

---

[1] 'Lingua Dei, lingua hominis: Sacred Language and Medieval Texts,' *Viator* 21 (1990): 51–74. All translations are mine unless otherwise indicated.

[2] The Christian pilgrim to Jerusalem, Ps.-Antoninus Placentinus and author of an *Itinerarium*, claims to have seen the *titulus* there; see *Itinerarium* 20, 12–16, in *Itineraria et alia geographica*, CCSL 175 (Turnholt: Brepols, 1965), 139. Although the martyr Antoninus visited Jerusalem during the second half of the sixth century, this text may date from centuries later. During restoration work at the end of the fifteenth century at the Basilica of Santa Croce in Gerusalemme in Rome, a leaden box was discovered bearing the inscription, *Titulus Crucis,* and a seal on the box can be traced to Pope Lucius II (1144–45), although the faithful regard this as an authentic relic of the True Cross. For a discussion of the claim, see Paul L. Maier, "The Inscription on the Cross of Jesus of Nazareth," *Hermes* 124, no. 1 (1996): 58–75, esp. 73–75. Radiocarbon dating of the wood of the relic suggests, in fact, a tenth- to twelfth-century origin. See Francesco Bella and Carlo Azzi, "^{14}C Dating of the 'Titulus Crucis,'" *Radiocarbon* 44, no. 3 (2002): 685–689.

[3] For medieval Jewish discussion of the claim that Hebrew is the original language, see, for example, Moshe Idel, "A la recherche de la langue originelle: le témoignage du nourisson," *Revue de l'histoire des religions* 213, no. 4 (1996): 415–42.

[4] On Hebrew as the *Endsprache* in some medieval Jewish sources, into which all other languages will collapse in the messianic age, see Moshe Idel, *Language, Torah, and Hermenuetics in Abraham Abulafia,* trans. Menahem Kallus (Albany, New York: SUNY Press, 1989), 25f. For Christian awareness of this tradition, see Claude Duret, *Thresor de l'histoire des langues de c'est univers* (Cologne: 1613), chap. 27, 259–61.

[5] Although, as Isidore of Seville notes, one can only speak of the "tongue" or language of angels equivocally, since (unembodied) angels do not have the physical requirements for speech. See *The Etymologies of Isidore of Seville,* eds. and trans. Stephen A. Barney, W. J. Lewis, J. A. Beach, and Oliver Berghof (Cambridge: Cambridge University Press, 2006), 9.1.1–14. Albert the Great also insists that angels communicate directly to one another, without audible speech – *sine voce prolato sermone.* See Albertus Magnus, *Summa Theologiae,* pars 2, tr. 9, q. 35, m.3 in ibid.,

thus, Dante affirmed that the first word Adam spoke was the Hebrew "El."[6] Hebrew was also sometimes privileged as the language spoken by Jesus himself.[7] These additional assertions strengthened Hebrew's claim to sacrality and helped to justify the inclusion of Hebrew words in the Christian liturgy.[8]

Nonetheless, Hebrew was also a language that had suffered corruption after Adam's fall and after the confusion of languages at Babel. In Latin astrological texts, Hebrew, like Jews themselves, is said to be subject to the influence of Saturn, a symbol of decline and decay.[9] Consequently, medieval Christian views

---

Opera omnia, ex editione lugdunensi, religiose castigata, vol. 32: *Summa Theologiae, secunda pars (quaest. I-LXVII)*, ed. Auguste Borgnet (Paris: Vivès, 1895), 381–82. For an overview of Scholastic discussions, see Bernd Rolling, "Angelic Language and Communication," in *A Companion to Angels in Medieval Philosophy*, ed. Tobias Hoffmann (Leiden: Brill, 2012), 223–260. Nonetheless, many traditions note that angels speak Hebrew as the language of revelation. In the book of Jubilees 12:25–26, God instructs an angel to speak in Hebrew, "the tongue of creation." For the text, see Nicholas de Lange, *Apocrypha: Jewish Literature of the Hellenistic Age* (New York: Viking, 1978), 57. Later Latin Christian theologians often affirm that the angels speak Hebrew – e.g., Hugh of St. Victor, *Miscellanea* 3.34 (PL 177: 655C). Cf. Arno Borst, *Der Turmbau von Babel*, 4 vols. (Stuttgart: Anton Hiersemann, 1957–1963), 2/2: 653f. In medieval Jewish sources, not only is Hebrew the official language of the celestial court, but, Trachtenberg maintains, "the angels are monolingual." Joshua Trachtenberg, *Jewish Magic and Superstition* (Philadelphia: University of Pennsylvania Press, 2004), 74. This point is also underscored by the mystical *Zohar* (1:75b), which records that the angels in the celestial court only understand and respond to the holy language. The confusion of tongues in the Tower of Babel episode in Gen. 11:6 resulted in deafness to the entreaties of the Tower's builders among the heavenly powers, because "the powers above know and recognize only the holy tongue," i.e., Hebrew. For this English translation, see *The Zohar: Pritzker Edition*, trans. Daniel C. Matt, vol. 1 (Stanford: Stanford University Press, 2004), 445; see also Raphael Patai, *Gates to the Old City* (New York: Avon, 1980), 477. For more on language and the angels, see Gabriel Wasserman's contribution in this volume.

6 Dante Aligheri, *De vulgari eloquentia* 1.4: "Quid autem prius vox primi loquentis sonaverit, viro sane mentis in promptu esse non titubo ipsum fuisse quod 'Deus' est, scilicet *El*, [. . .]," accessed August 31, 2019, http://www.thelatinlibrary.com/dante/vulgar.shtml#IV. Cf. idem, *Paradiso* 26, 124–126, where Adam reveals that "El" was second, and that "J[ehovah]" was first. See *The Divine Comedy* III: *Paradise*, trans. Louis Biancolli (New York: Washington Square Press, 1966), 107r.

7 Remigius of Auxerre, *Commentarius in Genesim* 10 (PL 131: 81B).

8 Iohannes Beleth, *Summa de ecclesiasticis officiis* 35b, CCCM 41A, ed. H. Douteil (Turnholt: Brepols, 1976), 64–65. Later the author also identifies Hebrew words in the liturgy as a *vox angelica*. Ibid., 79b, 146.

9 *Picatrix: The Latin Version of the Ghāyat Al-Hakīm*, 3.1, ed. David Pingree (London: The Warburg Institute, University of London, 1986), 91. For the influence of Saturn upon Jews and Judaism, see Eric Zafran, "Saturn and the Jews," *Journal of the Warburg and Courtauld Institutes* 42 (1979): 16–27; Irven M. Resnick, *Marks of Distinction: Christian Perceptions of Jews in the High Middle Ages* (Washington, DC: Catholic University of America Press, 2013), 215–67; and, Yvonne Owen, "The Saturnine History of Jews and Witches," *Preternature* 3, no. 1 (2014): 56–84.

of Hebrew seem caught between these two poles – the primordial language of humankind, the sacred language of God and the angels (*vox angelica*),[10] and its corrupt and degenerate successor. Moreover, medieval Latin Christians experienced profound anxiety, I maintain, because Jews were thought to possess a mastery of the Hebrew language, of which most Christians were ignorant. In addition, because medieval Jewish thinkers (e.g., Maimonides, Nachmanides, and Abraham Abulafia) routinely asserted the *superiority* of Hebrew as a sacred tongue – because it lacks a vocabulary for obscene and disgusting human functions,[11] or because it is the natural language, the holy language of all humanity before the episode at Babel,[12] the very language of God,[13] and the mother of all other languages[14] – Latin Christians sometimes engaged in a polemical effort to depict the Hebrew of medieval Jews as corrupted or diabolical while, at the same time, trying to reclaim a sacred Hebrew for Christians alone.[15]

---

10 Iohannes Beleth, *Summa de ecclesiasticis officiis* 79b, 146; Hugh of St. Victor, *Miscellanea* 3.34 (PL 177: 655C).
11 Maimonides, *Guide of the Perplexed* 3.8, trans. Shlomo Pines (Chicago: University of Chicago Press, 1964), 435–36.
12 See Rashi, *Commentaries on the Pentateuch*, trans. Chaim Pearl (New York: Viking Press, 1970), 38.
13 Ramban [Nachmanides], *Commentary on the Torah*, trans. Charles B. Chavel, 5 vols. (New York: Shilo Publishing House, 1971–76), 1: 519.
14 See esp. Moshe Idel, *Language, Torah, and Hermenuetics in Abraham Abulafia*, 12ff. For another medieval Jewish testimony to the sacrality of the *lingua adamica et angelica*, see Judah Halevi, *The Kuzari* 4.25, trans. Hartwig Hirschfeld (New York: Schocken, 1964), 229, 237. For a brief summary of medieval Jewish views of the origin of Hebrew language, see Alexander Scheiber, "Das Problem des Ursprungs der Sprache im Jüdischen Schriftum," *Magyar-zsido szemle* 53 (1937): 334–349.
15 This polemic was also sometimes directed internally against Christians who advocated strongly on behalf of the study of Greek and Hebrew. For example, see Philip of Harvengt, Abbot of Bonne-Esperance (d. 1183), and his Epist. 17, in which the author complains that one is much better served learning Latin, the language in which the true God is proclaimed, than Hebrew or Greek, which are renowned only for their antiquity (PL 203, 154A-C). Conversely, Peter Abelard strongly recommended the study of Hebrew, Greek and Latin, and held Heloise up as an example precisely because she was trained in all three languages. Peter Abelard, Epist. 9 [to the Virgins of the Paraclete]: *De studio litterarum* (PL 178, 333). See Constant J. Mews, "Abelard and Heloise on Jews and *Hebraica Veritas*," in *Christian Attitudes toward Jews in the Middle Ages: A Casebook*, ed. Michael Frassetto (New York, London: Routledge, 2007), 83–108.

1 Three, and Only Three, Sacred Languages

Although for medieval Christians Hebrew was one of *three* sacred languages, the early medieval western Church was principally concerned to promote the sacrality of Latin, whose last-place position on the *titulus* encouraged the view that among the sacred languages it was preeminent.¹⁶ Not only did its presence on the *titulus*, a sacred relic, help to establish Latin as a sacred language alongside Hebrew and Greek, but the appearance there of these three languages also contained a negative implication: viz., that all *other* languages are profane. This conclusion became prominent as elements within the Carolingian Church sought to establish the Latin liturgy as normative throughout Europe. Thus when Pope John VIII (r. 872–82) wrote to Methodius, Archbishop of Pannonia, who, along with his brother Cyril had instructed and evangelized the Slavs and created a Slavic liturgy, he ordered him to cease from celebrating mass in that language, and to "[chant it] either in the Latin or Greek language, just as the church of God ... chants it." Contrariwise, Pope John VIII accepted only the necessity of *preaching* in the vernacular for the benefit of the faithful.¹⁷

The pope's letter probably reflects the attitude of a majority of Frankish and Latin clerics. In the old Slavonic *Vita* of (Constantine-) Cyril, reference appears once more to this controversy. There, describing Cyril's efforts to create a Slavonic

---

16 See, for example, Pope Nicholas I's Epist. 86, *Ad Michaelem imperatorem* (PL 119, 932A), in which the Pope responds to the Byzantine emperor's complaint that Latin is a barbarous language by appealing to its pride of place on the titulus of the Cross. By contrast, medieval Jews typically asserted the sacred preeminence of Hebrew, as noted above.

17 "Audimus etiam, quod missas cantes in barbara, hoc est in Sclavina lingua, unde iam litteris nostris per Paulum episcopum Anconitanum tibi directis prohibuimus, ne in ea lingua sacra missarum sollempnia celebrares, sed vel in Latina vel in Greca lingua, sicut ecclesia Dei toto terrarum orbe diffusa et in omnibus gentibus dilatata cantat. Praedicare vero aut sermonem in populo facere tibi licet, quoniam psalmista omnes ammonet Dominum gentes laudare et apostolus: 'Omnis', inquit, 'lingua confiteatur, quia dominus Iesus in gloria est Dei patris.'" Pope John VIII, Epist. 201, in *Registrum Iohannis VIII*, ed. Erich Ludwig Eduard Caspar, *Epistolae karolini aevi*, 5, MGH Epp. 7 (Berlin: Weidmannsche Buchhandlung, 1928), 161, ll. 13ff. The dispute seems very much centered on language, since scholars have recognized that the formulary for the Mass that Cyril and Methodius used as the basis for their Slavonic liturgy may have been a Greek translation of a Latin formulary already in use in Moravia. Therefore, this was not principally a dispute over the *content* but over the appropriate language for the celebration of the mass. See Francis Dvornik, "The Significance of the Missions of Cyril and Methodius," *Slavic Review* 23, no. 2 (1964): 195–211, and esp. 201–202. For a brief recent discussion of the brothers' missionary effort to the Slavs, and western response, see Robert Louis Wilken, *The First Thousand Years: A Global History of Christianity* (New Haven: Yale University Press, 2012), 344–50.

liturgy for Moravia, the hagiographer remarks: "And he [the devil] began to rouse many, saying [...] 'only three languages, Hebrew, Greek, and Latin, were chosen as appropriate for rendering glory unto God.' These were the cohorts of the Latins speaking [...][and] Constantine [-Cyril] defeated them with words from the Scriptures, and called them trilinguists [...]"[18]

In contrast to Constantine-Cyril, then, who sought to defend a Slavonic liturgy, medieval "trilingualists" recognized the sacrality of *three and only three* languages for liturgical use: Hebrew, Greek, and Latin.

2 The Tetragrammaton, Magical Language, and the Demonic

Although "trilingualism" endorsed the sacral character of the Hebrew language, it seems that its sacrality was guaranteed only in certain contexts. Therefore, like other holy objects Hebrew is subject to misuse. We find a good example in the work of the eleventh-century north Italian *Wanderlehrer* and Milanese cleric, Anselm the Peripatetic. From about A.D. 1045 Anselm was a notary in the chancery of the emperor Henry III. Anselm is also the author of the unfinished *Rhetorimachia*, which was intended to illustrate his mastery of the principles of rhetoric and dialectic.[19] In it, Anselm attacked the alleged literary and moral failures of his cousin, Rotiland, whom he accused of pandering, necromancy, and several (unsuccessful) erotic adventures. Anselm describes a dream encounter he had with Rotiland's father, Robert, who revealed that on a certain night Rotiland led a young boy beyond the walls of the city into the meadow of St. John, where he buried the boy in a hole up to the waist, created a magic circle of stones around him, and tormented his eyes with smoke from an acrid incense. Rotiland kept vigil most of the night, during which he repeated these *sacred words* (*his sacris verbis*):

---

18 *Vita Constantini* 15, in *Medieval Slavic Lives of Saints and Princes*, trans. Marvin Kantor, Michigan Slavic Translations 5 (Ann Arbor: University of Michigan, 1983), 25–33 and 65–81. Although Rome would eventually confirm the use of Slavonic in the liturgy, it remained problematic: Pope Gregory VII in 1080 rejected a request from the Bohemian prince Uratislav that he be permitted to use it. See Pope Gregory VII, Epist. 7,11, in *Gregorii VII Registrum lib. V-IX*, ed. Erich Caspar, MGH, Epp. sel., vol. 2, part 2 (Berlin: Weidmannsche Buchhandlung, 1923), 474. For discussion of the early medieval debate over use of the vernacular in the liturgy, see also Angelus A. De Marco, *Rome and the Vernacular* (Westminster, MD: The Newman Press, 1961), chap. 2.

19 For discussion, see my "Anselm the Peripatetic (of Besate) and Humanism in the Eleventh Century," *Journal of Medieval Latin* 6 (1996): 1–12; Beth S. Bennett, "The Significance of the *Rhetorimachia* of Anselm of Besate to the History of Rhetoric," *Rhetorica* 5 (1987): 231–250.

As this youth has been bound in the ground on this spot, so [let] young girls be [bound] in my love. As he is encircled by a [stone] wall and a ditch, so too even [let them be] by my love. And as [his] eyes are weakened by the smoke [of the incense] so too [let] girls be by my absence. And he said these things with these words in the *Hebrew or rather diabolical [language]*.[20]

Anselm's tale points to an intriguing paradox. On the one hand, Rotiland uttered an incantation in Hebrew comprised of "sacred words"; on the other, these Hebrew words form a diabolical language, presumably because they were addressed to the devil, under whose tutelage all magical arts are practiced, according to Peter Lombard.[21] As such, this eleventh-century example of love magic provides an illustration of the abuse of the holy: Hebrew, a sacred language, is misused by Rotiland to invoke demons in order to achieve romantic control over women. Rotiland's incantation evokes a comparison too to the episode in the Garden of Eden in which Satan sought to seduce Eve, through his instrument the serpent, by uttering words presumably in Hebrew, the *lingua Adamica*.[22]

It seems worthy of note that in Anselm's text it is not a *Jewish* sorcerer but a Christian that is guilty of the abuse of the sacred, in contrast to the well-known role of the *Jewish* magician in the Theophilus legend that had circulated from the ninth century in Paul the Deacon's Latin text.[23] There, a Jewish sorcerer brokers

---

20 "'Ut est fixus adolescentulus in loco isto, sic puell[a]e in amore meo. Ut est precinctus muro et fossa, sic et ill[a]e dilectione mea. Et ut oculi consumuntur fumo, ita puellul(a)e abscessu meo.' Cum quibus verbis hec dicebat Hebraica vel potius diabolica." Anselm of Besate, *Rhetorimachia* 2.3, ed. Karl Manitius, MGH, Die deutschen Geschichtsquellen des Mittelalters 500–1500, 2 (Weimar: Hermann Böhlaus Nachfolger, 1958), 143, ll. 8–13. Italics are mine.
21 Peter Lombard, *Libri IV Sententiarum*, bk. II, dist. vii, cap. 6, 2nd ed. (Florence: Ex Typographia Collegii S. Bonaventurae, 1916), 1: 336–337, accessed September 1, 2019, https://archive.org/details/libriivsententia01pete/page/n3.
22 For some early Christians, the link between Satan and the serpent could be demonstrated linguistically. Thus, Justin Martyr offers the false etymology that even the name "Satan" is derived from the Hebrew *sata* ("apostate") and *nas* ("serpent"), suggesting an essential connection in the Hebrew language. See his *Dialogue with Trypho*, chap. 103, trans. Thomas B. Falls (Washington, DC: The Catholic University of America Press, 1965), 310. For medieval Latin tradition, Remigius of Auxerre reiterates a common view that it was the devil that spoke to Eve through the serpent; that the serpent itself had no capacity for understanding its own speech, just as individuals possessed by evil spirits (*energumenoi*) fail to understand the words they utter. See *Commentarius in Genesim* 3.1 (PL 131: 64B). Cf. Augustine, *De Genesi ad litteram libri duodecim* 11.27–29, CSEL 28.1, ed. J. Zycha, 360–62; Gregory the Great, *Moralium libri* 27.1 (PL 76: 399C); Peter Lombard, *Libri IV Sententiarum*, bk. II, dist. 21, cap. 4, p. 405; Thomas Aquinas, *Summa Theologica* 2.2, q. 165, art. 2 (Rome: Typographia Forzani et S., 1928), 3: 1079–1081.
23 Paul the Deacon. *Miraculum S. Mariae de Theophilo*. For the Latin text, see Robert Petsch, ed., *Theophilus, mittelniederdeutsches Drama in drei Fassungen* (Heidelberg: Carl Winters, 1908),

the contract between Theophilus and the devil.²⁴ Although Paul the Deacon's text does not claim that the Jewish sorcerer communicated with the devil in Hebrew, nonetheless, in the thirteenth-century Lambeth Palace Library Apocalypse, Theophilus is depicted sealing his pact with the devil whose scroll, according to Michael Camille, contains a "strange diabolic language," in what appears to be a pseudo-Hebrew.²⁵ In both texts, then, Hebrew – or rather pseudo-Hebrew – appears to be a diabolic language. This association may also be implied in the illustration accompanying Psalm 52 in the mid-thirteenth century Amesbury Abbey Psalter, in which Jesus – anachronistically – speaks Latin, but Satan speaks Hebrew, or a pseudo-Hebrew, suggesting to Ruth Mellinkoff that "Satan and the Jews are linked by their common language."²⁶ It is unsurprising that Jews,

---

1–10. On the Jewish magician or sorcerer generally in Christian sources, see the classic work by Joshua Trachtenberg, *Jewish Magic and Superstition*, passim.

24 On the development of the Theophilus legend in medieval texts, see Moshe Lazar, "Theophilus: Servant of Two Masters. The Pre-Faustian Theme of Despair and Revolt," *Modern Language Notes* 87, no. 6 (1972): 31–50. According to the Theophilus legend, the Virgin Mary intervenes to void the contract with the devil. See Adrienne Williams Boyarin, *Miracles of the Virgin in Medieval England: Law and Jewishness in Marian Legends* (Cambridge: D.S. Brewer, 2010), 42–103. For a good illustration in the De Brailes Hours (ca. 1240), see British Library, Add MS 49999, fol. 40v, accessed June 5, 2014, http://www.bl.uk/manuscripts/Viewer.aspx?ref=add_ms_49999_f001r . At fol. 42v, the contract is clearly marked by the Latin "carta teofoli"; at fol. 40v, however, the letters present an odd mixture of Latin and nonsense symbols or letters.

25 See Michael Camille, "The Devil's Writing: Diabolic Literacy in Medieval Art," in *World Art: Themes of Unity in Diversity; Acts of the XXVth International Congress of the History of Art*, 3 vols., ed. by Irving Lavin (University Park, PA: Pennsylvania University Press, 1989), 2: 355–60, citing 356 and 358, n. 15. Pseudo-Arabic script is also attested elsewhere in visual depictions of Jews, for example in an illustration of Cantiga 25 in the *Cantigas de Santa Maria* (the Escorial Codex, Escorial T.I.1, fols. 38v-39r). Pamela Patton suggests that use of pseudo-Arabic is meant to conflate Jews and Muslims as enemies of the Christian faith. See her "Constructing the Inimical Jew in the *Cantigas de Santa Maria*: Theophilus's Magician in Text and Image," in *Beyond the Yellow Badge: Anti-Judaism and Antisemitism in Medieval and Early Modern Visual Culture*, ed. Mitchell B. Merback (Leiden: Brill, 2008): 233–56, citing 240. See 510, fig. 5, for a reproduction. In Renaissance art, pseudo-Arabic sometimes has positive connotations and is used to identify members of the Holy Family (i.e., Mary, Joseph, etc.). See Rosamund E. Mack, *Bazaar to Piazza: Islamic trade and Italian Art, 1300–1600* (Berkeley: University of California Press, 2001), 51, 62–3. See also Alexander Nagel, "Twenty-Five Notes on Pseudoscript in Italian Art," *Res* 59/60 (2011): 228–48. For discussion of anti-Jewish motifs in medieval apocalypses other than the Lambeth Palace Library Apocalypse, see Suzanne Lewis, "*Tractatus Adversus Judaeos* in the Gulbenkian Apocalypse," *Art Bulletin* 68 (1986): 543–566; eadem, "Exegesis and Illustration in Thirteenth-Century English Apocalypses," in *The Apocalypse in the Middle Ages*, ed. Richard K. Emmerson and Bernard McGinn (Ithaca: Cornell University Press, 1992), 259–75.

26 Ruth Mellinkoff, *Outcasts: Signs of Otherness in Northern European Art of the Late Middle Ages*, 2 vols. (Berkeley: University of California Press, 1993), 1: 105.

therefore, who Latin Christians assumed routinely used Hebrew as a liturgical (but not vernacular) language, should frequently be identified with both the devil and magic.[27]

Pseudo-Hebrew also appears in Anselm's text to illustrate Rotiland's diabolical "Hebrew" incantation. Once again, Rotiland is not a Jew, and therefore it is not because Jews use it that Hebrew is diabolical. Rather, it is Hebrew's functionality, as a language employed by Satan or to address Satan, that seems most important. This conclusion drawn from Anselm's text does not imply that Anselm knew Hebrew or had any accurate knowledge of the Hebrew language. Indeed, the modern editor suggests that Anselm renders all but the incantation's last seven characters (which are Latinate) in Greek majuscules.[28]

Anselm's claim that the characters reproduced in his text represent Hebrew characters, however, reflects enduring assumptions of the extraordinary power of Hebrew *voces magicae*.[29] Despite a decline in Hebrew knowledge in Christian Europe, a belief in the power of Hebrew (or pseudo-Hebrew) words flourished in theological works, in medieval magical texts and in alchemical treatises.[30] Their power, however, seemed to depend on correct vocalization. The importance of correct vocalization is also illustrated among Christian authors by the special importance attached to the Hebrew Tetragrammaton, which, as Trachtenberg

---

[27] Although note that Alphonse Buenhombre (d. 1353), the Spanish Dominican 'translator' of R. Samuel of Morocco's *Liber de adventu messiae praeterito*, contends in his preface that the Jewish convert to Christianity, Samuel, wrote his treatise in Arabic rather than Hebrew because Arabic is unknown to most Jews and Christians, and therefore Arabic was a more suitable linguistic vehicle for his theological "secrets" (PL 149: 335B-336A). For the extraordinary popularity of this text, see Ora Limor, "The Epistle of Rabbi Samuel of Morocco: A Best-Seller in the World of Polemics," in *Contra Iudaeos: Ancient and Medieval Polemics Between Christians and Jews*, ed. Ora Limor and Guy G. Stroumsa (Tübingen: J.C.B. Mohr, 1996): 177–194. While Samuel allegedly utilized Arabic to "conceal" his meaning, Alphonse Buenhombre acknowledged that, "The synagogue has but one tongue, bedecked as if with one color, to wit Hebrew." ("Synagoga vero non habuit nisi unam linguam, et ornatum suum quasi uno colore, scilicet Hebraea.") Ibid., cap. 22 (PL 149: 361B).
[28] See Karl Manitius, "Magie und Rhetorik bei Anselm von Besate," *Deutsches Archiv für Erforschung des Mittelalters* 12 (1956): 52–72, citing 59.
[29] Many *voces magicae* in late antique or medieval texts are, in fact, not Hebrew at all, but may be linguistic inventions that merely reveal a coincidental phonetic similarity to some Hebrew word or phrase. For a survey of efforts to identify the Jewish origins of *voces magicae* in late antiquity, see especially Gideon Bohak, "Hebrew, Hebrew Everywhere?: Notes on the Interpretation of *Voces Magicae*," in *Prayer, Magic, and the Stars in the Ancient and Late Antique World*, ed. Scott B. Noegel, Joel Walker and Brannon M. Wheeler (University Park, PA: Pennsylvania State University Press, 2003): 69–82.
[30] Raphael Patai, *The Jewish Alchemists: A History and Source Book* (Princeton: Princeton University Press, 1994), 59.

noted, is first in occult power.³¹ For Peter Damian (d. 1072) too, although the Tetragrammaton "consisted of only a few letters," it contains "a force of great meaning."³² The perceived power of the Tetragrammaton was only enhanced by the unusual treatment accorded to it by Jews, whose authorities forbade its pronunciation from at least the first century of this era;³³ for medieval Jewish commentators, moreover, merely pronouncing the Tetragrammaton constitutes a crime that excludes one from the world to come.³⁴ Thus, at the very beginning of the thirteenth century, Alexander Nequam remarks upon the fact that rabbinic Jews correctly write in their Torah the Hebrew letters of the Tetragrammaton (a name, he says, that is especially expressive of divine power) but refuse to vocalize it, substituting for it the name *Adonay*.³⁵ Thomas Aquinas was likewise aware of

---

31 Joshua Trachtenberg, *Jewish Magic and Superstition*, 90–91.
32 Peter Damian, *Die Briefe des Petrus Damiani*, vol. 1, Epist. 28.42, ed. Kurt Reindel, MGH, Epp. Kaiserzeit (Munich: MGH, 1983–93), 1: 270; cf. *The Letters of Peter Damian, 1–30*, trans. Owen J. Blum, Fathers of the Church, Mediaeval Continuation 1 (Washington, DC: The Catholic University of America Press, 1989), 279.
33 For Jewish and early Christian sources, see Antti Marjanen, "A Nag Hammadi Contribution to the Discussion about the Pronunciation of the Tetragrammaton," *Studia Orientalia* 99 (2004): 153–59, citing 153, n. 3. In the fourth century, Jerome had noted that among the Hebrews the Tetragrammaton constitutes the ineffable name of God. See his *Commentarioli in psalmos*, Ps. 8, ln. 7, CCSL 72, ed. G. Morin (Turnholt: Brepols, 1959); idem, Epist. 25 and Epist. 64.17, CSEL 54, ed. I. Hilberg (Vienna: F. Temsky, 1910), 219, 604, where Jerome adds that the ineffable name was inscribed on a golden plate (*lamina aurea*) on the forehead of the high priest in the Jerusalem Temple. For his treatment of the priestly vestments, see esp. Robert Hayward, "St Jerome and the Meaning of the High-Priestly Vestments," in *Hebrew Study from Ezra to Ben-Yehuda*, ed. William Horbury (Edinburgh: T&T Clark, 1999), 90–105. Also Rupert of Deutz indicates that the letters of the Tetragrammaton cannot be understood in a syllable or in formed or articulated speech: "quae in syllabam aut uocem articulatam comprehendi nequeunt"; see his *De sancta trinitate et operibus eius* 13: *In Exodum* 4, CCCM 22, ed. R. Haacke (Turnholt: Brepols, 1971), 779. But Bede notes that the Tetragrammaton is ineffable not because it cannot be pronounced, but because it cannot be understood by any creature. Bede, *De tabernaculo* 3, ln. 803, CCSL 119A, ed. D. Hurst (Turnholt: Brepols, 1969); and similarly William Durand, *Rationale diuinorum officiorum*, 2.1.8.119, CCCM, 140, ed. A. Davril and T. M. Thibodeau (Turnholt: Brepols, 1995); Peter of Celle, *Tractatus de tabernaculo* 2.5.269, CCCM 54, ed. G. de Martel (Turnholt: Brepols, 1983). For a detailed study of the Tetragrammaton and for discussion of its magical uses, see Robert J. Wilkinson, *Tetragrammaton: Western Christians and the Hebrew Name of God. From the Beginnings to the Seventeenth Century*, Studies in the History of Christian Traditions 179 (Leiden, Boston: Brill, 2015), *passim*.
34 Daniel J. Lasker, "Blasphemy: Jewish Concept," in *Encyclopedia of Religion*, 2nd ed. (Detroit: Macmillan Reference USA, 2005), 2: 970.
35 Alexander Nequam, *Speculum Speculationum*, 1.32.1–3, ed. Rodney M. Thomson (Oxford: Oxford University Press, 1988), 103. Nequam (or Neckam) had a good knowledge of Hebrew. See Raphael Lowe, "Alexander Neckam's Knowledge of Hebrew," in *Hebrew Study from Ezra to*

Maimonides' claim that the true pronunciation of the Tetragrammaton is a secret, for which reason its use is prohibited.[36] Because rabbinic Jews, it was thought, no longer possessed the correct vocalization of the Tetragrammaton (not to mention a correct understanding of its meaning),[37] its use was forbidden. By implication, then, incorrect Hebrew vocalization could have profound unintended consequences, whereas the search for the secret vocalization of the Tetragrammaton led later medieval Christian theologians to scour Kabbalah. Thus, according to Thorndike, Henry Cornelius Agrippa (d. 1535) "declared that whoever knew the true pronunciation of the name Jehovah had 'the world in his mouth.'"[38]

Conversely, correct Hebrew vocalization of the Tetragrammaton and of *voces magicae* endows the speaker with real power, as indicated above. Perhaps Rotiland's "Hebrew" was deficient in this regard, since Anselm implies that his Hebrew incantation failed and that he had little success with women. But it was likely a fear that Hebrew words could successfully invoke demons that led authorities in fourteenth-century Avignon to threaten punishment to any Jew who spoke Hebrew in the presence of the consecrated Host.[39] These demons were also a concern to the Christian priest Johannes of Scheven, who remarked in his fifteenth-century *Margarita exorcistarum* that he took Hebrew lessons from a Jew so that he could correctly pronounce the names of the demons, precisely so that he could expel them

---

Ben-Yehuda, ed. William Horbury (Edinburgh: T&T Clark, 1999), 207–223. For Jewish views on pronouncing the Tetragrammaton, see Daniel J. Lasker, "Blasphemy: Jewish Concept," 2: 969–72.
36 For Maimonides, see esp. *The Guide of the Perplexed* 1.61–64, 147–57. Maimonides notes that the priests had ceased to use the "articulated name," that is, the *Shem ha-Mephorash* or the Tetragrammaton, "because of the corruption of the people" (151). For Aquinas and his dependence on Maimonides, see Armand Maurer, "St. Thomas on the Sacred Name 'Tetragrammaton,'" *Mediaeval Studies* 34 (1972): 275–86, and esp. 283; also, Robert A. Herrera, "Saint Thomas and Maimonides on the Tetragrammaton: the 'Exodus' of Philosophy?" *The Modern Schoolman* 59 (1982): 179–93; and Kevin M. Staley, "On Talking About God in the Academy: Thomas Aquinas and the Tetragrammaton," *New Blackfriars* 88, no. 1016 (2007): 433–42.
37 See, for example, Peter of Blois, who reiterates the claim introduced by Petrus Alfonsi that the Tetragrammaton contains a hidden allusion to the Trinity. See his *Contra perfidiam Judaeorum* 5 (PL 207: 833A). For Petrus Alfonsi on the Tetragrammaton, see his *Dialogue against the Jews,* trans. Irven M. Resnick, The Fathers of the Church, Mediaeval Continuation 8 (Washington, DC: The Catholic University of America Press, 2006), 172–175.
38 Lynn Thorndike, *The Place of Magic in the Intellectual History of Europe* (New York: Columbia University Press, 1905), 21.
39 Miri Rubin, *Gentile Tales: The Narrative Assault on Late Medieval Jews* (New Haven: Yale University Press, 1999), 31.

in his exorcisms.⁴⁰ At least some medieval Christians remained convinced that the demons and fallen angels understand Hebrew and still can be bound by its power.

Just as the correct vocalization of the Hebrew names of demons during an exorcism might drive them from the body, so too the power of Hebrew might miraculously heal the body of a variety of ailments. A late thirteenth-century Hebrew Psalter of English provenance (Bodleian MS Laud Or. 174) contains Latin instructions to Christian physicians to chant certain passages in Hebrew in order to cure specific illnesses.⁴¹ This text assumes that the Latin physician can at least correctly vocalize the Hebrew,⁴² despite the lamentable state of contemporary Christian knowledge of Hebrew.⁴³ Although Christian Hebraism surely flourished in the Scholastic era,⁴⁴ producing numerous encounters between Christians and Jewish biblical exegetes, and by the fourteenth century chairs in Hebrew had been established at major European universities, still one should not forget Erasmus's caricature of English clerics at the beginning of the sixteenth century, in which he proclaims that "whatever they do not understand, they call Hebrew."⁴⁵

---

40 Bernhard Bischoff, "The Study of Foreign Languages in the Middle Ages," *Speculum* 36, no. 2 (1961): 209–224, citing 209.

41 Mark Zier, "The Healing Power of the Hebrew Tongue: An Example from Late Thirteenth-Century England," in *Health, Disease, and Healing in Medieval Culture*, ed. Sheila Campbell, Bert Hall, and David Klausner (Houndmills, Basingstoke, Hampshire: Macmillan, 1992): 103–118.

42 Roger Bacon, well known for his criticism of Latins who knew neither Hebrew nor Greek, made it a point to provide a chart of the Hebrew alphabet and to explain Hebrew grammar and vocalization. See *The "Opus Maius" of Roger Bacon* 3.3, ed. John Henry Bridges (London: Williams and Norgate, 1900), 3: 91–92. In fact, Bacon's Hebrew knowledge was quite rudimentary, and inferior to that of other English Hebraists. See Judith Olszowy-Schlanger, "Christian Hebraism in Thirteenth-Century England," in *Crossing Borders: Hebrew Manuscripts as a Meeting-place of Cultures*, ed. Piet van Boxel and Sabine Arndt (Oxford: Bodleian Library, 2010): 115–22; and Eva De Visscher, "Cross-religious Learning and Teaching: Hebraism in the Works of Herbert of Bosham, and Contemporaries," in *Crossing Borders*, 123–32.

43 Michael Signer shows that most twelfth-century Christian Hebraists possessed merely a "cultural" Hebraism because they remained dependent on their Jewish guides to Hebrew texts, and were incapable of independent Hebrew study. See Michael Signer, "Polemic and Exegesis: The Varieties of Twelfth-Century Hebraism," in *Hebraica Veritas? Christian Hebraists and the Study of Judaism in Early Modern Europe*, ed. Allison P. Coudert and Jeffrey S. Shoulson (Philadelphia: University of Pennsylvania Press, 2004): 21–32. The situation begins to improve in certain learned circles during the thirteenth century.

44 For the early fourteenth-century Hebraist Nicholas of Lyra, see Deeana Copeland Klepper, *The Insight of Unbelievers: Nicholas of Lyra and Christian Reading of Jewish Text in the Later Middle Ages* (Philadelphia: University of Pennsylvania Press, 2007).

45 *Peregrinatio religionis ergo*, in Desiderius Erasmus, *The Colloquies of Erasmus*, trans. Craig R. Thompson (Chicago and London: University of Chicago Press, 1965), 289, cited in Boyarin, *Miracles of the Virgin in Medieval England*, 166.

Although any attempt to vocalize the Tetragrammaton entailed great risk, it was widely held that not only its correct vocalization but even the accurate *transcription* of the Hebrew Tetragrammaton, as well as other names,[46] conveyed great power. This is also evident in medieval Jewish polemics, since in the *Toledot Yeshu* there appears a tale in which Jesus steals the Tetragrammaton from the Temple, writing it on a parchment which he then inserted into the flesh of his leg, enabling him to perform acts of magic.[47] Not only might the divine name inserted under the flesh confer a magic power or ward off evil, but in the eleventh-century Byzantine *Chronicle of Ahimaaz*, Ahimaaz encountered a young Jew whose very life was sustained by an inscribed Tetragrammaton, which had been inserted into the flesh of his arm.[48]

Similarly, some medieval Jewish texts proclaim that the body of every Jew is inscribed with the Hebrew Tetragrammaton, or with another name for God, *Shaddai*. *Midrash Tanhuma*, a medieval homiletic collection on the Pentateuch, asserts that:

> the holy one blessed be He, has placed his name in Israel so that they will enter the Garden of Eden [. . .]. It is the name Shaddai (שדי). He placed the *shin* (ש) in the nose, the *dalet* (ד) in the hand and the *yod* (י) on the (place of) circumcision. Therefore when a Jew dies there is an appointed angel in the Garden of Eden who receives every circumcised Jew [. . .].[49]

In this instance it is not the Tetragrammaton but the name *Shaddai* (Almighty) that was inscribed in the flesh to serve as a protective marker or key to the gates of Eden. The thirteenth-century kabbalist Joseph of Hamadan, who lived in Spain, similarly understood that through ritual circumcision Jews are "imprinted" with the divine name in Hebrew as a sort of prophylactic device.[50]

While *Midrash Tanhuma* emphasizes that the *yod* completes the name *Shaddai*, German pietists of the thirteenth century connected the *yod* of circumcision to the

---

46 Even the name of Jesus! See Peter Schäfer, *Jesus in the Talmud* (Princeton: Princeton University Press, 2007), 39, 60.
47 For this and similar tales of the magical power of the Tetragrammaton, see Stephen Benin, "Jews, Muslims, and Christians in Byzantine Italy," in *Judaism and Islam: Boundaries, Communications, and Interaction: Essays in Honor of William M. Brinner*, ed. Benjamin H. Hary, John L. Hayes, and Fred Astren (Leiden: Brill, 2000): 27–36, citing 31–33.
48 *Chronicle of Ahimaaz*, trans. Marcus P. Salzman (New York: AMS Press, 1966), 66.
49 *Midrash Tanhuma* Shemini 8, cited in Elisheva Baumgarten, "Marking the Flesh: Circumcision, Blood, and Inscribing Identity on the Body in Medieval Jewish Culture," in *Micrologus: Natura, scienze e società medievali. Nature, Sciences and Medieval Societies*, 13: *La pelle umana; The Human Skin* (2005): 322–23.
50 Joseph Hamadan, *Sefer Ta'ame ha-Miswot*, ed. M. Meier (PhD diss.; Brandeis University, 1974), 242, cited by Elliot R. Wolfson, "Circumcision and the Divine Name: A Study in the Transmission of Esoteric Doctrine," *Jewish Quarterly Review* 78, no. 1–2 (1987): 77, n. 1.

first letter of the Tetragrammaton, whose apotropaic power seemed assured.[51] At times, the *yod* stood alone as an abbreviation for the Tetragrammaton.[52] In this way, the late fourteenth-century Spanish kabbalist Samuel ibn Matut related the appearance of the circumcised phallus to the letter *yod* and, therefore, to the Tetragrammaton.[53] Circumcision marked Jews in the flesh, then, with the Hebrew divine name or one of the divine attributes, whereby the divine word became flesh in an altogether novel way to distinguish medieval Jews from their uncircumcised neighbors.

Such traditions were certainly known to Christians. The sixteenth-century Johannes Buxtorf (1564–1629) acknowledged that the Jews say that with circumcision the name of God – *Shaddai* – is perfected in their flesh, with the letters *shin, dalet* and *yod*. The uncircumcised Christians lack the final letter, *yod*, and therefore they only have the letters *shin* and *dalet*, to produce "sched" or "devil," indicating that they are the sons of the devil, and not members of a holy people.[54] Here the absence of a single Hebrew letter – that is, incorrect transcription – just as with an improper vocalization, evinces a power that is not divine but diabolic.

Christians may have sought to respond by emphasizing a symbolic link between the Tetragrammaton and the Cross. Thus, Peter Damian avowed, just as the Tetragrammaton has four letters, which were inscribed on the forehead of the High Priest in the Temple on a *lamina* or gold plate, so too the Cross has four corners.[55] Since Jesus is the new High Priest, Rupert of Deutz adds, he was given this name, the Tetragrammaton, and its power.[56] Therefore, when the sign

---

51 Elliot R. Wolfson, "Circumcision and the Divine Name: A Study in the Transmission of Esoteric Doctrine," 88 and 97.
52 Not unlike the use of *nomina sacra* – abbreviations for sacred words, and especially for divine names – in early Christian MSS. It is often suggested that Christian practice derived from the Jewish custom of employing substitutes for the Tetragrammaton. See for example L. W. Hurtado, "The Origin of the Nomina Sacra: A Proposal," *Journal of Biblical Literature* 117, no. 4 (1998): 655–673.
53 Israel Moshe Sandman, "The Mašōbēb Natībōt of Samuel Ibn Matut ('Motot'): Introductory Excursus, Critical Edition, and Annotated Translation," vol 2; part 2, chap. 6 (PhD diss., University of Chicago, 2006), 2: 490.
54 Johannes Buxtorf, *Synagoga Judaica*, cap. 4 (Basil: E. König, 1680; reprint Hildesheim; New York: G. Olms, 1989), 87. Because the absence of the *yod* led to the word for a devil or demon, rabbinic Judaism avoided abbreviating the name *Shaddai*, whereas there were various abbreviations used to indicate the Tetragrammaton. See Jacob Z. Lauterbach, "Substitutes for the Tetragrammaton," *Proceedings of the American Academy for Jewish Research* 2 (1930–1931): 39–67, citing 44.
55 Peter Damian, *Sermones*, 39, ln. 204, ed. G. Lucchesi, CCCM 57 (Turnholt: Brepols, 1983). The text at PL 144: 715A shows a slight variation, since in Lucchesi's text the word Tetragrammaton is represented by the letters Iava.
56 Rupert of Deutz, *In Zachariam Prophetam Commentariorum* 2.3 (PL 168: 742C-D); idem, *In Apocalypsim Joannis Apostoli Commentariorum* 9.14 (PL 169: 1101B).

of the Cross is traced with holy chrism on the forehead of Christians, the power of the Tetragrammaton seems inscribed there as well.[57] While Christians may lack the *yod* imprinted upon Jews with circumcision, they have the ineffable name imprinted upon them by the sign of the Cross. To my knowledge, this argument does not appear in Christian anti-Jewish polemics. Christian anxiety with respect to a mastery of the Hebrew language persisted, however, and an awareness of a language deficit endured. Moreover, especially when employing *voces magicae,* a Hebrew language deficit could be quite dangerous.

3 Pseudo-Hebrew and Nonsense Hebrew

What were some effects of this language deficit? Christian ignorance of Hebrew could not be permitted to privilege the Jews with access to the sacred language, nor to the *Hebraica Veritas*, that is, the textual and exegetical traditions of the Hebrew Bible. Neither could the assertion remain unanswered that the Jews' flesh was inscribed with the Hebrew divine name, while Christians, because they failed to perform ritual circumcision, were inscribed with the name of the devil or with a diabolic form of Hebrew. With respect to the textual tradition of the Hebrew Bible, medieval Christians pursued two strategies: one entailed introducing corrections to the Vulgate, and the other produced the charge that where the Vulgate and the Hebrew text disagreed, Jews were responsible for having intentionally falsified and corrupted the Hebrew biblical text.[58]

Similarly, the appearance of pseudo-Hebrew in Christian texts and visual art may have sought to respond to the claim that the Jews have inscribed in their flesh the Hebrew divine name, since pseudo-Hebrew in Christian art and illuminations may have implied that Jews had also corrupted Hebrew itself, just as they were said to have intentionally falsified and corrupted the Hebrew Bible. A corrupted name, as we have seen, conveys no divine power at all.

I shall offer some comments concerning the symbolic significance of pseudo-Hebrew script, although these must remain quite speculative. As already seen, Anselm's incantation constitutes an early textually based example of pseudo-Hebrew which, alongside nonsense or meaningless Hebrew script, is well docu-

---

[57] Honorius of Autun, *De missae sacrificio et de ministris ecclesiae* 1, cap. 222 (PL 172: 611C).
[58] See my "Falsification of Scripture and Medieval Christian-Jewish Polemics," *Medieval Encounters* 2, no. 3 (1996): 345–380.

mented in Christian magical and alchemical texts,[59] in later medieval drama,[60] and in the visual art of the later Middle Ages.[61] Although examples of authentic Hebrew script in Christian visual art do appear from the beginning of the fifteenth-century,[62] earlier one finds only pseudo-Hebrew, indecipherable Hebrew letters, or nonsense Hebrew in Christian art. This phenomenon needs to be considered alongside any discussion of a rise of medieval Christian Hebraism.

I would define pseudo-Hebrew as those words or phrases in medieval Christian texts or illustrations that are not, in fact, in Hebrew characters at all, like

---

59 For an example of a late medieval Christian magical text that employs numerous allegedly Hebrew names, words, and pseudo-Hebrew script, see Richard Kieckhefer, *Forbidden Rites: A Necromancer's Manual of the Fifteenth Century* (University Park, PA: Pennsylvania State University Press, 1998).

60 For examples from medieval drama, see the late fifteenth-century Digby saint's play *Mary Magdalene*, in which, according to Anthony Bale, "the Jewish 'prysbyter' and his boy conjure up the spirit of 'Sentt Coppyn' (the imputed Jewish murderer of Little Hugh of Lincoln) and speak a scatological mock-Hebrew." See Bale, *The Jew in the Medieval Book: English Antisemitisms, 1350–1500* (Cambridge: Cambridge University Press, 2006), 141. Other interpreters have insisted that the passage constitutes a mangled Latin in mockery of the Church; see Matthew Boyd Goldie, "Audiences for Language Play in Middle English Drama," in *Traditions and Transformations in Late Medieval England*, ed. Douglas Biggs, Sharon D. Michalove, and A. Compton Reeves (Leiden: Brill, 2002): 200. Trachtenberg also remarked, however, that "when Jews are represented in the mystery plays as summoning their demonic confederates their charms are uttered in a gibberish that is intended to simulate Hebrew." Joshua Trachtenberg, *The Devil and the Jews: the Medieval Conception of the Jew and its Relation to Modern Antisemitism* (New Haven: Yale University Press, 1943), 61. Finally, Stephen Wright has noted that in the performance of the fourteenth-century *Ludus de assumptione Beatae Mariae Virginis*, the Jews are given a choral role with no specific rubric (l. 572), which may have been sung in an incomprehensible gibberish parodying Hebrew. See Stephen K. Wright, *The Vengeance of our Lord: Medieval Dramatizations of the Destruction of Jerusalem* (Toronto: Pontifical Institute of Mediaeval Studies, 1989), 42.

61 Pseudo-Hebrew script was a useful device to identify Jews – and often Jews as enemies of Christianity – in medieval visual art, and increasingly common from the thirteenth century. For Christian art, see especially Ruth Mellinkoff, *Outcasts*, 1: 97–108. Also see Heinz Schreckenberg, *The Jews in Christian Art: An Illustrated History* (New York: Continuum, 1996), 62, pl. 17 (Synagoga holding the tablets of the Law inscribed with pseudo-Hebrew); 111, pl. 55; 145, pl. 3; 146, pl. 4; 182, pl. 13; 186, pl. 20; 192, pl. 7; 210, pl. 27; 216, pl. 12; 221, pl. 9; 250, pl. 2; 308, pl. 1–2; 333, pl. 1; and, 347, pl. 3. For pseudo-Hebrew script in the fifteenth-century *Fountain of Grace and the Triumph of the Church over the Synagogue*, attributed to the school of Jan van Eyck, see also Achim Timmermann, "The Avenging Crucifix: Some Observations on the Iconography of the Living Cross," *Gesta* 40, no. 2 (2001): 156; and David Nirenberg, "The Judaism of Christian Art," in *Judaism and Christian Art: Aesthetic Anxieties from the Catacombs to Colonialism*, ed. Herbert L. Kessler and David Nirenberg (Philadelphia: University of Pennsylvania Press, 2011): 387–427, citing 404–405.

62 Gad B. Sarfatti, "Hebrew Script in Western Visual Arts," *Italia: Studi e ricerche sulla storia, la cultura e la letteratura degli Ebrei d'Italia* 13–15 (2001): 451–547, citing 451 and 453.

Anselm's incantation. Nonsense Hebrew, however, may be defined as those words or phrases that are in Hebrew characters, but which form unintelligible or meaningless words and phrases.[63] The *purpose(s)* behind such nonsense or pseudo-Hebrew text – when it does not merely reflect real ignorance of Hebrew – remain more elusive, although Alexander Nagel has helpfully suggested that, in late medieval Italian visual art, "the very unintelligibility of these scripts could be said, in some cases, to mark a gap between a fallen present and a sacred past" and to point to a "language beyond language."[64] That is, pseudo-Hebrew script need not imply the artist's inability to render correctly Hebrew characters, although in many cases this was undoubtedly so; in other instances, however, it may point to a primordial or meta-Hebrew. Such a notion conforms to Christian assumptions that Jews had introduced corruption to Hebrew. If *ab initio* Hebrew had been a perfect language, a *vox angelica*, then subsequent changes – whether in vocalization, transcription, or orthography – only implied decline and degeneration. Rupert of Deutz suggests as much when he notes that at the restoration of the Temple in Jerusalem God caused the scribe Ezra to introduce changes to Hebrew orthography in order to underscore the distance between the original Hebrew script that, previously, God had given to Moses and had used to write the tablets of the Law, and the later Hebrew language of the Jews.[65] Rupert remarks that this later language or orthography will undergo renewal, however – the old will pass away, and all will be made new – following the coming of the new High Priest, Jesus (cf. Heb. 9: 11). Nonsense or pseudo-Hebrew text, then, may be interpreted as a kind of visual allegory to evoke this perfect, primordial, sacred Hebrew, to which Christians have

---

63 For Renaissance art, Shalom Sabar expands this basic taxonomy to six: 1) pseudo-Hebrew script; 2) meaningless Hebrew script; 3) partially meaningful Hebrew script; 4) meaningful Hebrew script, usually based on older printed texts; 5) Latin and Greek texts correctly translated into (supposedly) ancient Hebrew; and, 6) original meaningful Hebrew inscriptions, created especially for the work of art. See his "Between Calvinists and Jews: Hebrew Script in Rembrandt's Art," in *Beyond the Yellow Badge: Anti-Judaism and Antisemitism in Medieval and Early Modern Visual Culture*, ed. Mitchell B. Merback (Leiden: Brill, 2008): 371–404, citing 374–75.
64 Alexander Nagel, "Twenty Five Notes," 229, 337.
65 On changes introduced to Hebrew orthography by the scribe Ezra, see Rabanus Maurus, *De inventio linguarum* (PL 112: 1579); and Rupert of Deutz, *De victoria verbi dei,* 3. 24 (PL 169: 1289A-C). For the claim that Ezra changed Hebrew script, see also the *Babylonian Talmud*, Tractate Sanhedrin 21b, accessed August 31, 2019, https://www.sefaria.org/Sanhedrin.21b.23?lang=bi&with=all&lang2=en. Although Rupert acknowledges that Moses produced Hebrew script and introduced the written language, it is nonetheless a script that God revealed to him. On Moses as the 'inventor' of Hebrew letters, see also Eugene of Toledo (b. 657), *Epitaphium proprium* 21 (PL 87: 366B). For various theories on the origin of Hebrew letters, see Claude Duret, *Thresor de l'histoire des langues de c'est univers* (Cologne: 1613), chap. 10.

access through Jesus, the Word and new High Priest, in the same way that through the sign of the Cross they are inscribed with the Tetragrammaton.

This is not to deny that in other instances of medieval Christian art, nonsense or pseudo-Hebrew reflects Christian perceptions of Hebrew's exotic, oriental character which, in some visual materials, could be used to encode and identify Jews.[66] At times these identifications are clearly polemical and suggest that just as a sacred Hebrew has suffered corruption, so too the Jews themselves are symbols of corruption and decline,[67] as suggested by Iberian illustrations from the thirteenth century that use pseudo-Hebrew lettering to identify heretics as well as Jews.[68] But if my suggestion above concerning a belief in the existence of a primordial Hebrew orthography is correct, then perhaps illustrations that depict a defeated *Synagoga* holding tablets of the Law with pseudo-Hebrew lettering can be interpreted in two ways: both as an allusion to the primordial script that existed on the tablets (and which was changed by Ezra later) and, more polemically, as an allusion to the Jews' failure to safeguard and preserve this linguistic heritage, especially when these tablets are depicted as falling from the hand of *Synagoga* or, when she holds the tablets firmly, she remains blind to the text displayed on them.[69]

---

[66] On pseudo-inscriptions in Renaissance art, especially pseudo-Hebrew and pseudo-Arabic, see also Moshe Barasch, "Some Oriental Pseudo-Inscriptions in Renaissance Art," *Visible Language* 23 (1989): 171–87. Although Barasch hesitates to speculate concerning the purposes behind pseudo-inscriptions, he does agree that they were likely intent upon providing "an authentic oriental air to biblical scenes . . ." (182).

[67] Mitchell Merback remarked "Hebrew letters, real and ersatz, were routinely employed by late medieval and Renaissance altar painters, often with no more profound an intention than to furnish an exotic, orientalizing design or to establish the biblical provenance of a particular figure, object, or scene. In other contexts Christian artists took over Hebrew words and letters to stigmatize the bearer as 'Jewish' or lend a mocking tone to a polemical image. In still other contexts it was the putative magical power of Hebrew script, corollary to the mystical formulas and 'name magic' that so intrigued hermeticists, that was being exploited." See his "Jewish Carnality, Christian Guilt, and Eucharistic Peril in the Rotterdam-Berlin Altarpiece of the Holy Sacrament," in *Judaism and Christian Art: Aesthetic Anxieties from the Catacombs to Colonialism*, 203–32, citing 220–21.

[68] See Pamela A. Patton, *Art of Estrangement: Redefining Jews in Reconquest Spain* (University Park, PA: Penn State University Press, 2012), 41–43, in which she analyzes the early thirteenth-century image of the heretic Helvidius holding a scroll with pseudo-Hebrew lettering in Ildefonsus's *Virginitate perpetua sanctae Mariae adversus tres infideles* found in Bib. Nacional de España, MS 10087; she also examines there a historiated initial from the book of Joshua (fol. 84r) in a late thirteenth-century Latin Bible from the Catalan city of Vic, in which Jews are depicted holding a scroll on which there appear tiny Hebrew letters, written from left to right.

[69] Cf. an illustration of *Synagoga* from the Altarpiece of the Mirror of Salvation by Conrad Witz (ca. 1435), image II.34 in Ruth Mellinkoff's *Outcasts*; cf. also Heinz Schreckenberg, *The Jews in Christian Art*, 62, pl. 17.

Finally, pseudo-Hebrew letters may provide a visual allegory not only to a primordial and sacred language, but also to one with Satanic potential, as we saw was suggested in both Anselm's *Rhetorimachia* and in the Amesbury Abbey Psalter. Though, as noted, Mellinkoff concluded from this latter instance that "Satan and the Jews are linked by their common language,"[70] it is also possible that the pseudo-Hebrew on Satan's scroll is a reminder that when the devil spoke through the serpent to Eve in the Garden, he undoubtedly would have spoken Hebrew, the original language, despite the anachronism in this Psalter of Jesus speaking Latin.[71] One need not conclude that all Jews are Satanic simply because they use Hebrew, any more than one should conclude that all those who use Latin are good Christians: in what may be a late medieval protest against clerical abuse in the *Chester Mystery* cycle's English play "The Coming of Antichrist," Antichrist speaks a beguiling Latin, as do various devils intent upon deception.[72] Clearly, language selection also has political or national implications: Bischoff mentions that in the eighth-century poems of Saint Guthlac, "Anglo-Saxons thought that the devil spoke the detested language of the detested British."[73] The fact that Antichrist speaks Latin in the later English "The Coming of Antichrist" may have the same significance. Nonetheless, both the Amesbury Abbey Psalter and "The Coming of Antichrist" remind us that a sacred language – whether Hebrew or Latin – can, when misused, be transformed into its opposite.

In sum, then, pseudo-Hebrew, including Rotiland's 'Hebrew' incantation to invoke the aid of demons, may reflect enduring assumptions concerning Hebrew's primordial nature as the *Ursprache* (and sometimes also the *Endsprache*)[74] – the language in which God and the angels spoke to Adam. The demons and fallen angels understand Hebrew and still can be bound by its power. Because Rotiland is not himself a Jew, Hebrew is not depicted in Anselm's text as diabolical *because the Jews use it*; in other instances, however, to the extent that Jews are held responsible for Hebrew's corruption, Mellinkoff may be correct that the Jews and Satan are linked by a common language, to reveal the darker side of a sacred tongue. This link of the Jews to Satan and to Hebrew's corruption has also been suggested

---

[70] Ruth Mellinkoff, *Outcasts*, 1: 105.
[71] Phillip of Harvengt links the language of the serpent in the Garden to the speech of pagans (*gentes*) and Jews when he describes their language as "serpentine" (*lingua serpentine*). See his *Commentaria in Cantica canticorum* 2.20 (PL 203: 284).
[72] See Richard K. Emmerson, "'Englysch Laten' and 'Franch' Language as a Sign of Evil in Medieval English Drama," in *The Devil, Heresy and Witchcraft in the Middle Ages: Essays in Honor of Jeffrey B. Russell*, ed. Alberto Ferreiro (Brill: Leiden, 1998): 305–26, citing 316 and 326.
[73] B. Bischoff, "The Study of Foreign Languages in the Middle Ages," 211.
[74] See n. 4, above.

by Bernhard Blumenkranz in connection with a study of Matfre Ermengaud's late thirteenth-century *Breviari d'amor*,[75] written in the langue d'Oc and distinguished by the presence of scriptural passages in Latin, Hebrew, and Occitan. In this long poetic text there appear also several miniatures of Jews who have been blindfolded by the devil, with accompanying text indicating that because of their relationship to the devil they do not even understand their own Hebrew.[76]

4 Adam of Bristol and Popular Christian Perceptions of Hebrew

My last example is from the late thirteenth century, and provides an interesting popular witness to how Christians who were *not* scholars (and perhaps not even clerics) perceived the Hebrew language. This example comes from the bizarre *Passion of Adam of Bristol*, a ritual crucifixion tale that alleges that the Jew Samuel and his family ritually murdered a young Christian boy, Adam of Bristol. The text pays much attention to language, since the various "actors" in the Passion text are differentiated by their knowledge of English, French, Irish, and Hebrew.

Although the Jewish perpetrators speak to their English neighbors using the vernaculars, rather unrealistically they use Hebrew among themselves as a language of concealment in order to hide their nefarious intentions. In this respect, these Bristol Jews appear not unlike the Jews in the fourteenth-century *Travels of Sir John Mandeville*, who everywhere use Hebrew, a dangerous language, so that they will be recognized by their co-religionists and co-conspirators who are bent upon destroying Christendom.[77] In like manner, Samuel of Bristol reveals to his wife *in Hebrew* his intention to take vengeance on the God of the Christians

---

75 A complete edition of the long poem was produced in two volumes by Gabriel Azaïs, *Le Breviari d'Amor, suivi de sa lettre a sa Soeur* (Geneva: Slatkine Reprints, 1977). A six-volume edition has begun to appear, edited by P. T. Ricketts, *Le Breviari d'Amor de Matfre Ermengaud* (Turnholt: Brepols, 1989–).
76 Bernhard Blumenkranz, "Écriture et image dans la polémique anti-juive de Matfre Ermengaud," in *Juifs et judaïsme de Languedoc*, Cahiers de Fanjeaux 12 (Toulouse: Édouard Privat, 1977): 295–318, citing 312–313.
77 On Hebrew language in Mandeville's text (and its various redactions) see esp. Marcia Kupfer, "'... lectres ... plus vrayes': Hebrew Script and Jewish Witness in the *Mandeville* Manuscript of Charles V," *Speculum* 83, no. 1 (2008): 58–111; and Miriamne Krummel, *Crafting Jewishness in Medieval England: Legally Absent, Virtually Present* (New York: Palgrave Macmillan, 2011), 78–87.

and on his mother, Mary, by murdering in ritual fashion the young Christian boy, Adam. To Adam, Samuel speaks only in French, which *was* the common vernacular of English Jews – although one that separated them culturally from their English neighbors and identified them with the ruling class – whereas Adam replies in English.

While the Jewish perpetrators in the *Passion of Adam of Bristol* speak Hebrew to one another in order to conceal their wicked intentions from Christians, at the same time, *God* speaks from the mouth of the victim *in Hebrew*, although in a Hebrew voice the Jews do not recognize even though they comprehend the meaning of what is said.[78] Although Samuel acknowledges that not a single Christian in Bristol knows the Hebrew language,[79] nonetheless he refuses to believe that the Christian God has spoken to him through the crucified victim, and insists instead that "Perhaps it was a phantasm."[80] For the unknown author of this text, Hebrew speech signifies the presence of the holy or the sacred, but one which the Jews have failed to recognize in the crucified victim, Adam, who represents the crucified Jesus. Ironically, the Jews in the text assume that the Hebrew voice they heard stems from something unsubstantial or even demonic, a *phantasm*. This completes the sacred-diabolic inversion: Hebrew is a sacred language, but it is also the language of Satan and demons; the Jews think that they hear a devil or phantasm speaking Hebrew, when in fact it is God who speaks. Their mastery of the Hebrew language does not lead to understanding, whereas the Christians, who suffer a Hebrew language deficit, seize upon the truth.

---

78 "'Samuel, why do you burn me all night? I am the God of Abraham and the God of Isaac and the God of Jacob, whom now for the fourth time you have affixed to the cross, and still you burn me. Desist, wretch, desist! It is the Almighty *whom you persecute.*' And the voice was silent. And the man and woman were stupefied, and they said: 'Now whose voice was that?' [. . .]. And the woman said: 'Who then has spoken to us in the Hebrew language? Have we not clearly heard the words of our own language?'" ("Samuel, quare me comburis tota nocte? Ego sum deus Abraham et deus Ysaac, et deus Jacob, quem quarto nunc cruci affixisti, et adhuc me comburis. Desine miser desine, omnipotens est *quem tu persequeris*! Et siluit vox. Et obstupuerunt vir et mulier, et dixerunt: 'Que nam hec vox est?' [. . .] Et ait mulier: 'Quis igitur locutus est nobis lingua ebrea? Nuncquid aperte audivimus verba lingue nostre?'") For the Latin text, see Christoph Cluse, "'Fabula ineptissima': Die Ritualmordlegende um Adam von Bristol nach der Handschrift London, British Library, Harley 957," *Aschkenas: Zeitschrift für Geschichte und Kultur der Juden* 5 (1995): 293–330, citing 310. The italics appear in the Latin.
79 "Not one single person in this entire town knows how to deliver a sermon like this in our Hebrew language . . ." ("Nec unus solus ex tota urbe ista sciret huius(modi) proferre sermonem in lingua nostra Hebrea [. . .]"). Cluse, "'Fabula ineptissima,'" 311.
80 "fortasse fantasma est." Cluse, "'Fabula ineptissima,'" 311.

This last illustration returns us to our earlier observation: Hebrew, as a sacred language, nevertheless can be used diabolically. Here the Jews use Hebrew among themselves to conceal their hatred of Christians and to conceal alleged, nefarious Jewish rituals. Although *God* also speaks in Hebrew, the "mother of all languages," contemporary Jews understand only the "letter" of the language, but have ceased to recognize its creator and author. In contrast, the town's Christians, who do not know Hebrew, nonetheless know the Hebrew God.

5 Conclusions

The texts I have cited suggest a few conclusions. First, I am convinced that many medieval Christians experienced acute anxiety because of their language deficit and ignorance of Hebrew, a sacred language. That ignorance of Hebrew, however, could not be permitted to privilege the Jews' access to the sacred language, nor to the *Hebraica Veritas*, i.e., the textual and exegetical tradition of the Hebrew Bible. As we have seen, Jews *know* Hebrew, at least according to the letter, but seem ignorant of its secrets and its truths. Although they can correctly vocalize it, this may only encourage their alliance with the demons, whereas it is Christians, like Johannes of Scheven, who would use Hebrew to expel demons. Jews copy Hebrew in their books, but they use a corrupt and degenerate script that in Christian texts and art is often countered by a *pseudo-Hebrew*.

Nonsense or pseudo-Hebrew text, then, may perhaps be interpreted as a kind of visual allegory to evoke this perfect, primordial, sacred Hebrew, to which Christians have been given access through Jesus, the new High Priest and the Word of God. By contrast, the Jews' understanding, which is marked by corruption and decline, is defeated by this meta-Hebrew. This interpretation of the symbolism of pseudo-Hebrew is highly speculative, of course. But it is deserving of further investigation.

In sum, then, medieval Christians avowed Hebrew's sacral character, recognized the Jews' use of Hebrew, but at the same time often sought to separate the Jews from the holy tongue and to link their use of Hebrew instead to magic, Satan, and the demons. At the same time, Christians may have sought to reclaim Hebrew for themselves through the use of pseudo-Hebrew text or inscriptions, intended as an allusion to a meta-Hebrew or language beyond language, which they alone possessed.

Abbreviations

CCCM   Corpus Christianorum. Continuatio Mediaevalis
CCSL   Corpus Christianorum. Series Latina
CSEL   Corpus Scriptorum Ecclesiasticorum Latinorum
MGH   Monumenta Germaniae Historica
PL   Patrologia Latina, 217 vols. Edited by J.-P. Migne. Paris, 1844-1855.

Bibliography

Albertus Magnus. *Opera omnia, ex editione lugdunensi, religiose castigata*. Vol. 32: *Summa Theologiae, secunda pars (quaest. I-LXVII)*, edited by A. Borgnet. Paris: L. Vivès, 1890–1899.

Anselm of Besate. *Rhetorimachia*, edited by Karl Manitius. MGH, Die deutschen Geschichtsquellen des Mittelalters 500–1500, 2. Weimar: Hermann Böhlaus Nachfolger, 1958.

Ps.-Antoninus Placentinus. *Itinerarium*. In *Itineraria et alia geographica*, 128–174. CCSL 175. Turnholt: Brepols, 1965.

Augustine. *De Genesi ad litteram libri duodecim*. CSEL 28.1, edited by J. Zycha. Vindobonae: F. Tempsky, 1894.

Azaïs, Gabriel. *Le Breviari d'Amor, suivi de sa lettre a sa Soeur*. Geneva: Slatkine Reprints, 1977.

Babylonian Talmud, Tractate Sanhedrin.

Bacon, Roger. *The "Opus Maius" of Roger Bacon*. Vol. 3, edited John Henry Bridges. London: Williams and Norgate, 1900.

Bale, Anthony. *The Jew in the Medieval Book: English Antisemitisms, 1350–1500*. Cambridge: Cambridge University Press, 2006.

Barasch, Moshe. "Some Oriental Pseudo-Inscriptions in Renaissance Art." *Visible Language* 23 (1989): 171–87.

Baumgarten, Elisheva. "Marking the Flesh: Circumcision, Blood, and Inscribing Identity on the Body in Medieval Jewish Culture." *Micrologus: Natura, scienze e società medievali. Nature, Sciences and Medieval Societies*, 13: *La pelle umana; The Human Skin* (2005): 313–330.

Bede. *De tabernaculo*. CCSL 119A, edited by D. Hurst. Turnholt: Brepols, 1969.

Beleth, Iohannes. *Summa de ecclesiasticis officiis*. CCCM 41A, edited by H. Douteil. Turnholt: Brepols, 1976.

Bella, Francesco and Carlo Azzi. "^{14}C Dating of the 'Titulus Crucis.'" *Radiocarbon* 44, no. 3 (2002): 685–689.

Benin, Stephen. "Jews, Muslims, and Christians in Byzantine Italy." In *Judaism and Islam: Boundaries, Communications, and Interaction: Essays in Honor of William M. Brinner*, edited by Benjamin H. Hary, John L. Hayes, and Fred Astren, 27–36. Leiden: Brill, 2000.

Bennett, Beth S. "The Significance of the *Rhetorimachia* of Anselm of Besate to the History of Rhetoric." *Rhetorica* 5 (1987): 231–250.

Bischoff, Bernhard. "The Study of Foreign Languages in the Middle Ages." *Speculum* 36, no. 2 (1961): 209–224.

Blumenkranz, Bernhard. "Écriture et image dans la polémique anti-juive de Matfre Ermengaud." In *Juifs et judaïsme de Languedoc*. Cahiers de Fanjeaux 12, 295–318. Toulouse: Édouard Privat, 1977.

Bohak, Gideon. "Hebrew, Hebrew Everywhere?: Notes on the Interpretation of *Voces Magicae*." In *Prayer, Magic, and the Stars in the Ancient and Late Antique World*, edited by Scott B. Noegel, Joel Walker and Brannon M. Wheeler, 69–82. University Park, PA: Pennsylvania State University Press, 2003.

Borst, Arno. *Der Turmbau von Babel,* 4 vols. Stuttgart: Anton Hiersemann, 1957–1963.

Boyd Goldie, Matthew. "Audiences for Language Play in Middle English Drama." In *Traditions and Transformations in Late Medieval England,* edited by Douglas Biggs, Sharon D. Michalove, and A. Compton Reeves, 177–216. Leiden: Brill, 2002.

Buxtorf, Johannes. *Synagoga Judaica.* Basil: E. König, 1680; reprint Hildesheim; New York: G. Olms, 1989.

Camille, Michael. "The Devil's Writing: Diabolic Literacy in Medieval Art." In *World Art: Themes of Unity in Diversity; Acts of the XXVth International Congress of the History of Art*, 3 vols., edited by Irving Lavin, 2: 355–60. University Park, PA: Pennsylvania University Press, 1989.

Chronicle of Ahimaaz, trans. Marcus P. Salzman. New York: AMS Press, 1966.

Cluse, Christoph. "'Fabula ineptissima': Die Ritualmordlegende um Adam von Bristol nach der Handschrift London, British Library, Harley 957." *Aschkenas: Zeitschrift für Geschichte und Kultur der Juden* 5 (1995): 293–330.

Copeland Klepper, Deeana. *The Insight of Unbelievers: Nicholas of Lyra and Christian Reading of Jewish Text in the Later Middle Ages.* Philadelphia: University of Pennsylvania Press, 2007.

Dante Aligheri. *De vulgari eloquentia.*

Dante Aligheri. *The Divine Comedy* III: *Paradise*, trans. Louis Biancolli. New York: Washington Square Press, 1966.

De Brailes Hours. British Library, Add MS 49999.

De Lange, Nicholas. *Apocrypha: Jewish Literature of the Hellenistic Age*. New York: Viking, 1978.

De Marco, Angelus A. *Rome and the Vernacular*. Westminster, MD: The Newman Press, 1961.

De Visscher, Eva. "Cross-religious Learning and Teaching: Hebraism in the Works of Herbert of Bosham, and Contemporaries." In *Crossing Borders, Hebrew Manuscripts as a Meeting-place of Cultures,* edited by Piet van Boxel and Sabine Arndt, 123–32. Oxford: Bodleian Library, 2010.

Durand, William. *Rationale diuinorum officiorum*. CCCM 140, edited by A. Davril and T. M. Thibodeau. Turnholt: Brepols, 1995.

Duret, Claude. *Thresor de l'histoire des langues de c'est univers*. Cologne: 1613.

Dvornik, Francis. "The Significance of the Missions of Cyril and Methodius." *Slavic Review* 23, no. 2 (1964): 195–211.

Emmerson, Richard K. "'Englysch Laten' and 'Franch' Language as a Sign of Evil in Medieval English Drama." In *The Devil, Heresy and Witchcraft in the Middle Ages: Essays in Honor of Jeffrey B. Russell,* edited by Alberto Ferreiro, 305–26. Leiden: Brill, 1998.

Erasmus, Desiderius. "*Peregrinatio religionis ergo.*" In *The Colloquies of Erasmus,* translated by Craig R. Thompson. Chicago and London: University of Chicago Press, 1965.

Eugene of Toledo. *Epitaphium proprium*. PL 87: 365–368.

Gregory the Great. *Moraliium libri*. PL 76: 9–782.

Gregory VII, Pope. Epist. 7. In *Gregorii VII Registrum lib. V-IX*, edited by Erich Caspar. MGH, Epp. sel. Vol. 2, part 2. Berlin Weidmannsche Buchhandlung, 1923.

Halevi, Judah. *The Kuzari*, translated by Hartwig Hirschfeld. New York: Schocken, 1964.
Hamadan, Joseph. *Sefer Ta'ame ha-Miswot*, edited by M. Meier. PhD diss., Brandeis University, 1974.
Herrera, Robert A. "Saint Thomas and Maimonides on the Tetragrammaton: the 'Exodus' of Philosophy?" *The Modern Schoolman* 59 (1982): 179–93.
Hayward, Robert. "St Jerome and the Meaning of the High-Priestly Vestments." In *Hebrew Study from Ezra to Ben-Yehuda*, edited by William Horbury, 90–105. Edinburgh: T&T Clark, 1999.
Honorius of Autun. *De missae sacrificio et de ministris ecclesiae.* PL 172: 543–615.
Hugh of St. Victor. *Miscellanea.* PL 177: 469–900.
Hurtado, L. W. "The Origin of the Nomina Sacra: A Proposal." *Journal of Biblical Literature* 117, no. 4 (1998): 655–673.
Idel, Moshe. "A la recherche de la langue originelle: le témoignage du nourisson." *Revue de l'histoire des religions* 213, no. 4 (1996): 415–42.
Idel, Moshe. *Language, Torah, and Hermenuetics in Abraham Abulafia*, translated by Menahem Kallus. Albany, New York: SUNY Press, 1989.
Isidore of Seville. *The Etymologies of Isidore of Seville,* edited and translated by Stephen A. Barney, W.J. Lewis, J.A. Beach, and Oliver Berghof. Cambridge: Cambridge University Press, 2006.
Jerome. *Commentarioli in psalmos.* CCSL 72, edited by G. Morin. Turnholt: Brepols, 1959.
Jerome. Epist. 25 and Epist. 64. CSEL 54, edited by I. Hilberg. Vienna: F. Temsky, 1910.
John VIII, Pope. Epist. 201. In *Registrum Iohannis VIII.* Epistolae karolini aevi 5, edited by Erich Ludwig Eduard Caspar. MGH, Epp. 7. Berlin: Weidmannsche Buchhandlung, 1928.
Justin Martyr. *Dialogue with Trypho,* translated by Thomas B. Falls. Washington, DC: The Catholic University of America Press, 1965.
Kieckhefer, Richard. *Forbidden Rites: A Necromancer's Manual of the Fifteenth Century.* University Park, PA: Pennsylvania State University Press, 1998.
Krummel, Miriamne. *Crafting Jewishness in Medieval England: Legally Absent, Virtually Present.* New York: Palgrave Macmillan, 2011.
Kupfer, Marcia. "'... lectres ... plus vrayes': Hebrew Script and Jewish Witness in the *Mandeville* Manuscript of Charles V." *Speculum* 83, no. 1 (2008): 58–111.
Lasker, Daniel J. "Blasphemy: Jewish Concept." In *Encyclopedia of Religion*, 2nd ed., 2: 970. Detroit: Macmillan Reference USA, 2005.
Lauterbach, Jacob Z. "Substitutes for the Tetragrammaton." *Proceedings of the American Academy for Jewish Research* 2 (1930–1931): 39–67.
Lazar, Moshe. "Theophilus: Servant of Two Masters. The Pre-Faustian Theme of Despair and Revolt." *Modern Language Notes* 87, no. 6 (1972): 31–50.
Lewis, Suzanne. "*Tractatus Adversus Judaeos* in the Gulbenkian Apocalypse." *Art Bulletin* 68 (1986): 543–566.
Lewis, Suzanne. "Exegesis and Illustration in Thirteenth-Century English Apocalypses." In *The Apocalypse in the Middle Ages*, edited by Richard K. Emmerson and Bernard McGinn, 259–75. Ithaca: Cornell University Press, 1992.
Limor, Ora. "The Epistle of Rabbi Samuel of Morocco: A Best-Seller in the World of Polemics." In *Contra Iudaeos: Ancient and Medieval Polemics Between Christians and Jews*, edited by Ora Limor and Guy G. Stroumsa, 177–194. Tübingen: J.C.B. Mohr, 1996.
Lowe, Raphael. "Alexander Neckam's Knowledge of Hebrew." In *Hebrew Study from Ezra to Ben-Yehuda,* edited by William Horbury, 207–223. Edinburgh: T&T Clark, 1999.

Mack, Rosamund E. *Bazaar to Piazza: Islamic trade and Italian Art, 1300–1600*. Berkeley: University of California Press, 2001.
Maier, Paul L. "The Inscription on the Cross of Jesus of Nazareth." *Hermes* 124, no. 1 (1996): 58–75.
Maimonides, Moses. *Guide of the Perplexed*, translated by Shlomo Pines. Chicago: University of Chicago Press, 1964.
Manitius, Karl. "Magie und Rhetorik bei Anselm von Besate." *Deutsches Archiv für Erforschung des Mittelalters* 12 (1956): 52–72.
Marjanen, Antti. "A Nag Hammadi Contribution to the Discussion about the Pronunciation of the Tetragrammaton." *Studia Orientalia* 99 (2004): 153–59.
Maurer, Armand. "St. Thomas on the Sacred Name 'Tetragrammaton.'" *Mediaeval Studies* 34 (1972): 275–86.
Mellinkoff, Ruth. *Outcasts: Signs of Otherness in Northern European Art of the Late Middle Ages*. 2 vols. Berkeley: University of California Press, 1993.
Merback, Mitchell. "Jewish Carnality, Christian Guilt, and Eucharistic Peril in the Rotterdam-Berlin Altarpiece of the Holy Sacrament." In *Judaism and Christian Art: Aesthetic Anxieties from the Catacombs to Colonialism*, edited by Herbert L. Kessler and David Nirenberg, 203–32. Philadelphia: University of Pennsylvania Press, 2011.
Mews, Constant J. "Abelard and Heloise on Jews and *Hebraica Veritas*." In *Christian Attitudes toward Jews in the Middle Ages: A Casebook,* edited by Michael Frassetto, 83–108. New York, London: Routledge, 2007.
Nagel, Alexander. "Twenty-Five Notes on Pseudoscript in Italian Art." *Res* 59/60 (2011): 228–48.
Nequam, Alexander. *Speculum Speculationum*, edited by Rodney M. Thomson. Oxford: Oxford University Press, 1988.
Nirenberg, David. "The Judaism of Christian Art." In *Judaism and Christian Art: Aesthetic Anxieties from the Catacombs to Colonialism,* edited by Herbert L. Kessler and David Nirenberg, 387–427. Philadelphia: University of Pennsylvania Press, 2011.
Olszowy-Schlanger, Judith. "Christian Hebraism in Thirteenth-Century England." In *Crossing Borders: Hebrew Manuscripts as a Meeting-place of Cultures,* edited by Piet van Boxel and Sabine Arndt, 115–22. Oxford: Bodleian Library, 2010.
Owen, Yvonne. "The Saturnine History of Jews and Witches." *Preternature* 3, no. 1 (2014): 56–84.
Patai, Raphael. *Gates to the Old City*. New York: Avon, 1980.
Patai, Raphael. *The Jewish Alchemists: A History and Source Book*. Princeton: Princeton University Press, 1994.
Patton, Pamela A. *Art of Estrangement: Redefining Jews in Reconquest* Spain. University Park, PA: Penn State University Press, 2012.
Patton, Pamela A. "Constructing the Inimical Jew in the *Cantigas de Santa Maria*: Theophilus's Magician in Text and Image." In *Beyond the Yellow Badge: Anti-Judaism and Antisemitism in Medieval and Early Modern Visual Culture,* edited by Mitchell B. Merback, 233–56. Leiden: Brill, 2008.
Paul the Deacon. "Miraculum S. Mariae de Theophilo." In *Theophilus, mittelniederdeutsches Drama in drei Fassungen*, edited by Robert Petsch, 1–10. Heidelberg: Carl Winters, 1908.
Peter Abelard, Epist. 9: *De studio litterarum*. PL 178: 325–336.
Peter of Blois. *Contra perfidiam Judaeorum*. PL 207: 825–870.

Peter of Celle. *Tractatus de tabernaculo*. CCCM 54, edited by G. de Martel. Turnholt: Brepols, 1983.
Peter Damian. *Die Briefe des Petrus Damiani*. Vol. 1, edited by Kurt Reindel. MGH, Epp. Kaiserzeit. Munich: Monumenta Germaniae Historica, 1983–93.
Peter Damian. *Sermones*, edited G. Lucchesi. CCCM 57. Turnholt: Brepols, 1983.
Peter Damian. *The Letters of Peter Damian*, 1–30, translated by Owen J. Blum. Fathers of the Church, Mediaeval Continuation 1. Washington, DC: The Catholic University of America Press, 1989.
Peter Lombard. *Libri IV Sententiarum*, 2nd ed. Florence: Ex Typographia Collegii S. Bonaventurae, 1916.
Petrus Alfonsi. *Dialogue against the Jews*, translated by Irven M. Resnick. The Fathers of the Church, Mediaeval Continuation 8. Washington, DC: The Catholic University of America Press, 2006.
Phillip of Harvengt. *Commentaria in Cantica canticorum*. PL 203: 181–490.
Phillip of Harvengt. Epistola 17. PL 203: 151–156.
Picatrix: The Latin Version of the Ghāyat Al-Hakīm, edited by David Pingree. London: The Warburg Institute, University of London, 1986.
Pope Nicholas I. Epistola 86, *Ad Michaelem imperatorem*. PL 119: 926–962.
Rabanus Maurus. *De inventio linguarum*. PL 112: 1579–1583.
Ramban [Nachmanides]. *Commentary on the Torah*, translated by Charles B. Chavel, 5 vols. New York: Shilo Publishing House, 1971–76.
Rashi. *Commentaries on the Pentateuch*, translated by Chaim Pearl. New York: Viking Press, 1970.
Remigius of Auxerre. *Commentarius in Genesim*. PL 131: 51–134.
Resnick, Irven M. "Anselm the Peripatetic (of Besate) and Humanism in the Eleventh Century." *Journal of Medieval Latin* 6 (1996): 1–12.
Resnick, Irven M. "Falsification of Scripture and Medieval Christian-Jewish Polemics." *Medieval Encounters* 2, no. 3 (1996): 345–380.
Resnick, Irven M. 'Lingua Dei, lingua hominis': Sacred Language and Medieval Texts." *Viator* 21 (1990): 51–74.
Resnick, Irven M. *Marks of Distinction: Christian Perceptions of Jews in the High Middle Ages*. Washington, DC: Catholic University of America Press, 2013.
Ricketts, P. T. *Le Breviari d'Amor de Matfre Ermengaud*. Turnholt: Brepols, 1989–.
Rolling, Bernd. "Angelic Language and Communication" In *A Companion to Angels in Medieval Philosophy*, edited by Tobias Hoffmann, 223–260. Leiden: Brill, 2012.
Rubin, Miri. *Gentile Tales: The Narrative Assault on Late Medieval Jews*. New Haven: Yale University Press, 1999.
Rupert of Deutz. *De sancta trinitate et operibus eius*. CCCM 22. Edited by R. Haacke. Turnholt: Brepols, 1971.
Rupert of Deutz. *De victoria verbi dei*. PL 169: 1217–1502.
Rupert of Deutz. *In Apocalypsim Joannis Apostoli Commentariorum*. PL 169: 827–1214.
Rupert of Deutz. *In Zachariam Prophetam Commentariorum*. PL 168: 699–814.
Samuel of Morocco. *Liber de adventu messiae praeterito*. PL 149: 335–368.
Sandman, Israel Moshe. "The Mašōbēb Natībōt of Samuel Ibn Matut ('Motot'): Introductory Excursus, Critical Edition, and Annotated Translation." Vol. 2. PhD diss., University of Chicago, 2006.

Sarfatti, Gad B. "Hebrew Script in Western Visual Arts." Italia: Studi e ricerche sulla storia, la cultura e la letteratura degli Ebrei d'Italia 13–15 (2001): 451–547.

Schäfer, Peter. *Jesus in the Talmud*. Princeton: Princeton University Press, 2007.

Scheiber, Alexander. "Das Problem des Ursprungs der Sprache im Jüdischen Schriftum." *Magyar-zsido szemle* 53 (1937): 334–349.

Schreckenberg, Heinz. *The Jews in Christian Art: An Illustrated History*. New York: Continuum, 1996.

Shalom, Sabar. "Between Calvinists and Jews: Hebrew Script in Rembrandt's Art." In *Beyond the Yellow Badge: Anti-Judaism and Antisemitism in Medieval and Early Modern Visual Culture,* edited by Mitchell B. Merback, 371–404. Leiden: Brill, 2008.

Signer, Michael. "Polemic and Exegesis: The Varieties of Twelfth-Century Hebraism." In *Hebraica Veritas? Christian Hebraists and the Study of Judaism in Early Modern Europe*, edited by Allison P. Coudert and Jeffrey S. Shoulson, 21–32. Philadelphia: University of Pennsylvania Press, 2004.

Staley, Kevin M. "On Talking About God in the Academy: Thomas Aquinas and the Tetragrammaton." *New Blackfriars* 88, no. 1016 (2007): 433–42.

The Zohar: Pritzker Edition, trans. Daniel C. Matt. Vol. 1. Stanford: Stanford University Press, 2004.

Thomas Aquinas. *Summa Theologica*. Vol. 3. Rome: Typographia Forzani et S., 1928.

Thorndike, Lynn. *The Place of Magic in the Intellectual History of Europe*. New York: Columbia University Press, 1905.

Timmermann, Achim. "The Avenging Crucifix: Some Observations on the Iconography of the Living Cross." *Gesta* 40, no. 2 (2001): 141–60.

Trachtenberg, Joshua. *Jewish Magic and Superstition*. Philadelphia: University of Pennsylvania Press, 2004.

Trachtenberg, Joshua. *The Devil and the Jews: the Medieval Conception of the Jew and its Relation to Modern Antisemitism*. New Haven: Yale University Press, 1943.

"Vita Constantini." In *Medieval Slavic Lives of Saints and Princes,* trans. Marvin Kantor. Michigan Slavic Translations 5. Ann Arbor: University of Michigan, 1983.

Wilken, Robert Louis. *The First Thousand Years: A Global History of Christianity*. New Haven: Yale University Press, 2012.

Wilkinson. Robert J. *Tetragrammaton: Western Christians and the Hebrew Name of God. From the Beginnings to the Seventeenth Century*. Studies in the History of Christian Traditions 179. Leiden, Boston: Brill, 2015.

Williams Boyarin, Adrienne. *Miracles of the Virgin in Medieval England: Law and Jewishness in Marian Legends*. Cambridge: D.S. Brewer, 2010.

Wolfson, Elliot R. "Circumcision and the Divine Name: A Study in the Transmission of Esoteric Doctrine." *Jewish Quarterly Review* 78, no. 1–2 (1987): 77–111.

Wright, Stephen K. *The Vengeance of our Lord: Medieval Dramatizations of the Destruction of Jerusalem*. Toronto: Pontifical Institute of Mediaeval Studies, 1989.

Zafran, Eric. "Saturn and the Jews." In *Journal of the Warburg and Courtauld Institutes* 42 (1979): 16–27.

Zier, Mark. "The Healing Power of the Hebrew Tongue: An Example from Late Thirteenth-Century England." In *Health, Disease, and Healing in Medieval Culture,* edited by Sheila Campbell, Bert Hall, and David Klausner, 103–118. Houndmills, Basingstoke, Hampshire: Macmillan, 1992.

Gabriel Wasserman
Aramaic – Between Heaven and Earth: On the Use of Aramaic in the Liturgical Life of Medieval European Jewry

Aramaic is a Northwest Semitic language, which was originally spoken by the so-called Aramean people, and subsequently served as the administrative language of the Babylonian Empire of Nebuchadnezzar and his successors (sixth century BCE), the Persian Empire of the Achaemenids (sixth to fourth centuries BCE), and the later Persian Empires of the Parthians (third century BCE to third century CE) and Sassanians (third to seventh centuries CE).[1] It was the regular spoken language in the Galilee during the Second Temple period, and among the majority of Jews from the mid-first century CE through the seventh-century Muslim conquest and beyond.[2]

By the High Middle Ages, most Jews no longer spoke Aramaic in their daily lives. In the Muslim world, it had been replaced by various Arabic and Persian dialects; in the Byzantine Empire, by Greek dialects; and in Western Christendom, by various Germanic and Romance dialects. (Romance dialects were also probably used in Muslim Andalusia for ordinary communication, despite the predominance of the Arabic language for high culture there.) Nonetheless, Aramaic continued to play a prominent role in the ritual and intellectual life of Jews throughout the world. This paper will focus specifically on the Jews of Western Christian Europe (Italy, Germany, and France) and their engagement with Aramaic texts in synagogue settings. I shall demonstrate that these Jews used Aramaic in the synagogue in two contexts: (a) situations in which use of the vernacular was to be expected, for there was a desire to have everyone in the synagogue understand; and (b) situations that were supposed to evoke mystical feelings of revelation, such that a language even more special than Hebrew was needed. In the second, more extensive, section of the paper, I will focus on a specific ritual that was practiced in the synagogues of many medieval European Jewish communities on certain holidays: the

---

[1] I would like to thank Daniel Stein Kokin for graciously inviting me to participate in the conference that lies at the root of this volume. I would also like to thank Ephraim Kanarfogel, Katja Vehlow, and Jen Taylor for reading previous drafts of this paper.
[2] Stephen A. Kaufman, "Aramaic," in Robert Hetzron, ed., *The Semitic languages* (London: Routlege, 1997): 114–130, especially 114–118. It is noteworthy that Aramaic words and sentences appear even in the Hebrew Bible, including entire chapters in the biblical books of Daniel (2:4b–7:28) and Ezra (4:8–6:18, 7:11–26).

reading of Aramaic translation, Targum, along with the Hebrew reading from the Torah. This ritual was practiced especially on the seventh day of Passover, known as Yom Vayyosha',[3] and on Shavu'oth (the Feast of Weeks, Pentecost). On these occasions, and periodically on others, the Torah and Hafṭara were read in the synagogue not only in Hebrew, but also accompanied by an Aramaic translation after each verse. I will argue that this ritual fits both of the two aforementioned situations, especially the desire to evoke mystical feelings.

Although the vast majority of their liturgy was in Hebrew, the Jews of Europe continued to recite a number of Aramaic liturgical texts – both regular daily ones, and special ones for occasional holidays or life cycle events. Traditional Aramaic liturgical passages include *Yequm purqan* and *Kol nidré*. *Yequm purqan* is a prayer, still recited in the Ashkenazic liturgy, which consists of two paragraphs: the first one prays for the welfare of the exilarch and other leaders of Babylonian Jewry; the second addresses the community directly, wishing for God to "bless you and make your lives long [. . .] and may you be rescued and spared from all distress [. . .]."[4] Because the prayer addresses members of the community in the second person, it makes sense that it would be recited in their vernacular language, so that they would be sure to understand it; the prayer mentions Babylonian Jewish positions of leadership, such as the exilarchate, pointing to Iraq as the location of its composition. *Kol nidré* is a legal declaration about the annulment of personal vows; in order for the legal declaration to be valid, it must be recited in a language that people can understand. *Kol nidré* is recited at the beginning of Yom Kippur in most Jewish rites; however, the Italian (Roman) and Greek (Romaniote) rites recite it in Hebrew, not Aramaic.[5]

---

3 *Yom Vayyosha'* (יום ויושע) is the name of the holiday on 21 Nisan (the seventh day of Passover), which celebrates the splitting of the sea and the original singing of the "Song of the Sea." (In the Diaspora, this holiday – like almost all holidays – is celebrated for two days, and thus continues until 22 Nisan.) Its name is taken from the initial word of Exodus 14:30, recounting the events on that date on the occasion of the Exodus from Egypt: ויושע יי ביום ההוא את ישראל מיד מצרים, *The Lord saved (vayyosha') Israel on that day, from the hand of Egypt*. Though the name appears primarily in Middle Eastern manuscripts found in the Cairo Geniza (see Ezra Fleischer, *Shirat ha-qodesh ha-'ivrit bimé ha-benayim* (Jerusalem: Keter Publishing House Ltd., 1975), 179 f.), I employ it in this paper in a European context in order clearly to distinguish the festival at the end of Passover from the first six days of the Passover week.

4 See any traditional Ashkenazic *siddur*, e.g. Seligman Baer, ed., *Seder 'avodath Yisra'el* (Roedelheim, 1868), 229 f.

5 For the Aramaic text of *Kol nidré*, according to the Ashkenazic rite, see Daniel Goldschmidt, ed., *Maḥzor for the Days of Awe* (Jerusalem: Koren, 1970), volume 2: Yom Kippur, 1; Sephardic versions are similar. For the Italian text in Hebrew, see Menachem Emmanuele Artom, ed., *Machazor di rito italiano completo*, vol. 3: Kippur (Jerusalem: Jerusalem Fine Art Prints, 2005, pp. 100 f.). Finally, for a Greek version in Hebrew, see *Siddur tefilloth ha-shana le-minhag qehilloth Roman-*

The Jews of Europe also continued to compose new liturgy in Aramaic. The largest corpus of Aramaic liturgy, at least in Italy, Germany, and France, consists of poems composed to adorn the aforementioned ritual of reciting Aramaic Targum during the public reading of the Torah on Yom Vayyosha' and Shavu'oth, though European poets occasionally wrote Aramaic liturgy for other occasions.[6]

Because Hebrew was the language of the vast majority of the Bible and most of the liturgy, and was considered *leshon ha-qodesh*, the sacred language, the presence of Aramaic in these elements of the liturgy posed a question: why were these Aramaic texts being recited long after Aramaic had fallen out of use as a spoken language in these Jewish communities?

The High Medieval Jewish writings tend to give one, or both, of two stock answers to this question. One answer reflects the memory that Aramaic was once the language of the commoners and was once universally understood; the language thus stands in a position much lower than Hebrew, functioning on the secular, rather than on the sacred plane. Though Aramaic was no longer the spoken language of the masses, the liturgy was very conservative, and had not been updated to reflect the current situation; rather than using French or German, the languages of the present day, it retained Aramaic, that of their ancestors.[7]

The second answer to the problem of Aramaic liturgy goes in the extreme opposite direction, and claims Aramaic not as a symbolic or historical vernacular, but as a holy language to rival Hebrew. According to this answer, Hebrew is the customary holy language, spoken by the angels, but Aramaic is a mystical, arcane language, which even the angels in heaven do not understand. To those who know this language, it offers a direct ticket to God, avoiding all angelic intermediaries.

---

ya (Venice, n.d. (ca. 1523), f. 329a), accessed November 19, 2015, http://aleph.nli.org.il/nnl/dig/books/bk001993278.html.

6 For an example of an Aramaic poem for a different occasion, see Isaac ibn Ghiyyāt's "*Yom purayya*," to be recited prior to reading of the Scroll of Esther on Purim. (Yonah David, ed., *Shiré R. Yiẓḥaq ibn Giyyat* (Jerusalem: Hoẓa'ath 'Akhshav, 1988), pp. 302 f.)

7 An instructive parallel to this, perhaps, is the practice in many American Orthodox Ashkenazic synagogues of making certain announcements, such as that of the *molad* (the exact time of the upcoming astronomical new moon), in Yiddish. Though the members of these communities tend not to understand much Yiddish, they know that their ancestors did, and that the original purpose of the announcement was that the masses, in their ancestors' time, should understand it. Yiddish thus functions as a "symbolic vernacular," though it is no longer spoken in the daily life of the community.

These two answers are jarringly juxtaposed in a number of medieval sources, including a commentary on the *Qaddish*[8] by Asher ben Sha'ul, the late twelfth-century Provençal author of *Sefer ha-minhagoth*:

הנה סיימנו תפלת ערבית ושחרית ועתה נדבר על הקדיש. וטעם הקדיש למה נאמ'
בלשון תרגום מצינו בהגדה כי לעתיד לבוא יהיו הצדיקים גדולים מן המלאכים [. . .] על
כן תקנו לאומרו בלשון ארמית שלא יכירו בו ויתפללו שיתאחר הקץ ולא ידל כבודם, וכן
אמרו רבי' מלאכי השרת אין מכירין בלשון ארמית.

ונראה בעיני מפני שרובן של ישראל מדברין בלשון ארמית אפי' עמי הארץ אפי' הערלים
מדברין הן בלשון ארמית. ובעבור שישמעו הכל ויבינו שעתיד הב"ה להתגדל ולהתקדש
לעיני עמים רבים לימות המשיח כמו שכתו' (והגדלתי) [והתגדלתי] והתקדשתי לעיני
עמים רבים על כן תקנוהו בלשון ארמית, וכן כל השטרות הן בלשון ארמית כדי שיבינו
בהם עמי הארץ.[9]

Now that we have concluded our discussion of the evening and morning prayers, let us speak about the Qaddish. Why is the Qaddish recited in the language of Targum [i.e., Aramaic]? We find in a *haggada*[10] that in the future, the pious will be greater than the angels [. . .] Therefore, it was instituted that the Qaddish should be recited in Aramaic, so that the angels will not understand [that it is a prayer for speedy arrival of the End of Days], and pray that the End of Days will not come, so that their status will not be demoted. As our sages say: *The ministering angels do not understand the Aramaic language.*[11]

And it seems to me that [the recitation of the Qaddish is in Aramaic also] is due to the fact that most Jews speak Aramaic, even the unlearned people, and even the gentiles. In order that all people should hear, and understand, that God will ultimately be magnified and sanctified before the eyes of many nations in the Days of the Messiah, as it is said, *And I shall become magnified and sanctified . . . before the eyes of many nations* [Ezekiel 38:23] – therefore, [the Sages] composed the Qaddish in Aramaic. And for the same reason, all legal documents are in Aramaic, so that the unlearned people will understand them.

---

8 The *Qaddish* is an Aramaic prayer, recited frequently in the Jewish liturgy, in various forms. Its primary content is praise of God.
9 *Sefer Ha-minhagoth*, 9b (text taken from Bar-Ilan Responsa Database). In this source, and in all other Hebrew sources that I cite in this paper, I have added punctuation to make the text easier for the reader to understand.
10 *Haggada* or *aggada*, literally "storytelling," refers to the non-legal parts of rabbinic literature. (The Passover Haggada — which shall be discussed below — is named after the storytelling component contained in it, though it also contains legal elements.) Note that I have not found this particular statement about the righteous and the angels in any source earlier than *Sefer ha-minhagoth*.
11 On this notion see below.

Asher here presents the two explanations side by side, to explain the same phenomenon: the Qaddish is in Aramaic so that the angels will not understand it, and thus not be jealous of, and seek to counter, its results; or, alternatively, it is in Aramaic so that the commoners will understand it.

One of the most famous presentations of this juxtaposition is in the commentary of R. David Abudarham (fourteenth-century Spain) on the opening passage of the Passover Haggada, *Ha laḥma 'anya* ("This is the bread of affliction"). In this passage, the master of the house, who is leading the *seder*, shows off the *maẓẓa*, declares that it is the bread that the Israelites ate in Egypt, invites "all who are hungry" to "come and eat," and states the hope that though this year we are enslaved in exile, next year we will be free in the Land of Israel:

> ומה שנהגו לאמרו בלשון ארמית לפי שכולם היו מדברים בלשון ארמית ואין עמי הארץ מבינים לשון הקדש. ד[בר] א[חר]: כדי שלא יכירו מלאכי השרת שאנו מתפארים בכל זה, ויקטרגו עלינו ויזכרו עונותינו שאין אנו ראויין להגאל, שאין מלאכי השרת מכירין לשון ארמית, כמו שפירשנו בקדיש.

> And why is it the custom to recite this in Aramaic? Because [at the time when this passage was written] everyone spoke Aramaic, and the unlearned people did not understand the holy language (i.e. Hebrew). Another explanation: It is so that the ministering angels will not hear that we are bragging about all this, lest they come and challenge us [in the heavenly courtroom], and mention our sins, [and say] that we are unworthy of being redeemed. For the angels do not understand Aramaic, as we have explained in [our commentary on] the *Qaddish* [prayer].[12]

From a historical point of view, the original reason for the recitation of *Ha laḥma* in Aramaic is presumably Abudarham's first one: this passage is an invitation made to the common Jews on the street, and presumably was composed in a community where their daily language would have been Aramaic.[13] Nonetheless, Abudarham's invocation of the trope of evading the angels is not entirely

---

12 David Abudarham, *Sefer Abudarham* (Venice, [5]326 (=1566)), in the section "Commentary on the Haggada," f. 81a, accessed November 18, 2015, http://hebrewbooks.org/44589. Note that Abudarham's explanation of the Aramaic of Qaddish, to which he refers here, can be found on folio 27b, and is identical to that of *Sefer ha-minhagoth*.

13 On the other hand, we must note that the passage does not yet appear in the version of the Passover Haggada contained in the prayerbook of Rav Se'adya Ga'on, from early tenth-century Babylonia, and it is hardly probable that Aramaic was the spoken language of any influential Jewish community after this period. (For Se'adya's text of the Passover Haggada, see Israel Davidson, Simḥa Assaf, and Issachar Joel, *Siddur R. Saadja Gaon* (Jerusalem: Mekize Nirdamim, 1941), 136.) Nonetheless, the passage may well have existed already before Se'adya's time, and just not been included in Se'adya's own particular rite.

surprising; for indeed, the passage *Ha laḥma ʿanya* is somewhat boastful. After the initial declaration about the historical significance of the *maẓẓa*, it makes the speakers appear both magnanimous and wealthy, by inviting hungry strangers to join the meal; and then states confidently that the Jews will have experienced redemption by next year. One would not want the angels to overhear such boasts and prevent them from being realized.

This trope about the angels can be traced to a passage in the Babylonian Talmud, Shabbath 12b:

אמ[ר] רבה בר בר חנה כי הוה אזילנא בתר ר׳ אלעזר לשיולי ביה בתפיחא,
זימנין אמ[רינן] ליה: המקום יפקדך בשלום ;זימנין אמ[רינן] ליה: רחמנא
לדכרינך בשלמא.
איני?! והאמ[ר] רב יהודה אמ[ר] רב: לעולם אל ישאל אדם צרכיו בלשון ארמי,
דאמ[ר] ר[בי] יוחנן: כל השואל צרכיו בלשון ארמי אין מלאכי שרת ניזקקין לו,
לפי שאין מלאכי השרת מכירין בלשון ארמי.
שאני חולה, דשכינה עמו.

> Rabba bar bar Ḥana[14] said: When we used to visit R. Elʿazar [ben Pedath], to ask about his convalescence, sometimes we would say to him, "May God take account of you to [give you] peace," in Hebrew, and other times we would say it in Aramaic.
> [The anonymous editor of the passage asks:] But how can this be? Did not Rav Yehuda say in the name of Rav: "One should never pray [lit., make petitions] for one's needs in Aramaic, for R. Yoḥanan said: Whoever prays in Aramaic, the ministering angels will not deal with him, for the ministering angels do not understand Aramaic."
> [The editor answers:] The case of a sick person is different, for the Divine Presence is with him.[15]

---

14 All the authorities named in this passage lived in the third century CE. R. Yoḥanan and his student R. Elʿazar ben Pedath lived in Palestine, and both died in the year 279 CE. Rav (died 247), R. Yehuda (died 299), and Rabba bar bar Ḥana all lived in Babylonia, though the last must have spent some time in Palestine if there is any historicity behind the claim that he paid a visit to R. Elʿazar's sickbed. (Dates taken from H. L. Strack and Günter Stemberger, *Introduction to the Talmud and Midrash*, trans. and ed. Markus Bockmuehl, 2nd ed. (Minneapolis: Fortress Press, 1996), 83 ff.) Modern scholarship, since David Weiss-Halivni, calls the anonymous editors of the Babylonian Talmud "Stammaim." The estimates for when they lived vary from the mid-fifth century to the latter half of the sixth century, and perhaps even beyond; see David Weiss-Halivni, *Introductions to "Sources and Traditions"* [in Hebrew] (Jerusalem: Magnes Press, 2009), vii, 207.
15 Babylonian Talmud, MS Toronto Friedberg 9-002, Shabbath 12b; accessed November 18, 2015, from the Talmud Text Databank of the Saul Lieberman Institute of Talmud Research of the Jewish Theological Seminary of America, http://www.lieberman-institute.com. According to the catalogue of the National Library of Israel (http://aleph.nli.org.il), the Toronto manuscript is from the twelfth or thirteenth century, in Byzantine/Italian script; it was found in the Cairo Geniza, and is the oldest manuscript of this section of Tractate Shabbath. In the standard printed Talmud, the text is fundamentally the same, except that Rabba bar bar Ḥana says not that "we" used to say certain prayers when visiting R. Elʿazar, but that an unidentified "he" used to do so.

In this Talmudic passage, of course, the angels' ignorance of Aramaic is used as a reason *not* to pray in Aramaic. Most likely, R. Yoḥanan's statement was originally meant to exclude all non-Hebrew prayer, and "Aramaic" was merely the most common non-Hebrew language known to the Jews of Late Antiquity. Nonetheless, the last line of our passage – in the voice of the later editors (Stammaim), not the third-century R. Yoḥanan – opens the door to the use of Aramaic prayer in exceptional situations, whereby one can bypass the angelic intercessors, and direct one's prayers straight to God, who, by virtue of His omniscience, understands all languages. The case mentioned here is prayer in the room of a sick individual, where God Himself is believed to be present. Another exceptional case in which Aramaic prayer is acceptable comes up in a different passage in the Babylonian Talmud (Soṭa 33a), namely the case of communal prayer. In a discussion of a ruling of the Mishna[16] that prayer may be recited in any language, the Stammaim bring up the restrictive statements of R. Yoḥanan and Rav Yehuda, that the angels do not understand Aramaic prayer, as a challenge to this ruling. They resolve this challenge by saying that the restriction applies only to an individual, but not to a community engaged in public prayer (הא ביחיד, הא בציבור). The Stammaim do not tell us why the case of communal prayer should be different; but presumably, the implication is that God hears the prayer of the community directly, without recourse to angelic intermediaries.

In these Talmudic passages, it seems that the justifications for using Aramaic prayer in certain situations merely grant permission to do so; they do not suggest that there is any benefit to having the angels not understand.[17] Because Aramaic was the vernacular, it was natural to use the language for certain prayers when there was no legal or theological impediment for doing so. However, in the medieval period, when the vast majority of Jews did not speak Aramaic in their daily interactions, nor was it their usual language in religious matters, the continued presence of Aramaic in certain traditional liturgical texts, such as *Ha laḥma 'anya* or the Qaddish doxology, needed special justification, as we have discussed above. The idea of the angels' non-comprehension of Aramaic, which emerged in Talmudic times as a deterrent from Aramaic prayer, now became a justification for it in situations in which it was preferable for the angels not to understand.

The sacral nature of Aramaic, the ancient vernacular, may be termed a paradox of sorts: The angels do not understand Aramaic because it is, or once

---

[16] The Mishna is a corpus of Jewish law completed in the early third century CE.
[17] Note that in the story about R. El'azar's illness, neither the characters in the story nor the stammaitic editors of the passage give any preference to the Aramaic prayer for the teacher's recovery; rather, the story reports that sometimes the students would pray for him in Hebrew, and other times in Aramaic, apparently indiscriminately.

was, a merely earthly, vernacular language; yet on the other hand, one cannot deny that God understands it, for He is omniscient. Thus, precisely the lowliest, most pedestrian of languages acquires a special heavenly status as a direct route to God. Paradoxically, the very lowly character of the vernacular contains the seeds of its potential hyper-sacralization.[18]

Medieval discussions of this type reveal that although the practice of reciting Aramaic was standard in this period, it caused medieval Jews pause, and required explanation and justification. Now that I have set the stage with this overview, and reflected on the self-awareness of medieval Jews regarding their liturgical use of Aramaic, I turn in the second half of the paper to the peculiar – yet widespread – practice of reciting Aramaic Targum on two holidays, Yom Vayyosha' and Shavu'oth, and to some possible reasons behind this practice.

On Yom Vayyosha', late antique Jewish tradition (both Palestinian and Babylonian) prescribes the liturgical reading of the story of the splitting of the sea and the "Song of the Sea," both of which are ascribed to this precise date (i.e. 21 Nisan).[19] On Shavu'oth, late antique tradition (again both Palestinian and Babylonian) prescribes the reading of the story of the theophany at Mt. Sinai and the Decalogue, which are dated to this day (6 Sivan). Though the association of Shavu'oth with the revelation at Sinai is not explicit in the Bible,[20] it emerges already in some Second Temple and rabbinic sources, and was the standard understanding of the holiday already by the early medieval period. The story of the Israelites at the sea, too, is associated with revelation, both in the biblical text (where it says that the Israelites "*saw* the heavy hand which the Lord had wrought

---

18 I thank Daniel Stein Kokin for formulating the paradox in the following terms: Aramaic becomes holy – and, indeed, especially holy – because it is forgotten as a vernacular. The people forget, God remembers, and the angels never learn.
19 See Chaim Milikowsky, ed., *Seder 'Olam* (Jerusalem: Yad Ben-Ẓvi, 2013), 235, lines 8–13 (chapter 5): "On the fourteenth of [Nisan], the Israelites slaughtered their paschal offerings; [. . .] that night, the [Egyptian] firstborns were struck dead. The next day [. . .] [the Israelites] traveled from Raamses to Sukkoth, and [on the next day] from Sukkoth to Etham, and [on the next day] from Etham to Pi ha-ḥiroth – this makes three days. On the fourth day, *it was told to the king of Egypt* [that they had traveled so far] (Exodus 14:5); on the fifth and sixth days, *the Egyptians chased after them* (Ex. 14:9). On the night before the seventh day, they all descended into the sea, and *there was cloud and darkness* (Ex. 14:20); and the next morning, they recited the Song: *Then sang Moses and the Israelites* (Ex. 15:1) – and that was the seventh day, the concluding festival day of [the] Passover [week]."
20 The book of Exodus dates the Sinai revelation to the third month after the Exodus, which fits with the date of Shavu'oth (in the rabbinic tradition, approximately the sixth of Sivan, the third month).

against the Egyptians"), and in the rabbinic tradition (according to which "A slave girl at the sea saw what even Ezekiel the prophet could not see"[21]).

On these two occasions, medieval Jewish communities recited Aramaic translation between the verses of their Hebrew Torah-reading; after each Hebrew verse read by the official reader, a second individual, called the *methurgeman* (literally: "translator"), would recite the Targum, the ancient Aramaic translation, of the verse. This had been the standard manner of ritual Torah reading, every Sabbath and festival morning (perhaps even on weekdays), throughout the Middle East in late antiquity, and is still practiced in Yemenite communities today, and probably had been so in Europe, as well, in hoary antiquity; however, in our earliest European evidence of the practice,[22] in the eleventh century, the reading of Targum is already limited practically[23] only to Shavu'oth and Yom Vayyosha'. While it is

---

[21] Haim Saul Horovitz and Israel Abraham Rabin, eds., *Mekhilta de-R. Yishma'el* (Frankfurt: Mekize Nirdamim, 1930), 126, line 19 f. (Shira §3).

[22] The earliest evidence is the composition of Aramaic Targum-poems (see below) by Meir bar Isaac in mid-eleventh-century Worms; these are specifically for Yom Vayyosha' and Shavu'oth. However, the fact that the recitation of Targum on specifically these days is attested not only in Germany and France, but also in Roman and Byzantine communities, indicates that it probably occurred already earlier than the eleventh century, in a period in which there was still extensive cross-pollination of liturgical material between these regions.

[23] Some other occasions are occasionally attested, as well, but less so than Yom Vayyosha' and Shavu'oth; and even these, at least for the Torah-reading (as opposed to the *haftara*) are all from outside of France and Germany. Shemu'el Ha-nagid (eleventh-century Granada), in a responsum that is preserved in Judah of Barcelona's early twelfth-century *Sefer ha-'ittim*, mentions a practice of reciting Targum with the *haftaroth* (readings from the prophets) on festivals in general, and on wedding Sabbaths, and of reciting Targum with the Torah reading on Simḥath Tora (the festival at the end of Sukkoth, when the annual cycle of reading the Torah is completed) – all "in order to beautify the ritual" (Jacob Schorr, ed., *Sefer ha-'ittim* (Cracow: Mekize Nirdamim, 1903), 267, §179.). The commentary of the Tosafists (twelfth- to thirteenth-century France and Germany) on the Babylonian Talmud, Megilla 23b and 24a (found in the usual printed editions of the Talmud) mentions a practice to recite Targum for all the *haftaroth* of Passover (not just the seventh day) and Shavu'oth; this tradition is found also in manuscripts and printed editions of the Italian Rite. The Nürnberg Maḥzor (MS Zurich Jeselsohn 9) contains Targum for the *haftaroth* of all festivals, including Rosh Hashana and Sukkoth. Manuscripts of the Italian Rite also contain Targum for the Torah reading of Simḥath Tora. Of all the liturgical occasions that we have mentioned in this footnote, only the Simḥath Tora reading in the Italian manuscripts was interwoven with liturgical hymns in Aramaic. In terms of practice, this is identical to the phenomenon that we see on Shavu'oth and Yom Vayyosha'. However, as opposed to what we will demonstrate concerning Yom Vayyosha' and Shavu'oth, the insertions on Simḥath Tora were probably intended merely to enhance the festivity of the occasion. In order to thoroughly address this issue, we would need to carefully analyze the texts of the Aramaic poems recited in the Targum on Simḥath Tora. In any event, this practice is limited to Italy and Greek lands, and not found in France or Germany.

possible that the practice had died out completely, and was only reinstated for these festive days as an innovation, it is more reasonable to suppose that there was continuity: first the Targum was read on a regular basis, and then communities became less and less committed to it as a regular practice, until ultimately it was in essence limited only to these especially significant days. Our evidence for this limited recitation of Targum in European countries, especially France and Germany (but also Rome and the Byzantine lands, and even beyond), continues past the eleventh century, through the fourteenth; after the fourteenth century, the practice seems to have fallen out of use entirely, as we shall discuss further on in this article. On these festive days, the French and German (and other) communities not only recited straight Aramaic translation of the Biblical text, but also supplemented it with long Aramaic insertions: texts from late antiquity, in both poetry and prose, but also new Aramaic poems, which European poets wrote following old models.

While a number of scholars have discussed these poems, the only scholar to deal with the question of *why* the European communities maintained this practice on Yom Vayyosha' and Shavu'oth is Jonah Fraenkel, who published over fifty of these Aramaic poems in the context of his editions of the Franco-Ashkenazic *Maḥzor* (festival prayerbook) for Passover and Shavu'oth.[24] Although Fraenkel devotes only a few brief notes to this question, the answers that he suggests are not consistent. Thus, on the one hand, in the introduction to his Passover *Maḥzor*, he writes:

> The common feature between the splitting of the sea [. . .] and the revelation at Sinai [. . .] is that they are considered in midrashic literature to be prominent experiences of divine revelation. It seems reasonable that there might have been a connection between the use of texts that were incomprehensible to the general public, such as the Aramaic *targumim*, and the arousal of mystical feelings of divine revelation. This is a possible explanation of the strange phenomenon that the communities recited Targum only on these specific days.[25]

---

24 J. Fraenkel, *Maḥzor for Passover, in accordance with the Ashkenazic Rite in all its branches* [in Hebrew] (Jerusalem: Koren, 1993), 608–661; ibid., *Maḥzor for Shavu'oth, in accordance with the Ashkenazic Rite in all its branches* [in Hebrew] (Jerusalem: Koren, 2000), pp. 385–593. At the time when I delivered this paper at the Greifswald conference, Prof. Fraenkel was among the living, and indeed, among the leading scholars in multiple fields of Jewish studies, including Talmud, *aggada* (non-legal materials from the Talmudic-era teachers), Rashi's commentaries, and *piyyuṭ* (liturgical poetry). His death, less than two months later, was a true loss for the field of Jewish studies, and he is sorely missed. May his memory be a blessing.

25 Fraenkel, *Passover*, p. xxi [כ]. Fraenkel's Hebrew is:

המשותף לאירועים של קריעת ים סוף [. . .] ו[. . .] מעמד הר סיני [. . .] הוא כי הם נחשבים במדרש למעמדות מובהקים של גילוי שכינה. מתקבל על הדעת שיש קשר בין העיסוק בטקסטים בלתי מובנים לקהל רחב, כגון התרגומים, לבין העלאת רגשות מיסטיים של גילוי שכינה ואולי זה מסביר את התופעה המוזרה של התרגומים דווקא בימים אלה.

On the other hand, in his article on the liturgy of the Nürnberg *Maḥzor*, he writes that the communities of Europe preserved the old, otherwise discarded custom of Targum on these holidays in order to add to the "festivity" of the ritual of reading, for the "Song of the Sea" (read on Yom Vayyosha') and the Decalogue (read on Shavu'oth) are "special" readings. This explanation would suggest that the presence of Aramaic is merely cosmetic. In other words, there might be no inherent value to the Aramaic language itself, but including this ancient, now rare, ritual is a way to make the Torah-reading more elaborate and beautiful.[26] This is clearly quite different from Fraenkel's other suggestion.

Is it plausible that European communities recited Targum in order to evoke a mystical feeling, as Fraenkel suggests? Of course, the answer to this question depends upon how we define the term *mysticism*. A comprehensive discussion of how to do so is beyond the scope of this paper, but Gershom Scholem's well-known definition represents a good place to start. At the beginning of his classic *Major Trends in Jewish Mysticism*, Scholem writes:

> Mysticism is a definite state in the historical development of religion. [. . .] The first stage [of religious consciousness, namely "monism"] represents the world as being full of gods whom man encounters at every step and whose presence can be experienced without recourse to ecstatic mediation. [. . . T]here is no room for mysticism as long as the abyss between Man and God has not become a fact of the inner consciousness.

The second state, which Scholem refers to as "standard religion," conceives of a great abyss between man and God, which is hardly crossed, except via occasional commands from God and prayer to Him. Thereafter, Scholem addresses the third period:

> And only now that religion has received [. . .] its classical expression [. . .] do we witness the phenomenon called mysticism; its rise coincides with what may be called the romantic period of religion. **Mysticism does not deny or overlook the abyss; on the contrary, it begins by realizing its existence, but from there it proceeds to a quest for the secret that will close it in, the hidden path that will span it.** [. . .][27]

With Scholem's definition in mind, we can, indeed, use the term "mysticism" as an appropriate category when describing the ritual recitation of Aramaic Targum. As we have seen, medieval Jews held the belief that Aramaic is the language that humans can use to bypass the ordinary, angelic channels to God, and reach God directly.

---

26 Jonah and Avraham Fraenkel, "Prayer and Piyyut in the Maḥzor Nuremberg" [in Hebrew], published online on the website of the National Library of Israel: http://jnul.huji.ac.il/dl/mss-pr/mahzor-nuremberg/pdf/fraenkel_j_a.pdf. An updated edition of this article will be published in English in a forthcoming volume on the Nürnberg Maḥzor.

27 Gershom Scholem, *Major Trends in Jewish Mysticism*, 2nd ed. (Jerusalem: Schocken, 1946), 7–8.

Do medieval sources support either of these claims, i.e. that the purpose of including Targum on these days was to evoke "mystical feelings of revelation" or "festivity"? The custom of reciting the Targum for hafṭaroth on Passover and Shavu'oth is discussed in a comment of the Tosafists on the Babylonian Talmud:[28]

> והא שאנו מתרגמין הפטרות של פסח ועצרת טפי משאר י[ום] ט[וב] לפי שהן
> מדברות בנס היום, כדי לפרסם הנס. וכן במתן תורה, כדי לפרסם הנס.

> Why do we recite the Targum of [lit. translate] the *hafṭaroth* of Passover and Shavu'oth, rather than [those of] any other festival? Because they speak about the miracles which occurred on those days. We want to publicize these miracles (לפרסם הנס). And similarly with regard to the giving of the Torah [i.e. the revelation at Sinai, as described in the Torah-reading on the first day of Shavu'oth], in order to publicize the miracle.

From a practical point of view, the explanation is difficult: How does an Aramaic Targum help "publicize the miracle" to people who understand Aramaic less than Hebrew? A possible answer is that the concept of publicizing the miracle refers not to telling the story of the miracle in words which the listeners will understand, but rather to performing a ritual action that will remind the participants of the story of the miracle, and put them into the frame of mind of people experiencing the miracle. In fact, the expression (in its Aramaic form, פַּרְסוֹמֵי נִיסָא, *parsomé nissa*) is used by the Babylonian Talmud with reference to the following rituals:[29] reciting Hallel (Berakhoth 14a),[30] reading the Scroll of Esther (Berakhoth 14a and Megilla 3b), kindling lights on Ḥanukka (Shabbath 23b), and drinking four cups

---

28 Printed Tosafoth commentary on bMegilla 24a. As noted by Ephraim Urbach, the printed Tosafoth on Tractate Megilla come from the school of R. Judah Sirilion, and thus can be located in early thirteenth-century northern France. Ephraim Elimelech Urbach, *The Tosafists: Their Lives, Works, and Approach* [in Hebrew], 4th ed. (Jerusalem: Bialik Institute, 1980), volume 2, 617 f.

29 Since this principle is not mentioned by Tannaim or Amoraim (the named authorities in Talmudic literature), both the expression *parsomé nissa* and the legal concept surrounding it appear to be innovations of the Stammaim. In any event, the Stammaim clearly consider it a very powerful principle, for whenever they bring it up, it is to defend why these rituals might take precedence over what are otherwise the most important halakhic activities: e.g., studying Torah; burying an abandoned corpse; or reciting *Qiddush*, the prayer that inaugurates the Sabbath over a cup a wine.

30 For the experiential value of "ecstatic joy," meant to accompany the recitation of Hallel (at least at the Passover seder), see yPesaḥim 7:11: דמתלין מתלא פיסחא כזיתא והלילה מתבר אגרייא – The popular expression says: "A bite of the paschal sacrifice and [the recitation of] Hallel used to break the roofs!"

of wine at the Passover *seder* (Pesaḥim 112a).³¹ Of all these activities, only the reading of the Scroll of Esther tells a story, and even this story does not include any overtly supernatural elements. All the other actions only recall miraculous events to people who already know the story, and already know the connection between the story and the ritual action. Thus, the recitation of Targum, as a ritual, *highlights* the readings on these special days which commemorate the miracles. Here is where Fraenkel's idea of the mystical experience of foreign languages fits in: in the same way that drinking wine at the Passover *seder* creates an experiential feeling of freedom, so too does listening to texts in Aramaic create an experiential feeling of revelation, such as Scripture says occurred at the splitting of the sea and the theophany at Sinai. The non-routine nature of the activity, and not the specific content, is what creates the experience.

Another possible answer, not contradictory to the first, is that although the masses do not actually understand the Aramaic translation, the ritual of reciting it represents *symbolically* the spreading of the story to the masses, because the community has maintained the memory that once upon a time, Aramaic was the language of the people. According to this understanding, too, the use of the term *publicizing the miracle* here means not explaining a story to people in a way that they will understand, but performing an action that will somehow evoke elements of the story in the communal consciousness, and perhaps highlight it through the very strangeness of the ritual action, in this case the use of texts in a language that most people do not understand.³²

---

31 bPesaḥim 108a-b indicates the experiential value of "freedom" meant to accompany the drinking of the four cups of wine at the Passover *seder*:

ואמר רבי יהושע בן לוי: נשים חייבות בארבעה כוסות הללו, שאף הן היו באותו הנס. אמר רב יהודה אמר שמואל: ארבעה כוסות הללו צריך שיהא בהן כדי מזיגת כוס יפה. שתאן חי [. . .], אמר רבא – ידי יין יצא, ידי חירות לא יצא. – R. Joshua ben Levi said: Women are obligated in the [drinking of the] four cups, for they too were present at the moment of the miracle [of the Exodus from Egypt]. Rav Judah said in the name of Shemuel: These four cups need to contain enough wine such that when they are mixed with water, they produce enough fluid for a full cup. If one drank them unmixed [in the form of a viscous syrup] . . . Rava said: Such a person has fulfilled the obligation of wine, but not the obligation of [experiencing a state of] "freedom".

32 As noted, our remarks here have focused on the Tosafist traditions that emerged in early thirteenth-century northern France. It is unclear whether the connection between "publicizing the miracle" and the practice of reciting Targum discussed here pre-dates this period. The connection does also appear in a parallel passage in the printed edition of *Maḥzor Vitry*, a twelfth-century legal-liturgical compilation from France by Simḥa of Vitry (Simon Hurwitz, ed., *Maḥzor Vitry* (Berlin: Mekize Nirdamim, 1893), p. 304, §106). However, Hurwitz's edition is based on the late thirteenth-century manuscript London British Library Add. 27200-01, and contains many accretions to the early twelfth-century text, so it is impossible, without consulting the various manuscripts, to know whether any particular line is authentically from the twelfth century. The

In short, consideration of this practice, along with the sources that present the two justifications for the liturgical use of Aramaic, leads to the conclusion that the recitation of Targum not only recalled the ancient purpose of making the text comprehensible, but also had a mystical component, serving to create a mystical experience during the synagogue service on these holidays. Let us now examine the ritual from another angle, by analyzing the texts of a few of the Aramaic liturgical poems (piyyuṭim) written by medieval European poets for use in the Torah readings on these holidays; these poems, too, attest that the communities thematized the language as revelatory. Reading these piyyuṭim alongside our other sources provides yet another perspective on the potentially mystical use of Aramaic during these two holidays.

Let us begin our study of the piyyuṭim with one composed by Meir bar Isaac in eleventh-century Worms. This piyyuṭ was written to be recited by the *methurgeman* after the first Hebrew verse of the Yom Vayyosha' Torah-reading, before the Targum of that same verse was read. The piyyuṭ opens with these lines:

אִילוּ פּוּמֵי נִימֵי // בְּנֵי נָשָׁא רָשְׁמֵי
גְּוִילֵי שְׁמַיָּא וּשְׁמֵי // דְּיוֹתָא כָּל יַמֵּי
הֲדַר מָרֵא עָלְמֵי // וְשַׁלִּיט בְּכָל תְּחוּמֵי
זְעֵיר סָפְקֵי סָכְמֵי // חֲדָא לְרִבְבָן קַמֵּי
טְפֵי טָבְוָן וְרַחֲמֵי // יִתּוּר חַסְדִּין דְּאַחֲמֵי
כְּדִי פְּרַק מֵעֲנָמֵי // לְעַם חַבִּיב כְּנַמֵּי

If all hairs were mouths // and all people were scribes,
And all heavens were parchment // and all seas were ink –
The glory of the world's Master, // Who rules over all regions
Would be insufficiently counted, // even one-hundredth of a percent.
His goodness was so great, // His kindness, which I saw,
When he redeemed, from the Egyptians, // his beloved people, as it is said.[33]

---

edition by Arye Goldschmidt (Jerusalem: Oẓar Ha-posqim, 2004) is too unsystematic to be useful in reconstructing the textual history of *Maḥzor Vitry*. On this text, see Justine Isserles, "Maḥzor Vitry: Étude d'un corpus de manuscrits hébreux ashkénazes de type liturgico-légal du XIIe au XIVe siècle" (PhD diss., École Pratique des Hautes Études, Paris and University of Geneva, 2012); this work is not a critical edition, but discusses the problems with the existing two printed editions of the text.

33 Fraenkel, *Passover*, p. 608. I have copied the texts and vocalization of all these piyyuṭim from Fraenkel. He notes that his vocalization is merely a first suggestion (הצעה ראשונה), because the study of the language of Medieval European Aramaic liturgical poetry is still in its infancy. I have also made great use of the Hebrew translations and notes which Fraenkel provides for the *piyyuṭim* in preparing my own English translations and interpretations of them. Perhaps I have overlooked certain other ways in which the texts could be understood.

These lines comment upon the inability of language, whether written or oral, to fully express the human experience of God's miraculous activity. Even if every hair on the head could speak, says the poet, and – in accordance with a late antique rabbinic trope[34] – all the heavens were parchment, and all the seas ink, this would still be insufficient to express the totality of God's deeds. Now, if ordinary language (Hebrew) is incapable of describing "the acts of kindness which I saw," perhaps an extra-ordinary language, Aramaic, can create a sense of the wondrous experience of them.

Meir wrote not only this one piyyuṭ for the Targum of the reading of Yom Vayyosha‘, but a sequence of three poems. The first poem, as we have seen, introduces the Targum of the first verse; the second introduces the Targum of Exodus 13:21, about God's physical manifestation in the pillar of cloud and pillar of fire, which led the Israelites in their wanderings;[35] and the last introduces the Targum of the "Song of the Sea" (beginning with 15:1), which concludes the story of the splitting of the sea. Of these, the first and last are obvious sites for poetic expansions of the Targum, for they introduce major sections: the beginning of the entire reading, and the reading of the "Song." The middle poem comes in a more unexpected place, but the content of the verse is about divine revelation in the cloud, a suitably mystical theme.

In the third poem of the sequence, introducing the "Song of the Sea," Meir begins by stating that he intends to sing praises of God (in the "Song"), and goes on to tell a parable, which he attributes to the Mekhilta:[36] when a human king enters a town, the residents of the town shower him with lavish praises, but these praises are false. However, when we praise God, the praises are true, and even these true praises are inadequate to capture God's actual glory. This trope fits well with our thesis that Aramaic is being used in order to transcend the limitations of the ordinary language, namely Hebrew.

Among the praises mentioned in the Mekhilta passage is that of the physical beauty of God. Meir follows his source very closely, and writes the following:

---

34 See Babylonian Talmud, Shabbath 11a; Avoth de-R. Nathan, Version A, chapter 25, folio 41a, ed. S. Schechter (Vienna, 1887).
35 Fraenkel, *Passover*, pp. 616 f.
36 In Meir's words: הֲלָא פְּרִישׁ יָאוּת לְגוֹ מְכִילְתָּא סְבִירָא, "is it not explained well in the Mekhilta, sensibly" (Fraenkel, *Passover*, p. 624, line 5). "Mekhilta" is the name of at least two works of rabbinic exegesis on the book of Exodus, one associated with the name of R. Ishmael, the other with the name of R. Simeon bar Yoḥai (both of second-century CE Palestine). This parable is found in the Mekhilta of R. Ishamel, *Shira*, §1 (ed. Horovitz–Rabin [see footnote 21, above], 119).

תְּקוֹף הֲדַר שׁוּפְרֵיהּ לָא לְדַמּוֹיֵי סִדְרָא
מְצַע אֵילֵי מְרוֹמָא שְׁחָקִים וּמְדוֹרָא
אָתָא הוּא בְּגוֹ רִבְוָן וְדוּגְמָא וְהֵכֵּירָא
יְקָרָא כְּעֵין דּוּגְמֵיהּ כִּבְשְׁבוּעָה חֲמִירָא
רְשִׁים בְּשֶׁבַח שְׁבָחִין דִּלְשְׁלֹמֹה אֲמִירָא

> One cannot describe the greatness of his beauty by any simile.
> Among the divine-like beings on high, in the heavens, His dwelling place,
> He is a sign amidst the myriads, and in prominent display.
> Glory like His appearance is [as binding as] a serious oath,
> As [He is] described in the Praise of Praises [Song of Songs], spoken by Solomon.[37]

Meir states here, in accordance with Isaiah 40:18,[38] that any similes that we might state about God's likeness – even the many similes that are used in the Song of Songs (which, as a biblical book, was presumably written under divine inspiration) – are inadequate to describe Him. Even the authors of Scripture were limited by ordinary language; how, then, is the poet to attempt adequate description? Perhaps the use of Aramaic Targum and *piyyuṭ* can enable this. Their literal content was barely understood in Europe because of the language barrier, and therefore, their recitation opened an avenue to pure mystical emotion and feelings of revelation.

Now let us turn to *Aqdamuth*, Meir's famous poem for Shavuʻoth, which introduces the recitation of the Targum of the reading for this holiday. Here, too, R. Meir emphasizes the inadequacy of language to describe God, but nonetheless proceeds to offer, ekphrastically, a visual description of God and His throne. Let us take a look at the opening section of the poem. In the first four lines (two beginning with *aleph* and two with *beth*), the poet/*methurgeman* asks for permission (*reshuth*) from God to discuss "two or three themes". Then (at the letter *gimmel*), he launches immediately into a discussion of the inadequacy of language to describe God's works:

אַקְדָּמוּת מִלִּין וְשָׁרָיוּת שׁוּתָא
אַוְלָא שָׁקֵלְנָא הַרְמָן וּרְשׁוּתָא.

---

37 Fraenkel, *Passover*, pp. 624 ff.
38 As Fraenkel notes in his commentary *ad locum*, the phrase לא לדמויי סדרא seems to be based on the Targum of Isaiah 40:18, ואל מי תדמיון אל ומה דמות תערכו לו (*And to whom could you compare God, and what image could you attribute to Him?*), namely: מסדרין . . . ומה . . . ולמאן אתון מדמין קדמוהי. We should note also that the Aramaic word סדרא, as well as the word ערך in the Hebrew of Isaiah, are both used in first-millennium-CE Hebrew to mean "a portion of Scripture." Our poet may therefore be implying that no passage of Hebrew Scripture can truly describe God.

בְּבָבֵי תְּרֵי וּתְלָת דְּאֶפְתַּח בְּנַקְשׁוּתָא
בְּבָרֵי דְבָרֵי וְטָרֵי עֲדֵי לְקַשִׁישׁוּתָא.
גְּבוּרָן עָלְמִין לַהּ וְלָא סְפֵק פְּרִישׁוּתָא
גְּוִיל אִלּוּ רְקִיעֵי, קְנֵי כָּל חוּרְשָׁתָא
דְּיוֹ אִלּוּ יַמֵּי וְכָל־מֵי כְנִישׁוּתָא
דָּיְרֵי אַרְעָא סָפְרֵי וְרָשְׁמֵי רַשְׁוָתָא
הֲדַר מָרֵי שְׁמַיָּא וְשַׁלִּיט בְּיַבֶּשְׁתָּא
הֲקִים עָלְמָא יְחִידַאי וְכַבְּשֵׁהּ בְּכַבְּשׁוּתָא.

> Before my words [of Targum], as I begin to speak,
> I start by asking permission and license.
> In two or three sections, I shall begin with trembling,
> With the permission of the Creator, who bears [everything] till old age.
> Eternal works are His, and there would not be sufficient [material] to recount them,
> If all the skies were parchment, and all the forests were writing-reeds,
> And all the seas were ink, and all pooled waters, too,
> And all inhabitants of the land were scribes, and writers of documents.
> [This would not be sufficient to recount] the beauty of the Master of Heaven, who rules also the land,
> Who set up the world on His own, and dominated it with his power.[39]

These lines are parallel to the first lines of Meir's opening *piyyuṭ* for Yom Vayyosha'. He even uses much of the same language in these two poems, based on the old trope of the inadequacy of all reeds, seas, and skies to write what one is trying to express. The difference is that in the poem for Yom Vayyosha', he is speaking of the inadequacy of language to describe God's specific miraculous activity in splitting the sea, whereas in *Aqdamuth*, he is speaking of the inadequacy of language to describe God's great works in general, or creation in particular. In each case, he is using the Aramaic language to tell how inadequate language is to describe God. As we have said above, this may imply that Aramaic is a mystical language, which is more capable of describing God than ordinary Hebrew is. Moreover, it is somehow fitting to convey the limitations of language by using a language that most listeners cannot understand.

Though the practice of reciting Targum on these holidays was still prevalent in French and German Jewry in the fourteenth century, as we see from manuscript *maḥzorim* from that century, the ritual eventually fell out of use. The early fifteenth-century Ashkenazic books of rituals, *Sefer Maharil* and *Sefer ha-minhagim*,[40] which

---

[39] Fraenkel, *Shavu'oth*, pp. 385 f.
[40] *Sefer Maharil* is by Zalman of St. Goar, and reports the practices of his teacher, Jacob ben Moses Mölin the Levite, known as Maharil; this text thus reflects the customs of Western Ashkenaz, i.e. the Rhineland. *Sefer ha-minhagim*, by Aizik Tyrnau, reports the practices of Eastern Ashkenaz, i.e. the eastern German and Slavic lands.

present detailed descriptions of the liturgy for every special occasion in the year, do not report any recitation of Targum or Aramaic *piyyuṭim* on Yom Vayyosha'.[41] Nonetheless, when describing the reading of the Torah and *hafṭara* on Shavu'oth, they do report the recitation of a few Aramaic *piyyuṭim*, though not of the Targum itself: *Aqdamuth* and *Arkhin* in the Torah reading of the first day, and *Yazziv pithgam* or *Atha ve-dugma*, given as alternatives for use in the *hafṭara* for the second day.[42]

In the twenty-first century, virtually all printed Ashkenazic prayerbooks, whether of Orthodox or Conservative rites, include *Aqdamuth*; and indeed, most of the communities that use these books still recite it on the first day of Shavu'oth. (This is in prominent contrast to dozens of other *piyyuṭim* that were printed in Ashkenazic prayerbooks throughout the twentieth century, and even in prayerbooks today, but are neglected by the vast majority of today's synagogues.) Many communities also recite *Yazziv pithgam* in the *hafṭara* of the second day of the holiday.[43] Thus, the *piyyuṭim* have long outlived the ritual of reciting Targum on

---

[41] Although the active use of Aramaic texts as liturgy on Yom Vayyosha' seems to have ceased by the fifteenth century, there are nonetheless many Ashkenazic *maḥzorim* from the period of print that present certain Targumic texts for this day. Thus, the *maḥzor* of the Eastern Ashkenazic Rite printed in Prague in 1606 includes the Targum of the first two verses of the day's Torah portion (Exodus 13:17–18), the Aramaic poem "Ezel Moshe" (cf. Yahalom-Sokoloff, pp. 82 ff.), an additional passage "Arba' Kittin" (found in manuscripts as a Targumic expansion on Exodus 15:3 or elsewhere in the passage), and the Targum of the entire *hafṭara* for the second day of Vayyosha' (Isaiah 10:32–12:5). All this material is presented in small cursive letters (the font known as "Rashi script"), without vowel-signs, in the margins of the Hebrew text of the Torah portion and on the subsequent page. It is highly unlikely that users of this volume treated these texts as liturgy, and it is quite possible that they were unaware that this had been their earlier function; it is more likely that they considered it a kind of a commentary, or a contemplative passage for readers to peruse. Other *maḥzorim* contain other selections of targumic texts for Yom Vayyosha'. In some more recent *maḥzorim*, the texts are mislabeled as "Zohar for the Seventh Day of Pesah," evidently by editors who did not recognize the texts, and assumed that because they were in Aramaic, they must be from the Zohar. (See *Maḥzor maṭṭé Levi for the Three Festivals*, Lemberg 1907; *Maḥzor divré Yo'el* for Shavu'oth, Kiryas Joel, 1992; in both cases, the texts are printed after the conclusion of the service for the first day of Yom Vayyosha'.) Thus, these texts continued to be printed, even when publishers and readers did not know what they were.

[42] Shlomo Shpitzer, ed., *Sefer Maharil* (Jerusalem: Machon Yerushalayim, 1989), 160 f.; ibid., ed., *Sefer ha-minhagim of Aizik Tyrnau* (Jerusalem: Machon Yerushalayim, 2000), 68 f. The text of *Aqdamuth* (from which we have already quoted extensively in this paper) can be found in Fraenkel, *Shavu'oth*, 385 f; *Arkhin* on p. 397; and *Yazziv pithgam* on 570. *Atha ve-dugma* can be found in Fraenkel, *Passover*, p. 634. Note that *Sefer ha-minhagim* reports the inclusion also of a third *piyyuṭ* for the Torah-reading on Shavu'oth, *Amar Yizḥaq le-Avraham* (printed in Fraenkel, *Shavu'oth*, 467); presumably, this reflects the eastern Ashkenazic practice of the time.

[43] This practice actually seems to have become more widespread over the past thirty years. (I have heard anecdotal reports from various people that their synagogues never used to recite

Shavu'oth, even though the poets wrote them to adorn this ritual. Nonetheless, through these *piyyuṭim*, the recitation of long texts in poorly-understood Aramaic has persisted into our own times.

Moreover, the connection between *Aqdamuth* and the trope about the angels has not been forgotten. In a number of printed *maḥzorim*, dating from the sixteenth through the late twentieth centuries, we find the following note, introducing *Aqdamuth*:

> ועשאו המחבר בלשון ארמי, לרוב חשיבות הפיוט, {ואולי כיוון לטעם האומר'
> שע"כ נתקן הקדיש בלשון ארמי} שלא יתקנאו בו מלאכי השרת. וראיה לדבר, כי
> לרוב חשיבות הפיוט אנו מפסיקין בו בקריאת התורה.

> The author wrote [this poem] in Aramaic, on account of the poem's great importance. {And perhaps he was thinking along the same lines as those that explain the reason for the Aramaic of Qaddish as being}[44] that the ministering angels should not [understand it and] be jealous of it. And the evidence of the poem's great importance is that we interrupt the reading of the Torah with it.

I have seen this comment in printed *maḥzorim* from 1568,[45] 1754,[46] 1795,[47] 1850,[48] and 1992;[49] further investigation would probably find it in many other *maḥzorim* from intervening years. The comment does not mention anything about the prac-

---

Yazziv pithgam, but have started doing so in the past few decades.) This seems to be a result of the popularity of the ArtScroll prayerbooks, which state: "In most congregations, יציב פתגם, *Yetziv Pisgam*, a song of praise, is inserted [. . .] at this point." (*The ArtScroll Siddur*, Rabbinical Council Edition (Brooklyn, NY: Mesorah Publications, 1991), 969). The same sentence, except for the word "communities" instead of "congregations," appears in *The Complete ArtScroll Machzor Shavuos: Nusach Ashkenaz* (Brooklyn, NY: Mesorah Publications, 1991), 526. This descriptive statement is on its way to becoming a self-fulfilling prophecy. It is a striking contrast to the usual practice in the past century, which has been to drop as many *piyyuṭim* as possible from the liturgy.

44 The words enclosed in angle brackets appear only in the 1568 printing; the brackets are my own.

45 *Maḥzor mi-kol ha-shana ke-minhag Qehilloth Qodesh Ashkenaz* (Venice, 1568), folio 239a, accessed November 25, 2015, http://books.google.com/books?id=bmxEAAAAcAAJ&pg=PT89.

46 *Maḥzor ke-minhag Qehilla Qedosha Ashkenazzim*, volume 2: Passover, Shavu'oth, and Sukkoth (Sulzbach, 1754): folio 212b.

47 *Maḥzor 'im kavvanath ha-payṭan*, volume 5: Shavu'oth (Sulzbach, 1795), folio 27a, accessed November 25, 2015, http://books.google.com/books?id=8NxRAAAAcAAJ&pg=PT184.

48 *Maḥzor*, volume 2: The Three Pilgrimage Festivals (Vilna, 1850), folio 156b, accessed November 25, 2015, http://books.google.com/books?id=3HNHAAAAYAAJ&pg=PA311.

49 Yaakov Weingarten, ed., *Ha-maḥzor ha-meforash le-ḥag ha-shavu'oth* (Jerusalem: Gefen, 1992), 347. In Weingarten's introduction, p. lxxxvii, he says that this note is found in "all the maḥzorim."

tice of reciting Targum, which was long dormant by the age of print, but retains a memory that the usage of Aramaic during the Torah-reading on Shavu'oth is a practice carried out to reach beyond the angels and straight to God.

Our study here of the recitation of Aramaic Targum and *piyyuṭim* has uncovered a new way of approaching the medieval European Jewish attitude toward Aramaic. Aramaic was not only an ancient language, the language of old venerated texts such as the Talmud, but also a useful language for connecting to the divine in contexts or at times in which the usual Hebrew was considered insufficient. This may be because Aramaic enabled a form of mystical experience, or because it was the secular spoken language of the ancestors, or because it was a unique holy language which could transcend the mediation of angels and directly reach God. In fact, these latter two ideas, which we have presented as stark opposites, may actually be connected: Aramaic may have become holy because it had been spoken by so many generations of the community's ancestors. If so, then perhaps precisely the rootedness of this holiness in its human and therefore informal, as opposed to ritual, use, accounts for its ability to transcend the rigid limitations of the formal language, Hebrew. The parallel of Yiddish in late twentieth-century America is instructive: it was not traditionally a language of ritual or scholarship, but a vernacular; descendants of Yiddish speakers, who no longer speak the language as their own vernacular, see a certain power in it, as a Jewish language that does not have the perceived formal rigidity of Hebrew.

The notion that these Aramaic poems participated in a mystical ritual in the synagogue service should teach us to consider the overall ritual context when examining other *piyyuṭim*. The study of *piyyuṭ* not only as literature, but also as ritual, promises very fruitful results. This paper also contributes to the increasingly prominent discussion of Jewish multilingualism, as evidenced, for example, in the work of Steven Fraade, a paper of whom is included in this volume.

In addition, the focus here on the role of Aramaic among Jews in twelfth- and thirteenth-century France, Germany, and Italy opens up paths for comparison and connections to other periods and regions. Might the mystical use of Aramaic in these communities have inspired, or contributed to, the choice of language of the authors of the Zohar in late thirteenth-century Spain?[50] Surprisingly little scholarship has been written on the choice of the Aramaic language for Zoharic writing. Gershom Scholem spends five whole pages analyzing the Aramaic of

---

[50] Zoharic literature is deeply influenced by Ashkenazic ritual practice, as shown by Yisrael Ta-Shma in his book *Ha-nigle sheba-nistar* (Tel Aviv: Hakibbutz Hameuchad Publishing House, Ltd., 2001). There are also certain peripheral attestations of the use of Targum in festival Torah readings in Iberian Jewish ritual, but they are from a much earlier period than the Zoharic literature. On this see above, note 23.

the Zohar, repeatedly criticizing the author for his "limited vocabulary," "motley display of different styles," and "syntax [that] is extremely simple, almost monotonous," yet never once stops to consider *why* the author (he of course believed that the Zoharic literature had a single author) might have decided to write in Aramaic.[51] Arthur Green does devote a few paragraphs to the question, in his introduction to Daniel Matt's translation of the Zohar.[52] His argument that "Aramaic was a mysterious and only vaguely understood language," which "shrouded [mystical ideas] in an obscuring veil," fits nicely with what we have written about the use of Targum on Yom Vayyosha' and Shavu'oth. Nonetheless, Green does not recognize that this usage of Aramaic in the Zohar is part and parcel of a long tradition: he writes that "even among rabbinic scholars, only very rarely was a short treatise or poem still written in Aramaic." On the other hand, Yehuda Liebes's brief article on the topic argues that the language of the Zohar fits right into an existing tradition of Jewish writing in Aramaic, especially in the field of mysticism.[53] Although Liebes is on the right track here, he adduces only scanty evidence, and does not mention the ritual of reciting Targum on Yom Vayyosha' or Shavu'oth, nor the mystically-themed Aramaic *piyyuṭim* that French and German Jews composed to insert into this recitation. For their part, Ada Rapaport-Albert and Theodore Kwasman write that they "intend to examine [. . . the] relationship of [Zoharic Aramaic] to the *Targumim* and the Aramaic elements of the midrashic corpus," and "propose to examine the relationship between the Aramaic of the Zohar and that of other types of Middle to Late Aramaic writings, for example, Aramaic *Piyyutim*, liturgy, magical texts, legal documents, and *Responsa*," but they do not raise the possibility that the European recitation of Targum and Aramaic *piyyuṭim* may have belonged to a mystical tradition or had a mystical aspect.[54] Charles Mopsik writes that the authors of Zoharic literature may have chosen Aramaic because, among other reasons, it was "at the same time [. . .] the language of the most authoritative legal and theological tradition, [. . .] the esoteric language *par excellence*, and [. . .] the only language unknown to the angels [. . .], which enables one to dodge their jealousy and to speak [. . .] directly

---

51 Scholem, *Major Trends*, 160–165. Despite all this verbal abuse, Scholem does admit that there are occasionally sentences of "sublime beauty" in the Zohar, alongside — to be sure — other sentences of "laboured tortuousness" (p. 160).
52 Arthur Green, "Introduction," in Daniel Matt, ed. and trans., *The Pritzker Zohar*, volume 1 (Stanford, California: Stanford University Press, 2004), lxxiv f.
53 Yehuda Liebes, "Hebrew and Aramaic as languages of the Zohar," *Aramaic Studies* 4 (2006): 35–52.
54 Ada Rapaport-Albert and Theodore Kwasman, "Late Aramaic: The Literary and Linguistic Context of the *Zohar*," *Aramaic Studies* 4 (2006): 5–19.

to God and to men without having to fear them[.]"⁵⁵ Although Mopsik, in discussing the Zohar, mentions some of the same ideas that we have raised in this paper with reference to Targum, he does not indicate any awareness of the European tradition of reciting Targum, or its connections to mysticism. I am therefore hopeful that this study will be a welcome addition to discussion of the mystical use of Aramaic in medieval Europe, whether with reference to Zoharic literature or to other texts. Finally, the analysis of the place of Aramaic in European Jewish culture may provide a fruitful point of comparison with other secondary learned languages in other, non-Jewish cultures, such as Greek, secondary to Latin in the Renaissance.

---

55 Charles Mopsik, "Late Judeo-Aramaic: The Language of Theosophic Kabbalah," *Aramaic Studies* 4 (2006): 21–33, especially 24.

Appendix

New Evidence: An Aramaic *Nishmath* Poem

In February 2017, as part of a project cataloguing the *piyyuṭim* found in French and Ashkenazic liturgical manuscripts, I came across a unique Aramaic text in MS Turin A II 25, which has never been noted in the scholarly literature; as we shall see, the poem speaks of angels, which is a link to the mystical elements that we have discussed in this paper. The selection of *piyyuṭim* in the Turin manuscript shows that it is of the Burgundian Rite, a local version of the French Rite.[56] The manuscript is in a very poor state, for it was apparently damaged in the great fire that ravaged the Turin Library in 1904; the volume has been torn apart into individual leaves; the leaves were arranged haphazardly when they were photographed in microfilm for the Institute of Microfilmed Hebrew Manuscripts of the National Library of Israel; and most of the pages in said microfilm are not numbered. In many pages there are tears and blurred letters; and, moreover, the bleed of the letters from one side of the leaf can always be seen on the other side, which makes it even more difficult to decipher the writing.

The manuscript contains a fairly large number of poems of the *nishmath* genre, which introduce the prayer "Nishmath Kol Ḥai" in the morning service, a genre that was very popular in Andalus, whence it spread both to Provence and to Northern France.[57] Among the Hebrew poems in a section devoted to this genre, the Turin manuscript presents one such poem in Aramaic, which we shall print and discuss in this appendix. The manuscript gives the text the generic heading *aḥer*, "another [poem of the same genre]," with no liturgical designation for any specific occasion; nonetheless, as we shall see, the text contains many references to the splitting of the sea, which, together with the fact that it is in Aramaic, makes it likely that it is intended for Yom Vayyoshaʻ. Although most of the poems in the manuscript are written with vowel-points, this one is left unvocalized, which suggests that it was not a part of the active liturgy of the community that produced or vocalized the manuscript.

---

[56] Leopold Zunz briefly discusses the Burgundian Rite in his book *Die Ritus des synagogalen Gottesdienstes* (Berlin, 1859), 63 f. I thank Avraham Levin for explaining to me the specific features of the Burgundian Rite, such as the selection of *maʻariv* poems recited on the evenings of the various festivals, and thus making it possible to identify the manuscript as belonging to this rite.

[57] For a discussion of the *nishmath* genre, see Fleischer, *Shirat Ha-qodesh*, 397 ff.

The text of the poem is as follows, based on the Turin manuscript.[58] The vocalization is my own. In a few places, I have emended the text; emendations are indicated with square brackets and explained in the critical apparatus, and deletions are indicated with parentheses. Where the manuscript presents a word in abbreviated form, I have spelled out the remainder of the word, in angle brackets. Letters whose decipherment is not entirely clear in the manuscript have been indicated here in outlined letters, thus.

נִשְׁמַת דְּחַיֵּי דְמַיָּא שִׁיתָא בְּשִׁתָּא גְפִין
תְּשַׁבְּחָךְ / בְּזַע יַמָּא לְשִׁקְעָא גֻּבְרִין חֲטוּפִין
אָתוֹהִי כַּמָּה רַבְרְבִין וְתִמְהוֹהִי כַּמָּה תַּקִּיפִין

נִ<שְׁ>מַת דִּי־קַדִּישֵׁי עֶלְיוֹנִים דִּמְשַׁמְּשִׁין בִּתְדָר
5 תַּמְלִיכָךְ / עָבֵיד שִׁמְשָׁא וְסִיהֲרָא, וְחֵילֵי שְׁמַיָּא אַסְדָּר
מַלְכוּתֵיהּ מַלְ[כוּת]‎ עָלַם וְשָׁלְטָנֵיהּ עִם (כל) דָּר וְדָר

נִשְׁ<מַת> דְּעִיר וְקַדִּישׁ תֻּשְׁבְּחָא כְּאַרְיָא יְנַהֲמוּן
תְּוָדְעָךְ / מְחָא חַרְטֻמַּיָּא וּבְיַמָּא יִתְרְמוּן
אֶלֶף אַלְפִין יְשַׁמְּשׁוּנֵּיהּ, וְרִיבּ[וֹא] רִבְבָן (מן) קֳדָמוֹהִי יְקוּמוּן

10 נִשְׁ<מַת> דִּפְרִיקִין דִּי־פְרִישִׁין, דַּחֲזוֹ אָתוֹהִי
תְּאַדְּרָךְ / אַשְׁדֵּי בְיַמָּא רְתִיכִין וְגִבְרִין בִּסְגִיאוּת תִּמְהוֹהִי
דְּשָׁלַח מַלְאֲכֵיהּ וְשֵׁזִיב לְעַבְדּוֹהִי

נִשְׁ<מַת> דִּי רוּחָא כָל־בִּישְׂרָא דְּאִיּשׁוּן עוֹבָדַיָּה
תְּלַבְּבָךְ / מְחָא רַשִּׁיעָא וְלִקְיָא וּבַעֲשַׂר גִּ[רִי]ן נְגַדְיֵהּ
15 וּכְמִצְבְּיֵהּ עָבֵיד בְּחֵיל שְׁמַיָּא וְדָיְירֵי אַרְעָא, וְלָא אִיתַאי דִּי יְמַחֵה בִּידֵיהּ

[נְ]שְׁ<מַת> כָּל־בִּרְיָּתָא דְּמִדְּחַלְתָּהּ רָגְזִין
תְּבָרְכָךְ / מְחָא מַלְכִין חֲסִינִין וְתַקִּיפִין כְּאַרְזִין
הוּא אֱלָ[הּ] אֱלָהִין וּמָרֵי מַלְכִין וְגָלֵי רָזִין

Critical Apparatus

6 **מַלְ[כוּת]**. בכה"י: מלך. ותיקנתי על פי הפסוק. **(כל)**. מחקתי על פי הפסוק. 9 **וְרִיבּ[וֹא]**. בכה"י: וריבו. ותיקנתי על פי הפסוק. 14 **(מן)**. מחקתי על פי הפסוק. **גִּ[רִי]ן**. בכה"י: גידון. ותיקנתי על פי סברא. 16 **[נְ]שְׁ<מַת>**. האות הראשונה של המילה לא שרדה, מפני קרע בדף. 18 **אֱלָ[הּ]**. בכה"י: אלהי. ותיקנתי על פי הפסוק.

---

[58] I would like to thank the Biblioteca Nazionale Universitaria di Torino for their permission to print this text.

Translation

	The soul of the [angelic] beings, [with] six wings to each, on the six days,
Praises You,	*/ who split the sea, to drown violent men.*
	His miracles are so great, and his wonders are so mighty.

The soul of the supernal holy ones, who serve [You] constantly,
Crowns You, / *who made the sun and the moon, and set up the hosts of heaven.* (5)
His kingdom is an eternal kingdom, and His dominion is over each generation.

The soul of the watcher and holy one, [who] roar praises like a lion,
Designates You, / *who smote the sorcerers, such that they were cast into the sea.*
A thousand thousands serve Him, and a myriad myriads stand before Him.

The soul of the rescued [people], of the separated [people], who saw His miracles, (10)
Glorifies You, / *who hurled chariots and mighty men into the sea, with His great wonders,*
Who sent His angel and rescued His servants.

The soul of the breath of all flesh, who are His handiwork,
Lauds You, / *who smote the wicked, and lashed him, and struck him with ten arrows,*
And who does as He desires to the host of heaven and the inhabitants of the earth, and there is no one that will prevent him. (15)

The soul of all creatures, which quiver from His tremendum,
Blesses You, / *who smote strong kings, mighty as cedars.*
He is the God of gods, and master of kings, and revealer of mysteries.

Commentary

(1) *The [angelic] beings, [with] six wings to each.* The term *ḥevé*, "beings" or "animals," for the angels, alludes to the cognate Hebrew term *ḥayyoth*, used in Ezekiel's vision of the chariot, in Ezekiel 1:5 ff. The description of the angels as having six wings alludes to Isaiah's vision of the seraphim, in Isaiah 6:2.
On the six days. A reference to the medieval tradition that the six-winged angels use one wing to praise God on each of the six weekdays, and are silent only on the Sabbath (when the Jews praise God on earth); cf. Isaac b. Moses of Vienna (thirteenth century), *Or Zarua'* §42, ed. Mechon Yerushalayim, 2010, p. 51, ¶4.
(3) *His miracles are so great, and his wonders are so mighty.* Daniel 3:33.
(4) *Supernal holy ones.* This term is from Daniel 7:18 ff., where it refers to the righteous Jews, who will ultimately take over earthly rule from the current corrupt empires. Our poet seems to be using it to refer to the angels, for both the previous and following stanzas speak unambiguously of angels.
(6) *His kingdom is an eternal kingdom, and His dominion is over every generation.* Daniel 3:33 (continuation of the verse cited in line 3).
(7) *The watcher and holy one.* Terms for angels, found in Daniel 4:10, 4:20.
(8) *Smote the sorcerers.* I.e. the Egyptians at the sea, probably specifically the magicians Jannes and Jambres, who flew in the sky in order to avoid drowning, but an angel cast them down into the sea (see Louis Ginzberg, *Legends of the Jews* (Philadelphia: JPS, 1909–1938), vol. 3, pp. 28 f., and the literature cited in the footnotes).
(9) *A thousand thousands serve Him, and a myriad myriads stand before Him.* Daniel 7:10.
(10) *The soul of the rescued [people], of the separated [people], who saw His miracles.* Here the poet moves from discussing angelic praise of God to discuss human, specifically Jewish, praise of God.
(11) *[Who] hurled chariots and mighty men into the sea.* Cf. Exodus 15:4; our poet uses language from the Aramaic version of this verse found in Targum Onqelos.
(12) *Who sent His angel and rescued His servants.* Daniel 3:28.
(13) *The soul of the breath of all flesh.* Here the poet turns to speak of the praise of God that is rendered not just by Jews, but by all people; he alludes to the opening of the "Nishmath Kol Ḥai" prayer: "The soul of all that lives renders blessing to Your name, O our God, and the breath of all flesh glorifies and exalts [every] mention of You . . ."
(14) *Struck him with ten arrows.* This evidently refers to the ten plagues, with which God beplagued Pharaoh and the Egyptians in the events that preceded

the splitting of the sea, in Exodus 8–12. The reading "arrows," *girin*, is an emendation; I have been unable to make sense of the reading in the manuscript, *gidun*.

(15) *And who does as He desires to the host of heaven and the inhabitants of the earth, and there is no one that will prevent him.* Daniel 4:32.

(16) *The creatures.* The inhabitants of the world, human and perhaps even animal.

(17) *Strong kings, mighty as cedars.* I.e. the Amorites, who are described thus in Amos 2:9.

(18) *He is the God of gods, and master of kings, and revealer of mysteries.* Daniel 2:47.

Analysis

This is the only known poem of the *nishmath* genre that is written in Aramaic, rather than Hebrew. In accordance with the conventions of the genre, each stanza concludes with a line taken from a biblical verse, known as a *siyyometh miqra'ith* ("scriptural conclusion"). Because the vast majority of the Hebrew Bible is written in Hebrew, we might expect that in the *siyyometh miqra'ith* lines our poet would relax his self-imposed restraint of writing in Aramaic; but, in fact, he is careful to select Aramaic scriptural verses, from Daniel.

In each stanza, there is a verb of praise in a fixed position, following a convention in the *nishmath* genre. This position is poised between the end of the first line and the beginning of the second; scholars tend to describe it as the end of the first line, but we print it here as the beginning of the second, in order to make the acrostic signature clearer.[59] For some of these verbs, our poet uses verbs that are otherwise attested only in Hebrew, not in Aramaic; morphologically, the forms could be either Hebrew or Aramaic, so they do not disrupt the Aramaic of the poem.[60]

---

59 The word properly belongs to neither line, but hovers between the two; Fleischer writes that it may have been intended to be a congregational response, recited after the cantor had finished reciting the first line, and before he had begun the second. (Fleischer, *Shirat Ha-qodesh*, loc. cit.)
60 The Hebraisms in the vocabulary are the verbs W-ʿ-D in the meaning "designate," ʾ-D-R in the meaning "to glorify," and L-B-B in the meaning "to laud"; these are not found in the Comprehensive Aramaic Lexicon (http://cal.huc.edu/, retrieved 14 August 2018). In line 5, the form תַּמְלִיכָךְ looks apparently Hebrew, for the expected Aramaic form would be תַּמְלְכָךְ; nonetheless, there are dialects of Aramaic that have *ḥireq* in the relevant position in *afʿel* forms, as well as dialects that use the letter *yod* to indicate the mobile *sheva*. I thank Binyamin Goldstein for clarifying this matter for me; he notes also that the use of Hebrew vocabulary is a regular feature of late Jewish liturgical Aramaic.

The acrostic, found in the second line of each stanza, reads *Shemu'el*, evidently the poet's name, Samuel. There may also be an acrostic *bar*, "son [of]," in the final stanza, but we cannot find any continuation with the name of the poet's father; if this *bar* is an authentic part of the acrostic, and not mere coincidence, then it is possible that the poem originally contained more stanzas, whose acrostic spelled the patronym, which have been left out of our one manuscript of the poem. Without additional information such as a patronym, it is impossible for us to identify the poet, for the name "Samuel" was common among medieval Jews. Because the manuscript is of the Burgundian Rite, and the poet writes in the *nishmath* genre, he seems to have been a French Jew, living some time after the middle of the eleventh century, when the *nishmath* genre spread from Andalus to France.

The references to the splitting of the sea point to Yom Vayyosha' as the liturgical occasion for the poem, but this on its own is not decisive. *Nishmath* poems lead into the line "If only our mouths were as full of praise as the sea [is full of water] . . . !" (*illu finu malé shira ka-yam*) in the fixed "Nishmath Kol Ḥai" prayer, so it would not be surprising to find allusions to the sea, even the splitting of the sea, in a *nishmath* poem for general use. However, when we take into consideration the fact that it is in Aramaic, it is highly likely that the poet intended it for Yom Vayyosha', to be the first Aramaic poem of the morning liturgy, and thus to set the tone for all the Aramaic texts of Targum and targumic *piyyuṭim* to be recited later in the morning, in the reading of the Torah and the *hafṭara*.

It is surprising to find our poet speak of the praise uttered by the "soul" of the angels; typically, *nishmath* poems speak of the praise that the Jewish people's soul renders to God. However, the insertion of angels into a *nishmath* poem is not entirely unprecedented: Solomon ibn Gabirol, in his *nishmath* poem whose surviving section begins "Nishmath Hamon Zoreaḥ," devotes the stanzas alternately to the soul of the angels and the soul of the Jewish people, each of whom render praise to God;[61] the mid-eleventh century French poet Joseph Ṭov 'Elem, who is the first French poet known to have written in the *nishmath* genre, follows Ibn Gabirol in this, in his poem "Nishmath Ṭakhsisim."[62] Avraham Levin notes that Ibn Gabirol's decision to include the angels in his *nishmath* poem fits the philosophical approach of Ibn Gabirol himself, who writes in his philosophical ode "Kether Malkhuth" that angels are "lofty souls," in contrast to earlier Jewish

---

[61] Dov Jarden, ed. *The Liturgical Poetry of Rabbi Solomon ibn Gabirol* [in Hebrew] (Jerusalem, 1971), vol. 1, 81 ff.
[62] Avraham Levin, "A Reconstructed Nishmath" [in Hebrew] (unpublished paper, 2010). The poem can be found in MS Columbia X 893 J 51 Q, folio 314.

literature, which does not speak of the angels as possessing souls.[63] Here, in our poem, the inclusion of stanzas about angelic praise of God situates it in the context of mystical discussions of the angels around the divine Throne of Glory, and thus fits with the mystical use of Aramaic that we have seen in this paper.

Bibliography

Abudarham, David. *Sefer Abudarham*. Venice, [5]326 (=1566).
Artom, Menachem Emmanuele, ed. *Machazor di rito italiano completo*. Vol. 3, Kippur. Jerusalem: Jerusalem Fine Art Prints, 2005.
Babylonian Talmud, Tractate Shabbath. MS Toronto Friedberg 9-002.
Baer, Seligman, ed. *Seder 'avodath Yisra'el*. Roedelheim, 1868.
David, Yonah, ed. *Shiré R. Yiẓḥaq ibn Giyyat*. Jerusalem: Hoẓa'ath 'Akhshav, 1988.
Davidson, Israel, Simḥa Assaf, and Issachar Joel. *Siddur R. Saadja Gaon*. Jerusalem: Mekize Nirdamim, 1941.
Fleischer, Ezra. *Shirat ha-qodesh ha-'ivrit bimé ha-benayim*. Jerusalem: Keter Publishing House Ltd., 1975.
Fraenkel, Jonah. *Maḥzor for Passover, in accordance with the Ashkenazic Rite in all its branches* [in Hebrew]. Jerusalem: Koren, 1993.
Fraenkel, Jonah. *Maḥzor for Shavu'oth, in accordance with the Ashkenazic Rite in all its branches* [in Hebrew]. Jerusalem: Koren, 2000.
Fraenkel, Jonah and Avraham Fraenkel. "Prayer and Piyyut in the Mahzor Nuremberg" [in Hebrew]. http://jnul.huji.ac.il/dl/mss-pr/mahzor-nuremberg/pdf/fraenkel_j_a.pdf.
Ginzberg, Louis. *The Legends of the Jews*. Philadelphia: Jewish Publication Society of America, 1909–1938.
Goldschmidt, Arye. *Maḥzor Vitry*. Jerusalem: Oẓar Ha-posqim, 2004.
Goldschmidt, Daniel, ed. *Maḥzor for the Days of Awe*. Jerusalem: Koren, 1970.
Green, Arthur. "Introduction." In *The Pritzker Zohar*. Vol. 1, edited and translated by Daniel Matt, XXXI-LXXXI. Stanford, California: Stanford University Press, 2004.
Horovitz, Haim Saul and Israel Abraham Rabin, eds. *Mekhilta de-R. Yishma'el*. Frankfurt: Mekize Nirdamim, 1930.
Hurwitz, Simon, ed. *Maḥzor Vitry* (Berlin: Mekize Nirdamim, 1893).
Isserles, Justine. "Maḥzor Vitry: Étude d'un corpus de manuscrits hébreux ashkénazes de type liturgico-légal du XIIe au XIVe siècle." PhD diss., École Pratique des Hautes Études, Paris and University of Geneva, 2012.
Jarden, Dov, ed. *The Liturgical Poetry of Rabbi Solomon ibn Gabirol*. Vol. 1 [in Hebrew]. Jerusalem, 1971.
Kaufman, Stephen A. "Aramaic." In *The Semitic languages*, edited by Robert Hetzron, 114–130. London: Routlege, 1997.
Levin, Avraham. "A Reconstructed Nishmath" [in Hebrew]. Unpublished paper, 2010.

---

[63] Levin, op. cit. The line in "Kether Malkhuth" is found in Jarden, *The Liturgical Poetry*, 52, §25, line 1 f.

Liebes, Yehuda. "Hebrew and Aramaic as languages of the Zohar." *Aramaic Studies* 4 (2006): 35–52.
Maḥzor divré Yo'el for Shavu'oth. Kiryas Joel, 1992
Maḥzor 'im kavvanath ha-payṭan. Vol. 5, Shavu'oth. Sulzbach, 1795.
Maḥzor ke-minhag Qehilla Qedosha Ashkenazzim. Vol. 2, Passover, Shavu'oth, and Sukkoth. Sulzbach, 1754.
Maḥzor maṭṭé Levi for the Three Festivals. Lemberg, 1907
Maḥzor mi-kol ha-shana ke-minhag Qehilloth Qodesh Ashkenaz. Venice, 1568.
Maḥzor. Vol. 2, The Three Pilgrimage Festivals. Vilna, 1850.
Milikowsky, Chaim, ed. *Seder 'Olam*. Jerusalem: Yad Ben-Zvi, 2013.
Mopsik, Charles. "Late Judeo-Aramaic: The Language of Theosophic Kabbalah." *Aramaic Studies* 4 (2006): 21–33.
Nürnberg Maḥzor. MS Zurich Jeselsohn 9.
Rapaport-Albert, Ada and Theodore Kwasman. "Late Aramaic: The Literary and Linguistic Context of the *Zohar*." *Aramaic Studies* 4 (2006): 5–19.
Schechter, Solomon, ed. *Avoth de-R. Nathan, Version A*. Vienna, 1887.
Scholem, Gershom. *Major Trends in Jewish Mysticism*. 2nd ed. Jerusalem: Schoken, 1946.
Schorr, Jacob, ed. *Sefer ha'ittim*. Cracow: Mekize Nirdamim, 1903.
Shpitzer, Shlomo ed. *Sefer ha-minhagim of Aizik Tyrnau*. Jerusalem: Machon Yerushalayim, 2000.
Shpitzer, Shlomo ed., *Sefer Maharil*. Jerusalem: Machon Yerushalayim, 1989.
Siddur Tefilloth ha-shana le-minhag qehilloth Romanya. Venice, n.d. (ca. 1523).
Strack, H. L. and Günter Stemberger. *Introduction to the Talmud and Midrash*, translated and edited by Markus Bockmuehl. 2nd ed. Minneapolis: Fortress Press, 1996.
Ta-Shma, Yisrael. *Ha-nigle she-banistar*. Tel Aviv: Hakibbutz Hameuchad Publishing House, Ltd., 2001.
The ArtScroll Siddur. Rabbinical Council Edition. Brooklyn, NY: Mesorah Publications, 1991.
The Complete ArtScroll Machzor Shavuos: Nusach Ashkenaz. Brooklyn, NY: Mesorah Publications, 1991.
Urbach, Ephraim Elimelech. *The Tosafists: Their Lives, Works, and Approach*. Vol. 2 [in Hebrew]. 4th ed. Jerusalem: Bialik Institute, 1980.
Weingarten, Yaakov ed. *Ha-maḥzor ha-meforash le-ḥag ha-shavu'oth*. Jerusalem: Gefen, 1992.
Weiss-Halivni, David. *Introductions to "Sources and Traditions"* [in Hebrew]. Jerusalem: Magnes Press, 2009.
Yahalom, Joseph, and Michael Sokoloff. *Shirat Bené Ma'arava [Jewish Palestinian Aramaic Poetry from Late Antiquity]*. Jerusalem: Israel Academy of Sciences and Humanities, 1999.
Zunz, Leopold. *Die Ritus des synagogalen Gottesdienstes*. Berlin, 1859.

Irene Zwiep
Choice and Determinism at the Crossroads of Early Modern Hebraism

1 Introductory Remarks

In the category "metaphors we live by," the image of the crossroads ranks high among the all-time favourites.[1] By conjuring up the memory of paths crossing and ways parting, it enables us to grasp the complex idea of cultural evolution, of encounter and exchange, and of the perpetual choice to either continue our course or change it as we see fit. In Latin poetry, the (urban) crossroads acquired a somewhat dismal reputation as the spot where illicit lovers meet.[2] In intellectual history, it represents points of cultural convergence, places that invite the traveller to pause, reorient, and perhaps reconsider his tracks. But how does that traveller decide whether to march straight ahead or explore alternative routes? Is it home, baggage and destiny that determine his course, or will his sense of adventure and, perhaps, expediency gain the upper hand? By drawing our gaze to this nexus of opportunities and by emphasizing the conflicting choices they present, the crossroads is an ideal vehicle for expressing the contested idea of cultural change and for articulating the dilemmas of conservation versus innovation, of choice and determinism, which govern its dynamic.

In this chapter, I propose to take a closer look at one such historical nexus: the confluence of Jewish and Christian Hebraism in the early decades of the sixteenth century, which opened up an unprecedented set of scholarly, religious and social avenues. One of the travellers whose journey we shall be monitoring is the Ashkenazi linguist and man of letters Elijah "Baḥur" Levita (1469–1549). Moving between Southern Germany and Italy, and obliging a broad and varied

---

[1] On conceptual metaphors, see George Lakoff and Mark Johnson's classic *Metaphors We Live By* (Chicago: University of Chicago Press, 1980). The crossroads as a conceptual metaphor is discussed at length in George Lakoff, "The Contemporary Theory of Metaphor," in *Metaphor and Thought*, 2nd ed., ed. Andrew Ortony (Cambridge: Cambridge University Press, 1993): 202–251.
[2] See most famously Catullus' *Carmen* 58: *illa Lesbia, quam Catullus unam plus quam se atque suos amavit omnes, nunc in quadriviis et angiportis glubit magnanimi Remi nepotes.* ("Lesbia, whom Catullus loved more than himself and all his friends, now at crossroads and in backstreets fools around with the grandsons of the magnanimous Remus.") The translation is mine.

Note: I would like to thank David Kromhout for his, as always, invaluable help in preparing this article.

readership, he found himself at an intricate junction of cities (from his native Neustadt, via Rome, Padua, Venice and Isny, back again to Venice), genres (grammar and *belles lettres*), languages (Hebrew and Yiddish), audiences (from Christian Humanists to Jewish ladies) and cultural traditions. In the present context, I merely wish to comment on one constant among all those variables: Levita's Ashkenazi origins, which provide a logical decor for his Yiddish output, but have been somewhat overlooked in previous scholarship on Levita the Hebraist. In the following, we will zoom in on the impact of Levita's Ashkenazi provenance on his rewriting of the Hebrew grammatical tradition. How much did his linguistic oeuvre, which is justly considered exceptional in its formal and thematic scope,[3] owe to the author's individual genius, and to what extent was it shaped by typically Ashkenazi concerns?

A good impression of Levita's Ashkenazi bias can be gained from his early linguistic work, *viz.* the *Sefer ha-baḥur* and *Pirqe 'Eliahu*, written in 1518 and 1520, respectively. Composed in Hebrew for a predominantly Christian readership, this early corpus was the outcome of a complex encounter. Traditionally, much attention has been paid to the meeting of Christian Renaissance Humanism and Jewish Hebraism. We should keep in mind, however, that in Levita's case that Hebraism was not so much Jewish, as *Ashkenazi* – a seemingly casuistic distinction that was of considerable consequence, as I hope to show.[4] Continuing a long tradition of Ashkenazi appropriations of Sephardi linguistic lore, Levita's approach to Hebrew was a hybrid one, combining the morphological finesse of the Andalusian-Provençal *medaqdeqim* (grammarians) with the attention to recitation and orthographic detail of the Ashkenazi *naqdanim* or punctators. As we shall see, the difference between Levita's system and that of his Ashkenazi predecessors was one of degree, timing and impact rather than form, content and method. His work not only left its mark on subsequent Christian descriptions of Hebrew, but in the rebound also laid the basis for a new, more grammatical type of Ashkenazi

---

[3] Besides morphological treatises (*Sefer ha-baḥur*, *Pirqe 'Eliahu*, the alphabetical *Sefer ha-harkavah* of 1518 and annotations to Moses Qimḥi and Abraham ibn Ezra [Venice, 1546]), Levita's Hebraist output included *Nimmuqim* to David Qimḥi's *Shorashim* (likewise included in the Venice 1546 edition), dictionaries of targumic Aramaic and rabbinic Hebrew (the *Meturgeman* and *Tishbi* of 1541), and various masoretic studies (*Masoret ha-masorah* 1538, *Tuv ta'am* 1539, and the unpublished concordance *Sefer ha-zikhronot*, ed. Frendsdorff, *Monastsschrift für Geschichte und Wissenschaft des Judentums* [1863]).

[4] Paul Fagius's suggestion (in the introduction to the *Tishbi*) that Levita's competence as a linguist was "rare among Jews, especially among the Jews of German lands" thus may have held true for the "average" Jew of his time, but did little justice to the indigenous tradition of linguistic studies that had nourished Levita's grammars, on which see below. See Elijah Levita, *Tishbi* (Isny, 1541), Intro., 3.

linguistics. Born at the crossroads of early modern Hebraism, both branches were as much a product of inter-religious conversation as of an inner-Jewish, "Ashkenazi-Sephardi" dialogue.

Levita's digests of the Hebrew tradition seem to support the case made by compatibilists from Rabbi Akiva to Daniel Dennett, who claim that but for a certain measure of choice everything in this world is determined.[5] If we transplant this philosophical insight into the realm of history, we may conclude that in cultural processes existing norms and patterns tend to nourish and shape new endeavours. To paraphrase a well-worn formula and apply it to our present case: even if we take the scholar out of Ashkenaz, we will not succeed in taking Ashkenaz quite out of the scholar. A traveller at a crossroads may change directions, but he will not leave behind his luggage. The following exploration of the Ashkenazi bias of early Christian Hebraism may serve as an illustration of this fundamental human insight. More importantly, however, it testifies to a tradition of Ashkenazi linguistics that has often been overlooked but in fact produced a sturdy line of Jewish *and* Christian offspring.

2 Levita Punctator

It is now time to move from the speculative to the technical, and to reconstruct the Ashkenazi lens through which Elijah Levita viewed the science of language. As mentioned above, his approach to grammar belonged to an extensive tradition of Ashkenazi scholarship that had absorbed the results of Iberian Hebrew linguistics into native Ashkenazi genres. In their search for biblical realia, medieval commentators from Rashi to Joseph Bekhor Shor had integrated the lexical data proffered by the "School of Cordoba" (ca. 950 and after) into their interpretations.[6] Likewise the *naqdanim*, whose task was to reconcile the Tiberian system of vocalization

---

5 M. Avot III.15 and Daniel Dennett, *The Elbow Room: The Varieties of Free Will Worth Wanting* (Oxford: Clarendon Press, 1984).
6 A reading of Rashi's commentary on the book of Psalms, which I undertook some fifteen years ago, seems to suggest that in *peshat* exegesis Sephardi lexicography was adduced in order to interpret words in terms of reference (i.e., as referring to objects in reality) rather than in terms of meaning. Thus an incipit like "'*al ha-gittit*" (Ps. 8:1) is first explained as *referring to* a musical instrument that had lent its name to a Temple melody. Only then does Rashi relate its *lexical meaning* to the threshing floor (*gat*) on which Rome, according to the *midrash*, will be crushed in Messianic times. This and other examples suggest that the *peshat-derash* opposition was one of extensionality (reference) versus intensionality (meaning) rather than literal versus homiletic interpretation. On this, see Irene Zwiep, "Magie, poëzie, exegese, geschiedenis: Een verkenning

with the traditional Ashkenazi pronunciation, referred to Sephardi morphology in their reconstructions of Hebrew phonetic rules and their exceptions. In each case, however, local concerns would set the agenda. If authors engaging in *peshat* exegesis showed a striking grasp of Andalusian grammatical techniques, it was always to shed light on an obscure biblical idiom, not to correct a contested morphological-semantic identification.[7] In a similar vein, the *naqdanim*'s priority lay with establishing concrete reading practices rather than abstract verbal patterns. Their treatises aimed at securing the correct recitation of Scripture and prayer; refining linguistic theory obviously came second to this religious task.[8]

On various occasions, Levita explicitly referred to works from this indigenous tradition.[9] More importantly, however, we find that his descriptive model was greatly indebted to its basic premise: the centrality of the *masorah*, especially of orthoepy, in the classification of the holy tongue. From the beginning, this preoccupation with correct pronunciation and recitation had determined both the form and the content of Ashkenazi linguistics. Early authors like Shimshon ha-Naqdan and his younger contemporary Yequtiel ben Judah ha-Kohen (also known as Salman ha-Naqdan) had composed bipartite treatises, in which a morphological outline preceded the actual masoretic section. In Shimshon ha-Naqdan's *Ḥibbur ha-qonim* a section on pronominal suffixes, verbs, nouns and vowels paved the way for five

---

van middeleeuwse joodse benaderingen van het boek Psalmen," *Amsterdamse Cahiers voor Exegese van de Bijbel en zijn Tradities* 18 (2000): 115–130.

7 A singular exception to this functional use of grammar was *The Book of Decisions* (*Sefer ha-hakhra'ot*) by Rabbenu Tam (ca. 1100–1171). Tam's belated attempt at defending Menachem ben Saruq's *Maḥberet* (*Book* [on Grammar], ca. 950) against its *Refutations* by Dunash ben Labrat testifies to his deep penchant for Sephardi literary culture.

8 For the background and use of masoretic literature in medieval and early modern Ashkenaz, see Stefan C. Reif, *Shabbethai Sofer and his Prayer-book* (Cambridge: Cambridge University Press, 1979), esp. chapter 4. Complementary surveys of the corpus can be found in Leopold Zunz, *Zur Geschichte und Literatur* (Berlin: Veit, 1845), 108–121; Cecil Roth, *The Intellectual Activities of Medieval English Jewry*. The British Academy Supplementary Papers 8 (London [1948]), 44ff.; Ilan Eldar, "The Grammatical Literature of Medieval Ashkenazi Jewry," in *Hebrew in Ashkenaz: A Language in Exile*, ed. Lewis Glinert (New York & Oxford: Oxford University Press, 1993), 26–45; Judith Olszowy-Schlanger, "The Science of Language among Medieval Jews," in *Science in Medieval Jewish Cultures: Madda'*, ed. Gad Freudenthal (Cambridge: Cambridge University Press, 2012): 359–424, *passim*.

9 Besides quoting Moses ha-Naqdan of London's *Darkhe ha-niqqud* (*Ways of Vocalisation*), Levita referred to Yequtiel ben Judah ha-Kohen's '*Ein ha-qore*' (*The Eye of the Reader*) in his *Masoret ha-masorah*; Zunz, *Zur Geschichte und Literatur*, 111, 115f.; Eldar, "The Grammatical Literature," 32. Although Levita introduces the Yahbi as a *naqdan mi-Prag*, it is more likely that this contemporary of Rabbenu Tam lived and worked in Northern France; cf. Olszowy-Schlanger (after Eldar), "The Science of Language," 395.

chapters on vocalization, the weak consonants (known by the acronym *Yehu*), *meteg* or secondary stress, cantillation, and the impact of the *dagesh*. The grammatical substance most likely was derived from Solomon ibn Parchon's *Maḥberet he-'arukh*, written in Salerno in 1161.[10] Yequtiel ha-Kohen likewise devoted the first part of his '*Ein ha-qore*' to morphological observations, before giving a detailed account of vocalization and accents, more specifically of the laws concerning penultimate and ultimate stress in ḥumash, haftarot, Lamentations and Esther, thus safeguarding the correct recitation of the most prominent liturgical portions of Scripture.[11] As a rule, the preliminary morphological considerations only played a minor role in the masoretic sequel, which concentrated on the *prima facie* interplay between Tiberian *niqqud* and *te'amim*.

Almost three and a half centuries later, Levita's *Sefer ha-baḥur* and *Pirqe 'Eliahu* faithfully mirror this traditional division of labour in Hebrew linguistic description. In four *ma'amarim*, each divided into thirteen '*iqqarim*, the *Baḥur* listed the various verbal classes and conjugations, followed by the regular nominal patterns and their irregular counterparts.[12] Even here, it must be said, Levita's morphology betrays the typical Ashkenazi preoccupation with vocalization. Inflection and conjugation are explained "from the vowel points" (*mi-tzad ha-nequdot*), with much room for elucidating their changing appearances (*be'ur hishtannut nequdot, sibbat hishtannut ha-nequdot*). In *Pirqe 'Eliahu*, explicitly presented by Levita as a supplement to the *Baḥur*,[13] vocalization takes up an even more prominent position. Again relying on the 4 x 13 format, the book contains information on the nominal categories (*pereq ha-minim*), the grammatical properties of the noun (*pereq ha-middot*) and the servile letters (*pereq ha-shimmushim*). These general observations are preceded by thirteen bulky stanzas on "all the laws on consonants and vowel points, with part of the laws on accents." Counting 98 pages, this exhaustive masoretic survey easily outnumbers the three remaining chapters, which together cover 76 pages.[14]

---

10 See Ilan Eldar, "Mi-kitve 'asqolat ha-diqduq ha-ashkenazit ha-shimshonit," *Leshonenu* 43 (1980): 100–111, 200–210.
11 '*Ein ha-qore*' was edited by Rivkah Yarkoni. See her "'*Ein ha-qore*' le-Yequtiel ha-Kohen" (PhD diss., Tel Aviv University, 1985).
12 NB: In obvious allusion to the articles of faith formulated by Maimonides, the thirteen paragraphs per chapter (adding up to a total of 52, the numerical value of the name Eliahu) betray the experimental artificiality of Levita's classifications. Simultaneously, the allusion to "Sephardic" dogma can be read as an expression of Levita's belief (without precedent in Ashkenazi scholarship) in grammar as a fundamentally scientific discipline.
13 In the general introduction, Levita stated that the book consisted of four chapters, which he had not, for lack of time, been able to include in the *Baḥur* at the time of its publication.
14 For the present article I have relied on the (Hebrew-Latin) Basel 1707 edition of *Pirqe 'Eliahu*.

Levita's characterization of the Hebrew learning process in *Pirqe 'Eliahu* also underlines the centrality of the *masorah* for his grammatical model. The holy tongue, he writes in the introduction to *pereq shirah*, should be conceptualized as a divine chariot (*merkavah*, or *currum* in Sebastian Münster's Latin translation), to which the student can gain access via a ladder of consonants (*sullam* or *scala*) that is kept together by the pegs (*yetedot* or *clavi*) of the vowels and their signs (*ha-tenu'ot ve-ha-nequdot*).[15] Within this divine structure, the masoretic accents do not deserve separate mention, but are treated in tandem with changes in vocalization. For Levita, this approach obviously represented a familiar routine – the use of phrases like "the *naqdanim* also used to . . . " suggests that he saw his work as the continuation of an established, living tradition.[16] Yet one cannot help wondering how a Christian novice to Hebrew will have read the lessons of the *punctatores*, who had chosen dots and dashes rather than roots and patterns as their basic units, and allowed an unwieldy mass of orthoepic minutiae to cloud the orderly deep structure of Hebrew that we know from the medieval Judaeo-Arabic grammars.

This brings us to a fundamental difference between the theoretical outlook of the Ashkenazi *naqdanim* and that of their colleagues living and working in the Arabic cultural sphere. The former, though deeply concerned with matters of actual recitation, approached Hebrew as an essentially written construct, a textual entity made up from consonants, vowel signs and auxiliary accents that demanded a correct performance in daily liturgical practice. By contrast, the *medaqdeqim* of Baghdad, the Maghreb, Sepharad and Provence, though mainly interested in abstract linguistic norms, described Hebrew as the product of sound (*qol* or *tenu'ah*) and articulation (the five *motza'e dibbur*) rather than as an ensemble of masoretic conventions. In this phonetic approach, the accents naturally tied in with exegesis and rhetoric rather than with *masorah*-based morphology.[17] Thus, somewhat ironically one might say, the more theoretical, pattern-based Sephardi tradition ultimately viewed "dead" Hebrew as a "spoken" language,

---

15 *Pirqe 'Eliahu, haqdamat pereq shirah*, [xiv] (unnumbered in the above-mentioned edition).
16 "Ha-naqdanim nohagim 'od" ("habent punctatores adhuc in usu"), 47–48 in the aforementioned edition.
17 Loci classici testifying to the exegetical and rhetorical use of the *te'amim* are Abraham ibn Ezra's exhortation to "always observe the way of the accents [in case of exegetical difficulties]" (in his Commentary on Isaiah 1:9) and of course Judah Halevi's vision of the masorah as a substitute for oral delivery in *Kuzari* II.68–72. Both views were explicitly instrumentalized in Profiat Duran's grammar *Ma'ase 'Efod* (1403), chapter 5. See Profiat Duran, *Ma'aseh 'Efod*, ed. Jonathan Friedländer and Jakob Kohn (Jerusalem, 1969).

whereas its more performance-oriented Ashkenazi counterpart treated it as the product of an intricate scribal tradition.[18]

It is a known fact that, for various historical reasons (including an enviable dose of self-promotion), the corpus of medieval Iberian, Rabbanite grammar came to be regarded as the superior, even canonical tradition of Jewish linguistic thinking. Yet we should realize that, in its denial of the grammatical potential of the *masorah*, it does somewhat represent a medieval *Alleingang*. In the Karaite academies of Jerusalem[19] and in the synagogues of Germany, Northern France and England, grammarians continued to use masoretic data. Given this tenacity of the *masorah*, it can hardly be called accidental that the Iberian "exile" Abraham ibn Ezra (1189/2–1164/7) listed the "Men of the Masorah" among the "Pillars of Language" in his linguistic debut *Moznayyim* (*The Book of Scales*; Rome, 1140), and that he gave center stage to the vowels in his *magnum opus* the *Sefer tzaḥot* (*The Book of Pure Speech*; Mantova, 1145).[20] Nor was it a coincidence that Levita chose both the *Moznayyim* and the *Tzaḥot* as the basis for his own linguistic annotations. In his collected notes or *nimmuqim*, published in Venice in 1546 under the title *Sefer diqduqim*, the mildly hybrid Ibn Ezra appears alongside David and Moses Qimḥi, whose work, thanks to Levita's brokerage, was likewise shown to possess sufficient overlap with the Ashkenazi tradition to become classics of early modern Ashkenazi commentary.[21]

---

18 Classifying the basic elements of language in terms of their physiological production, the Sephardi approach built on long-standing Stoic perceptions of language, which had also found their way into the Babylonian Talmud (bBer 61a). The *naqdanim* continued the Tiberian Masoretic view, which highlighted written language and reduced the role of articulation to "telling the meaning of the writing, which consists of words, which consist of letters, which have the form of written signs and are adorned with points" (*Diqduqe te'amim*, 6 § 5). See Irene E. Zwiep, *Mother of Reason and Revelation. A Short History of Medieval Jewish Linguistic Thought* (Amsterdam: Gieben, 1997), 14–16.
19 See the research conducted by Geoffrey Khan, most recently summarized in idem, "The Medieval Karaite Tradition of Hebrew Grammar," in *A Universal Art: Hebrew Grammar Across Disciplines and Faiths*, ed. Nadia Vidro et al. (Leiden: Brill, 2014): 15–33.
20 Ibn Ezra's poem on the semi-vowels and *matres lectionis Yehu* at the beginning of his Commentary on the Pentateuch may likewise represent an example of this linguistic compromise.
21 According to Levita, Moses Qimḥi's four-fold classification of the noun in the *Mahalakh shevile ha-da'at* adequately covered the essence of all nominal categories. He will have been no less enchanted, however, by the author's unusually prominent treatment of the *litterae bgdkft*, the *te'amim*, penultimate versus ultimate stress, and the extensive chapter on *niqqud* in the first book of the *Mahalakh*. Further glosses on the book were compiled by Solomon Ashkenazi of Posen and Shabtai Sofer, published in Cracow 1620 and Lublin 1622, respectively. Like Levita, Shabtai Sofer also wrote *nimmuqim* to David Qimḥi's *Shorashim*, now extant in MS Rosenthaliana

Summing up we can say that on the pages of the *Baḥur* and *Pirqe 'Eliahu* Levita meets us as a typical Ashkenazi *punctator*, for whom the correct reading of Scripture was an important starting point for grammatical description. In the following section, we shall briefly sketch the marks left by this "naqdanic" tradition on early modern Christian Hebrew scholarship. With that branch of Hebraism being bent on deciphering the language of Scripture (and not on studying Hebrew as such),[22] it should not surprise us that the masoretic-grammatical model was eagerly taken up by early Christian Humanists. Nor should we wonder that it was continued, with numerous major and minor adaptations, by Jewish grammarians until the Haskalah, when under the influence of the enlightened *Sprachwissenschaft* of Johann Christoph Adelung Ashkenazi linguists came to view biblical Hebrew as a language rather than as a technical scribal construct.[23]

3 Christian Afterlife

From Levita's *Baḥur* and *Pirqe 'Eliahu* various paper trails can be reconstructed. On the Jewish intellectual map, one obvious specimen runs from the *pereq ha-minim*, where Levita had outlined no less than thirteen nominal categories, to the thirteen-fold classification of the noun in Solomon Hanau's *Binyan Shlomo* of 1708.[24] In Central Europe, scholars supporting the educational reform of the Maharal of Prague (d. 1609) copied Levita's example by writing simple morphological textbooks, followed by short manuals on *niqqud* and *te'amim*.[25] On the

---

51 and analyzed in Stefan C. Reif, "A Defense of David Qimhi," *Hebrew Union College Annual* 44 (1973): 211–226.
22 Witness, e.g., the emphasis on reading in early works like Conrad Pellicanus' *De modo legendi et intelligendi Hebraeum* (Strassburg, 1504) and Johann Böschenstein's *Elementale introductorium in hebraeas literas* (Augsburg, 1514).
23 For a discussion of this development, see Irene Zwiep, "Imagined Speech Communities: Western Ashkenazi Multilingualism as Reflected in Eighteenth-Century Grammars of Hebrew," in *Speak Jewish – Jewish Speak: Multilingualism in Western Ashkenazic Culture*, ed., Shlomo Berger et al. (*Studia Rosenthaliana* 36, 2002–2003): 77–117.
24 Irene Zwiep, "The Impact of Teytsh on Diqduq, or: Why the Metaphor Became a Noun in Early Modern Ashkenazi Linguistics," in *A Universal Art*, 84–99.
25 The popular *Qol qore'* (1612/13), written by Joseph ben Elchanan Heilbronn of Posen as a supplement to his Hebrew-Yiddish primer *'Em ha-yeled* (1597), was an adaptation of Levita's *pereq shirah*. For the Christian impetus for these linguistic initiatives, see Andrea Schatz, *Sprache in der Zerstreuung: Die Säkularisierung des Hebräischen im 18. Jahrhundert* (Göttingen: Vandenhoeck & Ruprecht, 2009), 90–96. For a survey of other grammatical activities in the so-called "Ashkenazi Renaissance" (1550–1620), see Jacob Elbaum, *Petiḥut ve-histagrut: ha-yetzirah ha-ruḥanit*

Christian side, there is of course his well-documented collaboration with printers and scholars like Daniel Bomberg, Sebastian Münster and Paul Fagius.[26] Yet as always, the history of Hebraism followed a slightly more crooked path than these plain-cut paper trails suggest. The centrality of the Ashkenazi linguistic tradition, however, remains beyond dispute.

More than a decade before Levita published his *Sefer ha-Baḥur*, Johannes Reuchlin (1455–1522), who had studied Hebrew with the Ashkenazi court physician Jacob ben Yechiel Loans, had issued *De rudimentis hebraicis* (Pforzheim, 1506), a study of Hebrew based on the same version of Qimḥi's *Mahalakh* that Levita had used in his early teaching in Padua.[27] Issued by Soncino in 1488/89, Qimḥi's was the first Hebrew grammar to have been printed and thus constituted an obvious *Vorlage* for Jewish and Christian scholars alike.[28] Four years later, in 1510, Reuchlin supplemented his morphological survey, in good Ashkenazi fashion, with a separate tract on masoretic accentuation. Compared with Levita's *pereq shirah*, however, Reuchlin's *De accentibus et orthographia linguae hebraeae* strikes us as eminently systematic and comprehensive. Where Levita contented himself with setting up orthoepic rules and putting them to rhyme, Reuchlin not only listed the accents (book one), but also added discussions of the use of accents in biblical exegesis (book two) and their role in recitation, public as well as private (book three of *De accentibus*).[29] Students of Hebrew, he wrote, would do well to commit to heart one biblical verse a day, tropes and all.[30] In order to facilitate the memorizing process, he had included the musical notation for each

---

ha-sifrutit be-Polin u-ve-'artzot 'Ashkenaz be-shilhe ha-me'ah ha-shesh-'esreh (Jerusalem: Magnes Press, 1992), 260–273.

26 On Levita and Münster, please see the article by Melanie Lange in this volume.

27 Hermann Greive, "Die hebräische Grammatik Johannes Reuchlins *De rudimentis hebraicis*," *Zeitschrift für die Alttestamentliche Wissenschaft* 90 (1978): 395–409. On this work, please see Saverio Campanini's contribution in this volume.

28 Before being included in the 1546 *Diqduqim*, Levita's *nimmuqim* to the *Mahalakh*, noted down in 1504, were printed Pesaro 1508, in a pirate edition by Benjamin of Rome. That Levita used the printed edition of Qimḥi's grammar rather than his own manuscript version has been argued (contra Ginsburg) by Shimon Iakerson, "An Autograph Manuscript by Elijah Levita in St Petersburg," in *Omnia in Eo. Studies on Jewish Books and Libraries in Honour of Adri Offenberg*, ed. Irene E. Zwiep, et al. (*Studia Rosenthaliana* 38/39, 2006): 178–185.

29 "non tam ad grammaticum quam ad rhetorem ac musicum spectantia" (*De accentibus*, fol. 59b). See Johannes Reuchlin, *De accentibus et orthographia linguae Hebraicae* (Hagenau: In ædibus Thomæ Anshelmi Badensis, 1518).

30 *De accentibus*, fol. 81a.

accent in the book's final section – just as a *melammed* would append a *zarqa*-table to the *ḥumash* he used in his classroom.³¹

Reuchlin's exhaustive "bipartite grammar" obviously represented a new stage in the Christian ideal of *Hebraica Veritas*. His detailed attention to the *masorah* was not, however, a sign of exceptional diligence or curiosity, nor did it stem from the wish to share in an authentic Jewish biblical experience. In Ashkenazi Hebrew literacy, and in its early Christian offshoot, mastering the accents simply was part of mastering Hebrew. Even if the *te'amim* were said to be from Tiberias rather than from Sinai, they would always be an integral part of the language of Scripture. Though obviously shedding light on contemporary Jewish reading practices, Reuchlin's *Rudimentis* and *De accentibus* were thus grammars in content as well as method; they do not belong to the budding corpus of "Jewish ethnography" that originated alongside the Christian discovery of Jewish Hebraism.³²

If anything, Reuchlin's manuals neatly illustrate both the early Humanists' dependence on Ashkenazi linguistic models and their ability to absorb these models into their own idiom and taxonomies. Soon the Christian Hebraists would relinquish the Ashkenazi bipartite format, merging the masoretic bias of Ashkenazi grammar with their own (Latin) classifications of Hebrew. In 1524, Sebastian Münster had still followed Reuchlin in appending 23 folios on the *accentus grammatici*, *musici* and *rhetorici* to his *Institutiones grammaticae in Hebraeam linguam*. A century later, the complex interplay of consonants, accents and vocalization – a *res sollicita et operosa*, according to Johann Buxtorf³³ – had been thoroughly integrated into Hebrew morphology, or *etymologia* as it was called in the then-current Ramistic parlance. On a more speculative level, Christian theologians vehemently debated the pristine, divine origin of the masoretic notations; their Hebraist colleagues, on the other hand, limited themselves to briefly commenting on their form and function in relation to the *syllaba*, the unit that immediately preceded the *dictio* (word) that was their main concern. Reduced and simplified, and safely hidden among the preliminaries of Hebrew grammar, *niqqud* and *te'amim* were thus quietly absorbed into a more analytical brand of Hebrew description.³⁴ Having

---

31 For Christian interest in contemporary Ashkenazi classroom practice, see Hanoch Avenary, *The Ashkenazi Tradition of Biblical Chant Between 1500 and 1900: Documentation and Musical Analysis* (Tel Aviv University: Publications of the Department of Musicology and the Chaim Rosenberg School of Jewish Studies, 1978), 15.
32 For this corpus, see Yaacov Deutsch's fascinating *Judaism in Christian Eyes: Ethnographic Descriptions of Jews and Judaism in Early Modern Europe* (Oxford: Oxford University Press, 2011).
33 Johann Buxtorf, *Epitome grammaticae Hebraeae* (Franeker: Albertus Idzard, 1652), 129.
34 This conclusion is based on a check of the most representative Dutch Hebrew grammars of the seventeenth century (by Erpenius, Amama, Leusden and Van der Hoogt, 1621–1686), all written in the wake of Johann Buxtorf's *Epitome grammaticae Hebraeae* of 1613. On Buxtorf's Hebra-

retained this – preliminary but fundamental – position until this very day, they do testify, however, to a lasting Hebrew tradition that owes more to Ashkenazi linguistic thinking than has generally been acknowledged.

In conclusion we should say that, if the compass of early modern Hebraism was set by Christian Humanism, it was enterprising Ashkenazim who provided sustenance and guidance along the route. By acquitting themselves of this task they managed, in their turn, to enrich their own tradition of biblical scholarship. We have noted in passing how Elijah Levita's *Sefer ha-Baḥur* and *Pirqe 'Eliahu* nourished later (bipartite) Hebrew manuals, how his *Nimmuqim* inspired scribes in Poland to study Moses Qimḥi, and how his systematic introductions to the language of Scripture strengthened the commitment to biblical morphology in the prayer books, *ḥeders* and *yeshivot* of Ashkenaz. Perhaps we might go as far as to say that the Ashkenazi turn to the Hebrew Bible (away from Yiddish homily and traditional halakhic authority) during the eighteenth century was also – partly – indebted to the presence of men like Levita *in triviis*,[35] at the crossroads of early modern Hebraism.

Bibliography

Avenary, Hanoch. *The Ashkenazi Tradition of Biblical Chant Between 1500 and 1900: Documentation and Musical Analysis*. Tel Aviv University: Publications of the Department of Musicology and the Chaim Rosenberg School of Jewish Studies, 1978.

Alting, Jacob. *Fundamenta punctationis linguae sanctae*. Groningen: Lodovico Dolce, 1658.

Böschenstein, Johann. *Elementale introductorium in hebraeas literas*. Augsburg, 1514.

Burnett, Stephen. *From Christian Hebraism to Jewish Studies: Johannes Buxtorf (1564–1629) and Hebrew Learning in the Seventeenth Century*. Leiden: Brill, 1996.

Buxtorf, Johann. *Epitome grammaticae Hebraeae*. Franeker: Albertus Idzard, 1652.

Dennett, Daniel. *The Elbow Room: The Varieties of Free Will Worth Wanting*. Oxford: Clarendon Press, 1984.

Deutsch, Yaacov. *Judaism in Christian Eyes: Ethnographic Descriptions of Jews and Judaism in Early Modern Europe*. Oxford: Oxford University Press, 2011.

Duran, Profiat. *Maʿase 'Efod*, edited by Jonathan Friedländer and Jakob Kohn. Jerusalem, 1969.

Elbaum, Jacob. *Petiḥut ve-histagrut: ha-yetzirah ha-ruḥanit ha-sifrutit be-Polin u-ve-'artzot 'Ashkenaz be-shilhe ha-me'ah ha-shesh-'esreh*. Jerusalem: Magnes Press, 1992.

---

ism in context, see Stephen Burnett, *From Christian Hebraism to Jewish Studies: Johannes Buxtorf (1564–1629) and Hebrew Learning in the Seventeenth Century* (Leiden: Brill, 1996), 103–133; for the best-selling and influential *Epitome*, see 116. NB: A relative exception seems to be Jacob Alting's widely-read *Fundamenta punctationis linguae sanctae* (Groningen: Lodovico Dolce, 1658), which gave precedence to documenting the changes in Hebrew vocalization and retrieving their linguistic causes (*rationes*).

35 See Virgil, *Eclogue* III:26.

Eldar, Ilan. "Mi-kitve asqolat ha-diqduq ha-ashkenazit ha-shimshonit." *Leshonenu* 43 (1980): 100–111, 200–210.
Eldar, Ilan. "The Grammatical Literature of Medieval Ashkenazi Jewry." In *Hebrew in Ashkenaz: A Language in Exile*, edited by Lewis Glinert, 26–45. New York & Oxford: Oxford University Press, 1993.
Greive, Hermann. "Die hebräische Grammatik Johannes Reuchlins *De rudimentis hebraicis*." *Zeitschrift für die Alttestamentliche Wissenschaft* 90 (1978): 395–409.
Iakerson, Shimon. "An Autograph Manuscript by Elijah Levita in St Petersburg." In *Omnia in Eo. Studies on Jewish Books and Libraries in Honour of Adri Offenberg*, edited by Irene E. Zwiep, et al. *Studia Rosenthaliana* 38/39 (2006): 178–185.
Khan, Geoffrey. "The Medieval Karaite Tradition of Hebrew Grammar." In *A Universal Art: Hebrew Grammar Across Disciplines and Faiths*, edited by Nadia Vidro et al., 15–33. Leiden: Brill, 2014.
Lakoff, George. "The Contemporary Theory of Metaphor." In *Metaphor and Thought*, 2nd ed., edited by Andrew Ortony, 202–251. Cambridge: Cambridge University Press, 1993.
Lakoff, George and Mark Johnson. *Metaphors We Live By*. Chicago: University of Chicago Press, 1980.
Levita, Elijah. *Pirqe 'Eliahu*. Pisa: 1520.
Levita, Elijah. *Sefer ha-Baḥur*. Rome: 1518.
Levita, Elijah. *Tishbi*. Isny, 1541.
Olszowy-Schlanger, Judith. "The Science of Language among Medieval Jews." In *Science in Medieval Jewish Cultures: Madda'*, edited by Gad Freudenthal, 359–424. Cambridge: Cambridge University Press, 2012.
Pellicanus, Conrad. *De modo legendi et intelligendi Hebraeum*. Strassbourg, 1504.
Reif, Stefan C. "A defense of David Qimhi." *Hebrew Union College Annual* 44 (1973): 211–226.
Reif, Stefan C. *Shabbethai Sofer and his Prayer-book*. Cambridge: Cambridge University Press, 1979.
Reuchlin, Johannes. *De accentibus et orthographia linguae Hebraicae*. Hagenau: In ædibus Thomæ Anshelmi Badensis, 1518.
Roth, Cecil. *The Intellectual Activities of Medieval English Jewry*. The British Academy Supplementary Papers 8. London, 1948].
Schatz, Andrea. *Sprache in der Zerstreuung: Die Säkularisierung des Hebräischen im 18. Jahrhundert*. Göttingen: Vandenhoeck & Ruprecht, 2009.
Yarkoni, Rivkah. "'*Ein ha-qore*' le-Yequtiel ha-Kohen." PhD diss., Tel Aviv University, 1985.
Zunz, Leopold. *Zur Geschichte und Literatur*. Berlin: Veit, 1845.
Zwiep, Irene. "Imagined Speech Communities: Western Ashkenazi Multilingualism as Reflected in Eighteenth-Century Grammars of Hebrew." In *Speak Jewish – Jewish Speak: Multilingualism in Western Ashkenazic Culture*, edited by Shlomo Berger et al. *Studia Rosenthaliana* 36 (2002–2003): 77–117.
Zwiep, Irene. "Magie, poëzie, exegese, geschiedenis: Een verkenning van middeleeuwse joodse benaderingen van het boek Psalmen." *Amsterdamse Cahiers voor Exegese van de Bijbel en zijn Tradities* 18 (2000): 115–130.
Zwiep, Irene. *Mother of Reason and Revelation. A Short History of Medieval Jewish Linguistic Thought*. Amsterdam: Gieben, 1997.
Zwiep, Irene. "The Impact of Teytsh on Diqduq, or: Why the Metaphor Became a Noun in Early Modern Ashkenazi Linguistics." In *A Universal Art: Hebrew Grammar Across Disciplines and Faiths*, edited by Nadia Vidro et al., 84–99. Leiden: Brill, 2014.

Saverio Campanini
Learning Hebrew in the Renaissance: Towards a Typology

> Quicquid pracipies esto brevis, ut cito dicta
> Praecipiant animi dociles, teneantque fideles.
> Horace

The year 1500 saw the publication in Rome, for the printing press of Eucharius Silber, of the *De confutatione Hebraicae sectae* written by the Jewish convert of Spanish origin Johannes Baptista Gratia Dei.[1] It was dedicated to the Cardinal Bernardin de Carvajal, who was in turn instrumental in encouraging the future Cardinal Egidio da Viterbo to divulge the results of his Hebrew learning.[2] The book, a translation from Hebrew into Latin, as the author asserts in the dedication, is a collection of numerous passages from the Hebrew Bible, accompanied by a rich anthology of Jewish exegeses followed, no wonder, by a thorough refutation from the standpoint of Christian theology. In recommending the book, the author enlists among the reasons for reading it not only, as one might have expected, the opportunity to battle the Jews on the interpretation of their holy books and to ease the path of their conversion, taking advantage of the approaching Jubilee, but also the possibility that some readers, quite oddly, might feel the urge of learning Hebrew. In Gratia Dei's words:

> Excitabit quoque aliquos fortasse hebracis litteris vacare, quas ad Christianam veritatem perfecte adipiscendam non pauci iuvamenti esse censeo.[3]
>
> [Perhaps (the book) will also stimulate some (Christian) readers to learn Hebrew, which I deem very useful to obtain a perfect grasp of the Christian truth.]

It seems quite obvious that, even in a clearly polemical text, going back to a long tradition of disputations and *adversus Judaeos* treatises, the idea of praising it as a possible stimulus to the diffusion of Hebrew literacy among Christians, is testimony to a radical shift in the image of Hebrew, conceived here primarily as a language, and as a powerful tool for understanding more deeply the truth of Chris-

---

1 Johannes B. Gratia Dei, *Liber de confutatione hebraice secte* (Roma: Eucharius Silber, 1500). In the same year another edition was published by Martin Flach in Strasbourg.
2 Cf. Giuseppe Signorelli, *Il Cardinale Egidio da Viterbo. Agostiniano, umanista e riformatore* (Firenze: Libreria Editrice Fiorentina, 1929), 204.
3 Gratia Dei, *Liber de confutatione*, f. 1v.

tianity. I shall evoke here some instances of early modern learning of Hebrew in order to show how a choice which was new and somehow against the grain of an old tradition (with some exceptions, like the powerful but isolated outbursts of Hebraistic fervour so well documented and studied by Judith Olszowy-Schlanger[4]) came about and how it was implemented under different circumstances. We will see that the combinatory logic implied by the structure of this learning allows for at least four possible types of teacher-pupil relationship, but we will also have to take into account the always limited and provisional value of any classification, thus leading us to the core of the question: the individual and collective dimensions of the somehow unexpected Christian decision to learn Hebrew, which suddenly became en vogue, only in order to turn again, after a few decades of wide diffusion, into a rather seldom occurrence.

A further trait distinguishing the Renaissance from any earlier historical period concerning the concrete ways in which people approached the learning of Hebrew is the availability of copious sources of information. This novelty is due to the fact that, precisely at the dawn of the modern age, the practice of autobiographical writing was revived in a measure which remained unknown to the previous centuries. It was not only, according to the model suggested by Jacob Burckhardt, that the individual became the very centre of the humanistic Renaissance, starting early with Francesco Petrarca's *Secretum*; it was also, according to the model of the celebrated and widely read classical autobiographies, those of Augustine and Josephus, the emergence of a practice of writing as testimony, the documenting of a conversion or the recording of an event of lasting importance. To put it in context and to use the sensationalist style of

---

4 Judith Olszowy-Schlanger, "The Knowledge and Practice of Hebrew Grammar Among Christian Scholars in Pre-Expulsion England: The Evidence of 'Bilingual' Hebrew-Latin Manuscripts," in *Hebrew Scholarship and the Medieval World*, ed. Nicholas R. M. De Lange (Cambridge: Cambridge University Press, 2001): 107–28; Judith Olszowy-Schlanger, "A Christian Tradition of Hebrew Vocalisation in Medieval England," in *Semitic Studies in Honour of Edward Ullendorff*, ed. Geoffrey Khan (Leiden: Brill, 2005): 126–46; Judith Olszowy-Schlanger, "Rachi en latin. Les gloses latines dans un manuscrit du commentaire de Rachi et les études hébraïques parmi des chrétiens dans l'Angleterre médiévale," in *Héritages de Rachi*, ed. René-Samuel Sirat (Paris: Éditions de l'Éclat, 2006): 137–50; Judith Olszowy-Schlanger, "A School of Christian Hebraists in Thirteenth Century England: A Unique Hebrew-Latin-French and English Dictionary and its Sources," *European Journal of Jewish Studies* 1, no. 2 (2007): 249–77; Judith Olszowy-Schlanger, ed., *Dictionnaire hébreu-latin-français de la Bible hébraïque de l'Abbey de Ramsey (XIIIe siècle)* (Brepols: Turnout, 2008); Judith Olszowy-Schlanger, "Christian Hebraism in Thirteenth Century England. The Evidence of Hebrew-Latin Manuscripts," in *Crossing Borders. Hebrew Manuscripts as a Meeting-Place of Cultures*, ed. Piet van Boxel and Sabine Arndt (Oxford: Bodleian Library, 2009): 115–22.

contemporary low-brow publications, many an autobiographical memoir of the early Renaissance could be titled: "How Hebrew changed my life."[5] Some of the documents I am referring to are full-blown autobiographies, such as the *Chronikon* of Konrad Pellikan[6] and the rich and interesting autobiographical notices, reminding the reader rather of a diary, by the bishop of Liège, champion of Catholicism against the Reformation, Gerolamo Aleandro (Hieronymus Aleander),[7] but a treasure-trove of information can also be retrieved from sparse autobiographical annotations, which are particularly dense in the case of prefaces or prefatory epistles especially adorning grammatical works: only to name a few, the preface of Johannes Reuchlin to his *De rudimentis Hebraicis* (Pforzheim 1506),[8] the preface of François Tissard to his *Grammatica Hebraea* (Paris 1508),[9] or that of Matthäus Adrianus to his *Hora faciendi pro Domino* (Tübingen 1513).[10] A further set of sources, still underestimated and underrepresented in scholarly literature is humanist correspondence, some of which was written directly in

---

5 I have expanded on this point in Saverio Campanini, "Jews and Christian Hebraists in Renaissance Italy," in *The Renaissance Speaks Hebrew*, ed. Giulio Busi and Silvana Greco (Cinisello Balsamo: Silvana Editoriale, 2019): 184–195.
6 Cf. Bernhard Riggenbach, ed., *Das Chronikon des Konrad Pellikan. Zur vierten Säkularfeier der Universität Tübingen* (Basel: Bahnmaier's Verlag, 1877); Theodor Vulpinus, ed., *Die Hauschronik Konrad Pellikans von Rufach. Ein Lebensbild aus der Reformationszeit* (Strasbourg: J.H. Ed. Heitz, 1892); Frederick C. Ahrens, "The Chronicle of Conrad Pellican, 1478–1556" (PhD diss., Columbia University, 1950); further bibliography on the topic in Saverio Campanini, "Carta pecudina literis hebraicis scripta. The Awareness of the Binding Hebrew Fragments in History: An Overview and a Plaidoyer," in *Books within Books. New Discoveries in Old Book Bindings. European Genizah Texts and Studies 2*, ed. Andreas Lehnardt and Judith Olszowy-Schlanger (Leiden and Boston: Brill, 2014): 11–28, esp. 14.
7 See Henri Omont, *Journal autobiographique du Cardinal Jérôme Aléandre (1480–1530) publié d'après les manuscrits de Paris et d'Udine. Tiré des Notices et extraits des manuscrits de la Bibliothèque Nationale et d'autres bibliothèques (t. xxxv)* (Paris: C. Klincksieck, 1895); Jules Paquier, *L'humanisme et la réforme. Jérôme Aléandre de sa naissance à la fin de son séjour à Brindes (1480–1529), avec son portrait, ses armes, un fac-simile de son écriture et un catalogue de ses œuvres* (Paris: F. Leroux, 1900).
8 Hermann Greive, "Die hebräische Grammatik Johannes Reuchlins *De rudimentis hebraicis*," *Zeitschrift für alttestamentliche Wissenschaft* 90, no. 3 (1978): 395–409; cf. moreover Jean C. Saladin, "'Lire Reuchlin lire la Bible': sur la préface des 'Rudimenta Hebraica,'" *Revue de l'Histoire des Religions* 222, no. 3 (2005): 287–320.
9 Sophie Kessler-Mesguich, *Les études hébraïques en France de François Tissard à Richard Simon (1508–1680)* (Genève: Droz, 2013), esp. 99–120.
10 Thomas Anshelm, *Libellus hora faciendi pro domino scilicet filio virginis Mariae cuius mysterium in prologo patebit* (Tübingen, 1513). On Adriani, see now Saverio Campanini, "Una lettera in ebraico e una in latino da Matthaeus Adriani a Caspar Amman sul nome di Gesù," *Bruniana & Campanelliana* 24, no. 1 (2018): 25–47.

Hebrew. Here I refer not only to documents reflecting a completely new fashion of addressing Jews in their own language and, more often than not, even on their own terms, but also a widening phenomenon of using Hebrew, as had been the case previously with Greek, as one of the legitimate languages of correspondence between Christian humanists.[11]

Even from the Jewish side of this historical encounter there are quite a few documents and testimonies, once again in autobiographical mode: to mention only a few examples, one can recall the preface of Abraham De Balmes' Hebrew grammar, *Peculium Abrae*, published by Daniel Bomberg in 1523,[12] a letter by Obadiah Sforno to his brother and patron Chanan'el,[13] the colophons and the *Massoret ha-massoret* by Eliah Levita (Venice 1537).[14]

---

[11] Bernhard Walde, *Christliche Hebräisten Deutschlands am Ausgang des Mittelalters* (Münster: Aschendorff, 1916); Eric Zimmer, "Jewish and Christian Collaboration in Sixteenth Century Germany," in *Jewish Quarterly Review* 71, no. 2 (1980): 69–88; Eric Zimmer, "Hebrew Letters of Two Sixteenth Century German Humanists," in *Revue des Études Juives* 141 (1982): 379–86. I have edited the Hebrew letters written by Johannes Reuchlin in the four volumes of his correspondence; cf. Johannes Reuchlin, *Briefwechsel, Band I, 1477–1505*, ed. Stefan Rhein, Matthias Dall'Asta and Gerald Dörner (Stuttgart and Bad Cannstatt: Frommann-Holzboog, 1999), 192–95 and 338–39; Johannes Reuchlin, *Briefwechsel. Band II, 1506–1513*, ed. Matthias Dall'Asta and Gerald Dörner (Stuttgart and Bad Cannstatt: Frommann-Holzboog, 2003), 427–45; Johannes Reuchlin, *Briefwechsel. Band III, 1514–1517*, ed. Matthias Dall'Asta and Gerald Dörner (Stuttgart and Bad Cannstatt: Frommann-Holzboog, 2007), 263–67 and 410–15; Johannes Reuchlin, *Briefwechsel. Band IV, 1518–1522*, ed. Matthias Dall'Asta and Gerald Dörner (Stuttgart and Bad Cannstatt: Frommann-Holzboog, 2013), 354–56. For an early (ca. 1420) instance of correspondence in Hebrew between a Humanist and a Jewish intellectual, cf. Giulio Busi and Saverio Campanini, "Marco Lippomano and Crescas Meir. A Humanistic Dispute in Hebrew," in *Una manna buona per Mantova. Man-Tov le-Man Tovah. Scritti in onore di Vittore Colorni in occasione del suo 92° compleanno*, ed. Mauro Perani (Firenze: Olschki, 2004): 169–202. Already in that correspondence, the first issue discussed before the correspondence evolved into a religious disputation, was the possible exchange of books, concerning subjects such as philosophy, science and magic.

[12] Saverio Campanini, "*Peculium Abrae*. La grammatica ebraico-latina di Avraham de Balmes," *Annali di Ca' Foscari* 36, no. 3 (1997): 5–49.

[13] Studied in Saverio Campanini, "Un intellettuale ebreo del Rinascimento: 'Ovadyah Sforno e i suoi rapporti con i cristiani," in *Verso l'epilogo di una convivenza. Gli ebrei a Bologna nel XVI secolo*, ed. Maria Giuseppina Muzzarelli (Firenze: La Giuntina, 1996): 99–128; idem, "'Ovadyah Sforno: un banchiere filosofo ed esegeta," in *Cesena ebraica: Un percorso fra carte e codici*, ed. Marco Mengozzi (Cesena: Biblioteca Malatestiana, 2019): 103–118

[14] See the still unsurpassed Gérard E. Weil, *Élie Lévita. Humaniste et Massorète (1469–1549)* (Leiden: Brill, 1963).

Thanks both to this profusion of documents[15] as well as to the growing contemporary scholarly awareness of the phenomenon,[16] we are now in a position to sketch a typology, a synthetic yet reasoned description of the modes of learning Hebrew experimented with during the pioneering period of Christian Hebraism in the Renaissance, in particular between the end of the fifteenth century and the first decades of the sixteenth. After the publication of the grammatical works of Konrad Pellikan (1504), Johannes Reuchlin (1506 and 1518), François Tissard (1508), and especially after the publication of the *Miqneh Avram* of Abraham De Balmes (1523) and the many works of Sebastian Münster, the landscape changed dramatically. For the first time ever, due to the printing press and the Reformation, it became possible for Christians to be instructed in Hebrew by other Christians without recruiting Jewish teachers or even Jewish converts. This development, which led to an autonomous form of Christian Hebraism, marks the end of the phenomenon taken into consideration here.

1 Dogmatic or Theological Presuppositions

For a Christian to learn Hebrew was never, at least until the beginning of the Renaissance, a neutral act from a theological point of view. The same applies, although for different reasons, to its counterpart: for Jews to teach Hebrew to non-Jews, although never utterly forbidden, was always a problematic issue from a halakhic perspective, that is to say according to Jewish jurisprudence. For Christians it was more a matter of evaluation of the profit one could gain from this knowledge, normally related to the occult sciences or to the "fables and dreams" of the rabbis, as the parlance of anti-Jewish tracts termed the corpus of Jewish literature. Religious confrontation, and – especially from a Christian viewpoint – the

---

15 For a good overview of the phenomenon of Jewish teachers of Hebrew, see Stephen Burnett, "Jüdische Vermittler des Hebräischen und ihre christlichen Schüler im Spätmittelalter," in *Wechselseitige Wahrnehmung der Religionen im Spätmittelalter und in der Frühen Neuzeit. I. Konzeptionelle Grundfragen und Fallstudien (Heiden, Barbaren, Juden)*, ed. Ludger Grezmann, Thomas Haye, Nikolaus Henkel, and Thomas Kaufmann (Berlin and New York: De Gruyter, 2009): 173–88.
16 Cf. especially Stephen Burnett, *Christian Hebraism in the Reformation Era (1500–1660)* (Leiden and Boston: Brill, 2012); Dean P. Bell and Stephen Burnett, eds., *Jews, Judaism, and the Reformation in Sixteenth Century Germany* (Leiden and Boston: Brill, 2006); and Ilona Steimann, *Jewish Book – Christian Book: Hebrew Manuscripts in Transition Between Jews and Christians in the Context of German Humanism* (Brepols: Turnhout, 2020).

anticipated triumph resulting in conversion and baptism would always encumber the notion of a merely "cultural" transmission of information. There is probably never such a bare exchange of information without an implicit or explicit attempt at transforming the other, and the more or less unintended consequence of being transformed by the encounter. But in the case of the holy tongue, charged as it is with an immense religious potential, it was all the more difficult to imagine the simple activity of teaching or learning Hebrew without slippery or even dangerous overtones.

The autobiographical reports referred to earlier, however, are the testimony that this transformation (traditionally "conversion," in Greek *metanoia*, not necessarily in a religious sense) took place even before and not only after the encounter. Without the conviction that something important could be gained from learning the once-despised Hebrew language, this entire movement would not have taken place at all. This is not the occasion for expanding on the motivations for this shift in general attitude, but it will not come as a surprise that I would make a strong case for showing that it was the discovery of Kabbalah which determined the change, before an increasing interest in grammar in itself, as a consequence of the linguistic and philological battles around the Reformation, and a widespread mistrust in Kabbalah on the other hand, helped establish Christian Hebraism on a philological basis, resulting in the disappearance of almost all interest for Jewish mysticism.

It is precisely the status of Hebrew, a very much-discussed topic during and already before the Renaissance, especially as a part of the debate involving the value of the Vulgate, which reveals the authentic stakes of the movement toward a radical revision of a long-established tradition of suspicion, refusal and contempt.[17] In my opinion, nevertheless, the principle of the holiness of Hebrew, derived from rabbinic and kabbalistic ideology or logo-theology, was never fully accepted among the Christians for the very same reasons which, as we will see, conditioned the approach to the secret lore of Kabbalah. In the end, quite paradoxically, the Christians were left with the language (that is, its philology) but without the theological motivations justifying the centrality of Hebrew. In other words, philology, in the long run, substituted itself for theology as a secularized form of knowledge, aspiring to the leading function among sciences formerly occupied by theology itself.[18] Philology, in the end, was the discipline responsi-

---

[17] See Saverio Campanini, "Francesco Giorgio's Criticism of the Vulgata: Hebraica Veritas or Mendosa Traductio?" in *Hebrew to Latin – Latin to Hebrew. The Mirroring of two Cultures in the Age of Humanism*, ed. Giulio Busi (Turin: Nino Aragno, 2006): 206–231.
[18] I have expanded on this topic in Saverio Campanini, "Das Hebräische in Reuchlins Werk." In *Transcending Words. The Language of Religious Contact Between Buddhists, Christians and Mus-*

ble for sweeping out the claims to antiquity of the Kabbalah, a far more important result than anything "sacred philology" (*philologia sacra*) could achieve, considering that, as long as the "author" of the sacred text is God, no error can be ascertained as such, thereby discrediting the very method and instruments of textual criticism at their root.

The humanistic project of rediscovering the ancient languages reached its culmination with the addition of Hebrew, alongside Geek and Latin, to the linguistic canon of Christianity. The pedagogical shift implied by humanism, albeit only partly successful, brought about in turn a radical transformation: the Reform, both Catholic and Protestant, on one hand, and the limitation of the teaching of Hebrew among Christians to the Protestant theological faculties, on the other. There will be occasions, even further on here, to come back to this crucial point.

2 Anomaly and Analogy: How to Learn Hebrew

Having sketched the theological presuppositions and the historical-philological output of the lucid decision of learning Hebrew, the technical question needs to be asked: how did the humanists learn Hebrew? Concerning this specific problem we do not have as many relevant documents as for the general project of learning Hebrew or the difficulties accompanying this resolution, but some indications, alongside the obvious analogy with the techniques of learning Latin or Greek, have been preserved, as was shown in the precious studies of the late Sophie Mesguich-Kessler.[19] The two main features that emerge on the basis of the materials gathered so far is that Hebrew was learned on the basis of the *lexica* (more akin to a concordance than to a dictionary in the modern sense) and on the paradigms, the latter allowing the reader to make some sense out of the former. Not by chance, this follows an identical evolution within Jewish approaches to the grammatical consideration of Hebrew, the dominant tendency among the early Christian Kabbalists of the Renaissance being the use of the grammatical works of the Kimhi family, especially the *Mahalakh shevile ha-da'at* and the *Mikhlol*, of

---

lims in Premodern Times, ed. Görge K. Hasselhoff and Knut M. Stunkel (Bochum: Verlag Dieter Winkler, 2015).

[19] Sophie Kessler-Mesguich, "L'hébreu chez les hébraïsants chrétiens des XVIe et XVIIe siècles," in *Histoire Épistémologie Langage* 18, no. 1 (1996): 87–108; Sophie Kessler-Mesguich, "L'enseignement de l'hébreu et de l'araméen par les premiers lecteurs royaux (1530–1560)," in *Histoire du Collège de France,* vol. 1, ed. André Tuilier (Paris: Fayard, 2006): 257–82.

which the first part of Reuchlin's *De rudimentis hebraicis* represents an adaptation and an abridgement.

This holds true even in the case of Konrad Pellikan who, describing his painstaking endeavour to compile a concordance of the biblical text, reports that he started reading the Bible in Hebrew without almost any previous background. Although he managed to produce an extremely dependable concordance, he could not really achieve any significant progress (in terms of linguistic understanding) until Johannes Reuchlin taught him to analyze his random terms with the help of a paradigmatic morphological pattern.

Again, as we have seen before, we face the combination of the individual, the lexeme, and the general analogical rule or, in other words, the historical movement. As autobiography became fashionable and therefore far from individual, in the same way a language, even a sacred one, could be learned only by analyzing the individual shape of the words of the biblical text through the abstract model of morphology. One could argue therefore that the goal of the study of Hebrew was the ability to read the Bible or, *ce qui revient au même*, to criticize the Vulgate, but this would only partly be true, since the main point of the exercise was rather, as we will see, to grasp the meaning of the Bible, not just to master the subtleties of Hebrew morphology but rather to formulate a semantic approach with the broadest and deepest meaning possible. This peculiar movement guiding the appropriation of Hebrew among the Christians can be construed as a threefold dialectical model: the biblical text, which can be characterized as the raw individual fact, governed by the principle of anomaly, occupies the first place; then the facts are organized by the general rule, according to the principle of paradigmatic analogy; finally, the synthesis, that is the reverse movement of going back to the individual biblical text in order to understand its meaning, far beyond the boundaries of the mere literal sense.

The example of Egidio of Viterbo seems to me particularly appropriate for epitomizing this dialectical movement, bringing together many aspects of his personality: his Hebraic interests; his activity in favour of Hebrew learning among the clergy; his dual passion for Hebrew grammar and for Jewish esotericism. A brief manuscript annotation written in his own hand above the incipit of his[20] Latin translation of David Kimhi's *Sefer ha-shorashim* dictionary reads as follows:[21]

---

[20] Certainly in the sense that the book belonged to him. Whether he did execute the translation is rather unlikely, but still an open question.
[21] Rome, Biblioteca Angelica, ms. 3, f. 2r.

Curavit frater Aegidius Viterbiensis eremita, hoc haberi, tametsi inepta insulsa et minus latina, maluit tamen hec usui esse suis, quam contemnere,²² usui vero possunt esse non mediocri, si quis cum hebreo codice conferat, sine quo conferre possunt nihil. Id non omiserim, precepto domini obtemperari non posse sine his, cum scripturas scrutandas esse mandavit, quibus duo esse apud hebreos constat admodum necessarias et has grammatices institutiones ad linguam, et archanas commentationes ad intellectum.²³

[Brother Egidio of Viterbo of the Augustinians ordered this book to be kept, although its content is awkward, tasteless and less than correct; he preferred nevertheless that it be of use for his companions than just to despise it: these pages can be very useful indeed, if compared to the Hebrew original, without which they are useless. I would add that without them we cannot obey the Lord's precept, in which we are commanded to scrutinize Scripture, and for obtaining this goal it is held that there are two things among the Jews that are absolutely necessary: the principles of grammar, for language and the secret commentaries, for intellectual understanding].

If we are looking for a synthesis of the phenomenon which is described here, one could not have found, I believe, a more fitting slogan. Even talking about a no-nonsense dictionary of Hebrew, Egidio cannot forget the ultimate goal of the decision to translate a dictionary while admitting that it will be of no use without the original. But this brings us precisely to the core of the question: the arcane commentaries, that is to say the Kabbalah, provide the sense of the Bible and they lend meaning to the subversive idea of learning Hebrew not in order to make translations superfluous, but to abide with the original, piercing the screen between the reader and revelation. Only after having learned Hebrew will it become clear that Kabbalah is the answer, but in order to learn Hebrew an act of faith is needed, namely that the reward of the effort will be true Kabbalah, the authentic meaning of the word of God, no less.

From a typological point of view, the possible combinations offered by historical evidence are four: a Christian would-be Hebraist could, according to the different situations, learn Hebrew from an already knowledgeable fellow Christian (1), which implies also a sub-category, since a fellow Christian teacher could be, and in most cases was, a former Jew (2); he could teach himself Hebrew without a teacher, namely from books (3); or, finally, he could learn Hebrew from a Jew (4). For any of these types we can evoke a large number of examples but, since many cases have been already studied in detail, it will suffice to allude to some representative names, which will be listed in the following considerations. The

---

22 At first he wrote "contempnere" and afterwards corrected the orthography by marking two dots under the letter "p."
23 The annotation is already reproduced by Léon G. Pelissier, "Manuscrits de Gilles de Viterbe à la Bibliothèque Angélique (Rome)," *Revue des Bibliothèques* 2 (1892): 228–40, esp. 231.

last type (learning Hebrew from a Jew who stayed Jewish) is the most interesting, because of the theological problems we have recalled, and because of the humanistic persuasion that the purity of water, metaphorically, is functional to its closeness to the source.

A typology is certainly needed, but, as with any categorization, it is useful only to establish some lines or boundaries, even if these boundaries are there in order to be crossed. If we consider, for example, the experience of Konrad Pellikan,[24] it is easy to recognize that all four types are represented: he was certainly an autodidact, because, as he refers, he started reading every scratch of parchment upon which he could find Hebrew letters; he used the books available to him, in particular the *Stella Messiae* of the Dominican Petrus Nigri (Peter Schwarz), given to him, as chance has it, by Konrad Summenhart, a former pupil, together with Johannes Reuchlin, of Flavius Mithridates in Tübingen.[25] Afterwards, he crossed the border into other models. For example, he met a fellow Franciscan, Paul Pfedersheim, a former Jew from Mainz, and discussed Hebraistic matters also with him. Moreover, he had some meetings and *pourparlers* concerning possible collaboration, which did indeed, materialize, at least to a certain extent, with Johannes Reuchlin himself. Another important link for Pellikan, showing at the same time quite symbolically that at the beginning of Christian Jewish studies a sincere intellectual interest was hard to disentangle from a secular practice of persecution, is that with Johannes Bohem, who managed to acquire Hebrew grammatical books from the Jews of Ulm right before their expulsion from that southern German town.[26]

Given that the emergence of Hebrew learning among Christians is deeply rooted in Italian humanism, that the most important cases of collaboration in the early stage took place in Italy, that many Hebraists from other European countries,

---

[24] Cf. Saverio Campanini, "Carta pecudina," 11–28.
[25] Cf. Idem., "Mithridates deutsche Reise. Humanismus und Hebraistik zwischen Flucht und Ehrung," in *Buchkulturen des deutschen Humanismus (1430–1530): Netzwerke und Kristallisationspunkte*, ed. Anne Eusterschulte and Elke A. Werner (Leiden: Brill, in print).
[26] Eberhard Nestle, *Nigri, Böhm und Pellican. Ein Beitrag zur Anfangsgeschichte des hebräischen Sprachstudiums in Deutschland* (Tübingen: Heckenauer, 1893); Bernhard Walde, *Christliche Hebräisten*; Thomas Willi, "Hebraica Veritas in Basel: Christliche Hebraistik aus jüdischen Quellen," in *International Organization for the Study of the Old Testament. Congress (17th)*, ed. André Lemaire (Basel: Brill, 2001): 375–97; Beate Ego, "Konrad Pellican und die Anfänge der wissenschaftlichen christlichen Hebraistik im Zeitalter von Humanismus und Reformation," in *Humanismus und Reformation. Historische, theologische und pädagogische Beiträge zu deren Wechselwirkung*, ed. Reinhold Mokrosch and Helmut Merkel (Münster, Hamburg and, London: LIT Verlag, 2001): 73–84 and Steimann, *Jewish Book – Christian Book*.

such as the French Tissard and the German Reuchlin,[27] had to come to Italy to find Jews ready to instruct them, it has been assumed[28] that there was a specific Italian intellectual and political climate, in which the Jews were, for some reason, more prepared to teach Hebrew to non-Jews, but the reality on the ground looks rather more complex. If one excludes the countries where no real Jews were available, such as England, Northern France and, after 1492, Spain, the major European countries where the search for Hebrew teachers could find a fertile soil were Italy and Germany, and it would be far from correct to state that the availability of Jewish Hebrew teachers in Italy was in any way greater than in Germany. In the Bayerische Staatsbibliothek,[29] but also in the University Library of Munich,[30] several manuscripts preserved from the first decades of the sixteenth century attest a flourishing exchange of Hebrew letters, between Jews and Christians, but also among Christian humanists, trading information and grammatical works (among the most important, a series of treatises and abridged versions of the grammatical production of the Kimhi family, especially the *Sefer ha-shorashim*).[31] As opposed to this radically new phenomenon, what one observes in Italy is rather the classical medieval collaboration with Jewish converts, with a head start from the Dominicans, for example Johannes Gattus (Giovanni Gatti). This figure organized, most likely in the Sicilian town of Cefalù, with the help of some converted Jews, certainly Pablo de Heredia[32] and probably also with the above-mentioned Flavius Mithridates, an early example of a forgery factory, specifically of propagandistic and polemical *gematriot* aimed at the conversion of the Jews.[33]

---

[27] Saverio Campanini, "Reuchlins jüdische Lehrer aus Italien," in *Reuchlin und Italien*, ed. Gerald Dörner (Stuttgart: Jan Thorbecke Verlag, 1999): 69–85.
[28] For an example of this view, see Eric Zimmer, "Jewish and Christian Collaboration in Sixteenth Century Germany," esp. 81.
[29] For example, the MS Cod. hebr. 426, digitised and available online, accessed June 12, 2022, http://daten.digitale-sammlungen.de/~db/0008/bsb00082354/images/index.html.
[30] For example, Cod. or. 757. The manuscript, already known because it contains a very old rendition of a Jewish melody in Western musical transcription, would deserve a closer look for it bears further testimony to a climate of exchange between humanists and rabbis.
[31] Saverio Campanini, "'Thou bearest not the root, but the root thee': On the Reception of the *Sefer ha-Shorashim* in Latin," *Sefarad* 76, no. 2 (2016): 313–331.
[32] Gershom Scholem, "Zur Geschichte der Anfänge der christlichen Kabbala," in *Essays Presented to Leo Baeck on the Occasion of His Eightieth Birthday* (London: East and West Library, 1954): 158–93; François Secret, "L'Ensis Pauli de Paulus de Heredia," *Sefarad* 26 (1966): 79–102 and 253–71; Saverio Campanini, "Nottole ad Atene. La qabbalah cristiana e la conversione degli ebrei," *Materia Giudaica* 19 (2014): 81–101.
[33] For another example of forged texts eagerly copied by Christian readers, see Saverio Campanini, "Un frammento sconosciuto dello pseudo-Zohar nella Roma del Rinascimento," *Materia Giudaica* 22 (2017): 3–14.

The same applies to Pico della Mirandola in his formative years, when he was in contact with Jews and non-Jews, converted at least one of his teachers — Clemente Abramo (later teacher of Hebrew of Sante Pagnini) — but depended for his information, especially as far as Kabbalah is concerned, upon the baptised Jew Flavius Mithridates. The subsequent generation of Italian Hebraists was quite secretive concerning the identities of their Hebrew teachers. Apart from the name of yet another converted Jew of Spanish origin, Libertas Cominetti,[34] we still do not know much about exactly how important figures such as Agostino Giustiniani[35] and Pietro Galatino[36] acquired their knowledge. We know a little more from another Christian Hebraist who was in contact with Cominetti during the Lateran Council in Rome, I refer here to Teseo Ambrogio degli Albonesi who, in his *Introductio in Chaldaicam linguam*,[37] recalls several of his teachers *in Hebraicis* as well as *in Chaldaicis* (that is to say Aramaic and Syriac). Among them, if I am not mistaken, one could include Obadiah Sforno, referred to as "Abdia scholasticus," among the most prominent Roman Jews at the time.

An interesting case in point is represented by Francesco Giorgio: we still do not know much about his formative years, including from whom he acquired his remarkable Hebraistic education. Only fairly recently have new pieces of information emerged concerning the origins of his famous library, which was coveted all over Europe, as is very well known, and as the correspondence of Egidio da Viterbo (with Gabriele dalla Volta) and of Heinrich Cornelius Agrippa abundantly shows.[38] One central book in Giorgio's Kabbalistic library was no doubt the *Sefer*

---

34 Saverio Campanini, "La radice dolorante. Ebrei e cristiani alla scoperta del giudaismo nel Rinascimento, apparso," in *L'interculturalità dell'ebraismo*, ed. Mauro Perani (Ravenna: Longo, 2004): 221–47.
35 Cf. Saverio Campanini, "A Neglected Source on Asher Lemmlein and Paride da Ceresara: Agostino Giustiniani," *European Journal of Jewish Studies* 2, no. 1 (2008): 89–110.
36 Alba Palladino, *Il De arcanis di Pietro Galatino. Traditio giudaica e nuove istanze di riforma* (Galatina: Congedo, 2004); Saverio Campanini, "Quasi post vindemias racemos colligens. Pietro Galatino und seine Verteidigung der christlichen Kabbala," *Reuchlins Freunde und Gegner. Kommunikative Konstellationen eines frühneuzeitlichen Medienereignisses*, ed. Wilhelm Kühlmann (Ostfildern: Jan Thorbecke Verlag, 2010): 69–88.
37 *Introductio in Chaldaicam linguam, Syriacam, atque Armenicam, et decem alias linguas. Characterum differentium Alphabeta, circiter quadraginta, et eorundem invicem conformatio. Mystica et Cabalistica quamplurima scitu digna. Et descriptio ac simulachrum Phagoti Afranij*. Theseo Ambrosio ex comitibus Albonesii [. . . . . .] Authore, Papiae 1539, f. 14v. Cf. Eberhard Nestle, "Aus einem sprachwissenschaftlichen Werk von 1539," *Zeitschrift der deutschen Morgenländischen Gesellschaft* 58 (1904): 601–16.
38 I have expanded on Zorzi's library in Saverio Campanini, "Le fonti ebraiche del *De Harmonia mundi* di Francesco Zorzi," *Annali di Ca' Foscari* 38, no. 3 (1999): 29–74 and summarized the state

ha-Peliah. We have long been very well informed about the further destiny of this book, or, to be more precise, of its copy preserved at the Bodleian Library, made by the converted nephew of Eliah Levita, Vittorio Eliano, for the Knight of the Holy Sepulchre Thomas Markenfield. In the colophon Eliano states in Hebrew that he perused the copy (in 1565) which once belonged to the Franciscan friar of the Observance Francesco Giorgio. This information was very well known, as was the fact that Giorgio repeatedly used the *Sefer ha-Peliah*, consistently called by him "Elchana," in all his works, printed and unprinted, making it one of the pillars of his Kabbalistic worldview. What was not known, and Renata Segre deserves credit for her patient digging and sifting of the Venetian archives in order to find it out, is how (and when) Giorgio came to possess this precious kabbalistic book and to what extent he was able to read it. Now a document from the Archivio del Doge[39] informs us that Giorgio came to know that Damiano di Castiglia, a Jewish physician and refugee from Spain, possessed the manuscript. He arranged with the supreme authorities of the Republic to put at the disposal of this Spanish Jew an incredibly high amount of money (500 golden ducats) as a guarantee, so that he could borrow the book and copy it.[40] This short document, dated, as it appears, June 1506, contains two more elements worthy of our attention.

On one hand, it is clearly stated that Giorgio could count on the help of somebody for preparing the copy, probably a Jew, since this individual had easy access to Damiano's home and library. In the words of the document: "dominus Frater Franciscus qui habet secum personam doctissimam in lingua hebraica et propterea egregium interpretem et scriptorem" ["The reverend brother Franciscus, who has at his disposal a person, most learned in Hebrew and therefore an excellent translator and a copyist"], which is most likely also a reference to Giorgio's instructor in Hebrew. What we certainly know, from Marin Sanudo's chronicle, is that Giorgio was involved in the conversion of one Jew (a rabbi from Naples), who used to be at the service of the ambassador of Mantua in Venice. One is tempted to ask whether we are dealing here with one and the same person. The evidence is insufficient to prove this, but it is certainly possible, and would place Giorgio in good company among other Christian pupils who converted their Hebrew teach-

---

of our knowledge on the topic in Francesco Zorzi, *L'armonia del mondo*, Introduzione, traduzione e note di S. Campanini (Milano: Bompiani, 2010).
39 Archivio di Stato di Venezia, CCX, Notatorio, Reg. 3, ff. 207v–208r.
40 See now Saverio Campanini, "Elchana Hebraeorum doctor et cabalista: Le avventure di un libro e dei suoi lettori," in *Umanesimo e cultura ebraica nel Rinascimento italiano*, eds. Stefano Ugo Baldassarri and Fabrizio Lelli (Firenze: Angelo Pontecorboli Editore, 2016): 91–114.

ers, from Giannozzo Manetti[41] and Pico della Mirandola to, as we will see, the future cardinal Gerolamo Aleandro.

On the other, the document in question reveals a peculiar feature of the historical phenomenon depicted here: the highest authority of the city of Venice accepted involvement in a potentially risky affair, guaranteeing an enormous sum of money to protect the property of a Jew, and more precisely a book. Giorgio stated in his petition to the Doge that this rare book, called "Elchana," contains "very many secret doctrines of the Jews pertinent and worthy of being apprehended by Christians in order to disclose the truth and to sanctify our Christian faith" (*quamplurima secreta ipsorum hebreorum pertinentia et digna noticia christianorum ad declarationem veritatis et consecrationis fidei nostre christiane*). The importance of the book is clearly stated in the most classical terms of Christian Kabbalistic ideology: no effort should be spared for acquiring this secret knowledge, whose value for Christianity is incalculable.

The case of the Spanish exile Moshe Peretz allows us to examine, again from an autobiographical document,[42] a further example of the fourth type (instruction from a Jew), which represents an interesting and far from rare variant: the Jewish teacher converts to Christianity during or immediately after having imparted his Hebrew training. At the same time, it also enables us trace the spread of the conviction that Hebrew belongs to the central subjects of a well-rounded education, even in a region lacking a Jewish presence, following the tide of expulsions, executions and blood libels which characterized the second half of the fifteenth century. I am referring to the northern Italian region of Friuli, and to the experience of the young diplomat Gerolamo Aleandro. Though he was a man of the ecclesiastical hierarchy and a rather gifted Hellenist, he would never become a great Hebraist. However, in not being exceptional, he has the great advantage of helping us to set a typology, i.e. to determine the characteristic features of the average Hebraist. His Hebraistic education, carefully arranged by Aleandro's father to round out a well-conceived humanistic programme, had two consequences: the conversion of his teacher, on one hand, and, on the other, his entry into the job market for becoming a Hebrew teacher himself, after just one year of study. Here he did not have any success, due to the presence of too many destitute Jews who were willing to instruct the growing number of potential Christian pupils for less.

---

[41] Cf. Umberto Cassuto, *Gli ebrei a Firenze nell'età del Rinascimento* (Firenze: Tip. Galletti e Cocci, 1918), 275.
[42] See Henri Omont, *Journal autobiographique*, 37.

To sum up: as far as Italy is concerned, the only clear-cut[43] cases of Christians learning Hebrew from Jews who did not convert afterwards (at the latest) concern Obadiah Sforno, on one hand, who taught Reuchlin and yet another Christian pupil,[44] and, on the other, the celebrated encounter between Eliah Levita and Egidio of Viterbo. Interestingly, both cases, albeit in inverted directions, involve a German-Italian joint venture.

As to the motivations for converted Jews to enter this risky business, one does not need to insist much: they obviously had good reasons for attacking their former brethren. But at the same time, the changing climate among Christians frequently made them prisoners of their own discarded identity, in a way different but somehow parallel to the destiny of the more or less forcibly converted Jews of the Iberian Peninsula.

A different case altogether is represented by the motivations of the Jews involved in the process. In some cases, for example for Moshe Peretz, economic need and the brutal loss attendant upon the expulsion from Spain must have played a significant role. In some instances, such as in the case of Abraham De Balmes, it was the disappointment of a neglected scholar. In his preface to his *Miqneh Avram* (1523), published only in Hebrew in an otherwise completely bi-lingual Hebrew Grammar,[45] he praises Daniel Bomberg for his interest in Hebrew, polemically rebuking the Jews of Venice for their apathy as far as grammatical questions were concerned, concentrated as they were on the pursuit of material interests. In other cases, messianic expectations may have justified the favourable, perhaps even enthusiastic, response of some Jews to the increasing demand of Hebrew instruction. Eric Zimmer surmised that messianic reasons could have motivated Naftali Hirtz Treves, one of the most positively inclined correspondents with early German Hebraists – in particular with Caspar Amman and Johannes Reinhardt – to adopt an attitude of openness even in divulging kabbalistic secrets. Treves, who was the author of a kabbalistic commentary on the daily prayers, interestingly called *Diqduq tefillah* (Thiengen 1560), refers with an attitude of approval or at least of hope to his son's announcement in Cracow in 1531 of the beginning of redemption. Zimmer observes that the date recalls the

---

[43] The earlier case of Giannozzo Manetti, as far as our information reaches, is more complex because, as we have already mentioned, his biography credited him with the conversion of his Hebrew teacher, but also a fruitful intellectual relationship with "Manuello," that is to say Immanuel ben Abraham da San Miniato who did not convert, as far as we know, but should be seen rather as an informant than a teacher.

[44] Cf. Campanini, "Un intellettuale ebreo," 99–128 and idem, "'Ovadiah Sforno," 103–118 for further hypotheses as to his identity.

[45] Campanini, "Peculium Abrae," 5–49.

messianic activity of David Reuveni and Shelomoh Molko. It is interesting to note that according to the memoir of David Reuveni,[46] the Hebrew teacher of Reuchlin, Rabbi Obadiah Sforno, was briefly imprisoned at a dramatic juncture of the Reuveni affair in Rome. Perhaps he was not involved, but he may also very well have had reason in hindsight to keep silent about his enthusiasm for the pseudo-messiah, if he ever had been a follower of Reuveni. It is a fact, anyway, that Sforno underlines, upon translating his philosophical work (*Or 'ammim*) into Latin (*Lumen gentium*), that it is a pious deed to spread the light of Torah to the extreme boundaries of humanity. In his letter to his brother Chananel (Graziadio) announcing the completion of his Hebrew grammar to be printed in Latin (a project which did not succeed, but for which he had already obtained the permission of the Penitenzieria apostolica), he justifies his work by affirming that the superiority of Hebrew will be all the more evident if the speakers of Latin (*notzri*) will not be able to excuse themselves out of sheer ignorance. Moreover, a central tenet of his ideology is the diffusive character of the Torah, the providential explanation of Esau's domination over Israel, in order for Israel to be entirely devoted to contemplation.[47] And furthermore, at least implicitly, in his commentary on the tractate *Avot* of the Mishnah,[48] Sforno insists with pedagogical and homiletic skilfulness that the Torah is not a secure heritage for the Jews (*sheenah yerushah lakh*), but is rather open to a benign competition, and will belong to the ones who really love it.

From a halakhic point of view, concerning the question whether it should be acceptable for a Jew to teach Hebrew to non-Jews, there was not a prevailing consensus, at least not until the middle of the sixteenth century. Nevertheless, the dominant attitude is well exemplified by the *responsum* of Eliah Menachem Halfan.[49] Teaching Hebrew to non-Jews should not be entirely forbidden, but a distinction was prudently introduced: since Christians are obliged to obey the Noachic precepts, they need to be instructed to get acquainted with them. What they should not learn, however, are the *Sitre torah*, the secret lore of Kabbalah. The latter represents exactly, as I already pointed out, what the large majority of the early pioneers of Christian Hebraism were interested in. This paradox led to a peculiar situation and, perhaps, as I am inclined to believe, helped determine one historical outcome of the early season of Christian Hebraism before the success-

---

[46] Aaron Z. Aescoly, *Sippur David Reuveni* (Jerusalem: Ha-Ḥevrah ha-Erets Yisre'elit le-historyah ve-etnografyah, 1940), 47.
[47] Cf. *Commentary on the Pentateuch*, on Gen. 27:29.
[48] *Commentary on Mishnah Avot* 2:16.
[49] David Kaufmann, "Elia Menachem Chalfan on Teaching Hebrew to Non-Jews," *Jewish Quarterly Review* 9, no. 3 (1897): 500–08.

ful diffusion of Reformation in Central Europe. Many letters are preserved that show exactly the same kind of attitude established as normative by Halfan. One can refer, for example, to the polite but firm refusal to cede Kabbalistic books, on the pious ground that they were not available to him offered in response to Reuchlin's insistence[50] by Jakob Margalit, and to the letter written by Elijah Levita to Johann Albrecht Widmannstetter, containing a diplomatic refusal but also a skilful counter offer of less problematic books, mainly grammars.[51] The relevant examples could be easily multiplied. Rather rare, on the contrary, but quite influential, was the position of Shelomoh Luria, reinforced and even brought to the extreme by Isaiah Horowitz, that it should be forbidden for a Jew to teach anything religious to a non-Jew, in order to avoid giving birth to children of idolatry ('Avodah zarah).[52] Horowitz, fearing the ominous consequences for the Jews of sharing any religious information, even recommends to avoid teaching Christians the letters of the Hebrew alphabet!

A much later ruling, more representative of the consensus, is the one found in Isacco Lampronti's *Pachad Yitzchaq*, where he clarifies that while it should not be forbidden to a Jew to sell printed books to a Gentile, the opposite is true in the case of manuscripts. In other words, there is no prohibition against trading with Christians items they could get also without Jewish assistance, but by no means should the Jews give to Christians what they can only obtain from them.

This seems to me precisely one of the most paradoxical points of the much celebrated and often misunderstood relationship between Jews and Christians in the wake of the Reformation: what the Christian really desired from the Jews was the Kabbalah, and they were prepared, especially after Reuchlin, to take upon themselves the burden of learning Hebrew. In other words, the grammar was merely a means to a different end: the confirmation of Christianity, that is of their own tradition, by means of the secret lore of Judaism. For the Jews, in general, Hebrew grammar was the utmost they could offer without endangering a halakhic and prudential practice, lest the Christians would attain what they always claimed to possess, the Torah.

This situation might even be at the origin of one feature that characterised the parting of the ways between Protestants and Catholics. The latter chose tradition over philology, the Protestants, on the other hand, chose philology over tradition. This rough distinction must be further qualified but it captures somehow

---

50 Johannes Reuchlin, *Briefwechsel, Band I*, 192–95.
51 Joseph Perles, *Beiträge zur Geschichte der hebräischen und aramäischen Studien* (München: Theodor Ackermann, 1884), 158–59.
52 Cf., for this and the following rulings cited in the article Kaufmann, "Elia Menachem Chalfan," 502.

the turning point of the history I have tried to analyze here: both parties agreed very early to dispense with Jewish help, either clinging to the Vulgate or boasting to understand Hebrew better than the Jews, as a strong, specifically Protestant branch of the "theology of substitution" claimed.

Every encounter, even failed ones, brings about a transformation, and certainly a profound metamorphosis took place within Christianity in the sixteenth century. At the same time, one cannot fail to perceive the acute sense of a missed opportunity.

Bibliography

Aescoly, Aaron Z. *Sippur David Reuveni*. Jerusalem: Ha-Ḥevrah ha-Erets Yisre'elit le-historyah ve-etnografyah, 1940.

Ahrens, Frederick C. "The Chronicle of Conrad Pellican, 1478–1556." PhD diss., Columbia University, 1950.

Anshelm, Thomas. *Libellus hora faciendi pro domino scilicet filio virginis Mariae cuius mysterium in prologo patebit*. Tübingen, 1513.

Archivio di Stato di Venezia, CCX, Notatorio, Reg. 3, ff. 207v–208r.

Bell, Dean P., and Stephen Burnett, eds. *Jews, Judaism, and the Reformation in Sixteenth Century Germany*. Leiden and Boston: Brill, 2006.

Burnett, Stephen. *Christian Hebraism in the Reformation Era (1500–1660)*. Leiden and Boston: Brill, 2012.

Burnett, Stephen. "Jüdische Vermittler des Hebräischen und ihre christlichen Schüler im Spätmittelalter." In *Wechselseitige Wahrnehmung der Religionen im Spätmittelalter und in der Frühen Neuzeit. I. Konzeptionelle Grundfragen und Fallstudien (Heiden, Barbaren, Juden)*, edited by Ludger Grezmann, Thomas Haye, Nikolaus Henkel, and Thomas Kaufmann, 173–88. Berlin and New York: De Gruyter, 2009.

Busi, Giulio, and Saverio Campanini. "Marco Lippomano and Crescas Meir. A Humanistic Dispute in Hebrew." In *Una manna buona per Mantova. Man-Tov le-Man Tovah. Scritti in onore di Vittore Colorni in occasione del suo 92° compleanno*, edited by Mauro Perani, 169–202. Florence: Olschki, 2004.

Campanini, Saverio. "A Neglected Source on Asher Lemmlein and Paride da Ceresara: Agostino Giustiniani." *European Journal of Jewish Studies* 2, no. 1 (2008): 89–110.

Campanini, Saverio. "Carta pecudina literis hebraicis scripta. The Awareness of the Binding Hebrew Fragments in History: An Overview and a Plaidoyer." In *Books within Books: New Discoveries in Old Book Bindings. European Genizah Texts and Studies 2*, ed. Andreas Lehnardt and Judith Olszowy-Schlanger, 11–28. Leiden and Boston: Brill, 2014.

Campanini, Saverio. "Das Hebräische in Reuchlins Werk." In *Transcending Words: The Language of Religious Contact Between Buddhists, Christians and Muslims in Premodern Times*, edited by Görge K. Hasselhoff and Knut M. Stunkel. Bochum: Verlag Dieter Winkler, 2015.

Campanini, Saverio. "Elchana Hebraeorum doctor et cabalista: Le avventure di un libro e dei suoi lettori." In *Umanesimo e cultura ebraica nel Rinascimento italiano*, edited by Stefano Ugo Baldassarri and Fabrizio Lelli, 91–114. Firenze: Angelo Pontecorboli Editore, 2016.

Campanini, Saverio. "Francesco Giorgio's Criticism of the Vulgata: Hebraica Veritas or Mendosa Traductio?" In *Hebrew to Latin – Latin to Hebrew: The Mirroring of two Cultures in the Age of Humanism*, edited by Giulio Busi, 206–231. Turin: Nino Aragno, 2006.

Campanini, Saverio. "Jews and Christian Hebraists in Renaissance Italy." In *The Renaissance Speaks Hebrew*, edited by Giulio Busi and Silvana Greco, 184–195. Cinisello Balsamo: Silvana Editoriale, 2019.

Campanini, Saverio. "La radice dolorante. Ebrei e cristiani alla scoperta del giudaismo nel Rinascimento, apparso." In *L'interculturalità dell'ebraismo*, edited by Mauro Perani, 221–47. Ravenna: Longo, 2004.

Campanini, Saverio. "Le fonti ebraiche del *De Harmonia mundi* di Francesco Zorzi." *Annali di Ca' Foscari* 38, no. 3 (1999): 29–74.

Campanini, Saverio. "Mithridates deutsche Reise. Humanismus und Hebraistik zwischen Flucht und Ehrung." In *Buchkulturen des deutschen Humanismus (1430–1530). Netzwerke und Kristallisationspunkte*, edited by Anne Eusterschulte and Elke A. Werner. Leiden: Brill, in print.

Campanini, Saverio. "Nottole ad Atene. La qabbalah cristiana e la conversione degli ebrei." *Materia Giudaica* 19 (2014): 81–101.

Campanini, Saverio. "'Ovadyah Sforno: un banchiere filosofo ed esegeta." In *Cesena ebraica: Un percorso fra carte e codici*, edited by Marco Mengozzi, 103–118. Cesena: Biblioteca Malatestiana, 2019.

Campanini, Saverio. "Peculium Abrae. La grammatica ebraico-latina di Avraham de Balmes." *Annali di Ca' Foscari* 36, no. 3 (1997): 5–49.

Campanini, Saverio. "'Quasi post vindemias racemos colligens': Pietro Galatino und seine Verteidigung der christlichen Kabbala." In *Reuchlins Freunde und Gegner. Kommunikative Konstellationen eines frühneuzeitlichen Medienereignisses*, edited by Wilhelm Kühlmann, 69–88. Ostfildern: Jan Thorbecke Verlag, 2010.

Campanini, Saverio. "Reuchlins jüdische Lehrer aus Italien." In *Reuchlin und Italien*, edited by Gerald Dörner, 69–85. Stuttgart: Jan Thorbecke Verlag, 1999.

Campanini, Saverio. "'Thou bearest not the root, but the root thee': On the Reception of the *Sefer ha-Shorashim* in Latin." *Sefarad* 76, no. 2 (2016): 313–331.

Campanini, Saverio. "Un frammento sconosciuto dello pseudo-Zohar nella Roma del Rinascimento." *Materia Giudaica* 22 (2017): 3–14.

Campanini, Saverio. "Un intellettuale ebreo del Rinascimento: 'Ovadyah Sforno e i suoi rapporti con i cristiani." In *Verso l'epilogo di una convivenza. Gli ebrei a Bologna nel XVI secolo*, edited by Maria Giuseppina Muzzarelli, 99–128. Florence: Giuntina, 1996.

Campanini, Saverio. "Una lettera in ebraico e una in latino da Matthaeus Adriani a Caspar Amman sul nome di Gesù." *Bruniana & Campanelliana* 24, no. 1 (2018): 25–47.

Cassuto, Umberto. *Gli ebrei a Firenze nell'età del Rinascimento*. Florence: Tip. Galletti e Cocci, 1918.

Ego, Beate. "Konrad Pellican und die Anfänge der wissenschaftlichen christlichen Hebraistik im Zeitalter von Humanismus und Reformation." In *Humanismus und Reformation. Historische, theologische und pädagogische Beiträge zu deren Wechselwirkung*, edited by Reinhold Mokrosch and Helmut Merkel, 73–84. Münster, Hamburg and, London: LIT Verlag, 2001.

Gratia Dei, Johannes B. *Liber de confutatione Hebraicae sectae*. Roma: Eucharius Silber, 1500.

Greive, Hermann. "Die hebräische Grammatik Johannes Reuchlins *De rudimentis hebraicis*." *Zeitschrift für alttestamentliche Wissenschaft* 90, no. 3 (1978): 395–409.

Kaufmann, David. "Elia Menachem Chalfan on Teaching Hebrew to Non-Jews." *Jewish Quarterly Review* 9, no. 3 (1897): 500–08.
Kessler-Mesguich, Sophie. "L'enseignement de l'hébreu et de l'araméen par les premiers lecteurs royaux (1530–1560)." In *Histoire du Collège de France*. Vol. 1, edited by André Tuilier, 257–82. Paris: Fayard, 2006.
Kessler-Mesguich, Sophie. *Les études hébraïques en France de François Tissard à Richard Simon (1508–1680)*. Geneva: Droz, 2013.
Kessler-Mesguich, Sophie. "L'hébreu chez les hébraïsants chrétiens des XVIe et XVIIe siècles." In *Histoire Épistémologie Langage* 18, no. 1 (1996): 87–108.
Nestle, Eberhard. "Aus einem sprachwissenschaftlichen Werk von 1539." *Zeitschrift der deutschen Morgenländischen Gesellschaft* 58 (1904): 601–16.
Nestle, Eberhard. *Nigri, Böhm und Pellican. Ein Beitrag zur Anfangsgeschichte des hebräischen Sprachstudiums in Deutschland*. Tübingen: Heckenauer, 1893.
Olszowy-Schlanger, Judith. "A Christian Tradition of Hebrew Vocalisation in Medieval England." In *Semitic Studies in Honour of Edward Ullendorff*, edited by Geoffrey Khan, 126–46. Leiden: Brill, 2005.
Olszowy-Schlanger, Judith. "A School of Christian Hebraists in Thirteenth Century England: A Unique Hebrew-Latin-French and English Dictionary and Its Sources." *European Journal of Jewish Studies* 1, no. 2 (2007): 249–77.
Olszowy-Schlanger, Judith. "Christian Hebraism in Thirteenth Century England. The Evidence of Hebrew-Latin Manuscripts." In *Crossing Borders. Hebrew Manuscripts as a Meeting-Place of Cultures*, edited by Piet van Boxel and Sabine Arndt, 115–22. Oxford: Bodleian Library, 2009.
Olszowy-Schlanger, Judith. "Rachi en latin. Les gloses latines dans un manuscrit du commentaire de Rachi et les études hébraïques parmi des chrétiens dans l'Angleterre medieval." In *Héritages de Rachi,* edited by René-Samuel Sirat, 137–50. Paris: Éditions de l'Éclat, 2006.
Olszowy-Schlanger, Judith. "The Knowledge and Practice of Hebrew Grammar Among Christian Scholars in Pre-Expulsion England: The Evidence of "Bilingual" Hebrew-Latin Manuscripts." In *Hebrew Scholarship and the Medieval World*, edited by Nicholas R. M. De Lange, 107–28. Cambridge: Cambridge University Press, 2001.
Olszowy-Schlanger, Judith, ed. *Dictionnaire hébreu-latin-français de la Bible hébraïque de l'Abbey de Ramsey (XIIIe siècle)*. Brepols: Turnout, 2008.
Omont, Henri. *Journal autobiographique du Cardinal Jérôme Aléandre (1480–1530) publié d'après les manuscrits de Paris et d'Udine. Tiré des Notices et extraits des manuscrits de la Bibliothèque Nationale et d'autres bibliothèques (t. xxxv)*. Paris: C. Klincksieck, 1895.
Palladino, Alba. *Il De arcanis di Pietro Galatino. Traditio giudaica e nuove istanze di riforma*. Galatina: Congedo, 2004.
Paquier, Jules. *L'humanisme et la réforme. Jérôme Aléandre de sa naissance à la fin de son séjour à Brindes (1480–1529), avec son portrait, ses armes, un fac-simile de son écriture et un catalogue de ses œuvres*. Paris: F. Leroux, 1900.
Pelissier, Léon G. "Manuscrits de Gilles de Viterbe à la Bibliothèque Angélique (Rome)." *Revue des Bibliothèques* 2 (1892): 228–40.
Perles, Joseph. *Beiträge zur Geschichte der hebräischen und aramäischen Studien*. München: Theodor Ackermann, 1884.
Reuchlin, Johannes. *Briefwechsel, Band I, 1477–1505*, edited by Stephan Rhein, Matthias Dall'Asta and Gerald Dörner. Stuttgart and Bad Cannstatt: Frommann-Holzboog, 1999.
Reuchlin, Johannes. *Briefwechsel, Band I, 1477–1505*, edited by Stephan Rhein, Matthias Dall'Asta and Gerald Dörner. Stuttgart and Bad Cannstatt: Frommann-Holzboog, 1999.

Reuchlin, Johannes. *Briefwechsel. Band. II, 1506–1513*, edited by Matthias Dall'Asta and Gerald Dörner. Stuttgart and Bad Cannstatt: Frommann-Holzboog, 2003.
Reuchlin, Johannes. *Briefwechsel. Band III, 1514–1517*, edited by Matthias Dall'Asta and Gerald Dörner. Stuttgart and Bad Cannstatt: Frommann-Holzboog, 2007.
Reuchlin, Johannes. *Briefwechsel. Band IV, 1518–1522*, edited by Matthias Dall'Asta and Gerald Dörner. Stuttgart and Bad Cannstatt: Frommann-Holzboog, 2013.
Riggenbach, Bernhard, ed. *Das Chronikon des Konrad Pellikan. Zur vierten Säkularfeier der Universität Tübingen*. Basel: Bahnmaier's Verlag, 1877.
Saladin, Jean C. "'Lire Reuchlin lire la Bible': sur la préface des 'Rudimenta Hebraica.'" *Revue de l'Histoire des Religions* 222, no. 3 (2005): 287–320.
Scholem, Gershom. "Zur Geschichte der Anfänge der christlichen Kabbala." In *Essays Presented to Leo Baeck on the Occasion of His Eightieth Birthday*, 158–93. London: East and West Library, 1954.
Secret, François. "L'Ensis Pauli de Paulus de Heredia." *Sefarad* 26 (1966): 79–102 and 253–71
Signorelli, Giuseppe. *Il Cardinale Egidio da Viterbo. Agostiniano, umanista e riformatore*. Florence: Libreria Editrice Fiorentina, 1929.
Steimann, Ilona. *Jewish Book – Christian Book: Hebrew Manuscripts in Transition Between Jews and Christians in the Context of German Humanism*. Brepols: Turnhout, 2020.
Vulpinus, Theodor, ed. *Die Hauschronik Konrad Pellikans von Rufach. Ein Lebensbild aus der Reformationszeit*. Strassburg: J.H. Ed. Heitz, 1892.
Walde, Bernhard. *Christliche Hebräisten Deutschlands am Ausgang des Mittelalters*. Münster: Aschendorff, 1916.
Weil, Gérard E. *Élie Lévita. Humaniste et Massorète (1469–1549)*. Leiden: Brill, 1963.
Willi, Thomas. "Hebraica Veritas in Basel. Christliche Hebraistik aus jüdischen Quellen." In *International Organization for the Study of the Old Testament. Congress (17th)*, edited by André Lemaire, 375–97. Basel: Brill, 2001.
Zimmer, Eric. "Hebrew Letters of Two Sixteenth Century German Humanists." In *Revue des Études Juives* 141 (1982): 379–86.
Zimmer, Eric. "Jewish and Christian Collaboration in Sixteenth Century Germany." in *Jewish Quarterly Review* 71, no. 2 (1980): 69–88.
Zorzi, Francesco. *L'armonia del mondo*, Introduzione, traduzione e note di Saverio Campanini. Milan: Bompiani, 2010.

Ilona Steimann
Hebraism without Hebrew: Hartmann Schedel and the Conversion of his "Jewish" Books

The phenomenon of Hebraism has always been seen as closely connected to the study and some degree of mastery of the Hebrew language. In his article on the twelfth-century Hebraists, Michael Signer distinguished between "lexical Hebraism" and "cultural Hebraism," based upon whether Christian scholars could directly approach Hebrew texts themselves ("lexical Hebraism") or depended on Jewish interlocutors ("cultural Hebraism").[1] Similarly, regarding the seventeenth-century Christian Hebraists, Matt Goldish defined three levels of Hebraism, primary based on the degree of mastery of the Hebrew language. His categories encompassed Hebraists who could fluently read talmudic and rabbinic literature in its original Hebrew and Aramaic, those who had mastered biblical Hebrew but floundered in rabbinic writings, and those who could read some Hebrew but accessed Hebrew literature primarily in Latin and vernacular translations.[2] Finally, for Aaron Katchen, the term "Hebraist" refers to one interested in the Hebrew text of the Scripture and Jewish exegesis, regardless of whether he possesses any specific knowledge of the Hebrew tongue.[3]

Around 1500, when the key figure of this paper, the Nuremberg physician and humanist Hartmann Schedel (1440–1514), well known as the compiler of the Nuremberg *Weltchronik*, collected his Hebrew books, all levels of Christian Hebraism could be found in the German milieu. Its highest level was represented, for instance, by the famous German jurist, scholar, and Hebraist Johann Reuchlin (1455–1522), who had an excellent command of the Hebrew language, owned an impressive collection of Hebrew books, and published in 1506 a Hebrew grammar in Latin, *Rudimenta linguae hebraicae*.[4] Standing at the lowest level of Hebraism

---

[1] Michael Signer, "Polemic and Exegesis: The Varieties of Twelfth-Century Hebraism," in *Hebraica Veritas? Christian Hebraists and the Study of Judaism in Early Modern Europe*, eds. Allison Coudert and Jeffrey Shoulson (Philadelphia: University of Pennsylvania Press, 2004): 21.
[2] Matt Goldish, *Judaism in the Theology of Sir Isaac Newton* (Dordrecht: Klewer Academic Publishers, 1998), 17–19.
[3] Aaron Katchen, *Christian Hebraists and Dutch Rabbis: Seventeenth Century Apologetics and the Study of Maimonides' Mishneh Torah* (Cambridge, MA: Harvard University Press, 1985), 9.
[4] On Reuchlin's Hebrew books and Hebrew tutors, see Wolfgang von Abel und Reimund Leicht, eds., *Verzeichnis der Hebraica in der Bibliothek Johannes Reuchlins* (Ostfildern: Jan Thorbecke,

were figures such as Schedel himself, who, although he did not know Hebrew,[5] was highly interested in Hebrew books and purchased Reuchlin's *Rudimenta* for his library.[6]

In light of his lack of command of the Hebrew language, Schedel's enthusiasm for Jewish literature requires closer examination. In an attempt to define the purpose and use of the Hebrew codices in Schedel's library, this study analyzes how this lack of knowledge of Hebrew modelled Schedel's perception of the Hebrew book before and beyond its text, and how Hebrew codices were transformed in Schedel's hands in accordance with his ideas about Jews and Judaism. In order to provide a fuller picture of Schedel's collecting, the study also addresses the historical circumstances and literary climate with regard to the Jewish question in which Schedel's Hebraica collection emerged.

Schedel acquired his first two Hebrew books in 1501–1502 (a printed Bible and a manuscript prayer book),[7] whereas seven other manuscripts of prayer books and liturgical Pentateuchs entered his library as a group in 1504.[8] The Hebrew books

---

2005); Saverio Campanini, "Reuchlins Jüdische Lehrer aus Italien," in *Reuchlin und Italien*, ed. Gerald Dörner (Stuttgart: Jan Thorbecke, 1999): 69–85.

5 I am aware of no indication that Schedel had any direct knowledge of the Hebrew language. For further discussion, see Ilona Steimann, "Habent sua fata libelli: Hebrew Books from the Collection of Hartmann Schedel." (PhD diss., The Hebrew University, 2014), 20.

6 Neuburg an der Donau, Staatliche Bibliothek, no sign. Richard Stauber, *Die Schedelsche Bibliothek* (Freiburg im Breisgau: Herder, 1908), 50 and 145; Bernard Walde, *Christliche Hebraisten Deutschlands am Ausgang des Mittelalters* (Münster in Westphalia: Aschendorffsche Verlagsbuchhandlung, 1916), 186.

7 Munich, *Bayerische Staatsbibliothek* (henceforth BSB), Inc.c.a. 181 (Brescia, 1494) and Chm 410. *Gesamtkatalog der Wiegendrucke* (accessed July 27, 2022, https://www.gesamtkatalogderwiegendrucke.de/), 4200 and Moritz Steinschneider, *Die hebräischen Handschriften der K.Hof- und Staatsbibliothek in München* (Munich: Palm, 1895), 233, respectively. Stauber, *Die Schedelsche Bibliothek*, 50 and 149 (instead of Chm 410 it was identified erroneously as Chm 210); Paul Ruf, *Mittelalterliche Bibliothekskataloge Deutschlands und der Schweiz*, vol. 3, no. 1, *Bistum Augsburg* (Munich: C.H. Beck, 1932), 804 (following the error of Stauber, both manuscripts, Chm 210 and 410 were included); Walde, *Christliche Hebraisten Deutschlands*, 186–90. In Schedel's inscription in BSB, Chm 410, he dated its acquisition to 1502 (see note 13 below). I have dated all of Schedel's other acquisitions of Hebrew manuscripts on the basis of the manuscripts' new bindings, produced on Schedel's request immediately after the manuscripts were acquired. See Ilona Steimann, *Habent sua fata libelli*, 40–45. These two codices were bound by Francz Staindorffer in Nuremberg. Béatrice Hernad, ed., *Die Graphiksammlung des Humanisten Hartmann Schedel* (Munich: Prestel, 1990), 35; Ernst Kyriss, *Verzierte gotische Einbände im alten deutschen Sprachgebiet*, vol. 1 (Stuttgart: Max Hettler, 1954), no. 120.9 (the so-called Schedel Meister).

8 BSB Chm 14, 16, 21, 69, 88, 90, 298. Steinschneider, *Die hebräischen Handschriften*, 6, 7, 8, 46–47, 55–56 and 161. This group was bound in similar bindings by the successors of the monastic bindery, which belonged to the Order of Friars Minor (Franziskaner-Kloster) in Nuremberg.

in Schedel's collection were ordinary medieval biblical and liturgical codices, produced in the thirteenth to fifteenth centuries to meet the ritual needs of Ashkenazic Jewish communities and used in this context. They passed into Schedel's hands as a result of the persecutions and expulsions of Jews from German territories, namely from his hometown Nuremberg (1499)[9] and from Bamberg (1470s). The expulsion from Bamberg brought into Schedel's hands a tiny Siddur (BSB, Chm 410) that Schedel inscribed: "Iste liber hebraicus post expulsionem hebreorum ex Babenberga in sinagoga eorum (que postea consecrata fuit in pulchram capellam) repertus est. Hunc librum fratre ordinis praedicatorum mihi hartmanno Schedel doctori dono dederunt anno domini etc. 1502 die 27. Novembris Babenberge. Quem laceratum decorari feci ad laudem excelsi."[10]

Once in his possession, however, Hebrew books were not merely collectors' items: despite his ignorance of Hebrew, Schedel himself was actively involved in their "reshaping." He transformed his Hebrew codices, acquired in 1504, by adding both "prophetic" biblical verses, which according to Christian tradition announced the first coming of Christ, and typological-prefigurative printed images, which reflected a promise-fulfillment relationship between the Old and New Testaments.[11] These inscriptions and images were thus deployed to support the belief that Christ was Israel's promised Messiah.

Schedel wrote the inscriptions on the front and back flyleaves, which were added to his Hebrew manuscripts together with their new bindings as part of the process of adapting the codices for their new owner. In one of Schedel's Hebrew prayer books, originally produced in Franconia in the mid-thirteenth century (BSB, Chm 21), for instance, Schedel wrote at its beginning an inaccurate quotation from the Vulgate translation of Deuteronomy 28:36: "Ducet te dominus et

---

Ernst Kyriss, *Nürnberger Klostereinbände der Jahre 1433 bis 1525* (Erlangen: s.n., 1940), 74; Kyriss, *Verzierte gotische Einbände*, vol. 1, no. 121. 3, 7.

9 In the letter of Konrad Celtis to Schedel (BSB, Autogr. II A), to be discussed below, Celtis mentioned some Hebrew books, acquired by Schedel from an anonymous Nuremberg resident (see below in this paper). These were apparently the seven manuscripts acquired in 1504.

10 "This Hebrew book was discovered after the expulsion of the Jews from Bamberg in their synagogue (which afterwards was sanctified as a beautiful chapel). Monks of the Dominican order gave this book to me, Doctor Hartmann Schedel, as a gift on November 27, 1502 AD, in Bamberg. I have had this torn book restored in praise of the Sublime one" (BSB, Chm 410, fol. 262v).

11 Clearly manifested in Luke 24:44: ". . . everything written about me in the law of Moses, the prophets, and the psalms must be fulfilled." On typology, see Erich Auerbach, "Typological Symbolism in Medieval Literature," *Yale French Studies* 9 (1952): 3–10; Leonhard Goppelt, *Typos: The Typological Interpretation of the Old Testament in the New*, trans. Donald H. Madvig (Grand Rapids: William B. Eerdmans Publishing, 1982), 17–18; Robert Chazan, *Fashioning Jewish Identity in Medieval Western Christendom* (Cambridge: Cambridge University Press, 2004), 122.

regem tuu[m] quem constitue[ri]s sup[er] te in gentem qua[m] ignoras et patres."¹² Schedel used this verse, presented in Deuteronomy as Israel's punishment of exile for failure to fulfill the requirements of the covenant, apparently because of its "punishment" motif, suggesting that the expulsion of the Jews in Schedel's own time was a punishment for their stubbornness in not accepting the new covenant between God and Christians.

At the end of the same codex, Schedel misquoted Deuteronomy 18:15 (Vulgate): "Propheta[m] de medio tui de fratribus tuis sicut me sustitabit tibi d[omi]n[u]s de[us] tu[us] ip[su]m audies."¹³ In this verse God promised to Moses to raise up a prophet like him from among his brothers; not by chance a variation on this verse is also found in Acts 3:22, followed shortly thereafter by: "And all the prophets, as many as have spoken, from Samuel and those after him, also predicted these days" (Acts 3:24).¹⁴ This passage indicates, then, that this prophecy was fulfilled in Christ, who was the promised prophet like Moses. Deuteronomy 18:15 was understood in a similar sense in the writings of the Church Fathers, as for example in Eusebius' *Demonstratio evangelica* and in Ps.-Gregory of Nyssa's *Adversus Iudaeos*.¹⁵

The images inserted in Schedel's Hebrew books at the same time when the inscriptions were added also marked the beginning and end of the volumes, two in each, stuck to the first and last parchment leaves of the original corpus. Most of them were reprints from woodcut blocks originally carved in the atelier of Michael Wolgemut and Wilhelm Pleydenwurff to illustrate the incunabulum *Schatzbehalter oder Schrein der wahren Reichtümer des Heils und ewiger Seligkeit* (Treasure Keeper or Shrine of the True Richness of Salvation and Eternal Beatitude), which was published by Anton Koberger in Nuremberg in 1491.¹⁶ After the incunabulum was printed, the production of the *Schatzbehalter*'s reprints as single-leaf images was also, most likely, initiated by Koberger. To transform the *Schatzbehalter*'s

---

12 "The Lord will bring you, and the king whom you set over you, to a nation that neither you nor your ancestors have known." Here and elsewhere, biblical translations are based upon Michael Coogan, Marc Brettler and Carol Newsom, eds., *The New Oxford Annotated Bible with the Apocrypha* (Oxford: Oxford University Press, 2010). The inscription was cut from the front flyleaf, currently stuck on the pastedown of the front cover.
13 "The Lord your God will raise up for you a prophet like me from among your own people; you shall heed such a prophet." The inscription is written on the second back flyleaf^v.
14 See also in Acts 7:37.
15 Ivar August Heikel, ed., *Eusebius: Werke*, vol. 6, *Die Demonstratio evangelica* (Leipzig: J.C. Hinrichs'sche Buchhandlung, 1913), 17; Martin Albl, ed., *Pseudo-Gregory of Nyssa: Testimonies against the Jews* (Atlanta: Society of Biblical Literature, 2004), 17–20.
16 *Gesamtkatalog der Wiegendrucke*, 10329; Franz Stadler, *Michael Wolgemut und der Nürnberger Holzschnitt im letzten Drittel des XV. Jahrhunderts* (Strasbourg: Haitz, 1913), 2–28.

images from book illustrations into independently standing woodcuts, decorative borders were added. These were apparently intended to define the print as an object, differentiated from the text, and to elevate its status.[17] Koberger's printing shop was situated in Burgstraße, in the same area of Nuremberg where Schedel dwelled from 1488 on. Schedel therefore could easily have acquired these images from Koberger between 1491 and 1504.[18]

The text of the *Schatzbehalter* belongs to the genre of pious and moral guidance literature, which aimed to supply a lay audience with the means for contemplative practices.[19] It was composed of sermon-treatises written by the Franciscan friar Stephan Fridolin (1430–98),[20] who in the period of its creation was active as lector and preacher in the community of Poor Clares in Nuremberg.[21] The *Schatzbehalter* was composed of three books, which focused on the suffering of Christ (*Leiden Christi*). The second book constituted the main part of the work. It contained one hundred "objects" (*Gegenwürfe*; Latin *objecti*) from the Old and New Testaments, said to be related to the suffering of Christ.[22] This part of Fridolin's work was lavishly decorated with ninety-six images (of which five are repetitions), mostly depicting scenes from the Old and New Testaments. These images illustrate almost every one of the *Gegenwürfe*, which in turn include a

---

17 Marc P. McDonald, "'Extremely Curious and Important!': Reconstructing the Print Collection of Ferdinand Columbus," in *Collecting Prints and Drawings in Europe, c. 1500–1750*, eds. Christopher Baker, Caroline Elam and Genevieve Warwick (Aldershot: Ashgate, 2004): 38.
18 Sebastian Gulden, "An Ideal Neighborhood: The Physical Environment of the Early Dürer as a Space of Experience," in *The Early Dürer: Exhibition Organized by the Germanisches Nationalmuseum in Nuremberg, May 24 – September 2, 2012*, eds. Beate Böckem and Daniel Hess (Nuremberg: Verlag des Germanisches Nationalmuseum, 2012): 29–30; Hernad, ed., *Die Graphiksammlung*, 15.
19 Richard Bellm, *Der Schatzbehalter: ein Andachts-und Erbauungsbuch aus dem Jahre 1491* (Wiesbaden: Pressler, 1962), 1–2.
20 Although the author's name is not stated in the text, Fridolin's authorship can be established on the basis of an owner's inscription from 1498 in the copy from the Rebdorf monastery (today BSB, Rar. 293, front first flyleaf^v and fol. 350r), which attributes the *Schatzbehalter* to Stephan Fridolin. Ulrich Schmidt, *P. Stephan Fridolin: Ein Franziskaner Prediger des ausgehenden Mittelalters* (Munich: Lentner, 1910), 71–72. On Fridolin, see also Nicolaus Paulus, "Der Franziskaner Stephan Fridolin, ein Nürnberger Prediger," *Historisch-politische Blätter* 113 (1894): 465–83; Petra Seegets, *Passionstheologie und Passionsfrömmigkeit im ausgehenden Mittelalter: der Nürnberger Franziskaner Stephan Fridolin (gest. 1498) zwischen Kloster und Stadt* (Tübingen: Mohr Siebeck, 1998), 37–44.
21 Bert Roest, *Franciscan Literature of Religious Instruction before the Council of Trent* (Leiden: Brill, 2004), 83–84. Some scholars have also suggested that the *Schatzbehalter* was written specifically for this community. Seegets, *Passionstheologie und Passionsfrömmigkeit*, 178.
22 Stephan Fridolin, *Schatzbehalter oder Schrein der wahren Reichtümer des Heils und ewiger Seligkeit* (Nuremberg: Anton Koberger, 1491), fols. f iiii^v-H vi^v. For a detailed description of the *Schatzbehalter*'s content, see Seegets, *Passionstheologie und Passionsfrömmigkeit*, 292–306.

verbal description of the images to elucidate the depicted scenes.[23] According to Fridolin, the figurative representations were intended for the sake of lay people. They were to play an interpretive and mnemonic role, aiding in the better understanding and memory of the content.[24]

Out of the ninety-six woodcuts of the second part of Fridolin's work, Schedel had in his graphic holdings twenty-four images.[25] He used twelve of these in his Hebrew books,[26] thanks to Fridolin's typological-prefigurative interpretations of them. These interpretations were undoubtedly known to Schedel through the text of the *Schatzbehalter* itself, an entire copy of which he had in his library and which he possibly even used in his *Weltchronik*.[27]

For example, two images from the *Schatzbehalter*, inserted by Schedel in the aforementioned prayer book (BSB, Chm 21), depict the Midianites taking out Joseph from the cistern (based on Gen. 37:28) and the heroic deeds of Samson (based on Judg. 14:5–6, 15:4–6 and 15–16, and 16:1–3).

The first scene represents a cistern in the centre of a hilly landscape (Figure 1).[28] A Midianite takes Joseph out of the cistern. Behind the Midianite on the right is a

---

23 Andrea Thurnwald, "Zur Ikonographie der Capestrano-Tafel: Pater Stephan Fridolin als geistiger Urheber ihres theologischen Programms," in *Der Bußprediger Capestrano auf dem Domplatz in Bamberg: Eine Bamberger Tafel um 1470/75. Eine Didaktische Ausstellung des Historischen Museums Bamberg und des Lehrstuhls I für Kunstgeschichte an der Universität Bamberg*, ed. Hubert Russ (Bamberg: Historisches Museum, 1989): 19–48.
24 Fridolin, *Schatzbehalter*, fol. f iv^v.
25 The *Schatzbehalter*'s images from Schedel's collection which were not inserted in his books but were preserved as self-standing prints in the *Staatliche Graphische Sammlung* (henceforth SGS) in Munich: Inv. Nr. 171530a D, 118186 D, 118510 D, 118577 D, 171565 D, 118578 D, 118184 D, and four without a signature. In addition, the *Schatzbehalter*'s *Resurrection of Lazarus* was inserted by Schedel and remained in his copy of Marsilio Ficino's *Theologia Platonica de immortalitate animorum* (BSB, 2 Inc.c.a. 1204).
26 Most of the *Schatzbehalter* images were, however, removed from Schedel's Hebrew manuscripts in the course of the nineteenth-century for the purpose of separating genres. Except for two images in BSB, Chm 14, which remained in the manuscript, other images from the *Schatzbehalter* are presently preserved in SGS: Inv. Nr. 171521, 171522, 171523, 171524, 171525, 171526, 171527, 171528, 171529, 171530.
27 This copy has not survived, but is mentioned in Schedel's catalogue, compiled by him between 1498 and 1507: Berlin, *Preussische Staatsbibliothek*, MS germ. fol. 447, fol. 277r. Ruf, *Mittelalterliche Bibliothekskataloge*, vol. 3/1, *Bistum Augsburg*, 834; Stauber, *Die Schedelsche Bibliothek*, 137. See also Nikolaus Henkel, "Ein Zeugnis zum 'Schatzbehälter' des Stephan Fridolin in der deutschen Weltchronik Hartmann Schedels," in *500 Jahre Schedelsche Weltchronik*, ed. Stephan Füssel (Nuremberg: Hans Karl, 1994): 165–70.
28 Formerly a second front or first back flyleaf (unfortunately, in this case, it is unknown which image was added in the beginning and which one at the end of the manuscript), currently SGS, Inv. Nr. 171 524 D. Bellm, *Der Schatzbehalter*, 15–16; Hernad, ed., *Die Graphiksammlung*, 116.

Figure 1: *Midianites taking out Joseph from the cistern.* Nuremberg, after 1491. Staatliche Graphische Sammlung München, Inv. Nr. 171 524 D.

group of his people, whereas on the left another Midianite purchases Joseph from his brother. Also on the left is another group with camels and sheep in front of the well. The text in the *Schatzbehalter* that corresponds to this image (Figure 2) belongs to the second article of *Gegenwurf* 11, entitled *Alle Wirdigkeit hat Cristum bedeut* (Christ Sig-

Figure 2: *Midianites taking out Joseph from the cistern*. Fig. 14 in the Schatzbehalter. Nuremberg, 1491. Bayerische Staatsbibliothek München, Rar. 293.

nifies All Merits).[29] This text deals with Christ's merits as prefigured in the firstborn sons of the Old Testament. When discussing the matter of the "sale" (redemption) of the firstborn,[30] Fridolin explains that Christ had to be sold by priests to his mother. Similarly, he was sold by Judas at his betrayal. Regarding figure 14, Fridolin bases his

---

29 Fridolin, *Schatzbehalter*, fols. h v^v and h vi^r.
30 Based on Exodus 13:13–16 and Numbers 3:45–47.

commentary on Genesis 37:28, noting that Joseph was sold by his brothers and by the Midianites and Ishmaelites in Egypt in the same way that Christ also was sold. For Fridolin, Christ, the son of God, born before all creatures, occupied a similar position as Joseph, who was the actual firstborn son of Rachel – and also of Jacob, not chronologically, but from the point of view of his inheritance and dignity. Therefore, according to Fridolin, Joseph represented a prefiguration of Christ – as mentioned in the *Pascali sacramento* of Leo the Great, to which Fridolin referred.[31]

The second scene inserted in this prayer book portrays Samson carrying the gate of Gaza on his left shoulder and stepping on a lion with his left foot (Figure 3).[32] Behind him is a city, representing Gaza, in front of which is a wheat field burnt by Samson. In his right hand, Samson holds a donkey jaw, with which he killed a thousand Philistines, who lie prostrate on the right. This scene of Samson's heroic deeds and its clarification by Fridolin in the *Schatzbehalter* (Figure 4) were titled as the previous image, *Alle Wirdigkeit hat Cristum bedeut*.

It belongs to the first article of *Gegenwurf* 15, which deals with Nazirite dignity as prefigured in Old Testament figures and fulfilled in Christ.[33] In the text to this image, Fridolin wrote that Samson was usually remembered for his heroic deeds, but not for his Nazarene quality, i.e. his consecration to God by a vow from birth, which turned him into a holy person and prefiguration of Christ. Referring to Judges 13:5: ". . . for the boy shall be a Nazirite to God from birth," Fridolin compares this quality of Samson to that of Christ, in whose regard it was said in Matthew 2:23: "There he made his home in a town called Nazareth, so that what had been spoken through the prophets might be fulfilled, 'He will be called a Nazorean.'" "Nazareus" (or "Nazarenus," e.g. Mark 10:47) in the Gospel's case meant an inhabitant of the city of Nazareth – the place where Jesus grew up and part of Christological geography, based on its second, equally important meaning – a "Nazirite," from Hebrew *nazir* (devoted to God), a characteristic that described Christ and established his connection to the Old Testament Nazirites, particularly to Samson. Like Christ, Samson was conceived thanks to divine intervention and consequently became a holy person and redeemer of his

---

[31] "hic est qui in Abel occisus est, et in Isaac pedibus colligatus est, et in Jacob peregrinatus est, et in Joseph venundatus est . . ." (This is he [Christ] who was slain in Abel, and in Isaac was bound at his feet, and in Jacob wandered about, and in Joseph was sold . . .). Jacques-Paul Migne, ed. *Patrologia Latina*, vol. 56, Leo I, *Sermones* (Paris: Imprimerie Catholique, 1865), 1136.
[32] Formerly second front or first back flyleaf, currently SGS, Inv. Nr. 171 525 D. Bellm, *Der Schatzbehalter*, 17–18; Hernad, ed., *Die Graphiksammlung*, 65. The same single-leaf print with a different border is found in the collection of Ferdinand Columbus (1488–1539), British Museum, Department of Prints and Drawings, Inv. No. 2470. McDonald, "Extremely Curious and Important!," 38.
[33] Fridolin, *Schatzbehalter*, fol. k ii^v.

Figure 3: *Heroic deeds of Samson*. Nuremberg, after 1491. Staatliche Graphische Sammlung München, Inv. Nr. 171 525 D.

people.[34] The term "Nazareus" was interpreted in this sense by medieval theologians, for example by Remigius of Auxerre, who stated that "Nazareus" signified both someone from the city of Nazareth (the home of the young Jesus) and a holy person devoted to God by a vow (he mentioned Samson in this context in

---

34 James Sanders, "Ναζωραῖος in Matt 2:23," *Journal of Biblical Literature* 84, no. 2 (1965): 169–72.

Figure 4: *Heroic deeds of Samson*. Fig. 21 in the *Schatzbehalter*. Nuremberg, 1491. Bayerische Staatsbibliothek München, Rar. 293.

particular).³⁵ An additional meaning added by Remigius in this homily derived "Nazareus" from the Hebrew *netser*, having in mind Jerome's commentary on

---

35 Jacques-Paul Migne, ed. *Patrologia Latina*, vol. 131, Remigius Antissiodorensis, *Homiliae* (Paris: Imprimerie Catholique, 1853), 899.

Matthew 2:23 with his rendering of Isaiah 11:1, "Exiet virga de radice Jesse, et *Nazaraeus* de radice ejus conscendet,"[36] instead of the Vulgate's "Et egredietur uirga de radice Iesse et *flos* de radice eius ascendet" (italics mine).[37] In replacing "flos" by "Nazaraeus," Jerome claimed to be translating in accordance with the truth of the Hebrew original, basing his view on the phonetic similarity between *netser* and *Nazaraeus*. In this way, Jerome concretized the interpretation of this verse as particularly related to Jesus who was a *Nazaraeus* born to the royal line of David, and provided an important basis for its medieval interpreters.[38]

In these two examples, as well as in the others not represented here, the typological-prefigurative role of the *Schatzbehalter*'s woodcuts inserted in Schedel's Hebrew codices is quite obvious. But in contrast to the non-Hebrew books from Schedel's library, which were also lavishly decorated by him with images,[39] the prints in Schedel's Hebrew books, as in this case, had no direct relation to the books' texts. Similarly to his inscriptions placed at the beginning and end of the books, these images were associated with the books as a whole, addressing their contents in general. The definite typological-prefigurative meaning of the images, as clarified by Fridolin in the *Schatzbehalter*, suggested, in turn, that all the Hebrew Scriptures prefigure Christianity.

The typology of the *Schatzbehalter* and that of Schedel's additions to his Hebrew books were, however, instruments serving different goals. Speaking broadly, the purpose of Fridolin's use of typology in his work was didactic, intended to instruct his lay audience in piety. It focused not on giving Christian meaning to Old Testament events and figures, but rather on explaining Christian events, figures, and concepts by means of their Old Testament prototypes. In Schedel's case, by contrast, the juxtaposition of typological imagery with Hebrew text opposed in meaning to Christian dogma created a polemic with the Hebrew book itself. This dialogue aimed to demonstrate that the real meaning "hidden" in the Hebrew Scriptures predicted, prefigured, and symbolized Christianity. In other words, the role of typology in this case was indeed to be found in giving Christian meaning to the Old Testament events and figures. By adding prophetic inscriptions and typological woodcuts to his Hebrew books, therefore, Schedel actually engaged in a kind of anti-Jewish polemic. His additions evoked the idea

---

[36] "A shoot shall come out from the stump of Jesse, and a *Nazaraeus* shall grow out of his roots." Jacques-Paul Migne, ed. *Patrologia Latina*, vol. 26, Hieronymus Stridonensis, *Commentarium in Evangelium Matthaei* (Paris: Imprimerie Catholique, 1845), 29.
[37] "A shoot shall come out from the stump of Jesse, and a branch shall grow out of his roots."
[38] In the same vein, Schedel wrote out Isaiah 11:1 in the Vulgate translation on the second back flyleaf^v of one of his liturgical Pentateuchs (BSB, Chm 16).
[39] Hernad, ed., *Die Graphiksammlung*, 37–39.

of Jewish misunderstanding of the truth about the Messiah announced in the Old Testament, and the Hebrew book itself played the role of the Jew against whom Schedel polemicized.

The type of polemic represented in Schedel's Hebrew books via the addition of typological inscriptions and images used, then, biblical argumentation against the Jews, i.e., proofs, prophecies, and prefigurations taken from the Bible.[40] The notion of typological interpretation of the Old Testament was not new. The promise-fulfilment relation between the two Testaments was one of the basic Christian beliefs and often served also as one of the main Christian arguments in anti-Jewish polemics by the earliest Christian authors. The same was true of works by Schedel's contemporaries, such as the *Stern des Meschiah* (1477) of the Dominican preacher Peter Schwarz, alias Petrus Nigri (c. 1434–1483).[41] A copy of this work was found in Schedel's library.[42] By means of typological interpretation, Nigri demonstrated the main dogmas of the Christian faith and the punishment of the Jews for their unbelief.[43]

Jews were treated in a similar way by the Nuremberg barber-surgeon, Meistersinger, and printer Hans Folz (c. 1437–1513), whom Schedel perhaps knew personally.[44] Folz focused entirely on biblical argumentation in his *Fastnachtspiel*, *Kaiser Constantinus* (1473) and in *Reimpaarspruch, Christ und Jude* (1479), which

---

[40] Amos Funkenstein, "Basic Types of Christian Anti-Jewish Polemics in the Later Middle Ages," *Viator* 2 (1971): 374.

[41] Christopher Ocker, "German Theologians and the Jews in the Fifteenth Century," in *Jews, Judaism and the Reformation in Sixteenth-Century Germany*, eds. Dean Phillip Bell and Stephen Burnett (Leiden: Brill, 2006): 46–47.

[42] BSB, 4 Inc.c.a. 99m. It was included in Schedel's library register from c. 1498 (BSB, Clm 263, fol. 142r) and in its later version from c. 1507, which survived in a copy of Schedel's *Familienbuch* from 1552 (Berlin, Preußische Staatsbibliothek, MS germ. fol. 447, fol. 272v). Ruf, *Mittelalterliche Bibliothekskataloge* 3/1, *Bistum Augsburg*, 829; Stauber, *Die Schedelsche Bibliothek*, 129 and 197.

[43] The incarnation of Christ and redemption of Christians, for example, were foretold, according to him, in Jeremiah 14:7–9: ". . . wie gancz clerlich der prophet redet von der menschwerdung und von der armut des suns des almechtigen gottes der do also ersheinen ist auff der erden umb unser sünd willen die zu bueßen." (". . . how clearly the prophet speaks of the incarnation and poverty of the son of the almighty God, who appeared in the world to redeem us on account of our sins.") Petrus Nigri, *Stern des Meschiah* (Esslingen: Konrad Fyner, 1477); no original foliation; BSB, 4 Inc.c.a. 99m, fol. [41r].

[44] Folz was a close friend of the judge and member of the Nuremberg Great Council, Anton Haller, for whom he wrote the 1482 *Pestregimen in Prosa*. Schedel was Haller's son-in-law and through him was possibly acquainted with Folz. Hanns Fischer, "Hans Folz: Altes und Neues zur Geschichte seines Lebens und seiner Schriften," *Zeitschrift für deutsches Altertum und deutsche Literatur* 95, no. 3 (1966): 220–21.

drew heavily from *Kaiser Constantinus*. Both found in Schedel's library as well,[45] these works were written in the form of theological disputations, treating doctrinal issues such as the Trinity, the two natures of Christ, the virginity of Mary, Christ's passion, and the Eucharist. Like Nigri, in these works Folz especially emphasized that the Old Testament prefigures and confirms the New Testament – a concept clearly manifest in the following lines from *Kaiser Constantinus*: "Hör, Jüd, do merk pei und verstee, das alle geschicht der alten ee und aller propheten red gemein, ein figur der neüen ee ist allein."[46]

According to Christopher Ocker, this prevalent biblicism in German intellectual circles is to be linked to the expulsion of the Jews from German cities in the course of the fifteenth century. The diminishing Jewish urban presence, together with the threat emerging from other perceived enemies of the Christian faith (e.g., Hussites, heretics, witches), led to the Christian neglect of Jewish biblical commentaries, no longer deemed necessary for anti-Jewish polemic, and to their complete replacement by Christian commentaries concerned solely with the Christological meaning of the Holy Scriptures.[47]

Therefore, in spite of Nigri's good command of Hebrew, he used it in the *Stern des Meschiah* not to gain a deeper understanding of Jewish tradition, but rather only for access to biblical verses – translating, transliterating, and commenting on them in a typological sense. Regarding the purpose of his treatise, he noted

---

45 *Kaiser Constantinus*: BSB, Cgm 439, fols. 1r–19r. Karin Schneider, *Die deutschen Handschriften der Bayerischen Staatsbibliothek München, Cgm 351–500* (Wiesbaden: Harrassowitz, 1973), 258–62. This text was previously attributed to Folz's predecessor, Hans Rosenplut (Johann Andreas Schmeller, *Die deutschen Handschriften der K. Hof- und Staatsbibliothek zu München*, vol. 1. (Munich: Palm, 1866), 71–72), but recent publications have established the authorship of Hans Folz. See Helmut Lomnitzer, "Das Verhältnis des Fastnachtspiels vom 'Kaiser Constantinus' zum Reimpaarspruch 'Christ und Jude' von Hans Folz," *Zeitschrift für deutsches Altertum und deutsche Literatur* 92, no. 4 (1964): 277–78; Schneider, *Die deutschen Handschriften*, 258–59. On fol. 18r there is an ownership inscription of Anton Haller, from whom Schedel apparently received this codex. See above, note 47 and Fischer, "Hans Folz": 220. The text of the *Kaiser Constantinus* was published in Adelbert von Keller, ed., *Fastnachtspiele aus dem fünfzehnten Jahrhundert*, vol. 3 (Stuttgart: Literarischer Verein, 1853), 797–819. *Christ und Jude*: BSB, Rar. 182 Beibd. 4. Stauber, *Die Schedelsche Bibliothek*, 177. Published in Hanns Fischer, *Hans Folz: Die Reimpaarsprüche* (Munich: C. H. Beck, 1961), 226–42. See also Lomnitzer, "Das Verhältnis des Fastnachtspiels": 277–91.
46 "Hear, Jew, remember and understand that all stories of the Old Testament, and all that the prophets commonly said, is but a figure of the New Testament." BSB, Cgm 439, fol. 4v (Schedel's foliation: fol. 114v). Keller, ed., *Fastnachtspiele*, vol. 3, 801. See also Edith Wenzel, *"Do worden die Judden alle geschant": Rolle und Funktion der Juden in spätmittelalterlichen Spielen* (Munich: Fink, 1992), 226–27.
47 Ocker, "German Theologians and the Jews," 62.

that he wrote it to satisfy the spiritual hunger of the Jews,[48] and consequently used Hebrew as a missionary instrument. Nevertheless, his main audience in this case was Christian, in contrast to the sermons he delivered in Hebrew, which Jews were compelled to attend.[49] In the *Stern des Meschiah*, the Hebrew verses, therefore, were primarily intended to enhance the prestige of the author, whose knowledge of Hebrew was supposed to imply a more effective polemic.

The same can be said concerning Folz's use of Hebrew, of which he apparently had some knowledge. Folz transliterated and fairly accurately translated the Hebrew liturgical poem *Adon olam* (Lord of the Universe, or Eternal Lord) in his play, *Die alt und neu ee* (1473) in order to impress his audience with the authentic sound of the Jewish prayer service.[50] In the *Kaiser Constantinus* he also included a passage that was supposed to represent a Hebrew prayer, opening with "*Cados, cadas adanei . . .*" (Holy, holy, the Lord) – but it is actually merely a mixture of Hebrew, Greek, Latin, and undefined words.[51] Such pseudo-Hebrew was here intended to ridicule and satirize the language of the Jews and their rituals.[52]

Both Folz's literary activity as well as Nigri's sermons and tractates thus constituted works of a public character, performed in front of or read aloud by regular citizens. Nigri, who preached in Nuremberg in the same years in which Folz composed his early works, was possibly Folz's source of inspiration. He seems to have had an influence on the content and goals of Folz's works,[53] which aimed to provide instruction in apologetics to their lay audience and eventually to convince Jews to embrace Christianity.[54] However, in comparison to Folz's early

---

48 BSB, 4 Inc.c.a. 99m, fol. 5v.
49 Peter Browe, *Die Judenmission im Mittelalter und die Päpste* (Rome: Università Gregoriana, 1973), 69–70; Elisheva Carlebach, *Divided Souls: Converts from Judaism in Germany, 1500–1750* (New Haven & London: Yale University Press, 2001), 162.
50 Keller, ed., *Fastnachtspiele*, vol. 1, 7–8. David Price, "Hans Folz's Anti-Jewish Carnival Plays," *Fifteenth Century Studies* 19 (1992): 214–15. The suggestion of Caroline Huey that Folz probably used Schedel's library and that his *Adon olam* was translated from one of Schedel's Hebrew manuscripts does not seem to be correct, since Schedel acquired his Hebrew manuscripts in 1500 at the earliest, whereas *Die alt und neu ee* was written by Folz in 1474. Caroline Huey, *Hans Folz and Print Culture in Late Medieval Germany: The Creation of Popular Discourse* (Aldershot: Ashgate, 2012), 81; Wenzel, "Do worden die Judden alle geschant," 202.
51 BSB, Cgm 439, fols. 112r–112v. Keller, ed., *Fastnachtspiele*, vol. 3, 798.
52 Price, "Hans Folz's Anti-Jewish Carnival Plays," 215.
53 Lomnitzer, "Das Verhältnis des Fastnachtspiels," 290. Michael Toch connected Nigri's Nuremberg sermons from 1478 to Folz's works, written in the 1470s–1480s. Michael Toch, *Die Juden im mittelalterlichen Reich* (Oldenbourg: Wissenschaftsverlag, 2003), 65.
54 John Martin, "Dramatized Disputations: Late Medieval German Dramatizations of Jewish-Christian Religious Disputations, Church Policy, and Local Social Climates," *Medieval Encounters* 8, no. 2–3 (2002): 220.

works, which – as noted by John Martin – treat Jews "as tolerated outsiders who are also potential converts", his later plays convey that there was no place for the Jews in Christian society.[55] This shift was apparently related to the fact that despite all missionizing efforts and encouragement by the City Council, the actual rate of conversion in Nuremberg and neighboring cities was limited to a few individual cases only.[56] Hence, by the time of the expulsion of 1499 conversion was no longer perceived as a realistic alternative. It appears then that during the final period of the Jewish presence in Nuremberg, simultaneous conversion and expulsion attempts by the authorities ultimately meant that the Jews as "Jews" could not continue their existence in the city.

The specific motivation for the final expulsion of 1499, on the other hand, was not a result of the failure of conversion attempts, but was rather related to Jewish commercial activities, perceived by Nuremberg authorities and citizens as socially harmful. Previously Jews had practiced usury, forbidden to Christians according to canon law,[57] thereby fulfilling a necessary economic function in the Empire. In consideration of this function and due to the high taxes they paid, Jews were tolerated and given permission to live in Christian lands. However, in the fifteenth century, as a result of general socio-economic developments in German cities, they were pushed to the margins of local economic life, so much so that their presence in the cities was no longer considered necessary.[58] In Nuremberg, the expansion of non-Jewish banking together with increased demand for credit, which Jews were unable to meet, led to the loss by Jews of their high-ranking and patrician clients. As demonstrated by Michael Toch, the credit operations of the Nuremberg Jews between 1483 and 1499 were mainly limited to small loans, which

---

55 Martin, "The Depiction of Jews in the Carnival Plays and Comedies of Hans Folz and Hans Sachs in Early Modern Nuremberg," *Baylor Journal of Theatre and Performance* 3, no. 2 (2006): 46. See also in Martin, "Dramatized Disputations," 226. The relationship between Folz's anti-Jewish polemic and the policy of the Nuremberg Council has been discussed by some scholars. For example, Johannes Janota suggested that Folz, as a new citizen, was eager to be a part of the Council. See Johannes Janota, "Hans Folz in Nürnberg," in *Philologie und Geschichtswissenschaft. Demonstrationen literarischer Texte des Mittelalters*, ed. Heinz Rupp (Heidelberg: Quelle und Meyer, 1977), 76.
56 Mordechai Breuer, Yacov Guggenheim, and Arye Maimon, eds., *Germania Judaica*, vol. 3, no. 2 (Tübingen: Mohr Siebeck, 1995), 1012–13.
57 Guido Kisch, *The Jews in Medieval Germany. A Study of their Legal and Social Status* (New York: Ktav, 1970), 191–97.
58 Markus J. Wenninger, *Man bedarf keiner Juden mehr. Ursachen und Hintergründe ihrer Vertreibung aus den deutschen Reichsstädten im 15. Jahrhundert* (Vienna, Cologne & Graz: Böhlau, 1981), 137–45.

served customers from the lower and middle strata of society.⁵⁹ This "natural" decline of the economic activities of Nuremberg's Jewish community was fully supported by the authorities. In the 1470s, as part of the city's municipal law reform (*Stadtrechtsreformation*), which aimed to bring the traditional customs of German legislation into line with Roman law, the authorities restricted Jewish money lending to the point of prohibiting the charging of interest.⁶⁰

The alleged harmfulness of Jewish economic activities, then, was apparently a central issue in the expulsion of Jews from Nuremberg. It was also portrayed as such in a note that appears in two of Schedel's manuscripts, BSB, Clm 431 and Clm 951. Both manuscripts are miscellanies of texts, predominantly related to Nuremberg, and were copied by Schedel in the late fifteenth and early sixteenth centuries.⁶¹ The note opens: "De propulsione Iudeorum ex Nüremberga. Gens perfida Iudeorum crescens Nürembergae in personis ac malicia. Per plura dampna [damna] in usuris ac rebus mobilibus Christianos molenscans [molescens]."⁶² Although the source of Schedel's note is unknown, its content, which emphasizes the harm done by Jewish usury, is quite close to that of the imperial edict of 1498 that expelled the Jews.⁶³ Except for this note and Schedel's representation of the Jews in his *Weltchronik* as bloodthirsty people who murder Christian children and desecrate the Eucharistic host, which may well have reflected his literary sources more than his personal opinion,⁶⁴ Schedel did not address the Jewish question

---

59 Michael Toch, "Der jüdische Geldhandel in der Wirtschaft des Deutschen Spätmittelalters: Nürnberg 1350–1499." *Blätter für Deutsche Landesgeschichte* 1, no. 17 (1981): 306–10.
60 Michael Toch, "'Umb gemeyns Nutz und Nottdurfft willen': Obrigkeitliches und jurisdiktionelles Denken bei der Austreibung der Nürnberg Juden 1498–99." *Zeitschrift für historische Forschung* 1 (1984): 15–16. Some years before the expulsion, Peter Stahel, the legal adviser (*Syndikus*) of the city of Nuremberg, wrote to Willibald Pirckheimer his opinion that lending on interest to Christians is forbidden to Jews according to both the Torah and canon law. Emil Reicke, ed., *Willibald Pirckheimer: Briefwechsel*, vol. 1 (Munich: C. H. Beck, 1940), 295–96.
61 Karl Halm, Georg Laubmann, and Wilhelm Meyer, eds., *Catalogus codicum latinorum Bibliothecae Regiae Monacensis*, vol. 1, no. 1 (Wiesbaden: Harrassowitz, 1968), 117–18 and 214 respectively. In BSB, Clm 431 the note on the expulsion of the Jews was written on a piece of paper inserted between fols. 53 and 54 (as fol. 53a), suggesting that this version was earlier and served as a model for the nicely recopied version on the first folio of BSB, Clm 951.
62 "On the expulsion of the Jews from Nuremberg. The perfidious Jewish people of Nuremberg increased in number and wickedness. They oppressed Christians with many losses in interest and movables." BSB, Clm 431, fol. 53aᵛ and Clm 951, fol. 64v [1v].
63 Johann F. Böhmer, ed., *Regesta Imperii*, vol. 14, no. 2: *Ausgewählte Regesten des Kaiserreiches unter Maximilian I. 1493–1519* (Vienna, Cologne & Weimar: Böhlau Verlag, 1993), 404, no. 6459 and 409, no. 6491.
64 The majority of Schedel's *Weltchronik*, as noted already in Schedel's time by his friend Johannes Trithemius, derived from the *Supplementum chronicarum* (*Supplement to the Chronicles*)

directly. His attitude towards the Jews can therefore be deduced on the basis of indirect evidence only, such as facts from his biography and the treatment of his Hebrew books.

Schedel, who settled back in Nuremberg in 1481, found the city's government making efforts to expel the Jews. As the city physician and a respected resident, Schedel was made an appointee of the Nuremberg Great Council (Genannter des Großen Rates) in 1482,[65] and must have taken part in its anti-Jewish campaign. Despite a limited success of conversion and a certain suspicion vis-à-vis actual converts,[66] Jewish conversion to Christianity, as mentioned, remained the overarching goal in the years before the expulsion and generally guided the polemic. In this situation, the use of prefigurations and proofs taken from the Bible was considered the most effective means to enlighten "blind" Jews and bring them to accept baptism. The same type of anti-Jewish polemic was, not unexpectedly, demonstrated in Schedel's Hebrew books by means of "prophetic" inscriptions and typological images, but with a considerable difference in its aims. In 1501–1504, when Schedel collected his Hebrew books and added polemical inscriptions and images to them, the object of his polemics was absent, since there were no longer any Jews in his city. If the intended public function of Folz's works and Nigri's sermons, upon which his printed treatise was based, was quite obvious, the main recipient of Schedel's visual additions to his books seems to have been Schedel himself.[67] Naturally, his library also served his friends and possibly other scholars, but they were not the target audience of these additions, since his library was first of all a private collection and not a public place. With regard to both his Hebrew and non-Hebrew books, therefore, Schedel's artistic interventions were directed inwards, towards the books themselves, and were supposed to "improve"

---

of Jacopo Foresti of Bergamo, in its edition of 1490 (Venice). Christopher Reske, *The Production of Schedel's Nuremberg Chronicle* (Wiesbaden: Harrassowitz, 2000), 169.

65 Ferdinand Johann Roth, ed., *Verzeichnis aller Genannten des größern Raths: von den ältesten bis auf die neuesten Zeiten* (Nuremberg: Johann Georg Milbradt, 1802), 44. See also Stauber, *Die Schedelsche Bibliothek*, 44.

66 For instance, *Fortalitium fidei* (*Fortress of the Faith*), composed in 1460 by the Spanish Franciscan Alonso d'Espina, was known for its extreme position against the Jews and Spanish *conversos*. The author regarded *conversos* as secret Jews who tried to injure and destroy Christians. Benzion Netanyahu, "Alonso de Espina: Was He a New Christian?" *Proceedings of the American Academy for Jewish Research* 43 (1976): 108. The copy of this work mentioned in Schedel's catalogues has been lost, so it remains unknown which edition was in his possession. It is, however, known that one of its editions was printed in Nuremberg in 1485 by Koberger at his own expense. BSB, Clm 263, fol. 142r and PSB, MS germ. fol. 447, fol. 272v. Ruf, *Mittelalterliche Bibliothekskataloge*, vol. 3, no. 1, *Bistum Augsburg*, 828; Stauber, Die *Schedelsche Bibliothek*, 129.

67 Hernad, ed., *Die Graphiksammlung*, 66.

the books for their own sake, namely to make the books "better" in the sense of consummating their meaning, regardless of any intended or actual readers.

In the case of the Hebrew books, Schedel even went a step further. Since he was not really aware of their contents,[68] his perception of the Hebrew book was rather of the nature of a "Jewish object" per se, as opposed to of a specifically written source. The fact of their being "Jewish" rendered them in his eyes as representative of the Jews in general. Like the Jews, therefore, the books had to be converted – namely from a Jewish object into an object laden with Christian typological meaning. This goal was achieved via the addition of prophetic inscriptions and typological imagery at the beginning and end of the books, thereby applicable to the "Jewish object" as a whole. These additions surrounded all the books' contents, and suggested that the true spiritual meaning of everything written in these books in Hebrew was in fact to announce the new Christian dispensation. Pentateuchs and prayer books suit this interpretation well, even if Schedel was not aware of the contents of the Hebrew books he owned.

On the other hand, that Schedel treated his Hebrew books as "Jewish objects" in general was not an outcome of his lack of interest in their contents, but rather a function of his own ignorance of the Hebrew language, and of the absence of both Jewish interlocutors in his surroundings after the expulsion as well as qualified Christian Hebraists. Such an interest in Jewish literature regardless of the level of Hebrew mastery was not rare among Schedel's contemporaries. Two letters found in Schedel's library are highly indicative of what Hebrew manuscripts could ultimately mean for their Christian collectors who could not read them and were not even aware of their contents. One of them is the response of the monk (Cappelanus) Nonnosus from the Michaelsberg Convent in Bamberg to Schedel's request to restore a heavily damaged Hebrew manuscript that Schedel had sent to him in 1500.[69] In this letter, Nonnosus expressed regret at not being able to restore the manuscript. He therefore sent it back, which he would not

---

68 His owner inscription in BSB, Chm 410 (see note 14), opening with "Iste liber hebraicus" (This Hebrew book), suggests that he had no idea that this was a prayer book, otherwise he would presumably have written out its title, as he usually did in the case of his non-Hebrew books. Likewise, there is no sign of Schedel's awareness of the particular contents of his other Hebrew books, although it cannot be excluded that he had some general awareness thereof.

69 This manuscript has not survived. Walde, *Christliche Hebraisten Deutschlands*, 188–89. The letter was found in BSB, Chm 21, discussed previously. The monk Nonnosus was most probably Nonnosus Stettfelder, the secretary of the Michaelsberg Convent's abbot, Andreas Lang, about whose health Nonnosus informs Schedel at the end of his letter. Schedel and Lang maintained friendly relations, sharing a common love of books. In his *Reisetagebuch*, Schedel mentioned his visit to Lang that took place in 1488. Franz Fuchs, "Ein unbekanntes Reisetagebuch Hartmann Schedels aus dem Jahre 1488," in *Quellen in Geschichtswissenschaft und Geschichtsunterricht*.

have done had the manuscript been legible, as he had never possessed or even seen a Hebrew book before.⁷⁰ Regarding its condition, he referred to the opinion of the monastery *physicus* Eberhard, who insisted that the manuscript had been deliberately damaged by Jews in order to appear to Christians as an old codex containing Jewish secrets or antiquities.⁷¹

Although Nonnosus himself did not believe that the damage was intentionally caused and supposed that it was rather the result of storing the manuscript in a vessel sealed by pitch, he did believe in "Jewish secrets." He referred to a certain scholar who told him that he had read such secrets in a Hebrew book which he had examined with a certain Jew, and advised Schedel to visit a Franciscan in Nuremberg, who was knowledgeable in Hebrew.⁷² What kind of secrets Nonnosus meant is, however, not absolutely clear. These secrets could be related to alleged Jewish ritual practices, namely to the ritual murders and desecration of the Eucharistic host, accusations which were extremely widespread in this period and often used as a pretext for Jewish expulsions.⁷³ But the kabbalistic

---

Exemplarische Zugänge zur Rekonstruktion von Vergangenheit, ed. Helmut Beilner (Neuried: Ars Una, 2004), 43.

70 "Hunc tamen librum intactum remitto cum magna gratiarum actione; quod si legibilis fuisset, in instanti non remisissem, quia numquam potui aliquem hebraicum librum habere seu videre, quamquam multos habuerim labores." ("However, I send this book back untouched with much gratitude; but if it had been legible, I would not have sent it back immediately, since I have never been able to have or see a Hebrew book, although I made repeated attempts.") Regarding the various ways in which Christians could acquire Hebrew books, see Stephan Burnett, "Jüdische Vermittler des Hebräischen und ihre christlischen Schüler im Spätmittelalter," in *Wechselseitige Wahrnehmung der Religionen im Spätmittelalter und in der Frühen Neuzeit*, eds. Ludger Grenzmann, Thomas Haye, Nikolaus Henkel, Thomas Kaufmann (Berlin: Walter de Gruyter, 2009), 173–88.

71 "... id fore factum nequicia iudeorum, quia pergamenum apparet adhuc nouum et scriptura recens et valde exilis, non artificialis, et quod liber fuerit inutilis vel falsus, quem iudei nouiter absconderint, vt cum repertus per fideles existimen eum longo tempore fuisse absconditum et inibi contineantur secreta vel antiquitates eorum ..." ("... this was done by the wickedness of the Jews, since the parchment still appears new, and the script is fresh and very poor, not skillful, and this was a useless and even deceitful book which the Jews had recently concealed, so that when found by the faithful [i.e. Christians] they would surmise that it had been hidden for a long time and that the secrets or antiquities of the Jews are contained in it ...").

72 "Intellexi a quodam doctore ante biennium se vidisse aliquem librum cum quodam iudeo, in quo secreta aliqua legisset ... Est quidam minor nurmberge hebraico imbutus, hunc poterit r. v. [reverentia vestra] visitare." (I understood from a certain doctor two years ago that he had seen some book with a certain Jew, in which he read some secrets ... There is a certain Franciscan in Nuremberg, knowledgeable in Hebrew, whom you [your reverence] will be able to visit.)

73 For extensive literature on this topic, see, for example, Ronnie Po-chia Hsia. *The Myth of Ritual Murder: Jews and Magic in Reformation Germany* (New Haven & London: Yale University Press, 1988). Schedel's particular case is discussed in Chapter V.1 of my dissertation.

and magical connotations of these secrets seem to be more apparent, especially since the Kabbalah was one of the strongest motivations for Christian interest in Hebrew books.[74] The relationship of the Hebrew language to magical practices was clearly demonstrated also in a number of non-Hebrew books from Schedel's library.[75]

Judging from this letter, it seems that while none of the involved parties (i.e. Schedel, Nonnosus, and Eberhard) knew Hebrew, all of them presupposed the existence of such Jewish secrets. This assumption rendered Hebrew manuscripts even more attractive in their eyes and stimulated them to keep looking passionately for Hebrew books. On the other hand, the fact that Schedel personally attended to the material condition of his Hebrew codices reflects once again his approach towards the Hebrew book as a physical object whose importance extends beyond its text. By restoring the manuscript sent to Nonnosus, as well as the aforementioned Siddur (BSB, Chm 410), which was found in torn condition, Schedel demonstrated that such an object needs to be cultivated and carefully preserved in its wholeness. By adding the images, he also emphasized the object's artistic value, indeed elevating its status to that of an art object.

Another letter from Schedel's library, sent to Schedel by Konrad Celtis, reflects a similar enthusiastic search for Hebrew books.[76] Konrad Celtis (1459–1508) was a scholar, poet, and humanist who spent time in Nuremberg in the late fifteenth and early sixteenth centuries, and was even suggested by his patron, the Nuremberg patrician and councillor, Sebald Schreyer, to correct and enlarge Schedel's *Weltchronik*.[77] In his letter, Celtis asked Schedel to inform him whether or not

---

[74] See, for example, Saverio Campanini, "Die Geburt der Judaistik aus dem Geist der Christlichen Kabbalah," in *Gottes Sprache in der philologischen Werkstatt: Hebraistik vom 15. bis zum 19. Jahrhundert*, eds. Gerold Necker and Giuseppe Veltri (Leiden: Brill, 2004): 135–45.

[75] Especially BSB, Clm 276, fol. 96v and BSB, Clm 641, fol. 40r. This subject is extensively discussed in Chapter VII.2 of my dissertation. See also Bernhard Bischoff, "Study of Foreign Languages in the Middle Ages," *Speculum* 36, no. 2 (1961): 213; Bernhard Bischoff, "Übersicht über die nichtdiplomatischen Geheimschriften des Mittelalters," *Mitteilungen des Instituts für Österreichische Geschichtsforschung* 62 (1954): 133–34; David King, *The Ciphers of the Monks: A Forgotten Number-Notation of the Middle Ages* (Stuttgart: Franz Steiner, 2001), 121–23.

[76] BSB, Autogr. II A. Hans Rupprich, ed. *Konrad Celtis: Der Briefwechsel* (Munich: C. H. Beck, 1934), 599; Stauber, *Die Schedelsche Bibliothek*, 78; Walde, *Christliche Hebraisten Deutschlands*, 187. The letter is undated, but must have been written after 1504, when Schedel acquired the main group of his Hebrew manuscripts.

[77] Paul Joachimsen, *Geschichtsauffassung und Geschichtschreibung in Deutschland unter dem Einfluss des Humanismus* (Leipzig: Scientia Verlag Aalen, 1968), 155. Regarding Schedel's relations with Celtis, see in Lewis Spitz, *Conrad Celtis: The German Arch-Humanist* (Cambridge, MA: Harvard University Press, 1957), 7; Stauber, *Die Schedelsche Bibliothek*, 78; Walde, *Christliche Hebraisten Deutschlands*, 187–88.

the certain resident (obviously of Nuremberg) from whom Schedel had acquired his Hebrew books was still in possession of others, or to tell him about any other place where he might find Hebrew books.⁷⁸ In this letter, Celtis addressed Schedel as a person known for his interest in Hebrew books and for his Hebrew collection. Celtis's own knowledge of Hebrew was poor, if it existed at all, since he had studied the language with Rudolf Agricola in 1485 for less than half a year.⁷⁹ His search for Hebrew books did not reflect a strictly scholarly interest in their texts, but rather a general humanist appreciation for Hebrew literature.

The Hebrew book, then, was a desired object thanks to its high value for humanist scholarship, yet at the same time anti-Jewish tendencies and stereotypes turned it into a potentially dangerous object marked by secrecy and imbued with a magical and even demonic aura.⁸⁰ The absence of Jewish interlocutors, together with the collectors' own unfamiliarity with the Hebrew language and actual Jewish tradition, sharpened this confusion and general sense of uncertainty regarding Hebrew books. Since Christians such as Schedel could not use their Hebrew books in any constructive sense, there was no other use for them in Schedel's environment except to be refuted and converted, as was the case with the Jews themselves.

---

78 "Accepi clarissime domine doctor apud te esse hebrea quedam volumina eaque a Ciue quodam emisse. Oro si aliqua apud ciuem eundem quedam adhuc Inveniri possent, vt nomen Ciuis mihi significes aut vbi inveniri possent." ("I have heard, O most illustrious Lord doctor, that you have some Hebrew books and that you bought them from some citizen. If somehow that same citizen is still in possession of some [books], I ask you to indicate for me the name of the citizen or [the place] where the books can be found.")

79 Gustav Bauch, "Die Einführung des Hebräischen in Wittenberg," *Monatsschrift für Geschichte und Wissenschaft des Judentums* 48, no. 2 (1904): 83; Gustav Bauch, *Die Universität Erfurt im Zeitalter des Frühhumanismus* (Breslau: M. & H. Marcus, 1904), 68. See also Spitz, *Conrad Celtis*, 4; Walde, *Christliche Hebraisten Deutschlands*, 183.

80 In his panegyric to Nuremberg, *De origine, situ, moribus et institutis Norimbergae libellus*, written in 1485, Celtis described the Jews as sucking the blood of Christian children and desecrating the Eucharist. Albert Werminghoff, *Conrad Celtis und sein Buch über Nürnberg* (Freiburg im Breisgau: Julius Boltze, 1921), 198–99. Two copies of this work were preserved in Schedel's collection, both copied by Schedel himself, BSB, Clm 431, fols. 5r–52r and BSB, Clm 951, fols. 3r–54v.

List of Manuscripts

Berlin, Preuß. Staatsbibliothek, MS germ. fol. 447: Schedel's *Familienbuch*, including a catalogue of his library, 1552.
BSB, Cgm 439: *Fastnachtsspiel, Minnereden, Human-und Rossmedizin, Beichtspiegel*, Nuremberg, after 1473 and first half of the fifteenth century.
BSB, Clm 263: *Catalogue of Schedel's Library*, 1498.
BSB, Clm 276: *Compilation of Texts on Magic, Alchemy, Geomancy and Astrology*, fourteenth century.
BSB, Clm 431: *Compilation on Nuremberg*, Nuremberg, late fifteenth-early sixteenth century.
BSB, Clm 641: *Compilation of Hymns, Poems and Theological Extracts*, late fifteenth-early sixteenth century.
BSB, Clm 951: *Compilation on Nuremberg and Other German-Speaking Lands*, Nuremberg, 1497–9.
BSB, Cod. hebr. 14: *Liturgical Pentateuch*, Rhineland, ca. 1240–60.
BSB, Cod. hebr. 16: *Liturgical Pentateuch*, Ashkenazi and oriental scripts, thirteenth century.
BSB, Cod. hebr. 21: *Mahzor for Whole Year*, Franconia, ca. 1250–75.
BSB, Cod. hebr. 69: *Fragmented Siddur and Mahzor*, different Ashkenazi scripts, late thirteenth-early fourteenth centuries.
BSB, Cod. hebr. 88: *Mahzor for the High Holidays and Sukkot*, Ashkenazi scripts, late thirteenth and fourteenth centuries.
BSB, Cod. hebr. 90: *Fragmented Siddur*, Franconia, early fourteenth century.
BSB, Cod. hebr. 298: *Pentateuch*, Ashkenazi scripts, ca. 1400–50.
BSB, Cod. hebr. 410: *Siddur for Whole Year*, Franconia, fourteenth century.

List of Printed Books

BSB, 2 Inc.c.a. 1204: Marsilius Ficinus, *Theologia Platonica de immortalitate animorum*, Florence, 1482.
BSB, 4 Inc.c.a. 99 m.: Petrus Nigri, *Stern des Meschiah*, Esslingen, 1477.
BSB, Inc.c.a. 181: *Hebrew Bible*, Brescia, 1494.
BSB, Rar. 182: Hans Folz, *Krieg des Dichters wider einen Juden*, bound together with other Folz's works, Nuremberg, 1477.
BSB, Rar. 293: Stephan Fridolin, *Schatzbehalter oder Schrein der wahren Reichtümer des Heils und ewiger Seligkeit*, Nuremberg, 1491.
Neuburg an der Donau, Staatlische Bibliothek, no sign.: Johannes Reuchlin, *Rudimenta linguae hebraicae*, Pforzheim, 1506.

Bibliography

Abel, Wolfgang and Reimund Leicht, eds. *Verzeichnis der Hebraica in der Bibliothek Johannes Reuchlins*. Pforzheimer Reuchlinschriften 9. Ostfildern: Jan Thorbecke, 2005.
Albl, Martin, ed. *Pseudo-Gregory of Nyssa: Testimonies against the Jews*. Writings from the Greco-Roman World 5. Atlanta: Society of Biblical Literature, 2004.
Auerbach, Erich. "Typological Symbolism in Medieval Literature." *Yale French Studies* 9 (1952): 3–10.
Bauch, Gustav. "Die Einführung des Hebräischen in Wittenberg." *Monatsschrift für Geschichte und Wissenschaft des Judentums* 48, no. 2 (1904): 77–86.
Bauch, Gustav. *Die Universität Erfurt im Zeitalter des Frühhumanismus*. Breslau: M. & H. Marcus, 1904.
Bellm, Richard. *Der Schatzbehalter: ein Andachts-und Erbauungsbuch aus dem Jahre 1491*; mit 91 Holzschnitten und 2 Textseiten in Faksimile. Wiesbaden: Pressler, 1962.
Bischoff, Bernhard. "Study of Foreign Languages in the Middle Ages." *Speculum* 36, no. 2 (1961): 209–24.
Bischoff, Bernhard. "Übersicht über die nichtdiplomatischen Geheimschriften des Mittelalters." *Mitteilungen des Instituts für Österreichische Geschichtsforschung* 62 (1954): 1–27.
Breuer, Mordechai, Yacov Guggenheim, and Arye Maimon, eds. *Germania Judaica*. Vol. 3, no. 2. Tübingen: Mohr Siebeck, 1995.
Browe, Peter. *Die Judenmission im Mittelalter und die Päpste*. Rome: Università Gregoriana, 1973.
Burnett, Stephan. "Jüdische Vermittler des Hebräischen und ihre Christlischen Schüler im Spätmittelalter." In *Wechselseitige Wahrnehmung der Religionen im Spätmittelalter und in der Frühen Neuzeit*, edited by Ludger Grenzmann, Thomas Haye, Nikolaus Henkel, Thomas Kaufmann, 173–88. Berlin: Walter de Gruyter, 2009.
Böhmer, Johann F., ed. *Regesta Imperii*. Vol. 14, no. 2: *Ausgewählte Regesten des Kaiserreiches unter Maximilian I. 1493–1519*, eds. Hermann Wiesflecker and Manfred Hollegger. Vienna, Cologne & Weimar: Böhlau Verlag, 1993.
Campanini, Saverio. "Die Geburt der Judaistik aus dem Geist der Christlichen Kabbalah." In *Gottes Sprache in der philologischen Werkstatt: Hebraistik vom 15. bis zum 19. Jahrhundert*, edited by Gerold Necker and Giuseppe Veltri, 135–241. Leiden: Brill, 2004.
Campanini, Saverio. "Reuchlins Jüdische Lehrer aus Italien." In *Reuchlin und Italien*, edited by Gerald Dörner, 69–85. Pforzheimer Reuchlinschriften 7. Stuttgart: Jan Thorbecke, 1999.
Carlebach, Elisheva. *Divided Souls: Converts from Judaism in Germany, 1500–1750*. New Haven & London: Yale University Press, 2001.
Chazan, Robert. *Fashioning Jewish Identity in Medieval Western Christendom*. Cambridge: Cambridge University Press, 2004.
Coogan, Michael, Marc Brettler and Carol Newsom, eds. *The New Oxford Annotated Bible with the Apocrypha*, New Revised Standard Version. Fourth Edition. Oxford: Oxford University Press, 2010.
Estep, William. *Renaissance and Reformation*. Grand Rapids: William B. Eerdmans Publishing, 1986.
Fischer, Hanns. "Hans Folz: Altes und Neues zur Geschichte seines Lebens und seiner Schriften." *Zeitschrift für deutsches Altertum und deutsche Literatur* 95, no. 3 (1966): 212–36.
Fischer, Hanns. *Hans Folz: Die Reimpaarsprüche*. Munich: C.H. Beck, 1961.
Fridolin, Stephan. *Schatzbehalter oder Schrein der wahren Reichtümer des Heils und ewiger Seligkeit*. Nuremberg: Anton Koberger, 1491.

Fuchs, Franz. "Ein unbekanntes Reisetagebuch Hartmann Schedels aus dem Jahre 1488." In *Quellen in Geschichtswissenschaft und Geschichtsunterricht. Exemplarische Zugänge zur Rekonstruktion von Vergangenheit*, edited by Helmut Beilner, 40–50. Regensburger Beiträge zur Geschichtslehrerfortbildung 3. Neuried: Ars Una, 2004.

Funkenstein, Amos. "Basic Types of Christian Anti-Jewish Polemics in the Later Middle Ages." *Viator* 2 (1971): 373–82.

Goldish, Matt. *Judaism in the Theology of Sir Isaac Newton*. Dordrecht: Klewer Academic Publishers, 1998.

Goppelt, Leonhard. *Typos: The Typological Interpretation of the Old Testament in the New*, trans. Donald H. Madvig. Grand Rapids: William B. Eerdmans Publishing, 1982.

Gulden, Sebastian. "An Ideal Neighborhood: The Physical Environment of the Early Dürer as a Space of Experience." In *The Early Dürer: Exhibition Organized by the Germanisches Nationalmuseum in Nuremberg, May 24–September 2, 2012*, edited by Beate Böckem and Daniel Hess, 29–38. Nuremberg: Verlag des Germanisches Nationalmuseum, 2012.

Halm, Karl, Georg Laubmann, and Wilhelm Meyer, eds. *Catalogus codicum latinorum Bibliothecae Regiae Monacensis* (Reprint). Vols. 1–4. Wiesbaden: Harrassowitz, 1968–1969.

Heikel, Ivar August, ed. *Eusebius: Werke*. Vol. 6, *Die Demonstratio evangelica*. Die Griechischen Christlichen Schriftsteller 23. Leipzig: J.C. Hinrichs'sche Buchhandlung, 1913.

Henkel, Nikolaus. "Ein Zeugnis zum 'Schatzbehälter' des Stephan Fridolin in der deutschen Weltchronik Hartmann Schedels." In *500 Jahre Schedelsche Weltchronik*, edited by Stephan Füssel, 165–70. Pirckheimer-Jahrbuch 9. Nuremberg: Hans Karl, 1994.

Hernad, Béatrice, ed. *Die Graphiksammlung des Humanisten Hartmann Schedel*. Ausstellung in der Bayerischen Staatsbibliothek. München vom 20. Juni–15. September 1990. Munich: Prestel, 1990.

Hsia, Ronnie Po-chia. *The Myth of Ritual Murder: Jews and Magic in Reformation Germany*. New Haven & London: Yale University Press, 1988.

Huey, Caroline. *Hans Folz and Print Culture in Late Medieval Germany: The Creation of Popular Discourse*. Aldershot: Ashgate, 2012.

Janota, Johannes. "Hans Folz in Nürnberg." In *Philologie und Geschichtswissenschaft. Demonstrationen literarischer Texte des Mittelalters*, edited by Heinz Rupp, 74–91. Heidelberg: Quelle und Meyer, 1977.

Joachimsen, Paul. *Geschichtsauffassung und Geschichtschreibung in Deutschland unter dem Einfluss des Humanismus*. Leipzig: Scientia Verlag Aalen, 1968.

Joachimsen, Paul. "Humanism and the Development of the German Mind." In *Pre-Reformation Germany*, edited by Gerald Strauss, 162–224. New York: Harper & Row, 1972.

Katchen, Aaron. *Christian Hebraists and Dutch Rabbis: Seventeenth Century Apologetics and the Study of Maimonides' Mishneh Torah*. Harvard Judaic Texts and Studies 3. Cambridge, MA: Harvard University Press, 1985.

Keller, Adelbert, ed. *Fastnachtspiele aus dem fünfzehnten Jahrhundert*. Vol. 1. Bibliothek des literarischen Vereins in Stuttgart 28. Stuttgart: Literarischer Verein, 1853.

Keller, Adelbert, ed. *Fastnachtspiele aus dem fünfzehnten Jahrhundert*. Vol. 3. Bibliothek des literarischen Vereins in Stuttgart 30. Stuttgart: Literarischer Verein, 1853.

King, David. *The Ciphers of the Monks: A Forgotten Number-Notation of the Middle Ages*. Stuttgart: Franz Steiner, 2001.

Kisch, Guido. *The Jews in Medieval Germany. A Study of their Legal and Social Status*. New York: Ktav, 1970.

Kristeller, Paul Oskar. "The European Diffusion of Italian Humanism." *Italica* 39, no. 1 (1962): 1–20.
Kristeller, Paul Oskar. *Renaissance Thought: The Classic, Scholastic and Humanistic Strains.* New York, Evanston & London: Harper, 1961.
Kyriss, Ernst. *Nürnberger Klostereinbände der Jahre 1433 bis 1525.* Erlangen: s.n., 1940.
Kyriss, Ernst. *Verzierte gotische Einbände im alten deutschen Sprachgebiet.* Vol. 1. Stuttgart: Max Hettler, 1954.
Lomnitzer, Helmut. "Das Verhältnis des Fastnachtspiels vom 'Kaiser Constantinus' zum Reimpaarspruch 'Christ und Jude' von Hans Folz." *Zeitschrift für deutsches Altertum und deutsche Literatur* 92, no. 4 (1964): 277–91
Martin, John. "Dramatized Disputations: Late Medieval German Dramatizations of Jewish-Christian Religious Disputations, Church Policy, and Local Social Climates." *Medieval Encounters* 8, no. 2–3 (2002): 209–27.
Martin, John. "The Depiction of Jews in the Carnival Plays and Comedies of Hans Folz and Hans Sachs in Early Modern Nuremberg." *Baylor Journal of Theatre and Performance* 3, no. 2 (2006): 43–65.
Mcdonald, Marc. "'Extremely Curious and Important!': Reconstructing the Print Collection of Ferdinand Columbus." In *Collecting Prints and Drawings in Europe, c. 1500–1750*, edited by Christopher Baker, Caroline Elam and Genevieve Warwick, 37–51. Aldershot: Ashgate, 2004.
Migne, Jacques-Paul, ed. *Patrologia Latina*. Vol. 26, Hieronymus Stridonensis, *Commentarium in Evangelium Matthaei*. Paris: Imprimerie Catholique, 1845.
Migne, Jacques-Paul, ed. *Patrologia Latina*. Vol. 56, Leo I, *Sermones*. Paris: Imprimerie Catholique, 1865.
Migne, Jacques-Paul, ed. *Patrologia Latina*. Vol. 131, Remigius Antissiodorensis, *Homiliae*. Paris: Imprimerie Catholique, 1853.
Migne, Jacques-Paul, ed. *Patrologia Latina*. Vol. 167, Rupertus Tuitiensis. *In Jeremiam prophetam commentariorum*. Paris: Imprimerie Catholique, 1854.
Netanyahu, Benzion. "Alonso de Espina: Was He a New Christian?" *Proceedings of the American Academy for Jewish Research* 43 (1976): 107–65.
Nigri, Petrus. *Stern des Meschiah. In aller übung der vernunft ist die czu preysen vnd czu loben . . .* Esslingen: Konrad Fyner, 1477.
Ocker, Christopher. "German Theologians and the Jews in the Fifteenth Century." In *Jews, Judaism and the Reformation in Sixteenth-Century Germany*, edited by Dean Phillip Bell and Stephen Burnett, 33–65. Studies in Central European Histories 37. Leiden: Brill, 2006.
Paulus, Nicolaus. "Der Franziskaner Stephan Fridolin, ein Nürnberger Prediger." *Historisch-politische Blätter* 113 (1894): 465–83.
Price, David. "Hans Folz's Anti-Jewish Carnival Plays." *Fifteenth Century Studies* 19 (1992): 209–28.
Reicke, Emil, ed. *Willibald Pirckheimer: Briefwechsel*. Vol. 1. Munich: C. H. Beck, 1940.
Reske, Christopher. *The Production of Schedel's Nuremberg Chronicle*. Mainzer Studien zur Buchwissenschaft 10. Wiesbaden: Harrassowitz, 2000.
Roest, Bert. *Franciscan Literature of Religious Instruction before the Council of Trent*. Leiden: Brill, 2004.
Roth, Ferdinand Johann, ed. *Verzeichnis aller Genannten des größern Raths: von den ältesten bis auf die neuesten Zeiten*. Nuremberg: Johann Georg Milbradt, 1802.
Ruf, Paul. *Mittelalterliche Bibliothekskataloge Deutschlands und der Schweiz*. Vol. 3/1, *Bistum Augsburg*. Munich: C.H. Beck, 1932.

Rummel, Erika. *The Confessionalization of Humanism in Reformation Germany*. Oxford: Oxford University Press, 2000.
Rupprich, Hans, ed. *Konrad Celtis: Der Briefwechsel*. Veröffentlichungen der Kommission zur Erforschung der Geschichte der Reformation und Gegenreformation; Humanistenbriefe 3. Munich: C. H. Beck, 1934.
Sanders, James. "Ναζωραῖος in Matt 2:23." *Journal of Biblical Literature* 84, no. 2 (1965): 169–72.
Schmeller, Johann Andreas. *Die deutschen Handschriften der K. Hof- und Staatsbibliothek zu München*. Vol. 1. Munich: Palm, 1866.
Schmidt, Ulrich. *P. Stephan Fridolin: Ein Franziskaner Prediger des ausgehenden Mittelalters*. Veröffentlichungen aus dem Kirchenhistorischen Seminar München 3/11. Munich: Lentner, 1910.
Schneider, Karin. *Die deutschen Handschriften der Bayerischen Staatsbibliothek München, Cgm 351–500*. Editio altera. Wiesbaden: Harrassowitz, 1973.
Seegets, Petra. *Passionstheologie und Passionsfrömmigkeit im ausgehenden Mittelalter: der Nürnberger Franziskaner Stephan Fridolin (gest. 1498) zwischen Kloster und Stadt*. Tübingen: Mohr Siebeck, 1998.
Signer, Michael. "Polemic and Exegesis: The Varieties of Twelfth-Century Hebraism." In *Hebraica Veritas? Christian Hebraists and the Study of Judaism in Early Modern Europe*, edited by Allison Coudert and Jeffrey Shoulson, 21–32. Philadelphia: University of Pennsylvania Press, 2004.
Spitz, Lewis. *Conrad Celtis: The German Arch-Humanist*. Cambridge, MA: Harvard University Press, 1957.
Stadler, Franz. *Michael Wolgemut und der Nürnberger Holzschnitt im letzten Drittel des XV. Jahrhunderts*. Strasbourg: Haitz, 1913.
Stauber, Richard. *Die Schedelsche Bibliothek*. Freiburg im Breisgau: Herder, 1908.
Steinschneider, Moritz. *Die Hebräischen Handschriften der K.Hof-und Staatsbibliothek in München*. Catalogus codicum manuscriptorum Bibliothecae Monacensis 1/1. Munich: Palm, 1895.
Steimann, Ilona. "Habent sua fata libelli: Hebrew Books from the Collection of Hartmann Schedel." PhD diss., The Hebrew University, 2014.
Thurnwald, Andrea. "Zur Ikonographie der Capestrano-Tafel: Pater Stephan Fridolin als geistiger Urheber ihres theologischen Programms." In *Der Bußprediger Capestrano auf dem Domplatz in Bamberg: Eine Bamberger Tafel um 1470/75. Eine Didaktische Ausstellung des Historischen Museums Bamberg und des Lehrstuhls I für Kunstgeschichte an der Universität Bamberg*, edited by Hubert Russ, 19–48. Schriften des Historischen Museums Bamberg 12. Bamberg: Historisches Museum, 1989.
Toch, Michael. "Der jüdische Geldhandel in der Wirtschaft des Deutschen Spätmittelalters: Nürnberg 1350–1499." *Blätter für Deutsche Landesgeschichte* 1, no. 17 (1981): 283–310.
Toch, Michael. *Die Juden im mittelalterlichen Reich*. Oldenbourg: Wissenschaftsverlag, 2003.
Toch, Michael. "'Umb gemeyns Nutz und Nottdurfft willen': Obrigkeitliches und jurisdiktionelles Denken bei der Austreibung der Nürnberg Juden 1498–99." *Zeitschrift für historische Forschung* 1 (1984): 1–21.
Walde, Bernard. *Christliche Hebraisten Deutschlands am Ausgang des Mittelalters*. Münster in Westphalia: Aschendorffsche Verlagsbuchhandlung, 1916.

Wenninger, Markus J. *Man bedarf keiner Juden mehr. Ursachen und Hintergründe ihrer Vertreibung aus den deutschen Reichsstädten im 15. Jahrhundert*. Vienna, Cologne & Graz: Böhlau, 1981.

Wenzel, Edith. *"Do worden die Judden alle geschant": Rolle und Funktion der Juden in spätmittelalterlichen Spielen*. Munich: Fink, 1992.

Werminghoff, Albert. *Conrad Celtis und sein Buch über Nürnberg*. Freiburg im Breisgau: Julius Boltze, 1921.

Melanie Lange
Hebrew Caught Between?
Sebastian Münster's Edition of Elia Levita's *Sefer ha-Baḥur* as Evidence of Intercultural and Interreligious Dialogue

There is a typical German saying: "One does not talk about money." But despite this phrase, one focus of the following pages will be the man whose portrait decorated the 100 Deutsche Mark bill during the years 1962 to 1991: Sebastian Münster – a once famous German cosmographer, mathematician and Hebraist. The German federal bank settled upon this motif in the first place not because of Münster's scientific achievements but because of the fact that the portrait painted by Christoph Amberger in 1552 is so difficult to fake.[1] Admittedly, this circumstance does not necessarily point to great popularity. But it is nonetheless worth having a closer look at Münster's achievements, especially in the field of Hebrew studies.

During the age of Renaissance Humanism and the Protestant Reformation, scholars were driven by the appeal "ad fontes," and Martin Luther's principle "sola scriptura" led them to a new hermeneutics of biblical texts. But the road to this new Christian way of understanding Scripture was long and paved with many obstacles – most notably the language barrier. It was at this time that the modern history of philology began. Especially the study of the Hebrew language was affected by the evolving philological access and new methods of teaching within the tense atmosphere created by the intermixing of Christian theology, Jewish tradition and linguistic interest.

1 Vita Sebastian Münster

It was in this context that Sebastian Münster appeared on the scene. He was born in 1488 in the small town of Niederingelheim on the Rhine. His Christian religious career was by no means unique for the early sixteenth century: in 1507 Münster joined the Franciscan Order, a move which enabled him to pursue his studies at the lowest possible cost. Five years later he received his ordination. And finally, in 1529, he decided to leave the Franciscan Order and to convert to Protestantism.

---
[1] Cf. Karl H. Burmeister, *Sebastian Münster: Versuch eines biographischen Gesamtbildes* (Basel and Stuttgart: Helbing & Lichtenhahn, 1963), 199.

This step took him a relatively long time, and, significantly, the one whose face later graced the German 100 Mark bill first learned to handle money when he was past forty years of age (prior to that his order had attended to his subsistence).

Heidelberg, Leuven, Freiburg, Rouffach and Pforzheim: these are the places where Sebastian Münster dwelt to study philosophy, theology, mathematics, geography, astronomy and, last but definitively not least, the Hebrew language. Konrad Pellikan, with whom he remained close friends for the rest of his life, was his most famous and most important teacher.

In 1514 he began to work as a lecturer in philosophy and theology in Tübingen, and from 1518 on he did so at the University of Basel. But Münster despised metaphysical considerations.[2] His passion belonged to his geographical and Hebrew studies. *Epitome Hebraicae Grammaticae*, dating back to 1520, is the title that first won Münster a degree of fame in the field of Hebrew studies.

From 1524 to 1527 he was Professor of Hebrew at the University of Heidelberg, where he also became acquainted with Simon Grynaeus, the Greek scholar there, who exposed Münster to the works of Elia Levita.[3] During this period, Münster published a substantial amount of Hebrew study literature, and, as luck would have it, cultivated friendships with two of the most famous printers in Basel, Johannes Froben and Adam Petri.

In 1529 he received the professorship of Hebrew in Basel, where he had already lived for a number of years. So Münster succeeded his mentor and friend Konrad Pellikan, who himself had obtained the professorship of Hebrew in Zürich, in his chair. Münster's lectures became very popular among the students in Basel – and across Europe. John Calvin[4] as well as many of his later students came to Basel to learn Hebrew from Münster, as did people from as far away as Transylvania.[5] In May 1552 Sebastian Münster died of the plague. One of his former students and closest friends, Erasmus Oswald Schreckenfuchs, delivered the funeral oration – significantly, in Hebrew.[6]

---

2 Cf. Burmeister, *Sebastian Münster*, 23.
3 Elia Levita, *Grammatica Hebraica Absolutissima: sēfär haddiqdûq*, ed. Sebastian Münster (Basel: apvd Io. Frobenium, 1525), praef.
4 Cf. Theodor von Beza, *Johannis Calvini vita*, ed. Thomas Nickel (Güstrow: ex officina Ebertiana, 1862), 4.
5 Cf. Burmeister, *Sebastian Münster*, 67.
6 Erasmus O. Schreckenfuchs, *Trauerrede zum Gedächtnis seines Lehrers Sebastian Münster, Freiburg, 1552*, trans. Erwin Emmerling, Beiträge zur Ingelheimer Geschichte 12 (Ingelheim: Historischer Verein, 1960).

2 Münster Between Jews and Christians

Münster's predecessor in Hebrew studies in Heidelberg was Johannes Böschenstein, whom Münster, on the one hand, reproached because he provided inferior lessons at high cost and whom he insulted as a "baptized Jew."[7] On the other hand, several persons harshly criticized Münster himself even after his death for possessing occult books that they could not understand because of the unknown letters or that they condemned because they were written by Jews and conflicted with the Christian doctrine.[8] Such criticisms demonstrate that Christian Hebrew studies in the early sixteenth century were not free of prejudice in certain circles and even risked falling into the category of heresy on the Christian side.

But aside from these two examples, what was Münster's relationship to Jews like? As a teacher of the Hebrew language, he was supposed to debate with Jews about religious matters and even to do missionary work among them.[9] Münster was not afraid of interreligious contact. On the contrary, he sought dialogue with Jews, and visited synagogues and Jewish cemeteries, because he was convinced that only through the principle of "oculariter videre" "seeing with one's own eyes" can one obtain a better understanding of Judaism.[10]

Everything that Münster had expressed apologetically about Judaism, he ultimately summarized in two books: the *Evangelium secundum Matthaeum* (1537) and his *Messias Christianorum et Judaeorum* (1539). The latter text was originally intended for publication only in Hebrew, in what seems at first glance to indicate a Jewish target audience. But his attitude toward missionizing Jews was in fact rather resigned. He rejected the persecution of the Jews because he was of the

---

[7] Sebastian Münster, *Opus grammaticum consummatum: mĕläkät haddiqdûq haššālēm* (Basel: Henricum Petrum, 1542), praef.
[8] Cf. Burmeister, *Sebastian Münster*, 82. S. Burnett mentions that Münster possessed, for example, a copy of *Sefer Nizzahon*, an anonymous thirteenth-century Jewish polemical book against Christians. See Stephen G. Burnett, "Spokesmen for Judaism: Medieval Jewish Polemicists and their Christian Readers in the Reformation Era," in *Reuchlin und seine Erben. Forscher, Denker, Ideologen und Spinner*, ed. Peter Schäfer and Irina Wandrey (Ostfildern: Thorbecke, 2005): 48.
[9] Cf. the Councils of Vienne (1313) and Basel/Ferrara (1434), which established a canon of languages in academic education to advance missionizing.
[10] Cf. Sebastian Münster, *Biblia: miqdaš jahwē, 'äsrîm wĕ'arba' sifrê hammiqtāb haqqādôš, Hebrew-Latin with Annotations* (Basel: J. Bebel, 1534/1935), 141^v: "qui curiosior in his rebus cognoscendis esse voluerit, adeat Judaeos, praesertim in his locis, ubi habent synagogas et haec omnia oculariter videre poterit" ["he who should wish to know more inquisitively about these things, should go directly to the Jews, especially to those places, where they have synagogues and where one can see all these with one's own eyes." (This and all subsequent translations are by the author).

opinion that "Christ himself wanted the Jews to be disbelieving until the end of the world, as a negative example for the faithful and to fulfill Scripture."[11] For the most part, Münster's declarations about Judaism were responses to Christians who had requested statements from him. He did not have in mind to take strong measures against Jews. He strictly resisted the burning of Jewish books for he believed that medieval Jewish scholarship merited recognition alongside its Christian counterpart. This attitude led him to his many publications of rabbinic literature. Another remarkable point is the fact that he dated his publications as well as the matriculation register of Basel in 1547, during his tenure as rector of the university, according to the Christian *and* to the Jewish calendar.[12]

Nevertheless, although Münster seemed to be lacking any desire for missionary activity, the influence of his works on the Jewish mission – providing grist to the mill for the strict rejectors or persecutors of Judaism – should not be underestimated.

Thanks to both his rather tolerant attitude towards Jews and his conversion to Protestantism, most of Münster's books were placed on the index by Catholic authorities. As a result, much of Münster's work, especially in Hebrew studies, has become less important. Catholics regarded Münster as one of the most important Protestant theologians.[13] Yet although he maintained close friendships with several active reformers, Münster was nevertheless primarily a linguist and did not contribute anything to the systematic theology of the reformation movement.

Also on the Protestant side, there was not simply goodwill towards Münster. Indeed, for all Martin Luther's praise for Münster, his criticism of him is far more prominent. To his taste, Münster made too extensive use of rabbinic language in the Latin version of his *Hebraica Biblia* (1534/35), as indicated by his frequent Hebraisms.[14] But there is also criticism of the specific content of his works: Münster was happy to make use of rabbinical exegesis – so long as it did not contradict the Christian doctrine. As Luther himself commented: "I like Münster well, but I wish he would have been here and had conferred with us; it would have

---

11 Cf. Sebastian Münster, *Messias Christianorum et Judaeorum hebraicè & latinè* (Basel: Henricum Petrum, 1539), praef.
12 Hans G. Wackernagel, ed., *Die Matrikel der Universität Basel, vol. 2* (Basel: Verlag der Universitätsbibliothek, 1956), 50.
13 In 1556 Münster is mentioned in Q. Iacopo Moronessa da Lezze's catalogue of the most important heretics besides Melanchthon, Zwingli, Bucer, Farell, Pellikan and Oekolampad. Furthermore, he was listed on the Index librorum prohibitorum (1554) and mocked in an epigram by Andreas Frusius. See Andreas Frusius, *Epigrammata in Haereticos* (Köln: Bernhard Walter, 1600).
14 Martin Luther, *D. Martin Luthers Werke: kritische Gesamtausgabe*, vol. 3 (Weimar: Hermann Böhlau, 1883–2009), 362–63; Sebastian Münster, *Hebraica Biblia latina planeque nova* (Basel: J. Bebel, 1534–35).

helped him a lot, for he gives the Rabbis too much leeway, although he is hostile to the Jews, too, but not as much as I am."[15]

All in all, Münster's ambivalent attitude towards Judaism should not be equated with indifference. He had strong Christian beliefs and rejected the Jewish doctrine of the Messiah – but he did so no more than he disapproved the papacy.[16]

3 Münster's Relationship with Elia Levita

Aside from Münster's attitude towards Judaism in general, let us have a closer look at his personal relationships with individual Jews. Münster's work as a Hebraist can be divided between the time before and after his encounter with Elia Levita in 1525.[17] By re-editing Levita's books, by vocalizing them with vowel points and translating them into Latin, he made both Levita and himself famous throughout Central Europe.

But before I turn directly to Münster's relationship with Elia Levita, also known as Elia Baḥur or Elia Ben Asher Ashkenazi, a brief summary of Levita's eventful life is in order. Born in 1469 as the youngest of nine sons of Rabbi Asher Levita in the German town of Neustadt on the Aisch, Elia Levita's life was marked by several persecutions. In 1496 he emigrated to Venice and shortly thereafter to Padua. From 1509 on he had been living in Rome where he taught Cardinal Egidius da Viterbo, his most important patron, Hebrew. In 1527, in the course of the Sack of Rome, Levita lost all his property and many of his manuscripts, and had to escape to Venice, where he started to work as a corrector in the printing office of Daniel Bomberg. He spent the years 1540 to 1544 with the reformer Paul Fagius in the German Alpine town of Isny and in Constance. Together with him, Levita published some of his works. In the preface to one of those editions, Fagius wrote about his teacher Levita: "According to his faith, he is indeed still a Jew; but

---

15 "Munster gefelt mir wol, aber ich wolt, das er hie wer gewest und hett mitt uns hie conferiret; es solte im viel helffen. Denn er giebet den rabinis noch zu vil nach, wie wol er den Juden auch feind ist, abr er nimbt sichs so hefftig nicht an als ich." Luther, *D. Martin Luthers Werke*, vol. 5, 218.
16 Cf. Burmeister, *Sebastian Münster*, 106–07.
17 Cf. Thomas Willi, "Christliche Hebraistik aus jüdischen Quellen: Beobachtungen zu den Anfängen einer christlichen Hebraistik," in *Gottes Sprache in der philologischen Werkstatt. Hebraistik vom 15. bis zum 19. Jahrhundert*, ed. Giuseppe Veltri and Gerold Necker (Leiden and Boston: Brill, 2004): 44. Besides his correspondence with Levita, Münster also had contact with many other Jews, of whom Jakob Storck and Michael Adam are known by name, cf. Burmeister, *Sebastian Münster*, 75.

he is in truth not unfair to our faith and does not think spitefully about Christ our one and only Saviour."[18]

Among Levita's most famous publications are *Massoret ha-Massoret* (1538), *Sefer ha-Baḥur* (1517/18), *Meturgeman* (1541), *Tishbi* (1541) and several poetic works such as the *Bovo-Bukh* (1508) and *Paris un' Vienna* (1509), both written in Yiddish. He died in Venice in 1549.

Because of his extensive knowledge and his teaching abilities, he rapidly became a very popular teacher. He was in contact with Johannes Reuchlin and Andreas Osiander, and Philipp Melanchthon at least knew his books. Years later, the French King Francis I was so impressed by Levita's abilities that he offered him the professorship for Hebrew at the *Collège des trois langues* in Paris.[19] Levita turned the offer down, not wishing to be so removed from his co-religionists (there was no Jewish community at that time in Paris). But interestingly, Levita was similarly "caught between" like Münster. His orthodox brothers in faith resented Levita's cooperation with Christians. On the other side, Christians reproached him for proselytizing.

To sum up: we have here two men of different religions. Both had been critizised by their brothers in faith for working with "unbelievers." But at the same time, both were in need of each other: Münster needed Levita's Hebrew knowledge to instrumentalize it for Christian purposes, while Levita benefited from Münster making his books accessible to a broad, non-Jewish public.

We know that an intensive correspondence between Münster and Levita existed and it appears that Münster even wanted to publish it.[20] It would have been an invaluable resource for research into the roots of Christian Hebrew studies. But Münster had doubts as to the scholarly value of this material for his students and only one of these letters has survived down to the present. In this document, dated March 5, 1531, we can observe their respectful cooperation and even signs of a friendship between the two of them. Perhaps the mutual, in some way economic, dependence is the reason for the highly appreciative dealing with each other. But, possibly, the following remarks are also meant honestly, as Levita calls Münster an "intelligent and wise"[21] person and greets him with

---

18 "Religione quidem adhuc Judaeus est, sed qui vere non iniquus est in fidem nostram nec maligne sentiens de Christo unico redemptore nostro." In Elia Levita, *Tishbi* (Isny, 1541), praef.
19 Gérard E. Weil, *Élie Lévita. Humaniste et Massorète (1469–1549)* (Leiden: Brill, 1963), 237.
20 Sebastian Münster, *Perush al Amos ha-navi. Commentarivm Rabi Dauid Kimhi in Amos prophetam* (Basel: Apvd Henricum Petrum, 1531), praef.
21 "נבון וחכם" in: Moritz Peritz, "Ein Brief Elijah Levitas an Sebastian Münster. Nach der von letzterem 1531 besorgten Ausgabe desselben auf's Neue herausgegeben und mit einer deutschen

the words "May God [ha-Shem] grant you according to your request of heart [...] and may peace be with everything that is yours"[22] and in the letter's close: "Thus, farewell as you would like and as it is the wish of your friend, the man of your heart. Elijah Levi, Grammarian from Germany."[23] Levita and Münster probably never met personally. But Levita's desire for a visit becomes clear when he writes: "I wish I could be with you for one or two weeks and speak to you mouth to mouth."[24] On the other side, Münster offered similar praise of Levita: "In our Germany, a Jew who is an expert on grammar is not easy to find. Elia Levita, the German, who surpasses every Jew of our age through his studies, is unique."[25]

4 *The Sefer ha-Diqduq/Grammatica Hebraica Absolutissima*

Generally, a grammar is supposed to convey a certain norm of knowledge. But is this knowledge still the same when it is translated from one language, from one culture, from one religion into another? In addition to many other books of Elia Levita, Sebastian Münster translated his *Sefer ha-Baḥur* from Hebrew to Latin. This grammar, in Münster's edition entitled *Grammatica Hebraica Absolutissima*, shall be the subject of the following brief investigation. As we shall see, there are indications of Münster's Christian transformation of Levita's Jewish knowledge and evidence within the translation process concerning the relationship between Münster and Levita and also concerning his opinion of Judaism in general.

The *Grammatica Hebraica Absolutissima* was published by the printing press of Frobenius in Basel in 1525, eight years after Levita had written the original Hebrew text. Four further editions followed between 1532 and 1552. As is clear,

---

Uebersetzung und Anmerkungen versehen," *Monatsschrift für Geschichte und Wissenschaft des Judentums* 38 (N.F. 2), no. 6 (1894): 257.
22 "ושלום לכל אשר לך [...] יתן השם לך כלבבך" in: Peritz, "Ein Brief," 257.
23 "ובזה לך שלום כרצונך וכרצון אהובך איש כלבבך אליה לוי המדקדק אשכנזי", in: Peritz, "Ein Brief," 267.
24 "ומי יתן והייתי אצלך שבוע או שבועיים ופה אל פה אדבר בך" in: Peritz, "Ein Brief," 265–66.
25 "In nostra Germania, ubi non facilem Iudaeum aliquem invenies, qui grammaticae peritus sit. Unicus est Elias Levitas Germanus, qui suo studio facile superavit omnes nostrae aetatis Iudaeos." In Sebastian Münster, *Grammatica Rabbi Mosche Kimhi, iuxta hebraismum per Sebastianum Münsterum uersa. Accessit & utilissimum in eandem Eliae Levitae commentarium* (Basel: Andream Cratandrum, 1531), praef.

this grammar enjoyed great popularity – even after Münster had published a kind of "best-of" grammar of several of the Hebraist's works in 1542.[26]

The name ספר הבחור (*Sefer ha-Baḥur*), as Levita's grammar is originally called, can be translated in two different ways: "Book of the Youth" (as a subjective or objective genitive) or "The Choice Book." Münster decided for the latter variant and translated "Sefer ha-Baḥur" as "Liber electus." But there is yet a further difference between Levita's Hebrew text and Münster's Latin one concerning this title. In his preface, Levita explained the name as follows: "And, behold, I called this book with the name *Sefer ha-Baḥur*, and this for three reasons: first, for this book is excellent and good and totally pure; second, for it is written for every young man, so that he may learn with it in his days of youth, and it will be well in his heart in his last days; third, for this name is my peculiar nickname and with the name Baḥur I am called."[27]

That a translation can undermine the author-intended openness of a text can be seen when Münster belittles the choice of the name that Levita created in the homonym "baḥur." After having correctly translated Levita's first two explanations, Münster writes concerning the third one: "[. . .] so that the nickname is various, for that reason I name this (book) with the chosen name."[28] The reference to Levita's byname here is not as obvious anymore as it was in the Hebrew original. Contrary to his usual way of translation, Münster was not aware of the Hebrew forms in first person singular. Possibly, Levita's nickname was not familiar to him, since the *Sefer ha-Baḥur* was the first book of Levita with which Münster came into contact and in which Levita introduces himself as "Elijahu ha-Levi, called 'the German,'"[29] the name that can be found on the title page of Münster's edition of the *Sefer ha-Baḥur*.

From its very point of origin, the *Sefer ha-Baḥur* is evidence of intercultural and interreligious dialogue, for it was not Levita's idea to write it, but rather his patron, Cardinal Egidio da Viterbo, who inspired him to do so. For that reason and to express his thanks to him, Levita dedicated his Hebrew grammar to Egidio.[30] As such, the *Sefer ha-Baḥur* was intended for both Jewish and Christian students from the outset. Its importance for Hebrew studies on the Jewish side is reflected

---

26 Sebastian Münster, *Opus grammaticum consummatum* (Basel: Henricum Petrum, 1542).
27 והנה קראתי שם הספר הזה ספר הבחור וזה לשלש סבות האחת בהיות הספר הזה בחור וטוב וכולו סולת אין בו פסולת השנית בעבור היותו מחובר אל כל בחור ללמוד בו בימי בחרותו וייטב לבו באחריתו השלישית בעבור היות שם כנויי משונה ובשם בחור אכונה. In Levita, *Grammatica Hebraica Absolutissima*, praef.
28 "[. . .] ut sit cognomen varium, ideo nomine electo agnomino ipsum" Levita, *Grammatica Hebraica Absolutissima*, praef.
29 Elia Levita, *Sefer ha-Baḥur* (Rome, 1518), praef.
30 Levita, *Sefer ha-Baḥur*, praef.

by the fact that it – as the first book ever – got an official approbation by the Roman Rabbinical College.³¹

Levita's treatise is printed from right to left and divided into four parts. Each part is subdivided into thirteen sections, corresponding to the thirteen articles of the Jewish creed by Moses Maimonides.³² The entire number of sections, fifty-two, represents the numerical value of the name אליהו. The first part discusses the classification of Hebrew verbs, the second irregular verbs and the changes in the vowel points of different conjugations, the third regular nouns, and the fourth irregular ones. From the very beginning on, the *Sefer ha-Baḥur* was not written as a grammar with which students could learn Hebrew on their own. This is already clear from the fact that Levita's text is written in Hebrew only. Therefore, only students who had already learned the Hebrew alphabet and possessed a basic knowledge of grammar could use the *Sefer ha-Baḥur*. Levita himself admits: "[. . .] that [these matters], indeed, require extensive introduction, so we have left them aside and will talk with students about them directly (lit. mouth to mouth)."³³ So Münster supplemented the grammar with a general introduction at the beginning; and with explanations of the accents and conjugations, and declension tables in the appendix at the end. He thus made Levita's grammar accessible to a wider audience.

Before Münster became acquainted with the *Sefer ha-Baḥur*, he had planned to print the grammars by the brothers Kimḥi who, according to Münster, had the same stature in the field of Hebrew studies as Donatus and Priscianus for Latin.³⁴ But Münster did not carry out this plan, turning instead to the grammar by Abraham de Balmes that was recommended to him by a "rumor from Nuremberg."³⁵ However, while busy with that book, he realized: "Abraham de Balmes seems to me to do nothing else than continuously refute and assail the old teaching (lit. 'teaching of the ancients'); he is more involved in mocking than in teaching."³⁶ Thereafter, following the advice of his colleague Simon Grynaeus, the

---

31 J. Levi, *Elia Levita und seine Leistungen als Grammatiker* (Breslau: Schottlaender, 1888), 10.
32 Levita, *Sefer ha-Baḥur*, praef.
33 "[. . .] אבן היו צריכין להקדמות גדולות ולכן עזבנום ופה אל פה נדבר בם אל התלמידים [. . .]" resp. "[. . .] quae tamen indigent magnis praefationibus, ideo relinquimus ea, et ore ad os loquemur de eis ad discipulos." See Levita, *Grammatica Hebraica Absolutissima*, oratio prima, elementum quintum. Such remarks can be found more frequently within the grammar.
34 Levita, *Grammatica Hebraica Absolutissima*, praef.
35 See Levita, *Grammatica Hebraica Absolutissima*, praef. ("rumor allatus est ex Nuremberga").
36 "Abraham a Balmis nihil aliud agere mihi visus est, quam veterum doctrinam perpetuo convellere atque impugnare, magis in infectando occupatus quam in docendo." See Levita, *Grammatica Hebraica Absolutissima*, praef.

Professor of Greek in Heidelberg, Münster turned his attention to Levita's *Sefer ha-Baḥur* that was largely unknown in Germany at that time. Grynaeus was in raptures about Levita's grammar and, therefore, let Münster have his copy most willingly. Soon, Münster too was convinced by Levita's abilities. The title he gave to his edition of the *Sefer ha-Baḥur* attests his high opinion of this Jewish scholar: "The Most Perfect Hebrew Grammar by Elia Levita, the German; recently presented by Sebastian Münster in Latin alongside Hebrew, after which you reader will not without difficulty desire another one. Elementary introduction to the Hebrew language by the same author Sebast. Münster."[37]

This commendation of Levita continues in Münster's preface. He acknowledged Levita's achievements after he had been bitterly disappointed by the grammar of Abraham de Balmes: "I openly confess (and I am not ashamed to say it) that before I read this Elia I knew too little in grammatical matters; moreover that I owe much, nay rather very much, to his lucubrations. We had been teachers before we were students."[38] On the other hand, Münster's negative attitude towards Jewish methods of teaching Hebrew in general becomes obvious when he says: "It is a fact that the Jews thoroughly despise grammar. For they affirm that knowledge of their language is to be acquired not from rules but from constant reading of the Bible, just as if Cicero and Virgil among us or Lucianus and Homerus among the Greeks were to be continually offered to boys as needing to be learned instead of the rules of the grammarians. But we abandon the folly of the Jewish people."[39] The ambivalence of Münster's attitudes towards the Jews on a personal level and in general has already been noted.

---

[37] "Grammatica Hebraica Absolutissima, Eliae Levitae Germani: nuper per Sebastianum Munsterum iuxta Hebraismum Latinitate donata, post quam lector aliam non facile desiderabis. Institutio elementaria in Hebraicam linguam eodem Sebast. Munstero autore." Levita, *Grammatica Hebraica Absolutissima*, title page.

[38] "Ego sane fateor ingenue (nec dicere pudet) me priusquam Eliam istum legerem, in grammaticis parum scisse, multum autem imo plurimum huius lucubrationibus me debere. Fuimus praeceptores antequam discipuli." Levita, *Grammatica Hebraica Absolutissima*, praef.

[39] "Accedit quod Iudaei grammaticam plane contemptui habent. Neque enim ex regulis sed ex assidua lectione Bibliorum, suae linguae parandam cognitionem astruunt, perinde ac si apud nos Cicero & Virgilius, aut apud Graecos Lucianus & Homerus pueris statim discendi proponerentur non grammaticorum canones. Sed mittamus Iudaicae gentis ineptias." Levita, *Grammatica Hebraica Absolutissima*, praef.

5 Hebrew Between Faith and Knowledge? – The Propaedeutical Introduction to Münster's Edition of Levita's *Sefer ha-Baḥur*

How the approach to Hebrew by those students who worked with Münster's edition of Levita's *Sefer ha-Baḥur* was influenced by his Christian point of view shall now be shown with some examples from the *Elementaria Institutio in Hebraicam linguam*, written in Latin and in Hebrew, and presenting Hebrew phonetics and numerals. It is currently uncertain who might be the author of this text.[40] For the following considerations it may suffice to know that Münster – as editor and therefore responsible for the overall concept and structure of the *Grammatica Hebraica Absolutissima* – decided to prefix this *Institutio* to his edition of Levita's grammar.

In addition, the question of whether the Hebrew text is original – and the Latin version, consequently, merely a translation thereof – has remained unanswered down to the present. In light of the current state of research, I suspect that the elementary introduction was first written in Hebrew and then translated into Latin, because the examples given within the Latin text with Latin letters do not make sense for explaining grammatical phenomena, e.g ברוא is translated as "creatus" to illustrate the quiescent letter א. Thence, the Latin text seen without the Hebrew would be of little use. But it must be admitted that the introduction was written for non-Jewish students of Hebrew and that one cannot expect them to read Hebrew letters unassisted. Therefore, the combination of the Latin translation as it is printed opposite the Hebrew text is a helpful didactic method at least to allow simultaneous reading and thus to support learning initial vocabulary. Possibly both text versions were produced in parallel by one and the same author, who liked to assist students of the Hebrew language by presenting a bilingual text.

After the preface, in which Münster recounts his discovery of the *Sefer ha-Baḥur*, the elementary introduction begins with a list of the Hebrew alphabet, not by writing out letter after letter, but rather by giving the full names of each letter according to both the Latin and the Hebrew spelling. In what follows, the letters

---

40 Cf. Joseph Prijs and Bernhard Prijs, *Die Basler hebräischen Drucke (1492–1866)* (Olten: Urs Graf-Verlag, 1964), 34, who suspect that the Hebrew text of the introduction was written by an earlier, skillful Christian Hebraist (e.g. Johann Böschenstein or Matthäus Adrianus). This opinion competes with the information from the title indicating that Sebastian Münster himself is the author of the *Institutio elementaria in Hebraicam linguam*. However, this question seems to be more complex and has to be investigated on another occasion.

are classified as letters of the throat, palate, tongue, teeth and lips, and the rules of using the *dagesh*, a diacritic that indicates the doubling of a consonant or its particular pronunciation, are presented. Thereafter, the vowel points are listed and their names are explained. The rules of the *shewa* and the quiescent letters follow.

As indicated above, there is also a short paragraph about the Hebrew numeric system. As an example thereof, the author writes "the year of our Messiah" 1525 in Hebrew letters, old Roman capital numerals and Arabic numerals.[41] The reference to שנת המשיחנו resp. "annus Meschiae nostri" proves an incontestable Christian authorship.

The *Elementaria Institutio* ends with a short paragraph about the root and the servile letters in general. Münster also added a second section called *Explicatio compendiosa* that deals with the servile letters and syllables in detail and is written only in Latin, but offers examples in Hebrew letters. The further the text goes on, the longer the examples illustrating the grammatical characteristics of Hebrew become. And the longer the text, the more often the examples are translated and not just transcribed. As such, the author relies on the developing learning process of his students – learning letters turns into learning words.

The text provides examples from the entire Hebrew Bible. Sometimes the verses can be determined with ease,[42] as when the author uses rare forms or even *hapax legomena*; e.g. explaining that letters can be replaced, he quotes Ez 21:20 "אבחת חרב [the slaughter of the sword] instead of אבעת."[43] This example is taken from Ezekiel's judgement speech against Israel, the "Song of the Sword" in particular, in which God sends His all-devastating sword against Israel's officials and the entire people. Given the choice of example from such a severe passage against Israel, once can suspect an anti-Judaistic attitude in the Christian author. Another conspicuous example is found in the explanation that ה as characteristic of feminine gender at the end of a word may change into ת in several constructions: חטאת העם resp. "peccatum populi" ["sin of the people"]. This exact Hebrew form does not occur within the Hebrew Bible, while the term "peccatum

---

41 "[25] כה [1500] אקת or [25] כה [500] רש [1000] רתת" and in Latin "M. CCCCC. XXV. or 1525." Levita, *Grammatica Hebraica Absolutissima, Institutio elementaria*.

42 Unlike in the original *Sefer ha-Baḥur*, in which Levita notes the relevant book and chapter of every single biblical quote, the *Institutio elementaria* and the "Explicatio compendiosa" do not specify the origin of the biblical examples.

43 Levita, *Grammatica Hebraica Absolutissima, Institutio elementaria*. The form אבעט does not occur within the Hebrew Bible. "To slaughter" is typically represented by the root טבח, cf. the text-critical note to אבחת חרב in Ez 21:20 in the Biblia Hebraica Stuttgartensia. In general, the textual tradition of Ezekiel's "Song of the Sword" is very uncertain.

populi" appears frequently in the Vulgate.⁴⁴ As was the case with the example from Ezekiel, one could also here point to the anti-Judaistic views of the author. It seems probable that the author also shared the widespread accusation against Jews, characteristic among Christians of his age, of deicide⁴⁵ for having killed Jesus.⁴⁶

These examples are serious, although one must not forget that both are completely taken out of their biblical context. Likewise, the author has left his examples completely uncommented in terms of religious contents. It is not said that the "slaughter of the sword" was aimed against Israel, nor is העם resp. "populus" ["the people"] identified. In addition, most of the other examples within the particular context of the grammatical consideration⁴⁷ have no specific meaning for their content. Nonetheless, a theological sub-text cannot be ruled out – it is rather likely when we have a closer look at the following examples that are taken from the Hebrew Bible, but can clearly be placed in a Christian context without mentioning individuals from the New Testament by name, as for example אשה בבתוליה⁴⁸ "mulier in virginitatibus suis" ["a woman in her virginity"] as a reference to the Virgin Mary.⁴⁹ Or ⁵⁰מי יעלה השמימה "quis ascendet in coelum" ["who will go up to heaven"], alluding to the Ascension of Jesus.⁵¹ The form לחמנו, including the first person plural suffix occurs only four times in the Hebrew Bible,⁵² but its Latin translation "panis noster" ["our bread"] is a prominent part of the Lord's Prayer.⁵³ Another example is מסה במדבר, namely "temptatio in deserto" ["temptation in the desert"]. In the Hebrew Bible there is a brief reference to מסה at Exodus

---

44 Cf. Num 14:19; 1.Kings 8:34; Hos 4:8 and Dan 9:20 (cf. also Isa 1:4). With respect to the Hebrew example, there are similar constructions in Hos 4:8 (חטאת עמי), Jer 17:1 (חטאת יהודה) and Hos 10:8 (חטאת ישראל).
45 This term first appeared explicitly with Melito from Sardes in the late second century C.E. Cf. Nicholas R. M. De Lange, "Antisemitismus IV," in *Theologische Realenzyklopädie*, vol. 3, ed. Gerhard Müller, Horst Balz, James K. Cameron, Brian L. Hebbletwaite, and Gerhard Krause (Berlin and New York: De Gruyter, 1978), 128–37, esp. 130.
46 Well-known examples from this period of authors who engaged in the accusation of "deicide" against the Jews include Martin Luther ("Von den Jüden und ihren Lügen," 1543) and Johannes Reuchlin ("Tütsch Missiue. Warumb die Juden so lang im Ellend sind," 1505) – to name just two.
47 E.g. שינא resp. "somnus" [sleep], ילד resp. "puer" [child] or ירויון resp. "inebriabuntur" [they will drink plenty].
48 Lev 21:13.
49 Cf. Matt 1:23; Luke 1:27.
50 The object לנו is missing in the example which is taken from the pure Latin "Explicatio compendiosa" and originally written in Deut 30:12.
51 Cf. Luke 24:51; Acts 1:10f.
52 Num 14:9; Jos 9:12; Isa 4:1; Lam 5:9.
53 Cf. Matt 6:11; Luke 11:3.

17:7, where the Israelites, driven by their thirst for water, tempt the Lord in the desert. As a result, Moses calls the place Massa and Meribah ["temptation and strife"]. The wording of the example can be found in Ps 95:8, which refers to Ex 17:7. For Christian readers it is obvious that this example evokes Jesus' temptation in the desert in Mark 1:12. A final example for the author's implicit use of the Hebrew Bible in a Christian light is the quotation of Ps 22:2: למה עזבתני, i.e. "quare dereliquisti me" ["why have you forsaken me"].[54] Remarkably, Jesus' last words on the cross are also the last Hebrew words of the introductory part of the *Grammatica Hebraica Absolutissima*.

But the most glaring indication of the Christian approach to Hebrew in the *Elementaria Institutio* is found in the context of the author's declaration that this language has only consonant letters (as opposed to vowels), and thus that syllables can only be formed by combining letters and vowel-points. The example provided for this principle is nothing less than a Christian creed: אב בן רוח קדוש אל אחד (the Latin text transcribes it as "af ben ruah kadosch, el aehad" ["Father, Son, Holy Spirit, one God"]). This confessional formula is not a direct quotation of a biblical passage. No Jewish author would have written these words – especially not to express a grammatical norm of the holy language! Here is yet another indication that the author of the introduction to Münster's *Grammatica Hebraica Absolutissima* must have been Christian and of how he used his knowledge of Hebrew to disseminate the central planks of his Christian faith.

6 Conclusion

Translation is not just the transferring of information from one language into another but also the interpretation of the content. Sometimes, the translator also intentionally interferes in the text in order to adjust it to his own values and norms. As the translator of the *Sefer ha-Baḥur*, Sebastian Münster interpreted Elia Levita's work by prefixing to it a Christian propaedeutical introduction to Hebrew grammar. Thus, an originally Jewish grammar is now prefaced by a work that places the entire study of the Hebrew language in a markedly Christian light from the outset.

Münster's approach to the Hebrew language was ambivalent; perhaps we can say that he was caught between a Jewish and a Christian way of teaching Hebrew. As a Christian scholar, Münster read the Hebrew Bible from the perspective of the New Testament. But because of his immense interest in Hebrew, he sought out per-

---

54 Cf. Mark 15:34; Matt 27:46.

sonal contact with Jews. In addition, his own exegetical and commentary work on several biblical books furnishes evidence for his willingness to approach the other religion. Concerning Hebrew as well as the Bible, Münster's way of integrating rabbinic literature into source research was progressive and in a way pioneering for subsequent centuries, although many of his contemporaries disapproved of it. But today of it has become clear that interpretation of the New Testament without knowledge of talmudic literature is inconceivable, as is the case for biblical exegesis that excludes ancient Jewish texts, such as those found in Qumran.[55]

Bibliography

Burmeister, Karl H. *Sebastian Münster: Versuch eines biographischen Gesamtbildes.* Basel and Stuttgart: Helbing & Lichtenhahn, 1963.
Burnett, Stephen G. "Spokesmen for Judaism: Medieval Jewish Polemicists and their Christian Readers in the Reformation Era." In *Reuchlin und seine Erben. Forscher, Denker, Ideologen und Spinner,* edited by Peter Schäfer and Irina Wandrey, 41–52. Ostfildern: Thorbecke, 2005.
De Lange, Nicholas R. M. "Antisemitismus IV." In *Theologische Realenzyklopädie,* vol. 3, edited by Gerhard Müller, Horst Balz, James K. Cameron, Brian L. Hebbletwaite, and Gerhard Krause, 128–37. Berlin and New York: De Gruyter, 1978.
Frusius, Andreas. *Epigrammata in Haereticos.* Köln: Bernhard Walter, 1600.
Levi, J. *Elia Levita und seine Leistungen als Grammatiker.* Breslau: Nabu Press, 1888.
Levita, Elia. *Grammatica Hebraica Absolutissima: sēfär haddiqdûq,* ed. Sebastian Münster. Basel: Io. Frobenium, 1525.
Levita, Elia. *Sefer ha-Baḥur.* Rome, 1518.
Levita, Elia. *Tishbi.* Isny, 1541.
Luther, Martin. *D. Martin Luthers Werke: kritische Gesamtausgabe.* Weimar: Hermann Böhlau, 1883–2009.
Münster, Sebastian. *Hebraica Biblia latina planeque nova.* Basel: J. Bebel, 1534–35.
Münster, Sebastian. *Grammatica Rabbi Mosche Kimhi, iuxta hebraismum per Sebastianum Münsterum uersa. Accessit & utilissimum in eandem Eliae Levitae commentarium.* Basel: Andream Cratandrum, 1531.
Münster, Sebastian. *Messias Christianorum et Judaeorum hebraicè & latinè.* Basel: Henricum Petrum, 1539.
Münster, Sebastian. *Opus grammaticum consummatum: mĕläkät haddiqdûq haššālēm.* Basel: Henricum Petrum, 1542.
Münster, Sebastian. *Perush al Amos ha-navi. Commentarivm Rabi Dauid Kimhi in Amos prophetam.* Basel: Henricum Petrum, 1531.

---

[55] For further discussion of Sebastian Münster's edition of *Sefer ha-Baḥur,* see Melanie Lange, *Ein Meilenstein der Hebraistik: Der "Sefer ha-Bachur" Elia Levitas in Sebastian Münsters Übersetzung und Edition* (Leipzig: Evangelische Verlagsanstalt, 2018).

Peritz, Moritz. "Ein Brief Elijah Levitas an Sebastian Münster. Nach der von letzterem 1531 besorgten Ausgabe desselben auf's Neue herausgegeben und mit einer deutschen Uebersetzung und Anmerkungen versehen." *Monatsschrift für Geschichte und Wissenschaft des Judentums* 38 (N.F. 2), no. 6 (1894): 252–67.

Prijs, Joseph, and Bernhard Prijs. *Die Basler hebräischen Drucke (1492–1866)*. Olten: Urs Graf-Verlag, 1964.

Schreckenfuchs, Erasmus O. *Trauerrede zum Gedächtnis seines Lehrers Sebastian Münster, Freiburg, 1552*, trans. Erwin Emmerling. Beiträge zur Ingelheimer Geschichte 12. Ingelheim: Historischer Verein, 1960.

Von Beza, Theodor. *Johannis Calvini vita*, ed. Thomas Nickel. Güstrow: ex officina Ebertiana, 1862.

Wackernagel, Hans G., ed. *Die Matrikel der Universität Basel, vol. 2*. Basel: Verlag der Universitätsbibliothek, 1956.

Weil, Gérard E. *Élie Lévita. Humaniste et Massorète (1469–1549)*. Leiden: Brill, 1963.

Willi, Thomas. "Christliche Hebraistik aus jüdischen Quellen: Beobachtungen zu den Anfängen einer christlichen Hebraistik." In *Gottes Sprache in der philologischen Werkstatt. Hebraistik vom 15. bis zum 19. Jahrhundert*, edited by Giuseppe Veltri and Gerold Necker, 25–48. Leiden and Boston: Brill, 2004.

Stephen G. Burnett
Luther and Hebrew

1 Introduction

Statues of Martin Luther are a common sight in Germany. They are most frequently found in cities where he worked and lived, such as Eisenach and Wittenberg. Nearly all of these representations have Luther standing alone, one man on a pedestal. Even in the remarkable Worms Reformation monument with its crowd of reformers and their medieval predecessors, Luther's pedestal is higher than all of the others. In both popular presentations and even in scholarship, Luther is often treated as a uniquely important and gifted individual who had no peers.

Lutherans praise Luther as the one man most responsible for restoring the pure Gospel to the church after the long nightmare of medieval Catholicism. He had the courage to defy both Pope Leo X and Emperor Charles V, declaring at the Diet of Worms (1521),

> Unless I am convinced by the testimony of the Scriptures or by clear reason (for I do not trust either in the pope or in councils alone, since it is well known that they have often erred and contradicted themselves), I am bound by the Scriptures I have quoted and my conscience is captive to the Word of God. I cannot and I will not retract anything, since it is neither safe nor right to go against conscience. May God help me. Amen.[1]

Among his many achievements, Luther is remembered for translating the Bible into German, a translation that is still in use today, though it has been revised considerably since Luther's day. The act of remembering Luther's achievements has the effect of building his pedestal higher and higher, leaving us with the impression that he was like some kind of Olympic athlete who went from strength to strength throughout his career: "Citius, Altius, Fortius" (faster, higher, stronger).

The theme of Luther and Hebrew allows us to consider Luther's signature achievement, his German Bible, as a work of scholarship.[2] It allows us to take him off his pedestal and analyze his work, which he achieved in part by working closely with a team of Wittenberg colleagues. Luther would have liked this; he preferred company to solitude.

---

[1] Martin Brecht, *Martin Luther: His Road to Reformation 1483–1521*, trans. James L. Schaff (Philadelphia: Fortress Press, 1985), 460.
[2] Abbreviations: WA = *D. Martin Luthers Werke; kritische Gesamtausgabe* (Weimar: H. Bohlau, 1883–2001), 104 vols.; WA Br = *Briefwechsel*; WA TR = *Tischreden*; WA DB = *Deutsche Bibel*; LW = *Luther's Works* (Saint Louis: Concordia Publishing, 1955-2020), 82 vols.

2 Luther the Hebrew Student

Before the Reformation, a non-Jew in German-speaking Europe had great difficulty learning Hebrew. Johannes Reuchlin worked with three different Jewish tutors over the years, and Conrad Pellican's path to Hebrew knowledge was more difficult still. He had to learn the basics of Hebrew by comparing a literal Latin translation of the Prophets with the original Hebrew, and then figure out the grammar for himself. Not until a decade or so later was he able to study, however briefly, with the Jewish convert, Matthäus Adrianus, in Bruchsal.[3] At the time Luther began learning Hebrew, probably in 1509, he had only three possible choices of printed Hebrew grammars written in Latin: the short sketch of Hebrew printed as an appendix in Aldus Manutius' various grammars, Conrad Pellican's grammatical sketch first printed in 1504, and Reuchlin's *De Rudimenta* (1506).[4] He wisely picked Reuchlin's book, which contained both a Hebrew grammar and lexicon. Luther would continue to use it as his guide to Hebrew until the very end of his career, when he lectured on Genesis (1535–1545).[5] Until Philip Melanchthon came to Wittenberg in 1518, Luther apparently studied Hebrew by himself. Melanchthon, by contrast, had some instruction from his famous relative, Johannes Reuchlin. Melanchthon actually taught Hebrew at the University of Wittenberg when necessary, though he always preferred Greek to Hebrew.[6]

When Matthäus Aurogallus joined the Wittenberg faculty as professor of Hebrew in 1521, Luther gained not only an additional expert in Hebrew to work with, but one of the most important members of his "Biblical colloquium." Melanchthon and Aurogallus began working closely with Luther while he was revising his Pentateuch translation for publication in 1523.[7] He continued to consult these men and other scholars for almost two decades through both the first printing of

---

[3] Stephen G. Burnett, *Christian Hebraism in the Reformation Era: Authors, Books, and the Transmission of Jewish Learning* (Leiden: Brill, 2012), 52.

[4] Stephen G. Burnett, "Reassessing the 'Basel-Wittenberg Conflict': Dimensions of Reformation-Era Hebrew Scholarship," in *Hebraica Veritas? Christian Hebraists and the Study of Hebrew in Early Modern Europe*, ed. Allison P. Coudert and Jeffrey S. Shoulson (Philadelphia: University of Pennsylvania Press, 2004): 181–201, here 185–186.

[5] Siegfried Raeder, "The Exegetical and Hermeneutical Work of Martin Luther," in *Hebrew Bible/Old Testament: The History of its Interpretation*. Vol. 2, *From the Renaissance to the Enlightenment*, ed. Magne Sæbø (Göttingen: Vandenhoeck & Ruprecht, 2008): 363–406, here 397.

[6] Melanchton's copy of *De Rudimenta* has been preserved in the Rostock Universitätsbibliothek and contains a good deal of marginalia in his hand. Volker Gummelt, *Lex und Evangelium: Untersuchungen zur Jesajavorlesung von Johannes Bugenhagen*, Arbeiten zur Kirchengeschichte 62 (Berlin: Walter de Gruyter, 1994), 98.

[7] Raeder, "Exegetical and Hermeneutical Work," 397.

the entire German Bible in 1534, and then a complete revision of the translation from 1539–1541. Johannes Mathesius, one of Luther's former students, described Luther's meetings with his colleagues for the second revision of the Bible:

> Luther appointed the best men who were available. They came together in the Doctor's house once a week for some hours before supper, namely D. Johann Bugenhagen, D. Justus Jonas, D. Caspar Creutziger, Master Philipp Melanchthon and Matthaeus Aurogallus. Georg Roerer was also present. He was a corrector. Often foreign doctors and learned men came to this high work. . . . When Doctor [Luther] had checked the [printed] German Bible, he came into the consistorium, having his old [Latin] and new German Bible and in addition the Hebrew text [with him]. Master Philip brought the Greek text with him, Doctor Creutziger the Hebrew Bible and the Aramaic text. The professors had with them their Rabbis. D. Pommer [Bugenhagen] had before his eyes also a Latin text; he was very familiar with it. At first everybody had prepared for the text to be discussed and had looked into Greek, Latin and Jewish interpretations. Then Luther proposed a text and asked one after the other, what each of them wanted to say about it, according to the nature of the language or according to the interpretations of the old doctors. Wonderful and informative speeches were given about this work. Master Georg Roerer has written some of them down [1539–1541].[8]

As Mathesius noted, Luther and many members of his committee owned their own Hebrew Bibles. Luther probably acquired his first Hebrew Bible (Brescia, 1494) sometime between 1515 and 1518. It was a small book, easy to carry around, which may have been the reason that Luther held on to it until the end of his career.[9] Melanchthon owned at least two Hebrew Bibles, a Bomberg Rabbinic Bible (1517) and another one without commentaries, both purchased at the Leipzig book fair in 1518.[10] Caspar Cruciger also owned a Rabbinic Bible by 1540. Mathesius' phrase "The professors had their rabbis with them," may mean that the others brought Münster's *Hebraica Biblia* (1534–35) with its Hebrew text and annotations containing excerpts from Jewish Bible commentaries, or perhaps Nicholas of Lyra's Bible commentary. Although some of the men in the room, most notably Aurogallus, could read Jewish Bible commentaries in the Rabbinic Bible for themselves, Luther and most of the others were probably dependent upon summaries and digests such as Münster or Lyra for whatever knowledge of Jewish interpretation

---

8 Raeder, "Exegetical and Hermeneutical Work," 400. Johannes Mathesius, *Leben Dr. Martin Luthers, in Siebzehn Predigten*, ed. A.J.D. Rust (Berlin: Crantz, 1841), 281–282. Roerer's minutes are printed in: WA DB 3, 166–580; 4, 1–278.
9 Christoph Mackert, "Luthers Handexemplar der hebräischen Bibelausgabe von 1494 – objektbezogene und besitzgeschichtliche Aspekte," in *Meilensteine der Reformation: Schlüsseldokumente der frühen Wirksamkeit Martin Luthers*, ed. Irene Dingel and Henning P. Jürgens (Gütersloh: Gütersloher Verlagshaus, 2014): 70–78, with plates 4–8.
10 Philipp Melanchthon to [Georg Spalatin], *Melanchtons Briefwechsel. Kritische und Kommentierte Gesamtausgabe*, ed. Heinz Scheible (Stuttgart-Bad Cannstatt: Fromman-Holzboog, 1991), vol. 1, 75, l. 1–3 [letter 24].

they had. For Luther, in particular, it is important to remember that what he knew of Jewish biblical interpretation consisted of comments that had been excerpted and filtered by others. He was mostly reading passages and comments that other Christian scholars found useful for one reason or another, rather than the original texts themselves.

Luther depended upon Reuchlin's *De Rudimenta* (1506) and upon his colleagues' help for much of what he did, but there are two other facets of his Hebrew learning to consider: his willingness to use whatever Christian Hebraica was available, and his own decades-long disciplined reading of the Hebrew Bible. Luther and his colleagues were "early adopters" of the new Hebrew philology. Luther's revision of his Psalms translation around 1530 reflects in part his use of Martin Bucer's Psalms commentary (1529). When lecturing on Isaiah (1528–1530), he used Johannes Oecolampadius' Isaiah commentary (1525). Although Luther and his colleagues sharply disagreed with both Bucer and Oecolampadius on important issues such as the Eucharist, they were willing to seek help wherever they could find it when it came to reading and interpreting the Hebrew Bible. Luther's frequent references to Sebastian Münster's Bible translation and annotations, beginning in 1536 in the *Table Talk* and continuing through the 1540s, reflect Münster's importance to Luther as an interpretive resource and also his frequent disagreements with some of Münster's interpretations.[11] The Wittenberg University Library collection also attests to the eagerness of the Wittenbergers to stay abreast of the latest Hebrew scholarship, and the willingness of the Elector to fund it.[12]

Finally, an underappreciated part of Luther's encounter with the Hebrew Bible and Hebrew language was his decades-long study of the language by reading the Bible itself. Already in 1522, when Johannes Kessler and his friends found Luther (disguised as Junker Jörg) reading the Psalms in Hebrew in the public room of the Schwarzer Bär in Jena, Luther solemnly told them that the secret to learning Hebrew was to practice every day.[13] Luther read the entire Hebrew Bible all the way through at least three times as he prepared his German Bible translation and

---

[11] Burnett, "'Basel-Wittenberg Conflict'," 190. More recently, see Thomas Kaufmann, *Luthers "Judenschriften": Ein Beitrag zu ihrer historischen Kontextualisierung* (Tübingen: Mohr-Siebeck, 2011), 172–174.
[12] Burnett, "Basel-Wittenberg Controversy," 188.
[13] "Ir mögend es (Hebrew) wol ergrifen, wo ir anderst fliss anwenden; dann ich och beger witer zu erlernen und mich teglich herinn ub." Johannes Kessler, *Johannes Kesslers Sabbata mit kleineren Schriften und Briefe*, ed. Emil Egli and Rudolf Schoch (St. Gallen: Fehr'sche Buchhandlung, 1902), 78, 12.

its various revisions (1534, 1539–41).[14] Some books, such as the Psalms, Luther read and taught even more frequently.

Because Luther was involved in Bible translating for much of his career, he was not free to avoid difficult biblical passages; he had to try to understand them all. Luther had particular trouble reading Job. He wrote to Spalatin in February of 1524 that Job had suffered more from the attempts of his translators than from the bad advice of his friends.[15] In his *Open Letter on Translating* (1530), Luther recalled the troubles that he, Melanchthon, and Aurogallus had when they worked on the book of Job.

> I have constantly tried in translating to produce a pure and clear German, and it has often happened that for two or three or four weeks we have searched and inquired for a single word and sometimes have not found it even then. In translating Job, Master Philip, Aurogallus and I labored so that sometimes we scarcely handled three lines in four days.[16]

In light of Luther's Bible translation work, his constant complaints about the poor quality of the Hebrew reference books available to him become clearer. Luther felt duty bound to translate each and every word, expression, and sentence of the Bible as best he could. He was not very sympathetic or understanding when his reference books failed to do the same. This is also part of the reason why he criticized Jewish interpreters repeatedly.

3 Hebrew: The Language of the Jews

Luther's most memorable statement on Hebrew learning reflects his conflicting attitudes toward both the Hebrew language and the Jewish authorities who wrote about it. In 1532, Luther told his table companions, "If I wished to study Hebrew I would take and read the purest and best grammarians, David Kimhi and Moses Kimhi." But he then went on to say, "I am no Hebraist according to grammar and the rules, for I never allow myself to be bound [by them], but pass freely

---

[14] Most of Luther's Old Testament translation was printed between 1523–24, but the fourth part (Prophets) took much longer to complete. Luther and his colleagues revised the entire Bible from January to March 1534 before it was printed, and then again in 1539–41. Raeder, "Exegetical and Hermeneutical Work," 397–400.
[15] Luther to Spalatin, 23 February 1524. Quoted by Raeder, "Exegetical and Hermeneutical Work," 398 from WA DB 3, 249, 15–17.
[16] *On Translating-An Open Letter* (1530), WA 30.II:632–646 = LW 35:188.

through."[17] Luther was probably not declaring his independence from the Kimhis and their rules of grammar, but rather expressing his opinion about the limits of their Hebrew knowledge. He may also have been alluding to the importance of a Christo-centric interpretation of the Old Testament, something fundamentally important to Luther the Old Testament scholar.

Luther acknowledged that Hebrew was the language of the Jews, and that Christians first had to learn what the Kimhis and other Jewish experts could teach them about the language and its rules. Luther believed this until the very end of his life. In *On the Ineffable Name* (1543), he wrote:

> Learning their language and grammar from them is well and good, just as they do when they learn German from us, Italian from Italians, or the language of the land, wherever they are. However, they do not learn our faith and understanding of Scripture. In the same way, we, too, should learn their language from them but shun their faith and understanding, which God has condemned.[18]

Even in the midst of one of Luther's most vicious anti-Jewish works, he acknowledged Christian dependence upon Jewish instruction for learning Hebrew.

Luther was stating the obvious by acknowledging Jewish expertise. Reuchlin's *De Rudimenta* (1506) was essentially a Latin version of David Kimhi's *Michlol*, a combination grammar and dictionary.[19] Santes Pagninus was also heavily dependent upon David Kimhi's works for his own grammars and lexicons. Both Sebastian Münster and Paul Fagius translated the grammatical works of Elijah Levita into Latin, making them accessible to Christian students.

Luther had both philological and theological reasons to distrust Jewish scholarship although, as Siegfried Raeder pointed out, Luther tended to *identify* these two aspects of biblical scholarship rather than to *distinguish* between them.[20] Philologically, Luther had several reservations about the trustworthiness of Jewish linguistic scholarship. First, he believed that the Hebrew vowel points were not a part of the canonical biblical text, but rather an invention of the rabbis, and therefore could not be fully trusted. In his discussion of Psalm 22:16 in *Operationes in Psalmos* (1519–21), Luther asserted that the only philologically defensible explanation of the verse was the one reflected in the Septuagint and in the Vulgate: "they pierced

---

[17] WA, Ser 4: TR 1:525, #1040 (first half of 1530's = TR 3:243, #3271a, 9 August 1532). Translation from Jerome Friedman, *The Most Ancient Testimony. Sixteenth-Century Christian-Hebraica in the Age of Renaissance Nostalgia* (Athens OH: Ohio University Press, 1983), 128.
[18] WA 53:646, 13–15 = LW 61:502.
[19] Ludwig Geiger, *Das Studium der Hebräische Sprache in Deutschland vom Ende des XV. bis zur Mitte des XVI Jahrhunderts* (Breslau: Schletter, 1970), 35.
[20] Siegfried Raeder, *Grammatica Theologica: Studien zu Luthers Operationes in Psalmos* (Tübingen: Mohr, 1977), 4–6.

my hands and feet." Raeder commented here that for Luther it was clear "that the vowel points could not be trusted, because they were only invented later."[21] When commenting on Genesis 47:31 in his Genesis lectures, Luther discussed the age of the vowel points and their limitations as an exegetical aid.

> Somewhere Münster quotes a rabbi who says: "Holy Scripture cannot be understood without what is above and what is below," that is without the upper and lower points . . . It surely seems that at the time of Jerome points were not yet in use, but the whole Bible was read without them. But I do not agree with the Hebrews of more recent times. They arrogate to themselves the decisions regarding the true meaning and understanding of the language. But they are enemies of Scripture, not friends. Therefore I often pronounce contrary to the points, unless the previous meaning [their interpretation] agrees with the New Testament . . . Hence I do not worry much about the above and below of the rabbis. It would be better to read Scripture according to what is inside. And the New Testament gives us an inner understanding, not an upper or a lower one.[22]

For Luther, a Christocentric understanding of the text took precedence over its philological features.

In *On the Ineffable Name* (1543), Luther asserted that the true role of a Christian Hebrew scholar was to cleanse "the holy, ancient Bible from the Jews' peres [dung] and Judas-piss. Wherever they may amend and extricate the pointing, distinction, conjugation, construction, signification, and any other grammatical issues from the Jews' understanding so that it agrees and harmonizes with the New Testament."[23] The vowel points, however, were only one of Luther's concerns with Jewish linguistic scholarship. He also questioned the adequacy of their linguistic aids such as grammars and dictionaries.

Luther believed that much of what Jews had once known about the Hebrew language had been forgotten over the centuries. Through over twenty years of Bible translating and lecturing, Luther came to realize how woefully inadequate all existing Hebrew grammars and lexicons were in dealing with some Hebrew words and with figures of speech and proverbs.[24] On several occasions Luther

---

21 Raeder, *Grammatica Theologica*, 51.
22 WA 44:682, 33-683, 12 = LW 8:141.
23 "Darumb solten unsere Ebreisten (darumb ich sie auch hiemit wil umb Gottes willen gebeten haben) lassen ihn diese erbeit befolhen und angelegen sein, die heilige alte Bibel von der Jüden Peres und Judas pisse zu reinigen Wo sie die punct, distinction, coniugation, construction, signification und was mehr die Grammatica hat, kündten endern und von der Jüden verstand wenden, das sichs zum und mit dem newen Testament reimet . . . " *Vom Schem Hamphoras*, WA 53:646, 19-24 = LW 61:502.
24 See Gerhard Krause, *Studien zu Luthers Auslegung der Kleinen Propheten*, Beiträge zur Historischen Theologie 33 (Tübingen: Mohr Siebeck Verlag, 1962), 71-72, 199-202; and Dietrich Thyen, "Luthers Jesajavorlesung" (PhD diss., Universität Heidelberg, 1964), 109, 138, 170-186.

commented in the Genesis lectures that neither he nor the rabbis knew what particular words meant.²⁵ For example, when Luther commented on Genesis 25:30, the passage where Esau sells Jacob his birthright, he noted a *hapax legomenon*, a word that occurs once in the Bible.

> I commend this passage to the Hebrew grammarians for more careful explanation, for it is impossible to translate any language in such a way that all the emphases and forms of all words and sentences are preserved. The verb Esau uses in speaking to Jacob is *ha'liteni*, "feed me." It occurs in this passage only, but what its meaning is, neither the Jews nor I know.²⁶

On a darker note, Luther concluded his comment on the word *abaq*, "fine dust," in Genesis 32:24 by saying:

> However, I think that it is one of the words not adequately known, because the Hebrew language has not yet been perfectly restored. The Jews by their ambiguous interpretations have introduced many perversions, especially in the dark passages concerning the Messiah.²⁷

Ignorance of what many Hebrew words meant was troubling to Luther the Bible translator and scholar. When lecturing on Zephaniah 2:14 in 1527, Luther commented, "Up to this very day grammarians of the Hebrew language argue about the names of things, as important men have argued also about this matter. Because the Hebrew language is, to a great extent, lost to us, so that we can make no certain decision about many words, we follow that uncertain light whenever we can find nothing better."²⁸ He felt this lack keenly since it was only possible to render a passage into good German if one first understood the passage in good Hebrew, meaning Hebrew that reflected *usus loquendi* rather than the artificial grammar of grammarians.²⁹

Luther worked tirelessly to try and render Hebrew words as best he could into proper German. Perhaps the most famous story of Luther's willingness to spare no pains when seeking to translate Hebrew words involves his visiting a German butcher to learn the proper names of all the cuts of meat mentioned in the passages on animal sacrifices in the book of Leviticus.³⁰ Luther was also puzzled at times by the names of plants, animals, and tools.³¹ Luther wrote to

---

25 WA 43:206–207, 418–419, 659–660; 44:101–102, 248 = LW 4:99 (Gen 22:1–2), 393 (Gen 25:29–30); 5:335 (Gen 30:5–8); 6:136 (Gen. 32:25), 322 (Gen. 37:9).
26 LW 4:393.
27 LW 6:136.
28 WA 13:497, 22–26, translated in LW 18: *Lectures on the Minor Prophets*, 345.
29 Bengt Hägglund, "Martin Luther über die Sprache," *Neue Zeitschrift für Systematische Theologie und Religionsphilosophie* 26 (1984): 4.
30 Mathesius, *Leben Dr. Martin Luthers*, 281.
31 Krause, *Studien*, 66, 71.

Spalatin in December of 1522 about the difficulties he was having giving some birds and animals of the Bible their proper names. "I am all right on the birds of the night – owl, raven, horned owl, tawny owl, screech owl – and on the birds of prey – vulture, kite, hawk, and sparrow hawk. I can handle the stag, roebuck and chamois, but what in the devil am I to do with the taragelaphus, pygargus, oryx and camelopard (animal names from the Vulgate)?"[32] Luther keenly felt the lack of a good guide to figures of speech in Hebrew. Already by 1524 he had come to realize that Reuchlin's explanations of Hebrew words and expressions were simply not adequate for his purposes as a lecturer on the Hebrew Bible.

Luther believed that the Jews had forgotten a great deal about their own language, and much work remained to be done in order to restore a perfect knowledge of Hebrew.[33] He exhorted his students to consider choosing Hebrew philology as a field of study given that there was so much still to accomplish.[34]

Luther's theological objections to trusting too much in Jewish scholarship reflect both the kinds of objections that Christian scholars had long raised against Nicholas of Lyra's biblical commentaries, and also his own unique understanding that the texts of Scripture had a single meaning. The Jews, Luther believed, were blind to the true meaning of both the Hebrew Bible and their own history, not realizing that the entire purpose of the Old Testament was to prepare the way for the coming of Christ. He asserted that Christ's saving work was the subject matter (*res*) of Scripture. For a Christian to follow the lead of Jewish interpreters and to direct the reader away from the central message of Scripture was little short of criminal in Luther's mind.

4 Sebastian Münster and Luther

Luther's three notorious anti-Jewish polemics of 1543, *On the Jews and their Lies*, *On the Ineffable Name*, and *On the Last Words of David*, are primarily scathing, nasty polemics directed against Jews. But Luther also targeted Christian Hebraists in these works. In the last years of his life, Luther worried that Christians might be tempted to "judaize." In the *Judenschriften* of 1543, Luther was especially worried that Christians might be led astray by Jewish biblical interpretation.

---

32 Roland H. Bainton, *Here I Stand: A Life of Martin Luther* (New York and Nashville: Abingdon-Cokesbury Press, 1950), 327–328. Luther to Spalatin [Wittenberg, c.12 December 1522], WA Br 2:630, 14–631, 43.
33 WA 44:101–102, 135, 415–416 = LW 6:136 (Gen 32:25), 181–2 (Gen 33:18); 7:157 (Gen 41:33–36).
34 WA 44:170–171 = LW 6:230 (Gen 35:2).

Luther and his contemporaries had long worried about the degree to which Jewish interpretation had been incorporated into Christian biblical scholarship. Already in 1530 in his *Open Letter on Translation*, Luther wrote: "we have not acted out of a misunderstanding of the languages or out of ignorance of the rabbinical commentaries, but knowingly and deliberately."[35] Over the course of the 1530s, Luther became more and more concerned about this problem, as reflected both in his Genesis lectures and in his *Table Talk*, especially the passages where he quoted from or mentioned Sebastian Münster (1488–1552).

Sebastian Münster was one of the best-known and most respected Christian Hebraists of Luther's day. He taught Hebrew at the University of Basel from 1529 until his death in 1552.[36] He is best known today for his *Cosmographia*, a geographical work, but in his own day he made his reputation as an expert on Hebrew. He translated many of Elijah Levita's books into Latin, and he wrote a number of his own, including his *Hebraica Biblia* (1534–35; 1546) with its numerous biblical annotations. By 1536, the Wittenberg University Library contained no fewer than seventeen Hebrew books written or edited by Münster.[37]

Luther frequently criticized Münster in his Genesis lectures for failing to emphasize that Christ was the true subject (*res*) of Scripture. When discussing the nature of Abraham's faith in Gen 15:16, after quoting Jewish opinion on the passage (derived from Münster's commentary), Luther exploded: "Surely a thought worthy of the rabbis and enemies of Christ! For by it the entire sense is turned upside down, the promise and grace are excluded, and human righteousness is established—though Paul on the basis of this very passage most emphatically attacks this opinion as wrong and ungodly."[38] Luther felt that the revealed word of God in the Old Testament was consistent with the New Testament at the level of both doctrine and experience, and refusal to reflect this reality in translation and interpretation was unacceptable.

Luther repeatedly criticized Münster for his lack of concern in establishing the single, simple meaning of each and every biblical passage and instead giving credibility to multiple possibilities. Luther's commitment to "single meaning" reflected not only his position on the necessary relationship between the grammatical and theological meanings of particular passages but also his lifelong

---

35 Luther, *Ursachen des Dolmetschen*, WA 38:9, 9–14 = LW 35:209.
36 Karl Heinz Burmeister, *Sebastian Munster. Versuch eines biographischen Gesamtbildes*, Basler Beiträge zur Geschichtswissenschaft 91 (Basel: Helbing & Lichtenhahn, 1963).
37 Burnett, "The Basel-Wittenberg Conflict," 188. For more on Münster, including his relationship with Elijah Levita, see the article by Melanie Lange in this volume.
38 WA 42:563, 29–32 = LW 3:21 (Gen. 15:16); reflecting Münster, *Hebraica Biblia*, 23a, note c, quoting Rashi and Nahmanides ad loc.

work of Bible translation.[39] When commenting on the meaning of the Hebrew word *kibrat* (distance), Luther wrote that neither he nor the Jews knew what the word meant (Gen 35:16), but that ignorance spurred rather than stifled rabbinic creativity. "[W]hen the Jews have doubts about a word, they resort to equivocation and multiply meanings and make it more obscure by their glosses."[40] In his comment on Gen 48:22, Luther wrote that since "equivocation is always the mother of error" in interpretation, he hated the rabbinic fondness of equivocation.[41] Luther's source for Jewish opinion at this point, as in so many others, was Münster's annotations.[42]

Since Münster and other Christian Hebraists had given such credence to Jewish opinions, Luther felt obliged, however much he begrudged doing so, to discuss them. The rabbis, Luther said in his comments on Genesis 4:15,

> cause us double labor, for we are compelled to safeguard the text and to cleanse it from such distortions, and we must correct their very absurd comments. However, I am accustomed to quote them occasionally, to avoid the impression that we are treating them with haughty contempt and that we have either ignored or slighted their writings. *We read and understand them* [italics mine]; but we read them with critical judgment and do not permit them to obscure Christ or to distort the word of God.[43]

Luther believed that however good Münster's intentions were and however learned he was as a Hebraist, he was being misled by the Jews. He shared, to some extent, the Jews' inability to understand the subject matter of the Bible, he had a naive faith in Jewish grammatical scholarship, and he gave credence to what Luther considered "absurd" rabbinic comments that ran completely counter to the single, simple meaning of the biblical text. By refusing to identify the single meaning, and giving credence to the rabbis, "fine men" like Münster were making common cause with the enemies of God. On several occasions Luther wished Münster were in Wittenberg working with him and seeing how the job ought to be done: In 1535, in the Table Talk, he was quoted as saying: "Would that I were 100 Thaler in debt with Münster present while we translated, seeing us work, instead of flogging me with his Judaizing interpretations." Six years later, in late 1542, he said, "Münster's Bible pleases me, but I wish he had been here and conferred

---

39 See Armin Buchholz, *Schrift Gottes im Lehrstreit. Luthers Schriftverständnis und Schriftauslegung in seinen drei grossen Lehrstreitigkeiten der Jahre 1521–1528* (Frankfurt/Main: Peter Lang, 1993), 74–84, passim.
40 WA 44:197, 34ff = LW 6:266 (Gen 35:16).
41 WA 44:721, 32–33 = LW 8:195 (Gen 48:22).
42 Münster, *Biblia Hebraica*, 37b, 49a.
43 WA 42:223, 9 = LW 1:303 (Gen 4:15).

with us here.... It helped Dr. Forster and Ziegler very much that they talked with us here...."[44]

Luther's habit of identifying Christian Hebraists as "judaizers" and "rabbis," and even of addressing them in anti-Jewish treatises seems rather odd until we realize that Luther regarded these Christians as spokesmen for Jewish opinion. From Luther's references to Jews in the Genesis lectures it is clear that he feared the influence of Jewish biblical interpretation as much as the alleged malice of flesh and blood Jews.[45] Jewish biblical commentators possessed an enviable ability with the Hebrew language that gave them authority as guides for Christian biblical interpretation and thus, ultimately, for theological knowledge. Luther sought throughout his Genesis lectures to limit the authority of these Jewish experts by fencing them in with a ring of qualifications. The rabbis were, of course, incapable of speaking to the "subject matter" of Scripture as they denied Christ and the New Testament.[46] Their knowledge of the Hebrew language was far less certain than was often claimed, and even Jewish commentators were willing to admit on occasion that they had no idea what a particular word meant. By serving as an unreflective, uncritical mouthpiece for Jewish opinion, Münster and others like him were turning scholars away from the clear teaching of Scripture. At the end of *On the Ineffable Name* Luther singled out two Christian Hebraists for praise and blame:

> [T]he two admirable men, Sanctes [Pagnini] and [Sebastian] Münster, translated the Bible with incredible zeal and inimitable diligence and did much good thereby. However, the rabbis exerted too much influence over them in some places so that they even missed the analogy of faith and yielded too much to the rabbis' glosses.[47]

Luther criticized Nicholas of Lyra and even himself for being misled by the rabbis on occasion in *On the Last Words of David*:

---

[44] WA TR 3:362, 12–363, 6 (#3503), 12–16 December 1536; and WA TR 5:218, 8–14 (#5533), Winter 1542–3 = LW 54:445–6.
[45] Heiko A. Oberman, *The Roots of Anti-Semitism in the Age of Renaissance and Reformation*, trans. James I. Porter (Philadelphia: Fortress Press, 1984), 121–122.
[46] "Die Juden meinen, wir mussen von inen die bibliam studirn. Ja wol! Solten wir bibliam lernen ab eis, qui sunt summi hostes bibliae? Ich sehe wol, wo unser Hebrei hinaus wollen. Sie wolten gern, das wir unser neu testament solten vorliern und das niemer hetten. Drumb sehe ein ittlicher auff dasselbige uleissig. Das wirt in das alte wol lernen vorsthen. Wenn Moses sagt von dem Christo, so nem ich in an; sonst soll er mir nichts sein. So sagt Christus: in Moses und propheten de me scriptum est." TR 5:220, 25–31 (#5535), Winter 1542–3.
[47] WA 53:647, 27–31 = LW 61:503.

Still he [Nicholas of Lyra] surpasses all the others, both the old and the new Hebraists, who follow the rabbis altogether too strictly. Indeed in translating and expounding one need not intentionally strain oneself to transmit the concept of the rabbis and grammarians to us Christians. It is all too prone to stick to us of itself, automatically, just like pitch and glue, even if we deliberately guard against it. For the letters and the stories of the others blind the eyes and induce us occasionally to lose sight of the meaning of Christ where we should not, and thus the Jewish concept insinuates itself unawares, as every translator without exception has experienced. *I too was not exempt from it* [italics mine].[48]

5 Conclusion

Despite Luther's fame as a Bible translator, he was never famous for his expertise in Hebrew, even in his own day. He was an enthusiastic "early adopter" of the new Hebrew learning, and devoted decades of his life to reading, translating, and interpreting the Hebrew Bible for Christian readers and students. He believed that while Hebrew was the language of the Jews, it was also a holy language since the Holy Spirit revealed the word of God to the Israelites using their own language. Unlike many other thinkers, Luther did not believe that Hebrew was the language of creation or the oldest language of humankind; it was rather its status as a language of revelation that made it special.

The Jewish connection with Hebrew and the Bible was for Luther a source of greater or lesser scholarly tension throughout his working life. To what extent could the Jews be trusted both in their Hebrew fluency and in their ability to understand the revealed truth of God? The diligent work of Christian Hebraists such as Reuchlin and Münster made it possible for lesser figures such as Luther to learn Hebrew and pursue Hebrew scholarship. Reuchlin and Münster, not Luther, deserve to be put on pedestals for their expertise in Hebrew. Yet Luther believed that their willingness to trust Jewish learning too much also put them and their readers in spiritual danger.

Given Luther's own continued use of Hebrew to the very end of his life and his admonitions to his students to pursue Hebrew learning themselves in both the Genesis lectures and in *On the Last Words of David* (1543), it is incorrect to say that Luther had come to regret the scholarly world that he helped to create.[49] Throughout his life, however, Luther encountered Jewish opinions that contradicted both his own views and those historically confessed by the church as he prepared

---

48 LW 15:269.
49 Mickey L. Mattox, "From Faith to the Text and Back Again: Martin Luther on the Trinity in the Old Testament," *Pro Ecclesia* 13, no. 3 (2006): 281–303, here 283–284.

his theological lectures and his Bible translations. That Luther confronted these Jewish interlocutors in filtered form, mostly via excerpts selected and translated by other Christian scholars, merely adds new poignancy to the question posed by Stefan Schreiner in his well-known article "What could Luther have known about Judaism?"[50]

Bibliography

Bainton, Roland H. *Here I Stand: A Life of Martin Luther*. New York and Nashville: Abingdon-Cokesbury Press, 1950.

Brecht, Martin. *Martin Luther: His Road to Reformation 1483–1521*, trans. James L. Schaff. Philadelphia: Fortress Press, 1985.

Buchholz, Armin. *Schrift Gottes im Lehrstreit. Luthers Schriftverständnis und Schriftauslegung in seinen drei grossen Lehrstreitigkeiten der Jahre 1521–1528*. Frankfurt/Main: Peter Lang, 1993.

Burmeister, Karl Heinz. *Sebastian Munster. Versuch eines biographischen Gesamtbildes*. Basler Beiträge zur Geschichtswissenschaft 91. Basel: Helbing & Lichtenhahn, 1963.

Burnett, Stephen G. *Christian Hebraism in the Reformation Era: Authors, Books, and the Transmission of Jewish Learning*. Leiden: Brill, 2012.

Burnett, Stephen G. "Reassessing the 'Basel-Wittenberg Conflict': Dimensions of Reformation-Era Hebrew Scholarship." In *Hebraica Veritas? Christian Hebraists and the Study of Hebrew in Early Modern Europe*, edited by Allison P. Coudert and Jeffrey S. Shoulson, 181–201. Philadelphia: University of Pennsylvania Press, 2004.

Geiger, Ludwig. *Das Studium der Hebräische Sprache in Deutschland vom Ende des XV. bis zur Mitte des XVI Jahrhunderts*. Breslau: Schletter, 1970.

Gummelt, Volker. *Lex und Evangelium: Untersuchungen zur Jesajavorlesung von Johannes Bugenhagen*. Arbeiten zur Kirchengeschichte 62. Berlin: Walter de Gruyter, 1994.

Hägglund, Bengt. "Martin Luther über die Sprache." *Neue Zeitschrift für Systematische Theologie und Religionsphilosophie* 26 (1984): 1–12.

Kaufmann, Thomas. *Luthers "Judenschriften": Ein Beitrag zu ihrer historischen Kontextualisierung*. Tübingen: Mohr-Siebeck, 2011.

Kessler, Johannes. *Johannes Kesslers Sabbata mit kleineren Schriften und Briefe*, ed. Emil Egli and Rudolf Schoch. St. Gallen: Fehr'sche Buchhandlung, 1902.

Krause, Gerhard. *Studien zu Luthers Auslegung der Kleinen Propheten*. Beiträge zur Historischen Theologie 33. Tübingen: Mohr Siebeck Verlag, 1962.

Luther, Martin. *D. Martin Luthers Werke; kritische Gesamtausgabe*. Weimar: H. Bohlau, 1883–2001, 104 vols.

---

[50] Stefan Schreiner, "Was Luther vom Judentum wissen konnte?" in *Die Juden und Martin Luther – Martin Luther und die Juden*, ed. Heinz Kremers and Hannelore Siegele-Wenschkewitz (Neukirchen-Vluyn: Neukirchener Verlag, 1985): 58–71.

Luther, Martin. *Luther's Works*, 86 vols., ed. Jaroslav J. Pelikan, Helmut T. Lehmann, Christopher B. Brown, Benjamin T.G. Mays, et al. Saint Louis: Concordia Publishing House, 1955–.

Mackert, Christoph. "Luthers Handexemplar der hebräischen Bibelausgabe von 1494 – objektbezogene und besitzgeschichtliche Aspekte." In *Meilensteine der Reformation: Schlüsseldokumente der frühen Wirksamkeit Martin Luthers*, edited by Irene Dingel and Henning P. Jürgens, 70–78. Gütersloh: Gütersloher Verlagshaus, 2014.

Mathesius, Johannes. *Leben Dr. Martin Luthers, in Siebzehn Predigten*, ed. A.J.D. Rust, 281–282. Berlin: Crantz, 1841.

Mattox, Mickey L. "From Faith to the Text and Back Again: Martin Luther on the Trinity in the Old Testament." *Pro Ecclesia* 13, no. 3 (2006): 281–303.

Melanchthon, Philipp. *Melanchtons Briefwechsel. Kritische und Kommentierte Gesamtausgabe*, ed. Heinz Scheible. Stuttgart-Bad Cannstatt: Fromman-Holzboog, 1991.

Oberman, Heiko A. *The Roots of Anti-Semitism in the Age of Renaissance and Reformation*, trans. James I. Porter. Philadelphia: Fortress Press, 1984.

Raeder, Siegfried. *Grammatica Theologica: Studien zu Luthers Operationes in Psalmos*. Tübingen: Mohr, 1977.

Raeder, Siegfried. "The Exegetical and Hermeneutical Work of Martin Luther." In *Hebrew Bible/Old Testament: The History of its Interpretation*. Vol. 2, *From the Renaissance to the Enlightenment*, edited by Magne Saebø, 363–406. Göttingen: Vandenhoeck & Ruprecht, 2008.

Schreiner, Stefan. "Was Luther vom Judentum wissen konnte?" In *Die Juden und Martin Luther – Martin Luther und die Juden*, edited by Heinz Kremers and Hannelore Siegele-Wenschkewitz, 58–71. Neukirchen-Vluyn: Neukirchener Verlag, 1985.

Thyen, Dietrich. "Luthers Jesajavorlesung." PhD diss., Universität Heidelberg, 1964.

Guido Bartolucci
Hebrew in the Counter-Reformation: The Cases of Caesar Baronius and Gilbert Génébrard

1 Introduction

The Christian study of Hebrew represents a critical undertaking for any analysis and understanding of the history of European culture in the Counter-Reformation era. Attaining unprecedented prominence in the late fifteenth and early sixteenth centuries in the context of the humanist desire for direct access to the Sacred Scriptures and related sources, after the religious fracture of 1517 Hebrew learning played in addition a crucial role in the ensuing debate between clashing confessions which were concerned to develop and defend their respective identities.[1]

Previous research on Christian Hebraism in this period has focused on the Protestant world, thanks to the extensive and high-quality scholarship produced by Lutheran and Calvinist scholars. The situation concerning the Catholic world is quite different. Far too often, scholars have insisted on a decline in interest in the Hebrew language and Jewish tradition due primarily to mistrust of anything that could potentially threaten Catholic tradition and, after the Council of Trent, the sources upon which this tradition was based. To be sure, the burning of the Talmud in 1553 and the placement of the works of several Christian Hebraists on the "List of Prohibited Books" (Index Librorum Prohibitorum) clearly point to a changed atmosphere.[2] But matters are hardly as simple as this and in order

---

[1] On the origin and history of Christian Hebraism, see François Secret, *Les kabbalistes chrétiens de la Renaissance* (Paris: Dunod, 1964); Jerome Friedman, *The Most Ancient Testimony: Sixteenth-Century Christian-Hebraica in the Age of Renaissance Nostalgia* (Athens: Ohio University Press, 1983); Frank E. Manuel, *The Broken Staff: Judaism Through Christian Eyes* (Cambridge, MA: Harvard University Press, 1992); Saverio Campanini, "Die Geburt der Judaistik aus dem Geist der Chrislichen Kabbalah," in *Gottes Sprache in der philologischen Werkstatt: Hebraistik vom 15. bis zum 19. Jahrhundert*, ed. Giuseppe Veltri and Gerold Necker (Leiden: Brill, 2004): 135–241. For a comprehensive bibliography, see Stephen G. Burnett, *Christian Hebraism in the Reformation Era (1500–1660): Authors, Books, and the Transmission of Jewish Learning* (Leiden: Brill, 2012); Theodor Dunkelgrün, "The Christian Study of Judaism in Early Modern Europe," in *The Cambridge History of Judaism*, vol. 7: *The Early Modern World, 1500–1815*, ed. Jonathan Karp and Adam Sutcliffe (Cambridge: Cambridge University Press, 2017): 316–348.
[2] On the burning of the Talmud, see Fausto Parente, "The Index, the Holy Office, the Condemnation of the Talmud and Publication of Clement VIII's Index," in *Church, Censorship and Culture in*

fully to understand the Roman Catholic Church's stance towards Hebrew during this period it is necessary to distinguish between different geographic regions of the Catholic world. In each area of Europe that remained loyal to the Church of Rome there was a different attitude vis-à-vis the language, as Stephen Burnett has rightly pointed out in the cases of Spain, Italy, the Spanish Netherlands, and France.[3] However, an additional issue that has yet to receive sufficient attention is that in these countries in the first twenty and thirty years of the sixteenth century the first *collegia trilinguarum* were founded: the College of Alcalá in Spain, the College of Leuven in the Low Countries, and the Collège de France in Paris.[4] These institutions were mainly under the influence of the humanistic and especially Erasmian rethinking of Christian tradition, which necessarily required the study of sacred texts in their original languages. The peculiarity of these institutions is that they were all "private," i.e. founded independently of universities. This was due to the fact that the theology faculties – which remained loyal to Rome – could not accept that Hebraists were teaching and translating the Old Testament, thereby undermining the Catholic orthodoxy based on the transmission of the Latin text canonized by Jerome.

In spite of this, however, and notwithstanding the resultant limitation of Hebrew study (with rare exceptions, as we shall see), Catholic Hebraism did not disappear. Indeed, despite suspicions concerning the insufficient orthodoxy of some collaborators and related clashes with papal authority, the Antwerp Polyglot Bible (1572), edited by Benito Arias Montano, is an excellent example of the high scholarly level achieved in Europe by Catholic scholars.[5] In particular, the

---

Early Modern Italy, ed. Gigliola Fragnito; trans. Adrian Belton (Cambridge: Cambridge University Press, 2001): 163–193. On press control in the Catholic world, see Burnett, *Christian Hebraism*, 226–254.

3 Burnett, *Christian Hebraism*, 60–79.
4 Paul F. Grendler, "Italian Biblical Humanism and the Papacy, 1515–1535," in *Biblical Humanism and Scholasticism in the Age of Erasmus*, ed. Erika Rummel (Leiden: Brill, 2008): 227–276, esp. 247–251. See also Henry de Vocht, *History of the Foundation and the Rise of the Collegium Trilingue Lovaniense 1517–1550*, 4 vls. (Leuven: Bibliotèque de l'Université, 1951–1955); Jean Claude Margolin, "Érasme et le 'Collegium Trilingue Lovaniense'," in *Les origines du Collège de France (1500–1560)*: Actes du colloque international (Paris, décembre 1995), ed. Marc Fumaroli and Marianne Lion-Violet (Paris: Collège de France-Klincksieck, 1998): 257–278; Alfredo Alvar-Ezquerra, "Le modèle universitaire d'Alcalá de Henares dans la première moitié du XVIe siècle," in *Les origines du Collège de France*, 209–255.
5 See Robert J. Wilkinson, *Orientalism, Aramaic and Kabbalah in the Catholic Reformation: The First Printing of the Syriac New Testament*, Studies in the History of Christian Tradition 137 (Leiden: Brill, 2007); Robert J. Wilkinson, *The Kabbalistic Scholars of the Antwerp Polyglot*, Studies in the History of Christian Tradition 138 (Leiden: Brill, 2007). On Montano's life see Ben Rekers, *Benito Arias Montano (1527–1598)* (Leiden: Brill, 1972).

study and interpretation of the early history of the Church required the use of Jewish sources; even Catholic authors committed to writing works in defence of papal primacy could not avoid them. Debate concerning the use of these sources and the ability to interpret them thus became a central issue within the larger context of the controversy between the different Christian confessions.

A special case of such controversy, for example, is that which took place between the French Protestant scholar Isaac Casaubon and Cardinal Caesar Baronius. Their debate is particularly worthy of scholarly attention because it better enables us to evaluate the level of knowledge found in their respective confessional contexts.

2 Baronius, Casaubon, and the History of Christianity

> For no one can illuminate the institutions of the early Church, shed light on the Gospel History covered in these *Annales*, or illuminate the obscure writings of the Fathers and other writers, if he lacks skill in Hebrew and Greek and perfect mastery of all antiquities. For since this first volume, in particular, is stuffed with the testimonies of Hebrew and Greek writers, one might reasonably ask if [Baronius] had the linguistic skills and mastery of antiquities appropriate to the task. The *Annales* show, on almost every page, that he did not.[6]

The last work completed by the French scholar Isaac Casaubon in 1614 was the 800-page *De rebus sacris et ecclesiasticis exercitationes XVI*, which he composed to challenge almost line-for-line the first book of Caesar Baronius's *Annales*. Casaubon's critical effort (evident not only in the work itself, but also in the marginal notes of his copy of the *Annales*)[7] focused on Greek and Jewish sources. As we see in the above quotation, Casaubon maintained that nobody could shed light on the institutions of the early Church, the history of the Gospels, or the Church Fathers without knowledge of the Hebrew and Greek languages. Baronius, however, did not seem to know either one: he was therefore akin to a blind

---

6 Isaac Casaubon, *De rebus sacris et ecclesiasticis exercitationes XVI. Ad Cardinalis Baronii Prolegomena in Annales, et primam eorum partem, de Domini Nostri Iesu Christi nativitate, vita, passione, assuntione* (London: Norton, 1614), fol. A *recto*, cited in Anthony Grafton and Joanna Weinberg, *"I have always loved the Holy Tongue": Isaac Casaubon, the Jews, and a Forgotten Chapter in Renaissance Scholarship* (Cambridge, MA: The Belknap Press of Harvard University Press, 2011), 183.
7 On this copy, preserved today at the library of the Archbishop Marsh of Dublin, see Grafton and Weinberg, *"I have always loved the Holy Tongue,"* 164.

person attempting to distinguish colours.[8] Indeed, in Casaubon's work, the discussion of Jewish sources was crucial, not only for understanding individual episodes in the life of Jesus and of the time in which he lived, but also for analyzing critical issues such as the nature of the crucifixion or the date of the Passover on which Jesus was captured and condemned to death. In the *De rebus sacris*, the French scholar displays his extensive learning in this field of study, denouncing on the contrary the alleged incompetence of his opponent (Baronius). Moreover, Casaubon's critique of Baronius was no mere academic exercise: Casaubon believed the *Annales* had been written in support of papal tyranny and aimed to demonstrate that the Anglican church was closer to early Christianity than its Catholic rival.[9]

The theme of the role of Jewish sources as a tool in understanding the Christian past was well known to both Catholic and Protestant polemicists, but in the clash between the French scholar and the Cardinal of Sora, a sharp difference clearly emerges between the knowledge of Jewish sources in the Catholic and Protestant contexts. The burning of the Talmud in 1553, the censorship of Jewish books, and the general suspicion surrounding the erudites who studied the holy language had turned Catholic countries into an inhospitable place for the knowledge of Hebrew and its sources. But Baronius's references to Jewish works fit nicely with the use that authors from all Christian confessions made of Jewish tradition in the sixteenth century in order to reconstruct the origins of Christianity and illuminate the Jewish traditions described in the Gospels. Baronius knew no Hebrew – as Casaubon had charged – and thus used only secondary sources, including some which were rather uncommon. In addition, he could count on the presence, in the early years of his work, of Cardinal Guglielmo Sirleto, who was a decisive figure not only for introducing the historian to Greek literature, but also, probably, in suggesting Jewish sources that would be useful for his research.[10] Embracing both well-known, reliable sources and manifest forgeries, Baronius's use of Jewish tradition, which has not yet been the subject of study, is complex.

---

8 Cf. Grafton and Weinberg, *"I have always loved the Holy Tongue,"* 183; Causabon, *De rebus sacris et ecclesiasticis exercitationes XVI.*, fol. Ar.
9 On this see Grafton and Weinberg, *"I have always loved the Holy Tongue,"* 180–182.
10 Sirleto also collaborated on the Polyglot Bible edited by Benito Arias Montano. On his knowledge of Hebrew, see Mari del Carmen Álvarez Mulero, "Relaciones entre Benito Arias Montano y el cardenal italiano Guillermo Sirleti," in *Benito Arias Montano y los humanistas de su tiempo*, vol. 1, ed. José Maria Maestre Maestre et al., (Mérida: Editora Regional de Extremadura, 2006), 56.

To the first group belong, for example, the works of Giovanni Angelo Canini, Johannes Drusius or even Elijah Levita (1469–1549). In one case,[11] Baronius seeks to understand the meaning of the word "Hosanna," introduced in John 12:12, in the context of Jesus' triumphal entry into Jerusalem. He thus turns to Christian Hebraist studies, finding in the work of Canini (a teacher of Hebrew in Paris for some years) entitled *De locis Novi Testamenti* the correct solution that the term refers to the willow branch.[12] An even more interesting example comes to Baronius by way of a genuinely Jewish source, namely the grammatical work of Elijah Levita. Here the general topic is the sum of silver reportedly paid by the priests to Judas (Mt. 27:3–5), the specific question the monetary value of those 30 silver coins according to traditional Jewish interpretation. Baronius quotes Levita, who in his lexicon had given three distinct definitions of "silver" depending on the precise biblical context, e.g. Pentateuch, prophets or historical writings.[13] The peculiarity of this quotation is that the work of Elijah Levita, first published in Hebrew in Germany in 1536, had been translated and disseminated in Latin by a Lutheran professor of Oriental languages, Paulus Fagius.[14] Baronius did not forbear quoting the work

---

11 Caesar Baronius, *Annales ecclesiastici* (Venice: apud Haeredem Hieronymi Scoti, 1601), 99–100: "Nam 'Salva quaeso filio David' vitiosa esset locutio quae nullum congruentem refert sensum orationis, nisi dicere velimus esse Hebraismum idemque sonare, ac si diceretur, 'Salus nostra a filio David,' ut notat Ioannes Drusius." Johannes Drusius, or van der Drieschen (1550–1616), was one of the most well-known Hebraists of Louvain. Here Baronius is referring to Johannes Drusius, *Ad voces Hebraicas Novi Testamenti commentarius* (Antwerp: ex Christophori Palntini, 1582), 32–34. On Canini, see note 12; on Levita, note 13.

12 Baronius, *Annales*, 100: "Sed magis placente cum quae ipse ex Helia narrat, tum etiam quod Caninius rerum Hebraicarum peritissimus, ea refellens, ex Hebraicis fontibus tradit, Hosanna, non duas sed unam tantum esse dictionem eamdemque significare proprie ramos salicum." The reference is to Angelo Canini, *De locis sanctae Scripturae Hebraicis Angeli Caninii commentarius* (Antwerp: sumptibus viduae et haeredum Io. Belleri, 1600). On Canini, cf. Roberto Ricciardi, "Canini, Angelo," in *Dizionario Biografico degli Italiani*, vol. 18 (Roma: Istituto dell'Enciclopedia Italiana, 1975): 101–102. See also Grafton and Weinberg, *"I have always loved the Holy Tongue"*, 184–185.

13 Baronius, *Annales*, 103: "Aliam ergo putamus habendam esse rationem illorum triginta argenteorum, illam nempe quam Elias Levita Iudaeus in libro cuius est Titulus *Tisebi* ex maiorum diligenti observatione describit: nimirum hanc vocem argenteus, si posita reperiatur in Pentateucho selagh, hoc est siclum unum significare; si posita reperiatur in Prophetis, listrin, nempe libram intelligi debere, si autem in Hagiographis, eadem voce exprimi canterim, quod dicimus talentum, aliter cantarum."

14 *Opusculum recens Hebraicum a doctissimo Hebraeo Eliia Levita Germano grammatico elaboratum, cui titulum fecit tishby id est Thisbites, in quo 712 vocum quae sunt partim Hebraice, Caldaicae, Arabicae, Graecae et Latinae, quaeque in dictionariis non facile inveniuntur, per Paulum Fagium latinitae donatum* (Isnae in Algauia: Per Paulum Fagium, 1541). On Elija Levita and his influence on the Christian debate concerning the tradition of the Biblical text, cf. Stephen Burnett,

in order to lend authority to his treatment, thus overcoming the confessional barriers.

It thus appears that so long as citations were limited to the most authoritative sixteenth-century Christian Hebraica, the link between Baronius and Jewish sources did not pose any problem. However, there are sources that undermine the credibility of Baronius and it was on these that Casaubon concentrated his attention. An interesting case concerns the part of the work in which the historian, discussing the sensitive subject of the reliability of the Gospels and the Jewish institutions described therein, defines the function of the Sanhedrin during the period of the two high priests Annas and Caiaphas. The analysis of the Jewish Assembly offered by Baronius is highly ideological. He writes that the Sanhedrin, instituted by Moses on God's order, not only could judge the king, but was led by the high priest.[15] He then refers to an additional source to confirm his claim, namely the *De temporibus* of Pseudo-Philo. This work, however, was nothing but a fake, having been composed and published by the notorious quattrocento Dominican friar Giovanni Nanni, better known as Annio da Viterbo.[16] Furthermore, by the end of the sixteenth century, the period in which Baronius wrote (1588–1607), his unreliability had been recognized by numerous scholars of the *respublica litterarum*.[17] The reaction of Baronius's main foreign critic, Isaac

---

From Christian Hebraism to Jewish Studies: Johannes Buxtorf (1564–1629) and Hebrew Learning in the Seventeenth Century (Leiden: Brill, 1996); Stephen Burnett, *Christian Hebraism*, 136–137.

15 Baronius, Annales, I, 61: "Erat quidem apud Iudaeos ex senioribus atque magistris conflatum collegium, quod ad illis Synedrin dicebatur, constabatque ex septuagintaduobus viris. [...] Erat horum summa auctoritas, ut qui de lege cognoscerent, et de Propheta, ac simul de Regibus iudicarent. [...] At de horum munere pluribus acturi sumus inferius, modo autem (quod ad rem propositam pertinet) qui septuagintaduorum seniorum primus haberetur, idem princeps sacerdotum dicebatur, cum alioqui summus sacerdos primum omnium locum teneret, cunctisque praeesset principibus sacerdotum: seque habebat amborum perfunctio instar praefecturae Mosis et Aaron, quorum quamdam similitudinem exprimebant."

16 Berosus sacerdos Chaldaicus, *Antiquitatum libri quinque cum commentariis Ioannis Annii Viterbensis sacrae Theologiae professoris nunc primum in antiquitatum studiosorum commoditatem sub forma Enchiridii excusi et castigati* (Antwerp: In aedibus Ioannis Steelsii, 1545), 223–245. On Annius's writings, see Grafton, *Forgers and Critics: Creativity and Duplicity in Western Scholarship* (Princeton: Princeton University Press, 1990); Riccardo Fubini, "L'Ebraismo nei riflessi della cultura umanistica: Leonardo Bruni, Giannozzo Manetti, Annio da Viterbo," in Riccardo Fubini, *Storiografia dell'Umanesimo in Italia da Leonardo Bruni ad Annio da Viterbo* (Rome: Storia e Letteratura, 2003), 291–333. Baronius cites the following passage in this work: "Secundum ut praesset Zanedrim, id est collegio sacerdotum et doctorum legis, penes quos erat publica potestas iudiciorum et sceptrum occidendi et vivificandi, eligendi reges et deponendi, ut fecit Ioiada pontifex contra Athaliam." Berosus, *Antiquitatum libri quinque*, 231r.

17 See Anthony Grafton, *Forgers and Critics*, 110–115.

Casaubon, was predictably harsh, both as regards the jurisdictional powers of the Sanhedrin (which being a purely political – and not priestly – body did not possess the power to judge the King), and concerning the use of a source which had clearly been forged by Annius.[18]

But even if the misuse of some sources exposed him to Protestant attack, not all such criticism was legitimate, since the knowledge of Jewish sources was limited at the time even in the Protestant world. An exemplary case that demostrates the ambiguity of the Protestant criticism of the *Annales* (represented here by Casaubon) concerns the use made by Baronius of some rabbinic sources. In explaining the deposition of the body of Jesus in the sepulchre our Cardinal refers to "Rabbi Alphes" [Rabbi Isaac Alfasi (1013–1103)], Maimonides, and to a poorly identified Rabbi «Iacob Turim».[19] In the *Exercitationes* Casaubon did not miss the opportunity to attack him, arguing that the reference to «Iacob Turim» demonstrated Baronius's ignorance of this source, namely the *Arba'ah turim* (four rows), a code of Jewish law composed in the late thirteenth/early fourteenth centuries by Jacob ben Asher.[20] In fact, the criticism was disproportionate, because in other passages Baronius quoted the same source properly, indeed even on this very same page. But this, however, goes unacknowledged by Casaubon.[21] Thus, while it is correct to insist on Casaubon's superior knowledge with respect to Baronius, this superiority should not be exaggerated and needs to be subjected to critical inquiry.[22]

---

18 Isaac Casaubon, *De rebus sacris et ecclesiasticis exercitationes XVI* (Frankfort: typis Ioannis Bring, 1615), 178: "Vides quam imprudenter [Baronius] hic Pseudophilo Annii Viterbensis, praestigiatoris famosissimi, imposuerit."
19 Baronius, *Annales*, I, 630: "Ponendi autem in novo sepulchro Christi corporis quaenam ratio fuerit, colligitur ex compendio Thalmud, quod dicitur Alphesi, et Rabbinis Iacob Turim et Moyse Aegyptio."
20 Casaubon, *De rebus sacris*, 577: "Iudica nunc Lector de fide horum Annalium. [. . .] Quis autem ille est, quem nominat Baronius Iacobum Turim? Hic vero conditor Annalium hallucinatus est insigniter: perinde enim fecit, ut si quis inter auctores laudaret Tullium de natura, et M. Tullium intelligeret, qui scripsit de natura Deorum. R. Iacob, filius R. Asher, ante anno trecentos et quod excurrit. Librum scripsit *Sefer arba'ah turim*, sive quatuor ordines: opus est Talmudicum in quatuor partes divisum, quod titulus indicat."
21 Cf. Baronius, *Annales*, I, 630: "Addimus ad haec insuper quae Rabbi Iacob memoriae prodidit ex Rabbi Moyse Aegyptio." The marginal note reads: "Rabbi Iacob in Turim Iore Dogha [sic], c. 352," showing that Baronius was well aware of the difference between the name of the author and the title of the work. On this see Grafton and Weinberg, *"I have always loved the Holy Tongue"*, 183–184.
22 See, for example, Grafton and Weinberg, *"I have always loved the Holy Tongue"*, 183: "As Casaubon went through [Baronius's] work, he picked out point after point where the Oratorian revealed his ignorance of all things Jewish."

Another important element that emerges from the analysis of these sources is that the spectrum of Jewish texts Baronius used was extremely interesting and eccentric, especially considering the attitude at the time of the Church of Rome vis-à-vis the Talmud: it is sufficient to consider that the legal compendium of Alfasi quoted by the Catholic historian had itself been burned in 1553.[23] Baronius's quotation practice, then, does not reflect the official position of the Church of Rome towards rabbinic literature. Sirleto (already dead in 1585) was probably behind these references. He was protector of the house of Neophytes from 1567, i.e. during the pontificates of Pope Pius V (1566–1572) and Gregory XIII (1572–1585), and was interested in Jewish tradition both with regard to missionary activity, and understanding the Old and New Testaments.[24] It is thus interesting to note how interconfessional controversy concerning the first centuries of the Church and the use of rabbinic sources obliged even Counter-Reformation authors to use Jewish texts and to seek the cooperation of converts.[25] However, the case of Baronius contributes yet something further to reflection on the difference in Hebrew study between Catholic and Protestant countries. It is certainly true that the theological principle of *sola scriptura* promoted by Luther and Melanchthon gave a strong impulse to the study of the holy language and encouraged the establishment of university chairs for teaching it, and that, in contrast, the defence of tradition based on the *Vulgate* translation aroused in Catholic countries distrust of the original version of the Bible. But the story of the origins of Christianity represented, for Catholics and Protestants alike, a space within which the use of Hebrew and Jewish sources was decisive and in which, as in the case of Baronius, a different attitude towards these sources was not only permitted, but essential.

3 The Collège de France and Gilbert Génébrard

Rome, where Baronius wrote his works, was not a prominent center for the study of Hebrew in the second half of the sixteenth century, despite the presence of huge

---

[23] Fausto Parente, "La Chiesa e il 'Talmud': l'atteggiamento della Chiesa e del mondo cristiano nei confronti del 'Talmud' e degli altri scritti rabbinici, con particolare riguardo all'Italia tra XV e XVI secolo," in *Gli Ebrei in Italia*, vol. 1, ed. Corrado Vivanti, Storia d'Italia: Annali, 11 (Torino: Einaudi, 1996): 592.
[24] Cf. Parente, "La Chiesa e il 'Talmud'," 602–603.
[25] See, for example, the collaboration between Sirleto and the famous convert and preacher Andrea Del Monte in censoring Hebrew books. On this figure cf. Martine Boiteux, "Preaching to the Jews in Early Modern Rome: Words and Images," in *The Jewish-Christian Encounter in Medieval Preaching*, ed. Jonathan Adams and Jussi Hanska (New York: Routledge, 2015): 298–322.

collections of Hebrew manuscripts and important Christian Hebraists. At the same time, two other important centers for the study of Hebrew (Alcalá and Leuven) succumbed to the attacks of the theology faculties and the power of the ecclesiastical institutions.[26] The only *Collegium* that survived the age of confessionalization and maintained its independence in the Catholic world was the Collège de France in Paris. It remained a privileged place for the study and teaching of Hebrew throughout the sixteenth and seventeenth centuries.[27] One key reason for this was the fact that from the time of Francis I, who defended its prerogatives even in the midst of religious controversies, it had been an institution protected by the monarchy. The Collège was therefore one of the few places in Europe where the humanistic and Erasmian principles which had initially stimulated the study of Hebrew survived the diffusion of the Reformation; its professors, while mostly remaining faithful to the Church of Rome (except for Jean Mercier) continued to study Hebrew and to publish works that influenced the development of Christian Hebraism in later centuries.[28]

Gilbert Génébrard (1537–1597) was the last great exponent of the school of the Collège in the sixteenth century (where he was professor from 1567 to 1591). His loyalty to the Church of Rome was such that he sided openly with the Guise family's Catholic League during the last part of the French religious wars, and, after 1584, vigorously opposed the coronation of Henry IV, causing his removal as Bishop of Aix-en-Provence. Génébrard was born in Riom and took the Benedictine habit at the nearby Abbey of Mozac. He then studied Hebrew with the converted Jew Cesar Bras (Caesar Brancassius), rector of the Abbaye Saint-André, near Avignon. Thanks to the patronage of Guillaume du Prat, Bishop of Clermont, he subsequently moved to Paris and began his studies at the Collège, where he had as professors Andre Turnèbe for Greek, Jaques Charpentier for philosophy, and Claude de Sainctes for theology. He was declared a doctor on June 10, 1563.[29]

---

26 On these *collegia*, see above, n. 4. On Rome as a center for Jewish studies see also Burnett, *Christian Hebraism*, 66–67.
27 Sophie Kessler-Mesguich, "L'enseignement de l'hébreu et de l'aramée à Paris (1530–1560) d'après les œuvres grammaticales des lecteurs royaux," in *Les origines du Collège de France*, 366–368. On the study of Hebrew in France in this period see Sophie Kessler-Mesguich, *Les études hébraïques en France: de François Tissard à Richard Simon (1508–1680)* (Geneve: Droz, 2013); *Les hébraïsants chrétiens en France au XVIe siècle (Actes du Colloque de Troyes 2–4 septembre 2013)*, Édition coordonnée par Gilbert Dahan, Annie Noblesse-Rocher (Geneve: Droz, 2018).
28 On Mercier, see François Roudaut, ed., *Jean (c. 1525–1570) et Josias (c. 1560–1626) Mercier: l'amour de la philologie à la Renaissance et au début de l'âge classique*. Actes du Colloque d'Uzès (2 et 3 mars 2001) (Paris: Honoré Champion, 2006).
29 On Génébrard's life, see Pierre Claude Tailhand, *Étude sur Gilbert Génébrard, docteur de la Faculté de théologie de Paris (XVIe siècle)* (Riom: Ulysse Jouvet Imprimeur de la Cour, 1864); Pierre Feret, *La Faculté de Théologie de Paris et ses Docteurs les plus célèbres* (Paris: Picard 1901),

Unlike other French professors of Hebrew, such as Cinqarbres and Mercier, Génébrard did not study the language in Paris, but it was rather there that he for the first time became a theologian. His distinct scholarly profile refuted to some extent the accusation that professors from the Sorbonne had made against the first Hebraists at the founding of the Collège, namely that they were not qualified to teach Scripture and its interpretation because they lacked a theological education.[30] Extensive theological knowledge, skillful use of Hebrew, and a polemical spirit reflected in a sharp and at times explosive Latin jointly characterize Génébrard's extensive production.

Though Génébrard, like his predecessors, published useful tools for teaching the holy language,[31] he primarily used Hebrew as a means of challenging the cultural and theological positions of his opponents. With his biting Latin he attacked the theologians of the Sorbonne, who were unable to appreciate the value of Jewish sources for reconstructing the history of Christianity; the Antitrinitarians of Poland and Lithuania, who used rabbinic works to legitimize their heterodox positions;[32] the Calvinists of Geneva, in particular Theodore Beza;[33] Henry the IV and his Calvinist past; and indeed the very popes of the Roman Catholic Church, who had granted excessive privileges to the Crown over the Church in France.[34] One of Génébrard's particular interests was Jewish

---

tome second: époque moderne, 342–355; Jean-Pierre Rothschild, "La philologie de combat de Gilbert Génébrard (1535–1597)," in *Les hébraïsants chrétiens en France au XVIe siècle*, 363–421. Two other professors at the Collège also studied Hebrew in Avignon, François Vatable and Jean Mercier. On the peculiarity of the Hebrew of this community, see Simone Mreje-O'Hana, "À propos de l'Hébreu des 'quatre saintes communautés' du Comtat Venaissin et d'Avignon: lexique et grammaire," *Revue des études juives* 167 (2008): 121–152.

30 See above, notes 28–29.

31 See, for example, Gilbert Génébrard, *Hebraicum Alphabetum* (Paris: Apud Martinum Iuvenem, 1564).

32 Gilbert Génébrard, *De S. Trinitate libri tres contra huius aevi trinitarios, antitrinitarios et autotheanos. His praeposita est summa sessionum Synodi quam triennio superiore ministri Poloni cum trinitariis Petricoviae habuerunt, ex alicuius amici Poloni epistola* (Paris: apud J. Benenatum, 1569) (second edition in 1585); Gilbert Génébrard, *Ad Iacobum Schegkium Schorndoffensem philosophum et medicum assertionibus sacris de Deo sese temere immiscentem et tribus ipsius de S. Trinitate libris, modo pro Sabellianis, modo pro Trinitariis inconstantissime obtrectantem responsio* (Paris: apud Aegidium Gorbinum, 1575).

33 Gilbert Génébrard, *Canticum Canticorum Salomonis regis, cum commentariis trium rabbinorum, Salomonis Iarhii, Abrahami abben Ezrae et Innominati cuiusdam* (Paris: apud Martinum Iuvenem, 1570); Gilbert Génébrard, *Canticum Canticorum Salomonis versibus et commentariis illustratum Gilberto Genebrardo theologo Parisiensi, professore regio auctore. Adversus Trochaicam Theodori Bezae Paraphrasim* (Paris: apud Aegidium Gorbinum, 1585).

34 Gilbert Génébrard, *Psalmi Davidis vulgata editione, calendario Hebraeo, Syro, Graeco, Latino, argumentis et commentariis genuinum et primarium Psalmorum sensum, Hebraismosque lo-*

historiography, as attested by his translation and publication of *Seder Olam rabba*, *Seder Olam zuta*, and *Sefer ha-Qabbalah* (into Latin), and of Josephus Flavius (into French). These works were not only scholarly exercises or tools useful to his pupils for the study of Jewish tradition, but became the basis for constructing a world history that, though primarily based on classical texts, also made broad use of rabbinic sources.[35] At the same time, Génébrard was one of the first Christian scholars to become interested in Hebrew prosody extending beyond the Bible to encompass sources such as prayer books and even the epitaphs of the Jewish cemetery in Paris.[36]

---

cupletius, quam priore editione aperientibus, a Gilberto Genebrardo theologo parisiensi, divinarum Hebraicarumque literarum professore regio instructi (Paris: Oliva Petri L'Huillier, 1581; other editions in 1582, 1588 and 1592); Gilbert Génébrard, *De sacrarum electionum iure et necessitate ad Ecclesiae Gallicanae redintegrationem* (Lyon: apud Ioannem Philehotte, 1593). This work, composed after the coronation of Henry IV, denounced the appointment by the French kings of bishops, abbots, and other major ecclesiastical offices. Génébrard, in his letter of dedication to Cardinal Filippo Sega, papal legate of Piacenza, and Niccolò Pelevaeus, Archbishop of Rennes, constructs a parallel between the condition of the French clergy and the Babylonian exile of the Jews: "Hanc palmam ei supremus Deus, opinor designabat, ut captivitate hac plusquam babylonica 70 annorum nostratem ecclesiam liberaret. Instat enim septuagesimus ex quo Franciscus primus, circumscripto Leone 10 primum publicas vocationes sustulit et in suas privatas libidines convertit" (5).

35 Eldad Danius, *De Iudaeis clausis eorumque in Aethiopia beatissimo imperio* (Paris: apud Federicum Morellum, 1563); Gilbert Génébrard, *Hebraeorum breve chronicon, sive compendium de mundi ordina et temporibus ab orbe condito usque ad annum Christi 1112. Capita R. Mose ben Maiemon de rebus Christi Regis. Collectanea Eliae Levitis et R. Iacob Salomonis filii de eodem, quibus summatim explicatur* (Paris: apud Martinum Iuvenem, 1572); Gilbert Génébrard, *Chronologia Hebraeorum maior, quae Seder Olam Rabba inscribitur. Interprete Gilberto Genebrardo Theologo Parisiensi divinarum hebraicarum literarum professore regio* (Paris: apud Martinum Iuvenem, 1578); Flavius Josephus, *Histoire de Fl. Iosephe, sacrificateur hebrieu, mise en françois, reveuë sur le Grec et illustree de chronologie, figures, annotations et tables tant des chapitres, que des principales materies, par G. Génébrard, docteur en theologie de Paris*, 2 vols. (Paris: Pierre l'Huillier, 1578); Gilbert Génébrard, *Chronographia in duos libros distincta: prior est de rebus veteris populi* (Paris: apud Martinum Iuvenem, 1567; republished in 1570 and 1572); Gilbert Génébrard, *Chronographiae libri quatuor* (Paris: apud Martinum Iuvenem, 1580).

36 David ben Solomon Ibn Yaḥya, *De poetica hebraeorum, G. Genebrardo interprete. Adiecta sunt ad calcem in obscuriores locas scholia et nonnulorum canticorum latina conversio* (Paris: apud Guillelmum Morelium, 1562). At the same time while working on Jewish texts, Génébrard also published a translation of the complete works of Origen: Origen Adamantius, *Opera quae quidem proferri potuerunt omnia. Doctissimorum virorum studio iam olim translata et recognita, atque multiplice indice copiose locupletata. Nunc postremo a Gilberto Genebrardo partim cum graeca veritate collata, partim libris recens versis et e regia bibliotheca depromptis aucta*, 2 vols. (Paris: apud Guilielmum Chaudiere, 1572–1574).

4 Génébrard and Rabbinic Hebrew

One of the most interesting aspects of Génébrard's Hebraism is his commitment to the study of rabbinic Hebrew, of which he was the first to compose a specific grammar, initially entitled *Eisagoge ad legenda Rabbinorum commentaria* – incidentally the first work ever published by the Benedictine monk (in 1559). It was republished with additions and modifications in 1563, when he was still not yet a professor at the Collège, and once again in 1587.[37] This mode of operation was characteristic of Génébrard: he did the same with other works, such as the *Chronographia* and the commentary on the Psalms.[38]

The general scheme of the *Eisagoge*, constant throughout the three editions, was conceived mainly as a study tool for those wanting to read rabbinic biblical commentary.[39] The text is divided into three main parts.[40] The first is dedicated to the question of the origin of the Hebrew vowel points, the vocalisation of certain letters, and to nouns and verbs; while the second summarizes his analysis in a *tabula*.[41] In the third part of the work, Génébrard publishes as an exercise for his students a passage from the book of Joel together with a comment by David Kimḥi, accompanied by explanatory notes and references to the arguments developed in the grammar as a whole.[42]

The sources used by Génébrard for this unprecedented study of rabbinic Hebrew encompass both Christian Hebraist texts and works of Jewish authors. The first group includes Sebastian Münster, Conrad Pellikan, Agathius Guidac-

---

[37] Gilbert Génébrard, *Eisagoge ad legenda Rabbinorum commentaria* (Paris: apud Martinum Iuvenem, sub insigni Domini Christophori e regione gymnasii Cameracensium, 1559); Gilbert Génébrard, *Eisagoge ad legenda et intelligenda Rabbinorum commentaria* (Paris: apud Martinum Iuvenem, sub insigni Domini Christophori e regione gymnasii Cameracensium, 1563); Gilbert Génébrard, *Eisagoge ad legenda et intelligenda Hebraeorum et Orientalium sine punctis scripta. Ad Sanctum Patrem Sixtum V Pontificem Maximum* (Paris: apud Aegidium Gorbinum, sub insigne Spei, e regione gymnasii Cameracensium, 1587). (The three works will henceforth be identified as Génébrard, 1559; Génébrard, 1563; Génébrard, 1587). Cf. Sophie Kessler-Mesguich, "Gilbert Génébrard (1537–1597) et l'hébreu rabbinique," in *Sha'arei Lashon: Studies in Hebrew, Aramaic and Jewish Languages Presented to Moshe Bar-Asher*, ed. Aharon Maman, Steven E. Fassberg, and Yohanan Breuer, vol. 1 (Jerusalem: Bialik Institute, 2007): 101–116.
[38] See *supra* notes 35–36.
[39] Génébrard, 1559, 5. On the *Eisagoge*, see Kessler-Mesguich, ibid.
[40] The sections correspond respectively to Génébrard, 1559, 6–16; 16–18; and 18–25.
[41] Génébrard, 1559, 25–27.
[42] Génébrard, 1559, 27: "Ad usum et praxin praecedentium canonum, haec verba Ioëlis 2 cap. Cum scholiis R. David Kimhi examinabimus, ut habeas quod sequare. Ea vero typis Biblicis cudi mandavimus, ut notae arithmeticae insertae, quae te ad nostras meditationes numeris respondentes remittent, conspicuae magis essent."

erius, Cinqarbres and Jean Mercier. In the second, alongside the Targumim and Talmud, are numbered David Kimḥi's commentaries and the *Mikhlol*, Rashi, and especially Elijah Levita, of whom however only *Sefer ha-baḥur* is mentioned explicitly. The work is introduced by a letter, addressed in the 1559 edition to his patron Guillelme Du Prat, Bishop of Clermont (but in that of 1563 to Antoine du Prat, Abbot of Bonlieu[43]), in which Génébrard explains the reasons that led him to write this work, such as the desire to read rabbinic literature in order to clarify and interpret obscure passages of Scripture.[44]

The second edition of this work contains a series of interesting additions which presuppose Génébrard's close reading of Elijah Levita, particularly his *Massoreth ha-Massoreth*. The professor at the Collège drew especially upon Levita's work in support of the claim that the vowel points and accent marks of the Masoretic tradition were of human invention and first added to the Hebrew text of Scripture around the beginning of the 5th century CE.[45] Génébrard accepted the thesis of Elijah, categorically rejecting the hypothesis according to which the vowel and accent marks were either revealed directly at Sinai or instituted by Ezra.[46] The second edition was also enriched by new sources, for instance Samuel Ibn Tibbon's (1165–1232) Hebrew translation of Aristotle's *Physics*, and by a con-

---

[43] Génébrard, 1563, 3.
[44] Génébrard, 1563, 3: "Libellum de ratione legendi Hebraice sine punctis exaravi, cum ut ea quae superioribus annis observaveram in memoriam revocarem, tum ut plerisque prodessem, qui se queruntur destitui ratione legendi libros Rabbinorum. Etsi autem sciam aliquos istorum, qui cum sint bonarum artium rudes, doctuli et censores, si diis placet, aliorum haberi volunt, meis studis detracturos."
[45] Elijah Levita adopted this position in the third introduction to his work *Massoret ha-Massoret*, counting, in particular, 436 years from the destruction of the Second Temple in the year 70 CE. See Elias Levita, *The Massoreth ha-Massoreth*, edited and translated by Christian D. Ginsburg, in Jacob ben Chajim ibn Adonijah, *Introduction to the Rabbinic Bible*, ed. Christian D. Ginsburg (New York: Ktav Publishing House, 1968), 131: "The same was the case among us, prior to the invention of the points, and it continued till the time after the close of the Talmud, which took place in [the year] 3989 of the creation = 436 after the desctruction of the second Temple."
[46] Génébrard, 1563, 9: "Illud autem contigit apud Hebraeos, authore Elia, anno ab everso templo quadringentesimo trigesimosexto, qui est a Christo quadringentesimus septuagesimussextus. Ea enim aetate Tyberitae, qui inhabitabant Tyberiadem urbem Galilae a qua mare Tyberiadis in Evangelio et [. . .] thermae quaedam calidae celebratae in Talmud, ea inquam aetate non solum voces variis sonis distinxerunt, sed etiam puncta bibliis ad illam diversitatem significandam annotarunt, ut etiam illi errent vel turpissime, qui punctorum vocalium inventionem aut a monte Sina, aut ab Ezra concilioque eius repetunt." Note how Génébrard revises Levita's dating scheme, replacing the Temple with Christ as the chronological point of orientation. The reference to Christ must refer to his death, since $30 + 476 = 70 + 436$.

cluding discussion presenting the tools required for understanding the rabbinic lexicon, such as the dictionaries and works of Münster, Kimḥi and Levita.[47]

Génébrard's third edition was published more than twenty years after the second[48] and introduced further new features. In particular, he developed and expanded the final section on the specific vocabulary of rabbinic literature, creating a real dictionary divided into different topics, whether religious or philosophical, grammatical or rhetorical. To this dictionary he added a list of post-biblical Jewish works known to him, which in turn influenced the work of Buxtorf.[49] In addition, as an appendix, Génébrard published a short treatise on Hebrew poetry and prosody. The French professor clearly aimed to provide his students and, in general, all those who had an interest in studying rabbinic literature, with tools as complete and useful as possible.

In the course of its evolution, the work's introduction and overall significance also changed, as reflected in adjustments to its title. If in the two first editions there was an explicit reference to rabbinic literature (*Eisagoge de modo legendi Rabbinorum commentaria* and *De modo legendi et intelligendi Rabbinorum commentaria*), the 1587 title referred in more general terms to *ad legenda et interpretanda Hebraeorum et Orientalium sine punctis scripta*. In other words, by this point in time Génébrard intended for the manual to aid in the understanding not only of rabbinic literature, but of Hebrew in general, which was, according to him, a language written in its purest and most original form without dots and accents.[50] In addition, in the 1587 edition, Génébrard replaced the dedication to Du Prat with two letters, one to Pope Sixtus V, the other to the reader.[51]

In the latter, the French professor contextualizes his work within the tradition of Christian Hebraism that had preceded him. He explicitly mentions Von Campen,

---

47 Cf. Génébrard, 1563, 29.
48 Génébrard, 1587.
49 Burnett, *From Christian Hebraism to Jewish Studies*, 156–162.
50 The word "Orientalium" in the title was a reference to the other oriental languages to which Génébrard compared Hebrew. For example, in the Introduction, discussing the origins of the vowel points, Génébrard refers to the Oriental regions: "Quid igitur sunt scripta huius modi? Respondeo non abbreviationes, ut docui, non contractiones, non syllabaria, sed integrae dictiones et perfectae, constantes suis numeris, id est suis radicalibus et essentialibus litteris, exutae quidem externo illo et humano punctorum commento, quod anno quarter millesimo, trecentesimo ut minium anno ab orbe condito, excogitatum est ad stolidis et rudibus consulendum, sed vestitae rebus et ornamentis ad legendum necessariis, quibus contenti fuerunt olim docti, pariter et indocti, apud omnes Orientis Provincias." *Eisagoge* (1587), [*ivr].
51 Génébrard, 1587, *iir-v-[*iiir].

Clenard,[52] and Münster, criticizing their claim that Hebrew written without points was either a contracted, or abbreviated language, and of a minor status compared to Biblical Hebrew. He also attacks the Calvinist Hebraist Antoine Chevalier, who had not only demoted Hebrew written without vowel points, but had also claimed that these dots had been handed down from Moses along with the Old Testament.[53] By contrast, Génébrard states that he had written his work to demonstrate that the Hebrew language without the vowel points devised in the fifth century was a complete and legitimate language. Once again, Génébrard wished to assert that authentic Hebrew is that written without dots and that his work provides the keys to reading it.

In the former letter to Sixtus V, after praising the pope for his government of the Roman Church, Génébrard exalts the early Greek and Latin translations of the Bible as based on a Hebrew text written without vowels and, for this reason, superior to the Masoretic version of the Hebrew.[54] The new meaning that Génébrard attributed to his treatise, written in defence of the only biblical versions accepted by the Catholic Church, is explicit here. This letter takes on even greater significance when it is recalled that precisely at this time – and under the auspices of Sixtus V's pontificate – the new version of the *Vulgate* was being prepared.[55]

---

[52] On Nicolas Clenard (Cleynaerts), who published one of the first Hebrew grammars, cfr. Peter G. Bietenholz and Thomas Brian Deutscher, eds. *Contemporaries of Erasmus: A Biographical Register of the Renaissance and Reformation*, vol. 1 (Toronto: University of Toronto Press, 2003), 405; on Jean Campensis (Van Campen), professor of Hebrew in Louvain, see Peter G. Bietenholz and Thomas Brian Deutscher, *Contemporaries of Erasmus* I, 255–256. See also Sophie Kessler-Mesguich, "Deux hébraïsants à Louvain: Jean Campensis et Nicolas Clénard," *Helmántica* 154 (2000): 59–73.

[53] Génébrard, 1587, [*iiiv]: "Campensis, vir alioqui de lingua sancta optime meritus, Eliae Levitae discipulus, Clenardi praeceptor, qui Latinorum primus praeceptiones grammaticas satis obscure parum methodice a Sante Pagnino, Reuchlino Capnione et primis aliis Latinis Hebraicarum rerum tractatoribus explicatas, dilucide, methodice cum luce et ordine edidit ad Eliae Levitae praeceptoris imitationem. [. . .] Ab eo parum abscondit quidam Chevallerius apud suos et cacolycos alicuius nominis, apud Catholicos et doctos malus et indoctus, tum quasi communis sensus expers et vacuus, mancam scripturam appellat et imminutam eam, quae punctis caret, ut ideo audacter affirmet et contra omnium historiarum et seculorum fidem, puncta ab ipso Mose una cum literis sacris veteris testamenti in deserto fuisse tradita. [. . .] Munsterus in sua Chaldaica grammatica [tribuit] praeceptionibus Hebraicis et Chaldaicis ubi iis accesserit mediocris vocum perceptio et intelligentia."

[54] Génébrard, 1587, *iiv: "Adde veterum veteris testamenti, ut Septuaginta Seniorum, ut Hieronymi interpretationes inde copiosam lucem haustura. Ideo enim saepe obscuriores apparent, quod inspicienti puncta a recentioribus rabbinis, quos Masoretas appellant, elementis biblicis affixa, post eiusdem Hieronymi saeculum, non facile occurrat, quid maiores illi nostri legerint."

[55] Cf. Victor Baroni, *La Contre-Réforme devant la Bible: la question biblique: avec un supplément. Du XVIIIe siècle à nos jours* (Lausanne: La Concorde, 1943).

Génébrard clearly alludes here to the contemporary debate in the Roman curia on the need to revise the translation of Jerome, especially after the death of Cardinal Guglielmo Sirleto. Robert Bellarmine made an important contribution to this discussion which, after the publication of the Sistine version in 1592, continued in subsequent years under Pope Gregory XIV, and in which the claim as to the antiquity of the vowel points was used to legitimize new Latin translations.[56]

Even if Génébrard was not involved directly in the debate, his insistence on the importance of this early biblical tradition (that is without dots) and the opportunity to renew the *Vulgate* translation through the study of Greek and Hebrew was linked to his role as a Catholic Hebraist. Since the establishment of the Collège de France, in fact, the theologians of the Sorbonne had been suspicious about the study of Hebrew, particularly because the knowledge of the "holy tongue" represented a risk for the stability of the theological tradition, which was founded on the *Vulgate* text.[57] Within the Catholic world, Génébrard intended to defend the importance of the Hebrew language and Jewish tradition in the understanding of Christian and Catholic history.

But Génébrard's work can be better understood if we place it in the context of yet another debate, this time involving the French professor and the theologians of Geneva, in particular Theodore Beza. Génébrard first refers to this dispute with the successor to Calvin in 1579, in his second edition of the Psalms and, once again, in 1584, in the second edition of his commentary on the *Song of Songs*.[58] The main topic of disagreement was the proper versification of Latin biblical translations. Génébrard accused Beza of having used various lyrical meters when there was in fact only one sacred prosody suited to the Bible.[59] At issue here was

---

[56] Piet van Boxel, "Robert Bellarmine, Christian Hebraist and Censor," in *History of Scholarship: A Selection of Papers from the Seminar on the History of Scholarship held annually at the Warburg Institute*, ed. Christopher Ligota and Jean Louis Quantin (Oxford: Oxford University Press, 2006): 251–275; Richard Muller, "The Debate over the Vowel Points and the Crisis in Orthodox Hermeneutics," *The Journal of Medieval and Renaissance Studies* 10 (1980): 53–72, esp. 56–57.
[57] On these criticisms of the Sorbonne theologians, see Abel Lefranc, *Histoire du Collège de France* (Paris: Librarie Hachette, 1932), 122–23, 144–149, 404–405.
[58] Gilbert Génébrard, *Canticum Canticorum Salominis versibus et commentariis illustratum*.
[59] On this debate see Max Engammare, "Licence poétique versus métrique sacrée: la polémique entre Bèze et Génébrard au sujet des Psaumes et du Cantique des cantiques (1579–1586)," in *Théodore de Bèze (1519–1605): actes du colloque de Genève (septembre 2005)*, ed. l'Institut d'Histoire de la Réformation (Genève: Droz, 2007): 479–499; Max Engammare, "Licence poétique versus métrique sacrée (II): la polémique entre Bèze et Génébrard au sujet des Psaumes et du Cantique des cantiques (1579–1586)," *Revue de l'histoire des religions* 226, no. 1 (2009): 102–125.

the origin of the biblical text and the relationship between the three versions in Latin, Greek and Hebrew. In this context Génébrard attacked the Calvinist school of Geneva, maintaining the importance of the Greek version of the Bible, which for him also had a key role to play in understanding its Hebrew counterpart.[60]

In particular, Génébrard defended himself against accusations that he had ascribed too much importance to the Greek version of the Bible at the expense of the Hebrew one. In so doing, he insisted on the notion that since the Masoretic tradition was very recent, the Septuagint translation, made on the basis of a Hebrew version not vocalized by rabbis, was superior both in terms of antiquity and authority. In short, Génébrard's book was a lengthy critique of the alleged ancient origin of the vowel points based on the *auctoritas* of Elija Levita.

The debate as to the source of these points is well known. In the sixteenth century, following the publication of Elijah Levita's *Masoreth ha-Massoreth* and the Latin translation thereof by Sebastian Münster, a complicated and lengthy debate about the antiquity of the Hebrew vocalization and accents emerged. The issue became the pretext for a clash between the different confessions into which Europe was divided. Initially, both Catholics and Protestants had, in an anti-Jewish approach, embraced the idea of the 'imperfection' of the Hebrew text, arguing that the Jews had modified the biblical text to hide references to the true Messiah, i.e. Christ.[61]

In the second half of the sixteenth century, however, two distinct positions based on exclusively theological considerations began to emerge: on one side were Protestants who, in order to legitimize the principle of *sola scriptura*, necessarily supported the immutability of the biblical text and, as a result, the antiquity of vocalization; on the other were Catholics who, eager to strengthen the role of the tradition and interpretation taught by the Church, advocated the idea of the unreliability of the Masoretic Hebrew text, insisting instead on the relative "modernity" of Hebrew vocalization.

Génébrard asserted that the institutionalization of vocalization had also been discussed by many rabbis and Jewish scholars, such as Ibn Ezra and Kimḥi, and criticized the position of Antoine Chevalier, one of the Hebrew teachers in Geneva, a critique which was to be re-echoed in the *Eisagoge*: Génébrard referred to him not as a grammarian, but rather as an interpolator and plagiarist of gram-

---

60 Gilbert Génébrard, *Psalmi Davidis vulgata editione, calendario Hebraeo, Syro, Graeco, Latino* (1582), † iiiiv: "Sed interim tamen asperrimis illis locis sensum commodissimum attulerunt Septuaginta nostri Seniores, [...] et Rabbini aliqui, praecipue veteres, adhibuerunt, sequutique sunt, atque plena manu complexi."
61 On this topic, cf. Burnett, *From Christian Hebraism to Jewish Studies*, 203–239; Muller, "The Debate over Vowel Points."

marians, and as one who mantained that the points had been given to Moses together with the Law.⁶² In comparison with his Catholic companions, then, Génébrard adopted a different path, on one hand accepting the thesis of Elijah Levita and the position of the Catholic Church, but on the other providing the philological tools required to give assurance to the unvocalized Hebrew text. In so doing he introduced an important innovation into the Catholic tradition of biblical study and interpretation. Indeed, in teaching in his *Eisagoge* how to read unvocalized Hebrew, Génébrard implicitly rendered the Hebrew text of the Bible less "unstable" than the Catholic side had claimed it to be, thereby limiting the role of Church tradition in biblical exegesis. At the same time, Génébrard demonstrated that Hebrew study could be pursued in the context of Catholic orthodoxy at a level equally as high, if not higher, than that of the Protestant universities.

---

62 Gilbert Génébrard, *Psalmi Davidis vulgata editione*, 1582 *viv-*viiir: "Falso putant hebraicam veritatem sive fontem consistere in punctis, non in literis, nec vident puncta inventum esse humanum et quidem Iudaeorum, iam post quadringentos plus a Christo annos dispersorum et contra Christum Christianamque pietatem malevolentissime affectorum. Ideo enim istorum quidam Cevallerius Iudaei cuiusdam gener, non tam grammaticus, quam grammaticorum interpolator et plagiarius pertinacissime et stolidissime defendit puncta simul cum lege in monte Sinai data, eorum originem, effigiem, picturam, sonum a Deo *amesos* iam a primis illis seculis repetens." For Chevalier, see also note 53. The analysis of the vowel points tradition offers Génébrard the opportunity to introduce the subject of Kabbalah. He writes: "Masoreth enim nihil aliud est quam traditio grammatica de punctis, accentibus, syllabis, vocabulis et similibus minutiis, ac in eo differt a Cabbala, quod haec quidem traditio sit, verum theologica, deque rerum et verborum secretiore enuntiatione," Gilbert Génébrard, *Psalmi Davidis vulgata editione*, 1582 *viiv. A different conception of Kabbalah appears in Génébrard's *Chronographia*, where he writes: "R. Simeon ben Iohai auctor libri Zoar. Quo posuit fundamenta stultae et vanae artis illius Cabbalisticae, quae languet circa literarum apices, numeros, transpositiones, anagrammatismos, vocum inversiones, allusiones, amphibologias, homonymias. Nam eius vanitatis mysteria tribus precipue constant, quae indicantur voce GNT. Nempe geometria (sic imperite confunderunt geometriam cum arithmetica) quando literae expenditur numerus. Noteriacon quando litera ponitur pro integra dictione. Sic autem barbare dicitur a notariorum apicibus. Temurà, quae permutatio (elementorum) cum una litera pro altera substituitur. E duobus primis vocabulis, quorum unum est graecum, alterum semilatinum, intelligis, quo tempore tam inepta ars excogitata fuerit, nihilque minus esse quam Cabbalam, id est scientiam quae a maioribus per manum recepta sit. Preter istiusmodi ineptias continet multa impia et ex omni haeresum furfure constata. Constituit decem Sephirot sive numerationes, pro suo fundamento, quas sive statuant esse essentiam Dei, sive aliquid aliud extra Dei essentiam impie introductas ex eo apparet, quod in Deo numerum et multitudinem realem ponant. [...] Reuclinum Capnionem tribus libris harum nugarum gustum mundo praebuisse sine refutatione et Picum Mirandulanum se earum patronum constituisse equidem miror." (Gilbert Génébrard, *Chronographiae libri quatuor*, 168–169). Génébrard mantains that *Sefer ha-Zohar* was written in 87 B.C.E. In the 1567 edition Génébrard had only touched briefly upon the composition of the *Zohar*.

5 Conclusion

The lives and works of Caesar Baronius and Gilbert Génébrard are important because they help us rethink the place of knowledge of the Hebrew language within the post-Reformation Catholic world. Examination of Baronius's *Annales* reveals that the accusations brought against the work by Protestant scholars were not always well founded. The Roman cardinal, in fact, without knowing Hebrew, was able to make use of a substantial number of important Jewish sources (not all of which were secondary texts). To be sure, Rome in the second half of the sixteenth century was not a leading center for Hebrew studies. Nevertheless, Baronius managed to compose a set of texts to counter Protestant claims, aware that in order to fight effectively against his opponents he needed to resort to that kind of polemical activity.

Génébrard's textual production, on the other hand, is paradigmatic for the history of European Christian Hebraism in the sixteenth century. Conflicts between the different Christian confessions were also fought in the narrow field of Hebrew study and Génébrard was a formidable warrior in this arena: his works were deployed as weapons against Calvinism, Lutheranism, and other minor sects, such as the Antitrinitarians. However, his approach to Hebrew was opposed even by the Catholic theologians of the Sorbonne, as he insisted on using different versions of the Bible (for example, the Septuagint), thus straying far from tradition. Despite the great controversy it aroused, however, Génébrard's work is nevertheless of great scholarly importance. It demonstrates, in fact, that at least for the sixteenth and seventeenth centuries it is not entirely possible to distinguish between erudition and confessionalization when studying Christian Hebraism. Indeed, Génébrard's works would be used, in the following century, by a large number of Protestant scholars such as Casaubon and Buxtorf, precisely because they were essential tools for the study of Jewish sources, even if they were not born in an ivory tower, but rather crafted to defend elements of Catholicism against Lutherans and Calvinists. Most importantly, the lives and works of Génébrard and Baronius demonstrate that study and interest in Hebrew did not disappear from the Counter-Reformation world, but instead remained present and reached, in some cases, levels of knowledge, equal, if not superior, to that attained in Protestant countries.

Bibliography

Alvar-Ezquerra, Alfredo. "Le modèle universitaire d'Alcalá de Henares dans la première moitié du XVIe siècle." In *Les origines du Collège de France (1500–1560)*, edited by Marc Fumaroli, 209–255. Paris: Collège de France-Klincksieck, 1998.

Baroni, Victor. *La Contre-Réforme devant la Bible: la question biblique: avec un supplément. Du XVIIIe siècle à nos jours*. Lausanne: La Concorde, 1943.

Baronius, Caesar. *Annales ecclesiastici*. Venice: apud Haeredem Hieronymi Scoti, 1601.

Berosus sacerdos Chaldaicus. *Antiquitatum libri quinque cum commentariis Ioannis Annii Viterbensis sacrae Theologiae professoris nunc primum in antiquitatum studiosorum commoditatem sub forma Enchiridii excusi et castigati*. Antwerp: In aedibus Ioannis Steelsii, 1545.

Bietenholz, Peter G., and Thomas Brian Deutscher, eds. *Contemporaries of Erasmus: A Biographical Register of the Renaissance and Reformation*, vol. 1. Toronto: University of Toronto Press, 2003.

Boiteux, Martine. "Preaching to the Jews in Early Modern Rome: Words and Images." In *The Jewish-Christian Encounter in Medieval Preaching*, edited by Jonathan Adams and Jussi Hanska, 298–322. New York: Routledge, 2015.

Burnett, Stephen G. *Christian Hebraism in the Reformation Era (1500–1660): Authors, Books, and the Transmission of Jewish Learning*. Leiden: Brill, 2012.

Burnett, Stephen G. *From Christian Hebraism to Jewish Studies: Johannes Buxtorf (1564–1629) and Hebrew Learning in the Seventeenth Century* (Leiden: Brill, 1996)

Campanini, Saverio. "Die Geburt der Judaistik aus dem Geist der Christlichen Kabbalah." In *Gottes Sprache in der philologischen Werkstatt: Hebraistik vom 15. bis zum 19. Jahrhundert*, edited by Giuseppe Veltri and Gerold Necker, 135–241. Leiden: Brill, 2004.

Canini, Angelo. *De locis sanctae Scripturae Hebraicis Angeli Caninii commentaries*. Antwerp: sumptibus viduae et haeredum Io. Belleri, 1600.

Casaubon, Isaac. *De rebus sacris et ecclesiasticis exercitationes XVI. Ad Cardinalis Baronii Prolegomena in Annales, et primam eorum partem, de Domini Nostri Iesu Christi nativitate, vita, passione, assuntione*. London: Norton, 1614.

Casaubon, Isaac. *De rebus sacris et ecclesiasticis exercitationes XVI*. Frankfort: typis Ioannis Bring, 1615.

David ben Solomon Ibn Yaḥya. *De poetica hebraeorum, G. Genebrardo interprete. Adiecta sunt ad calcem in obscuriores locas scholia et nonnulorum canticorum latina conversion*. Paris: apud Guillelmum Morelium, 1562.

de Vocht, Henry. *History of the Foundation and the Rise of the Collegium Trilingue Lovaniense 1517–1550, 4 vols*. Leuven: Bibliotèque de l'Université, 1951–1955.

del Carmen Álvarez Mulero, Mari. "Relaciones entre Benito Arias Montano y el cardenal italiano Guillermo Sirleti." In *Benito Arias Montano y los humanistas de su tiempo*. Vol. 1, edited by José Maria Maestre Maestre et al., 51–56. Mérida: Editora Regional de Extremadura, 2006.

Drusius, Johannes. *Ad voces Hebraicas Novi Testamenti commentaries*. Antwerp: ex Christophori Palntini, 1582.

Dunkelgrün, Theodor. "The Christian Study of Judaism in Early Modern Europe." In *The Cambridge History of Judaism, vol. 7: The Early Modern World, 1500–1815*, edited by Jonathan Karp and Adam Sutcliffe, 316–348. Cambridge: Cambridge University Press, 2017.

Eldad Danius. *De Iudaeis clausis eorumque in Aethiopia beatissimo imperio*. Paris: apud Federicum Morellum, 1563.

Engammare, Max. "Licence poétique versus métrique sacrée: la polémique entre Bèze et Génébrard au sujet des Psaumes et du Cantique des cantiques (1579–1586)." In *Théodore de Bèze (1519–1605): actes du colloque de Genève (septembre 2005)*, edited by l'Institut d'Histoire de la Réformation, 479–499. Genève: Droz, 2007.

Engammare, Max. "Licence poétique versus métrique sacrée (II): la polémique entre Bèze et Génébrard au sujet des Psaumes et du Cantique des cantiques (1579–1586)." *Revue de l'histoire des religions* 226, no. 1 (2009): 102–125.

Feret, Pierre. *La Faculté de Théologie de Paris et ses Docteurs les plus célèbres*. Paris: Picard 1901.

Friedman, Jerome. *The Most Ancient Testimony: Sixteenth-Century Christian-Hebraica in the Age of Renaissance Nostalgia*. Athens: Ohio University Press, 1983.

Fubini, Riccardo. "L'Ebraismo nei riflessi della cultura umanistica: Leonardo Bruni, Giannozzo Manetti, Annio da Viterbo." In Riccardo Fubini, *Storiografia dell'Umanesimo in Italia da Leonardo Bruni ad Annio da Viterbo*, 291–333. Rome: Storia e Letteratura, 2003.

Génébrard, Gilbert. *Ad Iacobum Schegkium Schorndoffensem philosophum et medicum assertionibus sacris de Deo sese temere immiscentem et tribus ipsius de S. Trinitate libris, modo pro Sabellianis, modo pro Trinitariis inconstantissime obtrectantem responsio*. Paris: apud Aegidium Gorbinum, 1575.

Génébrard, Gilbert. *Canticum Canticorum Salomonis regis, cum commentariis trium rabbinorum, Salomonis Iarhii, Abrahami abben Ezrae et Innominati cuiusdam*. Paris: apud Martinum Iuvenem, 1570.

Génébrard, Gilbert. *Canticum Canticorum Salomonis versibus et commentariis illustratum Gilberto Genebrardo theologo Parisiensi, professore regio auctore. Adversus Trochaicam Theodori Bezae Paraphrasim*. Paris: apud Aegidium Gorbinum, 1585.

Génébrard, Gilbert. *Chronographia in duos libros distincta: prior est de rebus veteris populi*. Paris: apud Martinum Iuvenem, 1567.

Génébrard, Gilbert. *Chronographiae libri quatuor*. Paris: apud Mattinum Iuvenem, 1580.

Génébrard, Gilbert. *Chronologia Hebraeorum maior, quae Seder Olam Rabba inscribitur. Interprete Gilberto Genebrardo Theologo Parisiensi divinarum hebraicarum literarum professore regio*. Paris: apud Martinum Iuvenem, 1578.

Génébrard, Gilbert. *De sacrarum electionum iure et necessitate ad Ecclesiae Gallicanae redintegrationem*. Lyon: apud Ioannem Philehotte, 1593.

Génébrard, Gilbert. *De S. Trinitate libri tres contra huius aevi trinitarios, antitrinitarios et autotheanos. His praeposita est summa sessionum Synodi quam triennio superiore ministri Poloni cum trinitariis Petricoviae habuerunt, ex alicuius amici Poloni epistola*. Paris: apud J. Benenatum, 1569.

Génébrard, Gilbert. *Eisagoge ad legenda et intelligenda Hebraeorum et Orientalium sine punctis scripta. Ad Sanctum Patrem Sixtum V Pontificem Maximum*. Paris: apud Aegidium Gorbinum, sub insigne Spei, e regione gymnasii Cameracensium, 1587.

Génébrard, Gilbert. *Eisagoge ad legenda et intelligenda Rabbinorum commentaria*. Paris: apud Martinum Iuvenem, sub insigni Domini Christophori e regione gymnasii Cameracensium, 1563.

Génébrard, Gilbert. *Eisagoge ad legenda Rabbinorum commentaria*. Paris: apud Martinum Iuvenem, sub insigni Domini Christophori e regione gymnasii Cameracensium, 1559.

Génébrard, Gilbert. *Hebraeorum breve chronicon, sive compendium de mundi ordina et temporibus ab orbe condito usque ad annum Christi 1112. Capita R. Mose ben Maiemon de rebus Vhristi Regis. Collectanea Eliae Levitis et R. Iacob Salomonis filii de eodem, quibus summatim explicatur*. Paris: apud Martinum Iuvenem, 1572.

Génébrard, Gilbert. *Hebraicum Alphabetum*. Paris: Apud Martinum Iuvenem, 1564.

Génébrard, Gilbert. *Psalmi Davidis vulgata editione, calendario Hebraeo, Syro, Graeco, Latino, argumentis et commentariis genuinum et primarium Psalmorum sensum, Hebraismosque locupletius, quam priore editione aperientibus, a Gilbert Genebrardo theologo parisiensi, divinarum Hebraicarumque literarum professore Regio instructi*. Paris: Oliva Petri L'Huillier, 1581.

Génébrard, Gilbert. *Psalmi Davidis vulgata editione, calendario Hebraeo, Syro, Graeco, Latino, Argumentis et commentariis genuinum et primarium Psalmorum sensum, Hebraismoosque locupletius, quam priore editione aperientibus, a G. Génébrardo theologo parisiensi, divinarum Hebraicarumque literarum professore Regio instructi*. Paris: Oliva Petri L'Huillier, via Iacobaea, 1582.

Grafton, Anthony, and Joanna Weinberg. *"I have always loved the Holy Tongue": Isaac Casaubon, the Jews, and a Forgotten Chapter in Renaissance Scholarship*. Cambridge, MA: The Belknap Press of Harvard University Press, 2011.

Grafton, Anthony. *Forgers and Critics: Creativity and Duplicity in Western Scholarship*. Princeton: Princeton University Press, 1990.

Grendler, Paul F. "Italian Biblical humanism and the Papacy, 1515–1535." In *Biblical Humanism and Scholasticism in the Age of Erasmus*, edited by Erika Rummel, 227–276. Leiden: Brill, 2008.

Josephus Flavius. *Histoire de Fl. Iosephe, sacrificateur hebrieu, mise en françois, reveuë sur le Grec et illustree de chronologie, figures, annotations et tables tant des chapitres, que des principales materies, par G. Génébrard, docteur en theologie de Paris*. 2 vols. Paris: Pierre l'Huillier, 1578.

Kessler-Mesguich, Sophie. "Deux hébraïsants à Louvain: Jean Campensis et Nicolas Clénard." *Helmántica* 154 (2000): 59–73.

Kessler-Mesguich, Sophie. "Gilbert Génébrard (1537–1597) et l'hébreu rabbinique." In *Sha'arei Lashon: Studies in Hebrew, Aramaic and Jewish Languages Presented to Moshe Bar-Asher*, edited by Aharon Maman, Steven E. Fassberg, and Yohanan Breuer, vol. 1, 101–116. Jerusalem: Bialik Institute, 2007.

Kessler-Mesguich, Sophie. "L'enseignement de l'hébreu et de l'araméen à Paris (1530–1560) d'après les œuvres grammaticales des lecteurs royaux." In *Les origines du Collège de France (1500–1560): Actes du colloque international (Paris, décembre 1995)*, edited by Marc Fumaroli and Marianne Lion-Violet, 357–374. Paris: Collège de France-Klincksieck, 1998.

Kessler-Mesguich, Sophie. *Les études hébraïques en France: de François Tissard à Richard Simon (1508–1680)*. Geneve: Droz, 2013.

Lefranc, Abel. *Histoire du Collège de France*. Paris: Librarie Hachette, 1932.

Levita, Elijah. *Opusculum recens Hebraicum a doctissimo Hebraeo Eliia Levita Germano grammatico elaboratum, cui titulum fecit tishby id est Thisbites, in quo 712 vocum quae sunt partim Hebraice, Caldaicae, Arabicae, Graecae et Latinae, quaeque in dictionariis non facile inveniuntur, per Paulum Fagium latinitae donatum*. Isnae in Algauia: Per Paulum Fagium, 1541.

Levita, Elijah. *The Massoreth ha-Massoreth*, ed. and trans. Christian D. Ginsburg. In Jacob ben Chajim ibn Adonijah, *Introduction to the Rabbinic Bible*, ed. Christian D. Ginsburg. New York: Ktav Publishing House, 1968.

Manuel, Frank E. *The Broken Staff: Judaism Through Christian Eyes*. Cambridge, MA: Harvard University Press, 1992.
Margolin, Jean Claude. "Érasme et le 'Collegium Trilingue Lovaniense'." In *Les origines du Collège de France (1500–1560)*: Actes du colloque international, edited by de Marc Fumaroli and Marianne Lion-Violet, 257–278. Paris: Collège de France-Klincksieck, 1998.
Mreje-O'Hana, Simone. "À propos de l'Hébreu des 'quatre saintes communautés' du Comtat Venaissin et d'Avignon: lexique et grammaire." *Revue des études juives* 167 (2008): 121–152.
Muller, Richard. "The Debate over the Vowel Points and the Crisis in Orthodox Hermeneutics." *The Journal of Medieval and Renaissance Studies* 10 (1980): 53–72.
Origenis Adamantius, *Opera quae quidem proferri potuerunt omnia. Doctissimorum virorum studio iam olim translata et recognita, atque multiplice indice copiose locupletata. Nunc postremo a Gilberto Genebrardo partim cum graeca veritate collata, partim libris recens versis et e regia bibliotheca depromptis aucta*, 2 vols. Paris: apud Guilielmum Chaudiere, 1572–1574.
Parente, Fausto. "La Chiesa e il 'Talmud': l'atteggiamento della Chiesa e del mondo cristiano nei confronti del 'Talmud' e degli altri scritti rabbinici, con particolare riguardo all'Italia tra XV e XVI secolo." In *Gli Ebrei in Italia*. Vol. 1, edited by Corrado Vivanti, 521–643. Storia d'Itala: Annali 11. Torino: Einaudi, 1996.
Parente, Fausto. "The Index, the Holy Office, the Condemnation of the Talmud and Publication of Clement VIII's Index." In *Church, Censorship and Culture in Early Modern Italy*, edited by Gigliola Fragnito; trans. Adrian Belton, 163–193. Cambridge: Cambridge University Press, 2001.
Rekers, Ben. *Benito Arias Montano (1527–1598)*. Leiden: Brill, 1972.
Ricciardi, Roberto. "Canini, Angelo." In *Dizionario Biografico degli Italiani*. Vol. 18, 101–102. Roma: Istituto dell'Enciclopedia Italiana, 1975.
Rothschild, Jean-Pierre. "La philologie de combat de Gilbert Génébrard (1535–1597)." In *Les hébraïsants chrétiens en France au XVIe siècle* (Actes du Colloque de Troyes 2–4 septembre 2013), edited by Gilbert Dahan and Annie Noblesse-Rocher, 363–421. Geneve: Droz, 2018.
Roudaut, François, ed. *Jean (c. 1525–1570) et Josias (c. 1560–1626) Mercier: l'amour de la philologie à la Renaissance et au début de l'âge classique*. Actes du Colloque d'Uzès (2 et 3 mars 2001). Paris: Honoré Champion, 2006.
Secret, François. *Les kabbalistes chrétiens de la Renaissance*. Paris: Dunod, 1964.
Tailhand, Pierre Claude. *Étude sur Gilbert Génébrard, docteur de la Faculté de théologie de Paris (XVIe siècle)*. Riom: Ulysse Jouvet Imprimeur de la Cour, 1864.
van Boxel, Piet. "Robert Bellarmine, Christian Hebraist and Censor." In *History of Scholarship: A Selection of Papers from the Seminar on the History of Scholarship held annually at the Warburg Institute*, edited by Christopher Ligota and Jean Louis Quantin, 251–275. Oxford: Oxford University Press, 2006.
Wilkinson, Robert J. *Orientalism, Aramaic and Kabbalah in the Catholic Reformation: The First Printing of the Syriac New Testament*. Studies in the History of Christian Tradition 137. Leiden: Brill, 2007.
Wilkinson, Robert J. *The Kabbalistic Scholars of the Antwerp Polyglot*. Studies in the History of Christian Tradition 138. Leiden: Brill, 2007.

Stefan Schorch
The Peculiarities of Hungarian Christian Hebraism (16th and 17th Centuries)

In memoriam Géza György Xeravits (1971–2019)

Over the last several decades, Christian Hebraism has become the subject of broad and fruitful study. The focus of this research, however, seems to have been restricted to certain geographical and cultural areas of Europe, while other regions remained largely neglected, at least with regard to academic publications in English, and in the general perception of Christian Hebraism. Thus, despite an abundance of source material awaiting discovery and scholarly analysis, Christian Hebraism in Eastern Central Europe, i.e. the area covered today by the Baltic states, Poland, Belarus, Ukraine, the Czech Republic, Slovakia, Hungary, and Romania, has largely remained a *terra incognita*.[1]

The present article addresses this lacuna in scholarship by examining Hungarian Christian Hebraism.[2] When approaching this topic, one should of course

---

[1] The following more general publications in this field should be mentioned: Yuri Vartanov, "The Early Studies in Biblical Hebrew in Poland and Eastern Europe," *Kwartalnik Historii Żydów – Jewish History Quarterly* 3, no. 247 (2013): 511–23; Stefan Schorch and Johannes Thon, eds., *Christian Hebraism in Eastern Central Europe from the Renaissance to the Enlightenment* (forthcoming).

[2] Since the initial submission of this article, several important studies devoted to this topic have been published, especially in the framework of the extremely fecund research project "Magyar peregrinusok héber köszöntőversei a 17. században," headed by József Zsengellér and based at the Károli Gáspár University, with funding provided by the Hungarian National Research Development and Innovation Office for the period 2017–2021: Kornélia Koltai, "Hebrew Language Knowledge of Christian Hebraists Dealing with Hungarian Linguistics," *Studia Debreceni Teológiai Tanulmányok* 11 (2019): 9–23; Eadem, "Egy 17. századi héber carmen bemutatása – a carmenszerző héber grammatikája tükrében," in *A grammatikától a retorikáig: Nyelvészeti tanulmányok C. Vladár Zsuzsa tiszteletére*, ed. Ferenc Havas, Katalin Horváth, Éva Hrenek, and Mária

---

Note: I wish to thank my Hungarian colleagues Kornélia Koltai, Kövér András (both Eötvös Loránd University Budapest, Department of Assyriology and Hebrew), Katalin Rac (University of Florida, Gainesville), and Géza Xeravits† (Selye J. University Komarno, Reformed Theological Faculty) for carefully rechecking and correcting my translations from Hungarian sources and answering my questions. I also wish to express my appreciation to József Zsengellér (Károli Gáspár University of the Reformed Church in Hungary, Budapest, Theological Faculty) for countless interesting discussions in fields of joint interest throughout the many years of our friendship. This article is dedicated to the memory of our joint friend Géza ל״ז, one of the foremost Hungarian Christian Hebraists of our generation.

first inquire into the contours of the term "Hungarian." In other words, who can be called a Hungarian Hebraist in the 16th or 17th centuries? One might be inclined to reply, a scholar from Hungary. However, there is no clear-cut geographical region "Hungary," and the different political units associated with this name (especially the Kingdom of Hungary, which formally existed throughout the Middle Ages until 1946) changed their boundaries repeatedly and considerably throughout the ages, while their respective populations were always multiethnic, multicultural, and multilingual. Should we instead search for those who were Hungarian by self-definition, as indicated, for example, by the addition of the attribute "Ungaricus" to their names upon enrollment at a university? Yet individuals did not always behave consistently in this regard, and even those who did were not always Hungarians as we would probably understand it, i.e. they did not always speak Hungarian. It might therefore seem that use of the Hungarian language should serve as the litmus text for identifying a scholar as Hungarian. However, within the territories associated with Hungary the language of education was often not Hungarian, but German, and even with regard to popular vernaculars the Hungarian language had many competitors, especially Croatian, German, Polish, Romanian, Serbian, Slovakian, and Ukrainian.

In light of this situation, which makes a clear delimitation quite complicated, the most reasonable way of speaking of proper "Hungarian" Christian Hebraism still seems to be by referring to the Hungarian language, and I hope to demonstrate in this study *inter alia* that it does indeed makes sense to employ that category, since an impressive number of important Christian Hebraists used the Hun-

---

Ladányi (Budapest: ELTE BTK Alkalmazott Nyelvészeti és Fonetikai Tanszék, 2021): 43–52; József Zsengellér, "The Hebrew Language and Comparative Linguistics in the Early Centuries of Hungarian Protestantism," in *Protestantism, Knowledge and the World of Science*, ed. György Kurucz (Budapest: Károli Gáspár University of the Reformed Church in Hungary/L'Harmattan Publishing, 2017): 63–76; idem, "Franekeri héber carmina gratulatoria Martonfalvi György és diákjainak tollából [Hebrew Congratulatory Poems from Franeker by Georg Martonfalvi and His Students, in Hungarian]," *Református Szemle* 114 (2021): 125–158; idem, "Egy 17. századi héber vizsga margójára: Pontosítások és héber carmenek Tofeus Mihály váradi könyve alapján (RMK II. 764) [On the Margins of a 17th-Century Hebrew Exam: Precise Details and Hebrew Poems from Mihály Tofeus' Book from Várad, in Hungarian]," *Egyháztörténeti Szemle* 22 (2021): 5–28; idem, "*Carmina gratulatoria hebraica* és a héber nyelvoktatás a Nagyváradi Református Kollégiumban [Hebrew Congratulatory Poems and Hebrew Language Learning at the Reformed College in Nagyvárad, in Hungarian]," in *Ünnepi kötet Adorjáni Zoltán 65. születésnapja tiszteletére*, ed. Csaba Balogh and Vilmos József Kolumbán (Kolozsvár: Kolozsvári Protestáns Teológiai Intézet, forthcoming). I am grateful to Kornélia Koltai and József Zsengellér for kindly sharing with me the results of their work on this important research project. Unfortunately, it was not possible to fully integrate results from these and further publications that appeared after the submission of this article and to update it accordingly.

garian language within their academic work or otherwise established specific links between the Hungarian and the Hebrew languages. Therefore, the following discussion will be devoted to Hungarian-speaking Christian Hebraists, who were active in the context of primarily Hungarian-speaking communities in the 16th–17th centuries, which at that time lived especially in the regions of contemporary Hungary, as well as Eastern Slovakia, the Carpatho-Ukraine, and – most importantly for our subject – Transylvania.

Much more than in other European centres of Hebrew learning, it seems, Hungarian Christian Hebraism was dependent on influences from abroad: Many Hungarian students, especially students of theology, enrolled at universities outside the territories that were predominantly populated by Hungarian speakers.[3] Before the Protestant Reformation of the 16th century, the universities in Cracow, Prague, and Vienna were the primary destinations for these students. In the aftermath of the Reformation, however, the picture became more variegated, and a confessional difference emerged: While Roman Catholic students from Hungarian lands continued to populate the aforementioned universities, many Protestant students, and specifically those who wanted to study theology, matriculated at the University of Wittenberg,[4] which had been founded in 1502 and, with Luther and Melanchthon among its professors, soon became the most important university for Lutheran Protestantism. From the late-16th century onwards, however, when many Protestants in Hungary became followers of the Calvinistic confession,[5] the stream of students shifted to the Netherlands, mainly to the universities in Franeker and Utrecht.[6] As a result, the formation and devel-

---

3 For an overview, see Márta Fata, Gyula Kurucz, and Anton Schindling, eds., *Peregrinatio Hungarica: Studenten aus Ungarn an deutschen und österreichischen Hochschulen vom 16. bis zum 20. Jahrhundert*, Contubernium 64 (Stuttgart: Steiner, 2006).
4 See András Szabó, "Ungarische Studenten in Wittenberg 1555–1592," in *Iter Germanicum: Deutschland und die Reformierte Kirche in Ungarn im 16.–17. Jahrhundert*, ed. András Szabó (Budapest: Kálvin Kiadó, 1999): 154–68.
5 A short overview of confessionalization in Hungary can be found in Winfried Eberhard, "Voraussetzungen und strukturelle Grundlagen der Konfessionalisierung in Ostmitteleuropa," in *Konfessionalisierung in Ostmitteleuropa: Wirkungen des religiösen Wandels im 16. und 17. Jahrhundert in Staat, Gesellschaft und Kultur*, ed. Joachim Bahlcke and Arno Strohmeyer (Stuttgart: Steiner, 1999): 89–104, here: 90–91.
6 See Réka Bozzay, "The Influence of Dutch Universities on the Education of Seventeenth-Century Hungarian Intellectuals," in *A Divided Hungary in Europe: Exchanges, Networks and Representations, 1541–1699*, vol. 1: *Study Tours and Intellectual-Religious Relationships*, ed. Gábor Almási, Szymon Brzeziński, Ildikó Horn, Kees Teszelszky, and Áron Zarnóczki (Newcastle upon Tyne: Cambridge Scholars Publishing, 2014): 81–100; Gábor Kecskeméti, "The Effect of the Universities of the Low Countries on the Intellectual History of Hungary in the Early Modern Times," *Hungarian Studies* 26 (2012): 189–204.

opment of Hungarian Christian Hebraism was and remained dependent on academic traditions from foreign universities to a considerable extent, and it is therefore difficult from the outset to discern an "indigenous" Hungarian tradition of Christian Hebraism.[7]

Moreover, as there existed very few Protestant institutions of higher learning within the borders of Hungarian-speaking areas until the 19th century, while Hebrew, as an academic subject in Central Europe, was dominated by Protestant theologians, the study of Hebrew received much less attention in Hungarian lands than in other areas with a considerable Protestant population. This situation affected not only the study of the Hebrew language in the Hungarian academy, but also that of other Semitic languages until the 19th century, and it is therefore no coincidence that almost all the leading Hungarian orientalists of the 19th and early 20th century, who contributed to our knowledge of Hebrew and other Semitic languages, like Samuel Kohn (1841–1920), Ignaz Goldziher (1850–1921), Wilhelm Bacher (1850–1913), Immanuel Löw (1854–1944), or Ludwig Blau (1861–1936), were of Jewish origin and received their academic training mostly outside Hungary. The situation within Hungary only improved after the foundation of the Jewish Theological Seminary in Budapest (Hungarian: *Országos Rabbiképző-Intézet*, German: *Landesrabbinerschule*) in 1877.

But let us come back to Christian Hebraism: In spite of the lack of Hebrew learning in Hungarian universities, Hebrew was nevertheless taught and studied as a regular subject in quite a number of important institutions in the Hungarian lands beginning in the 16th century, especially in the reformed Protestant schools, which were established under the influence of Melanchthon's pedagogical vision.

The extent to which Hebrew was expected to be taught in the reformed schools of Hungarian Protestants is demonstrated by the 55th article of the Great Synod of the Reformed Church in Debrecen in eastern Hungary from 1567, where, circumstances permitting, Hebrew is listed as compulsory:[8]

---

[7] This is also demonstrated beyond doubt by the congratulatory poems that were penned by students from Hungarian speaking lands, as analysed by Kornélia Koltai and József Zsengellér (see above, footnote 2). The Hebrew language used in these poems exhibits no pecularities in comparison with congratulatory poems written by non-Hungarian students, but corresponds to the norm taught at the respective universities.

[8] Áron Kiss, *A XVI. században tartott magyar református zsinatok végzései* [The Decisions of the Hungarian Reformed Synode in the 16th Century, in Hungarian], A Magyarországi Protestansegylet kiadványai 19/Protestans theologiai könyvtár 16 (Budapest: Magyarországi Protestansegylet, 1881), 602.

Since the schools are the seedling nursery of God's word, it is from the schools that the Lord produces pastors and teachers, i.e. the educators of the church. Therefore, in Christian schools, languages, Latin and Greek grammar (and wherever possible also Hebrew), logic, rhetoric and further respected sciences, which are required for the understanding of theology, shall first of all be taught; thereafter theology and the Holy Scriptures in Greek and Latin shall be presented to the youth. ("Minthogy pedig az iskolák az isten igéjének veteményes kertjei, az iskolából is előállittatja az Ur a lelkipásztorokat, a tanitókat, az egyház oktatóit. Azért a keresztyének iskoláiban elsőben a nyelvek ismérete, latin s görög nyelvtan (a hol lehet zsidó is) észtan szónoklattan és más a theologia ismeretére megkivántató tisztességes tudományok tanittassanak, azután a hittudomány, a szent irás görög és latin nyelven adassanak elő az ifjuságnak.")

The cautious qualification added to the general ruling in favor of obligatory Hebrew lessons, "wherever possible," seems to reveal that this stipulation encountered difficulties – apparently qualified teachers were not always nor everywhere on hand, though the situation may have improved by the early 17th century, thanks to the large numbers of students who by then had already studied abroad in the learned centers of Lutheran Protestantism, mainly in Germany and specifically in Wittenberg,[9] and had returned with a good command of Hebrew. Moreover, there is clear evidence that at that time at least some of those who set out to study theology had already learned Hebrew before they entered the university.[10] The main fields in which Hungarian Christian Hebraists were active were 1) the teaching of Hebrew (primarily biblical, but to some degree also rabbinic) in schools as part of the humanistic and Protestant educational canon (though such instruction occurred on occasion even in Catholic schools),[11] and 2) the translation and learned exegesis of

---

[9] The University of Wittenberg, often referred to by its Greco-Latin name "Leucorea," in accordance with humanistic tradition, was the first (in 1518) in the German lands to establish a chair for the Hebrew language in 1518. On this, see Gianfranco Miletto and Giuseppe Veltri, "Hebrew Studies in Wittenberg (1502–1813): From Lingua Sacra to Semitic Studies," *European Journal of Jewish Studies* 6 (2012): 1–22, here: 9.
[10] For an overview of the study of Hebrew in Hungary in the early modern era, see Róbert Dán, *Humanizmus, reformáció, antitrinitarizmus és a héber nyelv Magyarországon* [Humanism, Reformation, Antitrinitarianism, and the Hebrew Language in Hungary], Humanizmus és reformáció 2 (Budapest: Akadémiai Kiadó, 1973), 25–36. In addition, several studies in Schorch and Thon, eds., *Christian Hebraism* (forthcoming) deal with local histories of Hebrew studies in certain universities or colleges, namely: Dénes Dienes, Mirjám Enghy, and Sándor Enghy, "Die hebräische Sprache im Reformierten Kollegium von Sárospatak im 16. und 17. Jahrhundert"; Zoltán Kustár, "Die Anfänge der Hebraistik in Debrecen und ihre Verbindung mit Wittenberg: Das Leben und Wirken von Péter Melius Juhász (1536–1572)"; János Molnár, "Unterricht in der hebräischen Sprache in Siebenbürgen im 17. Jahrhundert: Das Collegium Academicum und János Apáczai Csere."
[11] See Samuel Kohn, *Die Sabbatharier in Siebenbürgen: Ihre Geschichte, Literatur und Dogmatik. Mit besonderer Berücksichtigung des Lebens und der Schriften des Reichskanzlers Simon Péchi.*

the Hebrew Bible. As such, Hungarian Christian Hebraism does not appear to have differed much from Hebrew studies in other Protestant centers in Europe. Nevertheless, there are still some peculiar features of Hungarian Christian Hebraism, which are less prominent or even entirely absent in other regions. I refer here to the special role of Hebrew among the Sabbatarians in Transylvania, and to the importance of the Hebrew language with regard to the study of the Hungarian language. While the first phenomenon is connected to the important role antitrinitarian movements played in Eastern Central Europe, and specifically among Hungarian speakers in Transylvania, the second has to do with the pecularities of the Hungarian language itself, including its linguistic isolation.

1 The Use of Hebrew Among the Sabbatarians in Transylvania

Throughout the 16th and 17th centuries, Transylvania underwent an important change. A territory that had already been profoundly multiethnic (consisting mainly of Saxons, Hungarians, Szeklers,[12] and Romanians) as well as multilingual (German, Hungarian and Romanian were predominant) now also became increasingly multiconfessional. For the peculiar balance of political power that abided at the time thanks to the Ottoman control over large parts of Eastern Central Europe resulted in a broad acceptance of multiple Christian traditions there.

Indeed, in 1557/1558, the Diet of Torda decreed that "everyone shall practice the faith he desires, with new or with old ceremonies,"[13] though full acceptance was granted only to Calvinists, Lutherans, Roman Catholics, and Unitarians. Orthodox Christianity (to which most of the Romanian-speaking population belonged), Jews and Muslims were merely tolerated, but lacked legal guarantees. Thus the differ-

---

Ein Beitrag zur Religions- und Culturgeschichte der jüngsten drei Jahrhunderte (Budapest: Singer & Wolfner/Leipzig: Franz Wagner, 1894), 15. The German version is in fact a considerably shortened version of the original Hungarian monograph: Sámuel Kohn, *A szombatosok: Történetük, dogmatikájuk és irodalmuk. Különös tekintettel Péchi Simon főkanczellár életére és munkáira* (Budapest: Athenaeum, 1889). This article will refer primarily to the German translation, although the much more detailed Hungarian original will be quoted when necessary.

12 The Szeklers (Hungarian: *székely*) are a Hungarian-speaking ethnic group residing primarily in Transylvania.

13 István Keul, *Early Modern Religious Communities in East-Central Europe: Ethnic Diversity, Denominational Plurality, and Corporative Politics in the Principality of Transylvania, 1526–1691*, Studies in Medieval and Reformation Traditions 143 (Leiden and Boston: Brill, 2009), 243–44.

ent confessions and religions co-existed in Transylvania, but certainly not under equal rights.[14] As a result of this unique political and religious situation, which has been described as "contextual confessionalization,"[15] Transylvania gained a special place in the history of the Reformation.[16] One particular feature of early modern Transylvania was the enormous influence of Unitarianism, a strictly antitrinitarian branch of theology in the reformed tradition, which started to flourish there in the 1560s and soon attracted one of the largest groups of followers within this region.[17]

Transylvanian Sabbatarianism emerged as an offshoot of these prominent antitrinitarian traditions of Unitarianism at the end of the 16th century. Although its formative period occured in a multiethnic and multilingual context, and notwithstanding the fact that its first inspirer, Matthias Vehe-Glirius (1545–1590),[18] was a German who arrived in Transylvania as a refugee from religious persecution in the Electoral Palatinate of the Rhine, Transylvanian Sabbatarianism neverthe-

---

14 "Die Religionsgesetzgebung des Fürstentums Siebenbürgen im 16. und 17. Jh. war also [. . .] weit entfernt [. . .] davon, Ausdruck moderner Gleichberechtigung zu sein [. . .] Betrachtet man Toleranz als Voraussetzung von Religionsfreiheit, kann hier keineswegs von allgemeiner, sondern nur von relativer, abgestufter, ja selektiver Toleranz gesprochen werden. Diese Toleranz entsprang dabei nicht einer weltanschaulichen Überzeugung, sondern war das Ergebnis einer spezifischen [. . .] Machtstruktur, die den Ständen die Macht einräumte, ihre und ihrer Untertanen *religio* zu bestimmen." Walter Daugsch, "Toleranz im Fürstentum Siebenbürgen: Politische und gesellschaftliche Voraussetzungen der Religionsgesetzgebung im 16. Jahrhundert," *Kirche im Osten* 26 (1983): 35–72, here: 70. The Sabbatarian community (see below) was one of the Christian groups which suffered the most due to the imperfect degree of toleration, as was specially attested on the official level by a number of anti-Sabbatarian decrees, see Keul, *Early Modern Religious Communities*, 174–77.
15 Keul, *Early Modern Religious Communities*, 252–70.
16 See Volker Leppin, "Siebenbürgen: Ein kirchenhistorischer Sonderfall von allgemeiner Bedeutung," in *Konfessionsbildung und Konfessionskultur in Siebenbürgen in der Frühen Neuzeit*, ed. Volker Leppin and Ulrich A. Wien (Stuttgart: Franz Steiner Verlag, 2005): 7–13.
17 See Earl Morse Wilbur, *A History of Unitarianism: In Transylvania, England and America* (Cambridge, MA: Harvard University Press, 1952). Mihály Balázs has argued that a Unitarian "confessionalization," in the strict sense of the word, did not take place in 16th-century Transylvania, since no clear clerical hierarchy developed and no confessional documents gained universal acceptance. Mihály Balázs, "Gab es eine unitarische Konfessionalisierung im Siebenbürgen des 16. Jahrhunderts?" in *Konfessionsbildung und Konfessionskultur*, 135–52. Nevertheless, there is no doubt as to the enormous influence and success of Unitarian theology and thinking in Transylvania.
18 See Róbert Dán, *Matthias Vehe-Glirius: Life and Work of a Radical Antitrinitarian with His Collected Writings*, Studia Humanitatis 4 (Budapest: Akadémiai Kiadó/Leiden: Brill, 1982); Keul, *Early Modern Religious Communities*, 132.

less remained throughout its history an almost exclusively Hungarian-speaking movement,[19] and primarily restricted to the Szekler population.[20] The two first formative figures of this movement were the Szekler noblemen András Eössi (died ca. 1600)[21] and his successor Simon Péchi (1565/70–1643/44).[22] Eössi, a former Unitarian and as such convinced that Christ was man, not God, separated from the Unitarians in 1588 by claiming that Christ had not abolished the Torah but intended to introduce his non-Jewish followers to it, as expressed in one of the oldest Sabbatarian songs:[23]

[Jézus] zsidó volt nemzetben, mind vallás rendiben.	Jesus was Jewish by nation, And in all respects of his religion.
Ö a zsidó törvényt predikálotta, Mózesre és prófétákra Embert igazitta.	He preached the Jewish law, And towards Moses and the prophets He directed men.
Apostoli is mind zsidók voltanak Zsidó hitet tanitottak, Magok is tartottak.	His apostles too were all Jews, They taught the Jewish belief, Which they themselves kept.

As a consequence, the followers of Sabbatarianism observed the Jewish Sabbath, festivals and dietary laws. Circumcision did not become widespread among them, but was practiced by some.[24] Until the 19th century, the Sabbatarians remained an independent group and followed the perception that they were foreigners to the Jewish people and latecomers to the Jewish tradition:[25]

---

19 "Das Sabbathariertum in Siebenbürgen hatte von Anfang an ein rein magyarisches, richtiger: székler Gepräge, welches es auch bis zuletzt beibehalten hat." Kohn, *Die Sabbatharier*, 1.
20 For a short analysis of the special attraction the Szeklers seem to have felt towards Sabbatianism, see Keul, *Early Modern Religious Communities*, 129–31.
21 See Kohn, *Die Sabbatharier*, 39–45. Kohn's account of Eössi's life and oeuvre is still useful, although he seems to have overstated the latter's role in the foundation of Sabbatianism, see Keul, *Early Modern Religious Communities*, 131–32.
22 Kohn's book on the Sabbatarians was pioneering with regard to research on Péchi's life and especially his oeuvre. On this, see Kohn, *Die Sabbatharier*, 129–231 and 156–291. An updated account of Péchi and his influence can be found in Róbert Dán, *Az erdélyi szombatosok és Péchi Simon* [The Transylvanian Sabbatarians and Simon Péchi, in Hungarian], Humanizmus és reformáció 13 (Budapest: Akadémiai Kiadó, 1987), while the most recent overview is provided by Kornélia Koltai, "Simon Péchi, the Head of the Transylvanian Sabbatarian Movement (17th century)," in Schorch and Thon, eds., *Christian Hebraism* (forthcoming).
23 Kohn, *A szombatosok*, 63–64.
24 Kohn, *Die Sabbatharier*, 186 and 266.
25 See Kohn, *Die Sabbatharier*, 183–84. The original of this song is found in Kohn, *A szombatosok*, 89.

Mi – nem Ábrahám volt nekünk atyánk,	We – Abraham was not our father,
Sem maradéki vagyunk ő magvának,	And we are not from his seed,
De nemzetségi Jáfet házának	But from Japhet's house
Vagyunk, fiai tudatlan pogánynak.	We are, an ignorant heathen's children.

Nevertheless, the Sabbatarians prided themselves on joining biblical Israel by following Jewish law:[26]

Törvényed tartását azért választottuk,	We chose to keep your Law because
Izrael táborát kedveltük, javaltuk,	The camp of Israel we loved,
Magunk ahhoz adtuk,	And we devoted ourselves to it,
Nyomorult sorsával semmit nem gondoltunk.	Not caring for its distressful fate.

In early Sabbatianism Jesus was still regarded as a messianic figure, though salvation was understood to come through the observance of Jewish law alone:[27]

Az ki üdvözölni akar és élni,	Whoever wants to gain salvation and life,
Annak zsidó hitet kell tartani, nem egyebet.	Must follow the Jewish faith, no other.
Mostani zsidóktól külömbözni kell	From Jews today there is difference
Ez czikkelyben,	In this one point:
hogy az Jézust Krisztusnak ismerjük,	we accept Jesus as Christ.
De az üdvösségnek az ő utában	But on the way for salvation
Ez egy czikkely kivül, mondom,	Except from this one point, I tell,
most is egyesség kell.	even now unity is required.
Jó pogánynak úgy kell mint jó zsidónak	A good heathen must believe, live,
Hinni, élni és érteni üdvössége felöl.	And think about his salvation just like a good Jew.

If the christological element found in this text is characteristic of the early period of Transylvanian Sabbatianism, under the influence of Eössi and during the initial years of Péchi's leadership, it mostly disappeared after 1624 (i.e. in Péchi's later years as head of the Sabbatarians). In addition, Péchi greatly diminished the dogmatic importance of the New Testament and brought Sabbatianism much closer to Judaism, in terms of belief, religious practice and liturgy.[28] Nevertheless, the Sabbatarians remained an independent community, and it was only in 1868, after a long period of religious oppression which had led to a significant decline, and against the backdrop of the formal act of emancipation which was granted to the Jews by the Diet of Hungary in December 1867, that most members of the sole remaining community of Sabbatarians in Bözödujfalú (Romanian: Bezidu Nou), a village in Transylvania near Marosvásárhely (Romanian: Târgu

---

26 Kohn, *A szombatosok*, 88.
27 Kohn, *A szombatosok*, 88.
28 See Kohn, *Die Sabbatharier*, 188–97.

Mureș; German: Neumarkt am Mieresch), converted to Judaism.[29] Interestingly, the newly created Jewish congregation continued to insist on its proselyte identity, as attested e.g. by the official seal of the congregation, which in the Hebrew version reads קהל גרים עדת ישורון דק"ק ב' אויפאלא תרל"ד – "Congregation of proselytes Adat Yeshurun, of the holy congregation B. Ujfalú, year 5634 [= 1873/74]."[30] In the Shoah, almost all the Jewish inhabitants of Bözödujfalú were killed in the Auschwitz concentration camp.

Given their close attachment to the Hebrew Bible and Jewish traditions, it is no surprise that some of the formative figures of Sabbatarianism were eminent Hebraists. Miklós Bogáti Fazekas and Simon Péchi merit special mention in this regard; by contrast, András Eössi apparently did not know Hebrew.[31] Bogáti Fazekas (1548–d. between 1592 and 1598), a Unitarian minister, seems to have been one of the earliest followers and authors of the Sabbatarian movement in Transylvania. His most outstanding work as a Hebraist is the translation and poetic adaption of the book of Psalms into Hungarian *Magyar Zsoltár* (= "Hungarian Psalter"), in fact the very first full Hungarian translation of this biblical text.[32] Bogáti's intimate familiarity with Hebrew literature is revealed throughout this composition by his use of Jewish Midrashim and commentaries on the Psalms as well as by his specifications as to when certain psalms are to be recited. With regard to Bogáti's reliance upon Jewish Bible commentaries, the last stanza of his poetic adaption of Psalm 72 is particularly instructive:[33]

Csak halála előtt Dávid ezt megírá,	David wrote this psalm shortly before his death,
Fiát, Salamont hogy koronáztatá,	When he was going to crown Solomon, his son,
Jó szerencséjét jövendőben mondá,	Predicting his future fortune,
Hetvenkettedik énekben meghagyá.	In the seventy-second psalm he stated this.

Within the original text, no information is found which could be useful for a historical contextualization of the psalm, with the possible exception of the superscription לשלמה ("Of Solomon"), and the concluding subscript כלו תפלות דוד בן ישי ("End of the prayers of David son of Jesse"), the latter of which refers however to the whole preceeding collection of psalms. One might therefore ask for the source

---

29 See Kohn, *Die Sabbatharier*, 269–87. Nevertheless, not all of the remaining Sabbatarians became converts, and towards the end of the 19th century there were still five Sabbatarian families in Bözödujfalú. On this, see Kohn, *Die Sabbatharier*, 296.
30 Kohn, *A szombatosok*, 369.
31 Kohn, *Die Sabbatharier*, 43.
32 Kohn, *A szombatosok*, 140.
33 The Hungarian text follows Miklós Bogáti Fazekas, *Magyar zsoltár 151 verses parafrázisban* [Hungarian Psalter in a Paraphrase of 151 Verses, in Hungarian], ed. Gábor Gilicze (Budapest: Országos Széchényi Könyvtár, 2009), 143.

of Bogáti's indication that David wrote Psalm 72 on the occasion of his son Solomon's coronation. The most likely candidate is the explanation of the first word of the psalm in question as found in one of the classical and best-known Jewish commentaries to the book of Psalms, that of David Kimḥi, traditionally known as RaDaQ (1160–1235):[34]

זה המזמור חברו דוד על שלמה בנו, כשהמליכו, לפיכך אמר בסוף המזמור כלו תפלות בן ישי

> David wrote this psalm for Solomon his son, when he made him king, and accordingly he said at the end of the psalm: *End of the prayers of David son of Jesse* [Ps 72:20].

Bogáti clearly knew David Kimḥi's commentary, drawing on it time and again throughout his entire Hungarian psalter.[35] The fact that Kimḥi's Psalms commentary seems to have been a favourite of Bogáti is highly relevant for understanding the formation of Sabbatarian views, since this text is well known for its frequent polemical responses to the christological reading of psalms prominent in the Christian tradition.[36] Indeed, not a few of Kimḥi's anti-Christian statements found their way into Bogáti's psalter. However, Bogáti's use of Jewish psalm-commentary was by no means restricted to Kimḥi, but equally comprised Rashi, Ibn Ezra, and Midrash Tehilllim (*Šoḥer ṭov*).[37]

A telling example of Bogáti's specifications as to when a given psalm should be recited concerns Psalm 118, which in Bogáti's poetic adaption reads as follows:[38]

A húsvéti bárányt mikor zsidók ették, étel közben ezt mondták.	When the Jews ate the Easter lamb, they said this in the midst of the meal.
[...]	[...]
Marok zöld ágakkal sátoros ünnepen most is zsidó ezt mondja.	At the Feast of Booths, with green branches in their hands, Jews say this now too.

As is typically the case with Bogáti's specifications, these comments follow the Jewish tradition, according to which this Psalm is recited on both Pesach and Sukkot.[39]

The most important and probably most knowlegdable Hebrew scholar amongst the Transylvanian Sabbatarians seems, however, not to have been Bogáti, but rather

---

34 דוד בן יוסף קמחי, הפירוש השלם על תהילים (ירושלים: מוסד הרב קוק, תשל"א).
35 Kohn, *A szombatosok*, 144–46.
36 See Frank Talmage, "R. David Kimḥi as Polemicist," *Hebrew Union College Annual* 38 (1967): 213–35.
37 See Kohn, *A szombatosok*, 144–46.
38 Bogáti Fazekas, *Magyar zsoltár 151 verses parafrázisban*, 243.
39 Kohn, *A szombatosok*, 152.

Eössi's successor Simon Péchi. Péchi, who for some time served as the official state chancellor of the Hungarian Székely community in Transylvania, learnt Hebrew from Jewish teachers, mainly in Istanbul, the capital of the Ottoman Empire, of which the Principality of Transylvania was a vassal state during most of the 16th and 17th centuries. Subsequently, he became a prolific translator from Hebrew into Hungarian, creating a whole body of Sabbatarian literature in the Hungarian language.

Péchi translated the Hebrew Bible, wrote a Bible commentary[40] and translated *Pirqe Avot* on two separate occasions, first alongside Joseph ben Hayyim Jabez's commentary on *Pirqe Avot*, and afterwards together with Josef b. Abraham Hayyun's מילי דאבות.[41] Most prominently, however, he translated the *Siddur* and the *Mahzor*, adapting them to the Sabbatarian context. As Kornélia Koltai has pointed out, Péchi's translation of the Jewish prayer collections is the first comprehensive translation of the *Siddur* and *Mahzor* in any language.[42] Samuel Kohn, a graduate of the Jewish Theological Seminar in Breslau, chief rabbi of Budapest and himself an eminent scholar of the Hebrew language, is full of praise for Péchi's knowledge of the Hebrew language, and concludes that the latter's achievements in the field of Hebrew studies "earn him the foremost place among the Hebraists of his time, and reserve for him a distinguished position among the Hebraists of all times. Particularly among non-Jews there was probably no one until now who knew the post-Biblical Hebrew language so thoroughly [. . .]."[43]

In contrast to other contexts of Hungarian Christian Hebraism, the Transylvanian Sabbatarians have received rather substantial scholarly attention, beginning already in the 19th century. Landmarks are the aforementioned important monograph by Samuel Kohn, one of the outstanding personalities of the *Wissenschaft des Judentums* in Budapest, *The Sabbatarians: Their History, Their Dogmatics, and Their Literature, With Special Reference to the Chancellor Simon Péchi's Life and Work* (1889, in Hungarian; and 1894, in German translation); Mihály Guttmann's 1914 edition of the Sabbatarian prayerbook, undertaken on the initiative of the

---

40 See Kornélia Koltai, *Péchi Simon kiadatlan Biblia-fordítása (1634)* [Simon Péchi's Unedited Bible Translation (1634)], Hungaria Judaica 23 (Budapest: MTA Judaisztikai Kutatócsoport, 2011); Kornélia Koltai, "Péchi Simon Biblia-kommentárja" [Simon Péchi's Bible Commentary, in Hungarian], in *Vízió és valóság: A Pázmány Péter Katolikus Egyetemen 2010. október 28–29-én „A dialógus sodrában . . . " címmel tartott zsidó–keresztény konferencia előadásai*, ed. Károly Dániel Dobos and György Fodor (Budapest: Új Ember – Márton Áron Kiadó, 2011): 199–218.

41 The translation was edited and analysed in an important book by Kornélia Koltai, *Péchi Simon: Az Atyák mondásai* [Simon Péchi: Sayings of the Fathers, in Hungarian], Hungaria Judaica 11 (Budapest: MTA Judaisztikai Kutatócsoport, 1999).

42 Koltai, "Simon Péchi," 4.

43 Kohn, *Die Sabbatharier*, 229.

Neolog Jewish community in Budapest,[44] and an important monograph by Róbert Dán, *The Transylvanian Sabbatarians and Simon Péchi* (1987, in Hungarian). In the last decade, Kornélia Koltai published several editions of Péchi's works together with detailed analysis.[45]

Despite this impressive research, a number of important questions concerning the Hebraism of the Transylvanian Sabbatarians remain open, two of which I would like to point out here:

1) Transylvanian Sabbatarianism is closely linked with the religious and intellectual history of Central Europe in the 16th and 17th centuries. While this aspect is generally acknowledged in scholarship, the particular connections that abided between the Hebrew scholarship among the Transylvanian Sabbatarians and Christian Hebraism in other regions and milieus, especially in the core lands of the Lutheran reformation, remain largely unknown.

2) The overwhelming majority of Christian Hebraism in Europe developed within a Christian cultural and political environment. By contrast, Transylvanian Sabbatarianism uniquely emerged and developed at least partly under Muslim suzerainty, in the historical and geographical context of the Ottoman Empire. This fact points to generally more intellectual freedom and liberty on a local level in Transylvania than in other regions of contemporary Europe. To a large extent, Transylvanian Christian Hebraism resulted from the encounter between two religious minorities – Sephardic Jews and Protestant Christians – who could both follow their traditions largely in freedom. It was thanks to this very particular environment that Péchi was able to be in contact with Jews and to familiarize himself with Jewish daily life, with Jewish traditions of the Hebrew language and with Hebrew literature, without external disturbances and pressure from the political and clerical elite, and that his Jewish informants were able willingly to share their knowledge with a Christian without fear of denunication and abuse. Thus, Sabbatarian Hebraism emerged in a context in which there was far greater access to the liturgical and practical dimensions of Jewish culture – aside from its intellectual dimensions – than was generally the case in other manifestions of Christian Hebraism.

---

44 Mihály Guttmann and Sándor Harmos, eds., *Péchi Simon szombatos imádságos könyve* [Simon Péchi's Sabbatarian Prayerbook], Az Izraelita Magyar Irodalmi Társulat kiadványai 39 (Budapest: Izraelita Magyar Irodalmi Társulat, 1914).
45 See above.

2 The Role of Hebrew in Research Concerning the Hungarian Language

A second important and quite peculiar feature of Hungarian Christian Hebraism is the extensive use of Hebrew as a frame of reference in early research concerning the Hungarian language. Hebrew had been established as an integral part of the higher education system in many regions of Europe in the 16th century, was regarded as one of the "cardinal languages," most usually besides Latin and Greek, although this trio was sometimes expanded by further languages. Hebrew was often even regarded as the first and "mother of all languages," and therefore of special importance for the understanding of language in general, as well as of the commonalities and differences between individual languages.[46] Numerous lists and whole books were published which collected alleged cognate words between Hebrew and other languages, the most prominent and most influential among the earlier of these accounts probably being Georg Cruciger's *Harmonia linguarum quatuor cardinalium, hebraicae, graecae, latinae & germanicae* (Frankfurt: Tampachius, 1616). In this book, Cruciger attempts to delineate the relations between Hebrew, Greek, Latin and German words with the help of tree diagrams, each of which is devoted to one Hebrew primary root, provided in Hebrew letters. Cruciger's book comprises no less than 2100 such entries, which are numbered sequentially. Figure 1 below shows entry no. 1743, devoted to the root רחק and its derivatives:[47]

As can be seen in this image, Cruciger connects the Hebrew basic root רחק with direct derivatives in Hebrew (רָחוֹק), Greek (ῥύω), and German (*recken*), and additionally with a number of further derivatives in Greek, Latin and German, the emergence of which involves minor changes of the basic root (Greek ὀρέγω, Latin *arceo*, German *Erker*). Most obviously, the rationale for the construction of these connections was the coincidence of both phonetic and semantic similarities between the root and its supposed cognates.

Cruciger's book demonstrates that the use of Hebrew as a point of departure for the description and understanding of other languages was instrumental not only at the level of vocabulary and (speculative) etymology, but much beyond that as well, deeply affecting views of language structure and the methods of

---

46 See Wolf P. Klein, "Die ursprüngliche Einheit der Sprachen in der philologisch-grammatischen Sicht der frühen Neuzeit," in *The Language of Adam/Die Sprache Adams*, ed. Allison P. Coudert (Wiesbaden: Harrassowitz, 1999): 25–56, here: 26–32.

47 The image is taken from the digitized copy of Cruciger's book, kept in the Sächsische Landesbibliothek – Staats- und Universitätsbibliothek Dresden and accessible in the public domain under http://digital.slub-dresden.de/werkansicht/dlf/76251/5/0/ (accessed: 29/02/2016).

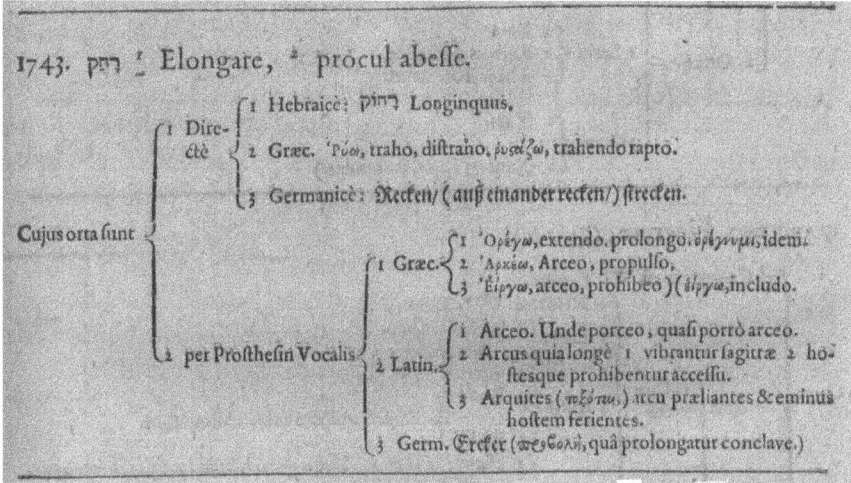

Figure 1: The entry for the root רחק from G. Cruciger, *Harmonia linguarum quatuor cardinalium* (1616).

their description and presentation. In this regard, the concept that the formation of words proceeds from a tri-literal root, became especially influential.[48]

While the comparison with Hebrew thus became rather common in the linguistic research of the early modern period, the comparison between Hungarian and Hebrew nevertheless involved a number of unique features. One concerns research into parallels between Hebrew and Hungarian grammar, while another is the construction of an exclusive relationship between these two languages, proceeding from the isolated situation of Hungarian in its cultural and linguistic environment.

The earliest attempt systematically to compare Hungarian and Hebrew seems to have been made by Ioannes (= Hungarian: János) Sylvester in his *Grammatica Hungarolatina*, published in 1539. This book is frequently regarded as the first grammar of the Hungarian language, at least among those which have been preserved,[49] although it must be admitted that Sylvester's book is not a full-fledged

---

[48] See Wolf P. Klein, "Was wurde aus den Wörtern der hebräischen Ursprache? Zur Entstehung der komparativen Linguistik aus dem Geist der etymologischen Spekulation," in *Gottes Sprache in der philologischen Werkstatt: Hebraistik vom 15. bis zum 19. Jahrhundert*, ed. Giuseppe Veltri and Gerold Necker (Leiden and Boston: Brill, 2004): 3–23, here: 14–22.

[49] There is the possibility that the first grammar of Hungarian was already written in the 15th century by the Hungarian humanist Janus Pannonius, but this work, if it ever existed, is not preserved. See István Bartók, ed., *Ioannes Sylvester: Grammatica Hungarolatina. Edidit, introduxit et commentariis instruxit Stephanus Bartók*, Bibliotheca Scriptorum Medii Recentisque Aevorum,

grammar in the modern sense, but rather a schoolbook aiming to teach grammar in general to Hungarian-speaking pupils through the use of Hungarian examples, *inter alia*. What makes this grammar relevant for research into Christian Hebraism, however, is the fact that Sylvester quite often cites Hebrew parallels to grammatical phenomena in the Hungarian language, in an attempt to explain the latter. Therefore, while the linguistic comparisons drawn between Hebrew and contemporary spoken languages were typically lexicographic in nature (as shown in the example from Cruciger's book above), Sylvester extended the comparative approach to grammar, and seems to have been pioneering in this regard. Moreover, with the help of this comparison, Sylvester seems to have been the first scholar successfully to discern some of the linguistic characteristics that distinguish Hungarian from most other languages in Europe.

One of these peculiarities is the use of possessive markers. Like in Ancient Hebrew, there is no independent possessive pronoun in the Hungarian language, and the notion of possession is expressed instead through suffixes attached to the noun. Thus, according to one of the examples provided by Sylvester, the Latin expression *pater tuus* would be rendered in Hungarian *at'ād* (in contemporary Hungarian: *atyád*), i.e. *atya* "father" with the suffix -*ad* "your." In his chapter on pronouns, Sylvester sets out to explain the Latin system of possessive pronouns, providing a table with the paradigm *Pater meus – Mater mea – Filius meus; Pater tuus – Mater tua*, etc., in which each expression is provided a translation into Hungarian. Thereafter he continues as follows:[50]

> From these [examples] it is easy to discern that the Latin language is completely without suffix pronouns, while our and the Hebrew language do have them, and it is therefore quite clear that Hebrew and ours are close [...] In the Greek and Latin language, the indication of person is separate, while in Hebrew and Hungarian it is attached. ("Ex his iam facile est cernere Latinam linguam affixis pronominibus prorsus carere, nostram vero illa perinde ac Hebraeam habere, quod ut sit manifestius, Hebraeam cum nostris coniungam. [...] In Graeco et Latino sermone personae subintelliguntur, in Hebraeo et Hungarico dictionibus includuntur.")[51]

Series Nova XV (Budapest: Akademia Kiadó/Argumentum Kiadó, 2006), 7. Moreover, there is also some indication that the Transylvanian nobleman Adrianus Wolphardus wrote a Hungarian grammar in 1512, but this claim cannot not be substantiated either. On this, see József Hegedűs, "Johannes Sylvester's Grammatical Legacy (1539) and its European Background," *Acta Linguistica Hungarica* 55 (2008): 41–57, here: 42.

50 Ioannes Sylvester, *Grammatica Hungarolatina in usum puerorum* (Neanesus [= Ujsziget-Sarvar], 1539), f. 26v.

51 Sylvester, *Grammatica*, f. 26v.

In order to illustrate this conclusion, Sylvester provides a table that juxtaposes the Hebrew paradigm אָבִי אָבִיךָ אָבִיו etc. with its equivalent in the contemporary Hungarian vernacular: *at'ām – at'ād – att'a* etc. (see Figure 2).[52] Thus, while grammars of Hebrew published by leading contemporary Christian Hebraists such as Sebastian Münster[53] aimed above all at teaching the Hebrew language *per se*, Sylvester turns Hebrew examples into a heuristic means to present language structure and grammar in general, a role which was usually played by Latin in the linguistics research and pedagogy of the time.

Sylvester goes even one step further in postulating that the usefulness of Hebrew for understanding the grammar of Hungarian is not mere coincidence, but rather demonstrates the close relationship between the two languages. This conclusion is most clearly conveyed in a paragraph devoted to the indication of the object as part of a verbal form. In certain cases Hungarian verbs can express not only the subject, but also the object of a given act, e.g. *szeretek* – "I love," *szeretem* – "I love it," *szeretlek* – "I love you." Sylvester seeks to elucidate this feature by quoting forms of the Hebrew verb פקד "to take care of," together with their Latin translation and Hungarian counterparts[54] (see Figure 3).

And he interprets the evidence presented in this table as follows:

> This feature demonstrates most clearly that there is a close affinity of our language with the holy language, which is Hebrew. Moreover, in order that this might be perfectly clear, we will conjugate our language together with Hebrew. ("Quae res manifestissime ostendit magnam nostrae linguae cum sacra illa, nimirum Hebraea esse affinitatem ut autem id cunctis sit manifestum nostram linguam cum Hebraea quoque coniungemus.")[55]

Thus, Sylvester describes the linguistic features shared by Hebrew and Hungarian as evidence for a special affinity of Hungarian with the holy language, ascribing to his and his pupil's mother tongue a special status, in comparison with Latin, or, for that matter, with other languages spoken in that region, especially German and possibly Slovakian.

The two grammatical features noted above – the use of nominal suffixes and the possibility of distinguishing with the help of verbal suffixes between different objects – are not the only cases in which Sylvester refers to Hebrew. On the contrary, quite a number of further references to Hebrew can be found throughout

---

52 The image is taken from the only known surviving copy of the book, found in the National Széchényi Library of Hungary in Budapest and made publically available at http://mek.oszk.hu/03400/03466/03466.pdf (accessed: 26/03/2016).
53 Sebastian Münster, מלאכת הדקדוק – *Institutiones grammaticae in Hebraeam linguam* (Basel: Johann Froben, 1524).
54 Sylvester, *Grammatica*, f. 31r.
55 Sylvester, *Grammatica*, f. 31r.

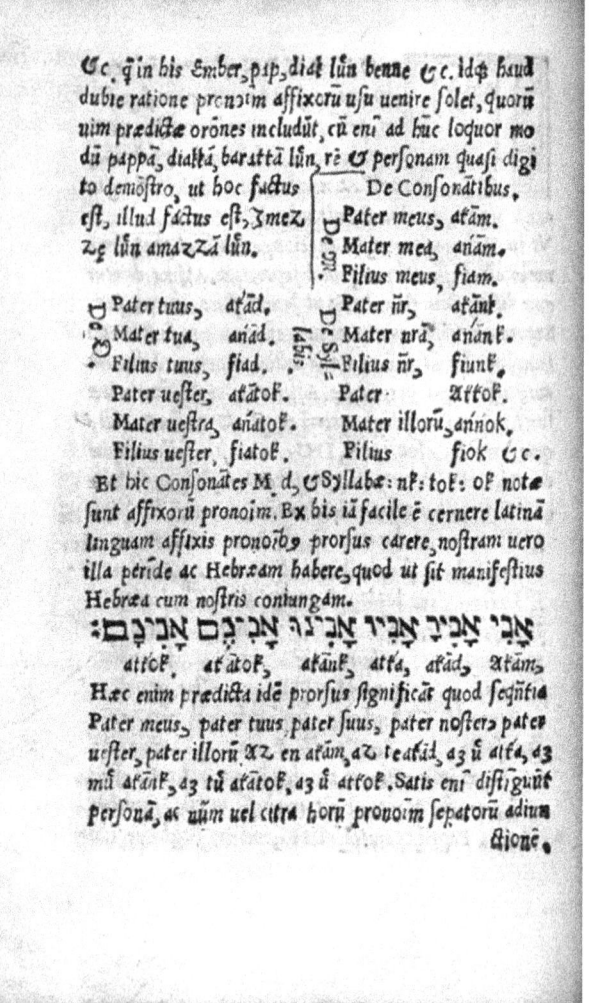

Figure 2: J. Sylvester, *Grammatica Hungarolatina* (1539), f. 26v.

his grammar. For instance, in the chapter "De orthographia hungarici sermonis" ("On the spelling of the Hungarian language"), which to a large extent deals with what we would generally today call "phonology," he remarks that the Hungarian language has three different "S"-consonants, like Hebrew, but unlike Latin.[56] In

---

[56] "While the Latin language has only one S, ours has three, which is in accordance with the Hebrew language." ("Cum latinus Sermo unum tantum S habeat, noster tria, idque iuxta Hebraeae linguae proprietatem.") See Sylvester, *Grammatica*, f. 8r.

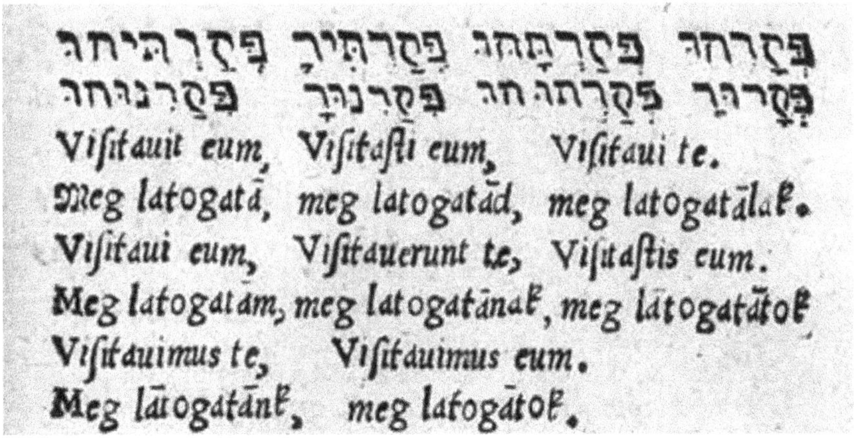

פְּקָרְחו פְּסָרְתָּחוּ פְּסָרְתָּחוּ פְּסָרְתִּיךָ פְּקָרְתִּיחֲ
פְּסָרְנוּחוּ פְּסָרְנוּךְ פְּסָרְתָּחֶם פְּסָרוּךְ
Viſitauit eum, Viſitaſti eum, Viſitaui te.
meg latogatá, meg latogatád, meg latogatálaẟ.
Viſitaui eum, Viſitauerunt te, Viſitaſtis eum.
Meg latogatam, meg latogatánaẟ, meg latogatátoẟ
Viſitauimus te, Viſitauimus eum.
Meg latogatánẟ, meg latogatoẟ.

Figure 3: J. Sylvester, *Grammatica Hungarolatina* (1539), f. 31r.

addition, in the chapter entitled "De articulo Hungarici sermonis" ("On the Pronunciation of the Hungarian Speech") we find the observation that the contrast in Biblical Hebrew between *Ketib* and *Qere* should be seen as but one instance of a phenomenon attested in many languages, according to which a distinction is drawn between the written form of a word and its pronunciation.[57] However, the two features considered in greater detail merit a special place in the present discussion, since they create the impression that the Hungarian and the Hebrew languages share linguistic features otherwise unknown in European languages, thereby setting the Hungarian language apart from the latter.

Sylvester[58] was born around 1504 in Szatmár County, today situated in northwestern Romania. In 1526, he enrolled at the University of Cracow and imbibed there the intellectual atmosphere of Erasmian Humanism; among his teachers there was the famous English humanist Leonard Cox (c. 1495–c. 1549). From 1527, Sylvester, as part of the humanist circle in Cracow, contributed to several editions of grammatical manuals and a school book for use in the classroom, the quite successful *Puerilium colloquiorum formulae*, which collected colloquial phrases

---

57 "Postremo, quod in omni fere lingua est quaedam in pronunciando varietas, ratio tamen Orthographiae apud omnes certa est. Hebraei scribunt יהוה et ייי proferunt autem non quod verba ipsa sonant, sed aliud quiddam." ("Finally, there is a certain variety in pronunciation in almost every language, while spelling in all languages is fixed. The Hebrews write יהוה and ייי, but do not utter what the words themselves would sound like, but something else.") Sylvester, *Grammatica*, f. 22r.
58 The following sketch of Sylvester's life and oeuvre generally follows Bartók's introduction to his edition of Ioannes Sylvester, *Grammatica Hungarolatina in usum puerorum* (Budapest: Akadémiai Kidó/Argumentum Kiadó, 2006), 7–14.

in Latin and several vernacular languages, especially Czech, Polish, and Hungarian; Sylvester was responsible for the latter. In 1529, he went from Cracow to the university in Wittenberg, where he became a student of Melanchthon (1497–1560) and the famous Hebraist Matthaeus Aurogallus (1490–1543). Thus, it seems that Sylvester acquired his familiarity with general linguistics in Cracow under Erasmian influence, while he gained most of his Hebrew knowledge in Wittenberg.[59]

The direct impact of both circles is clearly discernible in Sylvester's *Grammatica Hungarolatina*. Sylvester criticizes Melanchthon, whom he calls "our educator" ("praeceptor noster"), for his claim that only the German language possesses an equivalent to the Greek definite article and shows that the same is true for the Hungarian language.[60] And Sylvester's choice of the verb פקד for his paradigms betrays the influence of Aurogallus's *Compendium Hebreae Grammatices*,[61] at the time the foremost Hebrew primer of the Wittenberg school.[62]

The *Grammatica Hungarolatina* was printed in Sárvár in Western Hungary with the support of the nobleman Tamás Nádasdy, who became Sylvester's host and patron in 1534. In 1543, upon Nádasdy's recommendation, Sylvester received a position at the University of Vienna, initially teaching Hebrew, afterwards Greek. He died sometime before 1552.

With regard to our main topic, Sylvester's grammar demonstrates that Hebrew had already by 1539 become part of the educational canon for Hungarian pupils and the reference framework of education in at least some regions of Hungary, for otherwise the Hebrew parallels would not have made any sense. Moreover, one should be aware that Sylvester was indeed able to put his educational vision into practice, since he worked as a teacher in the elementary school of his patron's village.

Sylvester's aim seems to have been above all pedagogical in nature, and so was his use of Hebrew. However, as shown before, his references to the Hebrew language enabled him to discover and to describe important pecularities of the Hungarian language. Once again, this appears to have been the first time, not only in the Hungarian lands but in the context of European humanism in general,

---

59 Hegedűs, "Johannes Sylvester's grammatical legacy," 48.
60 Sylvester, *Grammatica*, f. 20v and compare Bartók, *Grammatica*, 9.
61 Róbert Dán, *Humanizmus*, 40–41; Matthaeus Aurogallus, *Compendium Hebreae Grammatices* (Wittenberg: Josef Klug, 1523). To be sure, the use of the root פקד as a verbal paradigm has a long pedigree. This root was apparently introduced into scholarship on Hebrew grammar by Moses Kimḥi in the 12th century and became a widely accepted standard through its use by his younger brother David Kimḥi. See Aaron D. Rubin, "The Paradigm Root in Hebrew," *Journal of Semitic Studies* 53 (2008): 29–41.
62 See Ludwig Geiger, *Das Studium der hebräischen Sprache in Deutschland: Vom Ende des XV. bis zur Mitte des XVI. Jahrhunderts* (Breslau: Schletter'sche Buchhandlung, 1870), 96.

that the broadening of linguistic horizons as expressed in the humanistic ideal of the *vir trilinguis* resulted in a practical contribution to the description of vernaculars, leading beyond the constraints of Latin grammar which generally dominated the contemporary linguistic thinking, especially through the humanistic reception of the Roman grammarian Donatus.[63] Later grammars of the Hungarian language, such as Albert Szenczi Molnár's *Novae grammaticae Ungaricae [. . .] libri duo* (1610),[64] often regarded as the first proper grammar of Hungarian, or György Csipkés Komáromi's *Hungaria illustrata* (1655) continued this use of Hebrew as a main part of the descriptive framework, on one hand, and as a heuristic device, on the other.[65]

Moreover, in line with the view expressed in Sylvester's *Grammatica Hungarolatina* that the Hungarian and Hebrew languages share certain grammatical features[66] not found in any other European language, during the second half of the 16th century and the first half of the 17th century the view of a special relationship and closeness between these two languages developed further. The first who appears to have had a comprehensive concept of Hebrew-Hungarian relatedness was the Transylvanian bishop and reformed theologian István Geleji Katona (1589–1649). In his book "Secret of secrets" (*Titkok titka*, Gyulafehérvár 1645), a polemical text against the Unitarian denial of the trinity, he states that the Hungarian language has no relation to other European languages, but rather belongs

---

[63] See Erika Ising, *Die Herausbildung der Grammatik der Volkssprachen in Mittel- und Osteuropa: Studien über den Einfluß der lateinischen Elementargrammatik des Aelius Donatus De octo partibus orationis ars minor*, Veröffentlichungen des Instituts für Deutsche Sprache und Literatur 4 (Berlin: Akademie-Verlag, 1970).

[64] Albert Szenczi Molnár, *Novae grammaticae Ungaricae succincta methodo comprehensae, et perspicuis exemplis illustratae libri duo* (Hannover: Typis Thomae Villeriani: impensis verè Conradi Biermanni & consort, 1610).

[65] Overviews of the emergence and the scholarly manifestations of linguistic comparison between Hungarian and Hebrew have been published by Lajos Venetianer, "A Héber-Magyar összehasonlító nyelvészet" [The Hebrew-Hungarian Comparative Linguistics], *IMIT Évkönyv* 7 (1898): 136–64; József Hegedűs, „A magyar nyelv összehasonlításának kezdetei az egykorú európai nyelvtudomány tükrében" [The Beginnings of the Comparative Study of the Hungarian Language in the Mirror of Linguistics at that Time], in *Nyelvtudományi értekesések* 56 (Budapest: Akadémiai Kiadó, 1966): 90–107; and József Zsengellér, "The Hebrew Language and Comparative Linguistics." In addition, Kornélia Koltai contributed an important article on the evidence emerging from "Hungarian linguistic literature written in Latin," namely Miklós Tótfalusi Kis' book *Ratiocinatio* (1684), devoted to orthography, and Miklós Révai's *Antiquitates* (1803), a work that deals with etymology. On this, see Koltai, "Hebrew Language Knowledge."

[66] As József Hegedűs has pointed out, Sylvester was the first European grammarian to base language comparison on grammatical structure (Hegedűs, "Johannes Sylvester's grammatical legacy," 49–50).

to the Oriental languages, and that this relationship goes back to the time of the confusion of the tongues following the destruction of the Tower of Babel (Gen 11:1–9).[67] An even more detailed and explicit account of this same concept can be found in György Csipkés Komáromi's Hungarian grammar, *Hungaria illustrata*.[68]

Before turning to this latter book, written by one of the most important Hungarian Christian Hebraists, however, and in order to be able fully to appreciate its significance, consequences, and overarching conception, a brief examination of common views at that time with regard to the relationship between different languages should first be undertaken. An especially illustrative impression may be gained from the *Thesaurus Polyglottus* of Hieronymus Megiser (c. 1554–1618/19), which was published in 1603 and 1613 in Frankfurt. Megiser's *Thesaurus* is basically a multilingual dictionary, one of many which were composed and published in the 16th and 17th centuries. The lemma or main entry is provided in Latin, ordered according to the Latin alphabet, and after the Latin lemma, equivalents in numerous other languages are quoted, as in the lemma "Abditus" (see Figure 4):[69]

The sheer range of languages quoted here is dazzling, and a tremendous amount of linguistic information is recorded in this dictionary for the first time. However, what seems particularly interesting in this context is the order in which the different languages appear, which remains consistent throughout the *Thesaurus*, though not every language is included in each lemma:

In the entry displayed below, after the Latin lemma "Abditus" the Hebrew equivalents ("*nistar, tsaphun*") come first; followed by "Syrochaldaic", i.e. Syriac; then classical and vernacular Greek; Latin, Italian, French, and Spanish come next; followed thereafter by German, English, Dutch, and Danish; then Slavonic, Croatian, Polish, and Czech; and, finally, Hungarian. Most obviously, thus, the languages mentioned here are arranged according to language families: Semitic languages – Greek – Latin and Romance languages – Germanic languages – Slavonic languages – Hungarian. Moreover, within these language families the author has established a clear hierarchy, heading each group by its primary language. This internal order follows the contemporary view of the so-called "cardi-

---

[67] Hegedűs, "A magyar," 97.
[68] Georgius Csipkes Comarinus, *Hungaria Illustrata. Hoc est, brevis, sed methodica naturae et genii, linguae Hungaricae, explicatio, anungaros in discenda lingua ista, facilitans, promovens, et Hungaros efficiens* (Ultrajecti [= Utrecht]: Joannis à Waesberge, 1655).
[69] Hieronymus Megiser, *Thesaurus Polyglottus vel Dictionarium multilingue* (Frankfurt 1613), 2–3. The image is taken from the copy kept in the Bayerische Staatsbibliothek and published in the public domain at: http://reader.digitale-sammlungen.de/en/fs1/object/display/bsb10927923_00005.html (accessed: 20/03/2016).

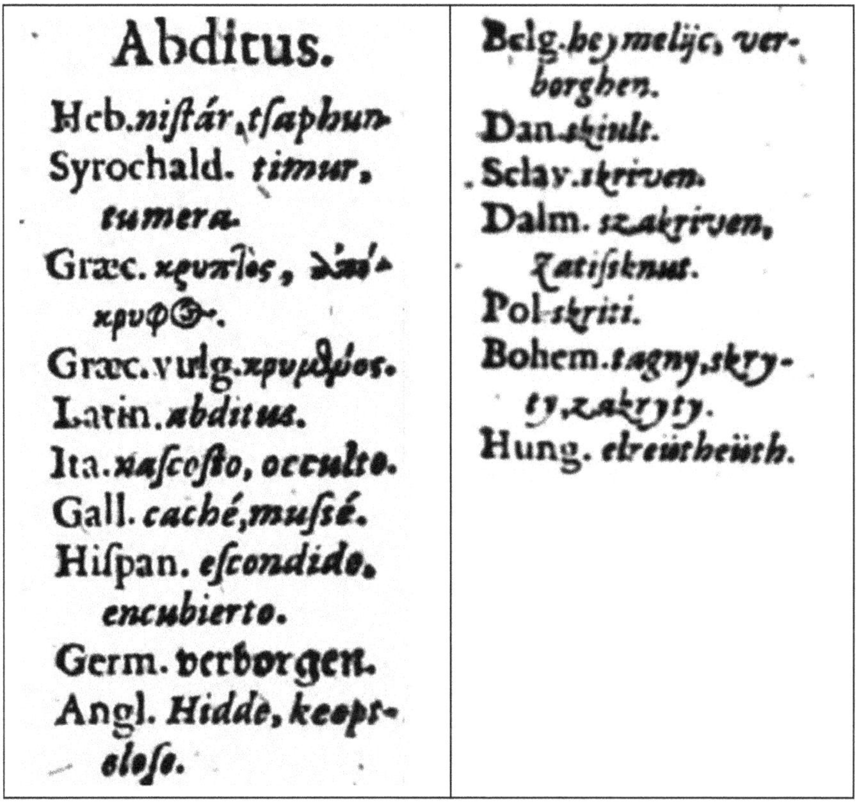

```
Abditus.
Heb. niſtár, tſaphun
Syrochald. timur,
    tumera.
Græc. κρυπ7ὸς, ἄλλ'
    κρυφῶ.
Græc. vulg. κρυμθμὸς.
Latin. abditus.
Ita. naſcoſto, occulto.
Gall. caché, muſsé.
Hiſpan. eſcondido,
    encubierto.
Germ. verborgen.
Angl. Hidde, keeps-
    cloſe.
```
```
Belg. heymelijc, ver-
    borghen.
Dan. skiult.
Sclav. skriven.
Dalm. szakriven,
    zatiſknut.
Pol. skriti.
Bohem. tagny, skry-
    ty, zakryty.
Hung. elreitheüth.
```

Figure 4: H. Megiser, *Thesaurus Polyglottus* (1603), entry "Abditus".

nal languages," i.e. the primary languages of each group, out of which additional, secondary dialects developed. Naturally, Hebrew introduces the first group, and the entry as a whole, since Hebrew is, according to the general view of that time, the first and original language of mankind. Classical Greek heads the Greek group, Latin the Romance languages, German the Germanic languages, and Church Slavonic the Slavic languages. At the end of the whole entry, the Hungarian language appears, without any further language connected to it. Thus, the author of this dictionary was not only familiar with some of the major language families (Semitic, Romance, Germanic, and Slavonic), but he is clearly of the view that Hungarian has no cognate among the languages included in his schema, and that it is therefore linguistically isolated.

Regarding the question as to which languages should be regarded as "cardinal languages," there seems to have been no clear consensus among scholars at that time. While Hebrew, Greek, and Latin were generally seen as belonging to this category, several additional languages were at times granted this status by different scholars. As already seen before, Cruciger in his famous *Harmonia linguarum quatuor cardinalium, hebraicae, graecae, latinae & germanicae* from 1616 included German, which was quite common at the time. Probably the most comprehensive attempt in this period to categorize languages was advanced by Joseph Justus Scaliger (1540–1609) in his treatise *Diatriba de europaeorum linguis*, published posthumously in 1610. Scaliger identifies eleven language groups ("matrices", i.e. "mothers"), among the languages spoken in Europe, which are not related one to the other and can be subdivided with respect to size into four major ("maiores matrices"), and seven minor, language groups ("minores matrices").[70] While the major language groups include Latin, Greek, German, and Slavonic, Hungarian is one of the minor language groups, placed alongside linguistically isolated languages such as Albanian, Tatar, Finnish (the linguistic relationship between Hungarian and Finnish was discovered only later[71]), Irish-Scotish, Breton, and Basque.[72] Megisser, in his *Thesaurus* from 1603, seems to proceed from the same or a very similar concept of separate and parallel language groups, with Hungarian forming an independent group.

The aforementioned István Geleji Katona and György Csipkés Komáromi combined the two lines of linguistic thinking described above – namely the view that Hungarian is linguistically independent from the other European languages, as indicated by Megisser and Scaliger, and the recognition of exclusive parallels between Hungarian and Hebrew first demonstrated by Sylvester, introducing a historical dimension into the synchronic perspective pursued by Megisser and Scaliger, and at the same time postulating that Hungarian is one of the cardinal languages.

György Csipkés Komáromi (1628–1678)[73] was a pupil of the important Hebraist Johann Leusden at Utrecht. After his return to Hungary, he became one of the translators of the Hungarian Bible and a professor at the Reformed college in

---

70 Joseph J. Scaliger, "Diatribae de europaeorum linguis," in *Opuscula varia antehac non edita* (Paris: Hadrianus Beys, 1610): 119–22; here: 119. Compare Thomas Paul Bonfiglio, *Mother Tongues and Nations: The Invention of the Native Speaker*, Trends in linguistics. Studies and monographs 226 (Berlin and New York: De Gruyter Mouton, 2010), 92.
71 The parallels between Finnish and Hungarian, as the basis for the notion of the Finno-Ugric language family, were discovered only in the second half of the 17th century. On this, see Bo Wickmann, "The History of Uralic Linguistics," in *The Uralic Languages: Description, History, and Foreign Influences*, ed. Denis Sinor (Leiden/New York/København/Köln: Brill, 1988): 792–818, here: 793–94.
72 Scaliger, "Diatribae," 121–22.
73 A detailed study of György Komáromi Csipkés' academic background in the Netherlands and his activity as a Christian Hebraist in Hungary is to be found in József Zsengellér, "György

Debrecen. In his *Hungaria illustrata*, he argues as follows with regard to the relation between Hungarian and Hebrew:

A) The Hungarian language did not evolve from any other language, but emerged immediately at Babel, in the context of the confusion of the tongues.

> With regard to origin and antiquity, it is not only probable, but necessary that the Hungarian language emerged at the time of the Babylonian confusion. Due to the fact that it is no other language's dialect, it is a cardinal language, a language mother, no less than German, Slavonic, Greek, Latin. ("Quantum ad originem et antiquitatem, linguam Hungaricam, tempore confusionis babilonicae, enatam esse, non solum probabile, sed et necessarium videtur. Quia nullius linguae dialectus est, sed lingua cardinalis, lingua Mater, non secus ac Germanica, Sclavonica, Graeca, Latina.")[74]

B) The Hungarian language does not contain any signs of a secondary development and has been influenced only very marginally by other languages. It thus has largely retained its original state, and the great measure of its pureness is unsurpassed by any other of the languages spoken in Europe:

> With regard to purity and the absence of mixture with other languages, the Hungarian language is pure and unpolluted by mixture with other other languages: it still has the pleasure of its own words, its own way of speaking, its own system of declination and conjugation. [. . .] Just as the mixing in of certain Aramaic words does not ruin the purity of Hebrew, just as the introduction of certain Syriac and Hebrew words does not ruin the purity of the Greek text of the New Testament, neither do some words from Slavonic, German, or Latin ruin the simple purity and chastity of the Hungarian language. ("Quantum ad puritatem, et à linguarum aliarum commixtione immunitatem, lingua Hungarica à commixtione, cum linguis aliis, casta est et pura: propriis adhuc gaudens vocibus; proprio loquendi modo; propria declinandi et conjugandi ratione. [. . .] Ut verò Hebraicę puritatem quarundam Chaldaicarum mixtura, Grecae Novi Testam. scripturae, quarundam Syriacarum et Hebraicarum interpositio, non tollunt, sic nec lingue Hungaricae simplicem puritatem et castitatem, voces aliquae Sclavonicae, Germanicae, et Latinae tollunt.")[75]

C) Unlike the other vernaculars in Europe, Hungarian is an oriental language[76] and its closest cognate among all other languages is Hebrew:

> As regards its similarity and agreement in relation to other languages, the Hungarian language is much closer to Hebrew, which is followed by Syriac, Aramaic, and, although more

---

Komáromi Csipkés (1628–1678) and the influence from the Netherlands on Christian Hebraism in Hungary," in Schorch and Thon, eds., *Christian Hebraism* (forthcoming).
74 György Csipkés Komáromi, *A magyar nyelv magyarázata – Hungaria illustrata*, ed. Zsuzsa C. Vladár (Budapest: A Magyar nyelvtudományi társaság, 2008), 62 (= p. 19 of the original edition from 1655).
75 Csipkés Komáromi, *A magyar*, 68 (= p. 22 of the original edition 1655).
76 Csipkés Komáromi, *A magyar*, 68 (= p. 20 of the original edition 1655).

remotely, Arabic, than it is to any other language under heaven. ("Quantum denique ad ejusdem, cum linguarum aliqua convenientiam et affinitatem, lingua Hungarica, nulli linguarum sub coelo tam est similis, ac Hebraicae; quam imitantur Syriaca, Chaldaica, et Arabica, quamvis longius.")[77]

For Csipkés Komáromi, therefore, Hungarian was a cardinal language, because it emerged as one of the first languages immediately after Babel, and has also largely retained its original character since then. Moreover, due to the association of the concept of cardinal languages with the events at Babel, Hebrew now hovers over these languages as the first language, with regard to history, and as a model for the most perfect language, with regard to quality. Csipkés Komáromi's views of the Hebrew language are fully in line with those of other Protestant scholars of his time, both abroad and in Hungary,[78] and appear most explicitly in the inaugural lecture that he delivered as professor at the Reformed college in Debrecen. The lecture was printed as an addendum to Csipkés Komáromi's Hebrew grammar *Schola hebraica* (1654),[79] which shows that his aims in this speech went far beyond one festive occasion, although the rhetoric is necessarily elevated, due to the genre:[80]

> All the other languages are punishment, while this one alone is the language of grace; the other were born through [the] confusion [of the tongues after Babel], but this one alone through God's divine disposition. [. . .] Therefore this holy language [i.e., Hebrew] is as superior to the other languages, as is the creator to his creation, holiness to the profane, divine order to confusion, grace to punishment. ("Aliae omnes sunt poena, haec sola est lingua gratiae; Aliae sunt nata per confusionem, haec sola per divinam Dei institutionem. [. . .] Unde lingua haec sancta, tanto reliquas, quanto creator creaturam, quanto sanctitas profanitatem, quanto ordo divinus confusionem, quanto gratia poenam excellit, antecellit."

Thus, if the Hungarian language is closer to Hebrew than any other of the living languages, as claimed by Csipkés Komáromi and a few scholars before him,

---

77 Csipkés Komáromi, *A magyar*, 70 (= p. 23 of the original edition 1655).
78 Compare e.g. the views concerning Hebrew found in István Geleji Katona's *Titkok tika* (1645), on which see Hegedűs, "A magyar," 97.
79 The full title of the book, which was printed in the Netherlands, refers to both parts: György Csipkés Komáromi, *Schola hebraica in qua theticè, et per breves positiones, ratio recte legendi, et fundamentaliter intelligendi, linguam hebraicam, ita traditur, ut quis etiam sine ullo praeceptore, privato studio, sufficientem linguae hebraeae cognitionem, ad intelligendum scripta ad scribendum intellecta, comparare possit auctore Georgio Csipkes Comarino [. . .] Accessit ejusdem autoris oratio inauguralis, de linguae hebraeae utilitate, dignitate, necessitate etc., habitâ ibidem Debrecini, anno gratia MDCLIII 8. Aug.* (Trajecti ad Rhenum [= Utrecht]: Gisbert à Zyll & Theodor ab Ackersdyck, 1654).
80 Csipkés Komáromi, *Schola hebraica*, 147.

especially István Geleji Katona, it obviously acquires a religious and theological quality not found elsewhere among the vernaculars. And Hebrew is not restricted to its role as heuristic or pedagocical reference framework, but has become a means of dignifying Csipkés Komáromi's own vernacular.

A few years before both his Hebrew and his Hungarian grammar were published, Csipkés Komáromi, then still a student of Johann Leusden (1624–1699) at the University of Utrecht, gave a public lecture at his *alma mater* with the title *Oratio Hebraea, continens Elogium Linguae Hebraeae*, i.e. "A Hebrew oration, containing a eulogy of the Hebrew language," which appeared in print in 1651, together with a Hebrew poem of his teacher Leusden.[81] As the title suggests, this lecture, comprising some nine and a half pages, is completely written in Hebrew, and thus shows that a very important part of Christian Hebraism, the active use of Hebrew and the composition of Hebrew texts, was present in Hungarian Christian Hebraism as well. Although somewhat clumsy, the oration is comprehensible and displays the notable measure of Csipkés Komáromi's command of Hebrew. Its language draws mainly on Biblical Hebrew, to some degree even on Biblical Aramaic, whereas the traces of Rabbinic Hebrew are slight. The character of a somewhat artificial *Gelehrtensprache* is revealed by the fact that a large number of the words which Csipkés Komárom employs are in fact *hapax legomena* in the Hebrew Bible, or at least are very rare. Most strikingly, the syntax of the text seems generally closer to Latin than to Hebrew, the possesive form של- is employed like the Greek genitiv, the demonstrative pronoun is used in the Latin way, the preposition ל- is stereotypically used where according to Latin syntax one would expect a dative, and so on. Thus, one may almost say that the text is Latin with Hebrew words.

Even in this speech, delivered in the Netherlands, Csipkés Komáromi makes a case for the closeness of Hungarian and Hebrew, although this time mainly on the lexical level, e.g.[82]

כִּי בִּלְשׁוֹן הַהוּנִּיִּים שֵׁם הַיּוֹלֵד Apa מֵאָב אוֹ אָבָה שֶׁל עִבְרִים

In the language of the Huns i.e., [the Hungarians[83]] the name for the father is *Apa*, from אב or אבה of the Hebrews.

---

81 György Csipkés Komáromi, *Oratio hebraea, continens Elogium Linguae Hebraeae* (Ultrajecti [= Utrecht]: Johannis à Waesberge, 1651).
82 Csipkés Komáromi, *Oratio hebraea*, 6r. Spelling and vocalization in the quote follow the original.
83 The relation between the Huns and the Hungarians was discussed already in the 16th century, as attested for instance in Sebastian Münster's *Cosmographia: Beschreibung aller Lender durch Sebastianum Munsterum, in welcher begriffen Aller völcker, Herrschafften, Stetten und namhafftiger flecken, herkommen: Sitten, gebreüch, ordnung, glauben, secten vnd hantierung, durch die gantze welt, vnd fürnemlich Teutscher nation. Was auch besunders in iedem landt gefunden, vnnd darin*

From the perpective of a modern linguist, this is of course an untenable etymological claim. Nevertheless, it demonstrates that the quest of Hungarian Christian Hebraists to create an exclusive relation between Hebrew and Hungarian related to all levels of these languages, including the lexicon. And, most obviously, together with the use of Hebrew among the Hungarian-speaking Sabbatarians in Transylvania, this endeavor is a typical peculiarity of Hungarian Christian Hebraism.

Bibliography

Aurogallus, Matthaeus. *Compendium Hebreae Grammatices*. Wittenberg: Josef Klug, 1523.
Balázs, Mihály. "Gab es eine unitarische Konfessionalisierung im Siebenbürgen des 16. Jahrhunderts?" In *Konfessionsbildung und Konfessionskultur in Siebenbürgen in der Frühen Neuzeit*, edited by Volker Leppin and Ulrich A.Wien, 135–52. Stuttgart: Franz Steiner Verlag, 2005.
Bartók, István, ed. *Ioannes Sylvester: Grammatica Hungarolatina. Edidit, introduxit et commentariis instruxit Stephanus Bartók*. Bibliotheca Scriptorum Medii Recentisque Aevorum. Series Nova XV. Budapest: Akademia Kiadó/Argumentum Kiadó, 2006.
Bogáti Fazekas, Miklós. *Magyar zsoltár 151 verses parafrázisban* [Hungarian Psalter in a Paraphrase of 151 Verses, in Hungarian], edited by Gábor Gilicze. Budapest: Országos Széchényi Könyvtár, 2009.
Bonfiglio, Thomas Paul. *Mother Tongues and Nations: The Invention of the Native speaker*. Trends in linguistics. Studies and monographs 226. Berlin and New York: De Gruyter Mouton, 2010.
Bozzay, Réka. "The Influence of Dutch Universities on the Education of Seventeenth-Century Hungarian Intellectuals." In *A Divided Hungary in Europe: Exchanges, Networks and Representations, 1541–1699*, vol. 1: *Study Tours and Intellectual-Religious Relationships*, edited by Gábor Almási, Szymon Brzeziński, Ildikó Horn, Kees Teszelszky, and Áron Zarnóczki, 81–100. Newcastle upon Tyne: Cambridge Scholars Publishing, 2014.
Csipkés Komáromi, György. *A magyar nyelv magyarázata – Hungaria illustrata*, ed. Zsuzsa C. Vladár. Budapest: A Magyar nyelvtudományi társaság, 2008.
Csipkés Komáromi, György. *Hungaria Illustrata. Hoc est, brevis, sed methodica naturae et genii, linguae Hungaricae, explicatio, anungaros in discenda lingua ista, facilitans, promovens, et Hungaros efficiens*. Ultrajecti [= Utrecht]: Joannis à Waesberge, 1655.
Csipkés Komáromi, György. *Oratio hebraea, continens Elogium Linguae Hebraeae*. Ultrajecti [= Utrecht]: Johannis à Waesberge, 1651.

---

beschehen sey. Alles mit figuren vnd schönen landt taflen erklert, vnd für augen gestelt (Basel: Petri, 1544). On this, see Hegedűs, "Johannes Sylvester's Grammatical Legacy," 48–49, with scholars at least partly affirming that Huns and Hungarians are the same. Csipkés Komáromi was obviously following this view.

Csipkés Komáromi, György. *Schola hebraica in qua theticè, et per breves positiones, ratio recte legendi, et fundamentaliter intelligendi, linguam hebraicam, ita traditur, ut quis etiam since ullo praeceptore, privato studio, sufficientem linguae hebraeae cognitionem, ad intelligendum scripta ad scribendum intellecta, comparare possit auctore Georgio Csipkes Comarino [. . .] Accessit ejusdem autoris oratio inauguralis, de linguae hebraeae utilitate, dignitate, necessitate etc., habitâ ibidem Debrecini, anno gratia MDCLIII 8. Aug.* Trajecti ad Rhenum [= Utrecht]: Gisbert à Zyll & Theodor ab Ackersdyck, 1654.

Dán, Róbert. *Az erdélyi szombatosok és Péchi Simon* [The Transylvanian Sabbatarians and Simon Péchi, in Hungarian]. Humanizmus és reformáció 13. Budapest: Akadémiai Kiadó, 1987.

Dán, Róbert. *Humanizmus, reformáció, antitrinitarizmus és a héber nyelv Magyarországon* [Humanism, Reformation, Antitrinitarianism, and the Hebrew Language in Hungary, in Hungarian]. Humanizmus és reformáció 2. Budapest: Akadémiai Kiadó, 1973.

Dán, Róbert. *Matthias Vehe-Glirius: Life and Work of a Radical Antitrinitarian with His Collected Writings*. Studia humanitatis 4. Budapest: Akadémiai Kiadó/Leiden: Brill, 1982.

Daugsch, Walter. "Toleranz im Fürstentum Siebenbürgen: Politische und gesellschaftliche Voraussetzungen der Religionsgesetzgebung im 16. Jahrhundert." *Kirche im Osten* 26 (1983): 35–72.

Eberhard, Winfried. "Voraussetzungen und strukturelle Grundlagen der Konfessionalisierung in Ostmitteleuropa." In *Konfessionalisierung in Ostmitteleuropa: Wirkungen des religiösen Wandels im 16. und 17. Jahrhundert in Staat, Gesellschaft und Kultur*, edited by Joachim Bahlcke and Arno Strohmeyer, 89–104. Stuttgart: Steiner, 1999.

Fata, Márta, Gyula Kurucz, and Anton Schindling, eds. *Peregrinatio Hungarica: Studenten aus Ungarn an deutschen und österreichischen Hochschulen vom 16. bis zum 20. Jahrhundert*. Contubernium 64. Stuttgart: Steiner, 2006.

Geiger, Ludwig. *Das Studium der hebräischen Sprache in Deutschland: Vom Ende des XV. bis zur Mitte des XVI. Jahrhunderts*. Breslau: Schletter'sche Buchhandlung, 1870.

Guttmann, Mihály, and Sándor Harmos, eds. *Péchi Simon szombatos imádságos könyve* [Simon Péchi's Sabbatarian Prayerbook, in Hungarian]. Az Izraelita Magyar Irodalmi Társulat kiadványai 39. Budapest: Izraelita Magyar Irodalmi Társulat, 1914.

Hegedűs, József. "A magyar nyelv összehasonlításának kezdetei az egykorú európai nyelvtudomány tükrében" [The Beginnings of the Comparative Study of the Hungarian Language in the Mirror of Linguistics at that Time, in Hungarian]. Nyelvtudományi értekesések 56, 90–107. Budapest: Akadémiai Kiadó, 1966.

Hegedűs, József. "Johannes Sylvester's Grammatical Legacy (1539) and its European Background." *Acta Linguistica Hungarica* 55 (2008): 41–57.

Ising, Erika. *Die Herausbildung der Grammatik der Volkssprachen in Mittel- und Osteuropa: Studien über den Einfluß der lateinischen Elementargrammatik des Aelius Donatus De octo partibus orationis ars minor*. Veröffentlichungen des Instituts für Deutsche Sprache und Literatur 4. Berlin: Akademie-Verlag, 1970.

Kecskeméti, Gábor. "The Effect of the Universities of the Low Countries on the Intellectual History of Hungary in the Early Modern Times." *Hungarian Studies* 26 (2012): 189–204.

Keul, István. *Early Modern Religious Communities in East-Central Europe: Ethnic Diversity, Denominational Plurality, and Corporative Politics in the Principality of Transylvania, 1526–1691*. Studies in Medieval and Reformation Traditions 143. Leiden and Boston: Brill, 2009.

Kiss, Áron. *A XVI. században tartott magyar református zsinatok végzései* [The Decisions of the Hungarian Reformed Synode in the 16th Century, in Hungarian]. A Magyarországi

Protestansegylet kiadványai 19/Protestans theologiai könyvtár 16. Budapest: Magyarországi Protestansegylet, 1881.

Klein, Wolf P. "Die ursprüngliche Einheit der Sprachen in der philologisch-grammatischen Sicht der frühen Neuzeit." In *The Language of Adam/Die Sprache Adams*, edited by Allison P. Coudert, 25–56. Wiesbaden: Harrassowitz, 1999.

Klein, Wolf P. "Was wurde aus den Wörtern der hebräischen Ursprache? Zur Entstehung der komparativen Linguistik aus dem Geist der etymologischen Spekulation." In *Gottes Sprache in der philologischen Werkstatt: Hebraistik vom 15. bis zum 19. Jahrhundert*, edited by Giuseppe Veltri and Gerold Necker, 3–23. Leiden and Boston: Brill, 2004.

Kohn, Sámuel. *A szombatosok: Történetük, dogmatikájuk és irodalmuk. Különös tekintettel Péchi Simon főkanczellár életére és munkáira*. Budapest: Athenaeum, 1889.

Kohn, Sámuel. *Die Sabbatharier in Siebenbürgen: Ihre Geschichte, Literatur und Dogmatik. Mit besonderer Berücksichtigung des Lebens und der Schriften des Reichskanzlers Simon Péchi. Ein Beitrag zur Religions- und Culturgeschichte der jüngsten drei Jahrhunderte*. Budapest: Singer & Wolfner/Leipzig: Franz Wagner, 1894.

Koltai, Kornélia. "Egy 17. századi héber carmen bemutatása – a carmenszerző héber grammatikája tükrében." In *A grammatikától a retorikáig: Nyelvészeti tanulmányok C. Vladár Zsuzsa tiszteletére*, edited by Ferenc Havas, Katalin Horváth, Éva Hrenek, and Mária Ladányi, 43–52. Budapest: ELTE BTK Alkalmazott Nyelvészeti és Fonetikai Tanszék, 2021.

Koltai, Kornélia. "Hebrew Language Knowledge of Christian Hebraists Dealing with Hungarian Linguistics." *Studia Debreceni Teológiai Tanulmányok* 11 (2019): 9–23.

Koltai, Kornélia. *Péchi Simon: Az Atyák mondásai* [Simon Péchi: Sayings of the Fathers, in Hungarian]. Hungaria Judaica 11. Budapest: MTA Judaisztikai Kutatócsoport, 1999.

Koltai, Kornélia. "Péchi Simon Biblia-kommentárja" [Simon Péchi's Bible Commentary, in Hungarian]. In *Vízió és valóság: A Pázmány Péter Katolikus Egyetemen 2010. október 28–29-én „A dialógus sodrában . . . " címmel tartott zsidó–keresztény konferencia előadásai*, edited by Károly Dániel Dobos and György Fodor, 199–218. Budapest: Új Ember – Márton Áron Kiadó, 2011.

Koltai, Kornélia. *Péchi Simon kiadatlan Biblia-fordítása (1634)* [Simon Péchi's Unedited Bible Translation (1634), in Hungarian]. Hungaria Judaica 23. Budapest: MTA Judaisztikai Kutatócsoport, 2011.

Koltai, Kornélia. "Simon Péchi, the Head of the Transylvanian Sabbatarian Movement (17th Century)." In *Christian Hebraism in Eastern Central Europa*, edited by Stefan Schorch and Johannes Thon (forthcoming).

Leppin, Volker. "Siebenbürgen: Ein kirchenhistorischer Sonderfall von allgemeiner Bedeutung." In *Konfessionsbildung und Konfessionskultur in Siebenbürgen in der Frühen Neuzeit*, edited by Volker Leppin and Ulrich A. Wien, 7–13. Stuttgart: Franz Steiner Verlag, 2005.

Megiser, Hieronymus. *Thesaurus Polyglottus vel Dictionarium multilingue*. Frankfurt, 1613.

Miletto, Gianfranco, and Giuseppe Veltri. "Hebrew Studies in Wittenberg (1502–1813): From Lingua Sacra to Semitic Studies." *European Journal of Jewish Studies* 6 (2012): 1–22.

Münster, Sebastian. *Cosmographia: Beschreibung aller Lender durch Sebastianum Munsterum, in welcher begriffen Aller völcker, Herrschafften, Stetten und namhafftiger flecken, herkommen: Sitten, gebreüch, ordnung, glauben, secten vnd hantierung, durch die gantze welt, vnd fürnemlich Teutscher nation. Was auch besunders in iedem landt gefunden, vnnd darin beschehen sey. Alles mit figuren vnd schönen landt taflen erklert, vnd für augen gestelt*. Basel: Petri, 1544.

Münster, Sebastian. מלאכת הדיקדוק – *Institutiones grammaticae in Hebraeam linguam*. Basel: Johann Froben, 1524.
Rubin, Aaron D. "The Paradigm Root in Hebrew." *Journal of Semitic Studies* 53 (2008): 29–41.
Scaliger, Joseph J. "Diatribae de europaeorum linguis." In *Opuscula varia antehac non edita*, 119–22. Paris: Hadrianus Beys, 1610.
Schorch, Stefan, and Johannes Thon, eds. *Christian Hebraism in Eastern Central Europa from the Renaissance to the Enlightenment* (forthcoming).
Sylvester, Ioannes. *Grammatica Hungarolatina in usum puerorum* (Neanesus [= Ujsziget-Sarvar], 1539).
Sylvester, Ioannes. *Grammatica Hungarolatina in usum puerorum*. Budapest: Akadémiai Kidó/ Argumentum Kiadó, 2006.
Szabó, András. "Ungarische Studenten in Wittenberg 1555–1592." In *Iter Germanicum: Deutschland und die Reformierte Kirche in Ungarn im 16.–17. Jahrhundert*, edited by András Szabó, 154–168. Budapest: Kálvin Kiadó, 1999.
Szenczi Molnár, Albert. *Novae grammaticae Ungaricae succincta methodo comprehensae, et perspicuis exemplis illustratae libri duo*. Hannover: Typis Thomae Villeriani: impensis verè Conradi Biermanni & consort, 1610.
Talmage, Frank. "R. David Kimḥi as Polemicist." *Hebrew Union College Annual* 38 (1967): 213–35.
Vartanov, Yuri. "The Early Studies in Biblical Hebrew in Poland and Eastern Europe." *Kwartalnik Historii Żydów – Jewish History Quarterly* 3/247 (2013): 511–523.
Venetianer, Lajos. "A Héber-Magyar összehasonlító nyelvészet" [Hebrew-Hungarian Comparative Linguistics, in Hungarian]. *IMIT Évkönyv* 7 (1898): 136–164.
Wickmann, Bo. "The History of Uralic Linguistics." In *The Uralic Languages: Description, History, and Foreign Influences*, edited by Denis Sinor, 792–818. Leiden/New York/ København/Köln: Brill, 1988.
Wilbur, Earl Morse. *A History of Unitarianism: In Transylvania, England and America*. Cambridge, MA: Harvard University Press, 1952.
Zsengellér, József. "*Carmina gratulatoria hebraica* és a héber nyelvoktatás a Nagyváradi Református Kollégiumban [Hebrew Congratulatory Poems and Hebrew Language Learning at the Reformed College in Nagyvárad, in Hungarian]." In *Ünnepi kötet Adorjáni Zoltán 65. születésnapja tiszteletére*, edited by Csaba Balogh and Vilmos József Kolumbán. Kolozsvár: Kolozsvári Protestáns Teológiai Intézet (forthcoming).
Zsengellér, József. "Egy 17. századi héber vizsga margójára: Pontosítások és héber carmenek Tofeus Mihály váradi könyve alapján (RMK II. 764) [On the Margins of a 17th-Century Hebrew Exam: Precise Details and Hebrew Poems from Mihály Tofeus' Book from Várad, in Hungarian]," *Egyháztörténeti Szemle* 22 (2021), 5–28.
Zsengellér, József. "Franekeri héber carmina gratulatoria Martonfalvi György és diákjainak tollából [Hebrew Carmina Gratulatoria from Franeker by Georg Martonfalvi and His Students, in Hungarian]," *Református Szemle* 114 (2021): 125–158;
Zsengellér, József. "György Komáromi Csipkés (1628–1678) and the Influence from the Netherlands on Christian Hebraism in Hungary." In *Christian Hebraism in Eastern Central Europa*, edited by Stefan Schorch and Johannes Thon (forthcoming).
Zsengellér, József. "The Hebrew Language and Comparative Linguistics in the Early Centuries of Hungarian Protestantism." In *Protestantism, Knowledge and the World of Science*, edited by György Kurucz, 63–76. Budapest: Károli Gáspár University of the Reformed Church in Hungary/L'Harmattan Publishing, 2017.

Yael Almog
Reasoning and Exegesis: Hamann and Herder's Notions of Biblical Hebrew

Late-eighteenth-century Germany displayed a fervent interest in Biblical Hebrew in the context of a general trend of admiration of the Old Testament. Prominent figures in this period's republic of letters, such as Johann Wolfgang Goethe and Johann Gottfried Herder, wrote about the language, often debating with one another as to the proper way to conceive of it.[1] In addition, specific genres of biblical literature, such as prophetic speech and the idyllic poetry found in the Psalter, were widely employed in new aesthetic enterprises, most prominently in the *Sturm und Drang* movement. This article describes how the debates concerning the reading of Biblical Hebrew shaped early philosophical positions in German idealism. I shall examine the work of two major late-eighteenth-century thinkers whose aesthetic theories were greatly informed by the question of how to read Biblical Hebrew: the theologian Johann Georg Hamann and his friend, Johann Gottfried Herder.

I shall begin by describing Hamann's vision of the revelatory potential of scriptural reading as a polemic against the scholarly approach to Biblical Hebrew advocated by his contemporary, the prominent philologist Johann David Michaelis. I will then demonstrate how Hamann's conception of Biblical Hebrew as a symbol for understanding that goes beyond the denotative meaning of words served Herder in formulating his own interventions into theology and textual interpretation. As Frederik Beiser has argued, "If we were to describe in a word how Herder assimilated Hamann's thought, then we would have to say that he secularized it. In other words, he explained it in naturalistic terms and justified it

---

1 See Maurice Olender, *The Languages of Paradise: Race, Religion, and Philology in the Nineteenth Century,* trans. Arthur Goldhammer (Cambridge, MA: Harvard University Press, 1992), 1–50; Daniel Weidner, *Bibel und Literatur um 1800* (München: Wilhelm Fink, 2011) offers a presentation of the engagement with the Bible during the late eighteenth and early nineteenth centuries. Weidner demonstrates that the cultural prevalence of the Bible is revealed not merely in correspondences with biblical motifs and narratives, but that it is evident as well in the overall literary production of the period – e.g. literary texts emulated biblical genres and literary interpretation built on the period's new approaches to scriptural exegesis.

Note: An earlier version of this article appeared in Spanish translation as "Estéticas de la Biblia: el imaginario del hebreo en las teorías de la interpretación de Hamann y Herder," *El Boletín de Estética es publicado* 31 (July 2015): 5–36.

https://doi.org/10.1515/9783110339826-013

in the light of reason."[2] Following this contention, I will show that Herder builds on Hamann's presentation of scriptural reading as a subjective and affective experience while at the same time promoting the view that readers should seek a deeper understanding of the Bible by reflecting on the text's historical and cultural origins. This latter notion of reasoning, which has become a pivotal direction in both theology and modern interpretation,[3] perpetuates the view of biblical interpretation as a revelatory experience, while combining this vision with the philological impetus of attaining an objective historical understanding of Scripture. I thus contend that Hamann and Herder's diverging approaches to Hebrew are emblematic of their respective positions in Enlightenment thought, particularly with regard to the role of reason in language use.[4]

My discussion focuses on two main texts by the above-mentioned authors that represent the salient differences between their approaches to Biblical Hebrew: Hamann's 1762 *Aesthetica in Nuce* and Herder's 1783 *On the Spirit of Hebrew Poetry*. In his provocative manifesto, Hamann proposed a new aesthetic theory based on his perspective on scriptural reading. A central principle of Hamann's approach is the notion of the reader's engagement with Scripture as an inspirational process of filling in the gaps in the so-called obscure text. Biblical Hebrew represents for Hamann a central platform on which to exemplify this approach. Hamann thus derides contemporary scholarly attempts to recover the original meaning of Hebrew words; for him, the merit of Hebrew lies precisely in its linguistic intricacy, which necessitates the reader's dynamic engagement with the biblical text.

By contrast, it was in the 1770s that Herder first began charting his distinct approach, which culminated with *On the Spirit of Hebrew Poetry*. This long essay celebrates Hebrew as a language with unique aesthetic merits and directly links the comprehension of the Hebrew text to the understanding of the culture that produced it, and of its religious, aesthetic, and social norms. As I shall show, Herder's interpretation theory builds on his distinction between the ancient Hebrews

---

[2] Frederick Beiser, *Enlightenment, Revolution, and Romanticism: The Genesis of Modern German Political Thought, 1790–1800* (Cambridge, MA: Harvard University Press, 1992), 195.

[3] On Herder's eminent part in a lineage of theologians who reconciled philological-historical approaches to the Bible with Protestant theology, and on the cultural prominence of this mediation, see Hans Frei, *The Eclipse of Biblical Narrative* (New Haven, CT: Yale University Press, 1974).

[4] I see Hamann as enhancing the congruence of Herder's theological efforts with central notions of reasoning in the late Enlightenment and in German idealism. In particular, I see this impact as ingrained in Hamann's presentation of reading as a platform for the reader's cognitive and affective experimentation. For a similar position – which depicts Hamann not merely as antagonistic to Enlightenment thought and to biblical philology, but as holding a constructive dialogue with them – see Jonathan Sheehan, "Enlightenment Details: Theology, Natural History, and the Letter h," *Representations* 61 (1998): 29–56.

and Judaism as a religion. He crystalizes the gap between the two in his praise of Hebrew as a unique aesthetic artifact of a national culture; the merits of the language were lost, he contends, during the diasporic stages of Judaism.

Notwithstanding the important differences between them, both Herder and Hamann were central proponents of a new approach to the Old Testament: the treatment of the Bible as an object whose supreme quality is the affective resonance it provokes in its readers owing to its style and use of literary devices. I wish to explore how the transformation of Scripture into a universal artifact relied on the transformation of Hebrew from a concrete language into a cultural artifact with symbolic presence. In this process, it was precisely the alleged difficulty of comprehending Hebrew literally, deemed a "problem" by all readers of Scripture, which gave rise to the conception of the language as a universal cipher. The reading of the Bible as an embodiment of God's word and the corresponding perception of the Bible as an object of worship were thus replaced with a new perception of Scripture as transcendent of confessional difference.

1 Enlightenment Theology and the Universalization of Scripture

The backdrop for the above theological developments was the emergence of the Bible as a crucible for new approaches to textual interpretation. As Jonathan Sheehan has shown, Protestant theologians reconstituted the Hebrew Bible as a cultural artifact to which each individual can relate. Sheehan describes how this modern reconceptualization of Scripture was fashioned through a broad wave of biblical translations, a practice essential to Protestant theology since its inception. In the second half of the eighteenth century, a wave of biblical translations "pluralized" Scripture, as the decision to translate the Bible became linked to individuals' own initiatives, ideologies, and motivations. According to Sheehan, it was, more specifically, a particular variant of Protestantism that made the Bible into a personalized object: the catalyst of biblical translation was a pietistic Bible project cultivating an "inspirational model of biblical translation."[5] Theories of textual interpretation played a seminal role in this cultural transformation as they rendered engagement with the Scripture a subjective enterprise that has an affective rapport with the individual.

---

5 Jonathan Sheehan, *The Enlightenment Bible: Translation, Scholarship, Culture* (Princeton, NJ: Princeton University Press, 2005), 67.

Sheehan's *The Enlightenment Bible* participates in a scholarly trend that emphasizes the salient role played by theology in the Enlightenment. Until recently, the dominant stream of scholarship on the German Enlightenment contended that the period's investigations into human reason were largely intertwined with "secularization," i.e., with a certain decline in the status of sectorial religious affiliations. This tendency is common in such historiographies as Peter Gay's *The Enlightenment* and Louis Dupré's *The Enlightenment and the Intellectual Foundations of Modern Culture*.[6] David Sorkin's 2008 *The Religious Enlightenment* has been influential in offering an alternative portrayal of the period in claiming that

> Contrary to our secular master narrative, the Enlightenment was not only compatible with religious belief but conducive to it. The Enlightenment made new iterations of faith. With the Enlightenment's advent, religion lost neither its place nor its authority in European society and culture. If we trace modern culture to the Enlightenment, its foundations were decisively religious.[7]

Sorkin emphasizes the proliferation of religious practices during the Enlightenment, and the congruence of these practices with ideals conceived as central to the Enlightenment heritage (e.g. religious toleration). He thus demonstrates that far from disappearing, religious practices were transformed during this period in ways that made them compatible with different faiths and diverging confessions:

> For Christians, the religious Enlightenment represented a renunciation of Reformation and Counter-Reformation militance, an express alternative to two centuries of dogmatism and fanaticism, intolerance and religious warfare. For Jews, it represented an effort to overcome the uncharacteristic cultural isolation of the post-Reformation period through appropriation of neglected elements of their own heritage and engagement with the larger culture.[8]

According to Sorkin, theology elicited a social turn in favor of moderation, which helped bring about nineteenth-century "cultural Protestantism."[9] The emergence of the notion of the public sphere enabled the establishment of religious tolerance in the Enlightenment's distinct national regimes. The ability of the "religious Enlightenment" to influence several different countries, religious groups, and social strata can thus be said to be reflected in modern notions of political

---

[6] Peter Gay, *The Enlightenment, An Interpretation: The Rise of Modern Paganism* (New York: W. W. Norton & Company, 1966); Louis Dupré, *The Enlightenment and the Intellectual Foundations of Modern Culture* (New Haven, CT: Yale University Press, 2004).
[7] David Sorkin, *The Religious Enlightenment: Protestants, Jews, and Catholics from London to Vienna* (Princeton: Princeton University Press, 2008), 3.
[8] Ibid., 4.
[9] Ibid., 313.

secularism. Sorkin's account thus offers an alternative model to the dismissal of religion from accounts of the Enlightenment by expanding the role of theology in shaping the Enlightenment public sphere. Treating such figures like William Warburton, Siegmund Jacob Baumgarten and Moses Mendelssohn, his *Religious Enlightenment* depicts how the interpretation of biblical and extra-biblical religious law builds on the notion of *sola scriptura* according to which every individual should be allowed to engage with the Scripture on his or her own terms.

In a similar manner, writings about Biblical Hebrew as a cultural asset could be seen as seminal in reconstituting the Bible as an object whose universal relevance derives not from its theological, juridical, and ritual standing, but from its cultural relevance to all readers. Close attention to the context in which Biblical Hebrew was dealt with highlights an additional – substantially different – facet of the Enlightenment's pluralistic approach to Scripture. Authors like Hamann and Herder represented early Romantic tendencies in their appreciation of Biblical Hebrew's "difficult" reading experience. Within this experience, they contended, the language serves to promote the subjective engagement with the text.

A major aspect of this pluralizing effect of Romantic reading was the abstraction of the language of Scripture from its confessional association. Hamann's theory of imaginative reading and Herder's hermeneutics of contextualization offer two ways of confronting the view of the Hebrew language as "Jewish knowledge," stressing, in Hamann's case, the revelatory potential that is unique to Christianity, and, for Herder, the need to rescue Hebrew from the damage of its circulation in Jewish contexts.

2 Hebrew beyond Confessional Difference

The Old Testament was the object of unprecedented interest in the German republic of letters between the years 1750–1780.[10] In such enterprises as the philological work of Johann David Michaelis, the culture of the ancient Hebrews exerted a major influence on legal and political norms in contemporary Germany. Michaelis had argued that the Hebrew language should be treated as a historical object, and developed critical scholarly approaches to the language accordingly. He advocated the study of Hebrew through comparative philology, claiming that consideration of other ancient languages like Arabic could hone the understanding

---

[10] For a recent account of the engagement with the Old Testament in this period, see Ofri Ilany, *In Search of the Hebrew People: Bible and Nation in the German Enlightenment* (Bloomington, IN: Indiana University Press, 2018).

of Hebrew, and called in his influential *Mosaisches Recht* (1770–1) to analyze the laws of the Israelites in light of the East's cultural norms. According to Michaelis, these norms had been determined by the area's climate, tribal customs, the influence of the surrounding oriental peoples and other factors. Michaelis conceived himself primarily not as a theologian, but as a philologist. As such, he saw his main task in the contextualization of the biblical sources:

> Es ist nöthig, daß ich hier die Lebensart erwähne, auf die Moses seinen ganzen Staat gründete, und zugleich anzeige, wie sich seine Gesetze gegen die übrigen Lebensarten verhielten. Weder die Regierungsform, noch auch das, was ich bisher von einigen Grundmaximen des Staats gesagt habe, werden wir hinlänglich verstehen, ohne den Israelitischen Bürger, ohne das Volk zu kennen, welches den Stoff des Staates ausmachte.[11]

> It is necessary that I mention here the way of life on which Moses has founded his entire state, and at the same time indicate how its laws relate to the other forms of life. We can adequately understand neither the form of government, nor what I have previously said concerning some basic principles of the state, if we do not know the Israelite citizens, the people who constituted the fabric of the state.

Michaelis conceived of the Bible as centered on Mosaic laws. He thus aimed at scrutinizing the premises and cultural norms that led to Moses's legal treatise. Moses's treatise has a reciprocal, dynamic relationship with the norms of the culture in which it emerges: it wishes to foster a certain way of life. At the same time, it is shaped and informed by the social norms of the society in which it was conceived. In that latter sense, law is constantly shaped by the people it addresses.

Michaelis's position was influential not only due to its provocative endorsement of an academic, philological approach to Scripture, but also because of the opposing stances that it provoked. Among these was the contention that the Bible should be read like a literary text, that is, regardless of the reader's philological or theological training. One of Michaelis's most vehement opponents was Johann Georg Hamann (1730–88). Hamann made a name for himself despite the fact that he did not complete his academic studies and never held a university position. Residing in Königsberg, home to the prominent philosopher Immanuel Kant, Hamann participated in several of the period's most prominent intellectual polemics. Much of Hamann's writing on Biblical interpretation sets itself in opposition to Michaelis's influential work. The notion that Biblical Hebrew should be restored via philology served as a major point of departure for Hamann, allow-

---

[11] Johann David Michaelis, *Mosaisches Recht*, vol. 1 (Frankfurt a. M.: J. Gottlieb Garbe, 1775), 234. All translations are mine unless otherwise indicated.

ing him to develop his alternative conception of the language as a catalyst of the human imagination in the course of the reading process.

In the context of their ongoing intellectual exchange, Hamann communicated his original notions of scriptural reading to Herder (1744–1803). Changing his place of residence several times – to Riga and Weimar, among others – in his pursuit of a career in the Church, Herder was exposed to the period's innovations in philosophy, literature, and aesthetics. He established his own influence on the aforementioned fields through his friendship and correspondence with such figures as Goethe and Mendelssohn. Herder's wide-ranging works encompassed attempts to clarify the course of world history, polemical writings on the period's aesthetic theory and literature, as well as translations of the Bible and other texts which he held in high regard.

While not discounting the significance of context for the understanding of the Old Testament, for Herder it was not primarily philological erudition that could hone knowledge of ancient Hebrew culture. Rather, he advocated for close attention to the social and cultural norms that led to the text's production. Herder can thus be said to reconcile, in his approach to Biblical Hebrew, Michaelis's perspective that the Hebrew texts could be restored through comprehension of the historical setting from which they emerged with Hamann's emphasis on the individual's engagement with the text. Herder presents scriptural reading as a process of close affective engagement with the Hebrew text in the course of which modern readers put themselves in the shoes of the ancient authors and try to understand the worldview of the target culture. Hamann's original approach to scriptural interpretation as a process whose significance lies in its status as a revelatory experience greatly influenced this intervention into theology.

3 Hamann's Notion of Biblical Hebrew: The Birth of Common Secrets

Describing biblical language as the language of creation, Hamann opens his essay *Aesthetica in Nuce* with the further identification of biblical poetry as the form of the language spoken during humankind's primordial stages. Poetry, writes Hamann in this manifesto, which had significant influence on the *Sturm und Drang* movement, is "the mother tongue of humankind."[12] This assertion emerges

---

[12] Johann Georg Hamann, *Aesthetica in Nuce*, ed. Sven-Aage Jørgensen (Stuttgart: Reclam, 1968), 81 ("Poesie ist die Muttersprache des menschlichen Geschlechts").

as a major presumption guiding Hamann's philosophy of language and approach to the Hebrew language – which have shaped, in turn, his understanding of the hermeneutic act. The moment of the creation of man was the pinnacle of the process of the world's creation, as man stands at its end as the pattern, or the copy, of divine characteristics: "Endlich krönte GOTT die sinnliche Offenbarung seiner Herrlichkeit durch das Meisterstück des Menschen. Er schuf den Menschen in Göttlicher Gestalt."[13] (Finally, God crowned the physical revelation of His grandeur with the masterpiece of man. He created man in the divine image.) At the center of Hamann's notion of creation is the parallel between God and man as creative entities.[14]

The beginning of Hamann's text demonstrates the significance of Hebrew. Hebrew is taken to be a "secret language" in the sense that its so-called incomprehensibleness is a constitutive all-human experience. This conception of the language reconstitutes biblical reading as a newly universal practice: due to Hebrew's initial unapproachability, all readers come to the Bible from a similar starting place.

A prominent aspect of Hamann's approach to Hebrew is related to his use of the word Kabbalah (the sub-title of *Aesthetica in Nuce* is "Eine Rhapsodie in Kabbalistischer Prose"). As noted by Betz, "The word ["Kabbalistic"] is perfectly suited for Hamann's sense of humor, evoking such notions, so antithetical to his 'enlightened' contemporaries, as 'hermeticism,' 'esotericism,' 'cryptography,' and, above all, 'darkness.'"[15] Despite its status as the divine language, the language of Scripture does not exclude the possibility of human comprehension, but is in fact tuned toward it. Hamann develops the notion, most frequently identified with its adaptation by his companion Herder, according to which the Bible should be read as meant for human eyes: "[F]or Hamann the humility of Scripture has another, plainly practical purpose, being suited precisely to accommodate our sensible nature and our intellectual weakness. This is why Scripture is written in a narrative form, and why Christ himself speaks in parables . . ."[16] The Bible represents an invitation to exercise the faith in God through a dynamic process of reading.

---

13 Ibid.
14 As Eva Kocziszky has noted, the creation topos in the text often describes God as a sculptor or a painter. As such, man's creation by God elevates the notion of flesh, thereby implicitly praising human sensuality. "Leib und Schrift in Hamanns *Aesthetica in Nuce*," in Bernhard Gajek, ed., *Die Gegenwärtigkeit Johann Georg Hamanns*, Regensburger Beiträge zur deutschen Sprach- und Literaturwissenschaft (Frankfurt a. M.: Peter Lang, 2005): 145–160.
15 John Betz, *After Enlightenment: The Post-Secular Vision of J.G. Hamann* (Oxford: Wiley-Blackwell, 2009), 101.
16 Ibid., 51.

Biblical interpretation transforms the inability to understand – a so-called human weakness – into a higher mode of "understanding."

Hamann opens the text with two epigraphs: the first from the book of Judges (from the "Song of Deborah"), the other from Job (Elihu's speech). The choice of these specific biblical excerpts underscores his approach to the Bible's so-called ambiguity. Taken from biblical poetry – a genre that is often archaic (or archaizing) – the citations are also enigmatic to readers of Hebrew and to biblical scholars, for they use several words in a manner at odds with their lexical meanings. And yet Hamann includes no translation to the epigrams.

Book of Judges, 5:30.
שלל צבעים רקמה
צבע רקמתים לצוארי שלל:

spoil of dyed stuffs embroidered,
two pieces of dyed work embroidered for my neck as spoil.[17]

Book of Job, 32:19–22.
הנה-בטני כיין לא־יפתח
כאבות חדשים יבקע:
אדברה וירוח לי
אפתח שפתי ואענה:
אל־נא אשא פני־איש
ואל־אדם לא אכנה:
כי לא ידעתי אכנה
כמעט ישאני עשני:

19 My heart is indeed like wine that has no vent;
   like new wineskins, it is ready to burst.
20 I must speak, so that I may find relief;
   I must open my lips and answer.
21 I will not show partiality to any person
   or use flattery towards anyone.
22 For I do not know how to flatter –
   or my Maker would soon put an end to me![18]

Hamann thus begins his own text with a performance of obscurity typical of his entire oeuvre.[19] Thereafter follows a third epigraph, a citation in Latin from the poet Horace: "Odi profanum vulgas et arceo." ("I hate the mob and distance

---

17 The translations to both biblical citations are from the New Revised Standard Version.
18 In *Aesthetica in Nuce*, 79.
19 On Hamann's own writing as performative, and on his original notion of textual interpretation and philology, see Eckhard Schumacher, *Die Ironie der Unverständlichkeit: Johann Georg*

myself from it.")²⁰ By playing familiarity against unfamiliarity, the text wishes to exclude precisely those readers who think that they understand a text by means of merely comprehending the language in which it is written. Hamann's many references to Michaelis in his oeuvre suggest that the target for his critique of the "mob" is this prominent philologist.[21] John Hamilton has argued that both the act of choosing to open his text with Hebrew fragments and the transition to the Horace citation embody the language philosophy that Hamann develops in his essay.[22] As Hamilton points out, Hamann dispels the ease embedded in the feeling of understanding a language: Latin-literate but Hebrew-illiterate readers would be made to feel that they are part of the vulgar crowd. In addition, one should note that in Hamann's text the transition away from Biblical Hebrew is a cipher for the shift from obscurity to clarity – or, at the least, the belief in such clarity. The Latin epigram is followed by Hamann's attack on the period's philologists, who aim to restore Scripture through the assembly of so-called remnants of ancient sources: "Heil dem Erzengel über die Reliquien der Sprache Kanaans!" ("Praise the archangel of the relics over the language of Canaan").

The "obscurity" of Hebrew thus emerges as a cultural trope, a representation with which the reader is now assumed to be familiar. The subsequent process of transcending the written letter builds on the presumption that the gaps in comprehension act as a barrier on a cognitive level, jeopardizing the understanding of the text for *all of its readers*. Hamann conceives of reading Hebrew as a cognitive mechanism relevant for the general audience. In other words, for both Hamann and Herder, the Hebrew Bible becomes a platform for explicating reading techniques as ingrained in a general theory of the reading process and its affective impacts. For Hamann, Hebrew embodies the obscurity of Scripture, an obscurity that continually challenges the confidence of the universal reader as to whether he in fact grasps its content, thereby eliciting understanding that is beyond the literal sense of the word.

The turning of Hebrew into a trope does not of course presume that every reader will now comprehend Hebrew letters, penetrating the Hebrew text and its secrets. It also does not imply that every reader could now understand Hamann's

---

Hamann, Friedrich Schlegel, Jacques Derrida, Paul de Man (Frankfurt a. M.: Suhrkamp, 2000), 109–22.
20 Carmina 3.1.1, in *Aesthetica in Nuce*, 81.
21 On Hamann's continual attacks on Michaelis's studies of the Hebrew language and their centrality to Hamann's rhetoric, see Michael C. Legaspi, *The Death of Scripture and the Rise of Biblical Studies* (Oxford: Oxford University Press, 2010), 162.
22 John Hamilton, "Poetica Obscura: Reexamining Hamann's Contribution to the Pindaric Tradition," *Eighteenth-Century Studies* 34 (2000): 93–115, especially, 93–5.

performative theory of reading. According to Betz, "Hamann was arguably the first to introduce into German letters an intentionally 'sublime style,' characterized like Hebrew poetry by elevated themes, a proliferation of symbolic figures, gnomic allusions, darkness, terseness, and vehemence of expression."[23] Robert Lowth's 1753 *Lectures on the Sacred Poetry of the Hebrews* deeply resonated with Hamann's efforts. Lowth was both a Bishop of the Church of England and a professor of poetry; accordingly, he examined the unique features of Hebrew verse – such as its parallelism, rhythm, and rhyme – as literary devices.[24] It was not only Lowth's methodology of reading the Bible that was received enthusiastically by German theologians, but also the premise that stands behind it: the contention that Hebrew poetry is a refined aesthetic creation.

The transition that takes place in *Aesthetica in Nuce*, via the aesthetic appraisal of the Bible, is the emergence of Hebrew as a trope that depicts the potential existence of a universal community of interpreters. Whereas the notion of Hebrew as a secret language was hardly new in the period, the case of the re-esotericization of the language in the mid-eighteenth century is telling. Against the backdrop of the period's description of human reason as universal, Hamann promotes a mirror phenomenon: an experience of obscurity, which he takes as shared by all readers of the biblical text.

Hamann composes the text as an aesthetic manifesto that connects his theory of an affective connection to Scripture to a theory of reading in general. It was already in his early writings that Hamann declared enthusiastically "Gott ein Schriftsteller!" ("God [is] an author"), and thereby compared the act of divine creation to writing.[25] *Aesthetica in Nuce* thus begins as an attack on the period's attempts to recover the world of the Bible – pertaining especially to the Old Testament – showing, through multiple references to Psalms, that the work of God the creator is shown in creation's fragmented structure. The Hebrew text is an epitome of God's work of creation. Treating Biblical Hebrew as a mere "relic" that could be restored, as does Michaelis, misses the point of recognizing an essential aspect of God's work.

Hamann's text exemplifies reading as a process that continually poses and challenges common assumptions regarding readers' identity and efforts. Hamann views the Bible not as a perfect divine object, but rather as a "human" transmission of the word of God in which errors, fragments, and gaps create moments

---

23 John Betz, *After Enlightenment*, 12.
24 Robert Lowth, *Lectures on the Sacred Poetry of the Hebrews*, ed. and trans. by G. Gregory (Boston: Crocker & Brewster, 1829).
25 Johann Georg Hamann, *Londoner Schriften*, ed. Oswald Bayer and Bernd Weissenborn (München: C.H. Beck, 1993), 59.

of incomprehension. The gaps in human understanding elicit a higher mode of conceiving cultural objects.[26] This mode of reading Scripture by confronting the lack of human knowledge can be described as a kind of leap of faith. A forerunner of religious existentialism (the Danish philosopher Søren Kierkegaard, the most notable representative of this stream of thought, quotes Hamann in an epigraph to his seminal text *Fear and Trembling*), Hamann praises the inspiration that emerges in the act of the creative reconciliation of textual gaps and difficulties through the use of one's imagination.

To Hamann, the interpreter of the Bible must have the courage to become a "Kabbalist," that is, to say more than the text does and utter what the author left unsaid. From the Kabbalah, Hamann derives the notion of the creative and imaginative reading of the Bible. According to his understanding of Kabbalistic reading techniques, interpretation is motivated by spiritual longing, which then yields powerful new connections to additional texts (including literary ones). In Hamann's mind, the power of the Bible lies in its position as an object that kindles the reader's imagination. Evoking this aspect of the Jewish practice of reading, Hamann forms a model of reading the Bible as a point of foci that activates and orchestrates human imagination. The recognition that the Bible is imperfect is highly important to Hamann. Indeed, this perception is a precondition for its role as a mediator of godly communication to humankind. As formulated by Dickson, for Hamann, "[t]he Bible, whatever the source of its inspiration, is written by human authors and is addressed to human beings to evoke a 'human' and personal response. Perfection [. . .] would be inappropriate [. . .] God communicates with us on *our* terms, in *our* fashion, within *our* limitations."[27]

Hamann's inspirational theory of reading embraced the conviction that every reader can engage in interpretation, as the "holy language" was taken to facilitate a common (if, yet, idealized or "sublime") starting-point for all readers. Thus, ironically, Hamman's radical theory of religious conduct through creative and inspirational imagination in fact constitutes a community, based on a presumed shared vocabulary, a vocabulary taken from religious practices – the reading of Hebrew, the secretiveness of the text, faith in God. It is precisely the esoteric and obscure character of Hebrew which invites a universal readership to grapple with its meaning and come to its own individual conclusions. The language points to a paradoxical notion that can be seen as salient to the Enlightenment heritage: that of a collective individuality.

---

26 See Gwen Griffith Dickson, *Johann Georg Hamann's Relational Metacriticism* (Berlin: Walter de Gruyter, 1995), 189.
27 Ibid., 132.

Hamann holds that one's perspective on the text is contingent upon one's particular life circumstances. He regards reading as a praxis that reciprocally constitutes the reader and the Bible. This radically "human" perception of divine language is, in effect, what mediated and enabled, in turn, Herder's famous and influential insistence upon reading the Bible as a "human" text. Hamann and Herder's mutual influence, the similarities and differences between their approaches, and their historical influence upon Enlightenment theology shed light on the cultivation of the Bible as a cultural artifact.

4 Herder's Notion of Biblical Reading: Between Theology and Anthropology

For both Hamann and Herder, it is the view of Hebrew as initially opaque that elicits a new, universalistic theory of reading. Whereas Hamann relies on this premise to develop a theory of a subjective and imaginative engagement with the Scripture, Herder, as we shall see, portrays Hebrew's enigmatic nature as a constructive challenge to human reason. In Herder's interpretation theory, Hebrew is emblematic of the need to understand a foreign culture in its historical and ethnographical context, in order to hone the comprehension of its cultural objects. Conceiving the Bible as a cultural object of universal relevance, Herder presents the question of how to read Hebrew as exemplary of the deciphering of an object foreign to the reader's own culture. In fact, it was already Hamann who defined in his early work on biblical interpretation the principle of empathy as seminal to reading in general. Written during the sudden religious conversion he experienced while in England in 1758, Hamann asserts in his London writings that affects should play a central role in biblical interpretation. Affect, in his view, is transferred between authors and readers through what Hamann describes as "Die Notwendigkeit uns als Leser in die Empfindung[en] des Schriftstellers, den wir vor uns haben, zu versetzen uns einer Verfaßung so viel möglich zu nähern. . . . ("the necessity as readers to immerse ourselves in the feeling[s] of the author whom we have before us, in order to come as close as possible to his state of mind").[28]

Furthermore, Hamann believes that "Einbildungskraft" (force of imagination) is a leading principle of this empathic process.[29] This conviction can be said

---

28 Johann Georg Hamann, *Londoner Schriften*, 66.
29 Ibid.

to have influenced Herder's more paradigmatic contention that the ancient, biblical text can and should be understood in the context in which it was composed. Despite its fragmented nature and linguistic obscurity, and notwithstanding the discrepancy between its cultural background and that of its modern readers, the Hebrew Bible can be made more approachable to the modern reader. Affective identification plays a seminal role in this process for Herder as well. Yet, a major difference between them lies in his view of biblical reading as a process that yields progress *toward an objective truth*, insofar as the reader gets closer to the authors' original meanings.

This view is expressed, for instance, in Herder's 1767–8 *Fragments on Recent German Literature*. Engaged with textual interpretation in general, this work explicates how the meaning of texts is modulated through time, through discussion of the difficulties of translating the Old Testament into German. Herder discusses Hebrew in the context of his thesis concerning the development of language from its childhood to its later stages. The early stages in a language's development parallel the primeval phase in the life of the nation that produced this language.[30] The antiquity of Hebrew thus results in meanings that are not immediately comprehensible to the modern reader. The ancient authors of the Bible scrupulously expressed with the vocabulary available to them their impressions of the world. Much of what they intended is no longer accessible to modern readers – a key example being their descriptions of nature and animals – which creates a problem for biblical translators.[31]

Another important principle that Herder shares with Hamann is the idea that the Bible is a text that was written for humans by humans, and that it should be read and interpreted as such. Herder thus develops an elaborate commentary on Hebrew poetry, applauding its aesthetic and historiographical value. His broad engagement with Hebrew verse, which extends to several volumes, thus strives to maintain the spiritual stature of the Bible, while at the same time developing a new, historiographical approach to the text. The divine, in this project, is embodied in the cognitive process of apprehending the thoughts of the ancient authors, witnessing God's greatness in His ability to be materialized in human form through the text of the Bible. Herder's view that the Bible should be read as a human artifact was strongly influenced by Hamann's earlier insistence that the Bible is a human text – a text that represents the divine at the same time that it addresses humankind, in its language. "[B]ei Gott ist Alles ein ewiger, vollkom-

---

[30] Johann Gottfried Herder, *Frühe Schriften 1764–1772*, ed. Ulrich Gaier (Frankfurt a. M.: Deutscher Klassiker Verlag [DKV], 1985), 182.
[31] Ibid., 195–197.

mener Gedanke: und in diesem Verstande einen Gedanken, ein Wort der Bibel Göttlich nennen, ist die größte Hyperbel von Anthropomorphismus," writes Herder at the beginning of his *On the First Document of Humankind*. ("With God, everything is an eternal and perfect thought, and in this sense, calling a word or a thought from the Bible divine is the grandest hyperbole of anthropomorphism.") Reading the Bible as God's word in its literality would thus be "Unsinn, Vergötterung einer Menschlichen Seele" ("nonsense, the divinization of the human soul"): an act that would contradict reason.[32] In light of the lack of means for understanding the divine, readers should instead seek a better understanding of the "human" aspects of the text: " . . . so lange wir keine Göttliche Grammatik, Logik, und Metaphysik haben; so lange wollen wir also auch Menschlich auslegen. Sprache, Zeiten, Sitten, Nation, Schriftsteller, Zusammenhang – alles, wie in einem Menschlichen Buche" ("so long as we do not have a godly grammar, logic, and metaphysics, we want to interpret [everything] in a human manner. Language, time, customs, nation, authors, context – everything, just like in a human book.")[33]

Understood via a process of reflection that does not require prior knowledge, the Hebrew language is a means of preserving both the "human" nature of the Bible, and its divine standing. Hebrew is a universal asset in the sense that it can be approached in the same manner by all readers, regardless of their level of education or ethnic identity. This feature of the language is shared between Hamann and Herder, insofar as it evokes a relational coexistence with God for Hamann, and insofar that for Herder the process of reading the Bible through reasoning is guided by the Protestant principle according to which the Bible itself holds the key to how it should be read.

As Spinoza demonstrated in his *Political-Theological Treatise*, human reason can be exercised through the reading of the Scripture. The success of Herder's hermeneutics lies in its ability to reconcile this contention with the religious view of the Bible as a divine artifact. The assumption that readers share similar tendencies – such as the understanding of a text in its cultural context – preconditions Herder's methodology. For this reconciliation to work, it was not enough to blur the distinction between factuality and fact-likeness, insisting that both should be interpreted in light of the cultural conventions at the time of the writing of the Hebrew Bible. A significant additional component of Herder's hermeneutics is an idealized conception of Hebrew and of philology. Herder holds that identifica-

---

32 Johann Gottfried Herder, *Schriften zum Alten Testament*, ed. Rudolf Smend (Frankfurt a. M.: Deutscher Klassiker Verlag [DKV], 1993), 28.
33 Ibid., 29.

tion with the Hebrews is essential to the "historical" understanding of the Bible. He thus echoes the period's philological attempts to offer new insight into the Old Testament, while yet preserving, through his notion of affective empathy, the standing of the text as supreme and faultless.

This effort reiterates the vision of philological recovery proposed by Michaelis. Nonetheless, there is a major difference between the two. In accordance with his position as a Protestant theologian, Herder's theory of biblical interpretation applies to each and every reader of the Bible. Thus, Herder's notion of the so-called historical understanding of Hebrew does not require the readers to learn the language. His proposed methodology of attending to authors' cultural norms and historical background can be followed by all readers. Similarly, the general reader is also capable of following Herder's aesthetic readings of biblical poetry by attending to such features as parallelism, repetition, and rhythm. In this way, Herder's examinations of Hebrew do not highlight its philological aspects, for they at the same time convey that the text can be interpreted by any reader, regardless of scholarly training, thanks to common-sense apprehension of the circumstances in which the text was produced. Hebrew consequently emerges as a language that is decipherable by all readers.

These interpretive principles reach their mature formulation in Herder's 1783 text *On the Spirit of Hebrew Poetry*. There, Herder contends that the Hebrews' "Denkart" (way of thinking) can be unveiled through the close examination of this people's poetry.[34] The presumption is that the Old Testament is a uniquely refined aesthetic artifact and that it can therefore serve effectively to examine the expression of a people's spirit. *On the Spirit of Hebrew Poetry* explains the purpose of studying the Old Testament in a dual apologia whose two parts are at odds with one another. First, Hebrew poetry, Herder explains, is not barbaric, primitive and inferior as one may think. It is an apt object for readers of poetry. Second, one should understand Hebrew poetry in order to understand the roots of the New Testament (whose importance to humanity Herder does not need to state): "Studiere man also das A.T., auch nur als ein menschliches Buch voll alter Poesien, mit Lust und Liebe; so wird uns das Neue in seiner Reinheit, seinem hohen Glanz, seiner überirdischen Schönheit von selbst aufgehn." ("If we study the Old Testament, even only as a human book filled with old poems, with love and desire, then the New [Testament] will rise for us by itself, in all its purity, high glory and celestial beauty").[35]

---

[34] Ibid., 666.
[35] Ibid., 670.

The text takes the form of a platonic dialogue between Alciphron, a young scholar who dismisses Hebrew as a barbaric language, and Eutyphron, who proves his companion wrong by pointing out to him Hebrew's various merits. Against the accusation of Hebrew's shortage in nouns, Eutyphron makes the point that their relatively small number only highlights the importance of verbs for this language. Hebrew thus appears to hold unique poetic attributes, since the high ratio of verbs to nouns fosters a feeling of continual motion ("Handlung," i.e., sustained development of the plot).[36] Similarly, the accusation that the parallelism of Hebrew poetry reflects simplicity of thought (and that it has a tedious effect on the reader) meets Herder's praise of symmetry as operating effectively on the human senses. Hebrew poetry exemplifies poetry's ability to provoke emotional rapport: "Für den Verstand allein dichtet die Poesie nicht, sondern zuerst und zunächst für die Empfindung" (Poetry does not resound for understanding alone, but first and foremost for feeling.).[37]

5 Judaism and the Command of Hebrew

In his writings on the Bible, Herder distinguishes between Hebrew as an ancient language, spoken by the ancient Hebrews, and the language's continued presence in modern Judaism. Thus, Eutyphron replies to his young companion's claim, according to which the language was preserved by the rabbis who kept speaking it, that it was not "pearls" that these had in their mouths:

> ... auch leider nicht nach dem Genius ihrer uralten Bildung. Das arme Volk war in die Welt zerstreut: Die meisten bildeten also ihren Ausdruck nach dem Genius der Sprachen, unter denen sie lebten, und es ward ein trauriges Gemisch, an das wir hier nicht denken mögen. Wir reden vom Ebräischen, da es die lebendige Sprache Kanaans war, und auch hier nur von ihren schönsten reinsten Zeiten ...[38]

And nor, unfortunately, were [their words] in accordance with the genius of their primeval education. The poor nation has been dispersed in the world: most of them thus shaped their way of expression according to the genius of the languages among which they lived, and it was a sad mixture, about which we would prefer not to think here. We are instead talking about Hebrew when it was the living language of Canaan, and even here, only about its most beautiful and purest times ...

---

36 Ibid., 674–675.
37 Ibid., 686.
38 Ibid., 678.

Herder's fullest account of the aesthetic supremacy of Hebrew thus distinguished between different cultural eras. Hebrew was at its peak when it functioned as a national language and it lost its beauty when the Jews were dispersed in the diaspora.

Expressed in many of his texts, and most famously in the *Treatise on the Origins of Language*, Herder described linguistic capacities as relying upon the bodily linguistic apparatus. The distinct bodily structure of a race – a structure that is shaped by many factors including climate and geography – is reflected in the particular structure of national languages. The statement that contemporary or medieval Jews do not use the same language as the ancient Hebrews thus marks them as inherently different and inferior from the ancient Hebrew people. This distinction thus seems at odds with Herder's treatment of Judaism elsewhere as a national entity that has existed since antiquity.[39]

As John Baildam has argued, "in an age which considered Hebrew poetry barbaric [...] Herder was unique with his plea that poetry in general was divine revelation, and that the Hebrew poetry of the Bible was the epitome of all poetry."[40] The important role that Hebrew plays in Herder's aesthetic theory marks nonetheless only a brief phase of the language's overall history: that which the theologian defines as the golden age of Hebrew poetry. This distinction is crucial in regard to Herder's perception of modern-day Jews. The Jews are guilty of linguistic hybridity, which disrupts the correlation of language to national culture.[41] Their daily use of the vernaculars of their respective places of residence interferes with their theological cultivation of Hebrew. Modern Jews weaken in this way Hebrew's national grounding and corrupt the language. Their linguistic hybridity is thus reflective of the deterioration of the Jews' national position: they are no longer members of an independent people nor are they fully immersed in modern states.

---

39 See F.M. Barnard, *Herder on Nationality, Humanity, and History* (Montreal: McGill-Queen's University Press, 2003), 17–20.

40 John D. Baildam, *Paradisal Love: Johann Gottfried Herder and the Song of Songs* (Sheffield: Sheffield Academic Press, 1999), 54.

41 Herder compares Jews elsewhere to nomadic peoples whose presence in Europe he sees as destructive: "Die Erhaltung der Juden erklärt sich eben so natürlich, als die Erhaltung der Bramanen, Parsen und Zigeuner" ["The preservation of the Jews can be explained just as naturally as the preservation of the Brahmans, Persians and Gypsies"] (Johann Gottfried Herder, *Ideen zur Philosophie der Geschichte der Menschheit*, ed. Martin Bollacher (Frankfurt a. M.: Deutscher Klassiker Verlag [DKV], 1989), 491. See ibid., 703 for a critique of the harmful presence of nomads on the European continent.

6 Conclusion

The treatment of Biblical Hebrew in early Romantic circles exemplifies, in sum, the intricacies of establishing the modern conception of humanity upon the globalization of theological practices, and, particularly, of scriptural interpretation. In his writings on Hebrew, Hamann insists on the role of imagination, personal inspiration, and faith, which readers employ as they fill in the gaps in the biblical text. Herder, on the other hand, presents biblical reading as a process of retrieving the particular historical conditions that led to the writing of the Bible. Herder developed a set of interpretive practices that aimed to scrutinize the cultural context of the composition of Hebrew Scripture. The attempts during the 1760s and 70s to reimagine and idealize the Hebrew language were essential steps in establishing a grand narrative of a system of nations. In this process, seemingly opposing approaches to the Hebrew Bible were combined with one another, creating an infrastructure that tethers interpretation to a universalistic understanding of biblical reading.

Insofar as it engaged with biblical interpretation continually, and expressed its innovations through biblical exegesis, late Enlightenment philosophy relied at its core upon religious ideology. Thus, as modern hermeneutics was becoming a dominant cultural practice, biblical interpretation served as the concrete field with which to establish reading as a form of interpersonal deciphering. The public appeal to dialogism is sustained through the belief in every person's aptitude to read and interpret, "abilities" that at times mask the fact that other conditions are required for embarking on a cultural dialogue. Readers of the Bible who used it to develop hermeneutics as a cultural phenomenon had to develop a Bible that everyone could interpret in the same manner: a Bible that could be a model for interpretation. The Bible could be perceived in the same manner "for everyone" through such means as emphasis on a text's style, literary devices, and the historical circumstances of its writing. The extensive engagement with the Hebrew language in the late eighteenth century was emblematic of this effort: it promoted a universalized approach to the language through such distinct forms as Hamann's construction of obscurity through Hebrew and Herder's new model of deciphering the Bible through the attention to its cultural context. The manifold perspectives on Hebrew as a cultural asset thus yielded two major stances in the period's philosophical climate: Hamann's invitation to endorse faith as an inseparable part of the human apparatus and Herder's model of adhering to affect as a companion to reason. Distinguishing himself from Hamann, Herder established his pivotal model of constructive intellectual reasoning: textual interpretation that promoted the period's interest in aesthetics, interpersonal exchange, and human empathy.

Bibliography

Baildam, John D. *Paradisal Love: Johann Gottfried Herder and the Song of Songs*. Sheffield: Sheffield Academic Press, 1999.
Barnard, F.M. *Herder on Nationality, Humanity, and History*. Montreal: McGill-Queen's University Press, 2003.
Beiser, Frederick. *Enlightenment, Revolution, and Romanticism: The Genesis of Modern German Political Thought, 1790–1800*. Cambridge, MA: Harvard University Press, 1992.
Betz, John. *After Enlightenment: The Post-secular Vision of J.G. Hamann*. Oxford: Wiley-Blackwell, 2009.
Dickson, Gwen Griffith. *Johann Georg Hamann's Relational Metacriticism*. Berlin: Walter de Gruyter, 1995.
Dupré, Louis. *The Enlightenment and the Intellectual Foundations of Modern Culture*. New Haven, CT: Yale University Press, 2004.
Frei, Hans. *The Eclipse of Biblical Narrative*. New Haven, CT: Yale University Press, 1974.
Gay, Peter. *The Enlightenment, An Interpretation*: *The Rise of Modern Paganism*. New York: W. W. Norton & Company, 1966.
Hamann, Johann Georg. *Aesthetica in Nuce*, ed. Sven-Aage Jørgensen. Stuttgart: Reclam, 1968.
Hamann, Johann Georg. *Londoner Schriften*, ed. Oswald Bayer and Bernd Weissenborn. München: C.H. Beck, 1993.
Hamilton, John. "Poetica Obscura: Reexamining Hamann's Contribution to the Pindaric Tradition." *Eighteenth-Century Studies* 34 (2000): 93–115.
Herder, Johann Gottfried. *Frühe Schriften 1764–1772*, ed. Ulrich Gaier. Frankfurt a. M.: Deutscher Klassiker Verlag [DKV], 1985.
Herder, Johann Gottfried. *Ideen zur Philosophie der Geschichte der Menschheit*, ed. Martin Bollacher. Frankfurt a. M.: Deutscher Klassiker Verlag [DKV], 1989.
Ilany, Ofri. *In Search of the Hebrew People: Bible and Nation in the German Enlightenment*. Bloomington, IN: Indiana University Press, 2018.
Kocziszky, Eva. "Leib und Schrift in Hamanns *Aesthetica in Nuce*." In *Die Gegenwärtigkeit Johann Georg Hamanns*, edited by Bernhard Gajek, 145–160. Regensburger Beiträge zur deutschen Sprach- und Literaturwissenschaft. Frankfurt a. M.: Peter Lang, 2005.
Legaspi, Michael C. *The Death of Scripture and the Rise of Biblical Studies*. Oxford: Oxford University Press, 2010.
Lowth, Robert. *Lectures on the Sacred Poetry of the Hebrews*, ed. and trans. G. Gregory. Boston: Crocker & Brewster, 1829.
Michaelis, Johann David. *Mosaisches Recht*, Vol. 1. Frankfurt a. M.: J. Gottlieb Garbe, 1775.
Olender, Maurice. *The Languages of Paradise: Race, Religion, and Philology in the Nineteenth Century*, trans. Arthur Goldhammer. Cambridge, MA: Harvard University Press, 1992.
Schumacher, Eckhard. *Die Ironie der Unverständlichkeit: Johann Georg Hamann, Friedrich Schlegel, Jacques Derrida, Paul de Man*. Frankfurt a. M.: Suhrkamp, 2000.
Sheehan, Jonathan. "Enlightenment Details: Theology, Natural History, and the Letter h." *Representations* 61 (1998): 29–56.

Sheehan, Jonathan. *The Enlightenment Bible: Translation, Scholarship, Culture*. Princeton, NJ: Princeton University Press, 2005.
Sorkin, David. *The Religious Enlightenment: Protestants, Jews, and Catholics from London to Vienna*. Princeton: Princeton University Press, 2008.
Weidner, Daniel. *Bibel und Literatur um 1800*. München: Wilhelm Fink, 2011.

Thomas Willi
Dalman als Aramaist: Auf der Suche nach der Sprache der neutestamentlichen Welt

1 Gustaf Dalman: Von Leipzig über Jerusalem nach Greifswald

Hebräische Sprache und jüdische Tradition im Spiegel christlicher Rezeption – das ist auch nach dem fulminanten Start im humanistischen Italien der Renaissance eine vielschichtige und tief gründende Geschichte geblieben. Wenn man von einem zweiten Höhepunkt des Prozesses im 17.-18. Jahrhundert, dem *Philosemitismus im Barock*,[1] sprechen kann, so folgt im 19. Jahrhundert die „dritte Welle". Ihr sind Franz Delitzsch und in seinem Gefolge auch Gustaf Hermann Dalman,[2] nach dem das ab Februar 1922 in Greifswald eingerichtete Institut[3] seit 1925 benannt ist, zuzurechnen. Sie sieht sich doppelt herausgefordert: Im Umfeld der christlichen Theologie löst sich das bislang unhinterfragt bestehende Band zwischen Bibelwissenschaft und Judaistik, im Blick auf das Judentum findet sie sich konfrontiert mit Emanzipation und Zionismus, aber auch einer neu entstehenden jüdischen Wissenschaft vom Judentum, wie sie in Deutschland durch Forscher wie Leopold Zunz, Abraham Geiger, Hirsch Heinrich Graetz, repräsentiert wird. Von besonderem Interesse sind daher die Kontakte Dalmans mit jüdischen Gelehrten in Europa und in Palästina (Immanuel Löw, Josef Klausner, Samuel

---

[1] H.J. Schoeps eröffnet seine Untersuchung *Philosemitismus im Barock* (1952) S. 1, indem er fünf Ausprägungen unterscheidet, nämlich die „christlich-missionarische", die „biblisch-chiliastische", die „utilitaristische", die „liberal-humanitäre" sowie den „religiösen Typus des Philosemitismus".
[2] Dalmans Leben und Wirken ist erschlossen durch J. Männchen. Neben einer Fülle von Einzeluntersuchungen und -aufsätzen sei hier nur verwiesen auf ihre grundlegenden Untersuchungen *Gustaf Dalmans Leben und Wirken in der Brüdergemeine, für die Judenmission und an der Universität Leipzig 1855–1902*: ADPV 9/1(1987); *Gustaf Dalman als Palästinawissenschaftler in Jerusalem und Greifswald: 1902–1941*: ADPV 9/2 (1993); „Gustaf Dalman – auf der Grenze : Leben und Forschen zwischen Kirche und Wissenschaft," in: T. Beyrich, I. Garbe, T. Willi (Hg.), *Greifswalder theologische Profile*: GThF 12 (2006), S. 109–126.
[3] Dazu J. Männchen, *Das Herz zieht nach Jerusalem – Gustaf Dalman zum 150. Geburtstag* (2005) S. 16–18.

Klein u. a.), wie sie durch Bezugnahmen, vor allem aber Briefe, Widmungen und Autoreneinträge[4] in den Bänden der Dalmansammlung dokumentiert sind.[5]

Überhaupt ist die kleine, aber feine Judaica-Bibliothek der Dalmansammlung der geeignetste Weg, um Dalman und sein Werk zu verstehen. Dalman tritt uns als eine höchst profilierte und eigenständige Persönlichkeit vor Augen. Zwei Faktoren haben dazu beigetragen. Da ist einmal sein *Verhältnis zur Herrnhuter Brüdergemeine*, aus der er kommt, und da ist zum anderen die *Beziehung zu Franz Delitzsch* (23.2.1813–4.3.1890), der sein väterlicher Mentor und Freund wird. Beide Faktoren spielen für Dalmans Zugang zum Judentum eine aussschlaggebende Rolle und können als „challenges" gelten, auf die Dalman mit seiner unverwechselbar eigenständigen „response" reagiert.

---

4 Dazu T. Willi, „Gustaf Dalman und Joseph Klausner. Christliche Judentums- und Palästinawissenschaft im Spiegel unveröffentlichter handschriftlicher Widmungen eines zeitgenössischen jüdischen Forschers", in: M. Witte/T. Pilger (Hg.), *Mazel tov*: SKI.NF 1, Leipzig (2012) 247–264.

5 Die Dalmansammlung hat auch ihre örtliche Vorgeschichte. Dazu gehören entsprechende Initiativen, die *vor* und insofern auch *hinter* der Einrichtung des Instituts stehen und die ihrerseits Schritte christlicher Aufnahme und Erforschung des Judentums repräsentieren. Eine Frucht des erwähnten barocken Philosemitismus war etwa die *Lehrsynagoge*, die Christoph Wallich im Übergang vom 17. zum 18. Jhd. im Auftrag des als Kämpfers gegen den noch jungen Pietismus bekannten Greifswalder Theologen Johann Friedrich Mayer (1650–1712) in dessen Haus am Platz des heutigen Universitätskanzleramts mit grösster halachischer Akribie aufgebaut, eingerichtet und in einem in Greifswald erschienenen Werk, einer Art „Synagogenführer", mit dem ausführlichen barocken Titel *Beyt ha-Kneset shel ha-Ga'on ha-Raw ha-Gadol Resch Metiwta we-Kohen Gadol Kawod Moreynu ha-Raw Rabbi Mayer Natrey Rachamana u-Barchey ha-Schochen beha-Jeschiwa Greifswalde, Oder Die Mayerische Synagoga in Greiffswalde zum Nutzen der studirenden Jugend auffgerichtet*, Greifswald, G.H. Adolphi (1708) ausführlich beschrieben hat. Eine zweite Auflage erschien 1712 in Helmstedt, eine dritte 1715 in Braunschweig, letztere mit einem „curieusen Anhang", einem Florilegium, „Darin 74. Talmudische Moralen, die mit Christi Lehr wohl übereinstimmen ... colligirt (und) in Ubersetzung" dargeboten und mit den einschlägigen Stellen des NTs verglichen werden. – Auch die mit dem Namen von Johann Gottfried Ludwig Kosegarten verbundene Greifswalder Orientalistik im beginnenden 19. Jhd hatte das Judentum mit im Blick; ihr ist wohl mindestens das eine der beiden Sifre Tora zu verdanken ist, die der Greifswalder Universitätsbibliothek gehören und die in einem Schrank der Abteilung „Altes Buch" bis vor etwa 20 Jahren durch einen Dornröschenschlaf vor den inzwischen über Land und Stadt hinweggezogenen mörderischen und vernichtenden Zeitläuften bewahrt waren. Vgl. dazu die grundlegende Studie von C. Böttrich, Die Geschichte der Mayerschen Lehrsynagoge, in: C. Böttrich/T. K. Kuhn/D. Stein Kokin (Hg.), *Die Greifswalder Lehrsynagoge Johann Friedrich Mayers: ein Beispiel christlicher Rezeption des Judentums im 18. Jahrhundert*, Leipzig 2016, 187–245.

a) Herrnhut

Den *herrnhutischen "approach"* zum Judentum hat der am 9. Juni 1855 in Niesky Geborene nie verleugnet. Der im dortigen Pädagogium Geschulte und am Theologischen Seminar in Gnadenfeld Ausgebildete und dort selbst von 1881 bis 1887 als Dozent Tätige hat ihm seinen Tribut gezollt in einer Studie über „Graf Zinzendorf und die Juden".[6] Darin schimmert insofern bereits Dalmans Position durch, wenn er zusammenfasst: „Zinzendorf (hat) das Judentum, *sofern es das Alte Testament repräsentiert,* anerkannt, zugleich aber geltend gemacht, das Wichtigste sei im Alten Testament, dass es die Menschwerdung Gottes ankündigt ... "[7] Was bei aller Seltsamkeit der bei den Herrnhutern gepflegten *philosemitischen* Tradition besonders im judaisierenden bzw. judenmissionarisch motivierten *Liedgut* gültig war und blieb, war der erklärte Wille, *über die Sprache* der jüdischen Tradition und dem aktuellen jüdischen Leben näher zu kommen, wodurch dann automatisch das überkommene antijüdische Ressentiment wenigstens ein Stück weit in Frage gestellt wurde.

Diese Glaubensprägung spornt denn auch den sehr früh alttestamentlich wie judaistisch hervortretenden Gustaf Dalman zu seinen hebraistischen und semitistischen Sprachstudien an.

b) Franz Delitzsch

Von ganz anderer Seite her, aber in gleicher Richtung, wirkte der schon vom Gymnasiasten Gustaf Marx[8] mit ersten Versuchen einer Übersetzung von Evangelientexten ins Hebräische 1871 gesuchte Kontakt zu Franz Delitzsch. Delitzsch, der nicht in der Brüdergemeine, sondern im konservativen Luthertum beheimatet war, wurde nicht bloss „mein bester Berater" für sein hebräisches Studium,[9] sondern begleitete ihn schon in der Gnadenfelder Zeit und bahnte ihm vor allem dann beim Ausscheiden aus der Brüdergemeine den Weg in die Judenmission und in die Universität. Dalman hat Delitzschs „theologische Grundhaltung", die, wie sein

---

6 Zuerst erschienen in: Saat auf Hoffnung 26 (1889) und 27 (1890), zum Gedenken von Zinzendorfs 200. Geburtstag 1900 wieder abgedruckt in: G. Dalman und A. Schulze, *Zinzendorf und Lieberkühn. Studien zur Geschichte der Judenmission: Schriften des Institutum Judaicum in Berlin* 32 (1903) S. 5–51.
7 A.a.O. S. 45 (Kursivierung tw).
8 Ab 1886 nennt sich der 1855 als Gustaf Marx Geborene aus Pietät gegenüber seiner 1870 verstorbenen Mutter und ihrer schwedischen Familie Gustaf Dalman.
9 G. Dalman in: Die Religionswissenschaft der Gegenwart, in *Selbstdarstellungen*, hrsg. von E. Stange (1928) Bd. 4 S. 4.

Biograph bemerkt, „Philologie sozusagen mit Theologie tauft",[10] grundsätzlich geteilt.[11]

Delitzsch seinerseits nimmt, zusammen mit einer Reihe namhafter Exegeten aus seiner Schule wie etwa Eduard König[12] oder Hermann L. Strack,[13] insofern eine zwar anachronistische, aber keineswegs eine überholte Position ein. Denn ihre *unzeitgemässen Forschungen* weisen – wenn man auf den Neuansatz christlicher Theologie nach dem Zweiten Weltkrieg und die ihr eigene Zuwendung zum Judentum blickt – durchaus avantgardistische Züge auf und bereiten *neuen judaistischen Fragestellungen* den Weg – verfrüht könnte man im Blick auf die Entwicklungen des 20. Jhd.s sagen.[14] Sie können jedenfalls als ein Fanal gegen eine isolierte, von der jüdischen völlig absehende Betrachtungsweise des Alten und *mutatis mutandis* des Neuen Testaments verstanden werden.

Delitzsch hat als den Schlüssel seiner biblisch-theologischen Haltung mit ihrer Zuwendung zum Judentum „diejenige Liebe zu Israel, welche Jesusliebe zu ihrer Wurzel hat ... " bezeichnet.[15] Das gilt für Dalman nicht weniger als für seinen

---

10 S. Wagner, *Franz Delitzsch. Leben und Werk* ¹(1978) S. 190. – Über dieses Standardwerk hinaus s. zu Delitzsch D. Mathias, „Das Alte Testament in Lehre und Forschung an der Theologischen Fakultät Leipzig", in: A. Gössner und A. Wieckowski (Hg.), *Die Theologische Fakultät der Universität Leipzig*: BLUWiG Reihe A Bd. 2 (2005) S. 397.400–404 und R. Smend, „Franz Delitzsch – Aspekte von Leben und Werk", in: A.C. Hagedorn und H. Pfeiffer (Hg.), *Die Erzväter in der biblischen Tradition*, FS M. Köckert: BZAW 400 (2009) S. 347–366, dem sich Delitzschs Bild streckenweise durchaus „verdunkelt", aber „gegen Ende wieder heller" wird (S. 354): vgl. zur Einschätzung Delitzschs vor allem das ausführliche Zitat von David Kaufmann S. (359) 360–362.
11 Zum Schritt von Gnadenfeld nach Leipzig, den dortigen akademischen Qualifikationen und einer Würdigung von Dalmans Tätigkeit an dem von Delitzsch 1886 gegründeten *Institutum Judaicum* vgl. neben den oben in Anm. 2 genannten Untersuchungen von J. Männchen noch T. Willi, „Christliche Rezeption des Judentums in Greifswald – Judenmission, Palästinawissenschaft und Aramaistik bei Gustaf Dalman": Judaica 66 (2010) 18–28.
12 Eine einfühlsame Skizze des fachlich, theologisch und menschlich bedeutenden Einzelgängers bei U. Rüterswörden, „Eduard König (1846–1936)", in: R. Schmidt-Rost, S. Bitter und M. Dutzmann (Hg.), *Theologie als Vermittlung. Bonner evangelische Theologen des 19. Jhds. im Porträt*, FS F. Wintzer: AThG 6 (2003) S. 172–177.
13 Zu ihm vgl. P. von der Osten-Sacken, „Liebe, mehr noch: Gerechtigkeit. Hermann Leberecht Strack und das Institutum Judaicum in Berlin in ihrem Verhältnis zum Judentum" : Judaica 66 (2010) 40–71.
14 Dazu W. Wiefel, „Von Strack zu Jeremias. Der Anteil der neutestamentlichen Wissenschaft an der Vorgeschichte der evangelischen Judaistik", in: K. Nowak/G. Raulet (Hg.), *Protestantismus und Antisemitismus in der Weimarer Republik* (1994) S. 95–125.
15 Christentum und jüdische Presse. Selbsterlebtes von F.D., in *Saat auf Hoffnung* 19 (1882) S. 83–146, separat erschienen Erlangen (1882); das Zitat a.a.O. S. 85f., vgl. S. Wagner, Franz Delitzsch S. 409.

Mentor. Dennoch schlägt er philologisch einen anderen Weg ein und vertritt eine alternative Position.

2 Aramaistik statt Hebraistik

Dalman kam zu einer Zeit nach Leipzig, als sich Delitzschs Leben bereits seinem Ende zuneigte, und dieser hat ihm das Herzstück seines Lebens und Wirkens als Vermächtnis überantwortet: die „judenmissionarisch" abgezweckte Übersetzung des Neuen Testaments ins Hebräische. Gerade dadurch ist Dalman paradoxerweise zum bahnbrechenden Aramaisten geworden! Die Auseinandersetzung ist keineswegs eine persönliche, sondern eine sachlich-wissenschaftliche, und sie wurzelt in einer Perspektive, die in die Anfangszeiten der neuzeitlichen Hebraistik *wie* der Aramaistik zurückreicht und die ihren Ausgang ganz konkret im Schaffen und Werk Sebastian Münsters nimmt.

a) Das Neue Testament auf Hebräisch – aber in welchem Hebräisch?

Die Vorgeschichte von Delitzschs *Ha-Brit ha-Ḥadaschah* reicht bis zu Sebastian Münster (1488–1552) zurück. 1537 veröffentlichte er in Basel das *Evangelium secundum Matthæum in lingua Hebraica* unter dem ominösen Titel Torat ha-Maschiaḥ.[16] In seinem Vorwort empfahl er diese sprachliche Form ausdrücklich als *nativa sua hoc est Hebraica lingua*.

Damit war nicht bloss eine Behauptung in die Welt gesetzt, sondern gleichzeitig eine Diskussion entfacht, die noch bei Delitzsch und Dalman nachwirkt und der unterschiedlichen Stellungnahme der beiden zugrunde liegt. Münsters Ausgabe gehört zu den drei von ihm veröffentlichten Werken mit christlich-apologetisch bzw. antijüdisch-polemischer Stossrichtung.[17] Das dürfte die im Titel

---

16 Bibliographie dazu und zu den weiteren Basler Auflagen von 1557 und 1582 bei J. Prijs und B. Prijs, *Die Basler hebräischen Drucke* (1964) Nr. 48 S. 82f.; Nr. 99 S. 143f.; Nr. 135 S. 228 sowie zur Herkunft des Textes Beilage 19 S. 500. – Zum Umfeld der Münsterschen Unternehmens wie zum Folgenden vgl. R. Flogaus, „Hebraica Christiana. Christliche Texte in hebräischer Sprache und ihre Verwendung in Schule und Mission (1475–1555)", in: M. Witte/T. Pilger (Hg.), *Mazel tov*, Leipzig (2012) 143–176. Füge Hinweis auf den Artikel von Lange in diesem Band ein!
17 Die beiden anderen sind seine Ausgabe des Alten Testaments (Basel 1534), die erste in Basel gedruckte vollständige hebräische Bibel, und die Schrift „Messias Christianorum et Iudaeorum hebraicè & latinè" (Basel 1539), vgl. dazu J. Prijs und B. Prijs, D*ie Basler hebräischen Drucke* (1964) S. 92 zu Nr. 57.

vertretene These mit motiviert haben, das *Hebräische* habe als die dem Neuen Testament aufgrund seiner jüdischen Herkunft *angeborene* (lat. *nativa*) Sprache zu gelten.

Der damit erhobene Anspruch hielt sich mehr oder minder bis zu Delitzschs Übersetzung.[18] Die Beweggründe, das Neue Testament ins Hebräische zu übersetzen, dürften wie schon bei Ibn Schaprut und Sebastian Münster unter den daran Beteiligten und im Laufe der Zeiten sehr unterschiedlich gewesen sein. Im 19. Jhd. suchen mehrere für das Judentum sensibilisierte Kreise, sei es in Grossbritannien, sei es auf dem europäischen Festland, das Neue Testament als die Grundlage ihres Glaubens den Juden auf Hebräisch zugänglich zu machen.[19] Die allererste neuzeitliche Judenmissionsgesellschaft, die 1808/09 in London entstandene *London Society for Promoting Christianity Amongst the Jews*, fasste, wie Delitzsch selber schreibt, „die Übersetzungsaufgabe als eine noch nicht vollkommen gelöste und doch unendlich wichtige ins Auge ... "[20] Sie wurde in folgenden Etappen angegangen:

- Die erste, von verschiedenen Übersetzern erarbeitete, Gesamtausgabe als Frucht der Londoner Bestrebungen erschien (1813) 1817; [2]1819; [3]1821; ihr einziges Ziel war, den „Israelitis diuturna cæcitate laborantibus" zur Klarheit, d. h. dann auch zur Bekehrung, zu verhelfen.[21]
- Eine Neubearbeitung wurde aber sehr bald nötig; sie erschien 1840 und dann 1846, 1852, 1853, 1863–1866 – hier bemängelt Delitzsch vor allem die Punktierung.
- Eine davon unterschiedene Ausgabe erschien schliesslich 1857–1863.

---

18 Abgesehen von der Frage der Zuschreibung hebräischer Textteile an den Verfasser des *Even Bohan*, Schemtob Ibn Schaprut (vgl. dazu D. Flusser, in: R.L. Lindsey, *A Hebrew Translation of the Gospel of Mark*, Jerusalem [2]1973, S. 67–69 sowie P. Lapide, *Hebräisch in den Kirchen*: FJCD 1, 1976, S. 71–75), ist in der Zwischenzeit neben Übertragungen einzelner Teile des Neuen Testaments (auch dazu P. Lapide a.a.O. S. 83) als ganze Übersetzung erschienen die von Elias Hutter 1599 herausgegebene (J. Chr. Wolff, Bibliotheca hebræa Bd. II S. 416), die durch den Cambridger Hebraisten Rev. William Robertson London 1661 und 1800 erneut durch Richard Caddick revidiert wurde; sodann – wieder nur die Evangelien – die Wiedergabe von Jehuda Jona (geb. 1581 in Safed, dann in Amsterdam, 1624 in Hamburg lebend, im folgenden Jahr 1624 getauft mit keinem Geringeren als König Sigismund III. als Taufpaten, ab 1638 in dem durch Papst Paul III. begründeten „Neofiti"-Unternehmen in Rom wirkend und in dieser Stellung Lehrer Bartoloccis: Sein *Avnei ha-Giljonim (Quattuor Evangelia Novi Testamenti)* betiteltes Werk erschien 1668 bei der Kongregation *De propaganda fide*. Vgl. D. Flusser a.a.O. 67 und P. Lapide a.a.O. 84–89.
19 Zum Folgenden vgl. P. Lapide a.a.O. S. 95–99.
20 Eine Übersetzungsarbeit von 52 Jahren (1891) S. 29.
21 *Brit Ḥadaschah al-pi Maschiaḥ*, London 1813, Widmung an die Bischöfe, Vorwort S. V.

Delitzsch selber fühlte sich durch die *Mängel* dieser Ausgaben zu seiner vieldiskutierten, aber insgesamt dennoch als Meisterleistung bezeichneten *Berit chadaschah* angestachelt, obwohl ihm von allem Anfang an klar war, dass diese neue Übersetzung „nicht das Werk eines Einzelnen sein" könne.[22] Sie war es denn auch nicht, obwohl sie verdientermassen unter Delitzschs Namen firmiert, denn schon bei dem Specimen 1Kor 13 hatte sein Lehrer, der berühmte Leipziger Orientalist und Bibliograph Julius Fürst (1805–1873),[23] sein Auge drauf. 1877 veröffentlichte die *British and Foreign Bible Society* die erste Auflage, die textlich im Grossen und Ganzen dem Codex Sinaiticus folgte, der dank Delitzschs Leipziger Kollegen Tischendorf grösstes Ansehen genoss, während dann die 2. Auflage 1878, im Jahr darauf, den Textus receptus zugrundelegte (^{3}1880, ^{4}1882). Alle folgenden Auflagen (^{5}1883, ^{6}1885, ^{7}1886, ^{8}1888, ^{9}1889, ^{10}1890) profitierten von der Mitwirkung des gelehrten Israel I. Kahan, besonders nachdem seit 1885 die neue Übersetzung von Isaac Edward Salkinson (1822–1883), die von Christian David Ginsburg (1831–1914) weiterbetreut wurde und überhaupt in England starke Förderung erfuhr, eine erneute Herausforderung darstellte.

Dennoch bleibt Delitzschs hebräische Wiedergabe des Neuen Testaments in ihrer Weise unübertroffen, auch und obwohl sie, vom heutigen Standpunkt aus gesehen, an einem mehrfachen Handicap zu leiden hatte. Die epochemachenden Funde der *Handschriften vom Toten Meer* liessen noch zwei Generationen auf sich warten; auch Dalman hat sie nicht mehr erlebt. Ein gründlicher philologischer Vergleich von Delitzschs hebräischem Neuen Testament mit dem Qumran-Hebräischen wäre nicht bloss wissenschaftsgeschichtlich von hohem Interesse und würde die Verdienste wie allenfalls die Schwächen der Übersetzung noch stärker hervortreten lassen. Zu berücksichtigen ist, dass Delitzsch noch nicht einmal über *verlässliche Konkordanzen* zur hebräischen (S. Mandelkern) und schon gar nicht zur griechischen Bibel Alten Testaments (E. Hatch – H.A. Redpath) verfügte; es gab zu seiner Zeit noch *kein Umfeld, das wie im heutigen Israel Hebräisch als allgemein gesprochene Sprache kennt*, und sein Unterfangen geschah zu *einer Zeit*, da „Dalman, Wellhausen, Burney, and Schlatter had not written".[24] Aber er hat diesen Forschern, die als Semitisten an das Neue Testament herangingen, den Weg geebnet, und wenn es nur dadurch geschah, dass er ihre Kritik und ihren Widerspruch herausforderte. Nirgends kommt das so eklatant zum Zuge wie bei seinem Lieblingsschüler Dalman.

---

22 F. Delitzsch, *Wissenschaft, Kunst, Judentum* (1838) S. 308f., vgl. P. Lapide a.a.O. 100f.
23 Zu ihm vgl. D. Mathias, „Das Alte Testament in Leipzig". S. 394, 396f.
24 D. Flusser a.a.O. 68.

Ihm vertraute Delitzsch im Februar 1890, schon auf dem Krankenbett, die Weiterarbeit an seinem Lebenswerk an. Schon 19 Jahre zuvor hatte der damalige Gymnasiast durch erste hebräische Übersetzungsversuche von Evangelientexten den Kontakt zu Delitzsch gesucht und gefunden.[25] Mit Sorgfalt und Respekt besorgte Dalman 1892 dann die 11. und 1901 die 12. Auflage, obwohl er dem Unterfangen Delitzschs, „nach eigenem Ermessen aus dem Hebräisch aller Perioden ... bis zum Abschluss der Mischna einen Dialekt zu bilden, welcher sich eigne, das Gefäss der neutestamentlichen Gedankenwelt zu werden",[26] grundsätzlich kritisch gegenüberstand. Aufschlussreich ist nun freilich die Begründung, die Dalman später, auf dem Übergang zu seinem neuen Lebensabschnitt, für den Kompromiss anführt, den er seinem philologischen Gewissen aus Pietät gegenüber Delitzsch zumutet. Seiner Meinung nach lässt sich die neutestamentliche Offenbarung nicht in alttestamentlichem Hebräisch wiedergeben. Die Wahl einer späteren Sprachstufe aber kommt deswegen nicht in Betracht, weil „ein heiliges Buch, die Vollendung der alttestamentlichen Offenbarung, aus Schicklichkeitsgründen nicht in das Gewand des rabbinischen Idioms gekleidet werden" kann, da es eben zwar mit dem Alten Testament, nicht aber mit Talmud und Midrasch ein Ganzes bilde![27] Diese Kritik und ihre mehr dogmatisch und geschmäcklerisch als historisch und philologisch gehaltene Begründung, die jeder soziolektalen Betrachtung zuwiderläuft, führt zu Dalmans dezidierter Mitteilung vom 3. Juli 1934, „dass er, seit 1901 die 12. Auflage von Delitzschs Hebräischem Neuen Testament erschien, nichts mehr mit diesem Werk zu tun hatte".[28]

So ergibt sich die nur auf den ersten Blick verwunderliche Tatsache, dass ausgerechnet der Testamentsvollstrecker Dalman der schärfste Kritiker des ihm von Delitzsch überantworteten hebräischen Neuen Testaments ist, während dieses im übrigen sehr positiv aufgenommen und rezensiert wurde, etwa durch Fachleute wie Emil Kautzsch, Hermann L. Strack, Samuel R. Driver, Carl Siegfried.[29]

---

25 J. Männchen, *Dalmans Leben und Wirken* S. 41, 53.
26 G. Dalman, *Das hebräische Neue Testament von Franz Delitzsch*: SaH 39 (1902) S. 154, vgl. J. Männchen, *Dalmans Leben und Wirken* S. 54.
27 A.a.O. S. 155, vgl. J. Männchen, *Dalmans Leben und Wirken* S. 54.
28 J. Boehmer, *Das Geheimnis um die Geburt von Franz Delitzsch* (1934) S. 22 Anm. 47. Mithin dürften die 1928 in Berlin erschienene 13. und die 1937 in London erschienene 14. Ausgabe (danach noch einmal London 1960) blosse Nachdrucke sein, gegen D. Flusser a.a.O 67: "The eleventh through the fourteenth editions are said to have been made under the supervision of Gustav [sic!] Dalman."
29 Vgl. S. Wagner, *Franz Delitzsch* S. 179 mit Anm. 207. Vgl. auch die positive Würdigung durch David Flusser a.a.O. – Eine interessante Detailkritik Dalmans findet sich schon in seiner *Grammatik des Jüdisch-Palästinischen Aramäisch*, J.C. Hinrichsche Buchhandlung Leipzig ¹(1894) S. 152 Anm. 3 zum Toponym Gethsemane.

In zweierlei Hinsicht hatte Dalman an Delitzschs Übersetzungswerk Kritik anzumelden. Wenn – mit Münster gesprochen – Hebräisch die *native* Sprache des Neuen Testaments war, so erhob sich sofort die Frage: Welches Hebräisch – etwa die literarische Hochsprache von Tora und Propheten? Dalman konnte sich in seiner eigenen, so ambivalent motivierten, Suche und mit seinen Zweifeln am *echten* sprachlichen und damit geistigen Hintergrund des Neuen Testaments durchaus auf einzelne Äusserungen Delitzschs stützen, wenn dieser das Neue Testament anlässlich seiner Römerbrief-Übersetzung – die mit ihren „Erläuterungen aus Talmud und Midrasch" auch Vor- und Urbild für den grossen Kommentar von Paul Billerbeck darstellt, der in dieser Zeit, Sommersemester 1874 bis Sommersemester 1875 bei Delitzsch studierte – mit der Mischna und dem Midrasch vergleicht: Obgleich unendlich verschieden von diesen Werken der Halacha und Haggada, „ist die neutestamentliche Schrift doch ein echtes und zwar das allerechteste Produkt jüdischen Geistes. Denn Jesus der Christ ist der Gipfelpunkt ... "[30] Dalman hat seinerseits später, 1928 im hohen Alter zurückblickend, immerhin die Möglichkeit reflektiert, das Hebräische *der Rabbinen* einer Übersetzung des Neuen Testaments zugrundezulegen.[31] Ahnt er hier etwas von der zwei Jahrzehnte danach getätigten Entdeckung des hebräischen Schrifttums in *Qumran* und am Toten Meer? Wie hat er, eine Generation jünger als Delitzsch, die Initiativen einer *Renaissance des Hebräischen* als lebendiger Umgangssprache beurteilt? Seine spürbare Distanzierung mag wohl weniger auf die Furcht vor einer Profanierung der Laschon ha-Kodesch, der „Heiligsprache", die jüdischerseits durchaus laut wurde, zurückzuführen sein als mit seiner Einschätzung des Zionismus zusammenhängen.[32] Er äussert sich jedenfalls kaum zu den Bestrebungen, das von Schalom Jakob Abramowicz (Pseudonym Mendele Moicher Sfurim, 1835–1917) geschaffene moderne Hebräisch zur gesprochenen Sprache zu machen, wie es durch Eliezer Jitzchak Perlman (Eliezer Ben Yehuda, 1858–1922) und den Kreis um den 1889 gegründeten Va'ad ha-Laschon ha-'Iwrit (Joseph Klausner, Jakob M.

---

30 Paulus des Apostels Brief an die Römer. Aus dem griechischen Urtext auf Grund des Sinai-Codex in das Hebräische übersetzt und aus Talmud und Midrasch erläutert. (Mit einem Rückblick auf die Übersetzungsgeschichte vom ersten bis zum neunzehnten Jahrhundert) (1870) S. 7–9, vgl. auch SaH 15 (1878) S. 223 und dazu S. Wagner, *Franz Delitzsch* S. 179 Anm. 207.
31 G. Dalman, *Religionswissenschaft der Gegenwart* S. 9: Bei einer solchen Übersetzung des Neuen Testaments war „ohne Anleihen aus dem Hebräischen der Mischna und des Midrasch nicht auszukommen ... Mir wäre es deshalb als eine wichtige Aufgabe erschienen, dies dem Neuen Testament in Stil und Wortbildung viel näherstehende Idiom zugrunde zu legen."
32 Dazu T. Willi, „Christliche Rezeption des Judentums in Greifswald – Judenmission, Palästinawissenschaft und Aramaistik bei Gustaf Dalman": Judaica 66 (2010) 22–26.

Pines, Zvi Yavetz, David Yellin u. a.) geschah.[33] Eine wirklich judenmissionarisch abgezweckte Übersetzung des Neuen Testaments hätte hier[34] oder noch eher beim Jiddischen[35] ansetzen müssen.

b) Aramäisch als Sprache Jesu – aber welches Aramäisch?

Dalmans zweiter Einwand gegenüber Delitzschs Lebenswerk gründet tiefer. Er berührt nicht einzelne stilistisch-sprachphänomenologische bzw. sprachhistorische Differenzierungen, sondern liegt im Ansatz als solchem. Könnte man Delitzschs Interesse etwas plakativ als literaturgeschichtlich und bibeltheologisch bezeichnen, so reiht sich Dalman als Kind seiner Zeit durchaus ein in den Historismus, der sucht, „wie es eigentlich gewesen ist" (Leopold von Ranke), und der Individualität und Persönlichkeit als geschichtswirksame Grössen hochschätzt. In diesem Zusammenhang ist Dalmans Kernanliegen die *ipsissima vox* Jesu. Nur auf den ersten Blick erscheint es daher paradox, dass er sich selber genau in der Zeit, wo er Delitzschs hebräisches Neues Testament zu betreuen hatte, einen ganz anderen Zugang zu Sprache und Welt Jesu und des Neuen Testaments erschloss: *die Erforschung des Aramäischen.*

---

33 Dazu E.Y. Kutscher, *A History of the Hebrew Language* (1982) Kap. 8, S. 183–196; A. Sáenz-Badillos, *A History of the Hebrew Language* (engl. transl. J. Elwolde, 1993) S. 269–287. – Mit Joseph Klausner, der fast unmittelbar nach seiner Alija am 17.12.1919 Sekretär des *Va'ad ha-Lašon*, der nationalen Sprachakademie in Jerusalem, wurde, verband Dalman gegenseitige Hochschätzung, vgl. T. Willi a.a.O. („Gustaf Dalman und Joseph Klausner") S. 4.

34 Erst 1969 wurde das Projekt der British and Foreign Bible Society einer modernen Wiedergabe des Neuen Testaments in Iwrit in Angriff genommen und unter der Federführung von Josef Atzmon durchgeführt, vgl. die Ausgabe *Ha-Brit ha-Ḥadaschah: Targum Ḥadasch* 1976 und P. Lapide, *Hebräisch in den Kirchen* S. 196–199.

35 Vgl. dazu die interessanten Hinweise bei R. Flogaus, „Hebraica Christiana. Christliche Texte in hebräischer Sprache und ihre Verwendung in Schule und Mission (1475–1555)", in: M. Witte/T. Pilger (Hg.), *Mazel tov*, Leipzig (2012) 165f. auf die erste, in Krakau 1540/41 durch den Konvertiten Paul Helicz gedruckte jiddische Übersetzung des NTs (ohne Offb). Sie hatte Nachfolgerinnen in den Ausgaben Amsterdam (1676–1678), Amsterdam (1679) und London (1821) sowie London (1872–1878). An modernen jiddischen Übersetzungen sind vor allem jene von Aaron Krolenbaum (1950) und Henry Einspruch (1959) zu erwähnen, vgl. E. Davis, Art. Bible, Jiddisch: EJ 4 (1971) Sp. 866–868 und W. Gundert, Art. Bibelübersetzungen in europäische Sprachen vom 17. Jh. bis zur Gegenwart: TRE 6 (1980) S. 280f. – Dalman selber hat sich kaum zum Jiddischen geäussert, wenn man absieht von den beiden Editionen *Jüdisch-deutscher Volkslieder aus Galizien und Russland*: Schriften des Institutum Judaicum in Leipzig, Nr. 20 und 21, Leipzig (1888) und *Jüdische Melodien aus Galizien und Russland: Zum ersten Male aufgezeichnet und unter Mitwirkung von Halfdan Jebe aus Drontheim herausgegeben*: Schriften des Institutum Judaicum in Berlin, Nr. 17, Leipzig (1893).

Das immer wieder kolportierte, auf der Einschätzung K.H. Rengstorfs[36] – der Dalman seine ersten Schritte *in rabbinicis* verdankt und sich nach dem Zweiten Weltkrieg mit dem Münsteraner Institutum Delitzschianum als Sachwalter der Leipziger Tradition geriert hat – beruhendes Urteil, Dalmans diesbezügliche Forschung müsse „als überholt" gelten,[37] bedarf einer sorgfältig abwägenden Revision.

Dalmans Leistung kann nur gewürdigt werden, wenn man sie in den grösseren Rahmen der *Erforschung des Aramäischen* stellt. Wiederum steht der Basler Sebastian Münster am Anfang. Auch die Frage nach der *Sprache Jesu*, die Dalman bewegt, hat eine längere Vorgeschichte.

Am 12. Tewet/16. Dezember 1526 erschien bei Johann Froben in Basel die *Chaldaica grammatica*, die unmittelbar nach dem aramäischen Haupttitel – er lautet Dikduk ha-Lishan Arami 'o ha-Kasra'ah – als absolute Pioniertat bezeichnet wird: „antehac a nemine attentata". In der *epistula nuncupatoria*, im ersten von zwei Widmungsschreiben,[38] rühmt sich Münster, dass er als „*primus inter mortales ... Chaldaicae linguae iacere fundamenta*", und er begründet das damit, dass er, anders als etwa Reuchlin bei seinen bahnbrechenden Hebräischstudien, nicht die geringste Hilfe von aussen empfangen habe, weder durch eine bestehende Grammatik noch durch einen sachkundigen Lehrer. Vielmehr habe er sich Regeln und Wortschatz der Sprache einzig durch intensive Lektüre der Targume erarbeitet, und nur für die Geschichte des Aramäischen *a docto quodam Judaeo* (den er wie andere jüdische Gewährsleute mit Ausnahme von Elia Levita nicht nennt) einige Hinweise empfangen.

Wohl auch aufgrund didaktischer Überlegungen geht Münster aus von verschiedenen „chaldäischen" Vokabeln und Eigennamen in den Evangelien; es folgt ein lexikalischer Vergleich zwischen Hebräisch, Aramäisch, Arabisch und Aethiopisch, je eine deutsch-jüdische und eine spanisch-jüdische Schrifttafel. Dem grammatischen Hauptteil (p. 19–140) ist eine Chrestomathie mit Beispielen aus den Targumen zu Dtn 5, Jos 24, Jes 42, Jer 23, Ez 18 und Ps 34 mit lateinischer Übersetzung beigegeben (p. 141–151). Als eigentlich zweiter Band sind p. 153–212

---

36 K. H. Rengstorf, „Gustaf Dalmans Bedeutung für die Wissenschaft vom Judentum": WZEMAU Greifswald, Jg. IV (1954/55), Gesellschafts- und sprachwiss. Reihe Nr. 4/5 S. 376: „Dennoch wird es dabei bleiben müssen, dass DALMANs Theorie über die sprachlichen Grundlagen einer Rückübertragung der Worte Jesu in ihre Ursprache als solche als überholt zu gelten hat ... "
37 K.H. Bernhardt, Art. Dalman, Gustaf: TRE 8 (1981) S. 322f.; J. Männchen, *Dalmans Leben und Wirken* S. 54 mit Anm. 212.
38 Fol. a 2ʳ, datiert Heidelberg 29. April 1526, wo Münster wie schon 1523 temporär als Professor wirkte.

ein beachtenswertes Spezialwörterbuch zu den rabbinischen Bibelkommentaren sowie ein Abbreviaturenlexikon angeschlossen.[39]

Es ist hier nicht der Ort, die Erforschung des Aramäischen bis zum aktuellen Stand darzustellen. Münsters Darstellung baute auf dem Sprachvergleich mit anderen semitischen Sprachen wie dem Hebräischen und dem Arabischen auf, wie sie die jüdischen Grammatiker des Mittelalters, denen natürlich auch die aramäischen Dialekte der Targume und der beiden Talmude vertraut waren, entwickelt und fruchtbar gemacht hatten. 1539 erschien die erste syrische Grammatik, 1555 die epochemachenden *editio princeps* eines syrischen (neutestamentlichen) Bibeltextes. In diesem Jahr, nachdem die Vorarbeiten am 10. August 1554 abgeschlossen waren, veröffentlichte Johann Albrecht Widmannstetter (1506–1557), ein Schüler Münsters, auf Rechnung von König Ferdinand I. in Wien die Handschrift des Moses von Mardin unter dem Titel *Liber sacrosancti Evangelii de Jesu Christo, Domino et Deo nostro*, bzw. *K⁽ᵉ⁾taba d-ewangelyon qaddischa de-maran w-alahan Yeschu' m⁽ᵉ⁾schicha*. Damit verband sich nahezu unmittelbar die Frage nach dem Verhältnis des aramäischen Dialekts von Urfa (antik Edessa) zu anderen Ausprägungen des Aramäischen und gleichzeitig bereits die Dalman beschäftigende *Frage nach der Sprache Jesu*. Widmannstetter selbst war nach dem Titel seiner *editio princeps* überzeugt, dass die „lingua Syra" die „Iesu Christo vernacula, Divino ipsius ore cōsecrata, et a Ioh. Evāgelista Hebraica dicta" sei, bzw. „Christo Jesu et eius matri domestica" sei.[40]

Bereits zwei Generationen später fällte Joseph Justus Scaliger in diesem Punkt das abschliessende Urteil, dass das Syrische des Neuen Testaments *nicht* die Sprache Jesu sei.[41] Diese Erkenntnis fand aber nur sehr selektive Aufnahme,[42]

---

39 Vgl. die genaue Beschreibung bei J. Prijs und B. Prijs, *Die Basler hebräischen Drucke* (1964) Nr. 23 S. 41–45.

40 Diese und reiche Hinweise zum Folgenden verdanke ich einer Präsentation von Aegidius Gutbiers *Novum Testamentum Syriacum* (Hamburg 1663) durch Hans Kurig im Hamburger Forschungscolloquium vom 20. 1. 2012. Vgl. weiter S. P. Brock, *An introduction to Syriac studies*. Gorgias Press, Piscataway (2006); R.J. Wilkinson, *Orientalism, Aramaic and Kabbalah in the Catholic Reformation: the first printing of the Syriac New Testament*: Studies in the History of Christian Tradition 137, Brill, Leiden (2007). Zu der Frage nach Jesu Muttersprache vgl. nach Widmannstetter auch Immanuel Tremellius in seiner in Heidelberg 1568 erschienenen Ausgabe des syrischen NT und Brian Walton in den Prolegomena zur syrischen Übersetzung in Bd. VI der Polyglotta Biblia Sacra, London (1657 = Ndr. Graz 1965) S. 91–96.

41 Epistola 449, in: J.J. Scaliger, Epistolae omnes quae reperiri potuerunt, nunc primum collectae et editae, Leiden, Elzevier (1627).

42 Im Blick auf Aegidius Gutbier und sein 1663 auf eigene Kosten in Hamburg ediertes *Novum Testamentum Syriacum* äussert sich Jacob Bernays in seiner Darstellung der Rezeption Scaligers: „Walton weiss über Scaliger Bescheid, der Deutsche [Gutbier] nicht.", vgl. ders., *Joseph Justus Scaliger*, Berlin, Hertz (1855) 64

neben Brian Walton etwa bei Hugo Grotius, der aus Matth. 27,46 und Mk. 15,34 den Schluss zog, Jesus habe einen Mischdialekt gespochen.

Aufgrund dieser Sachlage drängte sich eine sorgfältige Analyse der zeitlich wie regional so verschiedenen Ausprägungen des Aramäischen auf. Eine erste Schneise schlug der „treffliche [Samuel David] Luzzatto".[43] In seiner bereits 1832/33 ausgearbeiteten, aber erst 1865 erschienenen Abhandlung unterscheidet er schon im Titel: „Elementi grammaticali del Caldeo Biblico e del Dialetto Talmudico Babilonese",[44] d. h. separiert er das (heute als Spezialfall des sog. „Reichsaramäischen" geltenden) Biblisch-Aramäische vom späteren Jüdisch-Aramäischen. Hier setzt Dalman in seinen aramaistische Untersuchungen an. Für Franz Rosenthal in „Die Aramaistische Forschung seit Th. Nöldeke's Veröffentlichungen"[45] bleibt es sein Verdienst, die Tür zu den regionalen Ausprägungen des Aramäischen auf dem Übergang vom Mittel- (300 v. Chr.-200 n. Chr.) zum Spätaramäischen (200–700 n. Chr.) geöffnet zu haben. Seine „*Grammatik* des jüdisch-palästinischen Aramäisch"[46] von 1894 mit den sie ergänzenden „Aramäischen *Dialektproben*"[47] von 1896, sowie der schon im nächsten Jahr, 1897, veröffentlichte ʿArukh ha-ḥadasch, das „Aramäisch-neuhebräische [Hand-] *Wörterbuch* zu Targum, Talmud und Midrasch, mit Vokalisation der targumischen Wörter nach südarabischen Handschriften und besonderer Bezeichnung des Wortschatzes des Onkelostargums, Teil I-II"[48] erweisen sich im Überblick als umfassende Vorarbeiten. Das „Aramäisch-neuhebräische Wörterbuch" stellt einen in den Etymologien zurückhaltenden *Auszug* aus den grossen Wörterbüchern von Jacob Levy u. a. dar, der sich durch die *Kenntlichmachung des Onkelos-Gutes* sowie durch die *jemenitische Vokalisation* auszeichnet.[49] Alle diese Bücher werden bis heute immer neu aufgelegt. Natürlich differenziert die moderne Forschung in manchen Punkten heute anders als es Dalman tut. Nach den dreifachen Vorarbeiten erschien 1898 das *opus magnum* unter dem Titel: „Die Worte Jesu, mit Berücksichtigung des nachkanonischen jüdischen Schrifttums und der aramäischen Sprache erörtert.

---

43 Th. Nöldeke, *Mandäische Grammatik* (1875) S. V.
44 Padua 1865; zur langen Latenzzeit zwischen Konzipierung und Veröffentlichung S. 3. – Dalman selber urteilt in seiner *Grammatik des Jüdisch-Palästinischen Aramäisch*, J.C. Hinrichsche Buchhandlung Leipzig ¹(1894) S. 19 = ²(1905) S. 25: „Eine noch sehr unvollständige Grammatik für den aram. Dialekt des bab. Talmud schrieb *S.D.Luzzatto* ... Padua 1865, deutsch übersetzt von *M.S. Krüger*, Breslau 1873 (dazu *Nöldeke* Gött. Gel. Anz. 1868, 177–188)."
45 Als Preisaufgabe des 19. Orientalistenkongresses in Rom ausgeschrieben, erschien die Arbeit 1939 in Leiden.
46 ¹1894, ² erw. 1905 = 1960.1978.1981.1989; im Folgenden GJPA.
47 ¹1896, ² erw. 1927 = 1960.1978.1981.1989.
48 ¹1897–1901, ² verb. und erw. 1922, ³1938 = 1967.1987.1997 ... 2007.
49 F. Rosenthal, *Aramaistische Forschung* S. 117.

Bd. I Einleitung und wichtige Begriffe. Nebst Anhang (Messianische Texte)".[50] Darin kulminieren Dalmans aramaistische Untersuchungen, die über das letzte Jahrzehnt des 19. Jhd.s verteilt sind. Erst 1922, *nach* der seiner zweiten Lebenshälfte eine neue Richtung gebenden Wirksamkeit in Jerusalem, wird Dalman mit dem in Greifswald abgefassten „Jesus – Jeschua: die drei Sprachen Jesu – Jesus in der Synagoge, auf dem Berge, beim Passahmahl, am Kreuz"[51] die Thematik noch einmal angehen. Alle diese aramaistischen Forschungen Dalmans sind dabei von der Ausgangsfrage bestimmt, „wie die Worte Jesu in der Ursprache haben lauten müssen, und welchen Sinn sie in dieser Gestalt für den Hörer hatten".[52]

Dalman hat schon unmittelbar nach dem Erscheinen seiner „Grammatik des jüdisch-palästinischen Aramäisch" Anerkennung für seine aramaistischen Leistungen gefunden. Das zeigen zwei hier erstmals veröffentlichte Zeugnisse aus der Feder führender Semitisten, denen Dalman je ein Exemplar hatte zugehen lassen. Die zwei handschriftlichen Postkarten, beide adressiert an „Herrn Lic. (th.}Dr. Dalman, Leipzig, Brüderstr. 49" finden sich eingeklebt in Dalmans Handexemplar der Grammatik, heute im Gustaf-Dalman-Institut in Greifswald unter der Signatur *Da 12* aufbewahrt.

Die erste stammt von *Theodor Nöldeke* und ist abgestempelt „Strassburg/Els., 20.11.[18]94, 4–5 N.[achmittags] ". Sie lautet:

Sehr geehrter Herr Doctor!

Empfangen Sie schon jetzt m/n besten Dank für Ihre werthe Gabe. Ich habe bis jetzt nur ein paar Blicke in das Werk werfen können; die zeigen mir aber, dass ich es ernstlich studieren muß, und dazu habe ich wenigstens in der allernächsten Zeit noch keine Muße. Aber geschehen soll es, und ich werde mich dann weiter äußern. Nur die einleitenden §§ habe ich schon gelesen und daraus erkant, mit welcher Sorgfalt und welcher Gelehrsamkeit Sie verfahren. Daß ich in Bezug auf das relative Alter der Targume nicht gleich bekehrt werde, ist allerdings auch Ihnen schwerlich auffällig. Ich halte einstweilen daran fest, daß im jerus. Pent. Targ. sehr alte Reste sind, und daß Onkelos ein Kunstprodukt ist auf Grund einer älteren paläst. Targumschrift.

Da Sie einmal im Zuge sind, sollten Sie auch gleich eine ausführl. Grammatik des babyl. Aram., ich meine des bab. Talmudischen machen. Das traurige Buch von Siegfried und Strack muß möglichst bald beseitigt werden!

---

50 1898. – Das eine der im Dalman-Institut in Dalmans Handapparat vorhandenen Exemplare trägt die handschriftliche Widmung des Verfassers an seinen Vater.
51 1922.
52 Die Worte Jesu I (1898) S. 57, im Original gesperrt. Man vergleiche dazu die Nachricht, wonach letztlich die Frage, „was denn die Zuhörer Jesu unter Himmelreich verstanden hätten", Paul Billerbeck zu seinem Lebenswerk veranlasst habe, s. J. Männchen, Billerbeck, in: C. Böttrich, J. Thomanek, T. Willi (Hg.), Zwischen Zensur und Selbstbesinnung: GThF 17 (2009) S. 233.

Noch einmal besten Dank!

Ihr eg. [ergebener] ThNöldeke

Die zweite, von *Emil Kautzsch*, ist abgestempelt „Halle 22.11.[18]94, 11–12 V.[ormittags] ". Sie lautet

Halle, d. 21.11.94

Lieber Herr College! Durch die fr. Übersendung der aram. Gram. haben Sie mir eine freudige Überraschung bereitet. Ich ahnte nicht, daß Sie schon so weit damit zu Stande waren. Sie können sich denken, mit welchem Interesse ich nach so vielfacher Beschäftigung mit diesem Gegenstande das Buch zur Hand genommen habe, und jedenfalls darf ich Ihnen versichern, daß Sie nicht leicht einen aufmerksameren Leser haben sollen, dazu natürlich auch einen dankbaren, denn so viel sehe ich bereits, daß für die 2te Aufl. der Gram. [matik] des biblisch-Aram. , an die ich mit der Zeit denken muß, allerlei hier abfallen wird. Für heute mit meinem verbindlichen Dank herzl. Glückwunsch zu der glücklichen Beendigung des schwierigen Werks!

Mit collegial. Gruß

Ihr ergebenster E. Ktzsch

Kautzsch liess es nicht bei dieser Postkarte bewenden, sondern verfasste eine Rezension der Grammatik, die in ThLZ 20 (1895) Sp. 634–637 erschien.[53] Dalman wusste das zu schätzen, wie sich aus dem hinten im genannten Band *Da 12* eingelegten Entwurf einer Briefkarte ergibt, die in Dalmans charakteristisch hoher und steiler Handschrift geschrieben ist. Sie lautet:

Leipzig, 49 Brüderstr.
13. Dec. 1895

Sehr verehrter Herr Professor!

Nachdem meine Fahrt nach Halle leider ihren Zweck neulich verfehlte, möchte ich Ihnen nun schriftlich für Ihre freundliche Anzeige meiner Grammatik danken. Der Art der Vokalisierung der Paradigmata lag keine prinzipielle Erwägung, sondern nur der Wunsch, hier wenigstens das Abspringen der Vokale zu ... ten. Sollte das Buch noch einmal gedruckt werden, würde ich vielleicht die ganze obere Vokalisation in die niedere umschreiben. Die Korrektur war eine wahre Sisyphusarbeit. Aber ich hoffe, in diesem Fall das Bedürfnis des Schülers auch sonst besser wahrnehmen zu können.

In bezug auf Länge und Kürze der Vokale – nach der Intention der Vokalisatoren – gestehe ich, recht wenig zu wissen. Wer sagt uns, ob in q^{e}ṭalīt das Pathach wirklich kurz gesprochen

---

53 Weitere Rezensionen erschienen von M. Gaster im *Journal oft he Royal Asiatic Society* (1897) 158; von G.F. Moore in *The American Journal of Semitic Languages and Literatures* 15:2 (Jan. 1899) 116; von N. Porges in der *Revue des études juives* 52 (1906) 314; später dann von S. Wild in der *Zeitschrift der Deutschen Morgenländischen Gesellschaft* 113 (1963) 218.

> wurde, und ob das i nicht thatsächlich gedehnt war? Bei o und u im Impf. Peal, i und e im Pael entsteht mir dieselbe Frage. Mir scheint klar, was das Ursprüngliche gewesen sein muß, aber unklar, was der wirkliche Gebrauch war. Selbst bei den sogen. geschärften Sylben wäre doch, nachdem man aufgehört hatte, die Konsonanten doppelt zu sprechen, eine Dehnung der Vokale schon in älterer Zeit denkbar, wie die Juden sie jetzt anwenden. Für sie ist qiṭṭel = ḳīṭēl, qaṭṭel = ḳāṭēl. kᵉtabā kann sehr wohl kĕtābā́ gesprochen worden sein, kᵉtabīt kĕtābīt.

Dalman als Aramaist wird seinen Platz in der Wissenschaftsgeschichte schon aus den folgenden beiden Gründen behalten: Einmal macht er konsequent ernst mit der von Luzzato vorgenommenen elementaren *Differenzierung* zwischen dem (zum sog. Reichsaramäischen gehörenden) biblischen Aramäisch und dem Aramäischen der rabbinischen Traditionsliteratur. Zum Zweiten mahnt Dalman dringend kritische Textausgaben an und warnt vor einem Vorgehen wie dem von A. Merx in seiner „Chrestomathia Targumica".[54] An diesem Punkt kommen, was Druckausgaben betrifft, eine ganze Reihe von Judaica des Gustaf-Dalman-Instituts zu Ehren, die von Dalman in seinen Schriften akribisch konsultiert werden.[55] Gerade weil Dalman und seinen Zeitgenossen die Bedeutung und Dimension des Altaramäischen als dem Nährboden des Reichsaramäischen nicht bewusst war und nicht bewusst sein konnte, tat er gut daran, sich mit seiner bahnbrechenden „Grammatik des Jüdisch-Palästinischen Aramäisch" ganz auf den so definierten Bereich des Mittelaramäischen zu beschränken und ihn „nach Idiomen des palästinischen Talmud und Midrasch, des Onkelostargums (Cod. Socin 84) und der jerusalemischen Targume zum Pentateuch" darzustellen. Schon im Vorwort zur zweiten Auflage verwahrt sich Dalman gegen die "irrtümliche Annahme, als sähe ich darin ein in Judäa gesprochenes Aramäisch", und insofern geht der Vorwurf, dass seit Paul Kahle „der der Sprache Jesu am nächsten kommende Dialekt" am ehesten in den – dank den durch Salomon Schechter, d. h. ab 1897, langsam zugänglich werdenden – Fragmenten aus der Kairoer Geniza, besonders dem palästinischen Pentateuchtargum, zu finden sei, ins Leere.[56] Gewiss ist es für Dalman unverändert das „Interesse an der Sprache Jesu" und damit die

---

54 PLO 8 (1888), dazu kritisch Dalman, GJPA S. 13 Anm. 5.
55 Von den Bänden der Dalmansammlung, die Dalman für seine Aramäischstudien konsultierte, seien hier die Exemplare genannt, die in GJPA S. VII als „Druckausgaben" zusammengestellt sind: Pentateuch mit Targum Onkelos (von Lissabon 1491), Sabbioneta 1557: J I 14; Pentateuch mit drei Tagumen (Ed. princ. für Targum Jeruschalmi I), Venedig 1591: J I 15; Erst rabbinische Bibel (Ed. princ. für das Hagiographentargum und Targum Jeruschalmi II) [Felix Pratensis bei Daniel Bomberg], Venedig 1517: J I 25; Midrasch chamesch Megilloth, Pesaro 1519, Venedig 1545, Saloniki 1593: J VI 1; Midrasch [Ber.] rabba, Konstantinopel 1512: J VII 1; Midrasch Tehillim, Konstantinopel 1512, Venedig 1547: J VI 1; Jerusalemischer Talmud [Ed. princ.], Venedig 1523/24: J V 1; En Jaakob, Venedig 1546: J XIII 5; Aruk, Pesaro 1517: J XXI 50.
56 K. H. Rengstorf, „Gustaf Dalmans Bedeutung" S. 376.

„Erfassung des grössten Problems der Weltgeschichte, der Erscheinung Jesu",[57] das seine aramaistischen – wie später seine landeskundlichen – Forschungen antreibt. Er gelangt dabei zu Positionen, die zwar im einzelnen später durch die Forschungen v. a. Paul Kahles korrigiert werden, die aber mit ihren Fragestellungen und den Mitteln, sie zu lösen, gültig bleiben. Dazu gehört Dalmans durchaus zutreffende Empfindung, dass dem „westaramäischen" Sprachmaterial, dem sein Hauptaugenmerk gilt, durchaus eine einheitliche Vorstufe zugrundelag.[58]

Auch in weiteren – weitgehend von ihm eröffneten – Untersuchungsfeldern verdient seine Stimme nach wie vor Gehör: 1.) In der Frage nach der Sprache Jesu – wo Nöldekes Warnung vor einer zu sehr differenzierten Dialekteinteilung immer wichtig bleibt – war er es, der es „wohl als erster – mit der philologischen Seite des Problems wirklich genau nahm".[59] Im Disput mit J. Wellhausen und mit dem von diesem herkommenden F. Schulthess hielt Dalman an dem „als solide Arbeitsgrundlage in philologischer Hinsicht doch nur zu berechtigten Grundsatz ... : quod non est apud Rabbinos, non est judaicum" fest.[60] – 2.) Bei der Suche nach einer hinter den Evangelien liegenden „ursprünglichen" – aramäischen – Sprache war Dalman durchaus kritischer eingestellt als etwa E. Nestle oder J. Wellhausen, die beide mit einer aramäischen Quelle für Matthäus rechneten. – 3.) Im Gebiet der jüdisch-palästinischen aramäischen Literatur nahm Dalman, auch hier bahnbrechend, auf den einleitenden Seiten 6–39 seiner Grammatik (die leider die Syntax übergeht) eine Einteilung von drei Hauptgruppen vor, die sich als ganze bewährte: nämlich a) die *jüdischen d. h. judäischen Schriftdenkmäler*, zu denen er die aramäischen Partien des Alten Testaments, das aramäische Hasmonäerbuch,[61] die aramäischen Vokabeln im Neuen Testament und bei Josephus, die Megillat Ta'anit, alte Aussprüche, Urkundenformulare sowie das Onkelos- und Prophetentargum zählt (S. 6–16). b) Als *galiläisch* gelten ihm die aramäischen Partien im palästinischen Talmud, in den palästinischen Midraschim und die Mosaikinschrift im galiläischen Kafr Kenna. c) Die Gruppe der „Sprachdenkmäler *mit gemischtem Sprachtypus*" schliesslich erscheint sehr zusammengewürfelt und ist als solche denn auch durch Paul Kahle zu Recht als unbrauchbar erklärt worden; nach Dalman (S. 27–39) gehören dazu die palästinischen Pentateuch-

---

57 GJPA S. VII.X.
58 F. Rosenthal, *Aramaistische Forschung* S. 104 Anm. 2.
59 F. Rosenthal, *Aramaistische Forschung* S. 106.
60 F. Rosenthal, *Aramaistische Forschung* S. 107, unter Verweis auf die Gegenposition bei J. Wellhausen, *Einleitung in die drei ersten Evangelien* (1905) S. 41 und dann die ausführliche Begründung ebd. 2. Auflage (1911).
61 „Das er als eine Nachahmung in der aramäischen Sprachform des Alten Testaments erkannte, also ganz hätte aus dem Spiel lassen müssen", F. Rosenthal, *Aramaistische Forschung* S. 124.

argume, die Targume zu den Hagiographen, von denen Dalman selber freilich schon sagt, „dass sie nur Kunstprodukte sind"[62] und apokryphe aramäische Schriften wie der aramäische Tobit. In der Einschätzung dieses letztgenannten Werks, das Adolph Neubauer 1878 herausgegeben hatte, dürfte übrigens Dalman mit seiner Datierung „nicht vor dem siebenten Jahrhundert"[63] gegenüber Th. Nöldeke, der sein Idiom noch als „eine wirklich lebendige Sprache" einstufte und der es um 300 n. Chr. ansetzte,[64] im Recht bleiben. – 4.) Zum christlich-palästinischen Aramäisch hat sich Dalman aufgrund seiner eigenen Schwerpunktsetzung nur sporadisch und am Rande geäussert; ihm war wichtig, dass die seiner Zeit oft behauptete Beziehung zum galiläischen Dialekt nicht erweisbar sei, und er lehnt daher die von J. Wellhausen „aufgestellte Forderung, das Evangeliarium Hierosolymitanum bei der Erörterung der Muttersprache Jesu zu Grunde zu legen", rundweg ab.[65]

So, wie ihm im hebraistischen Bereich die Handschriftenfunde vom Toten Meer noch nicht zur Verfügung standen, fehlte ihm in der Aramaistik die seither zutage getretene umfangreiche epigraphische Dokumentation. Bezieht man die dadurch ermöglichte Erschliessung des Altaramäischen mit ein, so wird das bis heute lebendige Aramäische zu der am längsten kontinuierlich gesprochenen semitischen Sprache. In Ermangelung der Kenntnis der Frühstufen des Aramäischen stellte Dalman seine auf die Erhellung des jüdisch-palästinischen Aramäisch focussierten Forschungen in einen breiteren semitistischen Rahmen. Dafür legen nicht bloss seine aktiven Kenntnisse des Arabischen, besonders der „Volkssprache",[66] auf die er seine Sammeltätigkeit schon anlässlich seiner Nahostreise vom 10.3.1899 bis 12.6.1900 und dann in Jerusalem ausdehnte und in dem er sogar selber dichtete, Zeugnis ab, sondern auch seine Nabatäeruntersuchungen im Zusammenhang des zwischen 1904 und 1910 zehnmal besuchten Petra.[67] Die Aramaistik bildet überhaupt ein wichtiges *Continuum zwischen seiner Leipziger und seiner Jerusalemer Zeit*. Die mit sicherem Empfinden als den Ursprüngen am nächsten stehend eingeschätzte jemenitische Vokalisierung hat er für die zweite Auflage seiner Grammatik anhand einer jemenitischen Gen-Ex-Handschrift im

---

62 GJPA S. 35.
63 GJPA 37: „Die uns vorliegende Schrift ist nicht vor dem siebenten Jahrhundert entstanden in Kreisen, welche durch beide Talmude und die älteren Targume beeinflusst waren … "
64 Berichte über die Verhandlungen der königl. Akademie d. Wiss. zu Berlin (1879) S. 65–69, vgl. dazu F. Rosenthal, *Aramaistische Forschung* S. 125.
65 GJPA S. 41 mit Anm. 1.
66 „Die arabische Volkssprache, für welche mich Prof. Socin vor meiner Abreise in grosser Freundlichkeit noch privatim geschult hatte … ", Religionswissenschaft der Gegenwart S. 13.
67 F. Rosenthal, *Aramaistische Forschung* S. 86.

Besitz der Edler von Lämel-Schule[68] in Jerusalem und vor allem durch „praktische Kenntnisnahme der jemenischen Aussprache des Hebräischen und Aramäischen, zu welcher Jerusalem Gelegenheit bietet", verifiziert und bereinigt.[69]

3 Schluss

Dalman ist von allen Seiten als Palästinawissenschaftler gewürdigt worden. Das zeigte sich nicht zuletzt in der Feier zu seinem 70. Geburtstag, den er am 9. Juni 1925 in Jerusalem begehen konnte.[70] Demgegenüber sollte der *Aramaist* nicht vergessen werden. Denn auf diesem Weg ist Dalman zu dem *Judaisten* geworden, als den ihn einer, der es wissen musste, ehrt und würdigt. Joseph Klausner (1874–1958) hat Gustaf Dalman nahezu alle seine wichtigsten Veröffentlichungen geschenkt und vielfach mit Widmungen versehen. Die Bücher stehen in der Dalman-Bibliothek.[71] Die letzte Widmung, die alles noch einmal zusammenfasst, was Dalman für Klausner war, findet sich in: *Ha-bayit ha-sheni bi-gedulato. Sechs historische Untersuchungen.* Devir, Tel Aviv 1930 (J XVII B 46a). Sie lautet:

> Dem besten Kenner des Judentums und
> Palästinas des Zweiten Tempels,
> Prof. Gustaf Dalman,
> in grösster Verehrung
> vom Verfasser.

---

[68] Die 1856 gegründete Schule galt dem orthodoxen Jerusalem als Zentrum der Haskala, wozu auch die Tatsache beitrug, dass sie die erste war, an der einzelne Fächer in Iwrit unterrichtet wurde.
[69] GJPA S. VIII.
[70] Zu diesem Anlass wurde ihm durch Propst Wilhelm Hertzberg die Urkunde überreicht, durch die auf der Grundlage einer inner- und ausserhalb Deutschlands getätigten Geldsammlung, des Antrags der Greifswalder Theologischen Fakultät und der Bewilligung des Preussischen Kultusministeriums das „Gustaf-Dalman-Institut für Palästinawissenschaft" (ab 1946: „für biblische Landes- und Altertumskunde") ins Leben gerufen wurde. Der Anlass versammelte eine illustre Gesellschaft von Vertretern des diplomatischen, kirchlichen und akademischen Lebens des damaligen Jerusalem. Im Rückblick auf den Ehrentag in Jerusalem vermerkt Dalman selber nicht ohne Stolz und Genugtuung dass nicht nur „der Deutsche Konsul, der Leiter des Amerikanischen archäologischen Instituts, ein Vertreter der englischen Palästinawissenschaft ... und ein österreichischer Prälat, der Vikar des lateinischen Patriarchen ... das Wort" ergriffen, sondern auch „der Palästinologe und der Jesusforscher des heutigen Judentums". Mit dem „Palästinologen" ist Samuel Klein (1886–1940) gemeint, während sich hinter dem mit Achtergewicht genannten „Jesusforscher des heutigen Judentums" natürlich Josef Klausner verbirgt.
[71] Dazu T. Willi, „Gustaf Dalman und Joseph Klausner. Christliche Judentums- und Palästinawissenschaft im Spiegel unveröffentlichter handschriftlicher Widmungen eines zeitgenössischen jüdischen Forschers", in: M. Witte/T. Pilger (Hg.), *Mazel tov*: SKI.NF 1, Leipzig (2012) 247–264.

English abstract: Whosoever wishes to comprehend the fine little library of the Greifswald *Gustaf Dalman Institute* with its remarkable Jewish books, a good deal of them *editiones principes,* has to become acquainted with the life and work of its founder and collector, *Gustaf Dalman* (1855–1941). Dalman's scholarly work, including his Aramaic and Holy Land studies, must be seen against the background of his connections to the *Herrnhuter Brüdergemeine* from which he came, and of his relations with Franz Delitzsch (1813–1890), who was one of the outstanding conservative Bible scholars deeply engaged in Jewish life and Jewish studies. By dissociating himself from Delitzsch and his Hebrew translation of the New Testament, Dalman paved the way for future *Aramaic* studies. He appreciated the difference between Biblical and Rabbinic Aramaic, called for critical text editions, investigated the language of Jesus, searched for the Aramaic sources of the Gospels, and identified three main types of Jewish Aramaic.

Bibliography

Boehmer, Julius. *Das Geheimnis um die Geburt von Franz Delitzsch*. Kassel, 1934.
Brit Ḥadaschah al-pi Maschiaḥ. London: London Society for Promoting Christianity Amongst the Jews, 1813.
Bernays, Jacob. *Joseph Justus Scaliger*. Berlin: Hertz, 1855.
Bernhardt, Karl-Heinz. „Dalman, Gustaf." *Theologische Realenzyklopädie* 8 (1981): 322–323.
Böttrich, Christfried. „Die Geschichte der Mayerschen Lehrsynagoge." In *Die Greifswalder Lehrsynagoge Johann Friedrich Mayers: Ein Beispiel Christlicher Rezeption des Judentums im 18. Jahrhundert*, edited by Christfried Böttrich, Thomas K. Kuhn and Daniel Stein Kokin, 187–245. Leipzig: Evangelische Verlagsanstalt, 2016.
Brock, Sebastian P. *An introduction to Syriac studies*. Piscataway, NJ: Gorgias Press, 2006.
Dalman, Gustaf. *Das hebräische Neue Testament von Franz Delitzsch*: Saat auf Hoffnung 39 (1902): S. 154 Seitenangaben.
Dalman, Gustaf. *Die Worte Jesu, mit Berücksichtigung des nachkanonischen jüdischen Schrifttums und der aramäischen Sprache erörtert*, vol. 1. Leipzig: J.C. Hinrichs, 1898.
Dalman, Gustaf. „Graf Zinzendorf und die Juden." In *Zinzendorf und Lieberkühn: Studien zur Geschichte der Judenmission*, edited by Gustaf Dalman und Adolf Schulze, 5–51. Schriften des Institutum Judaicum in Berlin 32. Leipzig: J. C. Hinrichs, 1903.
Dalman, Gustaf. *Grammatik des Jüdisch-Palästinischen Aramäisch*. Leipzig: J.C. Hinrichsche Buchhandlung, 1894.
Dalman, Gustaf. *Jesus – Jeschua: die drei Sprachen Jesu – Jesus in der Synagoge, auf dem Berge, beim Passahmahl, am Kreuz*. Leipzig: J.C. Hinrichs, 1922.
Delitzsch, Franz. „Christentum und jüdische Presse: Selbsterlebtes von F.D." *Saat auf Hoffnung* 19 (1882): 83–146.
Delitzsch, Franz. *Paulus des Apostels Brief an die Römer: aus dem griechischen Urtext auf Grund des Sinai-Codex in das Hebräische übersetzt und aus Talmud und Midrasch erläutert*. Leipzig: Dörffling und Franke, 1870.

Delitzsch, Franz. *Wissenschaft, Kunst, Judentum*. Grimme: Gebhardt, 1838.
Flogaus, Reinhard. „Hebraica Christiana: Christliche Texte in hebräischer Sprache und ihre Verwendung in Schule und Mission (1475–1555)." In *Mazel Tov: Interdisziplinäre Beiträge zum Verhältnis von Christentum und Judentum. Festschrift anlässlich des 50. Geburtstages des Instituts Kirche und Judentum*, edited by Markus Witte and Tanja Pilger, 143–176. Studien zu Kirche und Israel, Neue Folge 1. Leipzig: Evangelische Verlagsanstalt, 2012.
Kautzsch, Emil. „Rezension: Gustaf Dalman, *Grammatik des Jüdisch-Palästinischen Aramäisch*." *Theologische Literaturzeitung* 20 (1895): 634–637.
Klausner, Joseph. *Ha-bayit ha-sheni bi-gedulato: shishah meḥkarim historiyim*. Tel Aviv: Devir, 1930.
Kutscher, Eduard Y. *A History of the Hebrew Language*. Jerusalem: The Magnes Press; Leiden: E.J. Brill, 1982.
Lapide, Pinchas E. *Hebräisch in den Kirchen*. Forschungen zum Jüdisch-Christlichen Dialog 1. Neukirchen, Vluyn: Neukirchener Verlag, 1976.
Lindsey, Robert Lisle. *A Hebrew Translation of the Gospel of Mark*. Forward by David Flusser. Jerusalem: Dugith Publishers, 1969.
Männchen, Julia. *Das Herz zieht nach Jerusalem: Gustaf Dalman zum 150. Geburtstag*. Greifswald: Universität Greifswald Theologische Fakultät, 2005.
Männchen, Julia. „Ernst Friedrich Paul Billerbeck (1853–1932): Stationen seines Lebens." In *Zwischen Zensur und Selbstbesinnung: Christliche Rezeptionen des Judentums*, edited by Christfried Böttrich, Judith Thomanek, and Thomas Willi, 215–288. Greifswalder theologische Forschungen 17. Frankfurt am Main: P. Lang, 2009.
Männchen, Julia. *Gustaf Dalman als Palästinawissenschaftler in Jerusalem und Greifswald (1902–1941)*. Abhandlungen des Deutschen Palästina-Vereins 9.2. Wiesbaden: Harrassowitz, 1993.
Männchen, Julia. „Gustaf Dalman – auf der Grenze: Leben und Forschen zwischen Kirche und Wissenschaft." In *Greifswalder theologische Profile: Bausteine zur Geschichte der Theologie an der Universität Greifswald*, edited by Imfried Garbe, Tilman Beyrich, and Thomas Willi, 109–126. Greifswalder theologische Forschungen 12. Frankfurt am Main: P. Lang, 2006.
Männchen, Julia. *Gustaf Dalmans Leben und Wirken in der Brüdergemeine, für die Judenmission und an der Universität Leipzig (1855–1902)*. Abhandlungen des Deutschen Palästina-Vereins 9.1. Wiesbaden: Harrassowitz, 1987.
Mathias, Dietmar. „Das Alte Testament in Lehre und Forschung an der Theologischen Fakultät Leipzig: Der Weg zu einer eigenständigen theologischen Disziplin im 19. Jahrhundert." In *Die Theologische Fakultät der Universität Leipzig: Personen, Profile und Perspektiven aus sechs Jahrhunderten Fakultätsgeschichte*, edited by Andreas Gössner und Alexander Wieckowski, 371–420. Beiträge zur Leipziger Universitäts- und Wissenschaftsgeschichte. Series A, Vol. 2. Leipzig: Evangelische Verlagsanstalt, 2005.
Merx, Adalbert. *Chrestomathia Targumica*. Porta Linguarum Orientalium 8. Berlin: H. Reuther, 1888.
Nöldeke, Theodor. *Mandäische Grammatik*. Halle: Verlag der Buchhandlung des Waisenhauses, 1875.
Osten-Sacken, Peter von der. „Liebe, mehr noch: Gerechtigkeit: Hermann Leberecht Strack und das Institutum Judaicum in Berlin in ihrem Verhältnis zum Judentum." *Judaica* 66 (2010): 40–71.
Prijs, Joseph und Bernhard Prijs. *Die Basler hebräischen Drucke*. Olten: Urs Graf-Verlag, 1964.

Rengstorf, K. H. „Gustaf Dalmans Bedeutung für die Wissenschaft vom Judentum."
    Wissenschaftliche Zeitschrift der Ernst Moritz Arndt Universität Greifswald 4 (1954/55),
    Gesellschafts- und Sprachwiss (Reihe 4/5): S. 376: [Seiten?]
Rosenthal, Franz. *Die Aramaistische Forschung seit Th. Nöldeke's Veröffentlichungen*. Leiden:
    Brill, 1939.
Rütersworden, U. „Eduard König (1846–1936)." In *Theologie als Vermittlung: Bonner
    evangelische Theologen des 19. Jahrhunderts im Porträt;* [Friedrich Wintzer zum 70.
    Geburtstag am 27. Juli 2003], edited by Reinhard Schmidt-Rost, Stephan Bitter und Martin
    Dutzmann, 172–177. Arbeiten zur Theologiegeschichte 6. Rheinbach: CMZ, 2003.
Sáenz-Badillos, Angel. *A History of the Hebrew Language*, trans. John Elwolde. Cambridge:
    Cambridge University Press, 1993.
Scaliger, Joseph Justus. *Epistolae omnes quae reperiri potuerunt, nunc primum collectae et
    editae*. Leiden: Elzevier, 1627.
Schoeps, Hans-Joachim. *Philosemitismus im Barock: Religions- und geistesgeschichtliche
    Untersuchungen*. Tübingen: J.C.B. Mohr, 1952.
Smend, Rudolf. „Franz Delitzsch: Aspekte von Leben und Werk." In *Die Erzväter in der
    biblischen Tradition: Festschrift für Matthias Köckert*, edited by A.C. Hagedorn und H.
    Pfeiffer, 347–366. Beihefte zur Zeitschrift für die Alttestamentliche Wissenschaft 400.
    Berlin: Walter de Gruyter, 2009.
Stange, Erich ed. *Die Religionswissenschaft der Gegenwart in Selbstdarstellungen*, vol. 4
    (Gustaf Dalman et al.). Leipzig: F. Meiner, 1928.
Wagner, Siegfried. *Franz Delitzsch: Leben und Werk*. Beiträge zur evangelischen Theologie, 80
    München: Kaiser, 1978.
Wellhausen, Julius. *Einleitung in die drei ersten Evangelien*. Berlin: G. Reimer, 1905.
Wellhausen, Julius. *Einleitung in die drei ersten Evangelien,* 2. Auflage. Berlin: G. Reimer, 1911.
Wiefel, W. „Von Strack zu Jeremias: Der Anteil der neutestamentlichen Wissenschaft an der
    Vorgeschichte der evangelischen Judaistik." In *Protestantismus und Antisemitismus in der
    Weimarer Republik*, edited by Kurt Nowak and Gérard Raulet, 95–125. Frankfurt am Main:
    Campus-Verlag; Paris: Editions de la Fondation Maison des Sciences de l'Homme, 1994.
Wilkinson, Robert J. *Orientalism, Aramaic and Kabbalah in the Catholic Reformation: The First
    Printing of the Syriac New Testament*. Studies in the History of Christian Tradition 137. Brill:
    Leiden, 2007.
Willi, Thomas. „Christliche Rezeption des Judentums in Greifswald: Judenmission,
    Palästinawissenschaft und Aramaistik bei Gustaf Dalman." *Judaica* 66 (2010): 18–28.
Willi, Thomas. „Gustaf Dalman und Joseph Klausner: Christliche Judentums- und
    Palästinawissenschaft im Spiegel unveröffentlichter handschriftlicher Widmungen eines
    zeitgenössischen jüdischen Forschers." In *Mazel Tov: Interdisziplinäre Beiträge zum
    Verhältnis von Christentum und Judentum. Festschrift anlässlich des 50. Geburtstages des
    Instituts Kirche und Judentum,* edited by Markus Witte and Tanja Pilger, 247–264. Studien
    zu Kirche und Israel, Neue Folge 1. Leipzig: Evangelische Verlagsanstalt, 2012.

Shalom Goldman
Apostasy, Identity, and Erudition: Paul Levertoff (1878–1954)

> The Sea of the Talmud has its Gulf Stream of mysticism
> (Paul Levertoff)

Born to a Hasidic family in White Russia, Feivel Levertoff was educated at home by his father and local rabbis, and as a teenager was sent to the renowned Talmudic academy at Volozhin. He arrived at the yeshiva with a considerable amount of prestige as he was a descendent of Rabbi Shneur Zalman of Liadi, the founder of the Habad-Lubavitch Hasidic dynasty. According to his daughter, poet Denise Levertov, he was the rabbi's great-grandson, tracing his lineage through one of Shneur Zalman's daughters. Other sources indicate that Feivel was the grandson of the Kapuster Rebbe, who had broken with the Lubavitch sect and formed his own group of Hasidim.[1] Levertoff was not the first apostate among the descendants of the Habad Rabbis; Moshe, son of Shneur Zalman of Liadi, the founder of the sect, apostasized to the Russian Orthodox Church in the early nineteenth century.[2]

The Yeshiva of Volozhin was founded at the beginning of the nineteenth century by students of the great Talmudist, the Gaon of Vilna (Rabbi Elijah of Vilna, 1720–1797), and by the time that Levertoff arrived in the 1890s it had become one of the great Talmudic academies of Europe. Though it was identified with the Mitnagdim initially, by the end of the nineteenth century many Hasidim studied there. The Yeshiva of Volozhin produced many eminent Talmudists. It also produced many famous (or infamous) rebels, heretics, and apostates, among them the Hebrew poet Hayyim Nahman Bialik (1837–1934). As Hebrew writer Yosef Hayyim

---

[1] Dana Greene, *Denise Levertov: A Poet's Life* (Urbana: University of Illinois Press, 2012). See also Paul Phillip Levertoff, *Love in the Messianic Age: Study Guide and Commentary*, ed. Toby Janicki, D. Thomas Lancaster, and Brian Reed (Marshfield, Missouri: Vine of David Publishers, 2009) and Anita Shapira, *Brener: sipur ḥayim* (Tel Aviv: ʿAm ʿoved, 2008), 74. According to these sources, Paul Levertoff was the grandchild, through his mother, of one of Rabbi Shneur Zalman's three brothers. The passage on Levertoff and the missionary activity in London directed towards Jews at the turn of the twentieth century is absent from the English translation of Shapira's biography. See Anita Shapira, *Yosef Haim Brenner: A Life*, trans. Anthony Berris, Stanford Studies in Jewish History and Culture (Stanford: Stanford University Press, 2015).
[2] See David Assaf, *Untold Tales of the Hasidim: Crisis and Discontent in the History of Hasidism* (Waltham, MA: Brandeis University Press, 2010), 29–96.

Brenner, who studied in another Lithuanian Yeshiva put it "from Volozhin great *shkotzim* (goyim, i.e. non-Jews) have emerged." Twenty years after both Levertoff and Brenner had left their respective yeshivot, they met in London and embarked on a correspondence about matters of faith, identity and Jewish nationalism.³

After a few years at the yeshiva, Feivel, a talented and precocious student, wished to attend a university to get a secular education, an opportunity denied to all but a small quota of Russian Jews. Feivel's father sent him to the University of Königsberg in Germany, a school open to Jewish applicants. At Königsberg, Levertoff had the opportunity to study the Gospels and Christian doctrine. On his first visit home, the young man, now eighteen years old, told his father about his "discovery of the Messiah." As Denise Levertov relates in her book *Tessarae*,

> Alas, his family was appalled. When my father met his father's fury staunchly, it was decided in despair that he must be mad, and he was locked into his bedroom. He climbed through the window in the middle of the night and caught the train to Petersburg, and so back to Königsberg.⁴

In 1894, at the age of seventeen, Levertoff was baptized into one of the Evangelical churches in Germany and soon afterwards moved to London to work for the LJS (the London Jews Society), whose formal name was the London Society for Promoting Christianity Among the Jews. At his baptism, Feivel Levertoff took the name Paul Phillip Levertoff. In his autobiographical writings, Levertoff described his decision to be baptized as the culmination of a process that had begun nearly a decade before he told his father of his "discovery of the Messiah," when he was just nine years old. It was then that he found and read a discarded page of a Hebrew translation of the Gospel according to Matthew. The story of the Jewish boy chosen by God to lead Israel and redeem the world took Levertoff by surprise – and he quickly realized that he had to hide his surprise and enthusiasm from his family. For his father, when presented with that page of the Gospels, destroyed the page by tearing it up and throwing the pieces in the fire. To burn a page of Hebrew writing was, as young Feivel knew, a very unusual act. What was so scandalous, he wondered, about the text on the page? His curiosity was piqued.

As in many conversion accounts, Levertoff's narrative of his "discovery" of Jesus as the Messiah has elements of both gradual change and sudden transformation. And, in Levertoff's case, as in many conversion stories, sacred text plays a pivotal role in the decision to leave one religious tradition and join another.

---

3 Jorge Quinonez, "Paul Levertoff: Pioneering Hebrew-Christian Scholar and Leader," *Mishkan* 37 (2002): 31, n. 65.
4 Denise Levertov, *Tesserae: Memories & Suppositions* (New York: New Directions, 1996), 7–8.

Three twentieth-century examples suggest themselves: for the philosopher Edith Stein, it was Teresa of Avila's autobiography, which she came across in a friend's house in 1922 and read through the night. For Donato Manduzio in 1920s rural Apulia, the text was a translation of the Old Testament into Italian (in a copy distributed by Protestant missionaries). He and his followers later converted to Judaism. For Rabbi Israel Zolli of Rome, the Gospel accounts of Jesus were pivotal. He had studied them for three decades before his conversion to Roman Catholicism in 1945. Study of the Old Testament-New Testament relationship brought him to Christianity.[5]

In the early twentieth century "Hebrew Christian" missionaries to Jews were a well-known and long-established phenomenon. Among the best known of these missionaries was Joseph Wolff (1795–1862). Like Levertoff, Wolff too was from a prominent rabbinical family. At age seventeen Wolff was baptized into the Roman Catholic Church, but after a few years found that he could not accept Catholic teachings. In the 1820's he was ordained as an Anglican priest and served for decades as a missionary to Jews, working for the London Jews Society, the same group that Paul Levertoff would serve seventy-five years later. Wolff's adventures, chronicled in his many widely-distributed books, were no doubt well-known to the young Paul Levertoff.

But unlike these better known converts who completely abandoned their previous religious identity, Levertoff insisted on maintaining and asserting his Jewish identity after his conversion to Christianity. Throughout his life he identified himself as a "Hebrew-Christian." His considerable intellectual abilities were directed toward creating a Hebrew-Christian liturgy and a Hebrew-Christian congregation. In his missionary activities, he sought to bring Jews into a religious life in which the two traditions were combined. And it is for that reason that, a half-century after his death, Levertoff was deemed a "pioneer of Hebrew Christianity" by the emergent Messianic Jewish movement in the United States. As Jorge Quinonez noted in 2002, Levertoff is "more relevant to us than he was seventy-five years ago when he seemed nothing more than a fringe theological curiosity ... he helped the Hebrew-Christian movement push in directions which reflected the modes of thought of traditional Judaism."[6]

Paul Levertoff, rejected by his family, persisted in the hope that they too would accept "the Christian Truth." Twenty years after his baptism, Levertoff dedicated one of his books, *Love and the Messianic Age*, to his father. The dedica-

---

[5] On Israel Zolli and his conversion, see Robert G. Weisbord and Wallace P. Sillanpoa, *The Chief Rabbi, the Pope, and the Holocaust: An Era in Vatican-Jewish Relations* (New Brunswick: Transaction Publishers, 1992).
[6] Quinonez, "Paul Levertoff," 32.

tion quoted the New Testament phrase "An Israelite in whom there was no guile." This is a well-known theme in modern conversion accounts: Jewish converts to Christianity persist in their hope that their parents (and/or siblings) will see the "Christian Truth" and convert. Rabbi Zolli of Rome hoped that his two daughters would follow him into the church (his wife had converted with him[7]). One of them did; the other did not.

In 1901, Paul Philip Levertoff left the London Jews Society and became a missionary for the Hebrew Christian Testimony to Israel, a London-based mission to the Jews. He was to work with the group's Jewish-born Christian missionaries for the next decade. In his first five years with the organization, Levertoff was stationed in London, where he wrote for the mission's publication, "The Scattered Nation," and produced Hebrew-language materials for its press, 'Edut le-Yisra'el ("Witness to Israel"). Among these materials were Hebrew-language tracts about Christianity that Levertoff and other missionaries authored. As his standing in the missionary organization grew, he was given more freedom and responsibility, and, by the middle of the decade, Levertoff was traveling to European Jewish communities as one of a number of Christian missionaries who directed their efforts towards both traditional and assimilated Jews. In 1908, accompanied by his fellow-convert and missionary-to-the-Jews David Baron, Levertoff embarked on a pilgrimage to the Holy Land. Baron was the founder of Hebrew Christian Testimony to Israel. Levertoff and Baron visited Palestine and Egypt, and both spent time teaching at Christian missions to the Jews in Jerusalem.

From 1901–1910, Levertoff was remarkably active as both a missionary and scholar. He produced a series of books on Christian themes, all written in Modern Hebrew, a language only then emerging as an instrument of general education, edification, and persuasion. These seven books included his own works on history and theology, and a translation of Augustine's *Confessions* into Hebrew, published in 1906. While the scholarly introduction to the *Confessions* was written in the Modern Hebrew idiom, Levertoff had translated Augustine's Latin into Rabbinic Hebrew. And the Biblical quotations quoted and referenced by Augustine are rendered in the original Hebrew. New Testament references in Augustine's text are presented in the German Lutheran theologian and Hebraist Franz Delitzsch's translations from Greek to Hebrew.[8] In all of these writings, Levertoff's Hebrew term for early Christianity is *Ha-'emunah ha-meshiḥit*, the Messianic faith.

---

[7] Weisbord and Sillanpoa, *The Chief Rabbi*, 135.
[8] On Delitzsch, see "Delitzch, Franz," *Encylopedia Judaica*, vol. 5 (Jerusalem: Keter Publishing House, 1972): 1474–1475.

When referring to the religion in subsequent historical periods, Levertoff uses the term *Natzrut*, the Nazarene faith.[9]

Levertoff's introduction to his translation of the *Confessions* concludes with an appeal to the skeptical Jewish reader, "who may be very distant from Christian thought in general and from the generation of Augustine in particular." He hopes that reader will find in this classic text "a human document which conveys an incisive portrait of a soul engaged in a profound struggle." And he notes that, in the *Confessions*, the Hebrew reader can recognize in Augustine the Christian monk and Catholic Saint "a soul close to his own." But beyond the attempt to persuade the modern Jewish reader that Augustine's writings have relevance, Levertoff also has a point to make about the canon of Hebrew literature, whose shape and content was, at the beginning of the twentieth century, being hotly debated. "The translator is quite sure that the discerning reader will bless him for his endeavor to introduce something fine into the canon of Hebrew literature, a literature very poor in translations from the classic writings of the world's religions."[10] Levertoff wrote this at the very time that the shapers of the Modern Hebrew canon were translating many of the classics of world literature into Modern Hebrew. But these were *literary* classics; sacred texts, he noted, were *not* translated. For the spirit of the *Haskalah* was overwhelmingly secular, and the religious texts of other traditions would have been perceived as a threat. And it is this perception of Christian texts as a threat to Jews and Judaism that Levertoff sought to challenge and counter.

Levertoff's *Ben ha-'Adam*, the first Modern Hebrew book about Jesus, was published in 1904. Its Hebrew subtitle was *Ḥayei Yeshuʻa ha-Mashiaḥ u-foʻalav*, and its English title was *The Son of Man: A Survey of the Life and Deeds of Jesus Christ*. *Ben ha-'Adam* was published by Hebrew Christian Testimony to Israel, the missionary organization that employed Levertoff. In the book's introduction, Levertoff refers to the growing interest in Jesus that he claimed was being expressed by many of his Jewish contemporaries. He presents his dense and scholarly book as "an innovation in Hebrew literature in which we will portray Jesus of Nazareth in the Hebrew language." In the book's introduction, Levertoff bemoans the general Jewish ignorance of the life of Jesus:

> But how then would a "simple Jew" know about Jesus? Have any of the writers who are promoting a return to Zion and the revival of our language written about the Jesus who sought to return us to our land and revive our people? Have any of our modern writers living in the

---

9 See Daniel Langton, *The Apostle Paul in the Jewish Imagination: A Study in Modern Jewish-Christian Relations* (Cambridge: Cambridge University Press, 2010), 139, n. 227.
10 *The Confessions of St. Augustine,* trans. Paul P. Levertoff (London: Luzac and Co., 1908), x.

new twentieth century sought to convey the ideas of the man from whose date of birth the centuries are counted? Have our Hebrew writers, who are lustily quoting Schopenhauer, Nietzsche, Kant and Tolstoy for our benefit, thought to quote the social ideas of Christian Messianism? Absolutely not! Yes, these writers have given us a Hebrew language life of Muhammad. A life of the Buddha will no doubt appear soon, as well as a book about the Mormons. But Jesus? Who would mention his name? Isn't this a great irony and a terrible tragedy? And at the same time it is a puzzle, one that is difficult to solve.[11]

From this attack on Jewish ignorance of — and hostility to — Jesus and Christianity, Levertoff moves to an attack on Jewish secularism, particularly as it was manifest in the Zionist movement. "These new 'enlightened' Jews," wrote Levertoff,

don't have a religion, rather, they have a nationalism. Their aim is not to protect the Talmud and the Commentaries, but maintain a peoplehood and its traditions. And from this we may conclude that our nationalists are just like the nationalists of other peoples – the Germans, the English and others. And if that is so, I have a simple question to ask our enlightened co-religionists: "Why then, my brothers, do you raise a ruckus when one of us leaves a 'religion,' which according to you doesn't really exist, and joins another faith community (Christianity), which you deem 'dangerous' . . . Is this the way enlightened nationalists in other countries would act? Is there a religion that a German or Englishman would have to practice in order for them to be deemed a proper patriot?"

Note the sarcastic, polemical tone of Levertoff's rhetoric, a tone well-honed by Hebrew writers of the period.

Less than a year after publishing *Ben ha-'Adam*, Levertoff wrote another Hebrew language book, *St. Paul: His Life, Works, and Travels* (London, 1905). As historian Daniel Langton has noted recently: "Effusive in his admiration for Paul, Levertoff regarded him as a Jewish hero who took Jesus' true Judaism or messianism to the Gentile World."[12]

Levertoff's identification with the apostle Paul colors the manner in which he constructed Paul's biography. He notes that "the Jewish people have considered Paul its greatest heretic." And he describes Paul's religious development in terms similar to his own: "Paul's family sends him to a yeshiva to study for the Rabbinate and later Paul may very well have studied in Tarsus' equivalent of a university, where he became familiar with Greek thought."[13]

In 1908 and 1909, Levertoff published two short Hebrew language tracts, each about thirty pages in length. *Yisra'el, emunato u-te'udato* [*Israel's Religion and Destiny: A Biblico-Historical Essay*] calls on maskilim to abandon Jewish nation-

---

[11] Paul P. Levertoff, *The Son of Man: A Survey of the Life and Deeds of Jesus Christ*, 2nd ed. (London: Hebrew Christian Testimony to Israel, 1911), iv–v.
[12] Langton, *The Apostle Paul*, 143.
[13] Ibid., 140.

alist ideas, particularly Zionism, and embrace the "messianic truth" of Christianity. In opposition to what Levertoff deems the false, secular ideas of the Zionists, he offers his readers the possibility of a spiritual redemption, a redemption that will come when "Israel recognizes its true faith and destiny."[14]

Hu' va-'ani: dapim mi-sefer zikhronotai [*He and I: Pages from My Memoirs*],[15] published in 1909, is a literary evocation of Levertoff's youth. It focuses on his contact with a fellow yeshiva student, Shmuel, whose intellectual and spiritual yearnings lead him to Christianity, and to rejection and humiliation by the local Jewish community.

In 1910, after a decade with the Hebrew Christian Testimony to Israel, David Baron's missionary group, Levertoff moved to Constantinople. There he served as a missionary to the Jews on behalf of the United Free Church of Scotland's "Jewish Committee." By the early twentieth century, the Scottish school in Constantinople was well established. It drew its teaching staff from England, Scotland, and Wales. Among the students in Constantinople were Muslims, Eastern Christians, and Jews from the Ottoman lands. Among the teachers was Beatrice Spooner-Jones of North Wales. Paul and Beatrice fell in love and were soon engaged to be married. As their daughter Denise Levertov put it, "Thus Celt and Jew met in Byzantium."[16]

After their 1911 wedding in England, the young couple went to Warsaw to serve as missionaries to that city's large Jewish population. But within a year they were called to Leipzig, where Paul Levertoff was offered a teaching position at the Institutum Judaicum (later named the Delitzschianum after its founder, the great scholar Franz Delitzsch). This institute trained Protestant missionaries to Jews and had from its inception a professorship in Hebrew and Rabbinics. In 1912, Levertoff assumed this teaching post and taught courses on biblical interpretation, Rabbinic texts, Jewish polemics, and the Yiddish language – subjects which the institute deemed useful for missionaries wishing to convert Jews to Christianity. Levertoff's predecessor in this professorship was Yechiel Lichtenstein, an Orthodox Rabbi who had converted to Christianity in the late nineteenth century.

In 1914, with the outbreak of World War I, Levertoff was placed under house arrest in Warsaw, as he was a Russian citizen. Despite this restriction, Levertoff wrote three scholarly books during this period, including a German translation of

---

14 Paul P. Levertoff, *Israel's Religion and Destiny: A Biblico-Historical Essay* (London: Hebrew Christian Testimony to Israel, 1908), 3.
15 Paul Levertoff, *Hu' va-'ani: dapim mi-sefer zikhronotai* (London: Edut le-Yisrael, 1909).
16 Levertov, *Tesserae*, 11.

selections from the Talmud.[17] These books were commissioned and published by the Institutum Judaicum.

Over the next decade, two daughters were born to the Levertoffs, Olga, born in 1914 in Germany, and Denise, born in 1923 in London. As a colleague of Levertoff's noted, "Both girls were intellectually precocious and encouraged to be old beyond their years."[18] Olga sought to become her father's intellectual and spiritual heir; Denise had artistic aspirations, which first expressed themselves in music and dance, and later in poetry and prose. Olga was to stay with her parents in England; Denise immigrated to the U.S.

Returning to England after the end of the First World War, the Levertoff family moved to Wales where Levertoff served as a church librarian while studying for the Anglican priesthood. In 1923 he was ordained as an Anglican priest by the Archbishop of Wales and soon afterwards moved back to London to establish a "Hebrew Christian Church" under the supervision of the English authorities. Officially, this church would be part of the Anglican Communion, but it would have a unique liturgy, a liturgy that would appeal to converts from Judaism. And once converted, those Jews would remain within this community. This was Levertoff's aim, but it did not work out in the manner he envisioned.

In shaping this new congregation, Levertoff sought to create a church in "a congenial Jewish traditional environment where the essentials of Christian Faith and worship are expressed, as much as possible, in Jewish terms."[19] For his Hebrew Christian congregation, Levertoff wrote a Hebrew and Aramaic prayer book that sought to blend Jewish and Christian liturgical traditions. Levertoff held the Hebrew service, which he titled *"Se'udata Demalka' Kadisha'"* ("The Meal of the Holy King," a Eucharistic service) on Saturdays, the Jewish Sabbath, not on Sundays. In the late 1930's, this service was held every Saturday in two London churches.[20] On Sundays, Levertoff would preach in other London churches about his missionary activities. Levertoff's new liturgy quoted from the Zohar and other Kabbalistic writings, and did so using the Aramaic originals, not their Hebrew translations. The name of Jesus was interpolated into traditional Jewish prayers. The Hebrew language instructions in the prayer book referred to the *Kohen* or

---

[17] Adolf Schlatter, *The Church in the New Testament Period*, trans. Paul P. Levertoff (London: S.P.C.K., 1955), ix-x.
[18] Paul Lacey, "An Afterword," in Denise Levertov, *Selected Poems* (New York: New Directions Pub. Corp., 2002), 204.
[19] Olga Levertoff, *The Wailing Wall* (London: Morehouse Pub. Co, 1937), 119. Here Olga Levertoff quotes the uncited words of her father.
[20] Ibid., 121–23.

priest, who was to lead the service. But the reference here was to an Anglican priest (in this case, Levertoff himself), not to a Jewish layperson of priestly origins.

Aramaic, both from the Zohar and other texts, is featured in these prayers. Levertoff's knowledge of the Aramaic of the Zohar was considerable, and he quotes freely from the Zohar and other Kabbalistic writings in his liturgical compositions. Because of his proficiency in Aramaic, he was later employed by the Soncino Press of London to collaborate on the English translation of the Zohar that was published in 1933.

It would be more than forty years after Levertoff created his liturgy that a similar effort to create a complete Hebrew Eucharistic service was made within the Roman Catholic Church. In the early 1960's, Brother Daniel of the Carmel monastery in Haifa translated the Latin Mass into Hebrew. This Hebrew Mass was approved by the Catholic Church (the Pope gave special permission for mass to be recited in Hebrew), and it has been used among Israeli "Hebrew Catholics" ever since.[21]

In addition to attending to his church duties, Levertoff cultivated contacts in scholarly circles, including the British universities. He served as an examiner in Hebrew and Old Testament theology at the University of Leeds, and on occasion was a guest lecturer at Lincoln, one of the Oxford Colleges. But his scholarly relationships were not limited to Christians or to other missionary converts to Christianity. Levertoff, unlike other Jewish apostates of the period, established and maintained contacts with many scholars within the Jewish world. Jewish scholars, aware of his considerable erudition in both Jewish and Christian texts, would consult with him, too.

While apostasy (or *shmad*) did constitute an act of "self-destruction" in the eyes of the Jewish community, each case differed and each individual "*meshummad*" fared differently. To some extent, this depended on the intentions of the apostate, and the social and political situation of the local Jewish community. Before the mid-nineteenth century, virtually all Jewish converts to Christianity were considered threats to both local Jews and the larger Jewish world. From the fifteenth century on, the stories of Jews, among them rabbis, who apostasized and then turned against their former co-religionists, were deeply embedded in Jewish lore and consciousness. They were "*meshummadim*" in two senses – they had destroyed themselves by turning to Christianity and they had attempted to destroy the community they had left. Levertoff was deeply aware of these atti-

---

21 See Pinhas E. Lapide, *Hebrew in the Church: The Foundations of Jewish-Christian Dialogue* (Grand Rapids, MI: Eerdmans, 1984), 128–129. There were, however, earlier, partial Hebrew translations of the mass prepared in the State of Israel. On this, see the sub-section "The Beginnings of the Roman Catholic Mass" in Lapide, 115–132.

tudes towards apostates, and he tried to avoid being identified with Jewish apostates of the past.

In this respect, his case recalls that of the renowned apostate Daniel Chwolson of late-nineteenth-century Russia, whose relationship with Jewish leaders remained close because he positioned himself as an advocate for Jewish causes and concerns. For example, when a blood libel accusation arose in the 1860's, Chwolson, at that time Professor of Semitic Languages at the University of St. Petersburg, informed the Czarist authorities that such an accusation was a libel, not a legitimate claim. Soon afterwards, Chwolson published a scholarly monograph refuting all claims that Jews used the blood of Christians in the Passover ritual. It did not stop future libels, but it influenced the Russian courts to not take these accusations seriously.[22]

Levertoff, resident in London, where Jews enjoyed religious freedom if not full social equality, did not have to defend Jews against blood libel accusations. But he did have to contend with a more genteel type of anti-Semitism. In addition, he wished to forge scholarly and social ties with members of a number of London's religious communities, Jews among them. For his Jewish interlocutors, these scholarly ties were not without encumbrances. For Levertoff did not hide his Christian missionary aims. Rather, he highlighted them. Nevertheless, his ties with Jewish scholars were maintained and in some cases strengthened during his thirty years in London. Like Professor Daniel Chwolson, Paul Phillip Levertoff was thought of by many Jews as what Shulamit Magnus has called a "good bad Jew." That is to say, although he had apostasized, and served as a missionary to Jews, he could still be of service and benefit to the local Jewish community.[23]

Levertoff's remarkable scholarly output of 1901–1910, consisting of seven books in Hebrew and German, was replicated in the 1920's and 30's, when he produced nine books in English. His accessible writing style in German and Hebrew had impressed many readers; his English style was equally fluent. The most daring, creative, and heretical of Levertoff's books appeared in a series on "Studies in Jewish and Christian Piety." Titled *Love and the Messianic Age in Hitherto Untranslated Hasidic Writings: with Special Reference to the Fourth Gospel*, this short book was based on lectures that Levertoff delivered to the Origen Society of Lincoln College, Oxford in 1920.

Acutely aware that the terms "Rabbinic" or "Pharisaic" had negative connotations for his Christian audience (he quotes Dr. Johnson's dictionary: "Phar-

---

[22] On Chwolson, see Shulamit S. Magnus, "Good Bad Jews" in *Boundaries of Jewish Identity*, ed. Susan A. Glenn and Naomi Sokoloff (Seattle: University of Washington Press, 2010): 142–6.
[23] Magnus, "Good Bad Jews," 149–150.

isaical (adjective) – externally religious: from the sect of the Pharisees, whose religion consists almost wholly in ceremonies."), Levertoff tells his readers that "I hope by means of this short study to prove that traditional Orthodox Judaism has no lack of spiritual fervour. Even 'the Sea of the Talmud' has its Gulf Stream of Mysticism."[24] Levertoff describes a Hasidic theology in which the mystic seeks "a knowledge of the inner being of God . . . a consummation which will not be reached until the Messianic Age . . . It is the business of the Hasid to live for the realization of this Messianic Age." The "Hasidic Theology" presented in *Love and the Messianic Age* draws on the Zohar and on the writings of Levertoff's ancestor Rabbi Shneur Zalman of Liadi: *Tanya'*, (1797) *Likkute Torah*, *Torah 'or* (1848), and on the Kabbalistic and Hasidic writings of other masters.[25] Levertoff displays a remarkable familiarity with and mastery of these esoteric writings. Anticipating mid-twentieth-century scholarship (especially that of Gershom Scholem) concerning Hasidic thought, Levertoff notes that "a great deal of Hasidic thought revolves around the consideration of the Messianic Age, which the theologians endeavor by their method to anticipate as far as may be."[26]

The book's epilogue, "Love in the Fourth Gospel" presents the experience of the members of the early Christian churches as "the realization of the highest ideal of the Hasidim – Achdut (unity)."[27] For Levertoff, "the most 'Hasidic' writing in the New Testament is *the Gospel According to John*."[28] In that gospel, we see that "Love is a reality only in the Messianic Community of the Church."[29]

Love and the Messianic Age was published in 1923, while Levertoff and his family were living in Hawarden, Wales, where he worked in a parish library and studied for the priesthood. His industriousness in scholarly production was not diminished in a period in which he was occupied with work and family. To the contrary, his scholarly output increased.

Thereafter, again in London, the Levertoffs purchased a small house where they spent the next thirty years, until Paul's death in 1954, during which period he served Holy Trinity, a small Anglican congregation in Shoreditch. A striking detail is that in Levertoff's home office he worked at a desk over which towered a larger-than-life statue of Jesus. Levertoff had spent the first four decades of his life on the move – in Russia, England, Palestine, Turkey, Poland, Germany, and

---

[24] Paul P. Levertoff, *Love and the Messianic Age: In Hitherto Untranslated Hasidic Writings; with Special Reference to the Fourth Gospel* (London: Episcopal Hebrew Christian Church, 1923), vii.
[25] Ibid., v.
[26] Ibid., 4.
[27] Ibid., 50.
[28] Ibid., 51.
[29] Ibid., 57.

Wales. Now, in London, he had a stable environment in which to think and write. It was in his London congregation that Levertoff created his Hebrew Christian Church. Its congregants would be, in his words,

> A group within the universal Church composed of racially, intellectually, and spiritually conscious Jews who, having accepted Christianity and become conscious Christians, refuse to renounce their Jewish identity, since they believe this to be entrenched and completed in Christ. But instead (they) demonstrate to the Jewish and Christian worlds the fact that Christ may be worshipped and his life lived in Jewish terms.[30]

The idea of a Hebrew Christian Church was heretical to both Jews and Christians.

With the rise of Nazism, many of the Jewish refugees fleeing Germany who settled in or passed through London sought Levertoff's company and counsel. And this despite the fact that he was well-known as a *meshummad*, an apostate. Like Daniel Chwolson in the nineteenth century, Levertoff was understood by many Jews as a friend of the Jewish community, not an adversary.

In 1926 Levertoff published *The Midrash Sifre on Numbers*, an annotated translation of a Rabbinic text previously unavailable in any European language. The text's scholarly introduction was by Herbert Box, Professor of Old Testament Exegesis at Kings College London. The translation is very faithful to the Hebrew original and Levertoff's scholarly footnotes make frequent reference to the New Testament. In his own introduction to the book, Levertoff mentions that he has almost completed English translations of the Mechiltah, the Sifra, and Sifre to Deuteronomy. These were never published and are not among his papers.

In the early 1930s, Paul Levertoff joined with two other scholars to produce the first English translation of the full text of the Zohar, the central text of the Jewish mystical tradition. His collaborators were the Jewish British scholars Maurice Simon and Harry Sperling, and there was no doubt some trepidation on their part and on the part of the publishers, the Soncino Press, about working with an apostate and missionary to the Jews. But Levertoff brought very rare skills to this translation project. For the Zohar is written in an Aramaic very different from that of Biblical or Talmudic Aramaic, and its world of ideas is complex, labyrinthine and inaccessible to most Judaica scholars. (This translation was done before the revolution in the study of Jewish mystical texts occasioned by the scholarly project of Gershom Scholem of the Hebrew University.) Levertoff knew the Zohar, and the Hasidic texts influenced by the Zohar, from his studies as a yeshiva student – and more directly from teachers within the tradition of his family – the descendants of Schneur Zalman of Liadi, the first Habad Rebbe.

---

30 Olga Levertoff, "Diary of an Optimist," *The Church and the Jews* 106 (Jan. 1936): 15.

According to Paul's wife Beatrice, the Soncino Press turned to her husband for assistance only after they had failed to find another competent translator. By the mid-1930s, when the Soncino Press embarked on the Zohar project, Levertoff was well known as an apostate and a missionary, and his name on the books' title page might have been an embarrassment. The press feared that "having his name on the publication would damage their credibility and feared that subscribers would cancel their subscriptions to the publication." But, as Mrs. Levertoff relates, her husband "insisted that if they used his work they place his name on the translation."[31]

Among the many Jewish figures that Levertoff was in contact with during his London years was Hans Herzl. Hans, the only son of Theodore Herzl, had been living in England since his youth. The Zionist organization had arranged for Hans to be educated at an English prep school and then at Cambridge University. Hans came to Paul Levertoff's church after having converted to Catholicism. Tragically, Hans Herzl later committed suicide after the death of his sister.

As he grew older, Paul Levertoff transmitted to his daughter Olga the essential elements of his Jewish-Christian synthesis. Though her unconventional and rebellious behavior disappointed both her parents, (they disapproved of her identification with the British Left and her volunteering to fight in the Spanish Civil War), Olga did write eloquently and forcefully about her father's ideas. She identified her own rebelliousness with his. "From the beginning he was a rebel," she wrote of her father. In her books and pamphlets she expounded on her father's observation that "Christianity is Judaism with its hopes fulfilled," and pointed out that, "from the age of eighteen . . . Paul Levertoff had been following a consistent path – the way of reconciliation between church and synagogue, between Jew and Gentile, between the Christianity influenced by Hellenistic concepts and the 'Jerusalem Church' from which it developed."

Olga Levertoff understood well the price her father had to pay for both his missionary activities and his attempts at shaping a Jewish-Christian synthesis – or, one might say, syncretism. Though some eminent Jewish scholars consulted with him, he was shunned by most British Jewish leaders. She wrote that, "From the day Levertoff became a Christian the enmity of the Jewish community was directed against him. The very fact that he is *sincere* in his profession made his apparent apostasy the more heinous a crime."[32] While the Jewish community shunned Paul Levertoff, his adopted Christian community was not completely at ease with him either. As Denise Levertoff's biographer Dana Greene has noted,

---

31 Quoted in Levertoff, *Love in the Messianic Age*, ed. Janicki, Lancaster, and Reed, 18.
32 Olga Levertoff, "Paul Levertoff and the Jewish-Christian Problem," in *Judaism and Christianity: Essays Presented to the Rev. Paul P. Levertoff, D.D.*, ed. Lev Gillet (London: J.B. Shears and Sons, 1940): 95.

"The Church of England did not quite know what to do with him. His vocation was both to Jews – to show that Christianity was not alien to them – and to Gentiles – to point out the Jewish origins of Christianity and thereby illustrate that anti-Semitism was incompatible with Christian life."[33]

Indications of antipathy to Levertoff persist in the *Encyclopedia Judaica*, published in Jerusalem in 1971–2. The entry for "Levertoff, Paul Philip" tells us much about the way he was remembered in "official" Jewish quarters. The entry opens with this description: "apostate and theologian. Levertoff, who was born in Orsha, Belorussia, into a Hasidic family, was converted to Christianity in 1895."[34]

Among the intellectual cultural figures that Levertoff was in contact with in his London years was the poet T.S. Eliot. They served together on a number of Church of England cultural committees. Levertoff gave some of his daughter Denise's early poems (she was 16 at the time) to Eliot, who wrote her a letter of encouragement,[35] though he declined to publish her early efforts.

It was only after her father's death in 1954 that Denise Levertov, then living in the U.S., began to take an interest in Hasidic thought – perhaps she felt released by her father's death to do so. She read carefully and deeply in Martin Buber's *Tales of the Hasidim* – and was especially pleased to find there stories of her father's ancestor, Rabbi Shneur Zalman.[36]

Writing of Denise Levertov's poetry of the late 1950's and early 1960's, Edward Zlotkowski noted that "throughout this period the importance of the Hasidic element in [her] background continues to unfold and make its influence felt both in her approach to art and in her understanding of reality in general."[37] Her father's "discovery" of Jesus was a recurring theme in her poems. Denise Levertov imagined the scene of her father's childhood "discovery" of Jesus as taking place in the deep of a Russian winter. In the late afternoon young Feivel was returning from playing with his friends on the icy banks of the Dnieper River.

> As he trudged homeward my father's eye was caught by a scrap of printed paper lying in the gray, trampled snow. Though he was a playful, disobedient boy like any other, he was also – like his playmates – a little Talmud scholar, respectful of words; and he saw at a glance, too, that this paper was not printed in Russian but in Hebrew. So he picked it up and began to read. Could it be a fragment of Torah? Never before had he read such a story: about a boy

---

33 Greene, *Denise Levertov*, 16.
34 "Levertoff, Paul Philip," *Encyclopedia Judaica*, vol. 11 (Jerusalem: Keter Publishing House, 1972), col. 71.
35 Greene, *Denise Levertov*, 19 and 38.
36 Ibid., 67–71.
37 Edward Zlotkowski, "Levertov and Christianity: A Journey Toward Renewal," *Christianity and Literature* 41.4 (1992): 447.

like himself who – it said – was found in the Temple expounding the scriptures to the old, reverent, important rabbis!

My father took the scrap – it was obviously a page from a book – home to his father. The effect was startling. No one asked him where he had been, so his disobedience – risking his life once more in the strictly prohibited game of ice-floe riding – went unnoticed. (He would not have lied.) Instead, his father became angry – not with him, exactly, but rather with the text he had brought to show him. He tore it into pieces and thrust them into the stove. My father was vehemently told to avoid such writings, utterly, if ever he should again encounter them; but just what they were, and how to tell them from holy writ, was not explained. My father was awed to see written words destroyed – Hebrew words. It was not as if it had been a mere scrap of Russian newspaper.

Secretly, he wished he had not given up the mysterious fragment. Who was the wise boy in the story? Yet he knew he ought not to wonder. It was wrong; but he could not forget it.[38]

In her poem "Wings in the Pedlar's Pack," Denise Levertov imagines her father going home from his studies at Königsberg University and telling his father of his "discovery of the Messiah":

You bore such news, so longed-for,
Fulfilling a hope so ancient
it had almost become dry parchment
not hope any more.

At the station you hailed a droshky
Greeted the driver like a brother.
At last there was the street,
There was the house:

But when you arrived
They would not listen
They laughed at you.
And then they wept.
But would not listen.[39]

For students of American literary history, Paul Levertoff's life and work is a reference point for understanding his daughter's poetry and prose. For students of American religion and the Christian-Jewish relationship in the U.S. and elsewhere, Levertoff's work has garnered attention because of the emergence of "Messianic Judaism." Levertoff's comparative study of Hasidism and Pauline thought, *Love*

---

38 Levertov, *Tesserae*, 4–5.
39 Levertov, *Selected Poems*, 167.

and the Messianic Age, has been adapted as a core text by some American Messianic congregations. And Levertoff's *yahrzeit*, the anniversary of his death, is now marked among both American and Israeli "meshiḥiyim" or "Messianic Jews."[40] As Boaz Michael wrote in 2009, when "Levertoff wrote *Love and the Messianic Age*, modern Messianic Judaism did not yet exist . . . [today it] is an important book for Messianic Judaism and Christianity both."[41]

Bibliography

Assaf, David. *Untold Tales of the Hasidim: Crisis and Discontent in the History of Hasidism*. Waltham, MA: Brandeis University Press, 2010.

Greene, Dana. *Denise Levertov: A Poet's Life*. Urbana: University of Illinois Press, 2012.

Lancaster, D. Thomas. "The Yahrzeit of Paul Phillip Levertoff."
http://ffoz.org/discover/messianic-luminaries/the-yahrzeit-of-paul-phillip-levertoff.html

Langton, Daniel R. *The Apostle Paul in the Jewish Imagination: A Study in Modern Jewish-Christian Relations*. 1st ed. Cambridge: Cambridge University Press, 2010.

Lapide, Pinhas E. *Hebrew in the Church: The Foundations of Jewish-Christian Dialogue*. Grand Rapids, MI: Eerdmans, 1984.

Levertoff, Olga. "Diary of an Optimist." *The Church and the Jews* 106 (Jan. 1936): 12–26.

Levertoff, Olga. "Paul Levertoff and the Jewish-Christian Problem." In *Judaism and Christianity: Essays Presented to the Rev. Paul P. Levertoff, D.D.*, edited by Lev Gillet, 93–110. London: J.B. Shears and Sons, 1940.

Levertoff, Olga. *The Jews in a Christian Social Order*. London: The Sheldon Press; New York: The Macmillan Company, 1942.

Levertoff, Olga. *The Wailing Wall*. London: Morehouse Pub. Co, 1937.

Levertoff, Paul P. *Hu' va-'ani: dapim mi-sefer zikhronotai*. London: Edut le-Yisrael, 1909.

Levertoff, Paul P. *Love and the Messianic Age: In Hitherto Untranslated Hasidic Writings; with Special Reference to the Fourth Gospel*. London: Episcopal Hebrew Christian Church, 1923.

Levertoff, Paul P. *Love and the Messianic Age: Study Guide and Commentary*," edited by Toby Janicki, D. Thomas Lancaster, and Brian Reed. Messianic Luminaries Series. Marshfield, Missouri: Vine of David Publishers, 2009.

Levertoff, Paul P. *The Christian Doctrine of God*. The Hebrew Library of the Christian Faith. London: The Sheldon Press, 1931.

Levertoff, Paul P. trans. *The Confessions of St. Augustine*. London: Luzac and Co., 1908.

Levertoff, Paul P. *The Messianic Hope: The Divine and Human Factors*. London: Thomas Murby & Co, 1938.

---

[40] For example, see D. Thomas Lancaster, "The Yahrzeit of Paul Phillip Levertoff," accessed Feb. 20, 2020, http://ffoz.org/discover/messianic-luminaries/the-yahrzeit-of-paul-phillip-levertoff.html.

[41] Boaz Michael, "Foreword," in Levertoff, *Love and the Messianic*, 7 and 9.

Levertoff, Paul P. *The Son of Man: A Survey of the Life and Deeds of Jesus Christ*. 2nd ed. London: Hebrew Christian Testimony to Israel, 1911.

Levertoff, Paul P. *Yisra'el, emunato u-te'udato*. London: Hebrew Christian Testimony to Israel, 1908.

Levertov, Denise. *Tesserae: Memories & Suppositions*. First Paperback Edition. New York: New Directions, 1996.

Levertov, Denise. *Selected Poems*. New York: New Directions Pub. Corp., 2002.

Levertov, Denise. *The Stream & the Sapphire: Selected Poems on Religious Themes*. New York: New Directions, 1997.

Magnus, Shulamit S. "Good Bad Jews." In *Boundaries of Jewish Identity*, edited by Susan A. Glenn and Naomi Sokoloff, 132–160. Seattle: University of Washington Press, 2010.

Quinonez, Jorge. "Paul Levertoff: Pioneering Hebrew-Christian Scholar and Leader." *Mishkan* 37 (2002): 21–34.

Schlatter, Adolf. *The Church in the New Testament Period*, trans. Paul P. Levertoff. London: S.P.C.K., 1955.

Shapira, Anita. *Brener: sipur ḥayim*. Tel Aviv: 'Am 'oved, 2008.

Shapira, Anita. *Yosef Haim Brenner: A Life*, trans. Anthony Berris. Stanford Studies in Jewish History and Culture. Stanford: Stanford University Press, 2015.

Sheleg, Yair. "Chabad's Lost Son." *Haaretz*, Dec. 26, 2002.

Weisbord, Robert G., and Wallace P. Sillanpoa. *The Chief Rabbi, the Pope, and the Holocaust: An Era in Vatican-Jewish Relations*. New Brunswick: Transaction Publishers, 1992.

Zlotkowski, Edward. "Levertov and Christianity: A Journey Toward Renewal." *Christianity and Literature* 41.4 (1992): 443–470.

Liora R. Halperin
Metaphors of the Sacred and Profane in Pre-State Zionist Hebrew Discourse

1 Introduction

"Flowing down from the hills of eternity, the Hebrew language has been set apart by God as the receptacle of truths destined to sway mankind and humanize the world," wrote the Livornese-American Rabbi Sabato Morais in 1876.[1] Hebrew was traditionally a holy language, marked for limited, exalted uses. The fascination it generated among both Jews and European Christians stemmed from its position as a holy tongue, the language of revelation and a space outside quotidian concerns.

Zionist cultural advocacy on behalf of Hebrew suggested that Hebrew's set-apart quality could and must be undermined so that the language would become suited for all purposes.[2] When Hebrew did not readily achieve full functional dominance in a society made up of Jewish immigrants from various points of origin, located under British mandatory rule, in the heart of the Arabic-speaking Middle East, activist organizations lamented and contested the apparent linguistic chaos. At the same time, however, a more limited conception of Hebrew's purview prevailed in practice. While official responses were based on the supposition that Hebrew was now a language for all activities and all times, other, less widely studied responses were based on the supposition that Hebrew remained a set-apart language, appropriate for particular spaces and times but not necessary in others. Just as users of Hebrew in pre-Zionist times understood that Hebrew would be used in some settings but not others, members of the Yishuv understood and played by a set of linguistic rules which required Hebrew in certain contexts, but condoned and sometimes encouraged the use of other languages in others.

Understanding the limits of Hebrew penetration in the Yishuv, some scholars have begun recently to question the realities of language practice as part of a broader turn to the cultural history of Zionism.[3] This article seeks to understand these

---

1 Cited in J.H. Hertz, *A Book of Jewish Thoughts Selected and Arranged by the Chief Rabbi* (Oxford: Oxford University Press, 1921), 13.
2 See, for example, Natan Efrati, *Mi-lashon yeḥidim le-lashon umah: ha-dibur ha-'Ivri be-Eretz Yisra'el ba-shanim 1882–1922* (Jerusalem: Hebrew Language Academy), 2004; Shmuel Morag, "Ha-'Ivrit ha-ḥadashah be-hitgabshutah: lashon ba-askpeklaryah shel ḥevrah," *Katedrah* 56 (1990): 70–92; Shlomo Karmi, *'Am eḥad ve-safah aḥat* (Jerusalem: Israel Ministry of Defense, 1997).
3 See Anat Helman, "Even the Dogs in the Street Bark in Hebrew: National Ideology and Everyday Culture in Tel Aviv," *Jewish Quarterly Review*, New Ser. 92, No. 3–4 (2002): 359–382; Liora R.

linguistic norms in light of a particular rhetoric long applied to Hebrew and its linguistic others: the language of sacredness and profaneness that had been modified in the context of modern nationalism, with the nation and its rituals now bearing the mantle of the sacred. The nation, it has been said, became the new repository of the sacred in modern times. We might also ask, in tandem, how this new conception of the sacred made room, as the sacred always makes room, for the profane. Were linguistic others impure forces that needed to be kept out at all costs, or were they rather simply profane sectors of a variegated system, inadmissible to certain sacred spaces, but conditionally acceptable within a complex social system?

As Jews in early-twentieth-century Palestine negotiated the place of Hebrew, they sometimes deployed a vocabulary of sacredness and profaneness both to define spheres outside the purview of Hebrew and to justify not using Hebrew at all places and at all times. On the one hand, the sacredness of national cultural practice and national loyalty was threatened and potentially displaced by the emergence (or persistence) of profane languages, whose profaneness was impure and ipso facto prohibited. As such, these profanities needed to be stamped out and isolated. On the other hand, the sacredness of Hebrew demanded that it be set apart within a social system that dictated special, respected functions for the language, against and alongside the profane, the neutral and unmarked stable state. Thus, these apparently contradictory forms of rhetoric – claims that other languages had no place and claims that other languages had real, if delimited, places, collectively constituted a shifting discourse about Hebrew's sacredness and the admissibility of other tongues. Ultimately, I argue, as the traditional discourse of sacred and profane was refigured in national terms, the emergent tension between the national sacred and the transnational or non-national profane, was a dominant feature of the linguistic discourse of the time. A division of linguistic labor required that other languages be granted real, if delimited, places at the boundaries of the nation.

2 Hebrew's Traditional Sacredness

In the traditional mode, Hebrew's sacredness lay in its separateness. This view was typical not only of Jews but also of Christian scholars who, at least since the early modern period, had accorded Hebrew the status of a primordial, sacred, and universal language. The Talmudic rabbis and medieval commentators had created a rich tradition of veneration for and protection of Hebrew, a linguistic stand-in for

---

Halperin, *Babel in Zionism: Jews, Nationalism, and Language Diversity in Palestine, 1920–1948* (New Haven, CT: Yale University Press, 2015).

the sacred more generally. Maimonides, influenced no doubt by the Muslim tradition concerning eloquent Arabic (*fusha*), spoke about the importance of *tzaḥut*, or purity, in language. On one level, the principles of corruption would apply to any language, "The root of the degradation of any language is the entrance of other languages into it."[4] But Hebrew was a language apart, thought Maimonides, it is "the language that the holy one, praised be he, speaks with his prophets and his people . . . and in which he created his world and gave names to the heavens and then earth and all that is in it."[5] Meanwhile, Christian Hebraists had embarked on the study of Hebrew, seeing it as a pathway to biblical truths and, moreover, a potential conduit to encouraging the conversion of Jews. Hebrew, the "mother of all languages" according to a tradition that stretched as far back as Jerome and Augustine, was potent, transcendent, and deserving of study because it was set aside for special purposes outside of the flow of daily life. Yiddish, on the other hand, was the quotidian language that was marked as alternately mundane and degenerate.[6]

The sacred, writes Mircea Eliade in his classic work on the topic, exists in a world profoundly divided between sacred and profane.[7] Hebrew – like sacred objects more generally – was associated with certain spaces, particularly the study hall and synagogue, and with certain times, particularly holidays and the Sabbath. The Sabbath marked the convergence point of time and space, as it was associated with special ritual requirements marking the traditional day of rest on which Jews were enjoined to desist from quotidian labor, known biblically as *melakhah*, and to spend time in the synagogue hearing the Torah read and reciting a mostly Hebrew liturgy.[8]

Noting this ritual place of Hebrew, individual early modern Rabbis went further and specifically recommended Hebrew speech on the Sabbath. The custom was apparently most widespread in Central Europe. The commentator Shene Luḥot ha-Berit (Yeshayah Ha-Levi Horovitz, 1558–1630) cited the Babylonian Talmud as justification of the practice (Sabbath 113b – "Make not your Sabbath speech like your profane speech"). R. Yitzḥak Lampronti (1679–1756) justified Hebrew speech in

---

4 Moses Maimonides, *Commentary on Nezirut*, 1:1.
5 Cited in Jacob S. Levinger, *Ha-Rambam ke-filosof ukhe-fosek* (Jerusalem: Bialik Institute, 1989), 94. Unless otherwise indicated, all translations are mine.
6 Sander L Gilman, *Jewish Self-Hatred: Anti-Semitism and the Hidden Language of the Jews* (Baltimore: Johns Hopkins University Press, 1986), 25–26; Aya Elyada, *A Goy Who Speaks Yiddish: Christians and the Jewish Language in Early Modern Germany* (Stanford, CA: Stanford University Press, 2012), 19–22; Stephen G. Burnett, *Christian Hebraism in the Reformation Era (1500–1660): Authors, Books, and the Transmission of Jewish Learning* (Leiden: Brill, 2012), 11–13.
7 Mircea Eliade, *The Sacred and the Profane; The Nature of Religion* (New York: Harper and Row, 1961), 20–21.
8 Exodus 20:8–11; Cf. Deuteronomy 5:12–15, which also references the Exodus from Egypt as a rationale for the observance of the Sabbath.

part by affirming that the medieval Kabbalists had done the same. Rabbi Nachman of Bratslav (1770–1881) cited Talmud Sotah 38a, which discussed the necessity of saying blessings in the holy tongue.⁹ This custom was also practiced by some religious women in Ottoman Jerusalem. Shim'on Berman, in his 1870 travel journal to Palestine, recalled a woman named Sheine Rivka Sheikovitz, who, though she spoke Yiddish normally, spoke Hebrew on the Sabbath.¹⁰ The workweek, it seemed clear, was the time for profane languages, whether European or Middle Eastern tongues or Jewish languages such as Ladino and Yiddish; the Sabbath, in contrast, would contain a flash of the sacred language amidst and against the profane.

The association of Hebrew with sacred or elevated spheres persisted into the period of the Haskalah. With the first stirrings of Modern Hebrew literature, Hebrew now was available to express non-religious matters and fictional plots. However, given a choice between Hebrew and German or Yiddish writing, the choice of Hebrew also set writing apart from the usual flow of life. In analyzing two works by Aaron Halle-Wolfssohn, one in Hebrew and one in German/Yiddish, Jeremy Dauber finds that the use of the sacred tongue located the Hebrew play "within not the actual world that he and his audience [inhabited], but a more epic, allegorical, typologically riven world. The world of the sacred is not merely different from that of the profane in speech, thought, and behavior, but is somehow more literary, more detached from reality."¹¹ Hebrew in the early days of Modern Hebrew literature also marked a world apart, a more formal world, a world defined by archetypes and aspirations rather than the quotidian world more readily described in Yiddish.

Part of the secularizing push of the modern era was to flatten the sacred into the perennial to create "the completely profane world, the wholly desacralized cosmos."¹² This is what Max Weber would call the "disenchantment of the world," the path towards moral perfection and technological progress.¹³ Benedict Anderson, considered among the "modernist" scholars of nationalism, holds that the decline of religion in Europe created the conditions for the emergence of national traditions. Part of this reorientation of religion was the desacralization

---

9 Simon Federbusch explored this tradition at some length in a 1967 study. Simon Federbusch, *Ha-lashon ha-'Ivrit be-Yisra'el uva-' amim* (Jerusalem: Rav Kook Institute, 1967), 325–327.
10 Margalit Shilo, *Princess or Prisoner?: Jewish Women in Jerusalem, 1840–1914*, 1st ed., Brandeis Series on Jewish Women (Waltham, MA: Brandeis University Press, 2005), 144.
11 Jeremy Dauber, "The City, Sacred and Profane: Between Hebrew and Yiddish in the Fiction of the Early Jewish Enlightenment," *Jewish Studies Quarterly* 12 (2005): 57–58.
12 Eliade, *The Sacred and the Profane; The Nature of Religion*, 13.
13 Max Weber, "Science as a Vocation," in David Owen and Tracy B. Strong, eds., *The Vocation Lectures*, trans. by Rodney Livingstone (Indianapolis, IN: Hackett, 2004), 30.

of language. Where, in the case of the Catholic Church, Latin had bound believers together and to the notions of sacred space and time, the emergence of a variety of vernaculars and the development of literary and journalistic traditions in those languages turned speakers and readers to new, more fragmented forms of collective identity.[14] In the European case, national languages (for example French, Italian, or Spanish) were distinct from the sacred language, Latin.

The secularization thesis has been challenged broadly as religion reasserts its place in national society and politics.[15] The paradigm in which the sacred is replaced by the vernacular was complicated in the Zionist case, where the emergent national language, retooled for everyday and continual use, was understood as a direct outgrowth of the sacred language (Hebrew has parallels with Arabic in this regard). In this case, the reconfiguration of the sacred language took the form of making the sacred perennial, not in desacralizing the sacred. To move toward the vernacular and towards a nation-based identity, in these cases, was not to abandon the sacred language and its associated religious practices, but to reclaim and exploit the sacred language for new, broader uses. This desacralized, but in fact re-sacralized, language existed in an intermediate space. As Todd Hasak-Lowy notes, if the sacred quality of Hebrew offered grounds for calling it abnormal, some writers sought a bridge to connect the sacred with the profane. S.Y. Agnon, he writes, charted out for himself a "conceptual no-man's-land positioned between the sacred and the profane."[16]

3 The National Context: The Sacred Becomes Perennial

In theory, this new Hebrew space, either all sacred or all profane, depending on one's perspective, was all-encompassing. In the Yishuv, the situation of Hebrew had theoretically been transformed. Refashioned as a vernacular, the language was tied not only to ritual but also to the ostensibly perennial work of building municipal, political, educational, and cultural institutions.

---

14 Benedict Anderson, *Imagined Communities: Reflections on the Origin and Spread of Nationalism* (London: Verso, 2006), 19.
15 See Erin K. Wilson, *After Secularism: Rethinking Religion in Global Politics* (New York: Palgrave MacMillan, 2012), 1–27.
16 Todd Hasak-Lowy, *Here and Now: History, Nationalism, and Realism in Modern Hebrew Fiction*, 1st ed., Judaic Traditions in Literature, Music, and Art (Syracuse, NY: Syracuse University Press, 2008), 98–99.

The concept of labor, *'avodah*, had been re-signified in Modern Hebrew to refer not only to one's personal work, but the collective effort of building a country, whether in agricultural fields, industrial factories, or cultural clubs. The word *'avodah* – which in the pre-modern period was used to describe Temple ritual and, later, prayer (*'avodah sheba-lev*) – was used frequently to describe culture and literature, for example in Ḥayim Naḥman Bialik's mention of "the labor of literature" in his speech to the Twelfth Zionist Congress in 1921 or the author Abraham Levinson's references to the "labor of [Hebrew] culture" at the Eighteenth Zionist Congress in 1933.[17] Carnivals, sports, books, theater and newspapers were all part of the Hebrew culture-building activities of the Yishuv.[18] The volitional quality of pioneering extended to the realm of language as well. Hebrew, both the chosen national language and a language that in practice required a degree of self-sacrifice, symbolized the laborious process of building a nation; using one's mother tongue, in contrast, appeared to embody a form of laziness. If Hebrew culture was to be the only culture, if Hebrew and Hebrew labor were to expand to encompass all elements of Zionist society,[19] Hebrew would become, as Natan Alterman wrote, "the language that does all the labor [*melakhah*] demanded of it."[20]

Transgressions now pertained not to traditional religious laws, promoted only by religiously orthodox elements, but to new, nationalist "laws" and cultural orthodoxies theoretically shared among all Jews. With respect to the Sabbath, the time of so much cultural activity, Zionists had less cast off the bonds of Sabbath restriction than recast them in the secular nationalist terms of Hebrew piety. Kibbutz movement leader Yitzhak Tabenkin felt that there was no place in the world where the Sabbath was as truly experienced as in Tel Aviv, secular kibbutzim, and moshavot. Israel Kolatt suggests that Tabenkin was promoting "a new mode of Sabbath observance," one closely bound up with a new orthodoxy.[21] The

---

17 Ḥayim Naḥman Bialik, "Ne'um ba-kongres ha-Tzioni ha-shenem 'asar be-Karlsbad, Elul 5681," accessed March 23, 2020, https://benyehuda.org/read/7293; Abraham Levinson, "Ha-tarbut ha-'Ivrit ba-golah," accessed March 23, 2020, https://benyehuda.org/read/2184.
18 Jacob Shavit, *Ha-historyah shel Tel-Aviv* (Tel Aviv: Ramot, Tel-Aviv University, 2001), 322–332.
19 "In the Land of Israel Hebrew became the language of entire lives: in theater and song, in literature and politics, in the sciences and in private reflections, in poetry and in signs on the street." Tamar Sovran, "Ha-'Ivrit ki-sefat tarbut," in *Ha-'agalah ha-mele'ah: me'ah ve-'esrim shenot tarbut Yisra'el*, ed. Yisrael Bartal (Jerusalem: Magnes Press, 2002), 52.
20 Nathan Alterman, *'Ir ha-yonah: shirim* (Tel Aviv: Maḥbarot le-sifrut, 1957), 265. Cited in Sovran, "Ha-'Ivrit ki-sefat tarbut," 52.
21 Israel Kolatt, "Religion, Society, and State during the Period of the National Home," in *Zionism and Religion*, ed. Shmuel Almog, Jehuda Reinharz, and Anita Shapira, The Tauber Institute for the Study of European Jewry Series 30 (Hanover, NH: University Press of New England, 1998), 291.

Sabbath was reconstructed as a secular festival in which Zionist ideals could be performed through communal rituals that replicated the sense of separateness and transcendence traditionally associated with the day of rest.[22] Schools created ceremonies for the Sabbath, usually performed on Fridays, some involving a ritual donation to the Jewish National Fund box and a "sermon" on the political issues of the day.[23] The Sabbath was also a time for organized cultural activities. In 1928, the American financier Samuel Simon Bloom funded the construction of Ohel Shem, a community center that Bialik hoped would provide cultural and educational programming on the Sabbath. Raphael Patai recalls lecture series on Sabbath mornings at the Beit Ha-ʻAm in Tel Aviv and the Edison Cinema in Jerusalem.[24] Such rituals and undertakings gave expression to "festive time," a lifestyle that exists beyond profane time and binds the group together. Significantly, the glue that bound them was their Hebrew language substrate: the Zionist Sabbath was a Hebrew Sabbath, not a Jewish Sabbath.

The supposition that the specialness associated with the promotion of Hebrew would suffuse all settings, work and leisure, home and outside, rested on a reorientation of Hebrew's purview and a repositioning of its relationship within the traditional dichotomy of sacred and profane languages. Concern about total secularization informed Gershom Scholem's cautionary comments, in a letter to Franz Rosenzweig, that the release of sacred Hebrew posed a danger greater than that of Zionist-Arab conflict:

> Many believe that the language has been secularized, and the apocalyptic thorn has been pulled out. But this is not true at all. The secularization of the language is only a *façon de parler*, a phrase! It is impossible to empty out words that are filled to the breaking point with specific meanings lest it be done at the sacrifice of the language itself.

In fact, "A generation that most fervently accepts the most fruitful of our holy tradition, cannot simply live without tradition, even if it might fervently wish to . . . .

---

[22] Anita Shapira stresses the religious, messianic overtones of labor ideology and, in particular, the transmutation of traditional Jewish holiday and Sabbath practices into Zionist rituals: "Basically," she writes, "the Palestine labor movement was a religious movement. It might be called a 'secular religion' or 'political messianism' . . . but it stands as a religious movement even without the secular modifiers" (254). Anita Shapira, "Religious Motifs of the Labor Movement," in *Zionism and Religion* (Hanover, NH: University Press of New England, 1998), 251–72.

[23] Chaya Naor and Jacob Shavit, *Staging and Stagers in Modern Jewish Palestine: The Creation of Festive Lore in a New Culture, 1882–1948*, Raphael Patai Series in Jewish Folklore and Anthropology (Detroit: Wayne State University Press, 2004), 65.

[24] Michael Brown, *The Israeli-American Connection: Its Roots in the Yishuv, 1914–1945*, America-Holy Land Monographs (Detroit: Wayne State University Press, 1996), 96; Raphael Patai, *Journeyman in Jerusalem: Memories and Letters, 1933–1947* (Salt Lake City: University of Utah Press, 1992), 213–216.

God will not remain silent in the language in which He has affirmed our life a thousand times and more."[25]

In his view, the eternal sacredness of Hebrew posed existential problems.

4 Pro-Hebrew Zealotry

Confronted with evidence of Hebrew's more limited scope, Hebrew's secular advocates often chastised non-conformists in national terms, calling users of other languages lazy or uncommitted, that is, haphazardly delinquent. What does it mean for Hebrew to be universal within Jewish society? In one understanding, it means that other languages are explicitly forbidden in any circumstance. The Yiddish poet Yehoash expressed a common ideological consensus when he used a metaphor taken from Jewish kashrut laws in describing language attitudes in Palestine: "Yiddish here is as impure as pork."[26] His utterance implies that the profane (*ḥol*) had taken on the qualities of the impure (*tame'*), that is, the ritually forbidden.

In practice, Hebrew was not so much desacralized as that its sacredness had been universalized across all realms of society. That which was in danger of defilement now was not the divine, but the nation, construed as sacred and as such requiring constant maintenance and oversight by its caretakers, the members of the nation. "The profane has overpowered the holy," wrote a proponent of socialist Zionist Hebrew culture in 1936, "Newspapers, meetings, and official business [take place] in Hebrew but profane life [*ḥaye ḥulin*] [takes place] in the language of inertia and routine."[27] Zionist work, he implies, was regularly taking place in Hebrew – the real threat to the language was arising during times away from work, times marked using the traditional Jewish notion of "profaneness" and defined by inertia and laziness. This haphazard disregard for the distinction between permitted and forbidden, pure and impure was frequently conceived of in terms of laziness. In a tract from 1921, Aharon Moshe Wizansky, a Zionist activist in Zurich who would soon after move to Palestine and teach at the elite Herzliyya Gymnasium in Tel Aviv, argued against the claim, then widespread in Europe, that Yiddish should be supported over Hebrew as a national

---

25 Cited in Udi Aloni, *What Does a Jew Want?: On Binationalism and Other Specters* (New York: Columbia University Press, 2011), 247–48.
26 Yehoash, "Fun New York biz Reḥovos un tsurik," 1:158. Cited in Benjamin Harshav, *Language in Time of Revolution* (Stanford, CA: Stanford University Press, 1999), 144.
27 Yehudah Gothelf, "Ba-ḥazit ha-tarbut ha-'Ivrit," *Ha-shomer ha-tza'ir*, November 1, 1936, 7.

language because it was less burdensome. But ease and comfort were not goals, insisted Yeḥieli: "not every unloading [of a burden] is liberation, just as not every loading [of a burden] is subjugation."[28] An article from 1936 spoke of the "inertia of adhering to Yiddish," saying that the new immigrant does not take up "the heavy burden of national values" but rather "the lighter rubbish."[29]

The degree of collective commitment, intimidation, and mutual censure surrounding these Hebrew leisure practices should be emphasized. Scholars have noted that totalitarian regimes are particularly distinguished by their attempts to intervene fully in leisure practices.[30] Stephen Kotkin uses a specifically linguistic metaphor to describe such a process in the Soviet State: "Publically expressing loyalty by knowing how to 'speak Bolshevik,'" he writes, "became an overriding concern."[31] Orit Rozin describes society during the Yishuv and early period of statehood as characterized by "a voluntary collectivism manifest in the willful recruitment of contemporaries to build a shared society and establish a shared identity."[32] Literary figures, leaders, and organizations collaborated in a shared cultural and linguistic project which largely transcended political divisions and which saw intimidation tactics not as a means of controlling foreign elements but, in general, as the cultivation of fellow citizens' true and authentic selves. This kind of ideological volunteerism correlated with strong collective censure of individual behaviors that seemed to transgress social norms. In the absence of an enforcement apparatus, the consequences of misbehavior, including linguistic misbehavior, were entirely in the realm of mutual critique and did not, for example, engage the legal or police system as was the case in the Soviet Union. Thus, the comparison is useful only to a certain extent. Nonetheless, the fantasy of social control – expressed in part as linguistic control – was palpable. The Yishuv, too, was a society deeply committed to a radical revision of both community life and the individual in the service of a new and better society, a society that saw it as

---

28 M.A. Yeḥi'eli [Shlomo Vaynshteyn], *Le-she'elat ha-safah* (Zurich: Ha-Mitzpah, 1921), 5.
29 Gothelf, "Ba-ḥazit ha-tarbut ha-'Ivrit," 7.
30 David Richard Leheny, *The Rules of Play: National Identity and the Shaping of Japanese Leisure*, Cornell Studies in Political Economy (Ithaca: Cornell University Press, 2003), 27; Anne White, *De-Stalinization and the House of Culture: Declining State Control Over Leisure in the USSR, Poland, and Hungary, 1953–89* (London: Routledge, 1990), 21–23. White cites Soviet politician Konstantin Chernenko's comment at a June 1983 plenum on ideology that socialization work "achieves lasting results ... when it encompasses all aspects of a person's life and world including their daily lives, their leisure and their family relations" (22).
31 Stephen Kotkin, *Magnetic Mountain: Stalinism as a Civilization* (Berkeley: University of California Press, 1995), 220.
32 Orit Rozin, *Ḥovat ha-ahavah ha-kashah: yaḥid u-kolektiv be-Yisra'el bi-shenot ha-ḥamishim* (Tel Aviv: 'Am 'Oved, 2008), 10.

absolutely reasonable (if impossible) to control not only what its members did on the job, but what they did during times of leisure.

While debauchery – or "deviant leisure" – tends normally to be associated with youth and its presumed deficient self-control, the discourse on deviant linguistic leisure in the Yishuv for the most part pertained to adults, who were labeled as petty criminals: "*portze gader*" (transgressors); promoters of "*hefkerut*" (lawlessness); and "*ḥotrim*" (saboteurs) for their tendency to use or access their mother tongues in leisure-time spaces. Children, schooled in Hebrew classrooms and indoctrinated young about the value of Hebrew, tended not to be linguistic offenders in this regard.[33] Much of the subtext of public debates about Hebrew leisure implies a generational conflict between children, who are true to the nation policing their parents, and these parents, whose leisure is seen as deviant. To the extent that most adults tried to perform a Hebrew identity in official or work settings, they seem to have fulfilled Goffman's notion of acting, in which "the surface of agreement, the veneer of consensus, [is] facilitated by each participant concealing his own wants behind statements which assert values to which everyone present feels obliged to give lip service."[34] Such apparent self-abnegation was by no means absolute: within any individual, the desire to participate in social activities, to demonstrate allegiance to a set of ideals, to fit in, could be as strong as a desire to indulge in the familiar, to be part of a subculture in another language. Moreover, individual self-censorship and occasional self-denial in the service of collective aims – oriented in these settings toward language – was at the heart of the Zionist conception of freedom.

5 A Sacred Realm and a Profane Realm

But a re-consideration of the rhetoric concerning linguistic discipline and license suggests that the traditional Jewish relegation of Hebrew to sacred realms persisted in the Yishuv, albeit in modified form. The social functions of language were not arbitrary, despite anxious descriptions of chaos. Rather, Hebrew, like other languages, tended to serve particular, delimited functions for those who did

---

[33] The discussion about children's speech pertained to the quality, tone, accent and vocabulary of their spoken Hebrew. For one such exploration, based on a study of children in the Yishuv, see Israel Rubin Rivkai, "'Al ha-spetzifiyut ha-leshonit be-fi yaldenu be-Eretz Yisraʾel," pts. 3–4 *Leshonenu* 5, no. 1 (Tevet 1933): 73–77; 5, no. 3–4 (Sivan-Elul 1933): 231–242. Also published in ibid., ʿ*Al sefat yeladenu ba-aretz: mikhtavim le-horim 2* (Tel Aviv: Mefits ha-sefer, 1938), 15–91.
[34] Erving Goffman, *The Presentation of Self in Everyday Life* (New York: Doubleday, 1959), 9.

not speak it natively: it was a language of official business, of work obligations and of Zionist cultural events; in other words, it was a language of national ritual.

In practice, the notion that Hebrew language use would be all-encompassing was not intuitively acceptable. The Yishuv was marked by the present of a refigured sacred but was not entirely suffused by it. As Giorgio Agamben has written, secularization created a change, but only a superficial one. It "may appear to liberate ideas and things from the sacred sphere in which they had dwelt, but, actually, that process only changes the location of the closed off area."[35] Was the new sacred a perennial state, a sort of all-sacred world? It may be more accurate to suggest, following Agamben, that the space of Hebrew was a new "closed-off area" within a broader system that included both sacred and profane elements.

Sources indicate that indeed, for many, Hebrew was not perennial but rather tended to exist in particular, protected spaces. This was true for national ritual in general. For example, Yoram Bar-Gal writes about the ritual conducted in Zionist schools on Fridays in which students would donate to the Jewish National Fund blue boxes as part of a (pre-) Sabbath ritual. On the one hand, "the JNF functionaries wanted the Box Work to be everywhere all the time, and they aspired to turn the ritual object into a Zionist icon, something that would be the hallmark of every Jewish home." At the same time, he writes, this Sabbath ritual was understood to be both sanctified and perennial: "elements of sanctity and separateness are evident [in the ritual of JNF donations on the Sabbath] . . . in schools the Blue Box was only taken out during ceremonies of greeting the Sabbath and was placed upon the table next to the lit candles."[36]

This division, along with its associated tension, pertained to language as well. As Bialik noted, a distinction was emerging between "Hebrew, which is the language of holidays and demonstrations in the schools, and other languages, which are the languages of ordinary (profane) days and regular use."[37] This division, too, reflects another reconfiguration of sacred and profane; in this case, not the presumption that the sacred should and would pervade all spaces (whether in the triumphant mode or in the potentially destructive mode that Scholem envisioned), but rather the presumption that sacred space and time, marked by Hebrew, would be set against other, permitted spaces, in which other languages would or could be allowed to reign.

---

35 Leland de la Durantaye, *Giorgio Agamben: A Critical Introduction* (Stanford, CA: Stanford University Press, 2009), 361–362.

36 Yoram Bar-Gal, *Propaganda and Zionist Education: The Jewish National Fund, 1924–1947* (Rochester, NY: University of Rochester Press, 2003), 106.

37 Ḥayim Naḥman Bialik, "Ha-zilzul ba-lashon ha-ʿIvrit ve-vaʿad ha-lashon," *Devarim she-beʿal peh*, vol. 2 (Tel Aviv: Devir, 1935), 132.

The leisure-time activities associated with the Sabbath were one such space, marked as a day apart by many modern, Hebrew-speaking Jews and attended to with the rhetoric of sacredness and profaneness. In this case, however, the linguistic referent had been inverted. If in the traditional setting Hebrew was the language associated with the Sabbath, in the Yishuv the Sabbath became a time and space in which Hebrew could be temporarily discarded. In a society where work had become a sacred national task, the day off from work was to be a day for languages other than Hebrew.

Two comical anecdotes illuminate the implicit existence of sacred and profane spheres in the linguistic practice of the Yishuv. A newspaper feature in the mid-1940s recounted the story of "a professor from among the German immigrants":

> He learned Hebrew, lectures in this language, and speaks it every day of the week. But on the Sabbath he speaks German. His friends asked him why. He said, "It says in our holy book, 'Do not do any sort of labor [on the Sabbath],' and I strictly observe this commandment."[38]

The story is an adaptation of a better-known anecdote about the writer Ḥayim Naḥman Bialik, who had died several years earlier in 1934:

> Once Bialik was found in his fallen state [be-kalkalato], speaking Yiddish on the Sabbath and they asked him "How can it be?" He replied: "Yiddish speaks itself and speaking Hebrew is labor [melakhah], and labor is forbidden on the Sabbath."[39]

Yerushalayim Segal, a filmmaker and translator of movie subtitles to Hebrew, remembers an event that occurred when he was spending time with his friends Mordekhai Noiman and Yehoshua Chechik, two of the founders of Mitzpah, the first private Hebrew publisher in Palestine, founded in 1925. As the three were riding on a bus, they began speaking Yiddish amongst themselves "without realizing it." As it happened, Itamar Ben-Avi, the son of the renowned modernizer of Hebrew Eliezer Ben-Yehuda, and a Hebrew journalist in his own right, got on the bus. When he heard Yiddish being spoken he came over and expressed his

---

[38] "Ha-profesor galui lev," Ha-'Erev [n.d.]. In Be'ayot lashon ve-tarbut: leket devarim she-ne'emru ve-nikhtevu be-ḥodshe Adar B-Nisan 5706 [1946], Jewish National Council Culture Department/Institute for Hebrew Language and Culture, 1946. CZA DD1/3250. I was unable to locate a publication called Ha-'Erev and thus do not know the source of the original publication.

[39] Nahum Hinitz, Gedole Yisra'el bi-vediḥah (Jerusalem: Kiryat Sefer, 1980), 20. Another version of the anecdote reads: "One Sabbath, friends came to visit Bialik at his home and found him speaking Yiddish. 'You, Bialik, speaking Yiddish!?' they asked him. 'Yiddish speaks itself,' he responded to them, 'and speaking Hebrew is difficult labor, which is forbidden on the Sabbath.'" Adir Kohen, ed., Sefer ha-humor ha-yehudi ha-gadol: otzar ha-bediḥah ha-Yehudit veha-Yisre'elit le-doroteha (Or Yehudah: Kineret, 2004), 256.

surprise: "Three good Jews, longstanding residents like yourselves, what's come over you [*mah pit'om*] that you are speaking Yiddish!?" Segal recalls that it was "only then" that they realized their linguistic shift "and, really, it wasn't pleasant." But Chechik recovered immediately and replied with a witty rejoinder: "But we were speaking in Latin letters!" Understanding the reference, Segal concludes his story, Itamar Ben-Avi returned to his seat.[40]

Segal recounts this story (which likely occurred sometime between 1925 and 1933, when Noiman and Chechik were partners at the Mitzpah publishing house) after discussing Ben-Avi's (never enacted) suggestion that Zionists should follow the recent example of the Turks and write Hebrew in Latin letters in order to make the language more intelligible to Westerners – Yiddish in Latin letters, the humorous rejoinder implies, would be preferable over Yiddish in Hebrew letters.[41] More than a conversation about orthography, however, this is an exchange about the use of Yiddish in public. Segal, Noiman, and Chechik were among the most important promoters of Hebrew in the realm of leisure-time activities – that is, they saw leisure as a space for the work of Hebrew promotion. Segal made his mark by providing accurate Hebrew titles for films, and Noiman and Chechik brought Hebrew reading materials to the general public through their publishing activities. Segal adds, moreover, that all three had been members of the most zealous pro-Hebrew organization at the time, the Battalion of the Defenders of the Hebrew Language, though the language he uses, "*meshuḥrarim*" (demobilized), indicates that they had finished their "service" in that quasi-military organization.

Nonetheless, foreign languages were often used on the streets defiantly or indifferently – Noiman and Chechik may have seen the bus ride as a rare opportunity to relax from their ardent devotion to Hebrew leisure. With the distance of sixty-five years (the memoir was published in 1993), Segal appears ashamed about Yiddish: at three points during the story he indicates that the use of Yiddish constituted a kind of unconscious act, a linguistic lapse ("I don't know why," "without realizing it," "it was only then that I realized it"). In effect, one promoter of Hebrew culture was policing others by pointing out their lapses. Chechik's response, however, is the most interesting part of the story. Rather than admit failure or wrongdoing, he answers with a joke, the Yiddish we were speaking wasn't really Yiddish; it was Yiddish in Latin letters. By evoking a small debate

---

[40] Yerushalayim Segal, *Zikhronot Yerushalayim be-Tel Aviv* (Tel Aviv: Moledet, 1993), 266.
[41] Ilker Ayturk describes the efforts of Itamar Ben-Avi, the prodigal son of Eliezer Ben-Yehuda, to promote the Latinization of Hebrew in order to avoid the isolation and stagnation of the Jewish people and promote a connection with the West. Ilker Ayturk, "Attempts at Romanizing the Hebrew Script and Their Failure: Nationalism, Religion, and Alphabet Reform in the Yishuv," *Middle Eastern Studies* 43, no. 4 (July 2007): 625–45.

in the language politics of the day, a discussion about the merits of transcribing Hebrew in Latin script, he lightened the weight of the linguistic offense, appealing to a shared sense that the "laws" of Hebrew were not as far-reaching as it might have seemed.

We would be incorrect to assume that anyone, Bialik included, made a rigid distinction between Sabbath and weekday language use; the absurd strictness of the distinction is part of what makes these anecdotes function as jokes. The joke, based on rigid oppositions or absurd juxtapositions, functions as a mirror in which societies see themselves and becomes thus a point of entry for the cultural historian.[42]

Bialik's friends respond to his linguistic deviance with a mix of condemnation and laughter – a double move of license and control. When the friends enter, they deem Bialik in a fallen state and act surprised. Bialik's response, however, elicits a form of empathetic laughter from the reading audience and, implicitly, from those who visited him – his transgression was familiar; moreover, it fit within the unwritten rules dictating the boundaries of language use in the Yishuv. Bialik as an individual had a particular role in the imagination of the Yishuv. As Miryam Segal points out, he was the emblematic Hebrew writer who never entirely spoke fluent Hebrew and who did not cease speaking other languages.[43] This contradiction, if projected onto Bialik, was familiar to many, who, despite their interest in and commitments to Hebrew in theory, were not interested in using it exclusively. Speaking Yiddish (or German, in the professor's case), could be construed as both an unforgivable breach and an entirely unremarkable activity, one particularly characteristic of the Sabbath, the day of rest. This combination of shock and acquiescence, of damning scowls and knowing winks, is laced through the sources on language and leisure in the Yishuv.

---

42 "Of all informing details," writes Joseph Boskin, "few more readily offer insight into societal affairs than people's laughter." Joseph Boskin, *Rebellious Laughter: People's Humor in American Culture*, 1st ed. (Syracuse, NY: Syracuse University Press, 1997), 202. Robert Darnton suggests that jokes or proverbs meaningful to "natives" can be among the "best points of entry" into the historical past, the points at which one can "grasp a foreign system of meaning in order to unravel it." Robert Darnton, *The Great Cat Massacre and Other Episodes in French Cultural History* (New York: Basic Books, 2009), 78.

43 Segal focuses on the irony that Bialik was crowned national poet despite the fact that he continued to write poetry in the earlier Ashkenazic accent (which produced a particular poetic meter) rather than a version of the Sephardic accent, usually with ultimate stress. "The national poet did not cover the distance between exile and homeland so much as dedicate himself to that distance" (148). Miryam Segal, *A New Sound in Hebrew Poetry: Poetics, Politics, Accent* (Bloomington, IN: Indiana University Press, 2010), 139–148.

Were these practices – Bialik's individual "relapse" into Yiddish, or the general practice of using other languages outside school and ceremonies – basically acceptable or basically unacceptable? On the face of it and from an official perspective, these manifestations were clearly unacceptable. Leisure is a sphere in which social norms are enacted and national ideals are performed, and in which elites can exert control over the masses by encouraging or requiring certain collective pursuits. The common Zionist term "*tarbut meguyeset*," culture mobilized to the interests of the nation, evokes military conscription and the foreswearing of individual freedom.[44] Official interest in leisure derives precisely from its independent nature; leisure invites concern "because it ostensibly represents the area of activity in which people can most be themselves."[45] Controls on leisure, ultimately, are designed to shape "the kind of people that citizens are supposed to be when they are being themselves."[46]

The interplay of license and control, central to scholars' descriptions of the paradox of modern leisure,[47] was pervasive in authorities' dealings with language transgression. The contestation over Sabbath language practices captured in the Bialik joke resonated in a society negotiating the terms of Sabbath observance, which, along with Hebrew language, were the pillars of the Yishuv's "Hebrew character" (the term joined together both culturally Jewish and linguistically Hebrew features).[48] The secularly oriented members of the Yishuv did not tend to observe traditional Sabbath restrictions: "In their eyes adherence to *halakhah* [Jewish law] retarded both individual and communal development and repre-

---

[44] On "mobilized culture," most often discussed with regard to literature, see Michael Gluzman, *The Politics of Canonicity: Lines of Resistance in Modernist Hebrew Poetry* (Stanford, CA: Stanford University Press, 2003).; Eric Stephen Zakim, *To Build and Be Built: Landscape, Literature, and the Construction of Zionist Identity* (Philadelphia: University of Pennsylvania Press, 2006).

[45] Leheny, *The Rules of Play*, 20. The tension between "recruited culture" and "free culture" is nicely summarized in Shavit, *Ha-historyah shel Tel-Aviv*, 312–316.

[46] Leheny, *The Rules of Play*, 31. This imperative is visible in the 1941 report prepared for the American Youth Commission which, while promoting the expression of "individuality," insists that youth "need guidance" to cultivate the right kind of individuality, lest they yield to deleterious influences, delinquency, crime, and debauchery. C. Gilbert Wrenn and Dudley Lee Harley, *Time on Their Hands; a Report on Leisure, Recreation, and Young People* (Washington, D. C: American Council on Education, 1941), xix, 25; E.P. Thompson discusses a similar exercise of leisure controls in early industrial Britain. See, for example, his discussion of leisure and the English working class, *The Making of the English Working Class* (London: V. Gollancz, 1963), 57–59.

[47] For an overview of the field of Leisure Studies, see the exchange in *Past and Present* 146 (1995) and 156 (1997). Many have seen Victorian England as a *locus classicus* for the articulation of leisure time as a site for the cultivation of individual and national identity.

[48] This point is made by Maoz Azaryahu, *Tel Aviv: Mythography of a City* (Syracuse, NY: Syracuse University Press, 2006), 79.

sented the negative aspect of *galut* society."[49] Religious Jews, oriented towards the traditional ban on *melakhah* – labor – on the Sabbath, were interested in curtailing traveling, cooking, and the use of money, electricity, and musical instruments on the Sabbath. Community committees, in Haifa for example, worked hard to prevent desecration.[50] In the case of secular Hebrew promotion, however, the mode of transgression and resignification was the norm – to break or modernize the Sabbath was not to transgress Zionism; it was in the eyes of many the definition of upholding it.

Anat Helman outlines the "sanctions" imposed against transgressors of Modern Hebrew, including "social pressure, cultural exclusion, derogatory jokes, and even discrimination."[51] But the intense and real censure of language diversity by members of the Yishuv coexisted with a great deal of license, license that made visible the limits of Hebrew hegemony and challenged its status as the dominant language. Many were demonstrably nonchalant about instances in which leisure time was spent in languages other than Hebrew – in many cases, lip service apparently did not need to be paid at all and the reality of multilingualism was freely accepted. "Time off," in the scholarly literature on leisure, can be conceived as time in which social norms can be discarded or even mocked. To adopt again the language of Erving Goffman, leisure-time activities have the potential to occur "backstage," which he defines as "a place, relative to a given performance, where the impression fostered by the performance is knowingly contradicted as a matter of course."[52] In a society characterized by programmatically announced social expectations, leisure time offered a way not only to relax into alternative practices – including linguistic ones – but also to poke fun at official strictures by exploring and enacting cultural alternatives. In a highly ideological, collectivist social context, Goffman's notion of a leisurely "backstage" free from performance needs to be modified, however. We are better off thinking of a social setting that is both separate from and continually monitored by an apparatus consisting of both individual citizens and citizen organizations concerned with policing social norms. These organizations and individuals, lacking real powers of enforcement,

---

49 Kolatt, "Religion, Society, and State during the Period of the National Home," 277.
50 Part of the Haifa Sabbath-related activism is found in the *Protocols of the Vaʿadah le-havtaḥat ha-tzivyon ha-ʿIvri shel ha-shekhunah, 1942–1949*. HMA (Haifa Municipality Archive) 6075-00312/19.
51 Anat Helman, "Even the Dogs in the Street Bark in Hebrew: National Ideology and Everyday Culture in Tel Aviv," 367.
52 Goffman, *The Presentation of Self in Everyday Life*, 112. Goffman, concerned with gestures and physical cues, does not consider the possibility that using a dominant language can itself be a social performance. Other writers, have, however, applied Goffman's terminology to multi-lingual situations in which "backstage" language use serves as a source of solidarity between minority actors.

have been referred to as the "informal state," a term particularly relevant in this pre-state context.⁵³ Nonetheless, even the most heavily monitored societies maintain "backstage" spaces of linguistic deviance. In the controlled environment of Soviet Magnitogorsk, where workers could be fired for lack of loyalty, "a person could 'speak Bolshevik' one moment, 'innocent peasant' the next, begging indulgence for a professed inability to master fully the demanding new language and behavior."⁵⁴ In this non-state context as well, public censure over multilingual leisure was combined with a repeated tendency to beg – and to grant – indulgence for linguistic deviance.

6 Conclusion: National Boundaries, or Border Zones

The metaphorical language that defined Hebrew's purview had changed. On one level, the sacred had become national rather than religious for many. What remained unclear and thus negotiable, however, is how the profane was defined in this new configuration. Could the profane exist only beyond the margins of that national society, or did the profane exist within the national cultural space, albeit in a space whose existence was accepted, if constantly contested? Is the linguistic-other to be considered ipso facto a threat to the coherence of the nation? In a multinational world, does national difference serve to shore up the borders and coherence of national groups that are always inherently artificial, or does it primarily allow nations to create internal spaces that can accommodate difference? Linda Colley has argued, in the case of the British, that "men and women decide who they are by reference to who and what they are not. Once confronted with an alien 'Them' an otherwise diverse community can become a reassuring or merely desperate "Us." British identity, she argues, was formed in contact with "The Other."⁵⁵ Zionists were also engaged in several levels of oppositional iden-

---

53 Such organizations have been referred to as the "informal state," a collection of commissions, boards, and organizations "either pressing for a change to the status quo or seeking to sustain a status quo that is in danger of being eroded." Morality is a common target of these efforts: such organizations were founded in numerous settings to combat prostitution, gaming, and Sabbath-breaking, for instance. The Hebrew enforcement apparatus can logically be understood in this vein. Eva Codo, *Immigration and Bureaucratic Control: Language Practices in Public Administration* (Berlin: Mouton de Gruyter, 2008).
54 Kotkin, *Magnetic Mountain*, 220.
55 Linda Colley, *Britons: Forging The Nation, 1707–1837* (New Haven, CT: Yale University Press, 2005), 6.

tity formation, with Yiddish, Arabic, German, and English as the shifting markers of cultural spaces against which the Hebrew community would be defined.

But the nation was not clearly demarcated by language, as many (most) Jews shared native languages with those outside the nation. Zionists might be more fruitfully compared to those, particularly in Central and Eastern Europe, who sat on national border lines, whose loyalties were subject to negotiation, and whose multilingual abilities in practice provided opportunities to act in different ways or in alliance with different groups at different times, sometimes seeming to undermine national unity but sometimes seeming to strengthen it, or at least not to trouble it.[56]

Bibliography

Aloni, Udi. *What Does a Jew Want?: On Binationalism and Other Specters*. New York: Columbia University Press, 2011.

Alterman, Nathan. *'Ir ha-yonah: Shirim*. Tel Aviv: Maḥbarot le-sifrut, 1957.

Anderson, Benedict. *Imagined Communities: Reflections on the Origin and Spread of Nationalism*. London: Verso, 2006.

Ayturk, Ilker. "Attempts at Romanizing the Hebrew Script and Their Failure: Nationalism, Religion, and Alphabet Reform in the Yishuv." *Middle Eastern Studies* 43, no. 4 (July 2007): 625–45.

Azaryahu, Maoz. *Tel Aviv: Mythography of a City*. Syracuse, NY: Syracuse University Press, 2006.

Bar-Gal, Yoram. *Propaganda and Zionist Education: The Jewish National Fund, 1924–1947*. Rochester, NY: University of Rochester Press, 2003.

Be'ayot lashon ve-tarbut: leket devarim she-ne'emru ve-nikhtevu be-ḥodshe Adar ve-Nisan 5706 [1946], Jewish National Council Culture Department/Institute for Hebrew Language and Culture, 1946. CZA (Central Zionist Archives) DD1/3250.

Bialik, Ḥayim Naḥman. "Ha-zilzul ba-lashon ha-'Ivrit ve-va'ad ha-lashon." *Devarim she-be'al peh*, vol. 2, 131–33. Tel Aviv: Devir, 1935.

Bialik, Ḥayim Naḥman. "Ne'um ba-kongres ha-Tzioni ha-shenem asar be-Karlsbad, Elul 5681." https://benyehuda.org/read/7293.

Boskin, Joseph. *Rebellious Laughter: People's Humor in American Culture*, 1st ed. Syracuse, NY: Syracuse University Press, 1997.

Brown, Michael. *The Israeli-American Connection: Its Roots in the Yishuv, 1914–1945*. America-Holy Land Monographs. Detroit: Wayne State University Press, 1996.

Burnett, Stephen G. *Christian Hebraism in the Reformation Era (1500–1660): Authors, Books, and the Transmission of Jewish Learning*. Leiden: Brill, 2012.

---

[56] See Pieter M. Judson, *Guardians of the Nation: Activists on the Language Frontiers of Imperial Austria* (Cambridge, MA: Harvard University Press, 2006); Tara Zahra, *Kidnapped Souls: National Indifference and the Battle for Children in the Bohemian Lands, 1900–1948* (Ithaca: Cornell University Press, 2008).

Codo, Eva. *Immigration and Bureaucratic Control: Language Practices in Public Administration*. Berlin: Mouton de Gruyter, 2008.

Colley, Linda. *Britons: Forging The Nation, 1707–1837*. New Haven, CT: Yale University Press, 2005.

Darnton, Robert. *The Great Cat Massacre and Other Episodes in French Cultural History*. New York: Basic Books, 2009.

Dauber, Jeremy. "The City, Sacred and Profane: Between Hebrew and Yiddish in the Fiction of the Early Jewish Enlightenment." *Jewish Studies Quarterly* 12 (2005): 43–60.

de la Durantaye, Leland. *Giorgio Agamben: A Critical Introduction*. Stanford, CA: Stanford University Press, 2009.

Efrati, Natan. *Mi-lashon yehidim le-lashon umah: ha-dibur ha-'Ivri be-Eretz Yisra'el ba-shanim 1882–1922*. Jerusalem: Hebrew Language Academy, 2004.

Eliade, Mircea. *The Sacred and the Profane; The Nature of Religion*. New York: Harper and Row, 1961.

Elyada, Aya. *A Goy Who Speaks Yiddish: Christians and the Jewish Language in Early Modern Germany*. Stanford, CA: Stanford University Press, 2012.

Federbusch, Simon. *Ha-lashon ha-'Ivrit be-Yisra'el uva-'amim*. Jerusalem: Rav Kook Institute, 1967.

Gilman, Sander L. *Jewish Self-Hatred: Anti-Semitism and the Hidden Language of the Jews*. Baltimore: Johns Hopkins University Press, 1986.

Gluzman, Michael. *The Politics of Canonicity: Lines of Resistance in Modernist Hebrew Poetry*. Stanford, CA: Stanford University Press, 2003.

Goffman, Erving. *The Presentation of Self in Everyday Life*. New York: Doubleday, 1959.

Gothelf, Yehudah. "Ba-ḥazit ha-tarbut ha-'Ivrit." *Ha-Shomer Ha-Tza'ir*, November 1, 1936, 7.

Halperin, Liora R. *Babel in Zion: Jews, Nationalism, and Language Diversity in Palestine, 1920-1948*. New Haven, CT: Yale University Press, 2015.

Harshav, Benjamin. *Language in Time of Revolution*. Stanford, CA: Stanford University Press, 1999.

Hasak-Lowy, Todd. *Here and Now: History, Nationalism, and Realism in Modern Hebrew Fiction*, 1st ed. Judaic Traditions in Literature, Music, and Art. Syracuse, NY: Syracuse University Press, 2008.

Helman, Anat. "Even the Dogs in the Street Bark in Hebrew: National Ideology and Everyday Culture in Tel Aviv." *Jewish Quarterly Review*, New Ser. 92, No. 3–4 (2002): 359–382.

Hertz, J.H. *A Book of Jewish Thoughts Selected and Arranged by the Chief Rabbi*. Oxford: Oxford University Press, 1921.

Hinitz, Nahum. *Gedole Yisra'el Bi-Vediḥah*. Jerusalem: Kiryat Sefer, 1980.

Judson, Pieter M. *Guardians of the Nation: Activists on the Language Frontiers of Imperial Austria*. Cambridge, MA: Harvard University Press, 2006.

Karmi, Shlomo. *'Am eḥad ve-safah aḥat*. Jerusalem: Israel Ministry of Defense, 1997.

Kohen, Adir. *Sefer ha-humor ha-Yehudi ha-gadol: otzar ha-bediḥah ha-Yehudit veha-Yisre'elit le-doroteha*. Or Yehudah: Kineret, 2004.

Kolatt, Israel. "Religion, Society, and State during the Period of the National Home." In *Zionism and Religion*, edited by Shmuel Almog, Jehuda Reinharz, and Anita Shapira, 273–301. The Tauber Institute for the Study of European Jewry Series 30. Hanover, NH: University Press of New England, 1998.

Kotkin, Stephen. *Magnetic Mountain: Stalinism as a Civilization*. Berkeley: University of California Press, 1995.

Leheny, David Richard. *The Rules of Play: National Identity and the Shaping of Japanese Leisure*. Cornell Studies in Political Economy. Ithaca: Cornell University Press, 2003.

Levinger, Jacob S. *Ha-Rambam ke-filosof ukhe-fosek*. Jersualem: Bialik Institute, 1989.
Levinson, Abraham. "Ha-tarbut ha-'Ivrit ba-golah." https://benyehuda.org/read/2184.
Maimonides, Moses. *Commentary on Nezirut*.
Morag, Shmuel. "Ha-'Ivrit ha-ḥadashah be-hitgabshutah: lashon ba-askpeklaryah shel ḥevrah." *Katedrah* 56 (1990): 70–92.
Naor, Chaya and Jacob Shavit. *Staging and Stagers in Modern Jewish Palestine: The Creation of Festive Lore in a New Culture, 1882–1948*. Raphael Patai Series in Jewish Folklore and Anthropology. Detroit: Wayne State University Press, 2004.
Patai, Raphael. *Journeyman in Jerusalem: Memories and Letters, 1933–1947*. Salt Lake City: University of Utah Press, 1992.
Protocols of the Va'adah le-havtaḥat ha-tzivyon ha-'Ivri shel ha-shekhunah, 1942–1949. HMA (Haifa Municipality Archive) 6075-00312/19.
Rivkai, Israel Rubin. "'Al ha-spetzifiyut ha-leshonit be-fi yaldenu be-Eretz Yisra'el," pts. 3–4. *Leshonenu* 5, no. 1 (Tevet 1933): 73–77; 5, no. 3–4 (Sivan-Elul 1933): 231–242.
Rivkai, Israel Rubin. *'Al sefat yeladenu ba-aretz: mikhtavim le-horim 2*. Tel Aviv: Mefits ha-sefer, 1938.
Rozin, Orit. *Ḥovat ha-ahavah ha-kashah: yaḥid u-kolektiv be-Yisra'el bi-shenot ha-ḥamishim*. Tel Aviv: 'Am 'Oved, 2008.
Segal, Miryam. *A New Sound in Hebrew Poetry: Poetics, Politics, Accent*. Bloomington, IN: Indiana University Press, 2010.
Segal, Yerushalayim. *Zikhronot Yerushalayim be-Tel Aviv*. Tel Aviv: Moledet, 1993.
Shapira, Anita. "Religious Motifs of the Labor Movement." In *Zionism and Religion*, edited by Shmuel Almog, Jehuda Reinharz, and Anita Shapira, 251–72. The Tauber Institute for the Study of European Jewry Series 30. Hanover, NH: University Press of New England, 1998.
Shavit, Jacob. *Ha-historyah shel Tel-Aviv*. Tel Aviv: Ramot, Tel-Aviv University, 2001.
Shilo, Margalit. *Princess or Prisoner?: Jewish Women in Jerusalem, 1840–1914*, 1st ed. Brandeis Series on Jewish Women. Waltham, MA: Brandeis University Press, 2005.
Sovran, Tamar. "Ha-'Ivrit ki-sefat tarbut." In *Ha-'agalah ha-mele'ah: me'ah ve-'esrim shenot tarbut Yisra'el*, edited by Yisrael Bartal, 52–61. Jerusalem: Magnes Press, 2002.
Thompson, E.P. *The Making of the English Working Class*. London: V. Gollancz, 1963.
Weber, Max. "Science as a Vocation." In *The Vocation Lectures*, edited by David Owen and Tracy B. Strong; translated by Rodney Livingstone, 1–31. Indianapolis, IN: Hackett, 2004.
White, Anne. *De-Stalinization and the House of Culture: Declining State Control Over Leisure in the USSR, Poland, and Hungary, 1953–89*. London: Routledge, 1990.
Wilson, Erin K. *After Secularism: Rethinking Religion in Global Politics*. New York: Palgrave MacMillan, 2012.
Wrenn, C. Gilbert and Dudley Lee Harley. *Time on Their Hands; a Report on Leisure, Recreation, and Young People*. Washington, D.C.: American Council on Education, 1941.
Yehi'eli, M.A. [Shlomo Vaynshteyn]. *Le-she'elat ha-safah*. Zurich: Ha-Mitzpah, 1921.
Zahra, Tara. *Kidnapped Souls: National Indifference and the Battle for Children in the Bohemian Lands, 1900–1948*. Ithaca: Cornell University Press, 2008.
Zakim, Eric Stephen. *To Build and Be Built: Landscape, Literature, and the Construction of Zionist Identity*. Philadelphia: University of Pennsylvania Press, 2006.

List of Contributors

Yael Almog is Assistant Professor of German at Durham University in the United Kingdom.

Guido Bartolucci is Associate Professor of Early Modern History in the Department of History, Cultures, and Civilizations of the Alma Mater Studiorum – Università di Bologna.

Stephen G. Burnett is the Hymen Rosenberg Professor in Judaic Studies at the University of Nebraska in Lincoln, Nebraska.

Saverio Campanini is Professor of Hebrew Language and Literature in the Department of History, Cultures, and Civilizations of the Alma Mater Studiorum – Università di Bologna.

Steven D. Fraade is the Mark Taper Professor of the History of Judaism at Yale University.

Shalom Goldman is the Pardon Tillinghast Professor of Religion at Middlebury College.

Liora R. Halperin is Associate Professor of International Studies, History, and Jewish Studies, and the Jack and Rebecca Benaroya Endowed Chair in Israel Studies, at the University of Washington.

Melanie Lange completed her PhD dissertation on Sebastian Münster's edition of Elia Levita's *Sefer ha-Baḥur* at the University of Rostock. She currently works as a parish educator and volunteer pastor in West Mecklenburg, Germany.

Irven M. Resnick is Professor of Philosophy and Religion, and Chair of Excellence in Judaic Studies, at the University of Tennessee at Chattanooga.

Alison G. Salvesen is Professor of Early Judaism and Christianity at the Oriental Institute, University of Oxford, and Polonsky Fellow at the Oxford Centre for Hebrew and Jewish Studies.

Stefan Schorch teaches at the Martin-Luther-Universität in Halle–Wittenberg, where he holds the Chair for Hebrew Bible.

Ilona Steimann is a post-doctoral researcher at the Hochschule für Jüdische Studien Heidelberg.

Daniel Stein Kokin is a Visiting Researcher at Arizona State University and was previously Junior Professor of Jewish Literature and Culture at the University of Greifswald in Germany.

Gabriel Wasserman recently completed a postdoctoral fellowship at The Hebrew University of Jerusalem and is currently a senior editor at The Karaite Press.

Thomas Willi is Professor Emeritus of Old Testament and Judaism in the Theology Faculty of the University of Greifswald, where he also served as director of the Gustaf Dalman Institute.

Irene Zwiep is Professor of Hebrew and Jewish Studies at the University of Amsterdam.

www.ingramcontent.com/pod-product-compliance
Lightning Source LLC
Chambersburg PA
CBHW050513170426
43201CB00013B/1937